Reading Matters

A COLLECTION OF READINGS FOR WRITERS

The Freshman English Program: University of New Orleans

third edition

Edited by Inge Fink and Gabrielle Gautreaux

Pearson
Custom
Publishing

Cover Art: "Eden," by Gregory Kitterle.

Printed in the United States of America

10 9 8 7 6 5 4 3 2 1

Please visit our web site at www.pearsoncustom.com

ISBN 0–536–62384–8

BA 992846

PEARSON CUSTOM PUBLISHING
75 Arlington Street, Boston, MA 02116
A Pearson Education Company

Acknowledgments

We are grateful to many for their contributions to this new version of *Reading Matters*: to our colleagues in the English Department, whose support, suggestions, and submissions have given us the energy to proceed with a third edition. Many brought to our attention new material, including their own students' writing, or shared assignments: Anne Charles, Kurtis Clements, Scott Farrin, Roslyn Foy, Jane Haspel, Lydia Hopkins, Jennifer Kuchta, Joe Letter, Catherine Loomis, Gary Richards, Patricia Roger, David Rutledge, Marcia Wall, Donna Woodford. We could not have met our deadline without Rolanda Lacy, who offered her professional typing skills, even at the eleventh hour. Our student workers, Tamika Maracalin and Ingrid Hughes, copied expertly—and cheerfully—throughout the project. We would also like to thank our friends in the Women's Center and in Women's Studies who contributed selections on violence against women. As always, we appreciate the support of John Cooke, our department chair.

Special thanks are due Angie Smajstrla and the folks at Pearson for their patience and expertise.

Finally, thanks to our students, past and present, who challenge us, who force us always to read anew, who remind us daily that our work matters.

Copyright Acknowledgments

Contents

Contents

Contents

Introduction

We start again with the central truth of our experience in the writing classroom: reading matters. Ask writers how they got to be writers and, invariably, they will tell you they started by reading. They remember the fairy tales their parents read them or the endless treasures they discovered in the public library; they recall a favorite aunt's gift of a prized book or the salve of a good novel. But they all recognize that reading uncovers new worlds and provides their most valuable, most varied, experience.

The readings gathered here—classic to contemporary, introspective to academic—cover a range of purpose, style, and subject. New voices join those of the "masters" to share an impressive breadth of experience and opinion. We hope that in these readings our students will discover experience for their own convictions, strategies for shaping their own arguments.

This edition contains 75 readings: roughly a third of those come from the previous edition; the rest are new. In cooperation with the Leanne Knot Violence Against Women Project, we have included several readings concerning the abuse of women. Following our colleagues' suggestions, we have retained a wide range of authors, periods, and styles. Appendix A, with the exception of one student essay, is entirely fresh. Two new features have been added to make *Reading Matters* more user-friendly: a list of questions following each reading selection, to encourage analysis and spark discussion, and a third appendix, with suggested writing assignments.

While students will find many good models of argument in these pages, *Reading Matters* aims to be more than a collection of models, aspiring instead to inform, inspire, and provoke, to provide new ways of thinking, and to help produce intelligent college writing—writing that matters.

*B*orn *and raised in Harlem, James Baldwin (1924–1987) educated himself by reading voraciously throughout his adolescence. After a brief evangelical ministry, Baldwin left Harlem and eventually sailed to Europe, settling finally in Paris, where he lived most of his adult life. In most of his writing, with brutal honesty and a keen political consciousness, Baldwin attacks ill-conceived social programs and paternalistic hypocrisy for perpetuating racial inequality. Rejecting the ghetto as one great failed project in* Fifth Avenue, Uptown: A Letter from Harlem, *from his essay collection* Nobody Knows My Name (1961), *Baldwin reminds us, "in the face of one's victim, one sees oneself."*

Fifth Avenue, Uptown: A Letter from Harlem

James Baldwin

There is a housing project standing now where the house in which we grew up once stood, and one of those stunted city trees is snarling where our doorway used to be. This is on the rehabilitated side of the avenue. The other side of the avenue—for progress takes time—has not been rehabilitated yet and it looks exactly as it looked in the days when we sat with our noses pressed against the windowpane, longing to be allowed to go "across the street." The grocery store which gave us credit is still there, and there can be no doubt that it is still giving credit. The people in the project certainly need it—far more, indeed, than they ever needed the project. The last time I passed by, the Jewish proprietor was still standing among his shelves, looking sadder and heavier but scarcely any older. Farther down the block stands the shoe-repair store in which our shoes were repaired until reparation became impossible and in which, then, we bought all our "new" ones. The Negro proprietor is still in the window, head down, working at the leather.

These two, I imagine, could tell a long tale if they would (perhaps they would be glad to if they could), having watched so many, for so long, struggling in the fishhooks, the barbed wire, of this avenue.

The avenue is elsewhere the renowned and elegant Fifth. The area I am describing, which, in today's gang parlance, would be called "the turf," is bounded by Lenox Avenue on the west, the Harlem River on the east, 135th Street on the north, and 130th Street on the south. We never lived beyond these boundaries; this is where we grew up. Walking along 145th Street—for example—familiar as it is, and similar, does not have the same impact because I did not know any of the people on the block. But when I turn east on 131st Street and Lenox Avenue, there is first a soda-pop joint, then a shoeshine "parlor," then a grocery store, then a dry cleaner's, then the houses. All along the street there are people who watched me grow up, people who grew up with me, people I watched grow up along with my brothers and sisters; and, sometimes in my arms, sometimes underfoot, sometimes at my shoulder—or on it—their children, a riot, a forest of children, who include my nieces and nephews.

When we reach the end of this long block, we find ourselves on wide, filthy, hostile Fifth Avenue, facing that project which hangs over the avenue like a monument to the folly, and the cowardice, of good intentions. All along the block, for anyone who knows it, are immense human gaps, like craters. These gaps are not created merely by those who have moved away, inevitably into some other ghetto, or by those who have risen, almost always into a greater capacity for self-loathing and self-delusion; or yet by those who, by whatever means—World War II, the Korean War, a policeman's gun or billy, a gang war, a brawl, madness, an overdose of heroin, or, simply, unnatural exhaustion—are dead. I am talking about those who are left, and I am talking principally about the young. What are they doing? Well, some, a minority, are fanatical churchgoers, members of the more extreme of the Holy Roller sects. Many, many more are "moslems," by affiliation or sympathy, that is to say that they are united by nothing more—and nothing less—than a hatred of the white world and all its works. They are present, for example, at every Buy Black street-corner meeting—meetings in which the speaker urges his hearers to cease trading with white men and establish a separate economy. Neither the speaker nor his hearers can possibly do this, of course, since Negroes do not own General Motors or RCA or the A & P, nor, indeed, do they own more than a wholly insufficient fraction of anything else in Harlem (those who do own anything are more interested in their profits than in their fellows). But these meetings nevertheless keep alive in the participators a certain pride of bitterness without which, however futile this bitterness may be, they could scarcely remain alive at all. Many have given up. They stay home and watch the TV screen, living on the earnings of their parents, cousins, brothers, or uncles, and only leave the house to go to the movies or to the nearest bar. "How're you making it?" one may ask, running into them along the block, or in the bar. "Oh, I'm TV-ing it"; with the saddest, sweetest, most shamefaced of smiles, and from a great distance. This distance one is compelled to respect; anyone who has traveled so far will not easily be dragged again into the world. There are further retreats, of course, than the TV screen or the bar. There are those who are simply sitting on their stoops, "stoned," animated for a moment only, and hideously, by the approach of someone who may lend them the money for a "fix." Or by the approach of someone from whom they can purchase it, one of the shrewd ones, on the way to prison or just coming out.

And the others, who have avoided all of these deaths, get up in the morning and go downtown to meet "the man." They work in the white man's world all day and come home in the evening to this fetid block. They struggle to instill in their children some private sense of honor or dignity which will help the child survive. This means, of course, that they must struggle, stolidly, incessantly, to keep this sense alive in themselves, in spite of the insults, the indifference, and the cruelty they are certain to encounter in their working day. They patiently browbeat the landlord into fixing the heat, the plaster, the plumbing; this demands prodigious patience; nor is patience usually enough. In trying to make their hovels habitable, they are perpetually throwing good money after bad. Such frustration, so long endured, is driving many strong, admirable men and women whose only crime is color to the very gates of paranoia.

One remembers them from another time—playing handball in the playground, going to church, wondering if they were going to be promoted at school. One remembers them going off to war—gladly, to escape this block. One remembers their return. Perhaps one remembers their wedding day. And one sees where the girl is now—vainly looking for salvation from some other embittered, trussed, and struggling boy—and sees the all-but-abandoned children in the streets.

Now I am perfectly aware that there are other slums in which white men are fighting for their lives, and mainly losing. I know that blood is also flowing through those streets and that the human damage there is incalculable. People are continually pointing out to me the wretchedness of white people in order to console me for the wretchedness of blacks. But an itemized account of the American failure does not console me and it should not console anyone else. That hundreds of thousands of white people are living, in effect, no better than the "niggers" is not a fact to be regarded with complacency. The social and moral bankruptcy suggested by this fact is of the bitterest, most terrifying kind.

The people, however, who believe that this democratic anguish has some consoling value are always pointing out that So-and-So, white, and So-and-So, black, rose from the slums into the big time. The existence—the public existence—of, say, Frank Sinatra and Sammy Davis, Jr. proves to them that America is still the land of opportunity and that inequalities vanish before the determined will. It proves nothing of the sort. The determined will is rare—at the moment, in this country, it is unspeakably rare—and the inequalities suffered by the many are in no way justified by the rise of a few. A few have always risen—in every country, every era, and in the teeth of regimes which can by no stretch of the imagination be thought of as free. Not all of these people, it is worth remembering, left the world better than they found it. The determined will is rare, but it is not invariably benevolent. Furthermore, the American equation of success with the big times reveals an awful disrespect for human life and human achievement. This equation has placed our cities among the most dangerous in the world and has placed our youth among the most empty and most bewildered. The situation of our youth is not mysterious. Children have never been very good at listening to their elders, but they have never failed to imitate them. They must, they have no other models. That is exactly what our children are doing. They are imitating our immorality, our disrespect for the pain of others.

All other slum dwellers, when the bank account permits it, can move out of the slum and vanish altogether from the eye of persecution. No Negro in this country has ever made that much money and it will be a long time before any Negro does. The Negroes in Harlem, who have no money, spend what they have on such gimcracks as they are sold. These include "wider" TV screens, more "faithful" hi-fi sets, more "powerful" cars, all of which, of course, are obsolete long before they are paid for. Anyone who has ever struggled with poverty knows how extremely expensive it is to be poor; and if one is a member of a captive population, economically speaking, one's feet have simply been placed on the treadmill forever. One is victimized, economically, in a thousand ways—rent, for example, or car insurance. Go shopping one day in Harlem—for anything—and compare Harlem prices and quality with those downtown.

The people who have managed to get off this block have only got as far as a more respectable ghetto. This respectable ghetto does not even have the advantages of the disreputable one—friends, neighbors, a familiar church, and friendly tradesmen; and it is not, moreover, in the nature of any ghetto to remain respectable long. Every Sunday, people who have left the block take the lonely ride back, dragging their increasingly discontented children with them. They spend the day talking, not always with words, about the trouble they've seen and the trouble—one must watch their eyes as they watch their children—they are only too likely to see. For children do not like ghettos. It takes them nearly no time to discover exactly why they are there.

The projects in Harlem are hated. They are hated almost as much as policemen, and this is saying a great deal. And they are hated for the same reason: both reveal, unbearably, the real attitude of the white world, no matter how many liberal speeches are made, no matter how many lofty editorials are written, no matter how many civil-rights commissions are set up.

The projects are hideous, of course, there being a law, apparently respected throughout the world, that popular housing shall be as cheerless as a prison. They are lumped all over Harlem, colorless, bleak, high, and revolting. The wide windows look out on Harlem's invincible and indescribable squalor: the Park Avenue railroad tracks, around which, about forty years ago, the present dark community began; the unrehabilitated houses, bowed down, it would seem, under the great weight of frustration and bitterness they contain; the dark, the ominous schoolhouses from which the child may emerge maimed, blinded, hooked, or enraged for life; and the churches, churches, block upon block of churches, niched in the walls like cannons in the walls of a fortress. Even if the administration of the projects were not so insanely humiliating (for example: one must report raises in salary to the management, which will then eat up the profit by raising one's rent; the management has the right to know who is staying in your apartment; the management can ask you to leave, at their discretion), the projects would still be hated because they are an insult to the meanest intelligence.

Harlem got its first private project, Riverton[1]—which is now, naturally, a slum—about twelve years ago because at that time Negroes were not allowed to live in Stuyvesant Town. Harlem watched Riverton go up, therefore, in the most violent bitterness of spirit, and hated it long before the builders arrived. They began hating it at about the time people began moving out of their condemned houses to make room for this additional proof of how thoroughly the white world despised them. And they had scarcely moved in, naturally, before they began smashing windows, defacing walls, urinating in the elevators, and fornicating in the playgrounds. Liberals, both white and black, were appalled at the spectacle. I was appalled by the liberal innocence—or cynicism, which comes out in practice as much the same thing. Other people were delighted to be able to point to proof positive that nothing could be done to better the lot of the colored people. They were, and are, right in

4

one respect: that nothing can be done as long as they are treated like colored people. The people in Harlem know they are living there because white people do not think they are good enough to live anywhere else. No amount of "improvement" can sweeten this fact. Whatever money is now being earmarked to improve this, or any other ghetto, might as well be burnt. A ghetto can be improved in one way only: out of existence.

Similarly, the only way to police a ghetto is to be oppressive. None of the Police Commissioner's men, even with the best will in the world, have any way of understanding the lives led by the people they swagger about in twos and threes controlling. Their very presence is an insult, and it would be, even if they spent their entire day feeding gumdrops to children. They represent the force of the white world, and that world's real intentions are, simply, for that world's criminal profit and ease, to keep the black man corralled up here, in his place. The badge, the gun in the holster, and the swinging club make vivid what will happen should his rebellion become overt. Rare, indeed, is the Harlem citizen, from the most circumspect church members to the most shiftless adolescent, who does not have a long tale to tell of police incompetence, injustice, or brutality. I myself have witnessed and endured it more than once. The businessmen and racketeers also have a story. And so do the prostitutes. (And this is not, perhaps, the place to discuss Harlem's very complex attitude toward black policemen, nor the reasons, according to Harlem, that they are nearly all downtown.)

It is hard, on the other hand, to blame the policeman, blank, good-natured, thoughtless, and insuperably innocent, for being such a perfect representative of the people he serves. He, too, believes in good intentions and is astounded and offended, when they are not taken for the deed. He has never, himself, done anything for which to be hated—which of us has?—and yet he is facing, daily and nightly, people who would gladly see him dead, and he knows it. There is no way for him not to know it: there are few things under heaven more unnerving than the silent, accumulating contempt and hatred of a people. He moves through Harlem, therefore, like an occupying soldier in a bitterly hostile country; which is precisely what, and where, he is and is the reason he walks in twos and threes. And he is not the only one who knows why he is always in company; the people who are watching him know why, too. Any street meeting, sacred or secular, which he and his colleagues uneasily cover has as its explicit or implicit burden the cruelty and injustice of the white domination. And these days, of course, in terms increasingly vivid and jubilant, it speaks of the end of that domination. The white policeman standing on a Harlem street corner finds himself at the very center of the revolution now occurring in the world. He is not prepared for it—naturally, nobody is—and, what is possibly much more to the point, he is exposed, as few white people are, to the anguish of the black people around him. Even if he is gifted with the merest mustard grain of imagination, something must seep in. He cannot avoid observing that some of the children, in spite of their color, remind him of children he has known and loved, perhaps even of his own children. He knows that he certainly does not want *his* children living this way. He can retreat from his uneasiness in only one direction: into a callousness which very shortly becomes second nature. He becomes more callous, the population becomes more hostile, the situation grows more tense, and the police force is increased. One day, to everyone's astonishment, someone

drops a match in the powder keg and everything blows up. Before the dust has settled or the blood congealed, editorials, speeches, and civil rights commissions are
loud in the land, demanding to know what happened. What happened is that
Negroes want to be treated like men.

Negroes want to be treated like men: a perfectly straightforward statement, containing only seven words. People who have mastered Kant, Hegel, Shakespeare,
Marx, Freud, and the Bible find this statement utterly impenetrable. The idea seems
to threaten profound, barely conscious assumptions. A kind of panic paralyzes
their features, as though they found themselves trapped on the edge of a steep
place. I once tried to describe to a very well-known American intellectual the conditions among Negroes in the South. My recital disturbed him and made him indignant; and he asked me in perfect innocence, "Why don't all the Negroes in the
South move North?" I tried to explain what *has* happened, unfailingly, whenever
a significant body of Negroes move North. They do not escape Jim Crow: they
merely encounter another, not-less-deadly variety. They do not move to Chicago,
they move to the South Side; they do not move to New York, they move to Harlem.
The pressure within the ghetto causes the ghetto walls to expand, and this expansion is always violent. White people hold the line as long as they can, and in as many
ways as they can, from verbal intimidation to physical violence. But inevitably the
border which has divided the ghetto from the rest of the world falls into the hands
of the ghetto. The white people fall back bitterly before the black horde; the landlords make a tidy profit by raising the rent, chopping up the rooms, and all but dispensing with the upkeep; and what has once been a neighborhood turns into a
"turf." This is precisely what happened when the Puerto Ricans arrived in their
thousands—and the bitterness thus caused is, as I write, being fought out all up and
down those streets.

Northerners indulge in an extremely dangerous luxury. They seem to feel that
because they fought on the right side during the Civil War, and won, they have
earned the right merely to deplore what is going on in the South, without taking
any responsibility for it; and that they can ignore what is happening in Northern
cities because what is happening in Little Rock or Birmingham is worse. Well, in
the first place, it is not possible for anyone who has not endured both to know
which is "worse." I know Negroes who prefer the South and white Southerners,
because "At least there, you haven't got to play any guessing games!" The guessing
games referred to have driven more than one Negro into the narcotics ward, the
madhouse, or the river. I know another Negro, a man very dear to me, who says,
with conviction and with truth, "The spirit of the South is the spirit of America."
He was born in the North and did his military training in the South. He did not,
as far as I can gather, find the South "worse"; he found it, if anything, all too
familiar. In the second place, though, even if Birmingham *is* worse, no doubt Johan-
nesburg, South Africa, beats it by several miles, and Buchenwald was one of the
worst things that ever happened in the entire history of the world. The world has
never lacked for horrifying examples; but I do not believe that these examples are
meant to be used as justification for our own crimes. This perpetual justification
empties the heart of all human feeling. The emptier our hearts become, the greater
will be our crimes. Thirdly, the South is not merely an embarrassingly backward

region, but a part of this country, and what happens there concerns every one of us.

As far as the color problem is concerned, there is but one great difference between the Southern white and the Northerner: the Southerner remembers, historically and in his own psyche, a kind of Eden in which he loved black people and they loved him. Historically, the flaming sword laid across this Eden is the Civil War. Personally, it is the Southerner's sexual coming of age, when, without any warning, unbreakable taboos are set up between himself and his past. Everything, thereafter, is permitted him except the love he remembers and has never ceased to need. The resulting, indescribable torment affects every Southern mind and is the basis of the Southern hysteria.

None of this is true for the Northerner. Negroes represent nothing to him personally, except, perhaps, the dangers of carnality. He never sees Negroes. Southerners see them all the time. Northerners never think about them whereas Southerners are never really thinking of anything else. Negroes are, therefore, ignored in the North and are under surveillance in the South, and suffer hideously in both places. Neither the Southerner nor the Northerner is able to look on the Negro simply as a man. It seems to be indispensable to the national self-esteem that the Negro be considered either as a kind of ward (in which case we are told how many Negroes, comparatively, bought Cadillacs last year and how few, comparatively, were lynched), or as a victim (in which case we are promised that he will never vote in our assemblies or go to school with our kids). They are two sides of the same coin and the South will not change—*cannot* change—until the North changes. The country will not change until it reexamines itself and discovers what it really means by freedom. In the meantime, generations keep being born, bitterness is increased by incompetence, pride, and folly, and the world shrinks around us.

It is a terrible, and inexorable, law that one cannot deny the humanity of another without diminishing one's own: in the face of one's victim, one sees oneself. Walk through the streets of Harlem and see what we, this nation, have become.

Endnote

1. The inhabitants of Riverton were much embittered by this description; they have, apparently, forgotten how their project came into being; and have repeatedly informed me that I cannot possibly be referring to Riverton, but to another housing project which is directly across the street. It is quite clear, I think, that I have no interest in accusing any individuals or families of the depredations herein described: but neither can I deny the evidence of my own eyes. Nor do I blame anyone in Harlem for making the best of a dreadful bargain. But anyone who lives in Harlem and imagines that he has *not* struck this bargain, or that what he takes to be his status (in whose eyes?) protects him against the common pain, demoralization, and danger, is simply self deluded. [author's note]

Questions for Reading and Analysis

1. What is the significance of Baldwin's title?

2. Cite examples from the essay that reveal Baldwin's intended audience.

3. How does the tone and mood shift in the second section of the essay (at paragraph 11)?

4. Baldwin points to not only the failure but the immorality of the American Dream. Does he support his argument? Is it convincing?

5. What does Baldwin mean when he writes, "in the face of one's victim, one sees oneself"?

*S*hannon Bell, a "heavily tattooed woman," explores American tattoo culture, arguing that, for some, the act of getting tattooed is more important than the image in the tattoo. The subversive act and its permanent mark reflect an individual's commitment to "live in truth for eternity." Bell's article was published in the Summer 1999 issue of Journal of American Culture.

Tattooed: A Participant Observer's Exploration of Meaning

Shannon Bell

As a heavily tattooed woman, the depth, complexity and variation of meaning ascribed to tattoos fascinate me. This essay will explore this variation through a discussion of the subculture of tattooed people and the relationship of tattoos to identity. Although the scope of this paper can only scratch the surface of the meaning associated with tattoos, I hope to be able to shed some light on these interpretations through my fifteen years of living with tattoos and tattooed people. I am primarily concerned with American and Western tattoo culture, since aboriginal tattooing has been covered extensively in the anthropological literature and for other reasons which will become clear through the course of this essay. I will begin my discussion with a brief history and overview of tattooing in different cultures to put this intriguing and complex American subculture into context.

Contextual Background

Tattooing has been widely documented in numerous ancient and aboriginal cultures from the Coptics to the Maoris to the Celts, from Brazil to Africa to Japan. The purpose of the tattoo (customarily done by hand, and not machine, in aboriginal cultures) is usually ornamental, ritual, or identity-oriented in nature. Many tattoos cover a large part of the body and are received during rites of passage to manhood, marriage, or as marks of affiliation, age, and wisdom (Sanders 8). In New Zealand's Maori tribes the *moko*, a facial tattoo, was a direct representation of identity, in that each family had a personal moko that was further personalized for individual family members. In this way, their moko was like a signature, which they actually used when signing documents; that is, instead of signing their names they drew their moko, which was a true representation of self. Aboriginal tattooing is generally abstract; they rarely use literal images per se, their tattoos being primarily composed of geometric shapes, dots, and lines that may have meaning to them but are not always exact representations of *things*.

One of the most artistically advanced forms of tattooing is found in the Japanese culture. For hundreds of years the practice of tattooing has been passed down from *Hori* (tattoo mentor) to student. Japanese tattoos use Japanese mythology as subject matter and are conventionally done as entire *body suits* (covering most of the body). Images are chosen from a proscribed set of imagery although artistic interpretation of the mythological characters may vary. There was a time when warriors and elites were tattooed in Japan, but currently only *Yakuza* (gangsters) and the Japanese youth, who emulate a more American style to be discussed later, take part in this practice. There is an incredible stigma attached to tattoos in Japan today, so much so that the tattooed are segregated from the rest of society and must have their own bath houses, brothels, and bars (Troy Denning, tattoo artist: personal communication 1998).

American tattooing has been evolving since there has been an America to speak of. Its Anglo-Saxon form is thought to have derived from the ancient tribes of the British Isles and is noted to have been practiced at various times throughout history by the aristocracy. As folklore has it, Captain Cook coined the term "tattoo" during his voyage to the South Pacific in 1769; he derived it from the Tahitian word "ta-tu," meaning "to mark," also associated with the sound made by the Tahitian tattoo instrument (Sanders 14). American tattooing has always been unique, which is why it needs a separate discourse from ancient or aboriginal tattooing. American tattoos are image-oriented, being primarily literal interpretations of *things,* unlike aboriginal tattoos. For the most part, American tattooed people will have a variety of images (or a single image) that stand alone against the skin, unlike the Japanese body suit that is all-encompassing and of a single theme. As a consumer society, it is not surprising that we are attracted to images of *things* and have tattooed ourselves accordingly. Contemporary Japanese youth also tend to have this collage-like, literal, image-oriented type of American tattoos, as opposed to the traditional Japanese type described above. American tattooed people have historically been military personnel, convicts, circus freaks, bikers, and other marginal people, although the current popularity has associated tattoos with celebrities, models, and the middle class.

In the following discussion of tattooing in relation to subculture and identity, I work with my belief that, although the act of tattooing may be thought to have meaning that is separate from the chosen image itself, the two are inextricably linked and cannot be analyzed alone.

Subculture

Tattoos have long been associated with the exotic "other" and are therefore fodder for imagination and use by subcultures of all types. American greasers, bikers, hippies, and punks have all used tattoos as part of their anti-mainstream adornment. Tattoos, as a visual means to separate oneself from the normalized culture, can be thought of as a "loaded choice," a choice that draws attention to oneself intentionally (Hebdige 101). Although Dick Hebdige refers to specific images, clothing, and hairstyles as signs, I believe that the appearance of *any* permanent mark on the body is a sign to the mainstream culture of one's separation, whether one meant it as such or not, regardless of the chosen image. Imagery comes into play where specific and personal identity is concerned, but, in relation to normalization, a tattoo is enough to separate oneself from society at large.

This separation from society is an essential factor in my theory about tattoos and why people get them. Despite one's affiliation with a particular subculture, tattoos are a sure way to dissociate one from the rest of society; a dissociation tattooes themselves sometimes do not fully realize the impact of. A common theme in the literature (Demello, "Not Just for Bikers"; Sanders; Hewitt) is that tattooing is a struggle for individualization in a society that is increasingly impersonal. (This dissociative individuality can be used against you, as in television shows such as *America's Most Wanted*, where a tattoo is used to identify a fugitive.) Tattoos are seen as a physical, visual resistance to the virtual (impermanent) and conservative world that we are now living in. Although I did not appreciate it until well into my 20s, I now enjoy the idea that by having tattoos I assure myself that I will never be part of the "straight" world. To use Vaclav Havel's terminology, being tattooed is synonymous with "living in the truth," one's personal truth, my truth. The tattooed lifestyle will always be resistance-oriented, overlying and encompassing other subcultures because of its basic truthful nature. The act of being tattooed is, in itself, confrontational to the status quo, an idea to be discussed further when I speak about identity.

Tattooing as an art form is also a topic of interest when considering it as a subculture. Tattooing has changed over that last fifty years from less use of *flash* (stock designs) to more use of *custom* design work, collaborations of ideas with the customer that are realized by the artist. This has transformed the tattooist from a tradesman to an artist, and there has been much discussion of tattooing as a fine art. Although I, and numerous others, see it as a fine art due to its history, quality, and need for technical expertise, I do not believe it will ever be fully accepted as such, due to the nature of the medium. "The institutions and practices, genres and terms of high art are currently categories of exclusion more than inclusion" (Willis 1). Paul Willis discusses the need for "art" to be associated with artifacts that can be shown in museums and galleries. Even more than graffiti, tattoos are ephemeral; they are not usually signed or dated by the artist; no one owns them but the wearer with whom they will disappear with death, and they are not easily displayed. (The only known place where one can see skins of deceased tattooes is in Japan's Medical Museum and only doctors are allowed to study them.) There has been one major show of tattoo artwork called *Pierced Hearts and True Love*, which was shown at select galleries throughout the country in 1995 and 1996. This was the closest tattoos have come to being recognized as fine art. Nevertheless, the fact that the images were shown in the drawing (paper) stages and not on actual people disavows the primary quality of tattoos, that the medium used is *skin*. Photos of tattoos on people, another common display method, do not do them justice either because the three-dimensional nature of the work is lost. These three-dimensional surfaces are people who incorporate the tattoos into their identity in unique ways.

Identity

As we have seen, aboriginal cultures have used tattooing to mark themselves with their identity. Japanese Yakuza tattoos can also be thought of as identity markers since one is most likely a gangster if adorned with a *body suit*. Just as clothes and hairstyles allow us to decorate ourselves according to personal aesthetics and identity, choosing how we will be perceived by others, so does the permanent decoration of tattooing.

As an introduction, Paul Willis's theory on *symbolic creativity* is useful for this discussion on identity: "Most young people's lives are not involved with the arts and yet are actually full of expressions, signs, symbols through which individuals and groups seek creatively to establish their presence, identity and meaning" (1). Being tattooed as an act of symbolic creativity in everyday life is part of the common experience of some young people; youth being key to identity formation and when most people get their first tattoos, professionally or on the street (regardless of its illegality under the age of eighteen or total illegality in some states).

Young or old, symbolic creativity concerning the formation of identity is crucial. For some, tattoos are part of this identity and these tattoos can be symbolic of many things. Many choose to honor their family members and lovers by name, display their religious beliefs (ironically, and importantly, despite scripture's words against marking the body) or their association with the military, patriotism being a common theme of tattoos especially in the 1930s and '40s. Increasingly, tattoos have become more personal, with the advent of custom designs discussed above. (An example of extreme personal identity association is a friend of mine who is named "Alien Boy" because his entire upper body is tattooed like H. R. Geiger's biomechanical *Alien* creature of movie fame.) What I propose is that the motivation behind this symbolically creative act and subsequent choice of image varies from person to person, but, to begin my discussion of meaning, can be categorized and analyzed by gender and class.

In terms of gender, tattoos, which have been traditionally associated with men, can be seen as a resistance to the common ideals of female beauty. Tattooing has long been associated with maleness because of the stereotyped imagery of tattooed people and the pain involved in the process. The subject matter for women's tattoos, however, is usually decidedly different from men's. Women tend to choose flowers and softer, more personal images and put them in places like the lower back, shoulder, or ankle. Men, on the other hand, choose more obvious places, of these the most popular being the upper arm. Men often adorn themselves with macho imagery that associates them with a group, such as the Hell's Angels, or they choose decorative but strong imagery such as dragons and the like.

A discussion of class brings us to the inclusion of the most stereotypical, macho, tattooed person, the convict: "(A) person so low in class he is almost unclassifiable." Margo Demello's *Convict Body* clearly stipulates prison tattoos as identity claimers that include group and/or gang associations. The difference between an inmate and convict, according to Demello, is based on how covered with tattoos one is, this being a direct reflection of the acceptance of the convict lifestyle and lifelong marginalization. Demello points out that prison tattoos are technically different from other types of tattooing because of the makeshift technology used while incarcerated. Professional tattoos, done in tattoo parlors or shops, use color, which is unavailable in prison, and are not done with single needles. These differences in tattoo technique and imagery set up visible class markers between prison/street and professional tattooing.

Professional tattooers are thought of as having some sort of artistic talent and are legitimized by the costliness of their time (about $80–$125/hr). These differences make professional tattooing a pastime of the middle class. Because tattooing has had historic association with the lower class and deviant subculture, Demello suggests, in her 1995 article "Not Just for Bikers Anymore" (37), that the media and middle class have worked together to tame the image of tattoos. Before tattoos became trendy, there was an upsurge in the number of regular, "normal," people getting tattoos in the late '80s. At the same time, many books and articles associated current tattoo trends with primitivism of a modern nature (Vale; Hardy, *Tattoo Time/New Tribalism*). The recurrent theme was that the urge to be tattooed was *primitive, natural, and universal*. It was, and still is, constantly associated with deep, personal meaning, rites of passage and as a key to spiritual enlightenment through pain (Hewitt 27). Although these associations may be applicable and meaningful for tattooed people of all classes, it is primarily the middle class, customers of artists, which feels the need to emphasize this aspect of tattooing. This ascribed spiritual meaning softens the anti-establishment, crude stereotype of a tattooed person and has paved the way for what we now see as tattoos becoming increasingly popular in the mainstream.

Despite this softening and popularity, I argue that tattoos will never be fully accepted into the mainstream, and to illustrate this point, I would like to further differentiate between two types of tattooed people. Corresponding with the level of dedication to the marginalized lifestyle between inmate and convict, I propose a differentiation between people who *have tattoos* and *tattooed people*. People who "have tattoos" often have only one or two, and they are usually personal images in places easily hidden from view. These people avoid the label of "tattooed person" due to peer or family pressure and the negative societal associations made with tattoos. "Tattooed people," on the other hand, have many bright or bold tattoos in obvious places, closer to the idea of a Japanese body suit in terms of body coverage. These people have decided to cross that point of no return, usually choosing to socialize with tattooists and other tattooed people within the subculture, avoiding the stares and numerous questions of outsiders, fully embracing marginalization.

In addition, I suggest that the recent co-option by the media and trendiness of tattoos as fashion has driven some people who "have tattoos" to the act. These people may not have become tattooed if they did not believe that it was fully accepted by the mainstream. Although I am pleased by the open mindedness of these new recruits, and their recognition of tattoos as identity signifiers similar to clothing, I am concerned that they are being duped into believing that tattoos have lost their stigma. From my personal experience of travel within and outside the United States, this is far from true. The response to tattoos is still very strong and differs from culture to culture and city to city. It takes a strong will and *sense of self* (identity) to withstand the blatant and piercing stares. I feel that many people swept up in the tattoo trend are not always prepared to be separated from society in this way, or may not have thought about its meaning and consequences long enough beforehand (this may explain the rise of tattoo removal services). Being heavily tattooed, even during this trend, is cause for prying questions and mistreatment from curious and overzealous onlookers. Being tattooed is still a "Freak Show."

These above differentiations are not meant to put tattooed people and their identifying motivations on a judgmental continuum, but only to highlight that they come in many forms, have different reasons for their acts and ascribe different levels of meaning to their tattoos in the social context. The theories pertaining to why people get tattooed, and the associated meaning regarding identity, are endless. In Samuel Steward's 1990 book, *Bad Boys and Tough Tattoos,* he gives the most comprehensive of possible reasons that I have found: decoration, herd instinct, narcissism, exhibitionism, possession, sadomasochism, rivalry, homosexuality, crypto-homosexuality, manhood initiation rite, masculine status, an existential act, compensation, imitation, compulsion, celebration, aliveness, non-conformity and rebellion, gang membership, fetishism, pastime, utilitarian, guilt and punishment, advertisement, sentimentality, bravado, braggadocio and wickedness, magic and totemism, religion, consecration, stigmata and the messiah complex, national and/or ethnic origins (45).This list exemplifies the complexity and depth of individual choices when it comes to tattoos.

Discussion

To illustrate the melange of material discussed in this essay, I would like to point out two common myths about tattooed people and the meaning of tattoos. The first myth is that all people who have tattoos get them for the viewer or for the "outside gaze," that tattoos are some sort of personal advertisement. I will concede that the image chosen must represent *something* to the tattooed person about themselves and that they may want *some* other people to see and interpret these images. I emphasize the *some* because, as I discussed above, many people who have small tattoos get them in easily hidden places, so that they can fit into the mainstream when necessary by covering them at work or school, and so forth. This act implies that the tattoo may be primarily a symbol for themselves and for people who are known very intimately, which may or may not include their family. On the other hand, many people with tattoos *do* seem to get them primarily for the outside gaze, choose their images accordingly, and will take any opportunity to show their skin art.

More heavily tattooed people have a harder time covering their tattoos, which may lead one to assume that they like it that way and enjoy the attention. From my experience and interactions with numerous other heavily tattooed people over the years, this is not the case. I find that we tend to wear long sleeves to avoid the attention, at least until we are comfortable with the surroundings and feel assured that we can be ourselves without imposition or consequence. There are places where it is never acceptable to uncover your tattoos: most common is one's place of employment—you would be surprised how many businessmen and women have body suits under their business suits! The most comfortable place for us is within our own subculture, where all are the same and there are no gawkers, people grabbing you and asking obvious questions like, "Did that hurt?" For all types of tattooed people, the tattoo is personal and *also* for a particular group of viewers. What that symbolic meaning is to the tattooed person may be complex or it may be simply aesthetic, which brings me to the second myth.

I would like to challenge the idea, implicated in the first myth, that every tattoo *means* something explicit in terms of the chosen imagery. This is why I have put so much emphasis on the *act* of tattooing in this essay. "What does this mean?" is one of the most common questions posed to tattooed people. From my experience, the more tattoos that one has, the less literal meaning that is intended for oneself and for others. The need for each tattoo image to be an exacting identifier lessens as you become more comfortable with yourself and your tattoos. Conversely, it makes sense that if you plan to have only one or two tattoos, there is much at stake in these select images. Years of identity, past and future, must be expressed in the images because they will be limited. Heavily tattooed people, on the other hand, are always in the process of being tattooed; the meaning is in the act, and importance becomes placed on personal aesthetics. The question is "Will it be aesthetically pleasing when I'm sixty?" not always, "Will it be meaningful to me?" Meanings change, beauty and truth are eternal. (This may explain the rise in popularity of Japanese style tattoos in the United States; they are based on standard images of mythology that can be interpreted and represented in many ways while the meaning transcends time and culture.) The first tattoos of heavily tattooed people may have been literal but often the chosen images become more decoratively symbolic as the years pass and their body becomes more covered. I see people who have many tattoos as people whose identities are evolving, a fact that they are comfortable with and a fascinating process to watch.

In conclusion, I would like to explore the further emphasis on spirituality and primitivism by the middle class mentioned previously. I believe that it may be related to a fear that the American, consumer, visually based society is superficial in nature and to the belief that the act of tattooing must transcend this lack of depth in some way. This adds another dimension to my discussion of meaning and I hope to bring this important point to light. The unique quality of American tattooing, its imagery and literalness, is a product of this surface-oriented society:

> [Surface] is a characteristic of our fast-flowing time, where every-
> thing has to communicate fast and move on. . . . Depth is a cate-
> gory that pretends to penetrate surface. . . . First impressions are
> decisive [and] surface is individuated by apparel. . . . The human
> body is not very attractive compared to a cheetah, that's why we
> have fashion. . . The search for interiority merely creates more
> surface. (Blonsky 17)

Although Marshall Blonsky is referring to fashion, it is not a far leap to the permanent adornment of tattooing. Tattooing, however, sets up a unique dichotomy of *surface-permanence* unparalleled by other forms of adornment and decoration. Clothes allow people to change their mind, follow the fashion trends, and recreate their identity in a way that tattooing does not. Blonsky goes on: "The nude . . . only creates another garment, one slightly boring after a while. All attempts at depth end up in surface" (18). Perhaps this is why we decorate ourselves, to ease the boredom of the nude, to add visual depth to the common, which only brings us back again to the external and surface that are the images on our skin.

Finally, I draw attention to the recurring question, "Is it real?" and the increasing popularity of temporary tattoos and *Henna* (Indian tattoos that wear off). Together, these observations give credence to my disbelief that real tattoos will be accepted by the mainstream in the long term, since it was quickly figured out how to solve the permanence problem. "How much did that cost?" is another frequent question which, although it makes sense in our consumer-based society, boggles me when asked in regard to something that is a permanent mark on your skin, lasting a lifetime. These various questions exemplify the fear of permanence, which is the most common objection to tattoos. This says much to me about society and the unwillingness to commit to identity and accept the consequences. To do something permanent is to be unable to take it back—it is to live in truth for eternity.

Works Cited

Blonsky, Marshall. *American Mythologies*. New York: Oxford UP, 1992.

Demello, Margo. "The Convict Body: Tattooing Among Male American Prisoners." *Anthropology Today* 9.6 (Dec. 1993): 10.

___. "Not Just for Bikers Anymore: Popular Representations of American Tattooing." *Journal of Popular Culture* 29.3 (Winter 1995): 37–52.

Hardy, D. E., ed. *Pierced Hearts and True Love*. New York: The Drawing Center, and Honolulu: Hardy Marks Publications, 1995.

___. *Tattoo Time: New Tribalism*. Honolulu: Hardy Marks Publications, 1988.

Havel, Vaclav, and Jan Vladislav, ed. *Living in Truth*. London: Faber and Faber, 1989.

Hebdige, Dick. *Subculture: The Meaning of Style*. New York: Routledge, 1988.

Hewitt, Kim. *Mutilating the Body: Identity in Blood and Ink*. Bowling Green, OH: Bowling Green State University Popular Press, 1997.

Sanders, Clinton R. *Customizing the Body: The Art and Culture of Tattooing*. Philadelphia: Temple UP, 1989.

Steward, Samuel M. *Bad Boys and Tough Tattoos: A Social History of the Tattoo with Gangs, Sailors, and Street Corner Punks, 1950–1965*. New York/London: Harrington Park P, 1990.

Vale, V., and Andrea Juno, eds. *Re/Search#12: Modern Primitives*. San Francisco: Re/Search Publications, 1989.

Willis, Paul. *Common Culture: Symbolic Creativity at Play in the Everyday Cultures of the Young*. Buckingham, England: Open UP, 1993.

Shannon Bell received her BA in anthropology from the University of California-Berkeley. After graduating from UCB, she spent three months interning at the Smithsonian Institution's National Museum of American History in the Social History Department's Costume Collection, and another month at the Oakland Museum of California through a generous award from the Region-V Costume Society of America. Shannon recently relocated to New York City to pursue her MA in Visual Culture: Costume Studies at New York University and a career in the field of Costume History and Curation, Visual Culture and the Anthropology of Adornment. She is currently a curatorial intern at the Solomon R. Guggenheim Museum for the upcoming exhibit "Armani," an examination of work by Italian fashion designer Georgio Armani, opening in October 2000.

Questions for Reading and Analysis

1. What are some of the reasons, according to Bell, that people get tattoos? Despite those different reasons, what do tattooed people have in common?

2. Bell distinguishes between "people who *have tattoos* and *tattooed people.*" What does she see as the main difference?

3. How do tattoos challenge a "surface-oriented" society?

4. Do you agree with Bell that people who get tattoos—for whatever reasons—are separating themselves from society?

5. Bell uses several sources in her article. Does she use them well? Do they help further her argument?

In this essay, which appeared in the New York Times Magazine *in April 2000, Jane Bernstein, a creative writing teacher at Carnegie Mellon University and the sister of a murder victim, reflects on the rights and responsibilities of murder victims' families in determining whether or not murderers are paroled. "Allowing victims a role in the decision about a prisoner's release is just and humane," she concludes. "Giving us the power to dictate someone's fate is not."*

Victim of Circumstance

Jane Bernstein

In September 1966, my sister, Laura, a 20-year-old college student in Tempe, Ariz., was chaining her bike to a window grate when she was stabbed six times and left to die on the pavement. My parents did not discuss the murder, so for years, all I knew was that the killer, David Mumbaugh, was a teenager, like me, and a stranger to my sister, that he had confessed to the crime and that he had been sent to prison.

We never asked what became of Mumbaugh, and maybe it was just as well, because in 1966 criminal files were sealed and murder victims' families weren't informed of parole hearings, which inmates' families were encouraged to attend. It took 24 years before Arizona passed a Victims' Bill of Rights.

That was why in 1990 I was informed that Mumbaugh was petitioning for his release from prison and invited to write an "impact statement." I asked a lot of questions about this hearing—my first and Mumbaugh's 10th. The advocate assigned to my case tried to reassure me that the procedural details were unimportant. Just tell the board your feelings, she said. Your statement will be the single most important thing it will hear. Only you can say if Mumbaugh's debt has been paid.

Can a debt be paid for murder? The wardens, cops and prosecutors I asked all said, "An eye for an eye." One official said, "Your sister didn't get a chance, why should he?" Those in the "forgiveness community" talked about forgiveness's healing qualities. Anger and hate are corrosive, they said. Use mercy to turn tragedy into "a growth experience."

Neither of these positions addressed Mumbaugh or his 24 years behind bars—years in which I had gone from being a teenager to being the mother of a teenager. What if Mumbaugh had been psychotic when he murdered my sister and had been languishing in prison for decades, no longer sick? What if he had worked hard in prison and shown genuine remorse? I had read about such a man—James Hamm—who had served part of his sentence in the same facility as Mumbaugh. Hamm had enrolled in every work program, in stress-reduction and self-improvement

18

classes, had earned a B.A. with honors, had his sentence for first-degree murder commuted and was paroled after 17 years. Could I approve Mumbaugh's release if he had served his time this productively?

I obtained Mumbaugh's file and learned that he had served his time well, if quietly. But his record was marred by certain "self-injurious incidents": in 1984 he swallowed insecticide and in 1989 stabbed himself in the thigh. So I spoke against Mumbaugh's release, citing these bizarre acts to suggest that rage still percolated beneath his placid exterior. No debate or discussion followed. Mumbaugh was simply sent back to prison.

I attended a second hearing in 1993. This time two of the board members seemed eager to give Mumbaugh a chance. Again I voiced my opposition. The gate crashed down. Mumbaugh's petition was immediately and unanimously denied.

I was chilled by my power. Regardless of my reasons, or Mumbaugh's behavior over the last 27 years, my "no" was all the board had to hear. Two months later he was found dead, more than likely a suicide.

Had the system swung too far on the side of victims? I had been mulling this question when I saw a newspaper article about Hamm. Upon his release, he had enrolled in tax-supported public law school (at the same university my sister had attended at the time of her murder) and had thereby started a bitter controversy. I phoned him in 1994 to ask if we could talk. When we met, at a crowded restaurant he was wearing a T-shirt with "Law" emblazoned across his powerful chest.

Hamm would not speak about his past, only of the moment in prison when he acknowledged the "absolute irrevocability" of his actions and decided that serving his time well was a way of paying in the only coin he had.

Was he the same person who had committed the murder? I asked. He couldn't relate to that other self. What did he say to death-penalty proponents? It was their perspective. And victims—now that we had so much power, what responsibility did he feel we had?

His expression clouded, as if my question was distasteful. "You have no responsibility," he said.

For a moment I believed him. But when I stepped away, years away, I was struck by the carelessness of his words; for only a free man can wear his guilt as openly as a law-school T-shirt.

Murder is irrevocable. When Mumbaugh killed my sister, he put a knife into my family's heart. There is no full payment for all that we lost. And yet, I am part of a society that stopped throwing prisoners into dungeons to rot, part of a culture that claims to be humane. Allowing victims a role in the decision about a prisoner's release is just and humane. Giving us the power to dictate someone's fate is not.

Questions for Reading and Analysis

1. Twenty-four years after her sister's murder, Bernstein is admitted to the murderer's parole hearings. What prompts her to say "I was chilled by my power"?

2. How does Bernstein resolve the dilemma of criminals and victims, of crime and its punishment?

3. To whom does Bernstein's title "Victim of Circumstance" refer?

4. James Hamm tells Bernstein that for him "serving his time was a way of paying in the only coin he had." Do you agree that a criminal's rehabilitation is a form of payment for the crime?

5. "Only you can say if Mumbaugh's debt has been paid," Bernstein's advocate tells her about the power the victim's family has at parole hearings. Even though Bernstein emphasizes that "murder is irrevocable," she does not think she should have "the power to dictate [the criminal's] fate." With which side do you agree?

*B*est known for his 1990 bestseller Iron John: A Book About Men,
Robert Bly argues in "A World of Half-Adults" that our society
is crippled by our inability to mature, to become adults in the way
older cultures defined it.

A World of Half-Adults

Robert Bly

It's the worst of times; it's the best of times. That's how we feel as we navigate from a paternal society, now discredited, to a society in which impulse is given its way. People don't bother to grow up, and we are all fish swimming in a tank of half -adults. The rule is: Where repression was before, fantasy will now be; we human beings limp along, running after our own fantasy. We can never catch up, and so we defeat ourselves by the simplest possible means: speed. Everywhere we go there's a crowd, and the people all look alike.

We begin to live a lateral life, catch glimpses out of the corners of our eyes, keep the TV set at eye level, watch the scores move horizontally across the screen.

We see what's coming out the sideview mirror. It seems like intimacy; maybe not intimacy as much as proximity; maybe not proximity as much as sameness. Americans who are 20 years old see others who look like them in Bosnia, Greece, China, France, Brazil, Germany, and Russia, wearing the same jeans, listening to the same music, speaking a universal language that computer literacy demands. Sometimes they feel more vitally connected to siblings elsewhere than to family members in the next room.

When we see the millions like ourselves all over the world, our eyes meet uniformity, resemblance, likeness, rather than distinction and differences. Hope rises immediately for the long-desired possibility of community. And yet it would be foolish to overlook the serious implications of this glance to the side, this tilt of the head. "Mass society, with its demand for work without responsibility, creates a gigantic army of rival siblings," in German psychoanalyst Alexander Mitscherlich's words.

Commercial pressures push us backward, toward adolescence, toward childhood. With no effective rituals of initiation, and no real way to know when our slow progress toward adulthood has reached its goal, young men and women in our culture go around in circles. Those who should be adults find it difficult or impossible to offer help to those behind. That pressure seems even more intense than it was in the 1960s, when the cry "Turn on, tune in, drop out" was so popular. Observers describe many contemporaries as "children with children of their own."

"People look younger all the time." Photographs of men and women a hundred years ago—immigrants, for example—show a certain set of the mouth and jaws that says, "We're adults. There's nothing we can do about it."

By contrast, the face of Marilyn Monroe, of Kevin Costner, or of the ordinary person we see on the street says, "I'm a child. There's nothing I can do about it."

People watching Ken Burns' *History of Baseball* remarked that faces of fans even in the 1920s looked more mature than faces of fans now. Looking at those old photos, one sees men and women who knew how to have fun, but they had one foot in Necessity. Walk down a European street these days and you will see that American faces stand out for their youthful and naive look. Some who are 50 look 30. Part of this phenomenon is good nutrition and exercise, but part of it is that we are losing our ability to mature.

Perhaps one-third of our society has developed these new sibling qualities. The rest of us are walking in that direction. When we all arrive there may be no public schools at all, nor past paradigms, because only people one's own age will be worth listening to.

We know that the paternal society had an elaborate and internally consistent form with authoritative father reflected upward to the strong community leader and beyond him to the father god up among the stars, which were also arranged in hierarchical levels, called "the seven heavens." Children imitated adults and were often far too respectful for their own good to authorities of all kinds. However, they learned in school the adult ways of talking, writing, and thinking. For some, the home was safe, and the two-parent balance gave them maximum possibility for growth; for others, the home was a horror of beatings, humiliation, and sexual abuse, and school was the only safe place. The teaching at home and in school encouraged religion, memorization, ethics, and discipline, but resolutely kept hidden the historical brutalities of the system.

Our succeeding sibling society, in a relatively brief time, has taught itself to be internally consistent in a fairly thorough way. The teaching is that no one is superior to anyone else: high culture is to be destroyed, and business leaders look sideways to the other business leaders. The sibling society prizes a state of half-adulthood in which repression, discipline, and the Indo-European, Islamic, Hebraic impulse-control system are jettisoned. The parents regress to become more like children, and the children, through abandonment, are forced to become adults too soon, and never quite make it. There's an impulse to set children adrift on their own. The old (in the form of crones, elders, ancestors, grandmothers and grandfathers) are thrown away and the young (in the form of street children in South America, or latchkey children in the suburbs of this country, or poor children in the inner city) are thrown away.

When I first began to write about this subject, I found it hard to understand why a society run by adolescents should show so much disregard for children who are, in the mass, worse off under Bill Clinton than they were under Theodore Roosevelt or Warren Harding. And yet, in an actual family, adolescents do not pay much attention to the little ones or to the very old. Newt Gingrich's Contract with America is adolescent.

The deepening rage of the unparented is becoming a mark of the sibling society. Of course, some children in our society feel well parented, and there is much adequate parenting; but there is also a new rage. A man said to me, "Having made it to the one-parent family, we are now on our way toward the zero-parent family."

The actual wages of working-class and middle-class parents have fallen significantly since 1972, so that often both parents work, one parent the day shift, another at night; family meals, talks, reading together no longer take place.

What the young need—stability, presence, attention, advice, good psychic food, unpolluted stories—is exactly what the sibling society won't give them. As we look at the crumbling schools, the failure to protect students from guns, the cutting of funds for Head Start and breakfasts for poor children, cutting of music and art lessons, the enormous increase in numbers of children living in poverty, the poor prenatal care for some, we have to wonder whether there might not be a genuine anger against children in the sibling society.

If we think of catching these changes in story form, "Jack and the Beanstalk" immediately comes to mind. There a fatherless boy, Jack, living alone with his mother, climbs the stalk and finds himself in danger of being eaten by a cruel and enormous giant. Jack, from his hiding place in the kitchen, "was astonished to see how much the giant devoured, and thought he would never have done eating and drinking." That's the way the rest of the world thinks of the United States.

More specifically, the boy, as helpless and vulnerable as the young ones are today, finds himself faced with an enemy much stronger than he is. We could say that the giant represents the current emphasis on greed, violent movies, and pornographic advertising. The giant is television. It eats up more and more of childhood each year. In the original story Jack learns to steal back some of his family treasures—the gold and silver coins, the divine hen, the golden harp—from the giant. But we have not gotten to that part of the story in our time. We have no idea how to steal back "gold" from the giant. Rather than keeping the children hidden, the adults in the sibling society call the giant over to the cabinet where the children are hidden, open the door and say, "Here they are!" In the sibling society Jack gets eaten alive.

Television is the thalidomide of the 1990s. In 1995 American children spent about one-third of their waking hours out of school watching television. The National Assessment of Educational Progress reported that only 5 percent of high school graduates could make their way through college-level literature. A recent 1,200-subject study, supported by the National Institute of Mental Health and guided by Mihaly Csikszentmihalyi and Robert Kuby, found that more skill and concentration were needed to eat a meal than to watch television, and the watching left people passive, yet tense, and it left them unable to concentrate.

Television provides a garbage dump of obsessive sexual material inappropriate to the child's age, minute description of brutalities, wars, and tortures all over the world: an avalanche of specialized information that stuns the brain. Even lyrics of songs come too fast for the brain to hear.

Grade school teachers report that in recent years they have had to repeat instructions over and over, or look each child in the face and give instructions separately, which interrupts class work. We know that the sort of music children hear much of—characterized by a heavy beat—is processed mainly by the right brain, which hears the tune as a whole and doesn't see its parts or question it. The brain goes into an alpha state, which rules out active thinking or learning.

American movies in the late 1950s vividly brought forward an old theme of adolescence: the impulse not to defend common projects, common stories, common values. James Dean and Marlon Brando played the roles of young men who demonstrated this rebellion, and the theme began to have an edge on it. "What are you rebelling against?" a Brando character is asked. "What do you have?" is the witty reply.

Human beings often struggle to preserve a given cultural group through the stories it holds in common, its remembered history of fragments of it, and certain agreed-on values and courtesies. A gathering of novels, plays, poems, and songs—these days wrongly called "the canon," more properly 'the common stories"—held middle-aged people, elders, and the very young together.

That most adolescents these days reject the common stories is no surprise. More often than not, they reject them without having read or heard them. When adolescence lasted only three or four years, the youths' refusal to support the commonly agreed on novels and poems did not affect the long-range commitment of the group to this reservoir; but now, as American adolescence stretches from age 15 or so all the way to 35, those 20 years of sullen silence or active rejection of any commonality, in literature or otherwise, can have devastating results. One can say that colleges and universities are precisely where the gifts of the past are meant to be studied and absorbed, yet those very places are where the current damage to the common reservoir is taking place. Men and women in their 20s take teaching jobs, and if they are still adolescent in their 30s, their hostility to the group's literature and to the group itself becomes palpable.

We know it is essential to open the cabinet of common stories to include literature from other cultures besides the European, and to include much more women's literature than the old reservoir held. That is long overdue. But inclusion, one could say, is a job for adults. When the adolescent gets hold of it, a deep-lying impulse comes into play, and it says, "I'm taking care of people my age, and that's it! My needs are important, and if the group doesn't survive, it doesn't deserve to."

What is asked of adults now is that they stop going *forward*, to retirement, to Costa Rica, to fortune, and turn to face the young siblings and the adolescents—the thousands of young siblings we see around us. Many of these siblings are remarkable and seem to have a kind of emotional knowledge that is far older than they are. Some have sharper intuitions into human motives and people's relationships with each other than any of us had at that age. Some who expect to die early—as many do—see with a brilliant clarity into the dramas taking place all around them.

One can imagine a field with the adolescents on one side of a line drawn on the earth and adults on the other side looking into their eyes. The adult in our time is asked to reach his or her hand across the line and pull the youth into adulthood. That means of course that the adults will have to decide what genuine adulthood is. If the adults do not turn and walk up to this line and help pull the adolescents over, the adolescents will stay exactly where they are for another 20 or 30 years. If we don't turn to face the young ones, their detachment machines, which are louder and more persistent than ours, will say, "I am not a part of this family," and they will kill any relationship with their parents. The parents have to know that.

During the paternal society, there were "representatives" of the adult community: highly respected grade school and high school teachers, strong personalities of novels and epics, admired presidents and senators, Eleanor Roosevelts and Madame Curies, priests untouched by scandal, older men and women in each community, both visible and capable of renunciation, who drew young people over the line by their very example, But envy and the habit of ingratitude have ended all that.

The hope lies in the longing we have to be adults. If we take an interest in younger ones by helping them find a mentor, by bringing them along to adult activities, by giving attention to young ones who aren't in our family at all, then our own feeling of being adult will be augmented, and adulthood might again appear to be a desirable state for many young ones.

In the sibling society, as a result of the enormous power of the leveling process, few adults remain publicly visible as models. Because they are invisible, the very idea of the adult has fallen into confusion. As ordinary adults, we have to ask ourselves, in a way that people 200 years ago did not, what an adult is. I have to ask myself what I have found out in my intermittent, poem-ridden attempts to become an adult. Someone who has succeeded better than I could name more qualities of the adult than I will, but I will list a few.

I would say that an adult is a person not governed by what we have called pre-Oedipal wishes, the demands for immediate pleasure, comfort, and excitement. The adult quality that has been hardest to understand for me, as a greedy person, is renunciation. Moreover, an adult is able to organize the random emotions and events of his or her life into a memory, a rough meaning, a story.

It is an adult perception to understand that the world belongs primarily to the dead, and we only rent it from them for a little while. The idea that each of us has the right to change everything is a deep insult to them.

The true adult is the one who has been able to preserve his or her intensities, including those intensities proper to his or her generation and creativity, so that he or she has something with which to meet the intensities of the adolescent. We could say that an adult becomes an elder when he not only preserves his intensities but adds more. In the words of the Persian poet Ansari, an adult is a person who goes out into the world and "gathers jewels of feeling for others."

The hope lies in our longing to be adults, and the longing for the young ones, if they knew what an honorable adulthood is, to become adults as well. It's as if all this has to be newly invented, and the adults then have to imagine as well what an elder is, what the elder's responsibilities are, what it takes for an adult to become a genuine elder.

I will end with a Norwegian story. A man walking through the forest and in danger of dying from cold sees at last a house with smoke rising from the chimney. He sees a 30-year-old man chopping wood and says to him, "Pardon me, but I am a traveler who has been walking all day. Would it be possible for me to stay overnight in your house?" The man says, "It's all right with me, but I am not the father of the house. You'll have to ask my father." He sees a 70-year-old man standing just inside the door, and the man says, "Pardon me, but I am a traveler and have been walking all day. Would it be possible to stay overnight in your house?" The old man says, "It's all right with me, but I am not the father of this house. You'll have to ask my father, who is sitting at the table." He says to this man, who looks about a hundred years old, "Pardon me, but I am a traveler who has been walking all day. Would it be possible for me to stay overnight in your house?" The hundred-year-old says, "It's all right with me, but I am not the father of this house. You'll have to ask my father." And he gestures toward the fireplace. He sees a very old man sitting in a chair near the fire. He goes up to him and says, "I am a traveler, and I have been walking all day. Would it be possible for me to stay overnight in your house?" In a hoarse voice this old man says, "It's all right with me, but I am not the father of the house. You'll have to ask my father." The traveler glances at the boxed-in bed, and he sees a very, very old man who seems no more than four feet tall lying in the bed. He raises his voice and says to him, "Pardon me, I am a traveler, and I have been walking all day. Would it be possible for me to stay overnight in your house?" The little man in the bed says in a weak voice, "It's all right with me, but I am not the father of this house. You'll have to ask my father." Suddenly the traveler sees a cradle standing at the foot of the bed. In it, there is a very, very little man, hardly the size of a baby, lying curled in the cradle. The man says, "Pardon me, but I am a traveler. I have been walking all day. Would it be possible for me to stay at your house tonight?" In a voice so faint it can hardly be heard, the man in the cradle says, "It's all right with me, but I am not the father of this house. You'll have to ask my father." As the traveler lifts his eyes, he sees an old hunting horn hanging on the wall, made from a sheep's horn, curved like the new moon. He stands and walks over to it, and there he sees a tiny old man no more than six inches long with his head on a tiny pillow and a tiny wisp of white hair. The traveler says, "Pardon me, I am a traveler, and I have been walking all day. Would it be possible for me to stay overnight in your house?" He puts his ear down close to the hunting horn, and the oldest man says, "Yes."

We know there is a Seventh Mother of the House, who is also very small. Perhaps she is far inside the womb, or sitting in the innermost cell of our body, and she gives us permission to live, to be born, to have joy. Her contribution is life. The contribution of the Seventh Father is a house. Together they grant permission from the universe for civilization.

Questions for Reading and Analysis

1. What evidence does Bly give to support his point that Americans "are losing [the] ability to mature"?

2. Bly says that "television is the thalidomide of the 1990's." Having looked up "thalidomide," what do you think he means by this?

3. What does Bly propose to solve the problem of "half-adulthood"?

4. Bly tells several stories in the course of his essay. What is the purpose of his storytelling and how is it connected to the theme of the essay?

5. Do you agree with Bly's premise that our society is a "gigantic army of rival siblings," a culture in which there are not true adults to guide the young into adulthood?

A philosophy professor at Washington University in St. Louis, Angela Bolte argues in favor of legalizing same-sex marriage, refuting voices from the gay and lesbian community that reject civil marriage as a viable option. The article was first published in Social Theory and Practice *in 1998.*

Do Wedding Dresses Come in Lavender? The Prospects and Implications of Same-Sex Marriage

Angela Bolte

On 3 December 1996, a Hawaiian state court upheld the legalization of same-sex marriage, although the next day the presiding judge set the ruling aside pending the outcome of an appeal by the state. This ruling rekindled fears that exist regarding the potential legalization of same-sex marriage throughout the United States. To answer concerns regarding same-sex marriage, I will examine several issues. First, the concept of marriage must be defined. Opponents often argue that same-sex marriage violates the definition of marriage and, thus, same-sex marriage should not be legalized. Second, given the difficulty of defining the concept of marriage, I will undertake an examination of the features of marriage so as to illustrate the compatibility of same-sex marriage with those features. Third, I will examine traditional legal arguments against same-sex marriage for their validity. Fourth, I will evaluate Claudia Card's arguments against same-sex marriage and offer a response to these arguments. Finally, I will explore domestic partnerships as a potential alternative to same-sex marriage. Once these steps are completed, it will be seen that same-sex marriage would be beneficial, rather than harmful, to the institution of marriage.

1.

One of the most important issues surrounding the same-sex marriage debate is whether or not same-sex marriages can even exist. All too often, same-sex marriages are discounted as impossible because marriage is viewed as existing only between a man and a woman. Gays and lesbians cannot meet the definition of marriage and, thus, "same-sex marriage" is an oxymoron.

One method of providing evidence for the possibility of same-sex marriages involves recognizing what is meant by the definition of marriage. Richard Mohr illustrates the difficulty of this task by pointing out the following:

> *Most commonly, dictionaries define marriage in terms of spouses,*
> *spouses in terms of husband and wife, and husband and wife in terms*
> *of marriage. In consequence, the various definitions do no work in*
> *explaining what marriage is and so simply end up assuming or stipu-*
> *lating that marriage must be between people of different sexes.*[1]

It does seem that Mohr, for the most part, is correct. In most dictionaries marriage is defined in these terms, although at times any reference to "spouses" is dropped, but the point remains.[2] Dictionary definitions usually focus on the concepts of husband and wife and spend little time explaining anything about the actual nature of marriage.

The legal definition of marriage fares no better. Although the marriage laws in most states refer generically to spouses, *Black's Law Dictionary* relies on the 1974 case *Singer v. Hara* to express the legal definition of marriage as "the legal union of one man and woman as man and wife."[3] Since the legal definition of marriage specifically excludes same-sex marriage, the courts have successfully argued that same-sex marriages cannot be allowed because these unions would destroy the very notion of marriage.

Some courts have tried to place an additional stipulation on the definition of marriage; namely, that marriage is a vehicle for the creation and raising of children. This traditional argument against same-sex marriage is also inadequate. With the elimination of the fertility clause in the marriage laws, the courts have removed the raising of children from the core of marriage law and the ability of spouses to create children together is no longer considered a requirement of marriage.[4] Thus, there is no legitimate legal basis from which to deny the right of marriage to gays and lesbians because they cannot create children together. Moreover, if this were legitimate, withholding marriage licenses from elderly or infertile couples would also be legitimate. In each of these cases, the couple cannot create children together and, to be consistent, denying the right of marriage to all of them would be necessary on these grounds. Due to the revised marriage laws, such a position would have little, if any, legal support.

It is also unclear how the stipulation that marriage is for the creation and raising of children truly excludes gays and lesbians. Gays and lesbians are increasingly becoming parents through new avenues such as adoption or artificial insemination. Many gays and lesbians also have children from previous marriages. This occurrence is presently so widespread that some mainstream and gay media have labeled this phenomenon a "gay baby boom."

It is estimated that there are three to four million gay and lesbian parents raising between six and fourteen million children.[5] This number is especially significant if it is argued that one of marriage's goals is the protection and care of the children that exist within it. There is an expectation that children are to be protected and cared for by the spouses while a marriage exists and this is reflected in the legal process that occurs when a marriage ends. The divorce laws are devised to help protect children by ensuring that child support is paid if necessary for the welfare of a particular child. Moreover, when a spouse dies, custody of the children is designed to pass to the living spouse, thus ensuring that the children are not removed from a familiar environment.

While traditional arguments claim that same-sex marriages should be banned because the children within those families will be subject to harm both through ridicule and confusion over sexual roles, it is rather the case that children are directly harmed through the banning of same-sex marriages. Currently, when a same-sex relationship ends, no institutions are in place to ensure the protection of the children, as there are when traditional marriages dissolve. A partner who leaves a same-sex relationship is under no obligation to provide financial support for children that he or she may have cared for and supported for years. In a case where the biological parent dies, the children could be left without either parent, if the living partner had not adopted them in a second-parent adoption. Moreover, in most states the courts do not allow second-parent adoptions by gays and lesbians. Given the vast numbers of children with same-sex parents, by not allowing same-sex marriage, many children are adversely affected.

As for the traditional arguments against same-sex marriage, Fredrick Elliston states that "in the case of . . . homosexual marriage, the source of the harm to children is social prejudice" against gays and lesbians.[6] Elliston argues that if same-sex marriages were legalized, this social prejudice would be diminished. As for the second argument, that the children will suffer from confusion over sex roles, this is not necessarily a problem. According to feminist thinking, traditional sex roles are not desirable, and Elliston similarly argues that same-sex marriage "may help to combat this evil [of traditional sex roles]."[7]

Given the failure of legal definitions of marriage, perhaps sociology or anthropology would be a better source for a definition of marriage. Definitions from these areas are more informative, but do not provide a complete picture of marriage. For example, marriage is described in the following manner:

> [M]arriage has been defined as a culturally approved relationship of one man and one woman (monogamy); or of one man and two or more women (polygyny/polygamy), in which sexual intercourse is usually endorsed between the opposite sex partners, and there is generally an expectation that children will be born of the union and enjoy the full birth status rights of their society. These conditions of sexual intercourse between spouses and reproduction of legitimate and socially recognized offspring are not, however, always fulfilled.[8]

The most important aspect of the above definition is the suggestion that a culture can define what is considered a marriage. In fact, a society could define and redefine marriage as often as it chooses.

Given that marriage is a perpetually evolving notion, same-sex marriages would not necessarily have a "negative" impact on the institution of marriage. The fear of such a negative impact is seen in a traditional argument that claims that the recognition of same-sex marriage would lead to the recognition of multiple forms of marriage, such as polygamy or group marriage, and traditional Western marriages would eventually be eradicated. If same-sex marriages lead to the eradication of traditional Western marriages, there is no reason to believe that this would somehow be negative. A move away from traditional Western marriages could be positive and stabilizing for the community because all citizens would be accepted, no matter what form their marriage takes.

Another traditional argument worries: "What if everybody did that [i.e., entered a same-sex marriage]?"[9] Although there eventually could be heterosexuals who choose to marry someone of the same sex, this would not necessarily be "negative." In fact, such marriages could be used to help provide basic needs and protections for those who are unable to support themselves. Unfortunately, in our society numerous citizens do not have equal access to basic rights and protections such as adequate housing or health insurance, because access to these rights and protections is limited by financial resources. If an individual lacks the financial means necessary to attain these rights and protections, he or she is usually forced to do without or to accept a substandard replacement.

Moreover, same-sex marriages would grant to gays and lesbians the rights attached to marriage that are presently denied to them. Unlike married opposite-sex couples, gays and lesbians with children are unable to have custody automatically passed to their partner at their death. Similarly, without a will, gays and lesbians cannot ensure that their estates will pass to their partner. Without being married, gays and lesbians cannot even file joint tax returns. Finally, the right of gays and lesbians to live in the community of their choice is limited, if the community specifies by law that only married couples may purchase a house within it. The denial of such rights to these citizens, while presently legal, is heterosexist and unjust.

Same-sex marriage could be used to provide access to these basic rights and protections. For example, a same-sex couple could pool their resources and attain adequate health insurance, better housing, or simply provide themselves financial security. Presently, many gays and lesbians enter traditional marriages with a heterosexual or a friend who is gay or lesbian to obtain these basic rights and protections. Heterosexuals could join a same-sex marriage for the same reason and this would not "make" them homosexual; just as gays or lesbians who are presently in traditional marriages for similar reasons are not "made" heterosexual.[10]

Although some heterosexuals could choose to enter same-sex marriages, the percentage of heterosexuals and homosexuals would not change greatly as some opponents of same-sex marriage fear. Most estimates of the actual number of gays and lesbians in the United States range between one and ten percent. This number would most likely stay the same, although even if this number were to change, there is no reason to believe that this would be "negative."[11] If a person had not previously been attracted to someone of the same sex, the ability of gays and lesbians to marry would not alter the fundamental sexual behavior of this person. For example, with the advent of the gay and lesbian rights movement, gays and lesbians have become increasingly visible, but the percentage of gays and lesbians has not radically changed. What has happened is that gays and lesbians who had felt compelled to live a "straight" life have become more visible. If the legalization of same-sex marriage were to occur, the same phenomenon would be likely, with some gays and lesbians leaving, or not choosing, heterosexual marriages because of the more acceptable alternative.

Some might worry that by legalizing same-sex marriage, the number of children raised in such households would increase and those children would be more likely to be gay or lesbian. Given studies on the sexual orientation of the children of gays and lesbians, these children are no more likely to be gay or lesbian than other children. Moreover, it is unclear why an increase in the number of gays and lesbians would be a "negative." If those who construe the increase of gays and lesbians as negative are actually concerned about the extinction of the human race, it is unclear why this would necessarily happen. The increasing number of gays and lesbians with children illustrates that a reproductive drive exists within gays and lesbians and there is no reason to think that humans would disappear if everyone was gay or lesbian.

2.

Although society can redefine what is meant by the concept of marriage, it is possible that same-sex marriage can be accepted while retaining the key features of marriage as it is presently known within Western society. Although describing marriage is difficult, the following list of features can be obtained.

> [Marriage] is usually a temporally extended relationship between or among two or more individuals; this usually involves (1) a sexual relationship; (2) the expectation of procreation; (3) certain expectations or even agreements to provide economic, physical, or psychological support for one another; and (4) a ceremonial event recognizing the condition of marriage.[12]

Palmer points out, however, that "none of these is a *necessary* condition, and if they are logically *sufficient* conditions when taken jointly it is probably because of the inclusion of feature number four."[13]

Richard Mohr characterizes marriage similarly. He believes that marriage is "intimacy given substance in the medium of everyday life, the day-to-day. Marriage is the fused intersection of love's sanctity and necessity's demand."[14] This characterization appears adequate to explain an institution infused with vagueness. Taken together, Palmer's and Mohr's conditions for marriage cover what the partners in a contemporary Western marriage generally expect. Moreover, their conditions for marriage dovetail with the definition from sociology and anthropology, but the following reduction is possible: an adequate level of commitment between partners; the joint raising of children, if the partners want them; and love. Although this reduction can be made, it is uncertain what each of these conditions entails for same-sex marriages.

The issue of commitment in marriage is interesting, yet controversial, and upon its discussion, questions concerning both the required amount of commitment and how best to define commitment immediately arise. These questions can be reduced to the following: either a committed marriage must be monogamous or it may be non-monogamous.[15] In the traditional Western view of marriage, monogamy in the form of sexual exclusivity is an essential ingredient in all marriages. Since gays and lesbians are often thought, under this traditional Western view, to be incapable of being sexually exclusive, it is claimed that they should not be allowed to marry, because they cannot meet a "necessary condition" of marriage.[16]

Although it is unclear that gays and lesbians are any less sexually exclusive or monogamous than heterosexuals, no marriage must be totally monogamous. If the partners in a marriage choose to have an "open" marriage, this does not mean that their marriage is somehow voided. The marriage is not voided, because monogamy is not a requirement of marriage; in fact, many types of marriage are non-monogamous by definition, such as polygamy or group marriage. Moreover, with the advent of no-fault divorce laws, the lack of monogamy within a marriage is no longer even legal ground for divorce. This shift in the law may be due to a recognition of the fact that the majority of society no longer considers monogamy a necessary condition of marriage. Therefore, if neither of the partners is coerced into giving assent to an open marriage, this decision should be respected.

Simultaneously, a decrease in monogamy need not amount to a decrease in commitment. While it is the case that a partner who is "cheating" on his or her partner most likely is guilty of a lack of commitment, if the relationship is open, a decrease in commitment is not necessary. While judging the degree of commitment in an open marriage is almost impossible, one indicator of commitment could simply be the continuation of the marriage.

In fact, Richard Mohr believes that if same-sex marriages were legalized, the marriages of gay men would help to improve mainstream views about monogamy. Mohr believes that monogamy is not essential for love and commitment in marriage, as evidenced by many long-term gay male relationships that incorporate non-monogamy.[17] Instead, Mohr believes that traditional couples should look at the relationships of gay men to rethink the traditional Western model of the family. Mohr's basic position on monogamy and commitment seems correct. A lack of monogamy should not undermine commitment if the partners have agreed not to be monogamous.

Turning to the question of children, as argued above, no legitimate reason exists for preventing gays and lesbians from marrying simply because they are seen as "incapable" of having children. Moreover, nothing prevents gays and lesbians from having children; as previously mentioned, many gays and lesbians do have children. Finally, there is the condition of love. Although love is closely tied to the issue of commitment, love and monogamy are separate issues. Viewed on its own, love is probably the one issue where some agreement can be reached, because gays and lesbians can easily meet this feature of marriage.

With these partial characterizations of marriage, it can be seen that gays and lesbians can meet its features. This means that the courts should not dismiss cases regarding same-sex marriage because these marriages are viewed as impossible by virtue of being between same-sex couples. Instead, a rigorous examination of the legal arguments against same-sex marriage must be undertaken to see if legitimate legal and moral reasons exist for not allowing same-sex marriage.

3.

During the 1970s, several court cases were aimed directly at allowing same-sex marriage, but none succeeded.[18] Because of these failures, and the United States Supreme Court's majority opinion in *Bowers v. Hardwick*, no other major cases regarding same-sex marriage were filed until the early 1990s.[19] In 1993, *Baehr v. Lewin* was brought before the Hawaiian Supreme Court and the court sent the issue back to the lower courts, ruling that the state must demonstrate a compelling state interest to ban same-sex marriage.[20] In December of 1996, a Hawaiian state court ruled that compelling state interest was not illustrated.

With the state court's ruling, there has been enormous speculation as to its potential effect on the rest of the United States. In particular, it has been questioned whether the other forty-nine states will be forced to recognize same-sex marriages performed in Hawaii. A related concern is the impact this ruling will have on opening other states' marriage laws to similar challenges. Many legal scholars believe that most, if not all, states' marriage laws will be challenged and many of those states will eventually be forced to recognize same-sex marriages.

With the possibility of the legalization of same-sex marriage, many traditional legal arguments against same-sex marriages have resurfaced. For example, in discussions of sodomy laws, two traditional arguments are often raised against homosexuality. The first argument claims that homosexual sex is not "natural" because it does not consist of penile-vaginal intercourse. Connected to this argument is a second argument that claims that homosexuality is intrinsically tied to perversion because it involves a misuse of body parts.[21] These arguments can be linked to the idea of "legal moralism" as advocated by Lord Patrick Devlin. Legal moralism states that the law ought to be based on the morality of the majority of society. Moreover, if a society wishes to continue, it must defend its moral code or potentially be destroyed.

Legal moralism and its connected arguments underlie discussions of how states can avoid, through "choice-of-law theory," recognizing same-sex marriages performed in sister states. Under choice-of-law, "any time application of the foreign state's law would violate a substantial public policy of the forum, the foreign law need not be applied," although there are constitutional restrictions to this.[22] Given the wording of choice-of-law theory, the substantial public policy could simply be the morality of a given state as expressed in law. In fact, the sodomy laws, which legal theorists believe will be used in an attempt to illustrate a substantial public policy against same-sex marriage, can be construed as a legal expression of what is presumed to be the morality of the state's citizens.[23]

While sodomy laws perhaps could be viewed as a clear expression of public morality and opinion toward homosexuality, it is unclear why this method is available when applications of the actual sodomy laws are examined. Sodomy laws are not enforced with regard to either homosexuals or heterosexuals in consensual relationships and, consequently, might not be accurate expressions of public opinion and morality. Given that the sodomy laws are ignored (even in *Bowers*, where an individual was caught in the act of violating the law and yet never charged), the argument can be made that these laws are no longer a part of public policy. Perhaps these laws were once an expression of public morality, but, because these laws are not enforced, this connection no longer exists. Nevertheless, the alternative view must be examined, because the mere existence of these sodomy laws will no doubt be used to argue against the legalization of same-sex marriage.

While the sodomy laws might be viewed as an expression of public morality, the fact that these laws are applied differently to heterosexuals and homosexuals distorts their moral message. In fact, legal theorists argue that those states with sodomy laws that apply both to heterosexuals and homosexuals have a weaker ability to display a substantial public policy against same-sex marriage. This weaker ability is due to the fact that heterosexual couples in these states are subject to the sodomy laws and, presumably, some heterosexual couples also violate these laws; nevertheless, these couples are allowed to marry.

It may appear that *Bowers* allows such differential treatment with regard to sodomy laws, but this is not necessarily the case. In *Bowers*, the Supreme Court specifically held that there was no privacy right within the Constitution to homosexual sodomy, because the privacy rights of individuals are limited to the "liberties that are deeply rooted in this Nation's history and tradition," a clear statement of legal moralism.[24] At the same time, there is no explicit statement within *Bowers* that sodomy laws that pertain to heterosexuals are in violation of the right to privacy and thus violate the United States Constitution. This means that the sodomy laws ought to be equally applied to heterosexuals and homosexuals in all areas. For these states to disallow same-sex marriage because of broadly written sodomy laws "would be indicative of differential treatment based on sexual orientation and arguably would be actionable under the Fourteenth Amendment if characterized as sex discrimination."[25] This strategy would be similar to the method presently being used in *Baehr* and would be available if *Baehr* is upheld.

Some might argue that homosexual sex is inherently in violation of the sodomy laws while heterosexual sex is not, and consequently it is not legitimate to apply broadly written sodomy laws to heterosexuals. This would mean that these states should have a good method for displaying a substantial public policy against same-sex marriage, but this argument is not necessarily correct. Depending on the wording of the statute, homosexual sex need not always violate sodomy statutes. For example, some sodomy laws are worded so that only anal sex is in violation of the law. Other sodomy laws are written so as either to make all intercourse illegal that is not penile-vaginal or to make oral sex illegal. Although some sodomy laws bar all of the above, not all sodomy laws are broadly worded. Given the variation of the laws, homosexual sex would not always be in violation of the sodomy statutes. Second, the question remains as to why heterosexuals should not be punished for violating sodomy laws. It seems that if states with broad sodomy laws are concerned with the violation of these laws, they should attempt to prevent all sodomy and not just apply the laws to gays and lesbians.

Another factor that would limit the demonstration of a substantial public policy against same-sex marriage by some states, but not all, is the presence of laws that protect gays and lesbians. Most relevant are the eight states that have laws forbidding discrimination against gays and lesbians, but there are several other important laws.[26] The courts in eleven states have rejected presumption against gays and lesbians in custody cases.[27] Eight states and the District of Columbia allow custody to gays and lesbians in second-parent adoptions.[28] Finally, cities in ten states and the District of Columbia have domestic partnerships for gays and lesbians.[29] In each of these individual cases, the state would have a hard time proving a legitimate substantial public policy against gays and lesbians.

The presence of positive laws regarding homosexuality is particularly relevant when discussing legal moralism. Devlin's position relies on moral uniformity within society, but these laws illustrate that such uniformity does not exist. The law does not have a sound, uniform foundation that it can use to draw conclusions concerning homosexuality; thus, the law cannot be used for judging attitudes toward homosexuality. In addition, the law does not have a firm foundation concerning its position on sodomy for either homosexuals or heterosexuals. Most states have no laws concerning sodomy and only five have exclusively same-sex sodomy laws. If the law is to be based on the majority of society, the law ought to reflect the fact that most states do not hold any form of sodomy to be illegal. To base the law on the minority opinion that sodomy is immoral violates the basic tenets of legal moralism and, for that reason alone, ought to be rejected by advocates of legal moralism.

Moreover, as H.L.A. Hart pointed out regarding Devlin's argument, there is no way to judge if a society's morals have shifted or if the moral code has been destroyed.[30] The positive laws listed above, when conjoined with the elimination of the majority of state sodomy statutes, could illustrate that society's values regarding homosexuality have shifted and homosexuality is no longer viewed by the majority as abhorrent. This would mean that if same-sex marriage were legalized, the law would be in step with society's moral code.

Nevertheless, this does not mean that legal moralism is correct. Even if the law is in accord with society's moral code, this does not mean that the moral code is just. The moral code of a society must be subject to scrutiny, and cannot simply be relied upon to generate the law without such scrutiny. It is not enough for tradition to support or deny any right; instead, a more neutral conception of justice must be used. If tradition were enough to support the law, numerous practices, such as slavery, would still be considered just. This fact alone illustrates the failure of legal moralism.

While some states may affirm same-sex marriages, this will not necessarily occur in all states. It could be that all states will be able both to eliminate laws that protect gays and lesbians and to put the necessary legislation in place to display a substantial public policy against same-sex marriage. Another scenario could be that the courts would allow any state to bar same-sex marriage due to the heterosexist tradition that exists regarding marriage within the United States. Only real challenges to the marriage laws of numerous states can demonstrate what will actually occur.

4.

Many within the gay and lesbian community also have articulated concerns regarding the acceptance of same-sex marriage. Claudia Card voices many of those concerns in her recent article "Against Marriage and Motherhood." Card believes that while it is wrong for the state to ban same-sex marriages, gays and lesbians should not be eager to enter marriage, because same-sex marriages will create multiple problems for the gay and lesbian community. Card rejects same-sex marriage because of the possible intrusiveness of the state into same-sex relationships, and she raises four specific problems that she believes should concern advocates of same-sex marriage.[31] First, gays and lesbians might be pressured into marriage to receive benefits such as health insurance. Second, once gays and lesbians enter these relationships, they could find the negative consequences of divorce too high because they could lose some of their economic resources. Third, marriage, due to its monogamous nature, will be too limiting and will distort the actual nature of many gay and lesbian relationships. Finally, Card claims that the legal access granted to spouses by marriage could open the door to all types of same-sex partner abuse. According to Card, instead of embracing flawed traditions, gays and lesbians should create their own traditions.

The problems that Card points out are significant but not overwhelming. As to her first two concerns, these problems are not specifically gay or lesbian in nature.[32] Many of those working for same-sex marriage realize that basic benefits such as health care should be available to everyone. The expansion of such benefits to everyone, not just to those who are married, is a major goal of these activists. Although the lack of such benefits for everyone within society should be a concern, it need not be tied only to the movement for same-sex marriage.

The basic problem underlying Card's second objection is one that is not new to the gay and lesbian community. Presently, palimony lawsuits often take place when a same-sex partnership dissolves. Card briefly mentions this fact and states that palimony is problematic specifically because it both prevents a partner from easily leaving a same-sex relationship and applies "the idea of 'common law' marriage to same-sex couples."[33] Card suggests that instead of palimony or marriage, couples who want a "contractual relationship" should engage in developing a specific legal contract that defines their relationship.

Although Card may find the restrictions placed on relationships both by divorce and palimony too limiting, these legal structures serve to protect both partners in ways that individualized "relationship contracts" might not. First, for such a move to be equitable to both partners, each partner would require a lawyer to ensure that the contract was fair. While this might be a simple requirement for some, many would find the lawyers' fees to be a burden and would reject a move toward a contract for that reason. Presumably, under Card's position, if the partners do not have a relationship contract, there would be no system in place to ensure a fair division of assets following a separation.[34] Second, some might attempt to negotiate their own contracts, and such a move could easily lead to one partner unwittingly accepting an unfair contract. Third, even with a contract negotiated by a lawyer, there is no guarantee that one partner will not be taken advantage of by the other. Fraud and deception often arise in other contractual situations, and there is no reason to believe that relationship contracts would be immune to such problems. Finally, circumstances surrounding a relationship can easily change, and there is no guarantee that the legal contract that encompasses the relationship is flexible enough to span the changes or, if it is not, that it will be altered in response to the changes in the relationship. While a few relationships would not greatly change over time, it cannot be assumed that this would be true for all relationships. Relationship contracts require additional expense, have the potential for unfairness and fraud, and can be made irrelevant by changing circumstances. Most important, by making relationship contracts the sole option for same-sex couples, those who are unable or unwilling to have such a contract will lose their current protections. Thus, while divorce and palimony may have some negative consequences, eliminating these institutions would cause even greater harm.

Card's third problem regarding the limiting nature of marriage is a common concern of some within the gay and lesbian rights movement.[35] Many of those in the gay and lesbian rights movement who stand opposed to same-sex marriage worry that marriage would become even more entrenched as the only acceptable type of relationship. They are concerned that those who are at the fringes of the gay and lesbian rights movement would be excluded because they choose not to live the more "acceptable" life of marriage.

I believe that this fear of accelerated exclusion due to the legalization of same-sex marriage is overstated. The fringe elements of the gay and lesbian rights movement are excluded currently by both the traditional and the gay and lesbian mainstreams with the ban on same-sex marriage. Since these elements are currently ostracized, legalizing same-sex marriage could not do a great deal more to harm those who are excluded.

It could be that those gays and lesbians who choose not to be married will be discriminated against, at times. Single and especially young heterosexuals are often thought not to be as stable as their married peers, and are, at times, at a disadvantage because they are not married.[36] The same would likely hold true for gays and lesbians. Nevertheless, it does seem that, overall, the legalization of same-sex marriage would have a liberalizing influence rather than cause a move toward increased conservatism.[37]

The legalization of same-sex marriage would bring what had once been determined to be "other," that is, what had been determined to be separate and inferior, into the mainstream. In other words, legalizing same-sex marriage would allow one form of difference to be included in what is deemed acceptable. By broadening the definition of what is considered acceptable, other forms of difference could become more accepted. For example, the gay and lesbian rights movement illustrates this occurrence. As gays and lesbians have become more visible and accepted, many issues surrounding their community have moved from unthinkable to potentially realizable. In fact, same-sex marriage has moved from unthinkable thirty years ago to potentially being legalized. In this manner, the legalization of same-sex marriage would lead to more rather than less acceptance of difference, and should therefore be supported by the gay and lesbian community.

Finally, Card's fourth concern claims that same-sex marriage could allow an abusive partner to abuse his or her same-sex spouse easily. While same-sex marriages could potentially increase the control of an abusive partner, it is not clear that this would outweigh the potential benefit that marriage could bring to the issue of same-sex partner battering. Presently, gays and lesbians have difficulty finding help when they are in a battering relationship, for many reasons. Perhaps the main reason is the combination of homophobia and heterosexism. The gay and lesbian community does not wish to recognize the problem of same-sex partner battering, and for this reason "it is absolutely vital to work to eliminate homophobia and heterosexism in the shelter environment."[38] Although much of the theoretical groundwork on battering was done by lesbians, in conjunction with their work in developing many original shelters, these shelters are not always welcoming to those in the gay and lesbian community who need help.[39] Along with the fear and hatred of gays and lesbians that exists within the shelters, there is often disbelief that a woman could batter another woman or that a man could not defend himself against another man.

If same-sex marriages became widespread, there could be a profound effect on opinions regarding gays and lesbians, which would be beneficial for those gays and lesbians who are in battering relationships. Same-sex marriages could help to eliminate heterosexism and homophobia by elevating homosexuality to the level of acceptability. Through the legalization of same-sex marriage, gay and lesbian relationships would be acknowledged as legitimate. Moreover, gays and lesbians could become more visible due to the protections accorded to married couples.

This visibility would further increase acceptance of gays and lesbians throughout society. Attributing increased acceptance of gays and lesbians to their growing visibility does seem possible. The gay and lesbian rights movement itself provides similar evidence, because as gays and lesbians have left the "closet," there has been a corresponding increase in their acceptance by society. In addition, when at least some people are aware that someone they know is gay or lesbian, they can be more accepting of gays and lesbians in general.

Same-sex marriage could also revolutionize the institution of marriage with regard to gender roles that support heterosexism and homophobia. Nan Hunter theorizes that same-sex marriage will cause a "subversion of gender."[40] Hunter believes that statements made by opponents of same-sex marriage—such as "Who would be the husband?"—illustrate the fear that exists regarding the revolutionary power of same-sex marriages.[41] While such statements are meant to ridicule the very idea of same-sex marriages, they also illustrate the speaker's fear that he or she will no longer be able to depend on the power granted by a social category such as "husband." Hunter believes that the subversion of gender would revolutionize marriage as it is known today and would begin the process of moving marriage away from its oppressive roots.

If gender roles were eroded, heterosexism and homophobia would be reduced, which would directly benefit those who are in abusive same-sex relationships by making shelter workers more willing to recognize and help them. Thus, it is likely that legalizing same-sex marriage would have a positive impact on abused gays and lesbians, regardless of their marital status.

5.

Although Card is concerned with any type of state regulation of same-sex relationships, she views domestic partnerships as less problematic, in some ways, than same-sex marriage.[42] In this respect Card agrees with many of those in the gay and lesbian community who have turned away from marriage and have embraced domestic partnerships.[43] While Card is not truly supportive of domestic partnerships, she is mistaken to consider them as a possible alternative to marriage.

Domestic partnerships may appear to be an attractive alternative to same-sex marriage, but the benefits of these partnerships are usually limited in scope. Municipalities offering the option of a domestic partnership usually offer the same benefits to both partners and spouses of employees. Non-employees, on the other hand, generally only have access to family memberships at city-owned attractions or the right to hospital or jail visitations. Private sector businesses offering domestic partnership policies usually restrict benefits to health insurance, although sometimes they are restricted further.

Although domestic partnerships are presently limited in their scope, advocates are working to expand their coverage. Their goal is to have the benefits attached to domestic partnerships equivalent to the benefits attached to traditional Western marriages. If domestic partnerships are implemented and expanded to become marriages by a different name, no fundamental difference between marriages and domestic partnerships would exist, because, presumably, domestic partnerships would be just as difficult to leave as marriages. If there were no difference between the two practices, there would be no real method by which to distinguish them. It appears that these advocates are engaged in self-deception, in that they want the rights and benefits of marriage, but not the label.

Supporters of domestic partnerships often claim that the problems surrounding domestic partnerships should be overlooked because these partnerships could be used to generate some significant benefits. One argument claims that domestic partnerships would be beneficial because they could be used to help educate the public in an effort to "pave the way" for same-sex marriages. A second argument is based on the idea that there is a much more realistic chance that domestic partnerships will become widespread than there is that same-sex marriage will be implemented soon. By having same-sex domestic partnerships in place, gays and lesbians can enjoy some actual benefits within their lifetimes, a guarantee that cannot be made regarding same-sex marriage.

While supporters of domestic partnerships try to illustrate their potential benefits, these relationships remain extremely problematic and could potentially contribute to the unjust treatment of gays and lesbians. If domestic partnerships are expanded, these partnerships could be viewed as "separate, but equal" to marriages between opposite-sex couples. As the civil rights movement illustrates, such situations are very rarely equal. Gays and lesbians must not be taken in by possible benefits, but must examine all the possibilities. There is a very real chance that domestic partnerships could be used to sidestep justice issues regarding the treatment of gays and lesbians. If domestic partnerships were granted, any request for the legalization of same-sex marriage could be seen as unnecessary and selfish. Moreover, while there might be an attempt to increase the legal rights of domestic partnerships, such as adding adoption or tax rights, access to these rights would have to occur at a state or national level through the legislative process. The prospects for state or nationwide same-sex domestic partnerships at the legislative level are no greater than the legalization of same-sex marriage. Thus, any promise of faster access to these rights is unlikely to be realized. These problems illustrate that domestic partnerships are not a legitimate alternative to same-sex marriage and it is only through marriage that gays and lesbians will achieve the rights they deserve as citizens.

6.

While it has been shown that major changes will occur in marriage when same-sex marriage is legalized, I do not feel that this would lead to the destruction of the institution itself. While some practices that marriage supports will be affected, marriage itself will continue. The political right will argue that any change in marriage will serve to undermine the institution, but this argument is flawed. Change cannot simply be equated with undermining. If this were the case, then marriage has already been undermined. Marriage is significantly different from its original incarnation. Even in the past twenty years there have been many changes in marriage. From the elimination of fertility laws to the advent of no-fault divorce, marriage has changed, but it has not faded from existence. There is no legitimate reason to believe that by allowing gays and lesbians to marry, the institution of marriage will disappear. In fact, it could be that allowing everyone to marry the mate of his or her choice will strengthen marriage by furthering the natural evolution of this diverse and widespread institution.[44]

Endnotes

1. Richard D. Mohr, "The Case for Same-Sex Marriage," *Notre Dame Journal of Law, Ethics & Public Policy* 95 (1995): 215–39; p. 219.

2. For an example of this usage, see *The American Heritage Dictionary*, 2nd ed., s.v. "marriage."

3. *Blacks Law Dictionary*, 5th ed., s.v. "marriage." In *Singer v. Hara* [522 P.2d 1187 (Wash. 1974)], the court denied the following: The silence of the marriage statutes on this issue allowed same-sex marriage, denying that same-sex marriage violated Washington's Equal Rights Amendment, and a denial of the plaintiff's right to marry would violate the Eighth, Ninth, and Fourteenth Amendments to the Constitution.

4. In 1985, Hawaii became the last state to repeal this clause.

5. Deborah M. Henson, "Will Same-Sex Marriages Be Recognized in Sister States?: Full Faith and Credit and Due Process Limitations on States' Choice of Law Regarding the Status and Incidents of Homosexual Marriages Following Hawaii's *Baehr v. Lewin*," *University of Louisville Journal of Family Law* 32 (1994): 551–600; p. 576.

6. Fredrick Elliston. "Gay Marriage," in Robert Baker and Fredrick Elliston (eds.), *Philosophy and Sex,* 2nd ed. (New York: Prometheus Books, 1984). pp. 146–66; p. 154.

7. Ibid.

8. *Social Science Encyclopedia.* 1st ed., s.v. "marriage."

9. Elliston, p. 160.

10. Although it may appear by this statement that I am advocating the position that homosexuality is genetic in origin, I do not hold this position. The "nature vs. nurture" debate is a controversy that I wish to put aside. Nevertheless, I do believe that anyone can choose to self-define as gay or lesbian. Such self-definition is done occasionally by feminists as a means of moving away from the male community. This is similar to cases in which someone who is attracted to the same sex, for whatever reason, chooses to ignore this attraction.

11. Ten percent was the number arrived at by the Kinsey studies and is the percentage generally used by the gay and lesbian rights movement, but other studies have arrived at lower numbers. This variation in percentages can be traced to two basic problems. First, arriving at a representative sample is often difficult due to "passing" by gays and lesbians. Second, there are also conflicting opinions on how to define what it means to be gay or lesbian.

12. David Palmer, "The Consolation of the Wedded," in Baker and Elliston, *Philosophy and Sex,* pp. 119–29; p. 119.

13. Ibid.

14. Mohr, p. 227.

15. Here, I am using monogamy in its more popular usage. Strictly speaking, a monogamous marriage is one in which there are only two marriage partners. Popularly speaking, a monogamous marriage is one in which the two partners are sexually exclusive to each other.

16. This view is based on old stereotypes held by the heterosexual community that homosexuals are "sexual animals" who are incapable of controlling their sexual desires. This view contrasts directly with the stereotype within the gay and lesbian community that lesbian relationships tend eventually to suffer from "bed death," that is, lesbian relationships become less sexual with time. For a discussion of men, lesbians, and sex, see Sarah Lucia Hoagland, *Lesbian Ethics: Toward New Values* (Palo Alto: Institute of Lesbian Studies, 1988), pp. 164–78.

17. Mohr, pp. 233–36. Mohr is citing evidence from David P. McWhirter and Andrew M. Mattison, *The Male Couple: How Relationships Develop* (Englewood Cliffs: Prentice Hall, 1984).

18. The first of these cases was *Baker v. Nelson* [191 N.W.2d 185 (Minn. 1971). Appeal dismissed 409 U.S. 810 (1972)]. The court denied the following: that the silence surrounding same-sex marriage was equal to permission, the Due Process Clause allowed same-sex marriage, and that by not allowing same-sex marriage the Equal Protection Clause was violated.

   Two years later in *Jones v. Hallahwa* [501 S.W.2d 588 (Ky. 1973)], it was argued that the state's refusal of a marriage license to a same-sex couple denied the plaintiffs the following constitutional rights: the right to marry, the right of association, the free exercise of religion, and that a denial of a marriage license was cruel and unusual punishment. The court denied these claims and made the further claim that the state did not prevent the plaintiffs from marrying, instead, their sex did. The last major case in this era that attempted to allow same-sex marriage was *Singer v. Hara* (see n. 3).

19. 478 U.S. 186 (1986). Here, the United States Supreme Court upheld the constitutionality of the Georgia sodomy laws. The Court refused to include consensual homosexual sodomy in the zone of privacy identified as residing in the "penumbras" of the First, Third, Fourth, Fifth, and Ninth Amendments in the Court's ruling in *Griswold v. Connecticut* [381 U.S. 479 (1965)].

20. 852 P.2d 44 (Haw. 1993). The plaintiffs in *Baehr v. Lewin* had applied for a marriage license and were denied under the Hawaiian marriage statutes, HRS 572-1, which restrict marriage to a man and a woman. As a result, a complaint was filed stating that it was unconstitutional for the plaintiffs to be refused a marriage license solely because they were of the same sex. The Hawaiian Supreme Court ruled that the plaintiffs in *Baehr* qualified for relief from the restrictions of HRS 572-1 under both Hawaii's Equal Protection Clause and Equal Rights Amendment. The Hawaiian Supreme Court sent the issue back to a lower court in order to subject HRS 572-1 to a "strict scrutiny" standard. This means that statute would be found unconstitutional unless the state can display the following: "(a) the statute's sex-based classification is justified by compelling state interest and (b) the statute is narrowly drawn to avoid unnecessary abridgements of the applicant couple's constitutional rights"(67). The lower court upheld the legalization of same-sex marriage on 3 December 1996, but this ruling is subject to appeal.

21. Michael Levin. "Why Homosexuality Is Abnormal," in William H. Shaw (ed.). *Social and Personal Ethics* (Belmont: Wadsworth, 1993), pp. 350–57.

22. Henson, p. 553. There are limits to choice-of-law. The two main limits are the Full Faith and Credit and Due Process Clauses of the United States Constitution. The Full Faith and Credit Clause requires for purposes of regulating interstate commerce, in most cases, that sister states recognize each other's laws. The Due Process

Clause is relevant because, when a marriage is revoked, a host of other rights and benefits are revoked also and this potentially could violate a citizen's due process under the law. Although these restrictions exist, a state would not have to recognize a marriage that violated the state's substantial public policy. Choice of law in marriage is usually applied in the areas of incestuous and underage marriages.

23. Presently, only five states have exclusively homosexual sodomy laws, namely, Arkansas, Kansas, Missouri, Montana, and Oklahoma. Thirty states do not have sodomy laws and fifteen states have sodomy laws that pertain both to heterosexual and homosexual sodomy (Henson, p. 590).

24. Ibid., pp. 594–95.

25. Ibid., p. 590.

26. Ibid., p. 578. As of 1994, these states are Wisconsin, Massachusetts, Hawaii, Connecticut, New Jersey, Vermont, California, and Minnesota.

27. Jeffery J. Swart, "The Wedding Luau—Who is Invited?: Hawaii, Same-Sex Marriage, and Emerging Realities," *Emory Law Journal* 43 (1994): 1577–616; p. 1594. As of 1994, the states are Alaska, California, Indiana, Michigan, New Jersey, New York, South Carolina, Vermont, Washington, Massachusetts, and West Virginia. In New Mexico presumption was rejected in a custody case concerning a gay uncle. In Virginia, courts have both rejected and not rejected presumption against gay parents.

28. Ibid., p. 1597. As of 1994, the states are Alaska, Massachusetts, New York, California, Washington, Oregon, Vermont, and Minnesota.

29. Ibid., p. 1598. As of 1994, the states are Michigan, Georgia, Massachusetts, Connecticut, New York, California, Washington, Minnesota, Wisconsin, and Maryland.

30. H.L.A. Hart, "Immorality and Treason," in R.M. Dworkin (ed.), *The Philosophy of Law* (Oxford: Oxford University Press, 1977), pp. 83–88.

31. Claudia Card, "Against Marriage and Motherhood," *Hypatia* 11 (1996): 1–23; p. 8.

32. At the same time, it should be noted that Card's project is against marriage in general and not exclusively against same-sex marriage.

33. Card, p. 13.

34. In her proposal, Card would have legal contracts replace marriage and palimony for same-sex couples. Thus, the assumption that there would be no safety net of marriage and palimony laws for those rejecting relationship contracts is not far-fetched.

35. Paula L. Ettelbrick, "Since When Is Marriage a Path to Liberation?," in Suzanne Sherman (ed.), *Lesbian and Gay Marriage: Private Commitments, Public Ceremonies* (Philadelphia: Temple University Press, 1992), pp. 20–26.

36. For example, promotions are often granted in the corporate and academic world only if the employee is married. Marriage is taken to mean that the employee has "settled down" and is now more serious and stable.

37. It should be noted that Card holds a contrasting position. Card believes that marriage could have a conservative effect by potentially making gays and lesbians less liberal and thus more "acceptable" to mainstream society.

38. Linda Geraci, "Making Shelters Safe for Lesbians," in Kerry Lobel (ed.), *Naming the Violence: Speaking Out About Lesbian Battering* (Seattle: Seal Press, 1986), pp. 77–79; p. 77.

39. Donna J. Cecere, "The Second Closet: Battered Lesbians," in Lobel (ed.), *Naming the Violence,* pp. 21–31.

40. Nan D. Hunter, "Marriage, Law and Gender: A Feminist Inquiry," in David S. Caudill and Steven Jay Gold (eds.), *Radical Philosophy of Law: Contemporary Challenges to Mainstream Legal Theory and Practice* (Englewood Cliffs, N.J.: Humanities Press, 1995), pp. 221–33; p. 225.

41. Ibid., p. 225.

42. Card, p. 12. It should be noted that Card is less critical of domestic partnerships, not because of any benefits that can be attached to these partnerships, but because the State is less involved in their regulation and because they are more readily dissolved than marriages.

43. For a discussion of domestic partnerships, see Barbara Findlen, "Is Marriage the Answer?," *Ms.,* May/June 1995, pp. 86–91.

44. I thank Irene Appelbaum, Claudia Card, Marilyn Friedman, Larry May, and Mark Rollins for extensive comments and suggestions on earlier versions of this paper. Earlier versions of this paper were read at the Thirteenth Annual International Social Philosophy Conference and at the 1996 Annual Meeting of the Society for Social and Political Philosophy. I thank those audiences for their criticisms and suggestions.

Questions for Reading and Analysis

1. Make a list of the arguments against same-sex marriage that come from the legal/heterosexual community. How does Bolte refute each of these?

2. Make a list of the arguments against same-sex marriage that come from the homosexual community (from Claudia Card's "Against Marriage and Motherhood" in particular). How does Bolte refute each of these?

3. Why does Bolte not consider domestic partnerships a viable alternative to civil marriage?

4. Bolte uses refutation as her major technique to support her thesis. How does this compare with the "personal evidence" approach we see in essays like Lisa Duggan's "Abolish Marriage"? What does Bolte gain by her approach?

5. What is Bolte's strongest argument in favor of same-sex marriage? Why?

Wayne Booth's essay, adapted from a speech to the Illinois Council of College Teachers of English in 1963, outlines necessary aspects of a successful paper: the writer's knowledge of the subject, awareness of audience, and own voice.

Boring from Within:
The Art of the Freshman Essay

Wayne C. Booth

Last week I had for about the hundredth time an experience that always disturbs me. Riding on a train, I found myself talking with my seat-mate, who asked me what I did for a living. "I teach English." Do you have any trouble predicting his response? His face fell, and he groaned, "Oh, dear, I'll have to watch my language." In my experience there are only two other possible reactions. The first is even less inspiriting: "I hated English in school; it was my worst subject." The second, so rare as to make an honest English teacher almost burst into tears of gratitude when it occurs, is an animated conversation about literature, or ideas, or the American language—the kind of conversation that shows a continuing respect for "English" as something more than being sure about *who* and *whom*, *lie* and *lay*.

Unless the people you meet are a good deal more tactful or better liars than the ones I meet, you've had the two less favorable experiences many times. And it takes no master analyst to figure out why so many of our fellow citizens think of us as unfriendly policemen: it is because too many of us have seen ourselves as unfriendly policemen. I know of a high school English class in Indiana in which the students are explicitly told that their paper grades will not be affected by anything they say; required to write a paper a week, they are graded simply on the number of spelling and grammatical errors. What is more, they are given a standard form for their papers: each paper is to have three paragraphs, a beginning, a middle, and an end—or is it an introduction, a body, and a conclusion? The theory seems to be that if the student is not troubled about having to say anything, or about discovering a good way of saying it, he can then concentrate on the truly important matter of avoiding mistakes.

What's wrong with such assignments? What's wrong with getting the problem of correctness focused sharply enough so that we can really work on it? After all, we do have the job of teaching correct English, don't we? We can't possibly teach our hordes of students to be colorful writers, but by golly, we can beat the bad grammar out of them. Leaving aside the obvious fact that we *can't* beat the bad grammar out of them, not by direct assault, let's think a bit about what that kind of assignment does to the poor teacher who gives it. Those papers must be read, by someone, and unless the teacher has more trained assistance than you and I have, *she's* the victim. She can't help being bored silly by her own paper-reading, and we all know what an evening of being bored by a class's papers does to our attitude toward that class the next day. The old formula of John Dewey was that any teaching that bores the student is likely to fail. The formula was subject to abuse, quite obviously, since interest in itself is only one of many tests of adequate teaching. A safer formula, though perhaps also subject to abuse, might be: Any teaching that bores the teacher is sure to fail. And I am haunted by the picture of that poor woman in Indiana, week after week reading batches of papers written by students who or have been told that nothing they say can possibly affect her opinion of those papers. Could any hell imagined by Dante or Jean-Paul Sarte[1] match this self-inflicted futility?

I call it self-inflicted, as if it were a simple matter to avoid receiving papers that bore us. But unfortunately it is not. It may be a simple matter to avoid the *total* meaninglessness that the students must give that Indiana teacher, but we all know that it is no easy matter to produce interesting papers; our pet cures for boredom never work as well as they ought to. Every beginning teacher learns quickly and painfully that nothing works with all students, and that on bad days even the most promising ideas work with nobody.

As I try to sort out the various possible cures for those batches of boredom—in ink, double-spaced, on one side of the sheet, only, please—I find them falling into three groups: efforts to give the students a sharper sense of writing to an audience, efforts to give them some substance to express, and efforts to improve their habits of observation and of approach to their task—what might be called improving their mental personalities.

This classification, both obvious and unoriginal, is a useful one not only because it covers—at least I hope it does—all of our efforts to improve what our students can do but also because it reminds us that no one of the three is likely to work unless it is related to each of the others. In fact each of the three types of cure—"develop an awareness of audience," "give them something to say," and "enliven their writing personalities"—threatens us with characteristic dangers and distortions; all three together are indispensable to any lasting cure.

Perhaps the most obvious omission in that Indiana teacher's assignments is all sense of an audience to be persuaded, of a serious rhetorical purpose to be achieved. One tempting cure for this omission is to teach them to put a controversial edge on what they say. So we ask them to write a three-page paper arguing that China should be allowed into the UN or that women are superior to men or that American colleges are failing in their historic task. Then we are surprised when the papers turn out to be as boring as ever. The papers on Red China are full of abstract pomposities that the students themselves obviously do not understand or care about, since they have gleaned them in a desperate dash through the most readily available sources listed in the *Readers' Guide*. Except for the rare student who has some political background and awareness, and who thus might have written on the subject anyway, they manage to convey little more than their resentment at the assignment and their boredom in carrying it out. One of the worst batches of papers I ever read came out of a good idea we had at Earlham College for getting the whole student body involved in controversial discussion about world affairs. We required them to read Barbara Ward's *Five Ideas that Change the World;* we even had Lady Jackson[2] come to the campus and talk to everyone about her concern for the backward nations. The papers, to our surprise, were a discouraging business. We found ourselves in desperation collecting the boners that are always a sure sign, when present in great numbers, that students are thoroughly disengaged. "I think altruism is all right, so long as we practice it in our own interest." "I would be willing to die for anything fatal." "It sure is a doggie dog world."

It is obvious what had gone wrong: though we had ostensibly given the student a writing purpose, it had not become *his* purpose, and he was really no better off, perhaps worse, than if we had him writing about, say, piccolos or pizza. We might be tempted in revulsion from such overly ambitious failures to search for controversy in the students' own mundane lives. This may be a good move, but we should not be surprised when the papers on "Let's clean up the campus" or "Why must we have traffic fatalities?" turn out to be just as empty as the papers on the UN or the Congo. They may have more exclamation points and underlined adjectives, but they will not interest any teacher who would like to read papers for his own pleasure or edification. "People often fail to realize that nearly 40,000 people are killed on our highways each year. Must this carnage continue?" Well, I suppose it must, until people who write about it learn to see it with their own eyes, and hearts, instead of through a haze of cliché. The truth is that to make students assume a controversial pose before they have any genuine substance to be controversial about is to encourage dishonesty and slovenliness, and to ensure our own boredom. It may very well lead them into the kind of commercial concern for the audience which makes almost every *Reader's Digest* article intelligible to everyone over the chronological age of ten and boring to everyone over the mental age of fifteen. *Newsweek* magazine recently had a readability survey conducted on itself. It was found to be readable by the average twelfth grader, unlike *Time*, which is readable by the average eleventh grader. The editors were advised, and I understand are taking the advice, that by improving their "readability" by one year they could improve their circulation by several hundred thousand. Whether they will thereby lop off a few thousand adult readers in the process was not reported.

The only protection from this destructive type of concern for the audience is the control of substance, of having something solid to say. Our students bore us, even when they take a seemingly lively controversial tone, because they have nothing to say, to us or to anybody else. If and when they discover something to say, they will no longer bore us, and our comments will no longer bore them. Having something to say, they will be interested in learning how to say it better. Having something to say, they can be taught how to give a properly controversial edge to what will by its nature be controversial—nothing, after all, is worth saying that everybody agrees on already.

When we think of providing substance, we are perhaps tempted first to find some way of filling students' minds with a goodly store of general ideas, available on demand. This temptation is not necessarily a bad one. After all, if we think of the adult writers who interest us, most of them have such a store; they have read and thought about man's major problems, and they have opinions and arguments ready to hand about how men ought to live, how society ought to be run, how literature ought to be written. Edmund Wilson, for example, one of the most consistently interesting men alive, seems to have an inexhaustible flow of reasoned opinions on any subject that comes before him. Obviously our students are not going to interest us until they too have some ideas.

But it is not easy to impart ideas. It is not even easy to impart opinions, though a popular teacher can usually manage to get students to parrot his views. But ideas—that is, opinions backed with genuine reasoning—are extremely difficult to develop. If they were not, we wouldn't have a problem in the first place; we could simply send our students off with an assignment to prove their conviction that God does or does not exist or that the American high school system is the best on God's earth, and the interesting arguments would flow.

There is, in fact, no shortcut to the development of reasoned ideas. Years and years of daily contact with the world of ideas are required before the child can be expected to begin formulating his own ideas and his own reasons. And for the most part the capacity to handle abstract ideas comes fairly late. I recently saw a paper of a bright high school sophomore, from a good private school, relating the economic growth of China and India to their political development and relative supply of natural resources. It was a terrible paper; the student's hatred of the subject, his sense of frustration in trying to invent generalizations about processes that were still too big for him, showed in every line. The child's parent told me that when the paper was returned by the geography teacher, he had penciled on the top of one page, "Why do you mix so many bad ideas with your good ones?" The son was almost in tears, his father told me, with anger and helplessness. "He talks as if I'd put bad ideas in on purpose. *I* don't know a bad idea from a good one on this subject."

Yet with all this said, I am still convinced that general ideas are not only a resource but also a duty that cannot be dodged just because it is a dangerous one. There is nothing we touch, as English teachers, that is immune to being tainted by our touch; all the difference lies in how we go about it.

Ideas are a resource because adolescents are surprisingly responsive to any real encouragement to think for themselves, *if* methods of forced feeding are avoided. The seventeen-year-old who has been given nothing but commonplaces and clichés all his life and who finally discovers a teacher with ideas of his own may have his life changed, and, as I shall say in my final point, when his life is changed his writing is changed. Perhaps some of you can remember, as I can, a first experience with a teacher who could think for himself. I can remember going home from a conversation with my high school chemistry teacher and audibly vowing to myself: "Someday I'm going to be able to think for myself like that." There was nothing especially unconventional about Luther Gidding's ideas—at least I can remember few of them now. But what I cannot forget is the way he had with an idea, the genuine curiosity with which he approached it, the pause while he gave his little thoughtful cough, and then the bulldog tenacity with which he would argue it through. And I am convinced that though he never required me to write a line, he did more to improve my writing during the high school years then all of my English teachers put together. The diary I kept to record my sessions with him, never read by anyone, was the best possible writing practice.

If ideas, in this sense of speculation backed up with an attempt to think about things rigorously and constructively, are a great and often neglected resource, they are also our civic responsibility—a far more serious responsibility than our duty to teach spelling and grammar. It is a commonplace to say that democracy depends for its survival on an informed citizenry, but we all know that mere information is not what we are talking about when we say such things. What we mean is that democracy depends on a citizenry that can reason for themselves, on men who know whether a case has been proved, or at least made probable. Democracy depends, if you will forgive some truisms for a moment, on free choices, and choices cannot be in any sense free if they are made blind: free choice is, in fact, choice that is based on knowledge—not just opinions, but knowledge in the sense of reasoned opinion. And if that half of our population who do not go beyond high school do not learn from us how to put two and two together and how to test the efforts of others to do so, and if the colleges continue to fail with most of the other half, we are doomed to become even more sheeplike, as a nation, than we are already.

Papers about ideas written by sheep are boring; papers written by thinking boys and girls are interesting. The problem is always to find ideas at a level that will allow the student to *reason*, that is, to provide support for his ideas, rather than merely assert them in half-baked form. And this means something that is all too often forgotten by the most ambitious teachers—namely, that whatever ideas the student writes about must somehow be connected with his own experience. Teaching machines will never be able to teach the kind of writing we all want, precisely because no machine can ever know which general ideas relate, for a given student, to some meaningful experience. In the same class we'll have one student for whom philosophical and religious ideas are meaningful, another who can talk with confidence about entropy and the second law of thermodynamics, a third who can write about social justice, and a fourth who can discuss the phony world of Holden Caulfield.[3] Each of them can do a good job on his own subject, because he has as part of his equipment a growing awareness of how conclusions in that subject are related to the steps of argument that support conclusions. Ideally, each of these students ought to have the personal attention of a tutor for an hour or so each week, someone who can help him sharpen those connections, and not force him to write on topics not yet appropriate to his interests or experience. But when these four are in a class of thirty of forty others, taught by a teacher who has three or four other similar sections, we all know what happens: the teacher is forced by his circumstances to provide some sort of mold into which all of the students can be poured. Although he is still better able to adapt to individual differences than a machine, he is unfortunately subject to boredom and fatigue, as a machine would not be. Instead of being the philosopher, scientist, political analyst, and literary critic that these four students require him to be, teaching them and learning from them at the same time, the teacher is almost inevitably tempted to force them all to write about the ideas he himself knows best. The result is that at least three of the four must write out of ignorance.

Now clearly the best way out of this impasse would be for legislatures and school boards and college presidents to recognize the teaching of English for what it is: the most demanding of all teaching jobs, justifying the smallest sections and the lightest course loads. No composition teacher can possibly concentrate on finding special interests, making imaginative assignments, and testing the effectiveness and cogency of papers if he has more than seventy-five students at a time; the really desirable limit would be about forty-five—three sections of fifteen students each. Nobody would ever expect a piano teacher, who has no themes to read, to handle the great masses of pupils that we handle. Everyone recognizes that for all other technical skills individual attention is required. Yet for this, the most delicate of all skills, the one requiring the most subtle interrelationships of training, character, and experience, we fling students and teachers into hopelessly impersonal patterns.

But if I'm not careful I'll find myself saying that our pupils bore us because the superintendents and college presidents hire us to be bored. Administrative neglect and misallocation of educational funds are basic to our problem, and we should let the citizenry know of the scandal on every occasion. But meanwhile, back at the ranch, we are faced with the situation as it now is: we must find some way to train a people to write responsibly even though the people, as represented, don't want this service sufficiently to pay for it.

The tone of political exhortation into which I have now fallen leads me to one natural large source of ideas as we try to encourage writing that is not just lively and controversial but informed and genuinely persuasive. For many students there is obviously more potential interest in social problems and forces, political controversy, and the processes of everyday living around them than in more general ideas. The four students I described a moment ago, students who can say something about philosophy, science, general political theory, or literary criticism, are rare. But most students, including these four, can in theory at least be interested in meaningful argument about social problems in which they are personally involved.

As a profession we have tried, over the past several decades, a variety of approaches attempting to capitalize on such interests. Papers on corruption in TV, arguments about race relations, analyses of distortions in advertising, descriptions of mass communication—these have been combined in various quantities with traditional subjects like grammar, rhetoric, and literature. The "communications" movement, which looked so powerful only a few years ago and which now seems almost dead, had at its heart a perfectly respectable notion, a notion not much different from the one I'm working with today: get them to write about something they know about, and make sure that they see their writing as an act of communication, not as a meaningless exercise. And what better material than other acts of communication.

The dangers of such an approach are by now sufficiently understood. As subject matter for the English course, current "communications media" can at best provide only a supplement to literature and analysis of ideas. But they can be a valuable supplement. Analysis in class of the appeals buried in a *New Yorker* or *Life* advertisement followed by a writing assignment requiring similar analyses can be a far more interesting introduction to the intricacies of style than assignments out of a language text on levels of usage or emotion-charged adjectives. Analysis of a *Time* magazine account, purporting to be objective news but in actual fact a highly emotional editorial, can be not only a valuable experience in itself, but it can lead to papers in which the students do say something to us. Stylistic analysis of the treatment of the same news events by two newspapers or weeklies of different editorial policy can lead to an intellectual awakening of great importance, and thus to papers that will not, cannot, bore the teacher. But this will happen only if the students' critical powers are genuinely developed. It will not only do simply to teach the instructor's own prejudices.

There was a time in decades not long past when many of the most lively English teachers thought of their job as primarily to serve as handmaids to liberalism. I had one teacher in college who confessed to me that his overriding purpose was to get students to read and believe *The Nation* rather than the editorials of their daily paper. I suppose that his approach was not entirely valueless. It seems preferable to the effort to be noncontroversial that marks too many English teachers in the '60's, and at least it stirred some of us out of our dogmatic slumbers. But unfortunately it did nothing whatever about teaching us to think critically. Though we graduated from his course at least aware—as many college graduates do not seem to be today—that you can't believe anything you read in the daily press until you have analyzed it and related it to your past experience and to other accounts, it failed to teach us that you can't believe what you read in *The Nation* either. It left the job undone of training our ability to think, because it concentrated too heavily on our opinions. The result was, as I remember, that my own papers in that course were generally regurgitated liberalism. I was excited by them, and that was something. But I can't believe that the instructor found reading them anything other than a chore. There was nothing in them that came from my own experience, my own notions of what would constitute evidence for my conclusions. There I was, in Utah in the depths of the depression, writing about the Okies when I could have been writing about the impoverished farmers all around me. I wrote about race relations in the South without ever having talked with a Negro in my life and without recognizing that the bootblack I occasionally saw in Salt Lake City in the Hotel Utah was in any way related to the problem of race relations.

The third element that accounts for our boring papers is the lack of character and personality in the writer. My life, my observations, my insights were not included in those papers on the Okies and race relations and the New Deal. Every opinion was derivative, every observation second-hand. I had no real opinions of my own, and my eyes were not open wide enough for me to make first-hand observations on the world around me. What I wrote was therefore characterless, without true personality, though often full of personal pronouns. My opinions had been changed, my *self* had not. The style was the boy, the opinionated, immature, uninformed boy; whether my teacher knew it or not—and apparently he did not—his real job was to make a man of me if he wanted me to write like a man.

Putting the difficulty in this way naturally leads me to what perhaps many of you have been impatient about from the beginning. Are not the narrative arts, both as encountered in great literature and as practiced by the students themselves, the best road to the infusion of individuality that no good writing can lack? Would not a real look at the life of that bootblack, and an attempt to deal with him in narrative, have led to a more interesting paper than all of my generalized attacks on the prejudiced southerners?

I think it would, but once again I am almost more conscious of the dangers of the cure than of the advantages. As soon as we make our general rule something like, "Have the students write a personal narrative on what they know about, what they can see and feel at first hand," we have opened the floodgates for those dreadful assignments that we all find ourselves using, even though we know better: "My Summer Vacation," "Catching My First Fish," and "Our Trip to the Seattle World's Fair." Here are personal experiences that call for personal observation and narration. What's wrong with them?

Quite simply, they invite triviality, superficiality, puerility. Our students have been writing essays on such non-subjects all their lives, and until they have developed some sort of critical vision, some way of looking at the world they passed through on their vacations or fishing trips, they are going to feed us the same old bromides that have always won their passing grades. "My Summer Vacation" is an invitation to a grocery list of items, because it implies no audience, no point to be made, no point of view, no character in the speaker. A bright student will make something of such an invitation, by dramatizing the comic family quarrel that developed two days out, or by comparing his view of the American motel system with Nabokov's in *Lolita*, or by remembering the types of people seen in the campgrounds. If he had his own eyes and ears open he might have seen in a men's room in Grand Canyon last summer, a camper with a very thick French accent trying to convert a Brooklyn Jew into believing the story of the Mormon gold plates.[4] Or he could have heard, at Mesa Verde, a young park ranger, left behind toward the end of the season by all of the experienced rangers, struggling ungrammatically through a set speech on the geology of the area and finally breaking down in embarrassment over his lack of education. Such an episode, really *seen*, could be used narratively to say something to other high school students about what education really is.

But mere narration can be in itself just as dull as the most abstract theorizing about the nature of the universe or the most derivative opinion-mongering about politics. Even relatively skilful narration, used too obviously as a gimmick to catch interest, with no real relation to the subject, can be as dull as the most abstract pomposities. We all know the student papers that begin like *Reader's Digest* articles, with stereotyped narration that makes one doubt the event itself: "On a dark night last January, two teenagers were seen etc., etc." One can open any issue of *Time* and find this so-called narrative interest plastered throughout. From the March 29 issue I find, among many others, the following bits of fantasy: #1: "A Bolivian father sadly surveyed his nation's seven universities, then made up his mind. 'I don't want my son mixed up in politics.' . . . So saying, he sent his son off to West Germany to college." So writing, the author sends me into hysterical laughter: the quote is phony, made up for the occasion to disguise the generality of the news item. #2: "Around 12:30 P.M. every Monday and Friday, an aging Cubana Airlines turbo-prop Britannia whistles to a halt at Mexico City's International Airport. Squads of police stand by. All passengers . . . without diplomatic or Mexican passports are photographed and questioned. . . . They always dodge questions. 'Why are you here? Where are you going?' ask the Mexicans. 'None of your business,' answer the secretive travelers." "Why should I go on reading?" ask I. #3: "At 6:30 one morning early this month, a phone shrilled in the small office off the bedroom of Egypt's President . . . Nasser. [All early morning phones "shrill" for *Time*.] Already awake, he lifted the receiver to hear exciting news: a military coup had just been launched against the anti-Nasser government of Syria. The phone rang again. It was the Minister of Culture. . . . How should Radio Cairo handle the Syrian crisis?

'Support the rebels,' snapped Nasser." Oh lucky reporter, I sigh, to have such an efficient wiretapping service. #4: "In South Korea last week, a farmer named Song Kyu Il traveled all the way from the southern provinces to parade before Seoul's Duk Soo Palace with a placard scrawled in his own blood. . . . Farmer Song was thrown in jail, along with some 200 other demonstrators." That's the last we hear of Song, who is invented as an individual for this opening and then dropped. #5: "Defense Secretary Robert McNamara last spring stood beside President Kennedy on the tenth-deck bridge of the nuclear-powered carrier *Enterprise*. For as far as the eye could see, other U.S. ships deployed over the Atlantic seascape." Well, maybe. But for as far as the eye can see, the narrative clichés are piled, rank on rank. At 12:00 midnight last Thursday a gaunt, harried English professor could be seen hunched over his typewriter, a pile of *Time* magazines beside him on the floor. "What," he murmured to himself, sadly, "whatever can we do about this trashy imitation of narration?"

Fortunately there is something we can do, and it is directly within our province. We can subject our students to models of genuine narration, with the sharp observation and penetrating critical judgment that underlies all good story telling, whether reportorial or fictional.

> *It is a truth universally acknowledged, that a single man in posses-sion of a good fortune must be in want of a wife.*
>
> *However little known the feelings or views of such a man may be on his first entering a neighborhood, the truth is so well fixed in the minds of the surrounding families, that he is considered as the rightful property of someone or other of their daughters.*
>
> *"My dear Mr. Bennet," said his lady to him one day, "have you heard that Netherfield Park is let at last?"*

And already we have a strong personal tone established, a tone of mocking irony which leaves Jane Austin's Mrs. Bennet revealed before us as the grasping, silly gossip she is. Or try this one:

> *I am an American, Chicago-born—Chicago, that somber city—and go at things as I have taught myself, free-style, and will make the record in my own way: first to knock, first admitted; sometimes an innocent knock, sometimes a not so innocent. But a man's character is his fate, says Heraclitus, and in the end there isn't any way to disguise the nature of the knocks by acoustical work on the door or gloving the knuckles.*
>
> *Everybody knows there is no fineness or accuracy of suppression: if you hold down one thing you hold down the adjoining.*
>
> *My own parents were not much to me, though I cared for my mother. She was simple-minded, and what I learned from her was not what she taught. . . .*

Do you catch the accent of Saul Bellow here, beneath the accent of his Augie March? You do, of course, but the students, many of them, do not. How do you know, they will ask, that Jane Austen is being ironic? How do you know, they ask again, that Augie is being characterized by his author through what he says? In teaching them how we know, in exposing them to the great narrative voices, ancient and modern, and in teaching them to hear these voices accurately, we are, of course, trying to change their lives, to make them new, to raise their perceptions to a new level altogether. Nobody can really catch these accents who has not grown up sufficiently to see through cheap substitutes. Or, to put it another way, a steady exposure to such voices is the very thing that will produce the maturity that alone can make our students ashamed of beclouded, commercial, borrowed spectacles for viewing the world.

It is true that exposure to good fiction will not in itself transform our students into good writers. Even the best-read student still needs endless hours and years of practice, with rigorous criticism. Fiction will not do the job of discipline in reasoned argument and of practice in developing habits of addressing a living audience. But in the great fiction they will learn what it means to look at something with full attention, what it means to see beneath the surface of society's platitudes. If we then give them practice in writing about things close to the home base of their own honest observations, constantly stretching their powers of generalization and argument but never allowing them to drift into pompous inanities or empty controversiality, we may have that rare but wonderful pleasure of witnessing the miracle: a man and a style where before there was only a bag of wind or a bundle of received opinions. Even when, as with most of our students, no miracles occur, we can hope for papers that we can enjoy reading. And as a final bonus, we might hope that when our students encounter someone on a train who says that he teaches English, their automatic response may be something other than looks of pity or, cries of mock alarm.

Endnotes

1. Booth refers to the elaborately described hell of the *Inferno*, by the fourteenth-century Italian poet Dante Alighieri, and to the banal locked room in which the characters of Sartre's *No Exit* discover that hell is "other people."
2. Barbara Ward.
3. The hero of *The Catcher in The Rye*, by J. D. Salinger.
4. Bearing, according to Mormon tradition, the Book of Mormon, divinely revealed to the prophet Joseph Smith in Upstate New York in 1827.

Questions for Reading and Analysis

1. Why, according to Booth, are freshman papers often boring?
2. In what ways have teachers "taught" students to write boring papers?
3. How does Booth define "idea"? How can a student be taught to have ideas?
4. How can teachers teach students "character and personality in the writer"?
5. Why does Booth attack some *Time* magazine writers? What is it about their writing that "sends [him] into hysterical laughter"?
6. Who is Booth's audience? How do you know?

In a piece published in The New Yorker *in June 2000, Christopher Buckley takes a humorous look at the 25-year reunion of the class of '75—and at the values of higher education in the post-baby boom era.*

Reunion Schedule

Christopher Buckley

Thursday

1–4 P.M.: Registration: Welcome back! Discover that all the classmates you wanted to see have cancelled and aren't coming! Not to worry! Now you'll have plenty of time to get to know the ones you've spent the last twenty-five years avoiding!

6–7 P.M.: Drinking!

7 P.M.–midnight: Dinner and more drinking! A chance to "break the ice" by expressing joy over having travelled thousands of miles to spend time with people you no longer have anything in common with!

Friday

8–10 A.M.: Breakfast. "You'd better put something in your stomach!"

10–11 A.M.: Welcome talk by President Lootin: "The New Millennium and How Much More of Your Money We'll Need." President L. will explain what the university has been doing with the money you have already given, and why it desperately needs more despite the fact that its endowment tops seven billion dollars. During the talk, development officers will pass Bloody Marys and pledge cards.

11 A.M.–noon: Faculty lectures.

"Fund-Raising in Ancient Mesopotamia." Dr. Harmon Beedlemeyer, of the Archeology Department, will show slides of early cuneiform donor-pledge forms, which made Babylon U. the finest educational institution of the sixth century B.C.

"Sexual Potency and Philanthropy." Dr. Pashtar Singh, Professor of Behavioral Medicine, has spent the last twenty years studying the effect of giving away money on virility, and has discovered startling connections.

12–1:30 P.M.: "Puttin' On the Feed Bag!" (Lunch.) The same food you remember, only this time washed down with plenty of alcohol!

2–6 P.M.: Panel discussions. Classmates who have done better than you in their careers will discuss why, and whether it's too late for you to do something about it.

7–8:30 P.M.: "Booze Cruise!" Cocktails on board the good ship Alma Water.

8:30 P.M.: Dinner. A warm supper will be served by current financial-aid students who hate you. Our after-dinner speaker is author Blaise Waimerd, who will regale us with stories about famous authors she has slept with.

10 P.M.–midnight: "Hail! Hail! Rock and Roll!" Dance the night away at our authentic re-creation of a college mixer. This time, at the end of the evening, you're guaranteed sex. (As long as you go home with your spouse!)

Saturday

8–10 A.M.: Hangovers, recriminations, and a scathing lecture from your spouse.
10 A.M.–noon: More panel discussions.
"If Drugs Are So Bad, How Come We Had So Much Fun?" Dave (Nickel Bag) Bender leads a discussion. (Note: Space limited. Reservations required.)
"This Is It?" Dr. Jacques Rien, of the Philosophy Department, discusses why your life peaked twenty-five years ago and whether you should kill yourself
"Leave It to *Us*!" University lawyers explain the tax advantages of bequeathing your estate to the university, instead of to heirs who secretly despise you while pretending to love you.
12–2 P.M.: "Déjeuner sur Herb." The Old Quad is transformed into the French countryside, complete with cows and cow by-products. Catch up with old friends while drinking "blush" wine from the brand-new upstate New Hampshire vineyard of classmate Herb Risko.
2–5 P.M.: Seminars.
"La Cage au Moi!" Margot (Mark) Lanham discusses his transformation from shy English major to transgender night-club sensation. Don't miss his hilarious impression of Attorney General Janet Reno: "Elián! Elián! Auntie Janet, she is coming to get you!"
"We Regret to Inform." Julie Figg, Director of Admissions, discusses why your child didn't get in, despite all that money you've given. Julie will also explain why *you* wouldn't get in today, either.
"Winning Isn't Everything!" Coach Fred Putsolatso explains why the football team hasn't won a game since our fifth reunion. Jim Dimmer, from Alumni Development, will follow with a presentation showing how we *can* win—if we give the school more money, so it can recruit from among the nation's leading juvenile-detention facilities!
7–10 P.M.: Luau. Burmlee Dining Hall goes Hawaiian with (real!) sand and (fake!) palm trees. Extremely strong rum drinks will be served by Alumni Development officers, along with durable power-of-attorney instruments.

Sunday

Noon: "We'll Do Lunch!" Ceremonial exchange of numbers and promises to get together before another twenty-five years go by!
12–4 P.M.: Departures. Attorneys and security personnel from Alumni Development meet with you to go over your—irrevocable!—financial pledges. Once all instruments are signed (three witnesses, please!), notarized, and entered at the County Courthouse, you'll be given back the keys to your car. See you at the thirtieth!

Questions for Reading and Analysis

1. What is Buckley's thesis: What does he really think about 25-year college class reunions and the way colleges are run today?

2. Satire is a form of irony that works by exaggerating grotesquely an opinion the writer does not share. How does Buckley use this technique? Where do you detect the first hint of satire?

The title story from Carver's critically acclaimed 1981 collection, Cathedral, *explores the real meanings of blindness and sight as the narrator is forced to give up the comfort of his stereotypes. A prolific writer of short stories, Raymond Carver (1939–88), drew upon his blue-collar background to shape his fiction, noted for the way its ordinary lives are touched by extraordinary moments.*

Cathedral

Raymond Carver

This blind man, an old friend of my wife's, he was on his way to spend the night. His wife had died. So he was visiting the dead wife's relatives in Connecticut. He called my wife from his in-laws'. Arrangements were made. He would come by train, a five-hour trip, and my wife would meet him at the station. She hadn't seen him since she worked for him one summer in Seattle ten years ago. But she and the blind man had kept in touch. They made tapes and mailed them back and forth. I wasn't enthusiastic about his visit. He was no one I knew. And his being blind bothered me. My idea of blindness came from the movies. In the movies, the blind moved slowly and never laughed. Sometimes they were led by seeing-eye dogs. A blind man in my house was not something I looked forward to.

That summer in Seattle she had needed a job. She didn't have any money. The man she was going to marry at the end of the summer was in officers' training school. He didn't have any money, either. But she was in love with the guy, and he was in love with her, etc. She'd seen something in the paper: HELP WANTED— *Reading to Blind Man,* and a telephone number. She phoned and went over, was hired on the spot. She'd worked with this blind man all summer. She read stuff to him, case studies, reports, that sort of thing. She helped him organize his little office in the county social-service department. They'd become good friends, my wife and the blind man. How do I know these things? She told me. And she told me something else. On her last day in the office, the blind man asked if he could touch her face. She agreed to this. She told me he touched his fingers to every part of her face, her nose—even her neck! She never forgot it. She even tried to write a poem about it. She was always trying to write a poem. She wrote a poem or two every year, usually after something really important had happened to her.

When we first started going out together, she showed me the poem. In the poem, she recalled his fingers and the way they had moved around over her face. In the poem, she talked about what she had felt at the time, about what went through her mind when the blind man touched her nose and lips. I can remember I didn't think much of the poem. Of course, I didn't tell her that. Maybe I just don't understand poetry. I admit it's not the first thing I reach for when I pick up something to read.

Anyway, this man who'd first enjoyed her favors, the officer-to-be, he'd been her childhood sweetheart. So okay. I'm saying that at the end of the summer she let the blind man run his hands over her face, said good-bye to him, married her childhood etc., who was now a commissioned officer, and she moved away from Seattle. But they'd kept in touch, she and the blind man. She made the first contact after a year or so. She called him up one night from an Air Force base in Alabama. She wanted to talk. They talked. He asked her to send him a tape and tell him about her life. She did this. She sent the tape. On the tape, she told the blind man about her husband and about their life together in the military. She told the blind man she loved her husband but she didn't like it where they lived and she didn't like it that he was part of the military-industrial thing. She told the blind man she'd written a poem and he was in it. She told him that she was writing a poem about what it was like to be an Air Force officer's wife. The poem wasn't finished yet. She was still writing it. The blind man made a tape. He sent her the tape. She made a tape. This went on for years. My wife's officer was posted to one base and then another. She sent tapes from Moody AFB, McGuire, McConnell, and finally Travis, near Sacramento, where one night she got to feeling lonely and cut off from people she kept losing in that moving-around life. She got to feeling she couldn't go it another step. She went in and swallowed all the pills and capsules in the medicine chest and washed them down with a bottle of gin. Then she got into a hot bath and passed out.

But instead of dying, she got sick. She threw up. Her officer—why should he have a name? he was the childhood sweetheart, and what more does he want?—came home from somewhere, found her, and called the ambulance. In time, she put it all on a tape and sent the tape to the blind man. Over the years, she put all kinds of stuff on tapes and sent the tapes off lickety-split. Next to writing a poem every year, I think it was her chief means of recreation. On one tape, she told the blind man she'd decided to live away from her officer for a time. On another tape, she told him about her divorce. She and I began going out, and of course she told her blind man about it. She told him everything, or so it seemed to me. Once she asked me if I'd like to hear the latest tape from the blind man. This was a year ago. I was on the tape, she said. So I said okay, I'd listen to it. I got us drinks and we settled down in the living room. We made ready to listen. First she inserted the tape into the player and adjusted a couple of dials. Then she pushed a lever. The tape squeaked and someone began to talk in this loud voice. She lowered the volume. After a few minutes of harmless chitchat, I heard my own name in the mouth of this stranger, this blind man I didn't even know! And then this: "From all you've said about him, I can only conclude—" But we were interrupted, a knock at the door, something, and we didn't ever get back to the tape. Maybe it was just as well. I'd heard all I wanted to.

Now this same blind man was coming to sleep in my house.

"Maybe I could take him bowling," I said to my wife. She was at the draining board doing scalloped potatoes. She put down the knife she was using and turned around.

"If you love me," she said, "you can do this for me. If you don't love me, okay. But if you had a friend, any friend, and the friend came to visit, I'd make him feel comfortable." She wiped her hands with the dish towel.

"I don't have any blind friends," I said.

"You don't have *any* friends," she said. "Period. Besides," she said, "goddamn it, his wife's just died! Don't you understand that? The man's lost his wife!"

I didn't answer. She'd told me a little about the blind man's wife. Her name was Beulah. Beulah! That's a name for a colored woman.

"Was his wife a Negro?" I asked.

"Are you crazy?" my wife said. "Have you just flipped or something?" She picked up a potato. I saw it hit the floor, then roll under the stove. "What's wrong with you?" she said. "Are you drunk?"

"I'm just asking," I said.

Right then my wife filled me in with more detail than I cared to know. I made a drink and sat at the kitchen table to listen. Pieces of the story began to fall into place.

Beulah had gone to work for the blind man the summer after my wife had stopped working for him. Pretty soon Beulah and the blind man had themselves a church wedding. It was a little wedding—who'd want to go to such a wedding in the first place?—just the two of them, plus the minister and the minister's wife. But it was a church wedding just the same. It was what Beulah had wanted, he'd said. But even then Beulah must have been carrying the cancer in her glands. After they had been inseparable for eight years—my wife's word, *inseparable*—Beulah's health went into a rapid decline. She died in a Seattle hospital room, the blind man sitting beside the bed and holding on to her hand. They'd married, lived and worked together, slept together—had sex, sure—and then the blind man had to bury her. All this without his having ever seen what the goddamned woman looked like. It was beyond my understanding. Hearing this, I felt sorry for the blind man for a little bit. And then I found myself thinking what a pitiful life this woman must have led. Imagine a woman who could never see herself as she was seen in the eyes of her loved one. A woman who could go on day after day and never receive the smallest compliment from her beloved. A woman whose husband could never read the expression on her face, be it misery or something better. Someone who could wear makeup or not—what difference to him? She could, if she wanted, wear green eye-shadow around one eye, a straight pin in her nostril, yellow slacks, and purple shoes, no matter. And then to slip off into death, the blind man's hand on her hand, his blind eyes streaming tears—I'm imagining now—her last thought maybe this: that he never even knew what she looked like, and she on an express to the grave. Robert was left with a small insurance policy and half of a twenty-peso Mexican coin. The other half of the coin went into the box with her. Pathetic.

So when the time rolled around, my wife went to the depot to pick him up. With nothing to do but wait—sure, I blamed him for that—I was having a drink and watching the TV when I heard the car pull into the drive. I got up from the sofa with my drink and went to the window to have a look.

I saw my wife laughing as she parked the car. I saw her get out of the car and shut the door. She was still wearing a smile. Just amazing. She went around to the other side of the car to where the blind man was already starting to get out. This blind man, feature this, he was wearing a full beard! A beard on a blind man! Too much, I say. The blind man reached into the back seat and dragged out a suitcase. My wife took his arm, shut the car door, and, talking all the way, moved him down the drive and then up the steps to the front porch. I turned off the TV. I finished my drink, rinsed the glass, dried my hands. Then I went to the door.

My wife said, "I want you to meet Robert. Robert, this is my husband. I've told you all about him." She was beaming. She had this blind man by his coat sleeve.

The blind man let go of the suitcase and up came his hand.

I took it. He squeezed hard, held my hand, and then he let it go.

"I feel like we've already met," he boomed.

"Likewise," I said. I didn't know what else to say. Then I said, "Welcome. I've heard a lot about you." We began to move then, a little group, from the porch into the living room, my wife guiding him by the arm. The blind man was carrying his suitcase in his other hand. My wife said things like, "To your left here, Robert. That's right. Now watch it, there's a chair. That's it. Sit down right here. This is the sofa. We just bought this sofa two weeks ago."

I started to say something about the old sofa. I'd liked that old sofa. But I didn't say anything. Then I wanted to say something else, small-talk, about the scenic ride along the Hudson. How going *to* New York, you should sit on the right-hand side of the train, and coming *from* New York, the left-hand side.

"Did you have a good train ride?" I said. "Which side of the train did you sit on, by the way?"

"What a question, which side!" my wife said. "What's it matter which side?" she said.

"I just asked," I said.

"Right side," the blind man said. "I hadn't been on a train in nearly forty years. Not since I was a kid. With my folks. That's been a long time. I'd nearly forgotten the sensation. I have winter in my beard now," he said. "So I've been told, anyway. Do I look distinguished, my dear?" the blind man said to my wife.

"You look distinguished, Robert," she said. "Robert," she said. "Robert, it's just so good to see you."

My wife finally took her eyes off the blind man and looked at me. I had the feeling she didn't like what she saw. I shrugged.

I've never met, or personally known, anyone who was blind. This blind man was late forties, a heavy-set, balding man with stooped shoulders, as if he carried a great weight there. He wore brown slacks, brown shoes, a light-brown shirt, a tie, a sports coat. Spiffy. He also had this full beard. But he didn't use a cane and he didn't wear dark glasses. I'd always thought dark glasses were a must for the blind. Fact was, I wished he had a pair. At first glance, his eyes looked like anyone else's eyes. But if you looked close, there was something different about them. Too much white in the iris, for one thing, and the pupils seemed to move around in the sockets without his knowing it or being able to stop it. Creepy. As I stared at his face, I saw the left pupil turn in toward his nose while the other made an effort to keep in one place. But it was only an effort, for that eye was on the roam without his knowing it or wanting it to be.

I said, "Let me get you a drink. What's your pleasure? We have a little of everything. It's one of our pastimes."

"Bub, I'm a Scotch man myself," he said fast enough in this big voice.

"Right," I said. Bub! "Sure you are. I knew it."

He let his fingers touch his suitcase, which was sitting alongside the sofa. He was taking his bearings. I didn't blame him for that.

"I'll move that up to your room," my wife said.

"No, that's fine," the blind man said loudly. "It can go up when I go up."

"A little water with the Scotch?" I said.

"Very little," he said.

"I knew it," I said.

He said "Just a tad. The Irish actor, Barry Fitzgerald? I'm like that fellow. When I drink water, Fitzgerald said, I drink water. When I drink whiskey, I drink whiskey." My wife laughed. The blind man brought his hand up under his beard. He lifted his beard slowly and let it drop.

I did the drinks, three big glasses of Scotch with a splash of water in each. Then we made ourselves comfortable and talked about Robert's travels. First the long flight from the West Coast to Connecticut, we covered that. Then from Connecticut up here by train. We had another drink concerning that leg of the trip.

I remembered having read somewhere that the blind didn't smoke because, as speculation had it, they couldn't see the smoke they exhaled. I thought I knew that much and that much only about blind people. But this blind man smoked his cigarette down to the nubbin and then lit another one. This blind man filled his ashtray and my wife emptied it.

When we sat down at the table for dinner, we had another drink. My wife heaped Robert's plate with cube steak, scalloped potatoes, green beans. I buttered him up two slices of bread. I said, "Here's bread and butter for you." I swallowed some of my drink. "Now let us pray," I said, and the blind man lowered his head. My wife looked at me, her mouth agape. "Pray the phone won't ring and the food doesn't get cold," I said.

We dug in. We ate everything there was to eat on the table. We ate like there was no tomorrow. We didn't talk. We ate. We scarfed. We grazed that table. We were into serious eating. The blind man had right away located his foods, he knew just where everything was on his plate. I watched with admiration as he used his knife and fork on the meat. He'd cut two pieces of meat, fork the meat into his mouth, and then go all out for the scalloped potatoes, the beans next, and then he'd tear off a hunk of buttered bread and eat that. He'd follow this up with a big drink of milk. It didn't seem to bother him to use his fingers once in a while, either.

We finished everything, including half a strawberry pie. For a few moments, we sat as if stunned. Sweat beaded on our faces. Finally, we got up from the table and left the dirty plates. We didn't look back. We took ourselves into the living room and sank into our places again. Robert and my wife sat on the sofa. I took the big chair. We had us two or three more drinks while they talked about the major things that had come to pass for them in the past ten years. For the most part, I just listened. Now and then I joined in. I didn't want him to think I'd left the room and I didn't want her to think I was feeling left out. They talked of things that had happened to them—to them!—these past ten years. I waited in vain to hear my name on my wife's sweet lips: "And then my dear husband came into my life"— something like that. But I heard nothing of the sort. More talk of Robert. Robert had done a little of everything, it seemed, a regular blind jack-of-all-trades. But most recently he and his wife had had an Amway distributorship, from which, I gathered, they'd earned their living, such as it was. The blind man was also a ham radio operator. He talked in his loud voice about conversations he'd had with fellow operators in Guam, in the Philippines, in Alaska, and even in Tahiti. He said he'd have a lot of friends there if he ever wanted to go visit those places. From time to time, he'd turn his blind face toward me, put his hand under his beard, ask me something. How long had I been in my present position? (Three years.) Did I like my work? (I didn't.) Was I going to stay with it? (What were the options?) Finally, when I thought he was beginning to run down, I got up and turned on the TV.

My wife looked at me with irritation. She was heading toward a boil. Then she looked at the blind man and said, "Robert, do you have a TV?"

The blind man said, "My dear, I have two TVs. I have a color set and a black-and-white thing, an old relic. It's funny, but if I turn the TV on, and I'm always turning it on, I turn on the color set. It's funny, don't you think?"

I didn't know what to say to that. I had absolutely nothing to say to that. No opinion. So I watched the news program and tried to listen to what the announcer was saying.

"This is a color TV," the blind man said. "Don't ask me how, but I can tell."

"We traded up a while ago," I said.

The blind man had another taste of his drink. He lifted his beard, sniffed it, and let it fall. He leaned forward on the sofa. He positioned his ashtray on the coffee table, then put the lighter to his cigarette. He leaned back on the sofa and crossed his legs at the ankles.

My wife covered her mouth, and then she yawned. She stretched. She said, "I think I'll go upstairs and put on my robe. I think I'll change into something else. Robert, you make yourself comfortable," she said.

"I'm comfortable," the blind man said.

"I want you to feel comfortable in this house," she said.

"I am comfortable," the blind man said.

After she left the room he and I listened to the weather report and then to the sports roundup. By that time, she'd been gone so long I didn't know if she was going to come back. I thought she might have gone to bed. I wished she'd come back downstairs. I didn't want to be left alone with a blind man. I asked him if he wanted another drink, and he said sure. Then I asked if he wanted to smoke some dope with me. I said I'd just rolled a number. I hadn't, but I planned to do so in about two shakes.

"I'll try some with you," he said.

"Damn right," I said. "That's the stuff."

I got our drinks and sat down on the sofa with him. Then I rolled us two fat numbers. I lit one and passed it. I brought it to his fingers. He took it and inhaled.

"Hold it as long as you can," I said. I could tell he didn't know the first thing.

My wife came back downstairs wearing her pink robe and her pink slippers.

"What do I smell?" she said.

"We thought we'd have us some cannabis," I said.

My wife gave me a savage look. Then she looked at the blind man and said, "Robert, I didn't know you smoked."

He said, "I do now, my dear. There's a first time for everything. But I don't feel anything yet."

"This stuff is pretty mellow," I said. "This stuff is mild. It's dope you can reason with," I said. "It doesn't mess you up."

"Not much it doesn't, bub," he said, and laughed.

My wife sat on the sofa between the blind man and me. I passed her the number. She took it and toked and then passed it back to me. "Which way is this going?" she said. Then she said, "I shouldn't be smoking this. I can hardly keep my eyes open as it is. That dinner did me in. I shouldn't have eaten so much."

"It was the strawberry pie," the blind man said. "That's what did it," he said, and he laughed his big laugh. Then he shook his head.

"There's more strawberry pie," I said.

"Do you want some more, Robert?" my wife said.

"Maybe in a little while," he said.

We gave our attention to the TV. My wife yawned again. She said, "Your bed is made up when you feel like going to bed, Robert. I know you must have had a long day. When you're ready to go to bed, say so." She pulled his arm. "Robert?"

He came to and said, "I've had a real nice time. This beats tapes, doesn't it?"

I said, "Coming at you," and I put the number between his fingers. He inhaled, held the smoke, and then let it go. It was like he'd been doing it since he was nine years old.

"Thanks, bub," he said. "But I think this is all for me. I think I'm beginning to feel it," he said. He held the burning roach out for my wife.

"Same here," she said. "Ditto. Me, too." She took the roach and passed it to me. "I may just sit here for a while between you guys with my eyes closed. But don't let me bother you, okay? Either one of you. If it bothers you, say so. Otherwise, I may just sit here with my eyes closed until you're ready to go to bed," she said. "Your bed's made up, Robert, when you're ready. It's right next to our room at the top of the stairs. We'll show you up when you're ready. You wake me up now, you guys, if I fall asleep." She said that and then she closed her eyes and went to sleep.

The news program ended. I got up and changed the channel. I sat back down on the sofa. I wished my wife hadn't pooped out. Her head lay across the back of the sofa, her mouth open. She'd turned so that her robe had slipped away from her legs, exposing a juicy thigh. I reached to draw her robe back over her, and it was then that I glanced at the blind man. What the hell! I flipped the robe open again.

"You say when you want some strawberry pie," I said.

"I will," he said.

I said, "Are you tired? Do you want me to take you up to your bed? Are you ready to hit the hay?"

"Not yet," he said. "No, I'll stay up with you, bub. If that's all right. I'll stay up until you're ready to turn in. We haven't had a chance to talk. Know what I mean? I feel like me and her monopolized the evening." He lifted his beard and he let it fall. He picked up his cigarettes and his lighter.

"That's all right," I said. Then I said, "I'm glad for the company."

And I guess I was. Every night I smoked dope and stayed up as long as I could before I fell asleep. My wife and I hardly ever went to bed at the same time. When I did go to sleep, I had these dreams. Sometimes I'd wake up from one of them, my heart going crazy.

Something about the church and the Middle Ages was on TV. Not your run-of-the-mill TV fare. I wanted to watch something else. I turned to the other channels. But there was nothing on them, either. So I turned back to the first channel and apologized.

"Bub, it's all right," the blind man said. "It's fine with me. Whatever you want to watch is okay. I'm always learning something. Learning never ends. It won't hurt me to learn something tonight. I got ears," he said.

We didn't say anything for a time. He was leaning forward with his head turned at me, his right ear aimed in the direction of the set. Very disconcerting. Now and then his eyelids drooped and then they snapped open again. Now and then he put his fingers into his beard and tugged, like he was thinking about something he was hearing on the television.

On the screen, a group of men wearing cowls was being set upon and tormented by men dressed in skeleton costumes and men dressed as devils. The men dressed as devils wore devil masks, horns, and long tails. This pageant was part of a procession. The Englishman who was narrating the thing said it took place in Spain once a year. I tried to explain to the blind man what was happening.

"Skeletons," he said. "I know about skeletons," he said, and he nodded.

The TV showed this one cathedral. Then there was a long, slow look at another one. Finally, the picture switched to the famous one in Paris, with its flying buttresses and its spires reaching up to the clouds. The camera pulled away to show the whole of the cathedral rising above the skyline.

There were times when the Englishman who was telling the thing would shut up, would simply let the camera move around over the cathedrals. Or else the camera would tour the countryside, men in fields walking behind oxen. I waited as long as I could. Then I felt I had to say something. I said, "They're showing the outside of this cathedral now. Gargoyles. Little statues carved to look like monsters. Now I guess they're in Italy. Yeah, they're in Italy. There's painting on the walls of this one church."

"Are those fresco paintings, bub?" he asked, and he sipped from his drink.

I reached for my glass. But it was empty. I tried to remember what I could remember. "You're asking me are those frescoes?" I said. "That's a good question. I don't know."

The camera moved to a cathedral outside Lisbon. The differences in the Portuguese cathedral compared with the French and Italian were not that great. But they were there. Mostly the interior stuff. Then something occurred to me, and I said, "Something has occurred to me. Do you have any idea what a cathedral is? What they look like, that is? Do you follow me? If somebody says cathedral to you, do you have any notion what they're talking about? Do you know the difference between that and a Baptist church, say?"

He let the smoke dribble from his mouth. "I know they took hundreds of workers fifty or a hundred years to build," he said. "I just heard the man say that, of course. I know generations of the same families worked on a cathedral. I heard him say that, too. The men who began their life's work on them, they never lived to see the completion of their work. In that wise, bub, they're no different from the rest of us, right?" He laughed. Then his eyelids drooped again. His head nodded. He seemed to be snoozing. Maybe he was imagining himself in Portugal. The TV was showing another cathedral now. This one was in Germany. The Englishman's voice droned on. "Cathedrals," the blind man said. He sat up and rolled his head back and forth. "If you want the truth, bub, that's about all I know. What I just said. What I heard him say. But maybe you could describe one to me? I wish you'd do it. I'd like that. If you want to know, I really don't have a good idea."

I stared hard at the shot of the cathedral on the TV. How could I even begin to describe it? But say my life depended on it. Say my life was being threatened by an insane guy who said I had to do it or else.

I stared some more at the cathedral before the picture flipped off into the countryside. There was no use. I turned to the blind man and said, "To begin with, they're very tall." I was looking around the room for clues. "They reach way up. Up and up. Toward the sky. They're so big, some of them, they have to have these supports. To help hold them up, so to speak. These supports are called buttresses. They remind me of viaducts, for some reason. But maybe you don't know viaducts, either? Sometimes the cathedrals have devils and such carved into the front. Sometimes lords and ladies. Don't ask me why this is," I said.

He was nodding. The whole upper part of his body seemed to be moving back and forth.

"I'm not doing so good, am I?" I said.

He stopped nodding and leaned forward on the edge of the sofa. As he listened to me, he was running his fingers through his beard. I wasn't getting through to him, I could see that. But he waited for me to go on just the same. He nodded, like he was trying to encourage me. I tried to think what else to say. "They're really big," I said. "They're massive. They're built of stone. Marble, too, sometimes. In those olden days, when they built cathedrals, men wanted to be close to God. In those olden days, God was an important part of everyone's life. You could tell this from their cathedral-building. I'm sorry," I said, "but it looks like that's the best I can do for you. I'm just no good at it."

"That's all right, bub," the blind man said. "Hey, listen. I hope you don't mind my asking you. Can I ask you something? Let me ask you a simple question, yes or no. I'm just curious and there's no offense. You're my host. But let me ask if you are in any way religious? You don't mind my asking?"

I shook my head. He couldn't see that, though. A wink is the same as a nod to a blind man. "I guess I don't believe in it. In anything. Sometimes it's hard. You know what I'm saying?"

"Sure I do," he said.

"Right," I said.

The Englishman was still holding forth. My wife sighed in her sleep. She drew a long breath and went on with her sleeping.

"You'll have to forgive me," I said. "But I can't tell you what a cathedral looks like. It just isn't in me to do it. I can't do any more than I've done."

The blind man sat very still, his head down, as he listened to me.

I said, "The truth is, cathedrals don't mean anything special to me. Nothing. Cathedrals. They're something to look at on late-night TV. That's all they are."

It was then that the blind man cleared his throat. He brought something up. He took a handkerchief from his back pocket. Then he said, "I get it, bub. It's okay. It happens. Don't worry about it," he said. "Hey, listen to me. Will you do me a favor? I got an idea. Why don't you find us some heavy paper? And a pen. We'll do something. We'll draw one together. Get us a pen and some heavy paper. Go on, bub, get the stuff," he said.

So I went upstairs. My legs felt like they didn't have any strength in them. They felt like they did after I'd done some running. In my wife's room, I looked around. I found some ballpoints in a little basket on her table. And then I tried to think where to look for the kind of paper he was talking about.

Downstairs, in the kitchen, I found a shopping bag with onion skins in the bottom of the bag. I emptied the bag and shook it. I brought it into the living room and sat down with it near his legs. I moved some things, smoothed the wrinkles from the bag, spread it out on the coffee table.

The blind man got down from the sofa and sat next to me on the carpet.

He ran his fingers over the paper. He went up and down the sides of the paper. The edges, even the edges. He fingered the corners.

"All right," he said. "All right, let's do her."

He found my hand, the hand with the pen. He closed his hand over my hand. "Go ahead, bub, draw," he said. "Draw. You'll see. I'll follow along with you. It'll be okay. Just begin now like I'm telling you. You'll see. Draw," the blind man said.

So I began. First I drew a box that looked like a house. It could have been the house I lived in. Then I put a roof on it. At either end of the roof, I drew spires. Crazy.

"Swell," he said. "Terrific. You're doing fine," he said. "Never thought anything like this could happen in your lifetime, did you, bub? Well, it's a strange life, we all know that. Go on now. Keep it up."

I put in windows with arches. I drew flying buttresses. I hung great doors. I couldn't stop. The TV station went off the air. I put down the pen and closed and opened my fingers. The blind man felt around over the paper. He moved the tips of his fingers over the paper, all over what I had drawn, and he nodded.

"Doing fine," the blind man said.

I took up the pen again, and he found my hand. I kept at it. I'm no artist. But I kept drawing just the same.

My wife opened up her eyes and gazed at us. She sat up on the sofa, her robe hanging open. She said, "What are you doing? Tell me, I want to know."

I didn't answer her.

The blind man said, "We're drawing a cathedral. Me and him are working on it. Press hard," he said to me. "That's right. That's good," he said. "Sure. You got it, bub. I can tell. You didn't think you could. But you can, can't you? You're cooking with gas now. You know what I'm saying? We're going to really have us something here in a minute. How's the old arm?" he said. "Put some people in there now. What's a cathedral without people?"

My wife said, "What's going on? Robert, what are you doing? What's going on?"

"It's all right," he said to her. "Close your eyes now," the blind man said to me. I did it. I closed them just like he said.

"Are they closed?" he asked. "Don't fudge."

"They're closed," I said.

"Keep them that way," he said. He said, "Don't stop now. Draw."

So we kept on with it. His fingers rode my fingers as my hand went over the paper. It was like nothing else in my life up to now.

Then he said, "I think that's it. I think you got it," he said. "Take a look. What do you think?

But I had my eyes closed. I thought I'd keep them that way for a little longer. I thought it was something I ought to do.

"Well?" he said. "Are you looking?"

My eyes were still closed. I was in my house. I knew that. But I didn't feel like I was inside anything.

"It's really something," I said.

Questions for Reading and Analysis

1. What kind of person is the story's narrator? List examples of statements he makes that help establish his character.

2. Why is the narrator bothered by the visit from the blind man?

3. What kind of relationship does the narrator have with his wife?

4. How is the narrator's marijuana smoking different from Robert's?

5. Why, at the end of the story, does Robert tell the narrator to close his eyes? What is the significance of the narrator's decision to keep his eyes closed "a little longer"?

6. Explain Carver's use of the metaphor of blindness in the story.

Stuart Chase, a longtime business consultant to government agencies, continues his campaign to clean up muddy English. This piece is excerpted from his The Power of Words 1953–54, *one of several books on the subject of language.*

Gobbledygook

Stuart Chase

Said Franklin Roosevelt, in one of his early presidential speeches: "I see one-third of a nation ill-housed, ill-clad, ill-nourished." Translated into standard bureaucratic prose his statement would read:

> *It is evident that a substantial number of persons within the Continental boundaries of the United States have inadequate resources with which to purchase the products of agricultural communities and industrial establishments. It would appear that for a considerable segment of the population, possibly as much as 33.3333[1] percent of the total, there are inadequate housing facilities, and an equally significant proportion is deprived of the proper types of clothing and nutriment.*

This rousing satire on gobbledygook—or talk among the bureaucrats—is adapted from a report[2] prepared by the Federal Security Agency in an attempt to break out of the verbal squirrel cage. "Gobbledygook" was coined by an exasperated Congressman, Maury Maverick of Texas, and means using two, or three, or ten words in the place of one, or using a five-syllable word where a single syllable would suffice. Maverick was censuring the forbidding prose of executive departments in Washington, but the term has now spread to windy and pretentious language in general.

"Gobbledygook" itself is a good example of the way a language grows. There was no word for the event before Maverick's invention; one had to say: "You know, that terrible, involved, polysyllabic language those government people use down in Washington." Now one word takes the place of a dozen.

A British member of Parliament, A. P. Herbert, also exasperated with bureaucratic jargon, translated Nelson's[3] immortal phrase, "England expects every man to do his duty":

> *England anticipates that, as regards the current emergency, personnel will face up to the issues, and exercise appropriately the functions allocated to their respective occupational groups.*

A New Zealand official made the following report after surveying a plot of ground for an athletic field:[4]

> *It is obvious from the difference in elevation with relation to the short depth of the property that the contour is such as to preclude any reasonable developmental potential for active recreation.*

Seems the plot was too steep.

An office manager sent this memo to his chief:

> *Verbal contact with Mr. Blank regarding the attached notification of promotion has elicited the attached representation intimating that he prefers to decline the assignment.*

Seems Mr. Blank didn't want the job.

> *A doctor testified at an English trial that one of the parties was suffering from "circumorbital haematoma."*

Seems the party had a black eye.

> *In August 1952 the U.S. Department of Agriculture put out a pamphlet entitled: "Cultural and Pathogenic Variability in Single-Condial and Hyphaltip Isolates of Hemlin-Thosporium Turcicum Pass."*

Seems it was about corn leaf disease.

On reaching the top of the Finsteraarhorn in 1845, M. Dollfus-Ausset, when he got his breath, exclaimed:

> *The soul communes in the infinite with those icy peaks which seem to have their roots in the bowels of eternity.*

Seems he enjoyed the view.

A government department announced:

> *Voucherable expenditures necessary to provide adequate dental treatment required as adjunct to medical treatment being rendered a pay patient in in-patient status may be incurred as required at the expense of the Public Health Service.*

Seems you can charge your dentist bill to the Public Health Service. Or can you? . . .

Reducing the Gobble

As government and business offices grow larger, the need for doing something about gobbledygook increases. Fortunately the biggest office in the world is working hard to reduce it. The Federal Security Agency in Washington,[5] with nearly 100 million clients on its books, began analyzing its communication lines some years ago, with gratifying results. Surveys find trouble in three main areas: correspondence with clients about their social security problems, office memos, official reports.

Clarity and brevity, as well as common humanity, are urgently needed in this vast establishment which deals with disability, old age, and unemployment. The surveys found instead many cases of long-windedness, foggy meanings, clichés, and singsong phrases, and gross neglect of the reader's point of view. Rather than talking to a real person, the writer was talking to himself. "We often write like a man walking on stilts."

Here is a typical case of long-windedness:

> *Gobbledygook as found: "We are wondering if sufficient time has passed so that you are in a position to indicate whether favorable action may now be taken on our recommendation for the reclassification of Mrs. Blank, junior clerk-stenographer, CAF 2, to assistant clerk-stenographer, CAF 3?"*
>
> *Suggested improvement: "Have you yet been able to act on our recommendation to reclassify Mrs. Blank?"*

Another case:

> *Although the Central Efficiency Rating Committee recognizes that there are many desirable changes that could be made in the present efficiency rating system in order to make it more realistic and more workable than it now is, this committee is of the opinion that no further change should be made in the present system during the current year. Because of conditions prevailing throughout the country and the resultant turnover in personnel, and difficulty in administering the Federal programs, further mechanical improvement in the present rating system would require staff retraining and other administrative expense which would seem best withheld until the official termination of hostilities, and until restoration of regular operations.*

The F.S.A. invites us to squeeze the gobbledygook out of this statement. Here is my attempt:

> *The Central Efficiency Rating Committee recognizes that desirable changes could be made in the present system. We believe, however, that no change should be attempted until the war is over.*

This cuts the statement from 111 to 30 words, about one-quarter of the original, but perhaps the reader can do still better. What of importance have I left out?

Sometimes in a book which I am reading for information—not for literary pleasure—I run a pencil through the surplus words. Often I can cut a section to half its length with an improvement in clarity. Magazines like *The Reader's Digest* have reduced this process to an art. Are long-windedness and obscurity a cultural lag from the days when writing was reserved for priests and cloistered scholars? The more words and the deeper the mystery, the greater their prestige and the firmer the hold on their jobs. And the better the candidate's chance today to have his doctoral thesis accepted.

The F.S.A. surveys found that a great deal of writing was obscure although not necessarily prolix. Here is a letter sent to more than 100,000 inquirers, a classic example of murky prose. To clarify it, one needs to *add* words, not cut them:

In order to be fully insured, an individual must have earned $50 or more in covered employment for as many quarters of coverage as half the calendar quarters elapsing between 1936 and the quarter in which he reaches age 65 or dies, whichever first occurs.

Probably no one without the technical jargon of the office could translate this: nevertheless, it was sent out to drive clients mad for seven years. One poor fellow wrote back: "I am no longer in covered employment. I have an outside job now."

Many words and phrases in officialese seem to come out automatically, as if from lower centers of the brain. In this standardized prose people never *get* jobs, they "secure employment"; *before* and *after* become "prior to" and "subsequent to"; one does not *do*, one "performs"; nobody *knows* a thing, he is "fully cognizant"; one never *says*, he "indicates." A great favorite at present is "implement."

Some charming boners occur in this talking-in-one's-sleep. For instance:

The problem of extending coverage to all employees, regardless of size, is not as simple as surface appearances indicate.
Though the proportions of all males and females in ages 16–45 are essentially the same . . .
Dairy cattle, usually and commonly embraced in dairying . . .

In its manual to employees, the F.S.A. suggests the following:

INSTEAD OF	USE
give consideration to	consider
make inquiry regarding	inquire
is of the opinion	believes
comes into conflict with	conflicts
information which is of a confidential nature	confidential information

Professional or office gobbledygook often arises from using the passive rather than the active voice. Instead of looking you in the eye, as it were, and writing "This act requires . . ." the office worker looks out of the window and writes: "It is required by this statute that . . ." When the bureau chief says, "We expect Congress to cut your budget," the message is only too clear; but usually he says, "It is expected that the departmental budget estimates will be reduced by Congress."

Gobbled: "All letters prepared for the signature of the Administrator will be single spaced."
Ungobbled: "Single space all letters for the Administrator." (Thus cutting 13 words to 7.)

Only People Can Read

The F.S.A. surveys pick up the point . . . that human communication involves a listener as well as a speaker. Only people can read, though a lot of writing seems to be addressed to beings in outer space. To whom are you talking? The sender of the officialese message often forgets the chap on the other end of the line.

A woman with two small children wrote the F.S.A. asking what she should do about payments, as her husband had lost his memory. "If he never gets able to work," she said, "and stays in an institution, would I be able to draw any benefits? . . . I don't know how I am going to live and raise my children since he is disable to work. Please give me some information. . . ."

To this human appeal, she received a shattering blast of gobbledygook, beginning, "State unemployment compensation laws do not provide any benefits for sick or disabled individuals . . . in order to qualify an individual must have a certain number of quarters of coverage. . . ." et cetera, et cetera. Certainly if the writer had been thinking about the poor woman he would not have dragged in unessential material about old-age insurance. If he had pictured a mother without means to care for her children, he would have told her where she might get help—from the local office which handles aid to dependent children, for instance.

Gobbledygook of this kind would largely evaporate if we thought of our messages as two-way—in the above case, if we pictured ourselves talking on the doorstep of a shabby house to a woman with two children tugging at her skirts, who in her distress does not know which way to turn.

Results of the Survey

The F.S.A. survey showed that office documents could be cut 20 to 50 percent, with an improvement in clarity and a great saving to taxpayers in paper and payrolls.

A handbook was prepared and distributed to key officials.[6] They read it, thought about it, and presently began calling section meetings to discuss gobbledygook. More booklets were ordered, and the local output of documents began to improve. A Correspondence Review Section was established as a kind of laboratory to test murky messages. A supervisor could send up samples for analysis and suggestions. The handbook is now used for training new members; and many employees keep it on their desks along with the dictionary. Outside the Bureau some 25,000 copies have been sold (at 20 cents each) to individuals, governments, business firms, all over the world. It is now used officially in the Veterans Administration and in the Department of Agriculture.

The handbook makes clear the enormous amount of gobbledygook which automatically spreads in any large office, together with ways and means to keep it under control. I would guess that at least half of all the words circulating around the bureaus of the world are "irrelevant, incompetent, and immaterial"—to use a favorite legalism; or are just plain "unnecessary"—to ungobble it.

My favorite story of removing the gobble from gobbledygook concerns the Bureau of Standards at Washington. I have told it before but perhaps the reader will forgive the repetition. A New York plumber wrote the Bureau that he had found hydrochloric acid fine for cleaning drains, and was it harmless? Washington replied: "The efficacy of hydrochloric acid is indisputable, but the chlorine residue is incompatible with the metallic permanence."

The plumber wrote back that he was mighty glad the Bureau agreed with him. The Bureau replied with a note of alarm: "We cannot assume responsibility for the production of toxic and noxious residues with hydrochloric acid, and suggest that you use an alternate procedure." The plumber was happy to learn that the Bureau still agreed with him.

Whereupon Washington exploded: "Don't use hydrochloric acid; it eats hell out of the pipes!"

Endnotes

1. Not carried beyond four places. [Chase's note]
2. This and succeeding quotations from F.S.A. report by special permission of the author, Milton Hall. [Chase's note]
3. Horatio Nelson (1758–1805), English naval hero, victor over the French at Trafalgar.
4. This item and the next two are from the piece on gobbledygook by W. E. Farbstein, *New York Times*, March 29, 1953. [Chase's note]
5. Now the Department of Health, Education, and Welfare. [Chase's note] Since divided into two departments: Education, and Health and Human Services.
6. By Milton Hall. [Chase's note]

Questions for Reading and Analysis

1. In your own words, define the term "gobbledygook."
2. Why does gobbledygook enjoy such high prestige? What do writers gain by using it?
3. What does the example of the plumber at the end of the essay illustrate?

*Sandra Cisneros (b. 1954), chronicles the Latina experience in con-
temporary America in her fiction and poetry. The daughter of a
Mexican-American mother and a Mexican father, she grew up in
Chicago, frequently visiting her father's family in Mexico, always conscious of the pull of two cultures. In the title story from her 1991 collection,* Woman Hollering Creek, *a young Mexican bride crosses the
border, full of hope for a new life with her husband, only to face disappointment and disillusionment, punctuated by his physical and
verbal abuse, until she is saved by a stranger.*

Woman Hollering Creek

Sandra Cisneros

The day Don Serafín gave Juan Pedro Martínez Sánchez permission to take
Cleófilas Enriqueta DeLeón Hernández as his bride, across her father's
threshold, over several miles of dirt road and several miles of paved, over
one border and beyond to a town *en el otro lado*—on the other side—already did
he divine the morning his daughter would raise her hand over her eyes, look south,
and dream of returning to the chores that never ended, six good-for-nothing
brothers, and one old man's complaints.

He had said, after all, in the hubbub of parting: I am your father, I will never
abandon you. He *had* said that, hadn't he, when he hugged and then let her go. But
at the moment Cleófilas was busy looking for Chela, her maid of honor, to fulfill
their bouquet conspiracy. She would not remember her father's parting words until
later. *I am your father, I will never abandon you.*

Only now as a mother did she remember. Now, when she and Juan Pedrito
sat by the creek's edge. How when a man and a woman love each other, sometimes that love sours. But a parent's love for a child, a child's for its parents, is
another thing entirely.

This is what Cleófilas thought evenings when Juan Pedro did not come home,
and she lay on her side of the bed listening to the hollow roar of the interstate, a
distant dog barking, the pecan trees rustling like ladies in stiff petticoats—*shh-
shh-shh, shh-shh-shh*—soothing her to sleep.

In the town where she grew up, there isn't very much to do except accompany
the aunts and godmothers to the house of one or the other to play cards. Or walk
to the cinema to see this week's film again, speckled and with one hair quivering
annoyingly on the screen. Or to the center of town to order a milk shake that will
appear in a day and a half as a pimple on her backside. Or to the girlfriend's house

75

to watch the latest *telenovela* episode and try to copy the way the women comb their hair, wear their makeup.

But what Cleófilas has been waiting for, has been whispering and sighing and giggling for, has been anticipating since she was old enough to lean against the window displays of gauze and butterflies and lace, is passion. Not the kind on the cover of the *¡Alarma!* magazines, mind you, where the lover is photographed with the bloody fork she used to salvage her good name. But passion in its purest crystalline essence. The kind the books and songs and *telenovelas* describe when one finds, finally, the great love of one's life, and does whatever one can, must do, at whatever the cost.

Tú o Nadie. "You or No One." The title of the current favorite *telenovela.* The beautiful Lucía Méndez having to put up with all kinds of hardships of the heart, separation and betrayal, and loving, always loving no matter what, because *that* is the most important thing, and did you see Lucía Méndez on the Bayer aspirin commercials—wasn't she lovely? Does she dye her hair do you think? Cleófilas is going to go to the *farmacía* and buy a hair rinse; her girlfriend Chela will apply it—it's not that difficult at all.

Because you didn't watch last night's episode when Lucía confessed she loved him more than anyone in her life. In her life! And she sings the song "You or No One" in the beginning and end of the show. *Tú o Nadie.* Somehow one ought to live one's life like that, don't you think? You or no one. Because to suffer for love is good. The pain all sweet somehow. In the end.

Seguín. She had liked the sound of it. Far away and lovely. Not like *Monclova. Coahuila.* Ugly.

Seguín, Tejas. A nice sterling ring to it. The tinkle of money. She would get to wear outfits like the women on the *tele*, like Lucía Méndez. And have a lovely house, and wouldn't Chela be jealous.

And yes, they will drive all the way to Laredo to get her wedding dress. That's what they say. Because Juan Pedro wants to get married right away, without a long engagement since he can't take off too much time from work. He has a very important position in Seguin with, with . . . a beer company, I think. Or was it tires? Yes, he has to be back. So they will get married in the spring when he can take off work, and then they will drive off in his new pickup—did you see it?—to their new home in Seguin. Well, not exactly new, but they're going to repaint the house. You know newlyweds. New paint and new furniture. Why not? He can afford it. And later on add maybe a room or two for the children. May they be blessed with many.

Well, you'll see. Cleófilas has always been so good with her sewing machine. A little *rrrr, rrrr, rrrr* of the machine and *¡zas!* Miracles. She's always been so clever, that girl. Poor thing. And without even a mama to advise her on things like her wedding night. Well, may God help her. What with a father with a head like a burro, and those six clumsy brothers. Well, what do you think! Yes, I'm going to the wedding. Of course! The dress I want to wear just needs to be altered a teensy bit to bring it up to date. See, I saw a new style last night that I thought would suit me. Did you watch last night's episode of *The Rich Also Cry?* Well, did you notice the dress the mother was wearing?

La Gritona. Such a funny name for such a lovely *arroyo*. But that's what they called the creek that ran behind the house. Though no one could say whether the woman had hollered from anger or pain. The natives only knew the *arroyo* one crossed on the way to San Antonio, and then once again on the way back, was called Woman Hollering, a name no one from these parts questioned, little less understood. *Pues, allá de los indios, quién sabe*—who knows, the townspeople shrugged, because it was of no concern to their lives how this trickle of water received its curious name.

"What do you want to know for?" Trini the laundromat attendant asked in the same gruff Spanish she always used whenever she gave Cleófilas change or yelled at her for something. First for putting too much soap in the machines. Later, for sitting on a washer. And still later, after Juan Pedrito was born, for not understanding that in this country you cannot let your baby walk around with no diaper and his pee-pee hanging out, it wasn't nice, *¿entiendes? Pues.*

How could Cleófilas explain to a woman like this why the name Woman Hollering fascinated her. Well, there was no sense talking to Trini.

On the other hand there were the neighbor ladies, one on either side of the house they rented near the *arroyo*. The woman Soledad on the left, the woman Dolores on the right.

The neighbor lady Soledad liked to call herself a widow, though how she came to be one was a mystery. Her husband had either died, or run away with an icehouse floozie, or simply gone out for cigarettes one afternoon and never came back. It was hard to say which since Soledad, as a rule, didn't mention him.

In the other house lived *la señora* Dolores, kind and very sweet, but her house smelled too much of incense and candles from the altars that burned continuously in memory of two sons who had died in the last war and one husband who had died shortly after from grief. The neighbor lady Dolores divided her time between the memory of these men and her garden, famous for its sunflowers—so tall they had to be supported with broom handles and old boards; red red cockscombs, fringed and bleeding a thick menstrual color; and, especially, roses whose sad scent reminded Cleófilas of the dead. Each Sunday *la señora* Dolores clipped the most beautiful of these flowers and arranged them on three modest headstones at the Seguin cemetery.

The neighbor ladies, Soledad, Dolores, they might've known once the name of the *arroyo* before it turned English but they did not know now. They were too busy remembering the men who had left through either choice or circumstance and would never come back.

Pain or rage, Cleófilas wondered when she drove over the bridge the first time as a newlywed and Juan Pedro had pointed it out. *La Gritona,* he had said, and she had laughed. Such a funny name for a creek so pretty and full of happily ever after.

The first time she had been so surprised she didn't cry out or try to defend herself. She had always said she would strike back if a man, any man, were to strike her.

But when the moment came, and he slapped her once, and then again, and again; until the lip split and bled an orchid of blood, she didn't fight back, she didn't break into tears, she didn't run away as she imagined she might when she saw such things in the *telenovelas.*

In her own home her parents had never raised a hand to each other or to their children. Although she admitted she may have been brought up a little leniently as an only daughter—*la consentida,* the princess—there were some things she would never tolerate. Ever. Instead, when it happened the first time, when they were barely man and wife, she had been so stunned, it left her speechless, motionless, numb. She had done nothing but reach up to the heat on her mouth and stare at the blood on her hand as if even then she didn't understand.

She could think of nothing to say, said nothing. Just stroked the dark curls of the man who wept and would weep like a child, his tears of repentance and shame, this time and each.

The men at the ice house. From what she can tell, from the times during her first year when still a newlywed she is invited and accompanies her husband, sits mute beside their conversation, waits and sips a beer until it grows warm, twists a paper napkin into a knot, then another into a fan, one into a rose, nods her head, smiles, yawns, politely grins, laughs at the appropriate moments, leans against her husband's sleeve, tugs at his elbow, and finally becomes good at predicting where the talk will lead, from this Cleófilas concludes each is nightly trying to find the truth lying at the bottom of the bottle like a gold doubloon on the sea floor.

They want to tell each other what they want to tell themselves. But what is bumping like a helium balloon at the ceiling of the brain never finds its way out. It bubbles and rises, it gurgles in the throat, it rolls across the surface of the tongue, and erupts from the lips—a belch.

If they are lucky, there are tears at the end of the long night. At any given moment, the fists try to speak. They are dogs chasing their own tails before lying down to sleep, trying to find a way, a route, an out, and—finally—get some peace.

In the morning sometimes before he opens his eyes. Or after they have finished loving. Or at times when he is simply across from her at the table putting pieces of food into his mouth and chewing. Cleófilas thinks, This is the man I have waited my whole life for.

Not that he isn't a good man. She has to remind herself why she loves him when she changes the baby's Pampers, or when she mops the bathroom floor, or tries to make the curtains for the doorways without doors, or whiten the linen. Or wonder a little when he kicks the refrigerator and says he hates this shitty house and is going out where he won't be bothered with the baby's howling and her suspicious questions, and her requests to fix this and this and this because if she had any brains in her head she'd realize he's been up before the rooster earning his living to pay for the food in her belly and the roof over her head and would have to wake up again early the next day so why can't you just leave me in peace, woman.

He is not very tall, no, and he doesn't look like the men on the *telenovelas.* His face still scarred from acne. And he has a bit of a belly from all the beer he drinks. Well, he's always been husky.

This man who farts and belches and snores as well as laughs and kisses and holds her. Somehow this husband whose whiskers she finds each morning in the sink, whose shoes she must air each evening on the porch, this husband who cuts his fingernails in public, laughs loudly, curses like a man, and demands each course of dinner be served on a separate plate like at his mother's, as soon as he gets home, on time or late, and who doesn't care at all for music or *telenovelas* or romance or roses or the moon floating pearly over the *arroyo*, or through the bedroom window for that matter, shut the blinds and go back to sleep, this man, this father, this rival, this keeper, this lord, this master, this husband till kingdom come.

A doubt. Slender as a hair. A washed cup set back on the shelf wrong-side-up. Her lipstick, and body talc, and hairbrush all arranged in the bathroom a different way.

No. Her imagination. The house the same as always. Nothing.

Coming home from the hospital with her new son, her husband. Something comforting in discovering her house slippers beneath the bed, the faded housecoat where she left it on the bathroom hook. Her pillow. Their bed.

Sweet sweet homecoming. Sweet as the scent of face powder in the air, jasmine, sticky liquor.

Smudged fingerprint on the door. Crushed cigarette in a glass. Wrinkle in the brain crumpling to a crease.

Sometimes she thinks of her father's house. But how could she go back there? What a disgrace. What would the neighbors say? Coming home like that with one baby on her hip and one in the oven. Where's your husband?

The town of gossips. The town of dust and despair. Which she has traded for this town of gossips. This town of dust, despair. Houses farther apart perhaps, though no more privacy because of it. No leafy *zócalo* in the center of the town, though the murmur of talk is clear enough all the same. No huddled whispering on the church steps each Sunday. Because here the whispering begins at sunset at the ice house instead.

This town with its silly pride for a bronze pecan the size of a baby carriage in front of the city hall. TV repair shop, drugstore, hardware, dry cleaner's, chiropractor's, liquor store, bail bonds, empty storefront, and nothing, nothing, nothing of interest. Nothing one could walk to, at any rate. Because the towns here are built so that you have to depend on husbands. Or you stay home. Or you drive. If you're rich enough to own, allowed to drive, your own car.

There is no place to go. Unless one counts the neighbor ladies. Soledad on one side, Dolores on the other. Or the creek.

Don't go out there after dark, *mi'jita*. Stay near the house. *No es bueno para la salud. Mala suerte. Bad luck. Mal aire.* You'll get sick and the baby too. You'll catch a fright wandering about in the dark, and then you'll see how right we were.

The stream sometimes only a muddy puddle in the summer, though now in the springtime, because of the rains, a good-size alive thing, a thing with a voice all its own, all day and all night calling in its high, silver voice. Is it La Llorona, the weeping woman? La Llorona, who drowned her own children. Perhaps La

Llorona is the one they named the creek after, she thinks, remembering all the stories she learned as a child.

La Llorona calling to her. She is sure of it. Cleófilas sets the baby's Donald Duck blanket on the grass. Listens. The day sky turning to night. The baby pulling up fistfuls of grass and laughing. La Llorona. Wonders if something as quiet as this drives a woman to the darkness under the trees.

What she needs is . . . and made a gesture as if to yank a woman's buttocks to his groin. Maximiliano, the foul-smelling fool from across the road, said this and set the men laughing, but Cleófilas just muttered. *Grosero*, and went on washing dishes.

She knew he said it not because it was true, but more because it was he who needed to sleep with a woman, instead of drinking each night at the ice house and stumbling home alone.

Maximiliano who was said to have killed his wife in an ice-house brawl when she came at him with a mop. I had to shoot, he had said—she was armed.

Their laughter outside the kitchen window. Her husband's, his friends'. Manolo, Beto, Efraín, el Perico. Maximiliano.

Was Cleófilas just exaggerating as her husband always said? It seemed the newspapers were full of such stories. This woman found on the side of the interstate. This one pushed from a moving car. This one's cadaver, this one unconscious, this one beaten blue. Her ex-husband, her husband, her lover, her father, her brother, her uncle, her friend, her co-worker. Always. The same grisly news in the pages of the dailies. She dunked a glass under the soapy water for a moment—shivered.

He had thrown a book. Hers. From across the room. A hot welt across the cheek. She could forgive that. But what stung more was the fact it was *her* book, a love story by Corín Tellado, what she loved most now that she lived in the U.S., without a television set, without the *telenovelas*.

Except now and again when her husband was away and she could manage it, the few episodes glimpsed at the neighbor lady Soledad's house because Dolores didn't care for that sort of thing, though Soledad was often kind enough to retell what had happened on what episode of *María de Nadie,* the poor Argentine country girl who had the ill fortune of falling in love with the beautiful son of the Arrocha family, the very family she worked for, whose roof she slept under and whose floors she vacuumed, while in that same house, with the dust brooms and floor cleaners as witnesses, the square-jawed Juan Carlos Arrocha had uttered words of love, I love you, María, listen to me, *mi querida,* but it was she who had to say No, no, we are not of the same class, and remind him it was not his place nor hers to fall in love, while all the while her heart was breaking, can you imagine.

Cleófilas thought her life would have to be like that, like a *telenovela*, only now the episodes got sadder and sadder. And there were no commercials in between for comic relief. And no happy ending in sight. She thought this when she sat with the baby out by the creek behind the house. Cleófilas de . . . ? But somehow she would have to change her name to Topazio, or Yesenia, Cristal, Adriana, Stefania, Andrea, something more poetic than Cleófilas. Everything happened to women with names like jewels. But what happened to a Cleófilas? Nothing. But a crack in the face.

Because the doctor has said so. She has to go. To make sure the new baby is all right, so there won't be any problems when he's born, and the appointment card says next Tuesday. Could he please take her. And that's all.

No, she won't mention it. She promises. If the doctor asks she can say she fell down the front steps or slipped when she was out in the backyard, slipped out back, she could tell him that. She has to go back next Tuesday, Juan Pedro, please, for the new baby. For their child.

She could write to her father and ask maybe for money, just a loan, for the new baby's medical expenses. Well then if he'd rather she didn't. All right, she won't. Please don't anymore. Please don't. She knows it's difficult saving money with all the bills they have, but how else are they going to get out of debt with the truck payments? And after the rent and the food and the electricity and the gas and the water and the who-knows-what, well, there's hardly anything left. But please, at least for the doctor visit. She won't ask for anything else. She has to. Why is she so anxious? Because.

Because she is going to make sure the baby is not turned around backward this time to split her down the center. Yes. Next Tuesday at five-thirty. I'll have Juan Pedrito dressed and ready. But those are the only shoes he has. I'll polish them, and we'll be ready. As soon as you come from work. We won't make you ashamed.

Felice? It's me, Graciela.

No, I can't talk louder. I'm at work.

Look, I need kind of a favor. There's a patient, a lady here who's got a problem.

Well, wait a minute. Are you listening to me or what?

I can't talk real loud 'cause her husband's in the next room.

Well, would you just listen?

I was going to do this sonogram on her—she's pregnant, right?—and she just starts crying on me. *Híjole,* Felice! This poor lady's got black-and-blue marks all over. I'm not kidding.

From her husband. Who else? Another one of those brides from across the border. And her family's all in Mexico.

Shit. You think they're going to help her? Give me a break. This lady doesn't even speak English. She hasn't been allowed to call home or write or nothing. That's why I'm calling you.

She needs a ride.

Not to Mexico, you goof. Just to the Greyhound. In San Anto.

No, just a ride. She's got her own money. All you'd have to do is drop her off in San Antonio on your way home. Come on, Felice. Please? If we don't help her, who will? I'd drive her myself, but she needs to be on that bus before her husband gets home from work. What do you say?

I don't know. Wait.

Right away, tomorrow even.

Well, if tomorrow's no good for you . . .

It's a date, Felice. Thursday. At the Cash N Carry off I-10. Noon. She'll be ready.

Oh, and her name's Cleófilas.

I don't know. One of those Mexican saints, I guess. A martyr or something. Cleófilas. C-L-E-O-F-I-L-A-S. Cle. O. Fi. Las. Write it down.

Thanks, Felice. When her kid's born she'll have to name her after us, right?

Yeah, you got it. A regular soap opera sometimes. *Qué vida, comadre. Bueno* bye.

All morning that flutter of half-fear, half-doubt. At any moment Juan Pedro might appear in the doorway. On the street. At the Cash N Carry. Like in the dreams she dreamed.

There was that to think about, yes, until the woman in the pickup drove up. Then there wasn't time to think about anything but the pickup pointed toward San Antonio. Put your bags in the back and get in.

But when they drove across the *arroyo*, the driver opened her mouth and let out a yell as loud as any mariachi. Which startled not only Cleófilas, but Juan Pedrito as well.

Pues, look how cute. I scared you two, right? Sorry. Should've warned you. Every time I cross that bridge I do that. Because of the name, you know. Woman Hollering. *Pues,* I holler. She said this in a Spanish pocked with English and laughed. Did you ever notice, Felice continued, how nothing around here is named after a woman? Really. Unless she's the Virgin. I guess you're only famous if you're a virgin. She was laughing again.

That's why I like the name of that *arroyo*. Makes you want to holler like Tarzan, right?

Everything about this woman, this Felice, amazed Cleófilas. The fact that she drove a pickup. A pickup, mind you, but when Cleófilas asked if it was her husband's, she said she didn't have a husband. The pickup was hers. She herself had chosen it. She herself was paying for it.

I used to have a Pontiac Sunbird. But those cars are for *viejas*. Pussy cars. Now this here is a real car.

What kind of talk was that coming from a woman? Cleófilas thought. But then again, Felice was like no woman she'd ever met. Can you imagine, when we crossed the *arroyo* she just started yelling like a crazy, she would say later to her father and brothers. Just like that. Who would've thought?

Who would've? Pain or rage, perhaps, but not a hoot like the one Felice had just let go. Makes you want to holler like Tarzan, Felice had said.

Then Felice began laughing again, but it wasn't Felice laughing. It was gurgling out of her own throat, a long ribbon of laughter, like water.

Questions for Reading and Analysis

1. How does the first paragraph of the story establish Cleófilas's plight, her position in the world(s) in which she dwells?

2. What does the story illustrate about the reasons battered women stay with their batterers?

3. What is the significance of Cleófilas's name?

4. Why does Felice holler when she and Cleofilas cross the bridge over the creek?

5. How optimistic is the end of the story?

Harry Crews, American novelist and journalist, writes with hard-edged, often dark humor about the grotesque characters and decadent situations of the South. In this essay, which appears in slightly altered form in Crews's acclaimed evocation of his Georgia boyhood, A Childhood: The Biography of a Place *(1978), Crews debunks the myths of idyllic farm life perpetuated by television and film.*

Pages from the Life of a Georgia Innocent

Harry Crews

Not very long ago I went with my twelve-year-old boy to a Disney movie, one of those things that show a farm family, poor but God knows honest, out there on the land building character through hunger and hard work. The hunger and hard work seemed to be a hell of a lot of fun. The deprivation was finally so rewarding you could hardly stand it. The farm was full of warm, fuzzy, furry, damp-nosed creatures: bawling calves and braying mules and dogs that were treated like people. There was a little pain here and there but just so much as would teach important lessons to all of us. It sometimes even brought a tear to the eye, but not a real tear because a tear only served to prove that a family out in the middle of nowhere scratching in the earth for survival didn't have it so bad after all. Somebody was forever petting and stroking the plump little animals, crooning to them, as they were raised for strange, unstated reasons, but surely not to be castrated and slaughtered and skinned and eaten. They were, after all, friends.

If somebody got sick, he'd just pop into an old, rattling but trustworthy pickup truck and go off to town, where a kindly doctor would receive him immediately into his office and effect an instant cure by looking down his throat and asking him to say Ah. No mention was made of payment.

As my boy and I came out of the movie, blinking in the sunlight, it occurred to me that Disney and others—the folks who bring you *The Waltons*, say, or *The Little House on the Prairie*—had managed to sell this strange vision of poverty and country life not only to suburbanites, while the suburbanites stuffed themselves with malt balls and popcorn, but also to people in little towns throughout the South who had proof in their daily lives to the contrary.

All fantasy. Now there is nothing wrong with fantasy. I love it, even live off it at times. But driving home, the reality behind the fantasy began to go bad on me. It seemed immoral and dangerous to show so many smiles without an occasional glimpse of the skull underneath.

As we were going down the driveway, my boy, Byron, said: "That was a great movie, huh, Dad?"

"Yeah," I said. "Great."

"I wish I could've lived in a place like that," he said.

"No, you don't," I said. "You just think you do."

My grandmother in Bacon County, Georgia, raised biddies: tiny cheeping bits of fluff that city folk allow their children to squeeze to death at Easter. But city children are not the only ones who love biddies; hawks love them, too. Hawks like to swoop into the yard and carry off one impaled on their curved talons. Perhaps my grandmother, in her secret heart, knew that hawks even then were approaching the time when they would be on the endangered-species list. Whether she did or not, I'm sure she often felt she and her kind were already on the list. It would not do.

I'll never forget the first time I saw her get rid of a hawk. Chickens, as everybody knows, are cannibals. Let a biddy get a spot of blood on it from a scrape or a raw place and the other biddies will simply eat it alive. My grandmother penned up all the biddies except the puniest one, already half pecked to death by the other cute little bits of fluff, and she set it out in the open yard by itself. First, though, she put arsenic on its head. I—about five years old and sucking on a sugar-tit—saw the hawk come in low over the fence, its red tail fanned, talons stretched, and nail the poisoned biddy where it squatted in the dust. The biddy never made a sound as it was carried away. My gentle grandmother watched it all with satisfaction before she let her other biddies out of the pen.

Another moment from my childhood that comes instantly to mind was about a chicken, too; a rooster. He was boss cock of the whole farm, a magnificent bird nearly two feet tall. At the base of a chicken's throat is its craw, a kind of pouch into which the bird swallows food, as well as such things as grit, bits of rock and shell. For reasons I don't understand they sometimes become crawbound. The stuff in the craw does not move; it remains in the craw and swells and will ultimately cause death. That's what would have happened to the rooster if the uncle who practically raised me hadn't said one day: "Son, we got to fix him."

He tied the rooster's feet so we wouldn't be spurred and took out his castrating knife, honed to a razor's edge, and sterilized it over a little fire. He soaked a piece of fine fishing line and a needle in alcohol. I held the rooster on its back, a wing in each hand. With the knife my uncle split open the craw, cleaned it out, then sewed it up with the fishing line. The rooster screamed and screamed. But it lived to be cock of the walk again.

Country people never did anything worse to their stock than they sometimes were forced to do to themselves. We had a man who farmed with us, a man from up north somewhere who had drifted down into Georgia with no money and a mouth full of bad teeth. Felix was his name and he was good with a plow and an ax, a hard worker. Most of the time you hardly knew he was on the place, he was so quiet and well-mannered. Except when his teeth began to bother him. And they bothered him more than a little. He lived in a shedlike little room off the side of the house. The room didn't have much in it: a ladder-back chair, a kerosine lamp, a piece of broken glass hanging on the wall over a pan of water where he shaved as often as once a week, a slat-board bed, and in one corner a chamber pot—which we called a slop jar—for use in the middle of the night when nature called. I slept in a room on the other side of the wall from him. I don't remember how old I was the night of his terrible toothache, but I do remember I was still young enough to wear a red cotton gown with five little pearl buttons down the front my grandmother had made for me.

When I heard him kick the slop jar, I knew it was his teeth. I just didn't know how bad it was. When the ladder-back chair splintered, I knew it was a bad hurt, even for Felix. A few times that night I managed to slip off to sleep only to be jarred awake when he would run blindly into the thin wall separating us. He groaned and cursed, not loudly but steadily, sometimes for as long as half an hour. Ordinarily, my mother would have fixed a hot poultice for his jaw or at least tried to do *something*, but he was a proud man and when he was really dying from his teeth, he preferred to suffer, if not in silence, at least by himself. The whole house was kept awake most of the night by his thrashing and groaning, by the wash pan being knocked off the shelf, by his broken shaving mirror being broken again, and by his blind charges into the wall.

See, our kindly country dentist would not have gotten out of his warm bed for anything less than money. And Felix didn't have any money. Besides, the dentist was in town ten miles away and we didn't have a rattling, trustworthy old truck. The only way we had to travel was two mules. And so there was nothing for Felix to do but what he was doing and it built practically no character at all. Looking back on it now, I can see that it wasn't even human. The sounds coming through the wall sure as hell weren't human anyway. On a Georgia dirt farm, pain reduced everything—man and beast alike—to the lowest common denominator. And it was pretty low and pretty common. Not something you'd want to watch while you ate malt balls and popcorn.

I was huddled under the quilts shaking with dread—my nerves were shot by the age of four and so they have remained—when I heard Felix kick open the door to his room and thump down the wooden steps in his heavy brogan work shoes, which he'd not taken off all night. I couldn't imagine where he was going but I knew I wanted to watch whatever was about to happen. The only thing worse than my nerves is my curiosity, which has always been untempered by pity or compassion, a serious character failing in most societies but a sanity-saving virtue in Georgia when I was a child.

It was February and I went out the front door barefoot onto the frozen ground. I met Felix coming around the corner of the house. In the dim light I could see the craziness in his eyes, the same craziness you see in the eyes of a trapped fox when it has not quite been able to chew through its own leg. Felix headed straight for the well, with me behind him, shaking in my thin cotton gown. He took the bucket from the nail on the rack built over the open wall and sent it shooting down hard as he could to break the inch of ice that was over the water. As he was drawing the bucket up on the pully, he seemed to see me for the first time.

"What the hell, boy! What the hell!" His voice was as mad as his eyes and he either would not or could not say anything else. He held the bucket and took a mouthful of the freezing water. He held it a long time, spat it out, and filled his mouth again.

He turned the bucket loose and let it fall again into the well instead of hanging it back on the nail where it belonged. With his cheeks swelling with water he took something out of the back pocket of his overalls. As soon as I saw what he had I knew beyond all belief and good sense what he meant to do, and suddenly I was no longer cold but stood on the frozen ground in a hot passion waiting to see him do it, to see if he *could* do it.

He had a piece of croker sack about the size of a half-dollar in his left hand and a pair of wire pliers in his right. He spat the water out and reached way back in his rotten mouth and put the piece of sack over the tooth. He braced his feet against the well and stuck the pliers in over the sackcloth. He took the pliers in both hands and immediately a forked vein leapt in his forehead. The vein in his neck popped big as a pencil. He pulled and twisted and pulled and never made a sound.

It took him a long time and finally as he fought with the pliers and with himself his braced feet slipped so that he was flat on his back when the blood broke from his mouth, followed by the pliers holding a tooth with roots half an inch long. He got slowly to his feet, sweat running off his face, and held the bloody tooth up between us.

He looked at the tooth and said in his old, recognizable voice: *"Huh now, you sumbitch!"*

Questions for Reading and Analysis

1. Towards the end of his introduction, Crews says, "It seemed immoral and dangerous to show so many smiles without an occasional glimpse of the skull underneath." What does he mean by this? What is "immoral" or "dangerous" about shows like *The Waltons* or *The Little House on the Prairie*?

2. Cite examples of the reality of farm life. What important points about the reality of farm life do all the examples illustrate?

3. Where does Crews state his thesis?

4. How do we know that Crew's description of idyllic farm life *à la* Disney is not how he sees it? Point out the instances in his use of language that let you know he sees movie versions of farm life as kitschy and unrealistic?

Angela Davis, a well-known 1960s activist, is currently a professor at the University of California at Santa Cruz and has written extensively on race, gender, and class. The following essay, excerpted from her book Blues, Legacies and Black Feminism: Gertrude "Ma" Rainey, Bessie Smith, and Billie Holiday, examines the ways in which the blues as sung by women challenge traditional, stereotypical notions of women's roles within marriage and romantic relationships.

I Used to Be Your Sweet Mama: Ideology, Sexuality, and Domesticity

Angela Davis

You had your chance and proved unfaithful
So now I'm gonna be real mean and hateful
I used to be your sweet mama, sweet papa
But now I'm just as sour as can be.

"I Used To Be Your Sweet Mama"[1]

Like most forms of popular music, African-American blues lyrics talk about love. However, what is distinctive about the blues, particular in relation to other American popular music forms of the 1920s and 1930s, is its intellectual independence and representational freedom. One of the most obvious ways in which blues lyrics deviated from that era's established popular music culture was their provocative and pervasive sexual—including homosexual—imagery.[2]

By contrast, the popular song formulas of the period demanded saccharine and idealized non-sexual depictions of heterosexual love relationships.[3] Those aspects of lived love relationships that were not compatible with the dominant, etherealized ideology of love—such as extramarital relationships, domestic violence, and the ephemerality of many sexual partnerships—were largely banished from the established popular musical culture. These themes pervade the blues. What is even more striking is the fact that initially the professional performers of this music—the most widely heard individual purveyors of the blues—were women. Bessie Smith earned the title "Empress of the Blues" not least through the sale of three-quarters of a million copies of her first record.[4]

The historical context within which the blues developed a tradition of openly addressing both female and male sexuality reveals an ideological framework that was specifically African American.[5] Emerging during the decades following the abolition of slavery, the blues gave musical expression to the new social and sexual realities encountered by African Americans as free women and men. The former slaves' economic status had not undergone a radical transformation—they were no less impoverished than they had been during slavery.[6] It was the status of their personal relationships that was revolutionized. For the first time in the history of the African presence in North America, masses of black women and men were in a position to make autonomous decisions regarding the sexual partnerships into which they entered.[7] Sexuality thus was one of the most tangible domains in which emancipation was acted upon, and through which its meanings were expressed. Sovereignty in sexual matters marked an important divide between life during slavery and life after emancipation.

Themes of individual sexual love rarely appear in the music forms produced during slavery. Whatever the reasons for this—and it may have been due to the slave system's economic management of procreation, which did not tolerate, and often severely punished, the public exhibition of self-initiated sexual relationships—I am interested here in the disparity between the individualistic, "private" nature of sexuality and the collective forms and nature of the music that was produced and performed during slavery. Sexuality after emancipation could not be adequately expressed or addressed through the musical forms existing under slavery. The spirituals and the work songs confirm that the individual concerns of black people given musical expression during slavery centered on a collective desire for an end to the system declaring them unconditional slaves to their white masters. This does not mean there was an absence of sexual meanings in the music produced by African-American slaves.[8] It means that slave music—both religious and secular— was quintessentially collective music. It was collectively performed and it gave expression to the community's yearning for freedom.[9]

The blues, on the other hand, the predominant post-slavery African-American musical form, articulated a new valuation of individual emotional needs and desires. The birth of the blues was aesthetic evidence of new psychosocial realities within the black population. This music was presented by individuals singing alone, accompanying themselves on such instruments as the banjo or guitar. The blues therefore marked the advent of a popular culture of performance, with the borders of performer and audience becoming increasingly differentiated.[10] Through the emergence of the professional blues singer—a predominantly female figure accompanied by small and large instrumental ensembles—as part of the rise of the black entertainment industry, this individualized mode of presenting popular music crystallized into a performance culture that has had an enduring influence on African-American music.

The spirituals, as they survived and were transformed during the post-slavery era, were both intensely religious and the aesthetic bearers of the slaves' collective aspirations for worldly freedom.[11] Under changed historical circumstances in which former slaves had closer contact with the religious practices and ideologies of the dominant culture, sacred music began to be increasingly enclosed within institutionalized religious spaces. Slave religious practices were inseparable from other aspects of everyday life—work, family, sabotage, escape. Post-slavery religion gradually lost some of this fluidity and came to be dependent on the church. As sacred music evolved from spirituals to gospel, it increasingly concentrated on the hereafter. Historian Lawrence Levine characterizes the nature of this development succinctly. "The overriding thrust of the gospel songs," he writes,

> *was otherworldly. Emphasis was almost wholly upon God with whom Man's relationship was one of total dependence. . . . Jesus rather than the Hebrew children dominated the gospel songs. And it was not the warrior Jesus of the spirituals but a benevolent spirit who promised His children rest and peace and justice in the hereafter.*[12]

The blues rose to become the most prominent secular genre in early twentieth-century black American music. As it came to displace sacred music in the everyday lives of black people, it both reflected and helped to construct a new black consciousness. This consciousness interpreted God as the opposite of the Devil, religion as the not secular, and the secular as largely sexual. With the blues came the designations "God's music" and the "Devil's music." The former was performed in church—although it could also accompany work[13]—while the latter was performed in jook joints, circuses, and traveling shows.[14]

Despite the new salience of this binary opposition in the everyday life of black people, it is important to underscore the close relationship between the old music and the new. The new music had old roots, and the old music reflected a new ideological grounding of black religion. Both were deeply rooted in the same history and culture.

God and the Devil had co-habited the same universe during slavery, not as polar opposites, but rather as complex characters who had different powers and who both entered into relationships with human beings. They also sometimes engaged with each other on fairly equal terms. As Henry Louis Gates and others have argued, the Devil was often associated with the trickster god Legba or Eleggua in Yoruba religions.[15] Some of the folk tales Zora Neale Hurston presents in *Mules and Men* portray the devil not as evil incarnate, but as a character with whom it was possible to identify in humorous situations.[16]

In describing the religious household in which she was reared, veteran blueswoman Ida Goodson emphasizes that the blues were banned from her childhood home. Nevertheless, she and her playmates often played and sang the blues when her parents were away. On those occasions when the parents showed up unexpectedly, they easily made the transition to gospel music without missing a beat:

> *My mother and father were religious persons. And they liked music, but they liked church music. They didn't like jazz like we do. And of course we could not even play jazz in our home while they were there. But just the moment they would turn their back, go to their society or church somewhere or another, we'd get our neighborhood children to come in there and we'd get to playing the blues and having a good time. But still we'd have one girl on the door watching to see when Mr. Goodson's coming back home or Mrs. Goodson. Because I knew if they came and caught us what we would get. . . . Whenever we'd see my father or my mother coming*

back home, the girl be saying, "There come Mr. Goodson 'nem."
And they'd be so close up on us, we'd change the blues, singing
"Jesus keep me near the cross." After that my mother and father
would join us and we'd all get to singing church songs.[17]

As if reconciling the two positions—that of herself as a young musician and that of her religious parents—Goodson later explains that "The Devil got his work and God got his work."

During slavery, the sacred universe was virtually all-embracing. Spirituals helped to construct community among the slaves and infused this imagined community with hope for a better life. They retold Old Testament narratives about the Hebrew people's struggle against Pharaoh's oppression, and thereby established a community narrative of African people enslaved in North America that simultaneously transcended the slave system and encouraged its abolition. Under the conditions of US slavery, the sacred—and especially sacred music—was an important means of preserving African cultural memory. Karl Marx's comments on religion as the "opium of the people"[18] notwithstanding, the spirituals attest to the fact that religious consciousness can itself play a transformative role. As Sojourner Truth and other abolitionists demonstrated—as well as insurrectionary leaders Nat Turner and Denmark Vesey, and the Underground Railroad conductor Harriet Tubman—religion was far more than Marx's "illusory sun." Spirituals were embedded in and gave expression to a powerful yearning for freedom.[19] Religion was indeed, in Marx's words, the "soul" of "soulless conditions."[20]

The spirituals articulated the hopes of black slaves in religious terms. In the vast disappointment that accompanied emancipation—when economic and political liberation must have seemed more unattainable than ever—blues created a discourse[21] that represented freedom in more immediate and accessible terms. The material conditions for the freedom about which the slaves had sung in their spirituals seemed no closer after slavery than they had seemed before, but there were nevertheless distinct differences between the slaves' personal status under slavery and during the post-Civil War period. In three major respects, emancipation had radically transformed their personal lives: (1) there was no longer a proscription on free individual travel; (2) education was now a realizable goal for individual men and women; (3) sexuality could be explored freely by individuals who now could enter into autonomously chosen personal relationships. The new blues consciousness was shaped by and gave expression to at least two of these three transformations: travel and sexuality. In both male and female blues, travel and sexuality are ubiquitous themes, handled both separately and together. But what finally is most striking is the way the blues registered sexuality as a tangible expression of freedom; it was this dimension that most profoundly marked and defined the secularity of the blues.

James Cone offers the following definition of the blues, agreeing with C. Eric Lincoln's succinct characterization of them as "secular spirituals." Cone writes,

They are secular in the same sense that they confine their attention
solely to the immediate and affirm the bodily expression of black soul,
including its sexual manifestations. They are spirituals because they
are impelled by the same search for the truth of black experience.[22]

It is not necessary to accede to Cone's essentialist invocation of a single meta-physical "truth" of black experience to gain from it a key insight into why the blues were condemned as the Devil's music. It was because they drew upon and incorporated sacred consciousness and thereby posed a serious threat to religious attitudes.

Levine emphasizes the blurring of the sacred and the secular both in gospel music and in the blues. It may not have been the secularity of the blues that produced such castigation by the church, he argues, but rather, precisely their sacred nature. He writes,

> *The blues was threatening not primarily because it was secular;*
> *other forms of secular music were objected to less strenuously and*
> *often not at all. Blues was threatening because its spokesmen and*
> *its ritual too frequently provided the expressive communal channels*
> *of relief that had been largely the province of religion in the past.*[23]

Although both Cone and Levine make references to Mamie Smith, Ma Rainey, Bessie Smith, and other women who composed and performed blues songs, they, like most scholars, tend to view women as marginal to the production of the blues. Note that in the passage quoted above, Levine refers quite explicitly to the "spokesmen" of the blues. With the simple substitution of "spokeswomen," the argument he suggests would become more compelling and more deeply revealing of the new religious consciousness about which he writes.

Blues practices, as Levine asserts, did tend to appropriate previously religious channels of expression and this appropriation was associated with women's voices. Women summoned sacred responses to their messages about sexuality.[24] During this period, religious consciousness came increasingly under the control of institution-alized churches, and male dominance over the religious process came to be taken for granted. At the same time that male ministers were becoming a professional caste, women blues singers were performing as professional artists and attracting large audiences in revival-like gatherings. Gertrude "Ma" Rainey and Bessie Smith were the most widely known of these women. They preached about sexual love, and in doing so they articulated a collective experience of freedom, and gave voice to the most powerful evidence there was for many black people that slavery no longer existed.

The expression of socially unfulfilled dreams in the language and imagery of individual sexual love is, of course, not peculiar to the African-American experi-ence. As part of the capitalist schism between the public and the private realms within European-derived American popular culture, however, themes of romantic love had quite different ideological implications from themes of sexuality within post-slavery African-American cultural expression. In the context of the consoli-dation of industrial capitalism, the sphere of personal love and domestic life in mainstream American culture came to be increasingly idealized as the arena in which happiness was to be sought.[25] This held a special significance for women, since love and domesticity were supposed to constitute the outermost limits of their lives. Full membership in the public community was the exclusive domain of men. Therefore, European-American popular songs have to be interpreted within this context and as contributing to patriarchal hegemony.

The blues did not entirely escape the influences that shaped the role of romantic love in the popular songs of the dominant culture. Nevertheless, the incorporation of personal relationships into the blues has its own historical meanings and social and political resonances. Love was not represented as an idealized realm to which unfulfilled dreams of happiness were relegated. The historical African-American vision of individual sexual love linked it inextricably with possibilities of social freedom in the economic and political realms. Unfreedom during slavery involved, among other things, a prohibition of freely chosen, enduring family relationships. Because slaves were legally defined as commodities, women of childbearing age were valued in accordance with their breeding potential and were often forced to copulate with men—viewed as "bucks"—chosen by their owners for the sole purpose of producing valuable progeny.[26] Moreover, direct sexual exploitation of African women by their white masters was a constant feature of slavery.[27] What tenuous permanence in familial relationships the slaves did manage to construct was always subject to the whim of their masters and the potential profits to be reaped from sale. The suffering caused by forced ruptures of slave families has been abundantly documented.[28]

Given this context, it is understandable that the personal and sexual dimensions of freedom acquired an expansive importance, especially since the economic and political ingredients of freedom were largely denied to black people in the aftermath of slavery. The focus on sexual love in blues music was thus quite different in meaning from the prevailing idealization of romantic love in mainstream popular culture. For recently emancipated slaves, freely chosen sexual love became a mediator between historical disappointment and the new social realities of an evolving African-American community. Ralph Ellison alludes to this dimension of the blues, I think, when he notes that "their mysteriousness . . . their ability to imply far more than they state outright and their capacity to make the details of sex convey meanings which touch on the metaphysical." [29]

Sexuality was central in both men's and women's blues. During the earliest phases of their history, blues were essentially a male phenomenon. The archetypal blues singer was a solitary wandering man accompanied by his banjo or guitar, and, in the words of blues scholar Giles Oakley, his principal theme "is the sexual relationship. Almost all other themes, leaving town, train rides, work trouble, general dissatisfaction sooner or later reverts to the central concern."[30] In women's blues, which became a crucial element of the rising black entertainment industry, there was an even more pronounced emphasis on love and sexuality.

The representations of love and sexuality in women's blues often blatantly contradicted mainstream ideological assumptions regarding women and being in love. They also challenged the notion that women's "place" was in the domestic sphere. Such notions were based on the social realities of middle-class white women's lives, but were incongruously applied to all women, regardless of race or class.[31] This led to inevitable contradictions between prevailing social expectations and black women's social realities. Women of that era were expected to seek fulfillment within the confines of marriage, with their husbands functioning as provider and their children as evidence of their worth as human beings. The sparsity of allusions to marriage and domesticity in women's blues therefore becomes highly significant.

In Bessie Smith's rendition of "Sam Jones Blues"—which contains one of the few commentaries on the subject of marriage to be found in her body of work—the subject is acknowledged only in relation to its dissolution. Her performance of this song satirically accentuates the contrast between the dominant cultural construction of marriage and the stance of economic independence black women were compelled to assume for their sheer survival. Referring to a wandering husband, Bessie Smith sings,

> . . . *I'm free and livin' all alone*
> *Say, hand me the key that unlocks my front door*
> *Because that bell don't read "Sam Jones" no more*
> *No, you ain't talkin' to Mrs Jones, you speaking to Miss Wilson*
> *now.*[32]

Although the written lyrics reveal a conversation between "proper" English and black working-class English, only by listening to the song do we experience the full impact of Smith's manipulation of language in her recording. References to marriage as perceived by the dominant white culture are couched in irony. She mocks the notion of eternal matrimony—"I used to be your lofty mate"—singing genteel words with a teasing intonation to evoke white cultural conceptions. On the other hand, when she indicates the perspective of the black woman, Miss Wilson—who "used to be Mrs Jones"—she sings in a comfortable, bluesy black English. This song is remarkable for the way Smith translates into musical contrast and contention the clash between two cultures' perceptions of marriage—and particularly women's place within the institution. It is easy to imagine the testifying responses Smith no doubt evoked in her female audiences, responses that affirmed working-class black women's sense of themselves as relatively emancipated if not from marriage itself then at least from some of its most confining ideological constraints.

The protagonists in women's blues are seldom wives and almost never mothers. One explanation for the absence of direct allusions to marriage may be the different words mainstream and African-American cultures use to designate "male spouse." African-American working-class argot refers to both husbands and male lovers (and even in some cases female lovers) as "my man" or "my daddy." But these different linguistic practices cannot be considered in isolation from the social realities they represent, for they point to divergent perspectives regarding the institution of marriage.

During Bessie Smith's era most black heterosexual couples—married or not—had children. However, blues women rarely sang about mothers, fathers, and children. In the subject index to her book *Black Pearls*, black studies scholar Daphne Duval Harrison lists the following themes: advice to other women; alcohol; betrayal or abandonment; broken or failed love affairs; death; departure; dilemma of staying with man or returning to family; disease and afflictions; erotica; hell; homosexuality; infidelity; injustice; jail and serving time; loss of lover; love; men; mistreatment; murder; other woman; poverty; promiscuity; sadness; sex; suicide; supernatural; trains; traveling; unfaithfulness; vengeance; weariness, depression and disillusionment; weight loss.[33] It is revealing that she does not include children, domestic life, husband, and marriage.

The absence of the mother figure in the blues does not imply a rejection of motherhood as such, but rather suggests that blues women found the cult of motherhood irrelevant to the realities of their lives.[34] The female figures evoked in women's blues are independent women free of the domestic orthodoxy of the prevailing representations of womanhood through which female subjects of the era were constructed. . . .

The woman in Ma Rainey's "Lawd Send Me a Man Blues" harbors no illusions about the relationship she desires with a man. She is lonely and is wondering "who gonna pay my board bill now." Appealing for any man she can get, she pleads, singing with a bluesy zeal,

> *Send me a zulu, a voodoo, any old man*
> *I'm not particular, boys, I'll take what I can.*[35]

Bessie Smith's "Baby Doll" conveys a similar message:

> *I want to be somebody's baby doll*
> *So I can get my loving all the time*
> *I want to be somebody's baby doll*
> *To ease my mind.*[36]

These blues women had no qualms about announcing female desire. Their songs express women's intention to "get their loving." Such affirmations of sexual autonomy and open expressions of female sexual desire give historical voice to possibilities of equality not articulated elsewhere. Women's blues and the cultural politics lived out in the careers of the blues queens put these new possibilities on the historical agenda. . . .

By focusing on the issue of misogynist violence, the first activist moments of the contemporary women's movement exposed the centrality of the ideological separation of the public and private spheres to the structure of male domination. In the early 1970s women began to speak publicly about their experiences of rape, battery, and about the violation of their reproductive rights. Obscured by a shroud of silence, these assaults against women traditionally had been regarded as a fact of private life to be shielded at all costs from scrutiny in the public sphere. That this cover-up would no longer be tolerated was the explosive meaning behind feminists' defiant notion that "the personal is political."[37]

The performances of the classic blues women—especially Bessie Smith—were one of the few cultural spaces in which a tradition of public discourse on male violence had been previously established. One explanation for the fact that the blues women of the 1920s—and the texts they present—fail to respect the taboo on speaking publicly about domestic violence is that the blues as a genre never acknowledges the discursive and ideological boundaries separating the private sphere from the public. Historically, there has been no body of literature on battering because white, well-to-do women who were in a position to write about their experiences in abusive relationships have only recently been convinced that such privately executed violence is a suitable subject for public discourse.

There is, however, a body of preserved oral culture—or "orature," to use a term employed by some scholars[38]—about domestic abuse in the songs of blues women like Gertrude Rainey and Bessie Smith. Violence against women was always an appropriate topic of women's blues. The contemporary urge to break the silence surrounding misogynist violence, and the organized political movement challenging violence against women has an aesthetic precursor in the work of the classic blues singers.

Women's blues have been accused of promoting acquiescent and therefore anti-feminist responses to misogynist abuse. It is true that some of the songs recorded by Rainey and Smith seem to exemplify acceptance of male violence—and sometimes even masochistic delight in being the target of lovers' beatings. Such claims do not take into account the extent to which blues meaning is manipulated and transformed—sometimes even into its opposite—in blues performance. Blues make abundant use of humor, satire, and irony, revealing their historic roots in slave music, wherein indirect methods of expression were the only means by which the oppression of slavery could be denounced. In this sense, the blues genre is a direct descendant of work songs, which often relied on indirection and irony to highlight the inhumanity of slave owners so that their targets were sure to misunderstand the intended meaning.[39]

Bessie Smith sings a number of songs whose lyrics may be interpreted as condoning emotional and physical abuse as attendant hazards for women involved in sexual partnerships. But close attention to her musical presentation of these songs persuades the listener that they contain implicit critiques of male abuse. In "Yes Indeed He Do," Bessie Smith's sarcastic presentation of the lyrics transforms their observations on an unfaithful, abusive and exploitative lover into a scathing critique of male violence:

> *Is he true as stars above me? What kind of fool is you?*
> *He don't stay from home all night more than six times a week*
> *No, I known that I'm his Sheba and I know that he's my sheik*
> *And when I ask him where he's been he grabs a rocking chair*
> *Then he knocks me down and says it's just a love lick dear.*[40]

Edward Brooks, in *The Bessie Smith Companion,* makes the following comment about this song:

> *Bessie delivers the song with growling gusto, as if it were really a panegyric to an exemplary lover; she relates his wrongs with the approval of virtues and it comes as a jolt when the exultation in her voice is compared with her actual words.*[41]

Brooks's analysis assumes that Smith was unselfconscious in her performance of this song. He therefore misses its intentional ambiguity and complexity. Smith was an accomplished performer, actor and comedian and was therefore well acquainted with the uses of humor and irony. It is much more plausible to characterize her decision to sing "Yes Indeed He Do" with mock praise and elation as a conscious effort to highlight, in the most effective way possible, the inhumanity and misogyny of male batterers. . . .

The female characters memorialized in women's blues songs, even in their most despairing moods, do not fit the mold of the typical victim of abuse. The independent women of blues lore are women who do not think twice about wielding weapons against men who they feel have mistreated them. They frequently brandish their razors and guns, and dare men to cross the lines they draw. While acknowledging the physical mistreatment they have received at the hands of their male lovers, they do not perceive or define themselves as powerless in face of such violence. Indeed, they fight back passionately. In many songs Ma Rainey and Bessie Smith pay tribute to fearless women who attempt to avenge themselves when their lovers have been unfaithful. In "Black Mountain Blues," Bessie Smith sings:

> *He met a city gal and he throwed me down*
> *I'm bound for Black Mountain, me and my razor and my gun*
> *Lord I'm bound for Black Mountain, me and my razor and my gun*
> *I'm gonna shoot him if he stands still and cut him if he run.*[42]

In Smith's "Sinful Blues," a woman's rage also turns into violence:

> *Gonna get me a gun long as my right arm*
> *Shoot that man because he done me wrong.*
> *Lord, now I've got them sinful blues.*[43]

In Ma Rainey's "See See Rider Blues," the protagonist, who has discovered that her man has another woman friend, announces her intention to buy herself a pistol and to "kill my man and catch the Cannonball."[44] Her concluding resolution is: "If he don't have me, he won't have no gal at all." In Rainey's "Rough and Tumble Blues," the woman attacks not the man, but the women who have attempted to seduce him:

> *I got rough and killed three women 'fore the police got the news*
> *'Cause mama's on the warpath with these rough and tumble blues.*[45]

The lives of many of the blues women of the twenties resembled those of the fearless women memorialized in their songs. We know that at times Bessie Smith was a victim of male violence and also that she would not hesitate to hurl violent threats—which she sometimes carried out—at the men who betrayed her. Nor was she afraid to confront the most feared embodiments of white racist terror. One evening in July of 1927, robed and hooded Ku Klux Klansmen attempted to disrupt her tent performance by pulling up the tent stakes and collapsing the entire structure. When Smith was informed of the trouble, she immediately left the tent and, according to her biographer:

> *. . . ran toward the intruders, stopped within ten feet of them, placed one hand on her hip, and shook a clenched fist at the Klansmen. "What the fuck you think you're doin'," she shouted above the sound of the band. "I'll get the whole damn tent out here if I have to. You just pick up them sheets and run!"*
>
> *The Klansmen, apparently too surprised to move, just stood there and gawked. Bessie hurled obscenities at them until they finally turned and disappeared quietly into the darkness . . .*
>
> *Then she went back into the tent as if she had just settled a routine matter.*[46]

Blues women were expected to deviate from the norms defining orthodox female behavior, which is why they were revered by both men and women in black working-class communities. Ida Cox's "Wild Women Don't Have the Blues" became the most famous portrait of the nonconforming, independent woman, and her "wild woman" has become virtually synonymous with the blues queen herself:

Wild women don't worry, wild women don't have the blues
You never get nothing by being an angel child
You'd better change your ways and get real wild.[47]

"Prove It On Me Blues," composed by Gertrude Rainey, portrays just such a "wild woman" who affirms her independence from the orthodox norms of womanhood by boldly flaunting her lesbianism. Rainey's sexual involvement with women was no secret among her colleagues and her audiences. The advertisement for the release of "Prove It On Me Blues" showed the blues woman sporting a man's hat, jacket and tie and, while a policeman looked on, obviously attempting to seduce two women on a street corner. The song's lyrics include the following:

Went out last night with a crowd of my friends
They must've been women 'cause I don't like no men . . .

Wear my clothes just like a fan
Talk to the gals just like any old man.[48]

Sandra Lieb has described this song as a "powerful statement of lesbian defiance and self-worth."[49] "Prove It On Me Blues" is a cultural precursor to the lesbian cultural movement of the 1970s, which, it is interesting to note, began to crystallize around the performance and recording of lesbian-affirming songs. (In fact, in 1977, Teresa Trull recorded a cover of Ma Rainey's song for an album entitled *Lesbian Concentrate.*[50])

Hazel Carby has insightfully observed that "Prove It On Me Blues"

vacillates between the subversive hidden activity of women loving women [and] a public declaration of lesbianism. The words express a contempt for a society that rejected lesbians. . . . But at the same time the song is a reclamation of lesbianism as long as the woman publicly names her sexual preference for herself. . . .

Carby argues that this song "engag[es] directly in defining issues of sexual preference as a contradictory struggle of social relations."[51]

"Prove It On Me Blues" suggests how the iconoclastic blueswomen of the twenties were pioneers for later historical developments. The response to this song also suggests that homophobia within the black community did not prevent blues women from challenging stereotypical conceptions of women's lives. They did not allow themselves to be enshrined by the silence imposed by mainstream society.

The blues songs recorded by Gertrude Rainey and Bessie Smith offer us a privileged glimpse of the prevailing perceptions of love and sexuality in post-slavery black communities in the United States. Both women were role models for untold thousands of their sisters to whom they delivered messages that defined the male dominance encouraged by mainstream culture. The blues women openly challenged the gender politics implicit in traditional cultural representations of marriage and heterosexual love relationships. Refusing, in the blues tradition of raw realism, to romanticize romantic relationships, they instead exposed the stereotypes and explored the contradictions of those relationships. By so doing, they redefined women's "place." They forged and memorialized images of tough, resilient and independent women who were afraid neither of their own vulnerability nor of defending their right to be respected as autonomous human beings.

Endnotes

1. Bessie Smith, "I Used To Be Your Sweet Mama," Columbia 14292-D, Feb. 9, 1928. Reissued on *Empty Bed Blues,* Columbia CG 30450, 1972.

2. According to Hazel Carby, "[w]hat has been called the 'Classic Blues,' the women's blues of the twenties and early thirties, is a discourse that articulates a cultural and political struggle over sexual relations: a struggle that is directed against the objectification of female sexuality within a patriarchal order but which also tries to reclaim women's bodies as the sexual and sensuous objects of song." "It Just Be's Dat Way Sometime: The Sexual Politics of Women's Blues," *Radical America,* 20, no. 4 (June–July 1986), 12.

3. See Henry Pleasants, *The Great American Popular Singers* (New York: Simon & Schuster, 1974). According to Lawrence Levine, "the physical side of love which, aside from some tepid hand holding and lip pecking, was largely missing from popular music, was strongly felt in the blues." *Black Culture and Black Consciousness: Afro-American Thought from Slavery to Freedom* (New York: Oxford University Press, 1975), 279.

4. Bessie Smith's first recording, a cover of Alberta Hunter's "Down Hearted Blues," sold 780,000 copies in less than six months. Chris Albertson, *Bessie* (New York: Stein & Day, 1972), 46.

5. The central place of the blues in the elaboration of a post-slavery black cultural consciousness has been examined widely in works like LeRoi Jones's pioneering *Blues People* and Lawrence Levine's engaging study *Black Culture and Black Consciousness.* While both suggest important approaches to the understanding of racial dimensions of African-American culture, scant attention is accorded gender consciousness. Daphne Duval Harrison's trailblazing study *Black Pearls: Blues Queens of the 1920s* (New Brunswick: Rutgers University Press, 1988) reveals, in fact, how rich women's blues can be as a terrain for explorations of the place gender occupies in black cultural consciousness.

6. See W. E. B. Du Bois, *Black Reconstruction in America* (New York: Harcourt, Brace, 1935).

7. See Herbert Gutman, *The Black Family in Slavery and Freedom, 1750–1925* (New York: Pantheon, 1976), ch. 9.

8. Lawrence Levine cites a rowing song heard by Frances Kemble in the late 1830s and characterized by her as nonsensical, but interpreted by Chadwick Hansen as containing hidden sexual meanings.

   Jenny shake her toe at me,
   > Jenny gone away;
   Jenny shake her toe at me,
   > Jenny gone away.
   Hurrah! Miss Susy, oh!
   > Jenny gone away;
   Hurrah! Miss Susy, oh!
   > Jenny gone away.

   Levine, *Black Culture and Black Consciousness,* p. 11. (Frances Anne Kemble, *Journal of a Residence on a Georgian Plantation in 1838–1839* [1863; reprint,

New York: Knopf, 1961], 163–4.) "Chadwick Hansen [in "Jenny's Toe: Negro Shaking Dances in America," *American Quarterly*, 19 (1967), 554–63] has shown that in all probability what Miss Kemble heard was not the English word 'toe' but an African-derived word referring to the buttocks." The Jenny of whom the slaves were singing with such obvious pleasure was shaking something more interesting and provocative than her foot.

9. According to James Cone, "The spiritual . . . is the spirit of the people struggling to be free . . . [it] is the people's response to the societal contradictions. It is the people facing trouble and affirming, 'I ain't tired yet.' But the spiritual is more than dealing with trouble. It is a joyful experience, a vibrant affirmation of life and its possibilities in an appropriate esthetic form. The spiritual is the community in rhythm, swinging to the movement of life." *The Spirituals and the Blues: An Interpretation* (New York: Seabury, 1972), 32–3.

10. Popular musical culture in the African-American tradition continues to actively involve the audience in the performance of the music. The distinction, therefore, is not between the relatively active and relatively passive stances of the audience. Rather it is between a mode of musical presentation in which everyone involved is considered a "performer"—or perhaps in which no one, the song leader included, is considered a "performer"—and one in which the producer of the music plays a privileged role in calling forth the responses of the audience.

11. See James Cone's discussion of the liberation content of the spirituals. John Lovell, Jr (*Black Song: The Forge and the Flame*, New York: Macmillan, 1972) also emphasizes the relationship between the slave community's yearning for liberation and the music it produced in the religious tradition of Christianity.

12. Levine, *Black Culture and Black Consciousness*, 175.

13. Religious themes are to be found in some of the prison work songs recorded by folklorists such as Alan Lomax during the thirties, forties, and fifties.

14. See Giles Oakley, *The Devil's Music: A History of the Blues* (New York and London: Harcourt Brace Jovanovich, 1976), 97–9.

15. See Henry Louis Gates, Jr, *The Signifying Monkey: A Theory of African-American Literary Criticism* (New York: Oxford University Press, 1988), ch. 1.

16. See Zora Neale Hurston, *Mules and Men* (Bloomington: Indiana University Press, 1978), stories on Jack and the Devil, 164, and about "unh hunh" as a word the Devil made up, 169.

17. *Wild Women Don't Have the Blues,* dir. Christine Dall, Calliope Film Resources, 1989, videocassette.

18. When applied to the religious contours and content of slave-initiated cultural community, the infamous observation by the young Karl Marx that religion is the "opium of the people" elucidates the utopian potential of slave religion; but, in this context, Marx's observation simultaneously goes too far and not far enough.

 Religious suffering is at the same time an *expression* of real suffering and a protest against real suffering. Religion is the sigh of the oppressed creature, the sentiment of a heartless world, and the soul of soulless conditions. It is the *opium* of the people. . . . Religion is only the illusory sun around which man revolves so long as he does not revolve around himself.

Karl Marx, "The Critique of Hegel's Philosophy of Right," in Karl Marx, *Early Writings,* ed. T. B. Bottomore (New York: McGraw-Hill, 1963), 43–4.

Marx goes too far in the sense that he assumes a necessarily and exclusively ideological relationship between religious consciousness and material conditions, i.e., that religion is fundamentally false consciousness and that the "self" or community it articulates is necessarily an illusion. Such an all-embracing conception of religion cannot account for its extra-religious dimensions. On the other hand, he does not go far enough when he dismisses the revolutionary potential of religious consciousness.

19. See Lovell, *Black Song,* chs 17 and 18.

20. Marx, "Critique of Hegel's Philosophy," 44.

21. See Houston A. Baker, Jr, *Blues, Ideology, and Afro-American Literature* (Chicago: University of Chicago Press, 1984).

22. Cone, *The Spirituals and the Blues,* 112. C. Eric Lincoln originated the term "secular spirituals."

23. Levine, *Black Culture and Black Consciousness,* 237.

24. Julio Finn argues that "the jook joint is to the blues what the church is to the spiritual, and the bluesman on stage is in his pulpit. Contrary to the 'holy' atmosphere which reigns in the church, the jook joint is characterized by its rowdiness—the noise and smoke and drinking are necessities without which its character would be fatally altered, for that would alter the music, which is in no small way shaped by it." Julio Finn, *The Bluesman* (London: Quartet, 1986), 202. Unfortunately, Finn confines his discussion to blues men and does not consider the role of women.

25. See Joan Landes, "The Public and the Private Sphere: A Feminist Reconsideration," in Johanna Meehan (ed.), *Feminists Read Habermas* (London: Routledge, 1995). According to Aida Hurtado in "Relating to Privilege: Seduction and Rejection in the Subordination of White Women and Women of Color" (*Signs: A Journal of Women and Culture in Society,* 14, no. 4 [Summer 1989]), "the public/private distinction is relevant only for the white middle and upper classes since historically the American state has intervened constantly in the private lives and domestic arrangements of the working class. Women of Color have not had the benefit of the economic conditions that underlie the public/private distinction. Instead the political consciousness of women of Color stems from an awareness that the public is *personally* political."

26. Du Bois points out that in many border states, slave-breeding became a main industry: "The deliberate breeding of a strong, big field-hand stock could be carried out by selecting proper males, and giving them the run of the likeliest females. This in many Border States became a regular policy and fed the slave trade." *Black Reconstruction in America,* 44.

27. Gutman, *The Black Family,* 80, 388.

28. Slave narratives by Frederick Douglass, Solomon Northrup, and Harriet Jacobs contain poignant descriptions of family separations. See also Gutman, *The Black Family,* ch. 8.

29. Ralph Ellison, *Shadow and Act* (New York: Vintage, 1972), 245.

30. Oakley, *The Devil's Music,* 59.

31. Angela Y. Davis, *Women, Race, and Class* (New York: Random House, 1981).

32. Bessie Smith, "Sam Jones Blues," Columbia 13005-D, Sept. 24, 1923. Reissued on *Any Woman's Blues*, Columbia G 30126, 1972.

33. Harrison, *Black Pearls*, 287.

34. See Mary P. Ryan's discussion of the cult of motherhood in *Womanhood in America: From Colonial Times to the Present* (New York: Franklin Watts, 1975).

35. Gertrude "Ma" Rainey, "Lawd, Send Me a Man Blues," Paramount 12227, May 1924. Reissued on *Queen of the Blues*, Biograph BLP-12032, n.d.

36. Bessie Smith, "Baby Doll," Columbia 14147-D, May 4, 1926. Reissued on *Nobody's Blues but Mine*, Columbia CG 31093,1972.

37. See Sara Evans's study, *Personal Politics: The Roots of Women's Liberation in the Civil Rights Movement and the New Left* (New York: Knopf, 1979).

38. See Michere Githae Mugo, *Orature and Human Rights* (Rome: Institute of South African Development Studies, NUL, Lesotho, 1991).

39. See Oakley's discussion of work and song, *The Devil's Music,* 36–46.

40. Bessie Smith, "Yes, Indeed He Do."

41. Edward Brooks, *The Bessie Smith Companion* (New York: Da Capo, 1982), 143.

42. Bessie Smith, "Black Mountain Blues," Columbia 14554-D, June 22, 1930. Reissued on *The World's Greatest Blues Singer,* Columbia CG 33, 1972.

43. Bessie Smith, "Sinful Blues," Columbia 114052-D, Dec. 11, 1924. Reissued on *The Empress,* Columbia CG 30818, 1972.

44. Gertrude "Ma" Rainey, "See See Rider Blues," Paramount 12252, Dec. 1925. Reissued on *Ma Rainey,* Milestone M-47021, 1974.

45. Gertrude "Ma" Rainey, "Rough and Tumble Blues," Paramount 12303, 1928. Reissued on *The Immortal Ma Rainey,* Milestone MLP 2001, 1966.

46. Albertson, *Bessie,* 132–3.

47. Ida Cox, "Wild Women Don't Have the Blues," Paramount 12228, 1924. Reissued on *Wild Women Don't Have the Blues,* Riverdale RLP 9374, n.d.

48. Gertrude "Ma" Rainey, "Prove It On Me Blues," Paramount 12668, June 1928. Reissued on *Ma Rainey,* Milestone M-47021, 1974.

49. Sandra Lieb, 125.

50. *Lesbian Concentrate: A Lesbianthology of Songs and Poems.* Olivia Records MU 29729, 1977.

51. Carby, "It Just Be's Dat Way Sometime," 18.

Questions for Reading and Analysis

1. Why, according to Davis, are the blues preoccupied with sexual love?

2. How do women's blues in particular contradict mainstream assumptions about women and love?

3. How does Davis support her argument about the strong feminism inherent in women's blues?

A prolific essayist and keen observer of the cultural landscape, Joan Didion (b. 1934) muses about the meaning of self-respect, suggesting that it is primarily a lack of self-deception. Without self-respect, Didion writes, "one runs away to find oneself, and finds no one at home."

On Self-Respect

Joan Didion

Once, in a dry season, I wrote in large letters across two pages of a notebook that innocence ends when one is stripped of the delusion that one likes oneself. Although now, some years later, I marvel that a mind on the outs with itself should have nonetheless made painstaking record of its every tremor, I recall with embarrassing clarity the flavor of those particular ashes. It was a matter of misplaced self-respect.

I had not been elected to Phi Beta Kappa. This failure could scarcely have been more predictable or less ambiguous (I simply did not have the grades), but I was unnerved by it; I had somehow thought myself a kind of academic Raskolnikov, curiously exempt from the cause-effect relationships which hampered others. Although even the humorless nineteen-year-old that I was must have recognized that the situation lacked real tragic stature, the day that I did not make Phi Beta Kappa nonetheless marked the end of something, and innocence may well be the word for it. I lost the conviction that lights would always turn green for me, the pleasant certainty that those rather passive virtues which had won me approval as a child automatically guaranteed me not only Phi Beta Kappa keys but happiness, honor, and the love of a good man; lost a certain touching faith in the totem power of good manners, clean hair, and proven competence on the Stanford-Binet scale. To such doubtful amulets had my self-respect been pinned, and I faced myself that day with the nonplused apprehension of someone who has come across a vampire and has no crucifix at hand.

Although to be driven back upon oneself is an uneasy affair at best, rather like trying to cross a border with borrowed credentials, it seems to me now the one condition necessary to the beginnings of real self-respect. Most of our platitudes notwithstanding, self-deception remains the most difficult deception. The tricks that work on others count for nothing in that very well-lit back alley where one keeps assignations with oneself: no winning smiles will do here, no prettily drawn lists of good intentions. One shuffles flashily but in vain through one's marked cards—the kindness done for the wrong reason, the apparent triumph which involved no real effort, the seemingly heroic act into which one had been shamed. The dismal fact is that self-respect has nothing to do with the approval of others—

who are, after all, deceived easily enough; has nothing to do with reputation, which, as Rhett Butler told Scarlett O'Hara, is something people with courage can do without.

To do without self-respect, on the other hand, is to be an unwilling audience of one to an interminable documentary that details one's failings, both real and imagined, with fresh footage spliced in for every screening. *There's the glass you broke in anger, there's the hurt on X's face; watch now, this next scene, the night Y came back from Houston, see how you muff this one.* To live without self-respect is to lie awake some night, beyond the reach of warm milk, phenobarbital, and the sleeping hand on the coverlet, counting up the sins of commission and omission, the trusts betrayed, the promises subtly broken, the gifts irrevocably wasted through sloth or cowardice or carelessness. However long we postpone it, we eventually lie down alone in that notoriously uncomfortable bed, the one we make ourselves. Whether or not we sleep in it depends, of course, on whether or not we respect ourselves.

To protest that some fairly improbable people, some people who *could not possibly respect themselves,* seem to sleep easily enough is to miss the point entirely, as surely as those people miss it who think that self-respect has necessarily to do with not having safety pins in one's underwear. There is a common superstition that "self-respect" is a kind of charm against snakes, something that keeps those who have it locked in some unblighted Eden, out of strange beds, ambivalent conversations, and trouble in general. It does not at all. It has nothing to do with the face of things, but concerns instead a separate peace, a private reconciliation. Although the careless, suicidal Julian English in *Appointment in Samarra* and the careless, incurably dishonest Jordan Baker in *The Great Gatsby* seem equally improbable candidates for self-respect, Jordan Baker had it, Julian English did not. With that genius for accommodation more often seen in women than in men, Jordan took her own measure, made her own peace, avoided threats to that peace: "I hate careless people," she told Nick Carraway. "It takes two to make an accident."

Like Jordan Baker, people with self-respect have the courage of their mistakes. They know the price of things. If they choose to commit adultery, they do not then go running, in an access of bad conscience, to receive absolution from the wronged parties; nor do they complain unduly of the unfairness, the undeserved embarrassment, of being named co-respondent. In brief, people with self-respect exhibit a certain toughness, a kind of moral nerve; they display what was once called *character*, a quality which, although approved in the abstract, sometimes loses ground to other, more instantly negotiable virtues. The measure of its slipping prestige is that one tends to think of it only in connection with homely children and United States senators who have been defeated, preferably in the primary, for reelection. Nonetheless, character—the willingness to accept responsibility for one's own life— is the source from which self-respect springs.

Self-respect is something that our grandparents, whether or not they had it, knew all about. They had instilled in them, young, a certain discipline, the sense that one lives by doing things one does not particularly want to do, by putting fears and doubts to one side, by weighing immediate comforts against the possibility of larger, even intangible, comforts. It seemed to the nineteenth century admirable, but not remarkable, that Chinese Gordon put on a clean white suit and held Khartoum against the Madhi; it did not seem unjust that the way to free land in California involved death and difficulty and dirt. In a diary kept during the winter of 1846, an emigrating twelve-year-old named Narcissa Cornwall noted coolly: "Father was busy reading and did not notice that the house was being filled with strange Indians until Mother spoke about it." Even lacking any clue as to what Mother said, one can scarcely fail to be impressed by the entire incident: the father reading, the Indians filing in, the mother choosing the words that would not alarm, the child duly recording the event and noting further those particular Indians were not, "fortunately for us," hostile. Indians were simply part of the *donnée*.

In one guise or another, Indians always are. Again, it is a question of recognizing that anything worth having has its price. People who respect themselves are willing to accept the risk that the Indians will be hostile, that the venture will go bankrupt, that the liaison may not turn out to be one in which *every day is a holiday because you're married to me*. They are willing to invest something of themselves; they may not play at all, but when they do play, they know the odds.

That kind of self-respect is a discipline, a habit of mind that can never be faked but can be developed, trained, coaxed forth. It was once suggested to me that, as an antidote to crying, I put my head in a paper bag. As it happens, there is a sound physiological reason, something to do with oxygen, for doing exactly that, but the psychological effect alone is incalculable: it is difficult in the extreme to continue fancying oneself Cathy in *Wuthering Heights* with one's head in a Food Fair bag. There is a similar case for all the small disciplines, unimportant in themselves; imagine maintaining any kind of swoon, commiserative or carnal, in a cold shower.

But those small disciplines are valuable only insofar as they represent larger ones. To say that Waterloo was won on the playing fields of Eton is not to say that Napoleon might have been saved by a crash program in cricket; to give formal dinners in the rain forest would be pointless did not the candlelight flickering on the liana call forth deeper, stronger disciplines, values instilled long before. It is a kind of ritual, helping us to remember who and what we are. In order to remember it, one must have known it.

To have that sense of one's intrinsic worth which constitutes self-respect is potentially to have everything: the ability to discriminate, to love and to remain indifferent. To lack it is to be locked within oneself, paradoxically incapable of either love or indifference. If we do not respect ourselves, we are on the one hand forced to despise those who have so few resources as to consort with us, so little perception as to remain blind to our fatal weaknesses. On the other, we are peculiarly in thrall to everyone we see, curiously determined to live out—since our self-image is untenable—their false notions of us. We flatter ourselves by thinking this compulsion to please others an attractive trait: a gist for imaginative empathy, evidence of our willingness to give. *Of course* I will play Francesca to your Paolo, Helen Keller to anyone's Annie Sullivan: no expectation is too misplaced, no role too ludicrous. At the mercy of those we cannot but hold in contempt, we play roles doomed to failure before they are begun, each defeat generating fresh despair at the urgency of divining and meeting the next demand made upon us.

It is the phenomenon sometimes called "alienation from self." In its advanced stages, we no longer answer the telephone, because someone might want something; that we could say *no* without drowning in self-reproach is all idea alien to this game. Every encounter demands too much, tears the nerves, drains the will, and the specter of something as small as an unanswered letter arouses such disproportionate guilt that answering it becomes out of the question. To assign unanswered letters their proper weight, to free us from the expectations of others, to give us back to ourselves—there lies the great, the singular power of self-respect. Without it, one eventually discovers the final turn of the screw: one runs away to find oneself, and finds no one at home.

1961

Questions for Reading and Analysis

1. What is *your* definition of self-respect? What, according to Didion, is self-respect?

2. Why, according to Didion, is self-deception "the most difficult deception"?

3. Didion says of people with self-respect, "They know the price of things." What does she mean? Cite other places in the essay where she says basically the same thing, using different metaphors.

4. How do the key images in paragraphs 3 and 4 unify the paragraphs?

Annie Dillard (b. 1945, noted especially for her philosophical musing in exquisitely detailed nature writing, teaches writing at Wesleyan University. In her Pulitzer Prize-winning Pilgrim at Tinker Creek, *Dillard argues that a certain "poverty," what she calls the "artificial obvious," is necessary for true sight. With such untainted vision, she considers fundamentalist Christians in* Singing with the Fundamentalists.

Singing with the Fundamentalists

Annie Dillard

It is early spring. I have a temporary office at a state university on the West Coast. The office is on the third floor. It looks down on the Square, the enormous open courtyard at the center of the campus. From my desk I see hundreds of people moving between classes. There is a large circular fountain in the Square's center.

Early one morning, on the first day of spring quarter, I hear singing. A pack of students has gathered at the fountain. They are singing something which, at this distance, and through the heavy window, sounds good.

I know who these singing students are: they are the Fundamentalists. This campus has a lot of them. Mornings they sing on the Square; it is their only perceptible activity. What are they singing? Whatever it is, I want to join them, for I like to sing; whatever it is, I want to take my stand with them, for I am drawn to their very absurdity, their innocent indifference to what people think. My colleagues and students here, and my friends everywhere, dislike and fear Christian fundamentalists. You may never have met such people, but you've heard what they do: they pile up money, vote in blocs, and elect right-wing crazies; they censor books; they carry handguns; they fight fluoride in the drinking water and evolution in the schools; probably they would lynch people if they could get away with it. I'm not sure my friends are correct. I close my pen and join the singers on the Square.

There is a clapping song in progress. I have to concentrate to follow it:

Come on, rejoice,
And let your heart sing,
Come on, rejoice,
Give praise to the king.

> *Singing alleluia—*
> *He is the king of kings;*
> *Singing alleluia—*
> *He is the king of kings.*

Two song leaders are standing on the broad rim of the fountain; the water is splashing just behind them. The boy is short, hardfaced, with a mustache. He bangs his guitar with the backs of his fingers. The blonde girl, who leads the clapping, is bouncy; she wears a bit of makeup. Both are wearing blue jeans.

The students beside me are wearing blue jeans too—and athletic jerseys, parkas, football jackets, turtlenecks, and hiking shoes or jogging shoes. They all have canvas or nylon book bags. They look like any random batch of seventy or eighty students at this university. They are grubby or scrubbed, mostly scrubbed; they are tall, fair, or red-headed in large proportions. Their parents are white-collar workers, blue-collar workers, farmers, loggers, orchardists, merchants, fishermen; their names are, I'll bet, Olsen, Jensen, Seversen, Hansen, Klokker, Sigurdsen.

Despite the vigor of the clapping song, no one seems to be giving it much effort. And no one looks at anyone else; there are no sentimental glances and smiles, no glances even of recognition. These kids don't seem to know each other. We stand at the fountain's side, out on the broad, bricked square in front of the science building, and sing the clapping song through three times.

It is quarter to nine in the morning. Hundreds of people are crossing the Square. These passersby—faculty, staff, students—pay very little attention to us; this morning singing has gone on for years. Most of them look at us directly, then ignore us, for there is nothing to see; no animal sacrifices, no lynchings, no collection plate for Jesse Helms, no seizures, snake handling, healing, or glossolalia. There is barely anything to hear. I suspect the people glance at us to learn if we are really singing: How could so many people make so little sound? My fellow singers, who ignore each other, certainly ignore passersby as well. Within a week, most of them will have their eyes closed anyway.

We move directly to another song, a slower one.

> *He is my peace*
> *Who has broken down every wall;*
> *He is my peace,*
> *He is my peace.*

> *Cast all your cares on him,*
> *For he careth for you—oo—oo*
> *He is my peace*
> *He is my peace.*

I am paying strict attention to the song leaders, for I am singing at the top of my lungs and I've never heard any of these songs before. They are not the old American low-church Protestant hymns; they are not the old European high-church Protestant hymns. These hymns seem to have been written just yesterday, apparently by the same people who put out lyrical Christian greeting cards and bookmarks.

"Where do these songs come from?" I ask a girl standing next to me. She seems appalled to be addressed at all, and startled by the question. "They're from the praise albums!" she explains, and moves away.

The songs' melodies run dominant, subdominant, dominant, tonic, dominant. The pace is slow, about the pace of "Tell Laura I Love Her," and with that song's quavering, long notes. The lyrics are simple and repetitive; there are very few of them to which a devout Jew or Mohammedan could not give wholehearted assent. These songs are similar to the things Catholics sing in church these days. I don't know if any studies have been done to correlate the introduction of contemporary songs into Catholic churches with those churches' decline in membership, or with the phenomenon of Catholic converts' applying to enter cloistered monasteries directly, without passing through parish churches.

> *I'm set free to worship,*
> *I'm set free to praise him,*
> *I'm set free to dance before the Lord . . .*

At nine o'clock sharp we quit and scatter. I hear a few quiet "see you"s. Mostly the students leave quickly, as if they didn't want to be seen. The Square empties.

The next day we show up again, at twenty to nine. The same two leaders stand on the fountain's rim; the fountain is pouring down behind them.

After the first song, the boy with the mustache hollers, "Move on up! Some of you guys aren't paying attention back there! You're talking to each other. I want you to concentrate!" The students laugh, embarrassed for him. He sounds like a teacher. No one moves. The girl breaks into the next song, which we join at once:

> *In my life, Lord,*
> *Be glorified, be glorified, be glorified;*
> *In my life, Lord.*
> *Be glorified, be glorified today.*

At the end of this singularly monotonous verse, which is straining my tolerance for singing virtually anything, the boy with the mustache startles me by shouting, "Classes!"

At once, without skipping a beat, we sing, "In my classes, Lord, be glorified, be glorified . . ." I give fleet thought to the class I'm teaching this afternoon. We're reading a little "Talk of the Town" piece called "Eggbag," about a cat in a magic store on Eighth Avenue. "Relationships!" the boy calls. The students seem to sing "In my relationships, Lord," more easily than they sang "classes." They seemed embarrassed by "classes." In fact, to my fascination, they seemed embarrassed by almost everything. Why are they here? I will sing with the Fundamentalists every weekday morning all spring; I will decide, tentatively, that they come pretty much for the same reasons I do: Each has a private relationship with "the Lord" and will put up with a lot of junk for it.

I have taught some Fundamentalist students here, and know a bit of what they think. They are college students above all, worried about their love lives, their grades, and finding jobs. Some support moderate Democrats; some support moderate Republicans. Like their classmates, most support nuclear freeze, ERA, and an end to the draft. I believe they are divided on abortion and busing. They are not particularly political. They read *Christianity Today* and *Campus Life* and *Eternity*—moderate, sensible magazines, I think; they read a lot of C. S. Lewis. (One such student, who seemed perfectly tolerant of me and my shoddy Christianity, introduced me to C. S. Lewis's critical book on Charles Williams.) They read the Bible. I think they all "believe in" organic evolution. The main thing about them is this: There isn't any "them." Their views vary. They don't know each other.

Their common Christianity puts them, if anywhere, to the left of their classmates. I believe they also tend to be more able than their classmates to think well in the abstract, and also to recognize the complexity of moral issues. But I may be wrong.

In 1980, the media were certainly wrong about television evangelists. Printed estimates of Jerry Falwell's television audience ranged from 18 million to 30 million people. In fact, according to Arbitron's actual counts, fewer than 1.5 million people were watching Falwell. And, according to an Emory University study, those who did watch television evangelists didn't necessarily vote with them. Emory University sociologist G. Melton Mobley reports, "When that message turns political, they cut it off." Analysis of the 1982 off-year election turned up no Fundamentalist bloc voting. The media were wrong, but no one printed retractions.

The media were wrong, too, in a tendency to identify all fundamentalist Christians with Falwell and his ilk, and to attribute to them, across the board, conservative views.

Someone has sent me two recent issues of *Eternity: The Evangelical Monthly*. One lead article criticizes a television preacher for saying that the United States had never used military might to take land from another nation. The same article censures Newspeak, saying that government rhetoric would have us believe in a "clean bomb," would have us believe that we "defend" America by invading foreign soil, and would have us believe that the dictatorships we support are "democracies." "When the President of the United States says that one reason to support defense spending is because it creates jobs," this lead article says, "a little bit of *1984* begins to surface." Another article criticizes a "heavy-handed" opinion of Jerry Falwell Ministries—in this case a broadside attack on artificial insemination, surrogate motherhood, and lesbian motherhood. Browsing through *Eternity*, I find a double crosstic. I find an intelligent, analytical, and enthusiastic review of the new London Philharmonic recording of Mahler's *Second Symphony*—a review which stresses the "glorious truth" of the Jewish composer's magnificent work, and cites its recent performance in Jerusalem to celebrate the recapture of the Western Wall following the Six Day War. Surely, the evangelical Christians who read this magazine are not bookburners. If by chance they vote with the magazine's editors, then it looks to me as if they vote with the American Civil Liberties Union and Americans for Democratic Action.

Every few years some bold and sincere Christian student at this university disagrees with a professor in class—usually about the professor's out-of-hand dismissal of Christianity. Members of the faculty, outraged, repeat the stories of these rare and uneven encounters for years on end, as if to prove that the crazies are everywhere, and gaining ground. The notion is, apparently, that these kids can't think for themselves. Or they wouldn't disagree.

Now again the mustached leader asks us to move up. There is no harangue, so we move up. (This will be a theme all spring. The leaders want us closer together. Our instinct is to stand alone.) From behind the tall fountain comes a wind; on several gusts we get sprayed. No one seems to notice.

We have time for one more song. The leader, perhaps sensing that no one likes him, blunders on, "I want you to pray this one through," he says. "We have a lot of people here from a lot of different fellowships, but we're all one body. Amen?" They don't like it. He gets a few polite Amens. We sing:

> *Bind us together, Lord,*
> *With a bond that can't be broken;*
> *Bind us together, Lord,*
> *With love.*

Everyone seems to be in a remarkably foul mood today. We don't like this song. There is no one here under seventeen, and, I think, no one here who believes that love is a bond that can't be broken. We sing the song through three times; then it is time to go.

The leader calls after our retreating backs, "Hey, have a good day! Praise Him all day!" The kids around me roll up their eyes privately. Some groan; all flee.

The next morning is very cold. I am here early. Two girls are talking on the fountain's rim; one is part Italian. She says, "I've got the Old Testament, but I can't get the New. I screw up the New." She takes a breath and rattles off a long list, ending with "Jonah, Micah, Nahum, Habakkuk, Zephaniah, Haggai, Zechariah, Malachi." The other girl produces a slow, sarcastic applause. I ask one of the girls to help me with the words to a song. She is agreeable, but says, "I'm sorry, I can't. I just became a Christian this year, so I don't know all the words yet."

The others are coming; we stand and separate. The boy with the mustache is gone, replaced by a big, serious fellow in a green down jacket. The bouncy girl is back with her guitar; she is wearing a skirt and wool knee socks. We begin without any preamble, by singing a song that has so few words that we actually stretch one syllable over eleven separate notes. Then we sing a song in which the men sing one phrase and the women echo it. Everyone seems to know just what to do. In the context of our vapid songs, the lyrics of this one are extraordinary:

> *I was nothing before you found me.*
> *Heartache! Broken people! Ruined lives*
> *Is why you died on Calvary.*

The last line rises in a regular series of half-notes. Now at last some people are actually singing; they throw some breath into the business. There is a seriousness and urgency to it: "Heartache! Broken people! Ruined lives . . . I was nothing."

We don't look like nothing. We look like a bunch of students of every stripe, ill-shaven or well-shaven, dressed up or down, but dressed warmly against the cold: jeans and parkas, jeans and heavy sweaters, jeans and scarves and blow-dried hair. We look ordinary. But I think, quite on my own, that we are here because we know this business of nothingness, brokenness, and ruination. We sing this song over and over.

Something catches my eye. Behind us, up in the science building, professors are standing alone at opened windows.

The long brick science building has three upper floors of faculty offices, thirty-two windows. At one window stands a bearded man, about forty; his opening his window is what caught my eye. He stands full in the open window, his hands on his hips, his head cocked down toward the fountain. He is drawn to look, as I was drawn to come. Up on the building's top floor, at the far right window, there is another: An Asian-American professor, wearing a white shirt, is sitting with one hip on his desk, looking out and down. In the middle of the row of windows, another one, an old professor in a checked shirt, stands sideways to the open window, stands stock-still, his long, old ear to the air. Now another window cranks open, another professor—or maybe a graduate student—leans out, his hands on the sill.

We are all singing, and I am watching these five still men, my colleagues, whose office doors are surely shut—for that is the custom here: five of them alone in their office in the science building who have opened their windows on this very cold morning, who motionless hear the Fundamentalists sing, utterly unknown to each other.

We sing another four songs, including the clapping song, and one which repeats, "This is the day which the Lord hath made; rejoice and be glad in it." All the professors but one stay by their open windows, figures in a frieze. When after ten minutes we break off and scatter, each cranks his window shut. Maybe they have nine o'clock classes too.

I miss a few sessions. One morning of the following week, I rejoin the Fundamentalists on the Square. The wind is blowing from the north; it is sunny and cold. There are several new developments.

Someone has blown up rubber gloves and floated them in the fountain. I saw them yesterday afternoon from my high office window, and couldn't quite make them out: I seemed to see hands in the fountain waving from side to side, like those hands wagging on springs which people stick in the back windows of their cars. I saw these many years ago in Quito and Guayaquil, where they were a great fad long before they showed up here. The cardboard hands said, on their palms, HOLA GENTE, hello people. Some of them just said HOLA, hello, with a little wave to the universe at large, in case anybody happened to be looking. It is like sending radio signals to planets in other galaxies: HOLA, if anyone is listening. Jolly folk, these Ecuadorians, I thought.

Now, waiting by the fountain for the singing, I see that these particular hands are long surgical gloves, yellow and white, ten of them tied off at the cuff. They floated upright and they wave, *hola, hola hola*; they mill around like a crowd, bobbing under the fountain's spray and back again to the pool's rim, *hola*. It is a good prank. It is far too cold for the university's maintenance crew to retrieve them without turning off the fountain and putting on rubber boots.

From all around the Square, people are gathering for the singing. There is no way I can guess which kids, from among the masses crossing the Square, will veer off to the fountain. When they get here, I never recognize anybody except the leaders.

The singing begins without ado as usual, but there is something different about it. The students are growing prayerful, and they show it this morning with a peculiar gesture. I'm glad they weren't like this when I first joined them, or I never would have stayed.

Last night there was an educational television special, part of "Middletown." It was a segment called "Community of Praise," and I watched it because it was about Fundamentalists. It showed a Jesus-loving family in the Midwest; the treatment was good and complex. This family attended the prayer meetings, healing sessions, and church services of an unnamed sect—a very low-church sect, whose doctrine and culture were much more low-church than those of the kids I sing with. When the members of this sect prayed, they held their arms over their heads and raised their palms, as if to feel or receive a blessing or energy from above.

Now today on the Square there is a new serious mood. The leaders are singing with their eyes shut. I am impressed that they can bang their guitars, keep their balance, and not fall into the pool. It is the same bouncy girl and earnest boy. Their eyeballs are rolled back a bit. I look around and see that almost everyone in this crowd of eighty or so has his eyes shut and is apparently praying the words of this song or praying some other prayer.

Now as the chorus rises, as it gets louder and higher and simpler in melody—

> *I exalt thee,*
> *I exalt thee,*
> *I exalt thee,*
> *Thou art the Lord—*

then, at this moment, hands start rising. All around me, hands are going up—that tall girl, that blond boy with his head back, the red-headed boy up front, the girl with the MacDonald's jacket. Their arms rise as if pulled on strings. Some few of them have raised their arms very high over their heads and are tilting back their palms. Many, many more of them, as inconspicuously as possible, have raised their hands to the level of their chins.

What is going on? Why are these students today raising their palms in this gesture, when nobody did it last week? Is it because the leaders have set a prayerful tone this morning? Is it because this gesture always accompanies this song, just as clapping accompanies other songs? Or is it, as I suspect, that these kids watched the widely publicized documentary last night just as I did, and are adopting, or trying out, the gesture?

It is a sunny morning, and the sun is rising behind the leaders and the fountain, so those students have their heads tilted, eyes closed, and palms upraised toward the sun. I glance up at the science building and think my own prayer: Thank God no one is watching this.

The leaders cannot move around much on the fountain's rim. The girl has her eyes shut; the boy opens his eyes from time to time, glances at the neck of his guitar, and closes his eyes again.

When the song is over, the hands go down, and there is some desultory chatting in the crowd, as usual: Can I borrow your library card? And, as usual nobody looks at anybody.

All our songs today are serious. There is a feudal theme to them, or a feudal analogue:

> *I will eat from abundance of your household.*
> *I will dream beside your streams of righteousness.*
>
> *You are my king.*
>
> *Enter his gates*
> *with thanksgiving in your heart;*
> *come before his courts with praise.*
> *He is the king of kings.*
>
> *Thou art the Lord.*

All around me, eyes are closed and hands are raised. There is no social pressure to do this, or anything else. I've never known any group to be less cohesive, imposing fewer controls. Since no one looks at anyone, and since passersby no longer look, everyone out here is inconspicuous and free. Perhaps the palm-raising has begun because the kids realize by now that they are not on display; they're praying in their closets, right out here on the Square. Over the course of the next weeks, I will learn that the palm-raising is here to stay.

The sun is rising higher. We are singing our last song. We are praying. We are alone together.

> *He is my peace*
> *Who has broken down every wall* . . .

When the song is over, the hands go down. The heads lower, the eyes open and blink. We stay still a second before we break up. We have been standing in a broad current; now we have stepped aside. We have dismantled the radar cups; we have closed the telescope's vault. Students gather their book bags and go. The two leaders step down from the fountain's rim and pack away their guitars. Everyone scatters. I am in no hurry, so I stay after everyone is gone. It is after nine o'clock, and the Square is deserted. The fountain is playing to an empty house. In the pool the cheerful hands are waving over the water, bobbing under the fountain's veil and out again in the current, *hola*.

Questions for Reading and Analysis

1. What stereotypes about fundamentalists run through Annie Dillard's mind as she listens to the students sing? What makes her leave her office to join them?

2. What does she notice about their group dynamics on her first day of singing with them? What does she mean when she says "There isn't any 'them'"?

3. Dillard's essay is divided into sections. Each section presents a part of her insight. What partial insights does she present in these sections? To what overall conclusion does she come?

4. How does the detail about the hands floating in the fountain tie in with the conclusions she reaches about the significance of her and the students' singing? What is the significance of the greeting "hola" she attributes to these hands? (Note that she ends the essay with it.)

5. Do you agree with Dillard's implied suggestion that to understand a group of people (and maybe to enhance one's tolerance for different ways of doing things), one should participate in some of their activities? In what ways is this sound advice? In what ways could this be dangerous?

An ex-welfare mom from Vermont puts "a face" on the hotly-debated issue du jour, *welfare reform. Downey's essay first appeared in* Hip Mama, *an Oakland, California, zine and was printed in the May 1998 issue of* Harper's Magazine.

I Am Your Welfare Reform

Annie Downey

I am a single mother of two children, each with a different father. I am a hussy, a welfare rider—burden to everyone and everything. I am anything you want me to be—a faceless number who has no story.

My daughter's father has a job and makes over two grand a month; my son's father owns blue-chip stock in AT&T, Disney, and Campbell's. I call the welfare office, gather old bills, look for day care, write for my degree project, graduate with my son slung on my hip, breast-feeding.

At the welfare office they tell me to follow one of the caseworkers into a small room without windows. The caseworker hands me a packet and a pencil. There is an older woman with graying hair and polyester pants and the same pencil and packet. I glance at her, she looks at me; we are both ashamed. I try hard to fill out the packet correctly, answering all the questions. I am nervous. There are so many questions that near the end I start to get careless. I just want to leave. I hand the caseworker the packet in an envelope; she asks for my pencil and does not look at me. I exit unnoticed. For five years I've exited unnoticed. I can't imagine how to get a job. I ride the bus home.

After a few weeks a letter arrives assigning me to "Group 3." I don't even finish reading it. When my grandmother calls later to tell me that I confuse sex with love, I tell her that I am getting a job. She asks what kind. I say, "Any job."

It is 5:00 A.M. My alarm wakes up my kids. I try nursing my son back to sleep, but my daughter keeps him up with her questions: "What time is it? Who's going to take care of us when you leave?" I want to cry. It is still dark and I am exhausted. I've had three hours of sleep. I get ready for work, put some laundry in the washer, make breakfast, set out clothes for the kids, make lunches. I carry my son; my daughter follows. They cling to me. They cry when I leave. I see their faces pressed against the porch window and the sitter trying to get them inside.

I slice meat for $5.50 an hour for nine hours a day, five days a week. I barely feed my kids; I barely pay the bills.

I struggle against welfare. But I know that without welfare I would have nothing. On welfare I went from teen mom to woman with an education. I published two magazines, became an editor, a teacher. Welfare, along with Section 8 housing grants and Reach Up, gave my children a life. My daughter loves school and does well there. My son is round and at twenty months speaks wondrous sentences about the moon and the stars. Welfare gave me what was necessary to be a mother.

Still, I cannot claim it. There is too much shame in me: the disgusted looks in the grocery lines, the angry voices of Oprah panelists, the unmitigated rage of the blue and white collars. I'm not what those voices say I am. I never buy expensive ice cream in pints. I don't do drugs. I don't own a hot tub.

I am one of 12 million people who account for less than 1 percent of the federal budget. I am one of the 26 percent of the AFDC recipients who are mothers and the 36.6 percent who are white. I am one of the 68 percent of teen mothers who were sexually abused. I am $600 a month below the poverty level for a family of three. I am a hot political issue. I am 145-65-8563. Group 3.

I have brown hair and eyes. I write prose. My mother has been married and divorced twice. I have never been married. I love Pablo Neruda's poetry, Louise Glück's essays. I love my stepfather but not my real father. My favorite book is *Love in the Time of Cholera* by Gabriel García Marquez; my favorite movie, *The Color Purple*. I miss my son's father. I love jazz. I've always wanted to learn how to ballroom dance. I have a story, and a life, and a face.

Questions for Reading and Analysis

1. What is Downey's thesis? What is it she wants her readers to know?

2. Downey introduces herself as "a hussy, a welfare rider" in the first paragraph, followed by some details about her children's fathers. What does she accomplish with this juxtaposition of information?

3. In a similar fashion, Downey's last two paragraphs juxtapose statistics and personal information. What is she trying to tell her readers?

4. What is the significance of her title?

A journalist, activist, historian, and queer studies professor at New York University, Lisa Duggan suggests that the solution to the debate over same-sex marriage is to abandon civil marriage altogether.

Abolish Marriage!

Lisa Duggan

I'm scared by the push to include same-sex couples under marriage laws. Even the idea of "commitment" ceremonies makes me nervous; they remind me of lunacy inquisitions. We should be arguing to abolish marriage laws instead.

However, I understand why the issue is important for many queer folks. In our culture, marriage operates on at least two levels. Symbolically, marriage is a central form of recognition that integrates relationships into larger social networks. Materially, marriage provides a wide array of benefits and subsidies, from tax and estate matters to health insurance and housing provisions. Our exclusion from these benefits is devastating and discriminatory, oftentimes leading to horrible consequences. But we need to think twice about how marriage and family truly operate and what it is we're really asking for.

There is nothing inherently natural about marriage and family. Worldwide, kinship systems vary enormously, from matrilineal systems in which the father is not recognized, to various forms of polygamy and polyandry. American civil marriage is not the only way to organize kinship, dependency, and responsibility for children.

In America today, the legal structure of marriage and family assumes that a sexual relationship is the primary basis for forming a household. It assumes that this is the place where reproduction occurs and where responsibility for children is centered. It assumes that sexual and emotional ties are interdependent with economics, and that this sort of household is the route for inheritance. In reality, this structure is so unstable divorce law is far more complex than marriage law.

The question for us is: Does this set of assumptions define the way we really live? Can such arrangements meet our needs, symbolically and materially? I don't think so.

Squeezing our actual relationships into the framework of marriage would be like trying to fit my size 10 foot into a size 5 shoe. Look at me: I've been with my partner for 15 years, and during that time our relationship has been the primary sexual and emotional relationship for us both. We consider ourselves to be each other's next of kin. But we don't live together and have only a limited economic partnership. We're not monogamous, and we're not a reproductive unit. Symbolically and materially, marriage doesn't work for us. Even the current definition of domestic partnership doesn't work for us.

Domestic partnership arrangements are available through my city, New York, and my employer, New York University. I want these benefits: recognition as next of kin, hospital visitation rights, bereavement leave. I also want my partner to be able to use the university's gym and library. But in order to register for such benefits, I must prove that we live together.

In other words, I have to get creative.

We need to disentangle symbolic and material needs and benefits and contest the way they currently are conjoined to marriage and family law. We need to find ways to recognize next-of-kin relationships that aren't based on biological or sexual ties, as well as sexual relationships that aren't linked to economic interdependency. We need to demand that government agencies and our employers recognize that these relationships don't always go together.

Look at me again: I am the guardian of my sister's three children. In the event of divorce or catastrophe, I might become a co-parent in addition to an aunt. It would make sense, in that case, for me to establish a household with my sister and her children. I would gain economic benefits, subsidies, and responsibilities of marriage. My partner would remain my next of kin for most purposes, such as medical consent and hospital visitation, but my health insurance and tax returns would be tied to my household with my sister. Furthermore, why shouldn't I then be permitted to adopt my sister's children? It makes no sense to tie two-parent adoptions to sexual relationships.

At times in the debate over same-sex marriage, gay advocates are represented as pragmatists. But working out legal alternatives to marriage is the truly pragmatic path. It is pragmatic to meet our concrete and variable needs; given these needs, it can be unrealistic and ideological to support same-sex marriage. In some cases, the progay marriage front produces an image of a responsible, respectable, domestic homosexual, as opposed to the deviant, promiscuous, irresponsible queer. I find this frightening and dangerous. The campaign has become ideological—a morality crusade—and not a pragmatic move towards equality.

The lesbian and gay promarriage juggernaut also contributes to the image of the responsible homosexual who does the right thing by confining sex to marriage. This ideological campaign contributes to the policing and persecution of gays, especially those whose sexual practices are not solely or primarily domestic.

Another way in which the gay marriage campaign works ideologically is by accepting and then mystifying how straight marriage works. Marriage arrangements make the transmission of property from generation to generation within a family seem natural and fair; economic inequality for gay families is thus made to feel "natural."

Finally, it's important to note that the ways in which our lives diverge from the legal model of marriage and family is something we share with heterosexuals. Most straight relationships don't fit into current arrangements of economic partnership and responsibility for children. We ought to be talking to feminists who seek to reformulate the family.

I call for the abolition of state-regulated marriage, and I'm not alone: In a recent campaign, the governor of Hawaii suggested just that. Let marriage be a religious, purely symbolic institution. Instead of calling for inclusion in state-sanctified marriage, gays and lesbians should argue for creative new ways to institute flexible partnerships that respond to our real needs, relationships, responsibilities, and dependencies. We need to accommodate the lives we actually have, rather than support the fantasy household assumed by marriage and family law. We need to stop the state from legislating our sexual relationships and instead ask it to respond to our diverse needs.

Questions for Reading and Analysis

1. What are Duggan's reasons for abolishing state-regulated marriage? What alternatives does she envision in the absence of civil marriage?

2. Analyze the logic of Duggan's argument. Where are its flaws? How could these flaws be overcome without changing her basic thesis?

3. Looking at Duggan's essay from a gay/lesbian perspective, do you think her argument would ultimately help or hinder the fight for equal recognition of their unions?

This 1995 article from Moxie *summarizes the threat second-hand smoke poses to nonsmokers.*

Smoking for Others: Predicament of the Nonsmoker

Judith Dunaway and K.H. Ginzel

The unprecedented marketing boon and victory march of the cigarette across countries and continents, especially in the last half century when women joined the ranks of smokers in ever increasing numbers, has prompted an equally unparalleled global spread of smoking-related disease and death. But, unlike other drug addictions, tobacco smoking has brought along a new phenomenon, the forced participation by those who do not smoke.

About two thirds of the smoke of a cigarette, the sidestream smoke, accumulates in enclosed air spaces as "environmental tobacco smoke," ETS. Having to breathe the smoke of others is aptly called "involuntary smoking," also referred to as "passive smoking."

Although tobacco lobbyists still persist in questioning the harmfulness of active smoking, albeit with less feigned conviction than 40 years ago when the lung cancer connection first surfaced, they are now vehemently vociferous in denying the recently documented dangers of exposure to ETS and in opposing and discrediting every attempt to protect nonsmokers by banning smoking in enclosed work areas and public places. For them, ETS is a more serious challenge to the future of the tobacco business than the health problems of the smoker, whose addiction affords at least a degree of confidence in continued consumption. If, however, smoking is increasingly more restricted, especially in the workplace where much of the smoking occurs, cigarette sales could plummet.

The absence of smoking in public places, in turn, would be a disincentive to youngsters to think about, experiment with, and eventually start smoking.

Involuntary smoking is, as the term implies, a much more complex, issue than "voluntary" smoking, invoking not only the health aspect but, inevitably, opening a moral and also a legal dimension.

Obviously, it is one thing for a smoker to die from lung cancer, but quite another for a nonsmoker to succumb to a disease, fatal or otherwise, that was inflicted by someone else. Yet, even in the case of the smoker, an outside influence must be acknowledged. Since almost 90% of all adult smokers started as children who may have been lured by the deceitful promises and the slick imagery of advertising, compacted into what is amiably called "peer pressure," the buzzwords "adult choice" are dubious at best. That breathing would turn out to be injurious to health had to be anticipated long before the epidemiological evidence was forthcoming. For one, the 4,700 plus chemicals present in tobacco smoke, more than 40 of which are proven carcinogens, are not exclusive to the mainstream smoke inhaled by the smoker, but occur actually in much higher concentrations in the smoke released into the environment. In modern filter cigarettes, the distribution of poisons and carcinogens is even further shifted to the sidestream smoke, for the total smoke yield remains essentially the same. The myth of the "light" cigarette is also risky for the smoker, who compensates for the lowered yield of nicotine, so specified by a standardized smoking machine, by inhaling deeper, and smoking more cigarettes. According to a 1989 study from Boston University, women who smoked "light" cigarettes had a slightly higher risk of heart attack than those who smoked stronger brands.

For a poison to become effective, it has to enter the organism. When nicotine blood levels were determined in smokers for the first time, nonsmoking controls also presented with measurable amounts of the drug which could be traced to exposure of the control subjects to cigarette smoke. Since then numerous studies have revealed the presence of nicotine, its metabolic product cotinine, and various other poisons and carcinogens not only in smokers but also in ETS exposed nonsmokers, infants, toddlers, children and adults alike. Even the amniotic fluid of nonsmoking pregnant women who were exposed to ETS tested positive for nicotine. Passive smoke exposure in pregnancy was found to be responsible for as much as two thirds of the reduction in birth weight seen with active smoking.

The levels of ETS in our lives today far exceed legally tolerated levels of individual constituents. Thus, nonsmokers may be exposed to up to 10 to 200 times the "acceptable daily intake" of nicotine and numerous other poisons, as well as to levels of carcinogens which, if they occurred in isolation in a manufacturing process, would require the worker to don protective clothing and gas mask.

Although there are fewer smokers today than 30 years ago, their per capita consumption of cigarettes is actually higher, and in the majority of households children still live with one or more smokers.

In a recently released report, the Environmental Protection Agency, EPA, estimates that ETS annually causes frequent middle ear and upper respiratory tract infections, 150,000 to 300,000 cases of bronchitis and pneumonia in infants and young children, 8,000 to 20,000 new cases of childhood asthma, and the worsening of symptoms in up to one million children with previously existing asthma.

Worse still, ETS has been causally linked to a significant increase in childhood leukemia, brain tumors, adult lung cancer traced to early exposure, and to approximately 3,000 lung cancer deaths annually in U.S. nonsmokers. In the wake of extensive research by scientists at prestigious institutions all over the world, the EPA has finally classified ETS as a Class A Human Carcinogen, as asbestos, benzene, or arsenic. Notwithstanding the fact that the designation of tobacco smoke as a human carcinogen has been on the books of the World Health Organization's International Agency for Research on Cancer since 1986, and that it received endorsements by every major medical organization as well as the world's leading authority in epidemiology, Sir Richard Doll, the tobacco industry and their mercenaries launched a vitriolic attack against the EPA, denigrating its competence and demanding retraction of its ruling. The expectation that the EPA pronouncement eventually might have to usher in regulatory and/or legislative action on behalf of the nonsmoking majority is anathema to tobacco interests and those profiting from them. Traditionally, tobacco has enjoyed unequaled immunity from virtually all laws to which it should have been subjected.

Yet, it is not just the risks of cancer, respiratory disease and fetal growth retardation that require intervention. As is the case with smoking, the major impact of ETS exposure is on the cardiovascular system with 47,000 cardiac deaths and about 150,000 nonfatal heart attacks projected for this year.

To any unbiased observer, confronted with the palette of horrors enumerated above, it must be totally incomprehensible that neither active nor passive smoking, the number one and number three preventable causes of premature disease, disability and death in our society, have been dealt with in any remotely consistent, honest, intelligent, responsible and—pardon the expression—ethical manner. Almost 4,000 years ago, the code of Hammurabi decreed the penalty of death to anyone who would harm a child. In our advanced culture, however, child abuse starting in the womb is sanctioned and tolerated in the name of a distorted concept of individual right and freedom of choice, that is insidiously nurtured by those who find it a convenient front to conceal their ulterior motives.

On the contrary, true freedom flows from self-restraint, respect and compassion for other beings.

Questions for Reading and Analysis

1. The writers claim that second-hand smoking opens "a moral and also a legal dimension" of the smoking debate. What do they mean by this?

2. What do the writers try to accomplish with their argument? What is their thesis?

3. Do you think that smoking (provided one does not force others to smoke "passively") is largely an individual choice? Is living a healthy lifestyle (without substance abuse of any kind) a responsibility we have not just towards ourselves but to others as well?

*A professor at the University of Virginia, Mark Edmundson paints
a stark picture of today's college students: reared in a consumer
culture shaped by light entertainment, they see themselves as paying
customers of the university and expect to be treated accordingly. He
regrets that the curious student, who pursues learning for its own
sake, has become an endangered species, labeled "uncool" by his con-
formist peers. The article was first published in* Harper's Magazine *in
September 1997 alongside Earl Shorris's article, which treats the same
subject from a different angle (see page 393).*

On the Uses of a Liberal Education

As Lite Entertainment For Bored College Students

Mark Edmundson

Today is evaluation day in my Freud class, and everything has changed. The class meets twice a week, late in the afternoon, and the clientele, about fifty undergraduates, tends to drag in and slump, looking disconsolate and a little lost, waiting for a jump start. To get the discussion moving, they usually require a joke, an anecdote, an off-the-wall question—When you were a kid, were your Halloween getups ego costumes, id costumes, or superego costumes? That sort of thing. But today, as soon as I flourish the forms, a buzz rises in the room. Today they write their assessments of the course, their assessments of *me*, and they are without a doubt wide-awake. "What is your evaluation of the instructor?" asks question number eight, entreating them to circle a number between five (excellent) and one (poor, poor). Whatever interpretive subtlety they've acquired during the term is now out the window. Edmundson: one to five, stand and shoot.

And they do. As I retreat through the door—I never stay around for this phase of the ritual—I look over my shoulder and see them toiling away like the devil's auditors. They're pitched into high writing gear, even the ones who struggle to squeeze out their journal entries word by word, stoked on a procedure they have by now supremely mastered. They're playing the informed consumer, letting the provider know where he's come through and where he's not quite up to snuff.

But why am I so distressed, bolting like a refugee out of my own classroom, where I usually hold easy sway? Chances are the evaluations will be much like what they've been in the past—they'll be just fine. It's likely that I'll be commended for being "interesting" (and I am commended, many times over), that I'll be cited for my relaxed and tolerant ways (that happens, too), that my sense of humor and capacity to connect the arcana of the subject matter with current culture will come in for some praise (yup). I've been hassled this term, finishing a manuscript, and so haven't given their journals the attention I should have, and for that I'm called—quite civilly, though—to account. Overall, I get off pretty well.

Yet I have to admit that I do not much like the image of myself that emerges from these forms, the image of knowledgeable, humorous detachment and bland tolerance. I do not like the forms themselves, with their number ratings, reminiscent of the sheets circulated after the TV pilot has just played to its sample audience in Burbank. Most of all I dislike the attitude of calm consumer expertise that pervades the responses. I'm disturbed by the serene belief that my function—and, more important, Freud's, or Shakespeare's, or Blake's—is to divert, entertain, and interest. Observes one respondent, not at all unrepresentative: "Edmundson has done a fantastic job of presenting this difficult, important & controversial material in an enjoyable and approachable way."

Thanks but no thanks. I don't teach to amuse, to divert, or even, for that matter, to be merely interesting. When someone says she "enjoyed" the course—and that word crops up again and again in my evaluations—somewhere at the edge of my immediate complacency I feel encroaching self-dislike. That is not at all what I had in mind. The off-the-wall questions and the sidebar jokes are meant as lead-ins to stronger stuff—in the case of the Freud course, to a complexly tragic view of life. But the affability and the one-liners often seem to be all that land with the students; their journals and evaluations leave me little doubt.

I want some of them to say that they've been changed by the course. I want them to measure themselves against what they've read. It's said that some time ago a Columbia University instructor used to issue a harsh two-part question. One: What book did you most dislike in the course? Two: What intellectual or characterological flaws in you does that dislike point to? The hand that framed that question was surely heavy. But at least it compels one to see intellectual work as a confrontation between two people, student and author, where the stakes matter. Those Columbia students were being asked to relate the quality of the *encounter*, not rate the action as though it had unfolded on the big screen.

Why are my students describing the Oedipus complex and the death drive as being interesting and enjoyable to contemplate? And why am I coming across as an urbane, mildly ironic, endlessly affable guide to this intellectual territory, operating without intensity, generous, funny, and loose?

Because that's what works. On evaluation day, I reap the rewards of my partial compliance with the culture of my students and, too, with the culture of the university as it now operates. It's a culture that's gotten little exploration. Current critics tend to think that liberal-arts education is in crisis because universities have been invaded by professors with peculiar ideas: deconstruction, Lacanianism, feminism, queer theory. They believe that genius and tradition are out and that P.C., multiculturalism, and identity politics are in because of an invasion by tribes of tenured radicals, the late millennial equivalents of the Visigoth hordes that cracked Rome's walls.

But mulling over my evaluations and then trying to take a hard, extended look at campus life both here at the University of Virginia and around the country eventually led me to some different conclusions. To me, liberal-arts education is as ineffective as it is now not chiefly because there are a lot of strange theories in the air. (Used well, those theories *can* be illuminating.) Rather, it's that university culture, like American culture writ large, is, to put it crudely, ever more devoted to consumption and entertainment, to the using and using up of goods and images. For someone growing up in America now, there are few available alternatives to the cool consumer worldview. My students didn't ask for that view, much less create it, but they bring a consumer weltanschauung to school, where it exerts a powerful, and largely unacknowledged, influence. If we want to understand current universities, with their multiple woes, we might try leaving the realms of expert debate and fine ideas and turning to the classrooms and campuses, where a new kind of weather is gathering.

From time to time I bump into a colleague in the corridor and we have what I've come to think of as a Joon Lee fest. Joon Lee is one of the best students I've taught. He's endlessly curious, has read a small library's worth, seen every movie, and knows all about showbiz and entertainment. For a class of mine he wrote an essay using Nietzsche's Apollo and Dionysus to analyze the pop group The Supremes. A trite, cultural-studies bonbon? Not at all. He said striking things about conceptions of race in America and about how they shape our ideas of beauty. When I talk with one of his other teachers, we run on about the general splendors of his work and presence. But what inevitably follows a JL fest is a mournful reprise about the divide that separates him and a few other remarkable students from their contemporaries. It's not that some aren't nearly as bright—in terms of intellectual ability, my students are all that I could ask for. Instead, it's that Joon Lee has decided to follow his interests and let them make him into a singular and rather eccentric man; in his charming way, he doesn't mind being at odds with most anyone.

It's his capacity for enthusiasm that sets Joon apart from what I've come to think of as the reigning generational style. Whether the students are sorority/fraternity types, grunge aficionados, piercer/tattooers, black or white, rich or middle class (alas, I teach almost no students from truly poor backgrounds), they are, nearly across the board, very, very self-contained. On good days they display a light, appealing glow; on bad days, shuffling disgruntlement. But there's little fire, little passion to be found.

This point came home to me a few weeks ago when I was wandering across the university grounds. There, beneath a classically cast portico, were two students, male and female, having a rip-roaring argument. They were incensed, bellowing at each other, headstrong, confident, and wild. It struck me how rarely I see this kind of full-out feeling in students anymore. Strong emotional display is forbidden. When conflicts arise, it's generally understood that one of the parties will say something sarcastically propitiating ("whatever" often does it) and slouch away.

How did my students reach this peculiar state in which all passion seems to be spent? I think that many of them have imbibed their sense of self from consumer culture in general and from the tube in particular. They're the progeny of 100 cable channels and omnipresent Blockbuster outlets. TV, Marshall McLuhan famously said, is a cool medium. Those who play best on it are low-key and nonassertive; they blend in. Enthusiasm, à la Joon Lee, quickly looks absurd. The form of character that's most appealing on TV is calmly self-interested though never greedy, attuned to the conventions, and ironic. Judicious timing is preferred to sudden self-assertion. The TV medium is inhospitable to inspiration, improvisation, failures, slipups. All must run perfectly.

Naturally, a cool youth culture is a marketing bonanza for producers of the right products, who do all they can to enlarge that culture and keep it grinding. The Internet, TV, and magazines now teem with what I call persona ads, ads for Nikes and Reeboks and Jeeps and Blazers that don't so much endorse the capacities of the product per se as show you what sort of person you will be once you've acquired it. The Jeep ad that features hip, outdoorsy kids whipping a Frisbee from mountaintop to mountaintop isn't so much about what Jeeps can do as it is about the kind of people who own them. Buy a Jeep and be one with them. The ad is of little consequence in itself, but expand its message exponentially and you have the central thrust of current consumer culture—buy in order to be.

Most of my students seem desperate to blend in, to look right, not to make a spectacle of themselves. (Do I have to tell you that those two students having the argument under the portico turned out to be acting in a role-playing game?) The specter of the uncool creates a subtle tyranny. It's apparently an easy standard to subscribe to, this Letterman-like, Tarantino-like cool, but once committed to it, you discover that matters are rather different. You're inhibited, except on ordained occasions, from showing emotion, stifled from trying to achieve anything original. You're made to feel that even the slightest departure from the reigning code will get you genially ostracized. This is a culture tensely committed to a laid-back norm.

Am I coming off like something of a crank here? Maybe. Oscar Wilde, who is almost never wrong, suggested that it is perilous to promiscuously contradict people who are much younger than yourself. Point taken. But one of the lessons that consumer hype tries to insinuate is that we must never rebel against the new, never even question it. If it's new—a new need, a new product, a new show, a new style, a new generation—it must be good. So maybe, even at the risk of winning the withered, brown laurels of crankdom, it pays to resist newness-worship and cast a colder eye.

Praise for my students? I have some of that too. What my students are, at their best, is decent. They are potent believers in equality. They help out at the soup kitchen and volunteer to tutor poor kids to get a stripe on their résumés, sure. But they also want other people to have a fair shot. And in their commitment to fairness they are discerning; there you see them at their intellectual best. If I were on trial and innocent, I'd want them on the jury.

What they will not generally do, though, is indict the current system. They won't talk about how the exigencies of capitalism lead to a reserve army of the unemployed and nearly inevitable misery. That would be getting too loud, too brash. For the pervading view is the cool consumer perspective, where passion and strong admiration are forbidden. "To stand in awe of nothing, Numicus, is perhaps the one and only thing that can make a man happy and keep him so," says Horace in the *Epistles*, and I fear that his lines ought to hang as a motto over the university in this era of high consumer capitalism.

It's easy to mount one's high horse and blame the students for this state of affairs. But they didn't create the present culture of consumption. (It was largely my own generation, that of the Sixties, that let the counterculture search for pleasure devolve into a quest for commodities.) And they weren't the ones responsible, when they were six and seven and eight years old, for unplugging the TV set from time to time or for hauling off and kicking a hole through it. It's my generation of parents who sheltered these students, kept them away from the hard knocks of everyday life, making them cautious and over fragile, who demanded that their teachers, from grade school on, flatter them endlessly so that the kids are shocked if their college professors don't reflexively suck up to them.

Of course, the current generational style isn't simply derived from culture and environment. It's also about dollars. Students worry that taking too many chances with their educations will sabotage their future prospects. They're aware of the fact that a drop that looks more and more like one wall of the Grand Canyon separates the top of economic tenth from the rest of the population. There's a sentiment currently abroad that if you step aside for a moment, to write, to travel, to fall too hard in love, you might lose position permanently. We may be on a conveyor belt, but it's worse down there on the filth-strewn floor. So don't sound off, don't blow your chance.

But wait. I teach at the famously conservative University of Virginia. Can I extend my view from Charlottesville to encompass the whole county, a whole generation of college students? I can only say that I hear comparable stories about classroom life from colleagues everywhere in America. When I visit other schools to lecture, I see a similar scene unfolding. There are, of course, terrific students everywhere. And they're all the better for the way they've had to strive against the existing conformity. At some of the small liberal arts colleges, the tradition of strong engagement persists. But overall, the students strike me as being sweet and sad, hovering in a nearly suspended animation.

Too often now the pedagogical challenge is to make a lot from a little. Teaching Wordsworth's "Tintern Abbey," you ask for comments. No one responds. So you call on Stephen. Stephen: "The sound, this poem really flows." You: "Stephen seems interested in the music of the poem. We might extend his comment to ask if the poem's music coheres with its argument. Are they consistent? Or is there an emotional pain submerged here that's contrary to the poem's appealing melody?" All right, it's not usually that bad. But close. One friend describes it as rebound teaching: they proffer a weightless comment, you hit it back for all you're worth, then it comes dribbling out again. Occasionally a professor will try to explain away this intellectual timidity by describing the students as perpetrators of postmodern irony, a highly sophisticated mode. Everything's a slick counterfeit, a simulacrum, so by no means should any phenomenon be taken seriously. But the students don't have the urbane, Oscar Wilde-type demeanor that should go with this view. Oscar was cheerful, funny, confident, strange. (Wilde, mortally ill, living in a Paris flophouse: "My wallpaper and I are fighting a duel to the death. One or the other of us has to go.") This generation's style is considerate, easy to please, and a touch depressed.

Granted, you might say, the kids come to school immersed in a consumer mentality—they're good Americans, after all—but then the university and the professors do everything in their power to fight that dreary mind-set in the interested of higher ideals, right? So it should be. But let us look at what is actually coming to pass.

Over the past few years, the physical layout of my university has been changing. To put it a little indecorously, the place is looking more and more like a retirement spread for the young. Our funds go to construction, into new dorms, into renovating the student union. We have a new aquatics center and ever-improving gyms, stocked with StairMasters and Nautilus machines. Engraved on the wall in the gleaming aquatics building is a line by our founder, Thomas Jefferson, declaring that everyone ought to get about two hours exercise a day. Clearly even the author of the Declaration of Independence endorses the turning of his university into a sports-and-fitness emporium.

But such improvements shouldn't be surprising. Universities need to attract the best (that is, the smartest *and* the richest) students in order to survive in an ever more competitive market. Schools want kids whose parents can pay the full freight, not the ones who need scholarships or want to bargain down the tuition costs. If the marketing surveys say that the kids require sports centers, then, trustees willing, they shall have them. In fact, as I began looking around, I came to see that more and more of what's going on in the university is customer driven. The consumer pressures that beset me on evaluation day are only a part of an overall trend.

From the start, the contemporary university's relationship with students has a solicitous, nearly servile tone. As soon as someone enters his junior year in high school, and especially if he's living in a prosperous zip code, the informational material—the advertising—comes flooding in. Pictures, testimonials, videocassettes, and CD ROMs (some bidden, some not) arrive at the door from colleges across the country, all trying to capture the student and his tuition cash. The freshman-to-be sees photos of well-appointed dorm rooms; of elaborate phys-ed facilities; of fine dining rooms; of expertly kept sports fields; of orchestras and drama troupes; of students working alone (no overbearing grown-ups in range), peering with high seriousness into computers and microscopes; or of students arrayed outdoors in attractive conversational garlands.

Occasionally—but only occasionally, for we usually photograph rather badly; in appearance we tend at best to be styleless—there's a professor teaching a class. (The college catalogues I received, by my request only, in the late Sixties were austere affairs full of professors' credentials and course descriptions; it was clear on whose terms the enterprise was going to unfold.) A college financial officer recently put matters to me in concise, if slightly melodramatic, terms: "Colleges don't have admissions offices anymore, they have marketing departments." Is it surprising that someone who has been approached with photos and tapes, bells and whistles, might come in thinking that the Freud and Shakespeare she had signed up to study were also going to be agreeable treats?

How did we reach this point? In part the answer is a matter of demographics and (surprise) of money. Aided by the G.I. bill, the college-going population in America dramatically increased after the Second World War. Then came the baby boomers, and to accommodate them, schools continued to grow. Universities expand easily enough, but with tenure locking faculty in for lifetime jobs, and with the general reluctance of administrators to eliminate their own slots, it's not easy for a university to contract. So after the baby boomers had passed through—like a fat meal digested by a boa constrictor—the colleges turned to energetic promotional strategies to fill the empty chairs. And suddenly college became a buyer's market. What students and their parents wanted had to be taken more and more into account. That usually meant creating more comfortable, less challenging environments, places where almost no one failed, everything was enjoyable, and everyone was nice.

Just as universities must compete with one another for students, so must the individual departments. At a time of rank economic anxiety, the English and history majors have to contend for students against the more success-insuring branches, such as the sciences and the commerce school. In 1968, more than 21 percent of all the bachelor's degrees conferred in America were in the humanities; by 1993, that number had fallen to about 13 percent. The humanities now must struggle to attract students, many of whose parents devoutly wish they would study something else.

One of the ways we've tried to stay attractive is by loosening up. We grade much more softly than our colleagues in science. In English, we don't give many D's, or C's for that matter. (The rigors of Chem 101 create almost as many English majors per year as do the splendors of Shakespeare.) A professor at Stanford recently explained grade inflation in the humanities by observing that the undergraduates were getting smarter every year; the higher grades simply recorded how much better they were than their predecessors. Sure.

Along with softening the grades, many humanities departments have relaxed major requirements. There are some good reasons for introducing more choice into curricula and requiring fewer standard courses. But the move, like many others in the university now, jibes with a tendency to serve—and not challenge—the students. Students can also float in and out of classes during the first two weeks of each term without making any commitment. The common name for this time span—shopping period—speaks volumes about the consumer mentality that's now in play. Usually, too, the kids can drop courses up until the last month with only an innocuous "W" on their transcripts. Does a course look too challenging? No problem. Take it pass-fail. A happy consumer is, by definition, one with multiple options, one who can always have what he wants. And since a course is something the students and their parents have bought and paid for, why can't they do with it pretty much as they please?

A sure result of the university's widening elective leeway is to give students more power over their teachers. Those who don't like you can simply avoid you. If the clientele dislikes you en masse, you can be left without students, period. My first term teaching I walked into my introduction to poetry course and found it inhabited by one student, the gloriously named Bambi Lynn Dean. Bambi and I chatted amiably awhile, but for all that she and the pleasure of her name could offer, I was fast on the way to meltdown. It was all a mistake, luckily, a problem with the scheduling book. Everyone was waiting for me next door. But in a dozen years of teaching I haven't forgotten that feeling of being ignominiously marooned. For it happens to others, and not always because of scheduling glitches. I've seen older colleagues go through hot embarrassment at not having enough students sign up for their courses: they graded too hard, demanded too much, had beliefs too far out of keeping with the existing disposition. It takes only a few such instances to draw other members of the professoriat further into line.

And if what's called tenure reform—which generally just means the abolition of tenure—is broadly enacted, professors will be yet more vulnerable to the whims of their customer-students. Teach what pulls the kids in, or walk. What about entire departments that don't deliver? If the kids say no to Latin and Greek, is it time to dissolve classics? Such questions are being entertained more and more seriously by university administrators.

How does one prosper with the present clientele? Many of the most successful professors now are the ones who have "decentered" their classrooms. There's a new emphasis on group projects and on computer-generated exchanges among the students. What they seem to want most is to talk to one another. A classroom now is frequently an "environment," a place highly conducive to the exchange of existing ideas, the students' ideas. Listening to one another, students sometimes change their opinions. But what they generally can't do is acquire a new vocabulary, a new perspective, that will cast issues in a fresh light.

The Socratic method—the animated, sometimes impolite give-and-take between student and teacher—seems too jagged for current sensibilities. Students frequently come to my office to tell me how intimidated they feel in class; the thought of being embarrassed in front of the groups fills them with dread. I remember a student telling me how humiliating it was to be corrected by the teacher, by me. So I asked the logical question: "Should I let a major factual error go by so as to save discomfort?" The student—a good student, smart and earnest—said that was a tough question. He'd need to think about it.

Disturbing? Sure. But I wonder, are we really getting students ready for Socratic exchange with professors when we push them off into vast lecture rooms, two and three hundred to a class, sometimes face them with only grad students until their third year, and signal in our myriad professorial ways that we often have much better things to do than sit in our offices and talk with them? How bad will the student-faculty ratios have to become, how teeming the lecture courses, before we hear students righteously complaining, as they did thirty years ago, about the impersonality of their schools, about their decline into knowledge factories? "This is a firm," said Mario Savio at Berkeley during the Free Speech protests of the Sixties, "and if the Board of Regents are the board of directors, . . . then . . . the faculty are a bunch of employees and we're the raw material. But we're a bunch of raw material that don't mean . . . to be made into any product."

Teachers who really do confront students, who provide significant challenges to what they believe, can be very successful, granted. But sometimes such professors generate more than a little trouble for themselves. A controversial teacher can send students hurrying to the deans and the counselors, claiming to have been offended. ("Offensive" is the preferred term of repugnance today, just as "enjoyable" is the summit of praise.) Colleges have brought in hordes of counselors and deans to make sure that everything is smooth, serene, unflustered, that everyone has a good time. To the counselor, to the dean, and to the university legal squad, that which is normal, healthy, and prudent is best.

An air of caution and deference is everywhere. When my students come to talk with me in my office, they often exhibit a Franciscan humility. "Do you have a moment?" "I know you're busy. I won't take up much of your time." Their presences tend to be very light; they almost never change the temperature of the room. The dress is nondescript: clothes are in earth tones; shoes are practical—cross-trainers, hiking boots, work shoes, Dr. Martens, with now and then a stylish pair of raised-sole boots on one of the young women. Many, male and female both, peep from beneath the bills of monogrammed baseball caps. Quite a few wear sports, or even corporate, logos, sometimes on one piece of clothing but occasionally (and disconcertingly) on more. The walk is slow; speech is careful, sweet, a bit weary, and without strong inflection. (After the first lively week of the term, most seem far in debt to sleep.) They are almost unfailingly polite. They don't want to offend me; I could hurt them, savage their grades.

Naturally, there are exceptions, kids I chat animatedly with, who offer a joke, or go on about this or that new CD (almost never a book, no). But most of the traffic is genially sleepwalking. I have to admit that I'm a touch wary, too. I tend to hold back. An unguarded remark, a joke that's taken to be off-color, or simply an uncomprehended comment can lead to difficulties. I keep it literal. They scare me a little, these kind and melancholy students, who themselves seem rather frightened of their own lives.

Before they arrive, we ply the students with luscious ads, guaranteeing them a cross between summer camp and lotusland. When they get here, flattery and nonstop entertainment are available, if that's what they want. And when they leave? How do we send our students out into the world? More and more, our administrators call the booking agents and line up one or another celebrity to usher the graduates into the millennium. This past spring, Kermit the Frog won himself an honorary degree at Southampton College on Long Island; Bruce Willis and Yogi Berra took credentials away at Montclair State; Arnold Schwarzenegger scored at the University of Wisconsin—Superior. At Wellesley, Oprah Winfrey gave the commencement address. (*Wellesley*—one of the most rigorous academic colleges in the nation.) At the University of Vermont, Whoopi Goldberg laid down the word. But why should a worthy administrator contract the likes of Susan Sontag, Christopher Hitchens, or Robert Hughes—someone who might actually say something, something disturbing, something "offensive"—when he can get what the parents and kids apparently want and what the newspapers will softly commend—more lite entertainment, more TV?

Is it a surprise, then that this generation of students—steeped in consumer culture before going off to school, treated as potent customers by the university well before their date of arrival, then pandered to from day one until the morning of the final kiss-off from Kermit or one of his kin—are inclined to see the books they read as a string of entertainments to be placidly enjoyed or languidly cast down? Given the way universities are now administered (which is more and more to say, given the way that they are currently marketed), is it a shock that the kids don't come to school hot to learn, unable to bear their own ignorance? For some measure of self-dislike, or self-discontent—which is much different than simple depression—seems to me to be a prerequisite for getting an education that matters. My students, alas, usually lack the confidence to acknowledge what would be their most precious asset for learning: their ignorance.

Not long ago, I asked my Freud class a question that, however hoary, never fails to solicit intriguing responses: Who are your heroes? Whom do you admire? After one remarkable answer, featuring T.S. Eliot as hero, a series of generic replies rolled in, one gray wave after the next: my father, my best friend, a doctor who lives in our town, my high school history teacher. Virtually all the heroes were people my students had known personally, people who had done something local, specific, and practical, and had done it for them. They were good people, unselfish people, these heroes, but most of all they were people who had delivered the goods.

My students' answers didn't exhibit any philosophical resistance to the idea of greatness. It's not that they had been primed by their professors with complex arguments to combat genius. For the truth is that these students don't need debunking theories. Long before college, skepticism became their habitual mode. They are the progeny of Bart Simpson and David Letterman, and the hyper-cool ethos of the box. It's inane to say that theorizing professors have created them, as many conservative critics like to do. Rather, they have substantially created a university environment in which facile skepticism can thrive without being substantially contested.

Skeptical approaches have *potential* value. If you have no all-encompassing religious faith, no faith in historical destiny, the future of the West, or anything comparably grand, you need to acquire your vision of the world somewhere. If it's from literature, then the various visions literature offers have to be inquired into skeptically. Surely it matters that women are denigrated in Milton and in Pope, that some novelistic voices assume an overbearing godlike authority, that the poor are, in this or that writer, inevitably cast as clowns. You can't buy all of literature wholesale if it's going to help draw your patterns of belief.

But demystifying theories are now overused, applied mechanically. It's all logo-centrism, patriarchy, ideology. And in this the student environment—laid-back, skeptical, knowing—is, I believe, central. Full-out debunking is what plays with this clientele. Some have been doing it nearly as long as, if more crudely than, their deconstructionist teachers. In the context of the contemporary university, and cool consumer culture, a useful intellectual skepticism has become exaggerated into a fundamentalist caricature of itself. The teachers have buckled to their students' views.

At its best, multiculturalism can be attractive as well-deployed theory. What could be more valuable than encountering the best work of far-flung cultures and becoming a citizen of the world? But in the current consumer environment, where flattery plays so well, the urge to encounter the other can devolve into the urge to find others who embody and celebrate the right ethnic origins. So we put aside the African novelist Chinua Achebe's abrasive, troubling *Things Fall Apart* and gravitate toward hymns on Africa, cradle of all civilizations.

What about the phenomenon called political correctness? Raising the standard of civility and tolerance in the university has been—who can deny it?—a very good thing. Yet this admirable impulse has expanded to the point where one is enjoined to speak well—and only well—of women, blacks, gays, the disabled, in fact of virtually everyone. And we can owe this expansion in many ways to the student culture. Students now do not wish to be criticized, not in any form. (The culture of consumption never criticizes them, at least not *overtly*.) In the current university, the movement for urbane tolerance has devolved into an imperative against critical reaction, turning much of the intellectual life into a dreary Sargasso Sea. At a certain point, professors stopped being usefully sensitive and became more like careful retailers who have it as a cardinal point of doctrine never to piss the customers off.

To some professors, the solution lies in the movement called cultural studies. What students need, they believe, is to form a critical perspective on pop culture. It's a fine idea, no doubt. Students should be able to run a critical commentary against the stream of consumer stimulations in which they're immersed. But cultural-studies programs rarely work, because no matter what you propose by way of analysis, things tend to bolt downhill toward an uncritical discussion of students' tastes, into what they like and don't like. If you want to do a Frankfurt School-style analysis of *Braveheart*, you can be pretty sure that by mid-class Adorno and Horkheimer will be consigned to the junk heap of history and you'll be collectively weighing the charms of Mel Gibson. One sometimes wonders if cultural studies hasn't prospered because, under the guise of serious intellectual analysis, it gives the customers what they most want—easy pleasure, more TV. Cultural studies becomes nothing better than what its detractors claim it is—Madonna studies—when students kick loose from the critical perspective and groove to the product, and that, in my experience teaching film and pop culture, happens plenty.

On the issue of genius, as on multiculturalism and political correctness, we professors of the humanities have, I think, also failed to press back against our students' consumer tastes. Here we tend to nurse a pair of—to put it charitably—disparate views. In one mode, we're inclined to a programmatic debunking criticism. We call the concept of genius into question. But in our professional lives per se, we aren't usually disposed against the idea of distinguished achievement. We argue animatedly about the caliber of potential colleagues. We support a star system, in which some professors are far better paid, teach less, and under better conditions than the rest. In our own profession, we are creating a system that is the mirror image of the one we're dismantling in the curriculum. Ask a professor what she thinks of the work of Stephen Greenblatt, a leading critic of Shakespeare, and you'll hear it for an hour. Ask her what her views are on Shakespeare's genius and she's likely to begin questioning the term along with the whole "discourse of evaluation." This dual sensibility may be intellectually incoherent. But in its awareness of what plays with students, it's conducive to good classroom evaluations and, in its awareness of where and how the professional bread is buttered, to self-advancement as well.

My overall point is this: It's not that a left-wing professorial coup has taken over the university. It's that at American universities, left-liberal politics have collided with the ethos of consumerism. The consumer ethos is winning.

Then how do those who at least occasionally promote genius and high literary ideals look to current students? How do we appear, those of us who take teaching to be something of a performance art and who imagine that if you give yourself over completely to your subject you'll be rewarded with insight beyond what you individually command?

I'm reminded of an old piece of newsreel footage I saw once. The speaker (perhaps it was Lenin, maybe Trotsky) was haranguing a large crowd. He was expostulating, arm waving, carrying on. Whether it was flawed technology or the man himself, I'm not sure, but the orator looked like an intricate mechanical device that had sprung into fast-forward. To my students, who mistrust enthusiasm in every form, that's me when I start riffing about Freud or Blake. But more and more, as my evaluations showed, I've been replacing enthusiasm and intellectual animation with stand-up routines, keeping it all at arm's length, praising under the cover of irony.

It's too bad that the idea of genius has been denigrated so far, because it actually offers a live alternative to the demoralizing culture of hip in which most of my students are mired. By embracing the works and lives of extraordinary people, you can adapt new ideals to revise those that came courtesy of your parents, your neighborhood, your clan—or the tube. The aim of a good liberal-arts education was once, to adapt an observation by the scholar Walter Jackson Bate, to see that "we need not be the passive victims of what we deterministically call 'circumstances' (social, cultural, or reductively psychological-personal), but that by linking ourselves through what Keats calls an 'immortal free-masonry' with the great we can become freer to be ourselves, to be what we most want and value."

But genius isn't just a personal standard; genius can also have political effect. To me, one of the best things abut democratic thinking is the conviction that genius can spring up anywhere. Walt Whitman is born into the working class and thirty-six years later we have a poetic image of America that gives a passionate dimension to the legalistic brilliance of the Constitution. A democracy needs to constantly develop, and to do so it requires the most powerful visionary minds to interpret the present and to propose possible shapes for the future. By continuing to notice and praise genius, we create a culture in which the kind of poetic gamble that Whitman made—a gamble in which failure would have entailed rank humiliation, depression, maybe suicide—still takes place. By rebelling against established ways of seeing and saying things, genius helps us to apprehend how malleable the present is and how promising and fraught with danger is the future. If we teachers do not endorse genius and self-overcoming, can we be surprised when our students find their ideal images in TV's latest persona ads?

A world uninterested in genius is a despondent place, whose sad denizens drift from coffee bar to Prozac dispensary, unfired by ideals, by the glowing image of the self that one might become. As Northrop Frye says in a beautiful and now dramatically unfashionable sentence, "The artist who uses the same energy and genius that Homer and Isaiah had will find that he not only lives in the same palace of art as Homer and Isaiah, but lives in it at the same time." We ought not to deny the existence of such a place simply because we, or those we care for, find the demands it makes intimidating, the rent too high.

What happens if we keep trudging along this bleak course? What happens if our most intelligent students never learn to strive to overcome what they are? What if genius, and the imitation of genius, become silly, outmoded ideas? What you're likely to get are more and more one-dimensional men and women. These will be people who live for easy pleasures, for comfort and prosperity, who think of money first, then second, and third, who hug the status quo; people who believe in God as a sort of insurance policy (cover your bets); people who are never surprised. They will be people so pleased with themselves (when they're not in despair at the general pointlessness of their lives) that they cannot imagine humanity could do better. They'll think it their highest duty to clone themselves as frequently as possible. They'll claim to be happy, and they'll live a long time.

It is probably time now to offer a spate of inspiring solutions. Here ought to come a list of reforms, with due notations about a core curriculum and various requirements. What the traditionalists who offer such solutions miss is that no matter what our current students are given to read, many of them will simply translate it into melodrama, with flat characters and predictable morals. (The unabated capitalist culture that conservative critics so often endorse has put students in a position to do little else.) One can't simply wave a curricular wand and reverse acculturation.

Perhaps it would be a good idea to try firing the counselors and sending half the deans back into their classrooms, dismantling the football team and making the stadium into a playground for local kids, emptying the fraternities, and boarding up the student-activities office. Such measures would convey the message that American colleges are not northern outposts of Club Med. A willingness on the part of the faculty to defy student conviction and affront them occasionally—to be usefully offensive—also might not be a bad thing. We professors talk a lot about subversion, which generally means subverting the views of people who never hear us talk or read our work. But to subvert the views of our students, our customers, that would be something else again.

Ultimately, though, it is up to individuals—and individual students in particular—to make their own way against the current sludgy tide. There's still the library, still the museum, there's still the occasional teacher who lives to find things greater than herself to admire. There are still fellow students who have not been cowed. Universities are inefficient, cluttered, archaic places, with many unguarded corners where one can open a book or gaze out onto the larger world and construe it freely. Those who do as much, trusting themselves against the weight of current opinion, will have contributed something to bringing this sad dispensation to an end. As for myself, I'm canning my low-key one-liners; when the kids' TV-based tastes come to the fore, I'll aim and shoot. And when it's time to praise genius, I'll try to do it in the right style, full-out, with faith that finer artistic spirits (maybe not Homer and Isaiah quite, but close, close), still alive somewhere in the ether, will help me out when my invention flags, the students doze, or the dean mutters into the phone. I'm getting back to a more exuberant style; I'll be expostulating and arm waving straight into the millennium, yes I will.

Endnote

Mark Edmundson is a contributing editor of *Harper's Magazine*. He is the author of *Nightmare on Main Street*, a study of the gothic in contemporary culture, forthcoming in October from Harvard University Press.

Questions for Reading and Analysis

1. Why is Edmundson dissatisfied with the comments he gets from his students on the course evaluation forms? Why does it bother him that they compliment him for his sense of humor and his talent to make the class "enjoyable"?

2. What are the implications of Edmundson's claim that, according to one administrator, colleges "don't have admissions offices anymore, they have marketing departments"?

3. How has the attitude that "the customer is king" affected the power relationship between students and professors? How has it affected the way professors teach their classes?

4. What does Edmundson mean when he says that students lack the "confidence to acknowledge what would be their most precious asset for learning: their ignorance"?

5. How does the writer's spelling of "lite" in the subtitle foreshadow his argument?

6. Underline Edmundson's references to popular culture. How do these references contribute to the points he makes in his essay?

7. Edmundson draws a rather unfavorable picture of today's college students: they are listless, disinterested consumers who consider college a financial investment rather than an avenue to personal and intellectual growth. If you look around you at your friends and classmates, do you find his evaluation to be accurate?

Barbara Ehrenreich, a columnist for Time *and other magazines, has often used humor as a means of making people see what she has to show them. Her essay "Spudding Out" argues that couch potatoes "love television because television brings us a world in which television does not exist"; it comes from her 1990 collection* The Worst Years of Our Lives.

Spudding Out

Barbara Ehrenreich

Someone has to speak for them, because they have, to a person, lost the power to speak for themselves. I am referring to that great mass of Americans who were once known as the "salt of the earth," then as "the silent majority," more recently as "the viewing public," and now, alas, as "couch potatoes." What drives them—or rather, leaves them sapped and spineless on their reclining chairs? What are they seeking—beyond such obvious goals as a tastefully colorized version of *The Maltese Falcon?*

My husband was the first in the family to "spud out," as the expression now goes. Soon everyone wanted one of those zip-up "Couch Potato Bags," to keep warm in during David Letterman. The youngest, and most thoroughly immobilized, member of the family relies on a remote that controls his TV, stereo, and VCR, and can also shut down the neighbor's pacemaker at fifteen yards.

But we never see the neighbors anymore, nor they us. This saddens me, because Americans used to be a great and restless people, fond of the outdoors in all of its manifestations, from Disney World to miniature golf. Some experts say there are virtues in mass agoraphobia, that it strengthens the family and reduces highway deaths. But I would point out that there are still a few things that cannot be done in the den, especially by someone zipped into a body bag. These include racquetball, voting, and meeting strange people in bars.

Most psychologists interpret the couch potato trend as a negative reaction to the outside world. Indeed, the list of reasons to stay safely tucked indoors lengthens yearly. First there was crime, then AIDS, then side-stream smoke. To this list should be added "fear of the infrastructure," for we all know someone who rashly stepped outside only to be buried in a pothole, hurled from a collapsing bridge, or struck by a falling airplane.

But it is not just the outside world that has let us down. Let's face it, despite a decade-long campaign by the "profamily" movement, the family has been a disappointment. The reason lies in an odd circular dynamic: we watch television to escape from our families because television shows us how dull our families really are.

Compare your own family to, for example, the Huxtables, the Keatons, or the peppy young people on *thirtysomething*. In those families, even the three-year-olds are stand-up comics, and the most insipid remark is hailed with heartening outbursts of canned laughter. When television families aren't gathered around the kitchen table exchanging wisecracks, they are experiencing brief but moving dilemmas, which are handily solved by the youngest child or by some cute extraterrestrial house-guest. Emerging from *Family Ties* or *My Two Dads*, we are forced to acknowledge that our own families are made up of slow-witted, emotionally crippled people who would be lucky to qualify for seats in the studio audience of *Jeopardy!*

But gradually I have come to see that there is something besides fear of the outside and disgust with our families that drives us to spudhood—some positive attraction, some deep cathexis to television itself. For a long time it eluded me. When I watched television, mainly as a way of getting to know my husband and children, I found that my mind wandered to more interesting things, like whether to get up and make ice cubes.

Only after many months of viewing did I begin to understand the force that has transformed the American people into root vegetables. If you watch TV for a very long time, day in, day out, you will begin to notice something eerie and unnatural about the world portrayed therein. I don't mean that it is two-dimensional or lacks a well-developed critique of the capitalist consumer culture or something superficial like that. I mean something so deeply obvious that it's almost scary: when you watch television, you will see people doing many things—chasing fast cars, drinking lite beer, shooting each other at close range, etc. But you will never see people *watching television*. Well, maybe for a second, before the phone rings or a brand-new, multiracial adopted child walks into the house. But never *really watching*, hour after hour, the way *real* people do.

Way back in the beginning of the television era, this was not so strange, because real people actually did many of the things people do on TV, even if it was only bickering with their mothers-in-law about which toilet paper to buy. But modern people, i.e., couch potatoes, do nothing that is ever shown on television (because it is either dangerous or would involve getting up from the couch). And what they do do—watch television—is far too boring to be televised for more than a fraction of a second, not even by Andy Warhol, bless his boredom-proof little heart.[1]

So why do we keep on watching? The answer, by now, should be perfectly obvious: we love television because television brings us a world in which television does not exist. In fact, deep in their hearts, this is what the spuds crave most: a rich, new, participatory life, in which family members look each other in the eye, in which people walk outside and banter with the neighbors, where there is adventure, possibility, danger, feeling, all in natural color, stereophonic sound, and three dimensions, without commercial interruptions, and starring . . . us.

"You mean some new kind of computerized interactive medium?" the children asked hopefully, pert as the progeny on a Tuesday night sitcom. But before I could expand on this concept—known to our ancestors as "real life"—they were back at the box, which may be, after all, the only place left to find it.

Endnote

1. Artist and filmmaker Andy Warhol (1928–1987) became well-known for his use of popular culture for high art. Warhol's intentional repetition of images and deliberately boring recordings of mundane activities—such as *Empire*, which filmed the Empire State Building for 24 hours from a position across the street—led one critic to announce that "not one ounce of sentiment disturbs the numb silence of these images."

Questions for Reading and Analysis

1. What is the "mass agoraphobia" Ehrenreich talks about? What caused the phenomenon?

2. What is Ehrenreich's thesis?

3. How does Ehrenreich use the metaphor in the title throughout the essay? What is the significance of comparing people to root vegetables?

4. Point out the instances in Ehrenreich's essay that are funny. How does she use humor to drive home a point that is not terribly funny when looked at closely?

5. Do you think Ehrenreich's essay accurately describes American family life, or do you think she exaggerates the degree of "spudhood" we have achieved? Back up your answer with personal examples.

ouise Erdrich (b. 1954), novelist and essayist, is a member of the Turtle Mountain Band of Chippewa. Her Native American heritage and upper-midwestern upbringing inform much of her work. "Skunk Dreams," which first appeared in the Georgia Review *in 1994, is a testament to her attachment to the land, her need to get outside, whether in the wilds of North Dakota or the heavily-civilized New England landscape.*

Skunk Dreams

Louise Erdrich

When I was fourteen, I slept alone on a North Dakota football field under the cold stars on an early spring night. May is unpredictable in the Red River Valley, and I happened to hit a night when frost formed in the grass. A skunk trailed a plume of steam across the forty-yard line near moonrise. I tucked the top of my sleeping bag over my head and was just dozing off when the skunk walked onto me with simple authority.

Its ripe odor must have dissipated in the frozen earth of its winterlong hibernation, because it didn't smell all that bad, or perhaps it was just that I took shallow breaths in numb surprise. I felt him—her, whatever—pause on the side of my hip and turn around twice before evidently deciding I was a good place to sleep. At the back of my knees, on the quilting of my sleeping bag, it trod out a spot for itself and then, with a serene little groan, curled up and lay perfectly still. That made two of us. I was wildly awake, trying to forget the sharpness and number of skunk teeth, trying not to think of the high percentage of skunks with rabies, or the reason that on camping trips my father always kept a hatchet underneath his pillow.

Inside the bag, I felt as if I might smother. Carefully, making only the slightest of rustles, I drew the bag away from my face and took a deep breath of the night air, enriched with skunk, but clear and watery and cold. It wasn't so bad, and the skunk didn't stir at all, so I watched the moon—caught that night in an envelope of silk, a mist—pass over my sleeping field of teenage guts and glory. The grass in spring that has lain beneath the snow harbors a sere dust both old and fresh. I smelled that newness beneath the rank tone of my bag-mate—the stiff fragrance of damp earth and the thick pungency of newly manured fields a mile or two away—along with my sleeping bag's smell, slightly mildewed, forever smoky. The skunk settled even closer and began to breathe rapidly; its feet jerked a little like a dog's. I sank against the earth, and fell asleep too.

Of what easily tipped cans, what molten sludge, what dogs in yards on chains, what leftover macaroni casseroles, what cellar holes, crawl spaces, burrows taken from meek woodchucks, of what miracles of garbage did my skunk dream? Or

141

did it, since we can't be sure, dream the plot of *Moby-Dick*, how to properly age parmesan, or how to restore the brick-walled, tumbledown creamery that was its home? We don't know about the dreams of any other biota, and even much about our own. If dreams are an actual dimension, as some assert, then the usual rules of life by which we abide do not apply. In that place, skunks may certainly dream themselves into the vests of stockbrokers. Perhaps that night the skunk and I dreamed each other's thoughts or are still dreaming them. To paraphrase the problem of the Chinese sage, I may be a woman who has dreamed herself a skunk, or a skunk still dreaming that she is a woman.

In a book called *Death and Consciousness*, David H. Lund—who wants very much to believe in life after death—describes human dream-life as a possible model for a disembodied existence:

> *Many of one's dreams are such that they involve the activities of an apparently embodied person whom one takes to be oneself as long as one dreams. . . . Whatever is the source of the imagery . . . apparently has the capacity to bring about images of a human body and to impart the feeling that the body is mine. It is, of course, just an image body, but it serves as a perfectly good body for the dream experience. I regard it as mine, I act on the dream environment by means of it, and it constitutes the center of the perceptual world of my dream.*

Over the years I have acquired and reshuffled my beliefs and doubts about whether we live on after death—in any shape or form, that is, besides the molecular level at which I am to be absorbed by the taproots of cemetery elms or pines and the tangled mats of fearfully poisoned, too-green lawn grass. I want something of the self on whom I have worked so hard to survive the loss of the body (which, incidentally, the self has done a fairly decent job of looking after, excepting spells of too much cabernet and a few idiotic years of rolling my own cigarettes out of Virginia Blond tobacco). I am put out with the marvelous discoveries of the intricate biochemical configuration of our brains, though I realize that the processes themselves are quite miraculous. I understand that I should be self-proud, content to gee-whiz at the fact that I am the world's only mechanism that can admire itself. I should be grateful that life is here today, though gone tomorrow, but I can't help it. I want more.

Skunks don't mind each other's vile perfume. Obviously, they find each other more than tolerable. And even I, who have been in the presence of a direct skunk hit, wouldn't classify their weapon as mere smell. It is more on the order of a reality-enhancing experience. It's not so pleasant as standing in a grove of old-growth red cedars, or on a lyrical moonshed plain, or watching trout rise to the shadow of your hand on the placid surface of an Alpine lake. When the skunk lets go, you're surrounded by skunk presence: inhabited, owned, involved with something you can only describe as powerfully *there*.

I woke at dawn, stunned into that sprayed state of being. The dog that had approached me was rolling in the grass, half-addled, sprayed too. The skunk was gone. I abandoned my sleeping bag and started home. Up Eighth Street, past the tiny blue and pink houses, past my grade school, past all the addresses where I had baby-sat, I walked in my own strange wind. The streets were wide and empty, I met no one—not a dog, not a squirrel, not even an early robin. Perhaps they had all scattered before me, blocks away. I had gone out to sleep on the football field because I was afflicted with a sadness I had to dramatize. Mood swings had begun, hormones, feverish and brutal. They were nothing to me now. My emotions had seemed vast, dark, and sickeningly private. But they were minor, mere wisps, compared to skunk.

I have found that my best dreams come to me in cheap motels. One such dream about an especially haunting place occurred in a rattling room in Valley City, North Dakota. There, in the home of the Winter Show, in the old Rudolph Hotel, I was to spend a weeklong residency as a poet-in-the-schools. I was supporting myself, at the time, by teaching poetry to children, convicts, rehabilitation patients, high-school hoods, and recovering alcoholics. What a marvelous job it was, and what opportunities I had to dream, since I paid my own lodging and lived low, some-times taking rooms for less than ten dollars a night in motels that had already been closed by local health departments.

The images that assailed me in Valley City came about because the bedspread was so thin and worn—a mere brown tissuey curtain—that I had to sleep beneath my faux fur Salvation Army coat, wearing all of my clothing, even a scarf. Cold often brings on the most spectacular of my dreams, as if my brain has been incited to fevered activity. On that particular frigid night, the cold somehow seemed to snap boundaries, shift my time continuum, and perhaps even allow me to visit my own life in a future moment. After waking once, transferring the contents of my entire suitcase onto my person, and shivering to sleep again, I dreamed of a vast, dark, fenced place. The fencing was chain-link in places, chicken wire, sagging X wire, barbed wire on top, jerry-built with tipped-out poles and uncertain corners nailed to log posts and growing trees. And yet it was quite impermeable and solid, as time-tested, broken-looking things so often are.

Behind it, trees ran for miles—large trees, grown trees, big pines the likes of which do not exist on the Great Plains. In my dream I walked up to the fence, looked within, and saw tawny, humpbacked elk move among the great trunks and slashing green arms. Suave, imponderable, magnificently dumb, they lurched and floated through the dim-complexioned air. One turned, however, before they all van-ished and from either side of that flimsy-looking barrier there passed between us a look, a communion, a long and measureless regard that left me, on waking, with a sensation of penetrating sorrow.

I didn't think about my dream for years, until after I moved to New Hamp-shire. I had become urbanized and sedentary since the days when I slept with skunks, and I had turned inward. For several years I spent my days leaning above a strange desk, a green door on stilts, which was so high that to sit at it I bought a barstool upholstered in brown leatherette. Besides, the entire Northeast seemed like the inside of a house to me, the sky small and oddly lit, as if by an electric bulb. The sun did not pop over the great trees for hours—and then went down so soon. I was suspicious of Eastern land: the undramatic loveliness, the small scale, the lack of sky to watch, the way the weather sneaked up without enough warning.

The woods themselves seemed bogus at first—every inch of the ground turned over more than once, and even in the second growth of old pines so much human evidence. Rock walls ran everywhere, grown through and tumbled, as if the dead still had claims they imposed. The unkillable and fiercely contorted trees of old orchards, those revenants, spooked me when I walked in the woods. The blasted limbs spread a white lace cold as fire in the spring, and the odor of the blossoms was furiously spectral, sweet. When I stood beneath the canopies that hummed and shook with bees, I heard voices, other voices, and I did not understand what they were saying, where they had come from, what drove them into this earth.

Then, as often happens to sparring adversaries in 1940s movies, I fell in love.

After a few years of living in the country, the impulse to simply *get outside* hit me, strengthened, and became again a habit of thought, a reason for storytelling, an uneasy impatience with walls and roads. At first, when I had that urge, I had to get into a car and drive fifteen hundred miles before I was back in a place that I defined as *out*. The West, or the edge of it anyway, the great level patchwork of chemically treated fields and tortured grazing land, was the outside I had internalized. In the rich Red River Valley, where the valuable cropland is practically measured in inches, environmental areas are defined and proudly pointed out as stretches of roadway where the ditches are not mowed. Deer and pheasants survive in shelter belts—rows of Russian olive, plum, sometimes evergreen—planted at the edges of fields. The former tall-grass prairie has now become a collection of mechanized gardens tended by an array of air-conditioned farm implements and bearing an increasing amount of pesticide and herbicide in each black teaspoon of dirt. Nevertheless, no amount of reality changed the fact that I still *thought* of eastern North Dakota as wild.

In time, though, *out* became outside my door in New England. By walking across the road and sitting in my little writing house—a place surrounded by trees, thick plumes of grass, jets of ferns, and banks of touch-me-not—or just by looking out a screen door or window, I started to notice what there was to see. In time, the smothering woods that had always seemed part of Northeastern civilization— more an inside than an outside, more like a friendly garden—revealed themselves as forceful and complex. The growth of plants, the lush celebratory springs made a grasslands person drunk. The world turned dazzling green, the hills rode like comfortable and flowing animals. Everywhere there was the sound of water moving.

And yet, even though I finally grew closer to these woods, on some days I still wanted to tear them from before my eyes.

I wanted to *see*. Where I grew up, our house looked out on the western horizon. I could see horizon when I played. I could see it when I walked to school. It was always there, a line beyond everything, a simple line of changing shades and colors that ringed the town, a vast place. That was it. Down at the end of every grid of streets: vastness. Out the windows of the high school: vastness. From the drive-in theater where I went parking in a purple Duster: vast distance. That is why, on lovely New England days when everything should have been all right—a fall day, for instance, when the earth had risen through the air in patches and the sky lowered, dim and warm—I fell sick with longing for the horizon. I wanted the clean line, the simple line, the clouds marching over it in feathered masses. I suffered from horizon sickness. But it sounds crazy for a grown woman to throw herself at the sky, and the thing is, I wanted to get well. And so to compensate for horizon sickness, for the great longing that seemed both romantically German and prag-matically Chippewa in origin, I found solace in trees.

Trees are a changing landscape of sound and the sound I grew attached to, possible only near large deciduous forests, was the great hushed roar of thousands and millions of leaves brushing and touching one another. Windy days were like sitting just out of sight of an ocean, the great magnetic ocean of wind. All around me, I watched the trees tossing, their heads bending. At times the movement seemed passionate, as though they were flung together in an eager embrace, caressing each other, branch to branch. If there is a vegetative soul, an animating power that all things share, there must be great rejoicing out there on windy days, ecstasy, for trees move so slowly on calm days. At least it seems that way to us. On days of high wind they move so freely it must give them a cellular pleasure close to terror.

Unused to walking in the woods, I did not realize that trees dropped branches— often large ones—or that there was any possible danger in going out on windy days, drawn by the natural drama. There was a white pine I loved, a tree of the size foresters call *overgrown*, a waste, a thing made of long-since harvestable material. The tree was so big that three people couldn't reach around it. Standing at the bottom, craning back, fingers clenched in grooves of bark, I held on as the crown of the tree roared and beat the air a hundred feet above. The movement was frantic, the soft-needled branches long and supple. I thought of a woman tossing, anchored in passion: calm one instant, full-throated the next, hair vast and dark, shedding the piercing, fresh oil of broken needles. I went to visit her often, and walked onward, farther, though it was not so far at all, and then one day I reached the fence.

Chain-link in places, chicken wire, sagging X wire, barbed wire on top, jerry-built with tipped-out poles and uncertain corners nailed to log posts and growing trees, still it seemed impermeable and solid. Behind it, there were trees for miles: large trees, grown trees, big pines. I walked up to the fence, looked within, and could see elk moving. Suave, imponderable, magnificently dumb, they lurched and floated through the dim air.

I was on the edge of a game park, a rich man's huge wilderness, probably the largest parcel of protected land in western New Hampshire, certainly the largest privately owned piece I knew about. At forty square miles—25,000 acres—it was bigger than my mother's home reservation. And it had the oddest fence around it that I'd ever seen, the longest and the tackiest. Though partially electrified, the side closest to our house was so piddling that an elk could easily have tossed it apart. Certainly a half-ton wild boar, the condensed and living version of a tank, could have strolled right through. But then animals, much like most humans, don't charge through fences unless they have sound reasons. As I soon found out, because I nat-urally grew fascinated with the place, there were many more animals trying to get into the park than out, and they couldn't have cared less about ending up in a hunter's stew pot.

These were not wild animals, the elk—since they were grained at feeding sta-tions, how could they be? They were not domesticated either, however, for beyond the no-hunt boundaries they fled and vanished. They were game. Since there is no sport in shooting feedlot steers, these animals—still harboring wild traits and therefore more challenging to kill—were maintained to provide blood pleasure for the members of the Blue Mountain Forest Association.

As I walked away from the fence that day, I was of two minds about the place—and I am still. Shooting animals inside fences, no matter how big the area they have to hide in, seems abominable and silly. And yet, I was glad for that wilderness. Though secretly managed and off limits to me, it was the source of flocks of evening grosbeaks and pine siskins, of wild turkey, ravens, and grouse, of Eastern coyote, oxygen-rich air, foxes, goldfinches, skunk, and bears that tunneled in and out.

I had dreamed of this place in Valley City, or it had dreamed me. There was affinity here, beyond any explanation I could offer, so I didn't try. I continued to visit the tracts of big trees, and on deep nights—windy nights, especially when it stormed—I liked to fall asleep imagining details. I saw the great crowns touching, heard the raving sound of wind and thriving, knocking cries as the blackest of ravens flung themselves across acres upon indifferent acres of tossing, old-growth pine. I could fall asleep picturing how, below that dark air, taproots thrust into a deeper blankness, drinking the powerful rain.

Or was it so only in my dreams? The park, known locally as Corbin's Park, after its founder, Austin Corbin, is knit together of land and farmsteads he bought in the late nineteenth century from 275 individuals. Among the first animals released there, before the place became a hunting club, were thirty buffalo, remnants of the vast Western herds. Their presence piqued the interest of Ernest Harold Bayne, a conservation-minded local journalist, who attempted to break a pair of buffalo calves to the yoke. He exhibited them at country fairs and even knit mittens out of buffalo wool, hoping to convince the skeptical of their usefulness. His work inspired sympathy, if not a trend for buffalo yarn, and collective zeal for the salvation of the buffalo grew until by 1915 the American Bison Society, of which Bayne was secretary, helped form government reserves that eventually more than doubled the herds that remained.

The buffalo dream seems to have been the park's most noble hour. Since that time it has been the haunt of wealthy hunting enthusiasts. The owner of Ruger Arms currently inhabits the stunning, butter-yellow original Corbin mansion and would like to buy the whole park for his exclusive use, or so local gossip has it.

For some months I walked the boundary admiring the tangled landscape, at least all that I could see. After my first apprehension, I ignored the fence. I walked along it as if it simply did not exist, as if I really were part of that place which lay just beyond my reach. The British psychotherapist Adam Phillips has examined obstacles from several different angles, attempting to define their emotional use. "It is impossible to imagine desire without obstacles," he writes, "and wherever we find something to be an obstacle we are at the same time desiring something. It is part of the fascination of the Oedipus story in particular, and perhaps narrative in general, that we and the heroes and heroines of our fictions never know whether obstacles create desire or desire creates obstacles." He goes on to characterize the Unconscious, our dream world, as a place without obstacles: "A good question to ask of a dream is: What are the obstacles that have been removed to make this extraordinary scene possible?"

My dream, however, was about obstacles still in place. The fence was the main component, the defining characteristic of the forbidden territory that I watched but could not enter or experience. The obstacles that we overcome define us. We are composed of hurdles we set up to pace our headlong needs, to control our desires, or against which to measure our growth. "Without obstacles," Phillips writes, the notion of development is inconceivable. There would be nothing to master."

Walking along the boundary of the park no longer satisfied me. The preciousness and deceptive stability of that fence began to rankle. Longing filled me. I wanted to brush against the old pine bark and pass beyond the ridge, to see specifically what was there: what Blue Mountain, what empty views, what lavender hillside, what old cellar holes, what unlikely animals. I was filled with poacher's lust, except I wanted only to smell the air. The linked web restraining me began to grate, and I started to look for weak spots, holes, places where the rough wire sagged. From the moment I began to see the fence as permeable, it became something to overcome. I returned time after time—partly to see if I could spot anyone on the other side, partly because I knew I must trespass.

Then, one clear, midwinter morning, in the middle of a half-hearted thaw, I walked along the fence until I came to a place that looked shaky—and was. I went through. There were no trails that I could see, and I knew I needed to stay away from any perimeter roads or snowmobile paths, as well as from the feeding stations where the animals congregated. I wanted to see the animals, but only from a distance. Of course, as I walked on, leaving a trail easily back-tracked, I encountered no animals at all. Still, the terrain was beautiful, the columns of pine tall and satisfyingly heavy, the patches of oak and elderly maple from an occasional farmstead knotted and patient. I was satisfied, and sometime in the early afternoon, I decided to turn back and head toward the fence again. Skirting a low, boggy area that teemed with wild turkey tracks, heading toward the edge of a deadfall of trashed dead branches and brush, I stared too hard into the sun, and stumbled.

In a half crouch, I looked straight into the face of a boar, massive as a boulder. Cornfed, razor-backed, alert, sensitive ears pricked, it edged slightly backward into the convening shadows. Two ice picks of light gleamed from its shrouded, tiny eyes, impossible to read. Beyond the rock of its shoulder, I saw more: a sow and three cinnamon-brown farrows crossing a small field of glare snow, lit by dazzling sun. The young skittered along, lumps of muscled fat on tiny hooves. They reminded me of snowsuited toddlers on new skates. When they were out of sight the boar melted through the brush after them, leaving not a snapped twig or crushed leaf in his wake.

I almost didn't breathe in the silence, letting the fact of that presence settle before I retraced my own tracks.

Since then, I've been to the game park via front gates, driven down the avenues of tough old trees, and seen herds of wild pigs and elk meandering past the residence of the gamekeeper. A no-hunting zone exists around the house, where the animals are almost tame. But I've been told by privileged hunters that just beyond that invisible boundary they vanish, becoming suddenly and preternaturally elusive.

There is something in me that resists the notion of fair use of this land if the only alternative is to have it cut up, sold off in lots, condominiumized. Yet the dumb fervor of the place depresses me—the wilderness locked up and managed but not for its sake; the animals imported and cultivated to give pleasure through their deaths. All animals, that is, except for skunks.

Not worth hunting, inedible except to old trappers like my uncle Ben Gourneau, who boiled his skunk with onions in three changes of water, skunks pass in and out of Corbin's Park without hindrance, without concern. They live off the corn in the feeding cribs (or the mice it draws), off the garbage of my rural neighbors, off bugs and frogs and grubs. They nudge their way onto our back porch for catfood, and even when disturbed they do not, ever, hurry. It's easy to get near a skunk, even to capture one. When skunks become a nuisance, people either shoot them or catch them in crates, cardboard boxes, Havahart traps, plastic garbage barrels.

Natives of the upper Connecticut River valley have neatly solved the problem of what to do with such catches. They hoist their trapped mustelid into the back of a pickup truck and cart the animal across the river to the neighboring state— New Hampshire to Vermont, Vermont to New Hampshire—before releasing it. The skunk population is estimated as about even on both sides.

We should take comfort from the skunk, an arrogant creature so pleased with its own devices that it never runs from harm, just turns its back in total confidence. If I were an animal, I'd choose to be a skunk: live fearlessly, eat anything, gestate my young in just two months, and fall into a state of dreaming torpor when the cold bit hard. Wherever I went, I'd leave my sloppy tracks. I wouldn't walk so much as putter, destinationless, in a serene belligerence—past hunters, past death overhead, past death all around.

Questions for Reading and Analysis

1. What is the point of Erdrich's opening anecdote?

2. What is the "horizon sickness" that Erdrich suffers after moving to the northeast?

3. To what does Erdrich refer when, midway through her essay, she says, "then . . . I fell in love"?

4. Why does Erdrich have mixed feelings about the game park in New Hampshire? What, eventually, is the effect of the boundary around the park?

5. Why does Erdrich say that if she were to be an animal, she would choose to be a skunk? What qualities in a skunk does she admire?

"Blame it on Feminism" is an excerpt from Susan Faludi's controversial first book, Backlash: The Undeclared War Against American Women *(1991), which won the National Book Critics Circle award in 1992. A Harvard graduate and Pulitzer Prize-winning journalist, Faludi investigates the neoconservative backlash against the feminist movement. Faludi points out the underlying fallacy in the neoconservative argument: "what has made women unhappy in the last decade is not their 'equality'—which they don't have yet—but the rising pressure to halt, and even reverse, women's quest for that equality."*

Blame It on Feminism

Susan Faludi

To be a woman in America at the close of the twentieth century—what good fortune. That's what we keep hearing, anyway. The barricades have fallen, politicians assure us. Women have "made it," Madison Avenue cheers. Women's fight for equality has "largely been won," *Time* magazine announces. Enroll at any university, join any law firm, apply for credit at any bank. Women have so many opportunities now, corporate leaders say, that they don't really need opportunity policies. Women are so equal now, lawmakers say, that they no longer need an Equal Rights Amendment. Women have "so much," former president Ronald Reagan says, that the White House no longer needs to appoint them to high office. Even American Express ads are saluting a woman's right to charge it. At last, women have received their full citizenship papers.

And yet . . .

Behind this celebration of the American woman's victory, behind the news, cheerfully and endlessly repeated, that the struggle for women's rights is won, another message flashes: you may be free and equal now, but you have never been more miserable.

This bulletin of despair is posted everywhere—at the newsstand, on the TV set, at the movies, in advertisements and doctors' offices and academic journals. Professional women are suffering "burnout" and succumbing to an "infertility epidemic." Single women are grieving from a "man shortage." The *New York Times* reports: childless women are "depressed and confused" and their ranks are swelling. *Newsweek* says: unwed women are "hysterical" and crumbling under a "profound crisis of confidence." The health-advice manuals inform: high-powered career women are stricken with unprecedented outbreaks of "stress-induced disorders," hair loss, bad nerves, alcoholism, and even heart attacks. The psychology books advise: independent women's loneliness represents "a major mental-health problem today." Even founding feminist Betty Friedan has been spreading the word: she warns that women now suffer from "new problems that have no name."

How can American women be in so much trouble at the same time that they are supposed to be so blessed? If women got what they asked for, what could possibly be the matter now?

The prevailing wisdom of the past decade has supported one, and only one, answer to this riddle: it must be all that equality that's causing all that pain. Women are unhappy precisely because they are free. Women are enslaved by their own liberation. They have grabbed at the gold ring of independence, only to miss the one ring that really matters. They have gained control of their fertility, only to destroy it. They have pursued their own professional dreams—and lost out on romance, the greatest female adventure. "Our generation was the human sacrifice" to the women's movement, writer Elizabeth Mehren contends in a *Time* cover story. Baby-boom women, like her, she says, have been duped by feminism: "We believed the rhetoric." In *Newsweek*, writer Kay Ebeling dubs feminism the "Great Experiment That Failed" and asserts, "Women in my generation, its perpetrators, are the casualties."

In the eighties, publications from the *New York Times* to *Vanity Fair* to *The Nation* have issued a steady stream of indictments against the women's movement, with such headlines as "When Feminism Failed" or "The Awful Truth about Women's Lib." They hold the campaign for women's equality responsible for nearly every woe besetting women, from depression to meager savings accounts, from teenage suicides to eating disorders to bad complexions. The *Today* show says women's liberation is to blame for bag ladies. A guest columnist in the *Baltimore Sun* even proposes that feminists produced the rise in slasher movies. By making the "violence" of abortion more acceptable, the author reasons, women's-rights activists made it all right to show graphic murders on screen.

At the same time, other outlets of popular culture have been forging the same connection: in Hollywood films, of which *Fatal Attraction* is only the most famous, emancipated women with condominiums of their own slink wild-eyed between bare walls, paying for their liberty with an empty bed, a barren womb. "My biological clock is ticking so loud it keeps me awake at night," Sally Field cries in the film *Surrender*, as, in an all-too-common transformation in the cinema of the eighties, an actress who once played scrappy working heroines is now showcased groveling for a groom. In prime-time television shows, from *thirtysomething* to *Family Man*, single, professional, and feminist women are humiliated, turned into harpies, or hit by nervous breakdowns; the wise ones recant their independent ways by the closing sequence. In popular novels, from Gail Parent's *A Sign of the Eighties* to Stephen King's *Misery*, unwed women shrink to sniveling spinsters or inflate the fire-breathing she-devils; renouncing all aspirations but marriage, they beg for wedding bands from strangers or swing axes at reluctant bachelors. Even Erica Jong's high-flying independent heroine literally crashes by the end of the decade, as the author supplants *Fear of Flying*'s saucy Isadora Wing, an exuberant symbol of female sexual emancipation in the seventies, with an embittered careerist-turned-recovering-"codependent" in *Any Woman's Blues*—a book that is intended, as the narrator bluntly states, "to demonstrate what a dead end the so-called sexual revolution had become and how desperate so-called free women were in the last few years of our decadent epoch."

Popular psychology manuals peddle the same diagnosis for contemporary female distress. "Feminism, having promised her a stronger sense of her own identity, has given her little more than an identity *crisis*," the best-selling advice manual *Being a Woman* asserts. The authors of the era's self-help classic, *Smart Women/Foolish Choices*, proclaim that women's distress was "an unfortunate consequence of feminism" because "it created a myth among women that the apex of self-realization could be achieved only through autonomy, independence, and career."

In the Reagan and Bush years, government officials have needed no prompting to endorse this thesis. Reagan spokeswoman Faith Ryan Whittlesey declared feminism a "straitjacket" for women, in one of the White House's only policy speeches on the status of the American female population—entitled "Radical Feminism in Retreat." The U.S. attorney general's Commission on Pornography even proposed that women's professional advancement might be responsible for rising rape rates: with more women in college and at work now, the commission members reasoned in their report, women just have more opportunities to be raped.

Legal scholars have railed against the "equality trap." Sociologists have claimed that "feminist-inspired" legislative reforms have stripped women of special "protections." Economists have argued that well-paid working women have created a "less stable American family." And demographers, with greatest fanfare, have legitimated the prevailing wisdom with so-called neutral data on sex ratios and fertility trends; they say they actually have the numbers to prove that equality doesn't mix with marriage and motherhood.

Finally, some "liberated" women themselves have joined the lamentations. In *The Cost of Loving: Women and the New Fear of Intimacy*, Megan Marshall, a Harvard-pedigreed writer, asserts that the feminist "Myth of Independence" has turned her generation into unloved and unhappy fast-trackers, "dehumanized" by careers and "uncertain of their gender identity." Other diaries of mad Superwomen charge that "the hard-core feminist viewpoint," as one of them puts it, has relegated educated executive achievers to solitary nights of frozen dinners and closet drinking. The triumph of equality, they report, has merely given women hives, stomach cramps, eye "twitching" disorders, even comas.

But what "equality" are all these authorities talking about?

If American women are so equal, why do they represent two-thirds of all poor adults? Why are more than 70 percent of full-time working women making less than twenty-five thousand dollars a year, nearly double the number of men at that level? Why are they still far more likely than men to live in poor housing, and twice as likely to draw no pension? If women "have it all," then why don't they have the most basic requirements to achieve equality in the work force: unlike that of virtually all other industrialized nations, the U.S. government still has no family-leave and child-care programs.

If women are so "free," why are their reproductive freedoms in greater jeopardy today than a decade earlier? Why, in their own homes, do they still shoulder 70 percent of the household duties—while the only major change in the last fifteen years is that now men *think* they do more around the house? In thirty states, it is still generally legal for husbands to rape their wives; and only ten states have laws mandating arrest for domestic violence—even though battering is the leading cause of injury to women (greater than rapes, muggings, and auto accidents combined).

The word may be that women have been "liberated," but women themselves seem to feel otherwise. Repeatedly in national surveys, majorities of women say they are still far from equality. In poll after poll in the decade, overwhelming majorities of women said they need equal pay and equal job opportunities, they need an Equal Rights Amendment, they need the right to an abortion without government interference, they need a federal law guaranteeing maternity leave, they need decent child-care services. They have none of these. So how exactly have women "won" the war for women's rights?

Seen against this background, the much ballyhooed claim that feminism is responsible for making women miserable becomes absurd—and irrelevant. The afflictions ascribed to feminism, from "the man shortage" to "the infertility epidemic" to "female burnout" to "toxic day care," have had their origins not in the actual conditions of women's lives but rather in a closed system that starts and ends in the media, popular culture, and advertising—an endless feedback loop that perpetuates and exaggerates its own false images of womanhood. And women don't see feminism as their enemy, either. In fact, in national surveys, 75 to 95 percent of women credit the feminist campaign with *improving* their lives, and a similar proportion say that the women's movement should keep pushing for change.

If the many ponderers of the Woman Question really wanted to know what is troubling the American female population, they might have asked their subjects. In public-opinion surveys, women consistently rank their own *inequality*, at work and at home, among their most urgent concerns. Over and over, women complain to pollsters of a lack of economic, not marital, opportunities; they protest that working men, not working women, fail to spend time in the nursery and the kitchen. It is justice for their gender, not wedding rings and bassinets, that women believe to be in desperately short supply.

As the last decade ran its course, the monitors that serve to track slippage in women's status have been working overtime. Government and private surveys are showing that women's already vast representation in the lowliest occupations is rising, their tiny presence in higher-paying trade and craft jobs stalled or backsliding, their minuscule representation in upper management posts stagnant or falling, and their pay dropping in the very occupations where they have made the most "progress."

In national politics, the already small numbers of women in both elective posts and political appointments fell during the eighties. In private life, the average amount that a divorced man paid in child support fell by about 25 percent from the late seventies to the mid-eighties (to a mere $140 a month). And government records chronicled a spectacular rise in sexual violence against women. Reported rapes more than doubled from the early seventies—at nearly twice the rate of all other violent crimes and four times the overall crime rate in the United States.

The truth is that the last decade has seen a powerful counterassault on women's rights, a backlash, an attempt to retract the handful of small and hard-won victories that the feminist movement did manage to win for women. This counterassault is largely insidious: in a kind of pop-culture version of the big lie, it stands the truth boldly on its head and proclaims that the very steps that have elevated women's position have actually led to their downfall.

The backlash is at once sophisticated and banal, deceptively "progressive" and proudly backward. It deploys both the "new" findings of "scientific research" and the dime-store moralism of yesteryear; it turns into media sound bites both the glib pronouncements of pop-psych trend-watchers and the frenzied rhetoric of New Right preachers. The backlash has succeeded in framing virtually the whole issue of women's rights in its own language. Just as Reaganism shifted political discourse far to the right and demonized liberalism, so the backlash convinced the public that women's "liberation" was the true contemporary American scourge—the source of an endless laundry list of personal, social, and economic problems.

But what has made women unhappy in the last decade is not their "equality"—which they don't yet have—but the rising pressure to halt, and even reverse, women's quest for that equality. The "man shortage" and the "infertility epidemic" are not the price of liberation; in fact, they do not even exist. But these chimeras are part of a relentless whittling-down process—much of it amounting to outright propaganda—that has served to stir women's private anxieties and break their political wills. Identifying feminism as women's enemy only furthers the ends of a backlash against women's equality by simultaneously deflecting attention from the backlash's central role and recruiting women to attack their own cause.

Some social observers may well ask whether the current pressures on women actually constitute a backlash—or just a continuation of American society's long-standing resistance to women's equal rights. Certainly hostility to female independence has always been with us. But if fear and loathing of feminism is a sort of perpetual viral condition in our culture, it is not always in an acute stage; its symptoms subside and resurface periodically. And it is these episodes of resurgence, such as the one we face now, that can accurately be termed "backlashes" to women's advancement. If we trace these occurrences in American history, we find such flare-ups are hardly random; they have always been triggered by the perception—accurate or not—that women are making great strides. These outbreaks are backlashes because they have always arisen in reaction to women's "progress," caused not simply by a bedrock of misogyny but by the specific efforts of contemporary women to improve their status, efforts that have been interpreted time and again by men—especially men grappling with real threats to their economic and social well-being on other fronts—as spelling their own masculine doom.

The most recent round of backlash first surfaced in the late seventies on the fringes, among the evangelical Right. By the early eighties, the fundamentalist ideology had shouldered its way into the White House. By the mid-eighties, as resistance to women's rights acquired political and social acceptability, it passed into the popular culture. And in every case, the timing coincided with signs that women were believed to be on the verge of a breakthrough.

Just when the women's quest for equal rights seemed closest to achieving its objectives, the backlash struck it down. Just when a "gender gap" at the voting booth surfaced in 1980, and women in politics began to talk of capitalizing on it, the Republican party elevated Ronald Reagan and both political parties began to shunt women's rights off their platforms. Just when support for feminism and the Equal Rights Amendment reached a record high in 1981, the amendment was defeated the following year. Just when women were starting to mobilize against battering and sexual assaults, the federal government cut funding for battered-woman's programs, defeated bills to fund shelters, and shut down its Office of Domestic Violence—only two years after opening it in 1979. Just when record numbers of younger women were supporting feminist goals in the mid-eighties (more of them, in fact, than older women) and a majority of all women were calling themselves feminists, the media declared the advent of a younger "post-feminist generation" that supposedly reviled the women's movement. Just when women racked up their largest percentage ever supporting the right to abortion, the U.S. Supreme Court moved toward reconsidering it.

In other words, the antifeminist backlash has been set off not by women's achievement of full equality but by the increased possibility that they might win it. It is preemptive strike that stops women long before they reach the finish line. "A backlash may be an indication that women really have had an effect," feminist psychiatrist Dr. Jean Baker Miller has written, "but backlashes occur when advances have been small, before changes are sufficient to help many people. . . . It is almost as if the leaders of backlashes use the fear of change as a threat before major change has occurred." In the last decade, some women did make substantial advances before the backlash hit, but millions of others were left behind, stranded. Some women now enjoy the right to legal abortion—but not the forty-four million women, from the indigent to the military worker, who depend on the federal government for their medical care. Some women can now walk into high-paying professional careers—but not the millions still in the typing pools or behind the department-store sales counters. (Contrary to popular myth about the "have-it-all" baby-boom women, the largest percentage of women in this generation remain in office support roles.)

As the backlash has gathered force, it has cut off the few from the many—and the few women who have advanced seek to prove, as a social survival tactic, that they aren't so interested in advancement after all. Some of them parade their defection from the women's movement, while their working-class peers founder and cling to the splintered remains of the feminist cause. While a very few affluent and celebrity women who are showcased in news stories boast about going home to "bake bread," the many working-class women appeal for their economic rights— flocking to unions in record numbers, striking on their own for pay equity, and establishing their own fledgling groups for working-women's rights. In 1986, while 41 percent of upper-income women were claiming in the Gallup poll that they were not feminists, only 26 percent of low-income women were making the same claim.

Women's advances and retreats are generally described in military terms: battles won, battles lost, points and territory gained and surrendered. The metaphor of combat is not without its merits in this context, and, clearly, the same sort of martial accounting and vocabulary is already surfacing here. But by imagining the conflict as two battalions neatly arrayed on either side of the line, we miss the entangled nature, the locked embrace, of a "war" between women and the male culture they inhabit. We miss the reactive nature of a backlash, which, by definition, can exist only in response to another force.

In times when feminism is at a low ebb, women assume the reactive role—privately and, most often, covertly struggling to assert themselves against the dominant cultural tide. But when feminism itself becomes the tide, the opposition doesn't simply go along with the reversal: it digs in its heels, brandishes its fists, builds walls and dams. And its resistance creates countercurrents and treacherous undertows.

The force and furor of the backlash churn beneath the surface, largely invisible to the public eye. On occasion in the last decade, they have burst into view. We have seen New Right politicians condemn women's independence, antiabortion protesters firebomb women's clinics, fundamentalist preachers damn feminists as "whores." Other signs of the backlash's wrath, by their sheer brutality, can push their way into public consciousness for a time—the sharp increase in rape, for example, or the rise in pornography that depicts extreme violence against women.

More subtle indicators in popular culture may receive momentary, and often bemused, media notice, then quickly slip from social awareness: a report, for instance, that the image of women on prime-time TV shows has suddenly degenerated. A survey of mystery fiction finding the number of tortured and mutilated female characters mysteriously multiplying. The puzzling news that, as one commentator put it, "so many hit songs have the B word [bitch] to refer to women that some rap music seems to be veering toward rape music." The ascendancy of violently misogynist comics like Andrew Dice Clay, who calls women "pigs" and "sluts," or radio hosts like Rush Limbaugh, whose broadsides against "femi-Nazi" feminists helped make his syndicated program the most popular radio talk show in the nation. Or word that, in 1987, the American Women in Radio and Television couldn't award its annual prize to ads that feature women positively: it could find no ad that qualified.

These phenomena are all related, but that doesn't mean they are somehow coordinated. The backlash is not a conspiracy, with a council dispatching agents from some central control room, nor are the people who serve its ends often aware of their role; some even consider themselves feminists. For the most part, its workings are encoded and internalized, diffuse and chameleonic. Not all of the manifestations of the backlash are of equal weight or significance, either; some are mere ephemera thrown up by a culture machine that is always scrounging for a "fresh" angle. Taken as a whole, however, these codes and cajolings, these whispers and threats and myths, move overwhelmingly in one direction: they try to push women back into their "acceptable" roles—whether as Daddy's girl or fluttery romantic, active nester or passive love object.

Although the backlash is not an organized movement, that doesn't make it any less destructive. In fact, the lack of orchestration, the absence of a single string-puller, only makes it harder to see—and perhaps more effective. A backlash against women's rights succeeds to a degree that it appears *not* to be political, that it appears not to be a struggle at all. It is most powerful when it goes private, when it lodges inside a woman's mind and turns her vision inward, until she imagines the pressure is all in her head, until she begins to enforce the backlash, too—on herself.

In the last decade, the backlash has moved through the culture's secret chambers, traveling through passageways of flattery and fear. Along the way, it has adopted disguises: a mask of mild derision or the painted face of deep "concern." Its lips profess pity for any woman who won't fit the mold, while it tries to clamp the mold around her ears. It pursues a divide-and-conquer strategy: single versus married women, working women versus homemakers, middle versus working class. It manipulates a system of rewards and punishments, elevating women who follow its rules, isolating those who don't. The backlash remarkets old myths about women as new facts and ignores all appeals to reason. Cornered, it denies its own existence, points an accusatory finger at feminism, and burrows deeper underground.

Backlash happens to be the title of a 1947 Hollywood movie in which a man frames his wife for a murder he's committed. The backlash against women's rights works in much the same way: its rhetoric charges feminists with all the crimes it perpetrates. The backlash line blames the women's movement for the "feminization of poverty"—while the backlash's own instigators in Washington have pushed through the budget cuts that have helped impoverish millions of women, have fought pay-equity proposals, and undermined equal-opportunity laws. The backlash line claims the women's movement cares nothing for children's rights—while its own representatives in the capital and state legislatures have blocked one bill after another to improve child care, slashed billions of dollars in aid for children, and relaxed state licensing standards for daycare centers. The backlash line accuses the women's movement of creating a generation of unhappy single and childless women—but its purveyors in the media are the ones guilty of making single and childless women feel like circus freaks.

To blame feminism for women's "lesser life" is to miss its point entirely, which is to win women a wider range of experience. Feminism remains a pretty simple concept, despite repeated—and enormously effective—efforts to dress it up in greasepaint and turn its proponents into gargoyles. As Rebecca West wrote sardonically in 1913, "I myself have never been able to find out precisely what feminism is: I only know that people call me a feminist whenever I express sentiments that differentiate me from a doormat."

The meaning of the word "feminism" has not really changed since it first appeared in a book review in *The Athenaeum* on April 27, 1895, describing a woman who "has in her the capacity of fighting her way back to independence." It is the basic proposition that, as Nora put it in Ibsen's *A Doll's House* a century ago, "Before everything else I'm a human being." It is the simply worded sign hoisted by a little girl in the 1970 Women's Strike for Equality: "I AM NOT A BARBIE DOLL." Feminism asks the world to recognize at long last that women aren't decorative ornaments, worthy vessels, members of a "special-interest group." They are half (in fact, now more than half) of the national population, and just as deserving of rights and opportunities, just as capable of participating in the world's events, as the other half. Feminism's agenda is basic: It asks that women not be forced to "choose" between public justice and private happiness. It asks that women be free to define themselves—instead of having their identity defined for them, time and again, by their culture and their men.

The fact that these are still such incendiary notions should tell us that American women have a way to go before they enter the promised land of equality.

Questions for Reading and Analysis

1. Describing "fear and loathing of feminism" as a "perpetual viral condition in our culture," Faludi claims that outbreaks of anti-feminist sentiment (or "backlashes") occur at similar moments. What triggers backlashes? What triggered the backlash of the late eighties?

2. What is Faludi's in-a-nutshell definition of feminism? Why do you think she ended rather than started her essay with this definition?

3. What is the effect of juxtaposing the good news in the first paragraph with the bad presented in the third? What point does Faludi try to drive home with this technique?

4. Why is it harder for a woman to have a career and a family? What problems are there to be worked out? What suggestions do you have to solve these problems?

A novelist, critic, and essayist, E. M. Forster (1879–1970) is prob-
ably best known for his novels A Room with a View *(1908),*
Howard's End *(1910), and* A Passage to India *(1924). In this selection*
from his essay collection Two Cheers for Democracy *(1951), Forster*
enters a distinguished line of English cultural criticism suspicious of
democracy; writing on the eve of World War II, he calls for tolerance,
decency and "the holiness of the heart's affections" to combat the
cruelty and chaos of force.

What I Believe

E. M. Forster

I do not believe in Belief. But this is an age of faith, and there are so many militant creeds that, in self-defense, one has to formulate a creed of one's own. Tolerance, good temper and sympathy are no longer enough in a world which is
rent by religious and racial persecution, in a world where ignorance rules, and science, who ought to have ruled, plays the subservient pimp. Tolerance, good temper
and sympathy—they are what matter really, and if the human race is not to collapse they must come to the front before long. But for the moment they are not
enough, their action is no stronger than a flower, battered beneath a military jackboot. They want stiffening, even if the process coarsens them. Faith, to my mind,
is a stiffening process, a sort of mental starch, which ought to be applied as spar-
ingly as possible. I dislike the stuff. I do not believe in it, for its own sake, at all.
Herein I probably differ from most people, who believe in Belief, and are only
sorry they cannot swallow even more than they do. My law-givers are Erasmus and
Montaigne, not Moses and St. Paul. My temple stands not upon Mount Moriah
but in that Elysian Field where even the immoral are admitted. My motto is: "Lord,
I disbelieve—help thou my unbelief."[1]

I have, however, to live in an Age of Faith—the sort of epoch I used to hear
praised when I was a boy. It is extremely unpleasant really. It is bloody in every sense
of the word. And I have to keep my end up in it. Where do I start?

With personal relationships. Here is something comparatively solid in a world
full of violence and cruelty. Not absolutely solid, for Psychology has split and shattered the idea of a "Person," and has shown that there is something incalculable
in each of us, which may at any moment rise to the surface and destroy our normal
balance. We don't know what we are like. We can't know what other people are
like. How, then, can we put any trust in personal relationships, or cling to them in
the gathering political storm? In theory we cannot. But in practice we can and do.
Though A is not unchangeably A or B unchangeably B, there can still be love and
loyalty between the two. For the purpose of living one has to assume that the

personality is solid, and the "self" is an entity, and to ignore all contrary evidence. And since to ignore evidence is one of the characteristics of faith, I certainly can proclaim that I believe in personal relationships.

Starting from them, I get a little order into the contemporary chaos. One must be fond of people and trust them if one is not to make a mess of life, and it is therefore essential that they should not let one down. They often do. The moral of which is that I must, myself, be as reliable as possible, and this I try to be. But reliability is not a matter of contract—that is the main difference between the world of personal relationships and the world of business relationships. It is a matter for the heart, which signs no documents. In other words, reliability is impossible unless there is a natural warmth. Most men possess this warmth, though they often have bad luck and get chilled. Most of them, even when they are politicians, *want* to keep faith. And one can, at all events, show one's own little light here, one's own poor little trembling flame, with the knowledge that it is not the only light that is shining in the darkness, and not the only one which the darkness does not comprehend. Personal relations are despised today. They are regarded as bourgeois luxuries, as products of a time of fair weather which is now past, and we are urged to get rid of them, and to dedicate ourselves to some movement or cause instead. I hate the idea of causes, and if I had to choose between betraying my country and betraying my friend, I hope I should have the guts to betray my country. Such a choice may scandalize the modern reader, and he may stretch out his patriotic hand to the telephone at once and ring up the police. It would not have shocked Dante, though. Dante places Brutus and Cassius in the lowest circle of Hell[2] because they had chosen to betray their friend Julius Caesar rather than their country, Rome. Probably one will not be asked to make such an agonizing choice. Still, there lies at the back of every creed something terrible and hard for which the worshipper may one day be required to suffer, and there is even a terror and a hardness in this creed of personal relationships, urbane and mild though it sounds. Love and loyalty to an individual can run counter to the claims of the State. When they do—down with the State, say I, which means that the State would down me.

This brings me along to Democracy, "even Love, the Beloved Republic, which feeds upon Freedom and lives." Democracy is not a Beloved Republic really, and never will be. But it is less hateful than other contemporary forms of government, and to that extent it deserves our support. It does start from the assumption that the individual is important, and that all types are needed to make a civilization. It does not divide its citizens into the bossers and the bossed—as an efficiency-regime tends to do. The people I admire most are those who are sensitive and want to create something or discover something, and do not see life in terms of power, and such people get more of a chance under a democracy than elsewhere. They found religions, great or small, or they produce literature and art, or they do disinterested scientific research, or they may be what is called "ordinary people," who are creative in their private lives, bring up their children decently, for instance, or help their neighbors. All these people need to express themselves; they cannot do so unless society allows them liberty to do so, and the society which allows them most liberty is a democracy.

Democracy has another merit. It allows criticism, and if there is no public criticism there are bound to be hushed-up scandals. That is why I believe in the Press, despite all its lies and vulgarity, and why I believe in Parliament. Parliament is often sneered at because it is a Talking Shop. I believe in it *because* it is a talking shop. I believe in the Private Member who makes himself a nuisance. He gets snubbed and is told that he is cranky or ill-informed, but he does expose abuses which would otherwise never have been mentioned, and very often an abuse gets put right just by being mentioned. Occasionally, too, a well-meaning public official starts losing his head in the cause of efficiency, and thinks himself God Almighty. Such officials are particularly frequent in the Home Office. Well, there will be questions about them in Parliament sooner or later, and then they will have to mind their steps. Whether Parliament is either a representative body or an efficient one is questionable, but I value it because it criticizes and talks, and because its chatter gets widely reported.

So Two Cheers for Democracy: one because it admits variety and two because it permits criticism. Two cheers are quite enough: there is no occasion to give three. Only Love the Beloved Republic deserves that.

What about Force, though? While we are trying to be sensitive and advanced and affectionate and tolerant, an unpleasant question pops up: does not all society rest upon force? If a government cannot count upon the police and the army, how can it hope to rule? And if an individual gets knocked on the head or sent to a labor camp, of what significance are his opinions?

This dilemma does not worry me as much as it does some. I realize that all society rests upon force. But all the great creative actions, all the decent human relations, occur during the intervals when force has not managed to come to the front. These intervals are what matter. I want them to be as frequent and as lengthy as possible, and I call them "civilization." Some people idealize force and pull it into the foreground and worship it, instead of keeping it in the background as long as possible. I think they make a mistake, and I think that their opposites, the mystics, err even more when they declare that force does not exist. I believe that it exists, and that one of our jobs is to prevent it from getting out of its box. It gets out sooner or later, and then it destroys us and all the lovely things which we have made. But it is not out all the time, for the fortunate reason that the strong are so stupid. Consider their conduct for a moment in the Niebelung's Ring.[3] The giants there have the guns, or in other words the gold; but they do nothing with it, they do not realize that they are all-powerful, with the result that the catastrophe is delayed and the castle of Walhalla, insecure but glorious, fronts the storms. Fafnir, coiled round his hoard, grumbles and grunts; we can hear him under Europe today; the leaves of the wood already tremble, and the Bird calls its warnings uselessly. Fafnir will destroy us, but by a blessed dispensation he is stupid and slow, and creation goes on just outside the poisonous blast of his breath. The Nietzschean would hurry the monster up, the mystic would say he did not exist, but Wotan, wiser than either, hastens to create warriors before doom declares itself. The Valkyries are symbols not only of courage but of intelligence; they represent the human spirit snatching its opportunity while the going is good, and one of them even finds time to love. Brünnhilde's last song hymns the recurrence of love, and since it is the privilege of art to exaggerate, she goes even further, and proclaims the love which is eternally triumphant and feeds upon freedom, and lives.

So that is what I feel about force and violence. It is, alas!, the ultimate reality on this earth, but it does not always get to the front. Some people call its absences "decadence"; I call them "civilization" and find in such interludes the chief justification for the human experiment. I look the other way until fate strikes me. Whether this is due to courage or to cowardice in my own case I cannot be sure. But I know that if men had not looked the other way in the past, nothing of any value would survive. The people I respect most behave as if they were immortal and as if society was eternal. Both assumptions are false: both of them must be accepted as true if we are to go on eating and working and loving, and are to keep open a few breathing holes for the human spirit. No millennium seems likely to descend upon humanity; no better and stronger League of Nations will be instituted; no form of Christianity and no alternative to Christianity will bring peace to the world or integrity to the individual; no "change of heart" will occur. And yet we need not despair, indeed, we cannot despair; the evidence of history shows us that men have always insisted on behaving creatively under the shadow of the sword; that they have done their artistic and scientific and domestic stuff for the sake of doing it, and that we had better follow their example under the shadow of the aeroplanes. Others, with more vision or courage than myself, see the salvation of humanity ahead, and will dismiss my conception of civilization as paltry, a sort of tip-and-run game. Certainly it is presumptuous to say that we *cannot* improve, and that Man, who has only been in power for a few thousand years, will never learn to make use of his power. All I mean is that, if people continue to kill one another as they do, the world cannot get better than it is, and that since there are more people than formerly, and their means for destroying one another superior, the world may well get worse. What is good in people—and consequently in the world—is their insistence on creation, their belief in friendship and loyalty for their own sakes; and though violence remains and is, indeed, the major partner in this muddled establishment, I believe that creativeness remains too, and will always assume direction when violence sleeps. So, though I am not an optimist, I cannot agree with Sophocles that it were better never to have been born. And although, like Horace, I see no evidence that each batch of births is superior to the last, I leave the field open for the more complacent view. This is such a difficult moment to live in, one cannot help getting gloomy and also a bit rattled, and perhaps short-sighted.

In search of a refuge, we may perhaps turn to hero-worship. But here we shall get no help, in my opinion. Hero-worship is a dangerous vice, and one of the minor merits of a democracy is that it does not encourage it, or produce that unmanageable type of citizen known as the Great Man. It produces instead different kinds of small men—a much finer achievement. But people who cannot get interested in the variety of life, and cannot make up their own mind, get discontented over this, and they long for a hero to bow down before and to follow blindly. It is significant that a hero is an integral part of the authoritarian stock-in-trade today. An efficiency-regime cannot be run without a few heroes stuck about it to carry off the dullness—much as plums have to be put into a bad pudding to make it palatable. One hero at the top and a smaller one on each side of him is a favorite arrangement, and the timid and the bored are comforted by the trinity, and, bowing down, feel exalted and strengthened.

No, I distrust Great Men. They produce a desert of uniformity around them and often a pool of blood too, and I always feel a little man's pleasure when they come a cropper. Every now and then one reads in the newspapers some such statement as: "The coup d'état appears to have failed, and Admiral Toma's whereabouts is at present unknown." Admiral Toma had probably every qualification for being a Great Man—an iron will, personal magnetism, dash, flair, sexlessness—but fate was against him, so he retires to unknown whereabouts instead of parading history with his peers. He fails with a completeness which no artist and no lover can experience, because with them the process of creation is itself an achievement, whereas with him the only possible achievement is success.

I believe in aristocracy, though—if that is the right word, and if a democrat may use it. Not an aristocracy of power, based upon rank and influence, but an aristocracy of the sensitive, the considerate and the plucky. Its members are to be found in all nations and classes, and all through the ages, and there is a secret understanding between them when they meet. They represent the true human tradition, the one permanent victory of our queer race over cruelty and chaos. Thousands of them perish in obscurity, a few are great names. They are sensitive for others as well as for themselves, they are considerate without being fussy, their pluck is not swankiness but the power to endure, and they can take a joke. I give no examples—it is risky to do that—but the reader may as well consider whether this is the type of person he would like to meet and to be, and whether (going farther with me) he would prefer that this type should *not* be an ascetic one. I am against asceticism myself. I am with the old Scotsman who wanted less chastity and more delicacy. I do not feel that my aristocrats are a real aristocracy if they thwart their bodies, since bodies are the instruments through which we register and enjoy the world. Still, I do not insist. This is not a major point. It is clearly possible to be sensitive, considerate and plucky and yet be an ascetic too, if anyone possesses the first three qualities, I will let him in! On they go—an invincible army, yet not a victorious one. The aristocrats, the elect, the chosen, the Best People—all the words that describe them are false, and all attempts to organize them fail. Again and again Authority, seeing their value, has tried to net them and to utilize them as the Egyptian Priesthood or the Christian Church or the Chinese Civil Service or the Group Movement, or some other worthy stunt. But they slip through the net and are gone; when the door is shut, they are no longer in the room; their temple, as one of them remarked, is the Holiness of the Heart's Affection,[4] and their kingdom, though they never possess it, is the wide-open world.

With this type of person knocking about, and constantly crossing one's path if one has eyes to see or hands to feel, the experiment of earthly life cannot be dismissed as a failure. But it may well be hailed as a tragedy, the tragedy being that no device has been found by which these private decencies can be transmitted to public affairs. As soon as people have power they go crooked and sometimes dotty as well, because the possession of power lifts them into a region where normal honesty never pays. For instance, the man who is selling newspapers outside the Houses of Parliament can safely leave his papers to go for a drink and his cap beside them: anyone who takes a paper is sure to drop a copper into the cap. But the men who are inside the Houses of Parliament—they cannot trust one another like that, still less can the Government they compose trust other governments. No caps upon the pavement here, but suspicion, treachery and armaments. The more highly public life is organized the lower does its morality sink; the nations of today behave to each other worse than they ever did in the past, they cheat, rob, bully and bluff, make war without notice, and kill as many women and children as possible; whereas primitive tribes were at all events restrained by taboos. It is a humiliating outlook—though the greater the darkness, the brighter shine the little lights, reassuring one another, signalling: "Well, at all events, I'm still here. I don't like it very much, but how are you?" Unquenchable lights of my aristocracy! Signals of the invincible army! "Come along—anyway, let's have a good time while we can." I think they signal that too.

The Saviour of the future—if ever he come—will not preach a new Gospel. He will merely utilize my aristocracy, he will make effective the good will and the good temper which are already existing. In other words, he will introduce a new technique. In economics, we are told that if there was a new technique of distribution, there need be no poverty, and people would not starve in one place while crops were being ploughed under in another. A similar change is needed in the sphere of morals and politics. The desire for it is by no means new; it was expressed, for example, in theological terms by Jacopone da Todi over six hundred years ago. "Ordina questo amore, O tu che m'ami," he said; "O thou who lovest me—set this love in order." His prayer was not granted, and I do not myself believe that it ever will be, but here, and not through a change of heart, is our probable route. Not by becoming better, but by ordering and distributing his native goodness, will Man shut up Force into its box, and so gain time to explore the universe and to set his mark upon it worthily. At present he only explores it at odd moments, when Force is looking the other way, and his divine creativeness appears as a trivial byproduct, to be scrapped as soon as the drums beat and the bombers hum.

Such a change, claim the orthodox, can only be made by Christianity, and will be made by it in God's good time: man always has failed and always will fail to organize his own goodness, and it is presumptuous of him to try. This claim—solemn as it is—leaves me cold. I cannot believe that Christianity will ever cope with the present world-wide mess, and I think that such influence as it retains in modern society is due to the money behind it, rather than to its spiritual appeal. It was a spiritual force once, but the indwelling spirit will have to be restated if it is to calm the waters again, and probably restated in a non-Christian form. Naturally a lot of people, and people who are not only good but able and intelligent, will disagree here; they will vehemently deny that Christianity has failed, or they will argue that its failure proceeds from the wickedness of men, and really proves its ultimate success. They have Faith, with a large F. My faith has a very small one, and I only intrude it because these are strenuous and serious days, and one likes to say what one thinks while speech is comparatively free: it may not be free much longer.

The above are the reflections of an individualist and a liberal who has found liberalism crumbling beneath him and at first felt ashamed. Then, looking around, he decided there was no special reason for shame, since other people, whatever they felt, were equally insecure. And as for individualism—there seems no way of getting off this, even if one wanted to. The dictator-hero can grind down his citizens till they are all alike, but he cannot melt them into a single man. That is beyond his power. He can order them to merge, he can incite them to mass-antics, but they are obliged to be born separately, and to die separately, and, owing to these unavoidable termini, will always be running off the totalitarian rails. The memory of birth and the expectation of death always lurk within the human being, making him separate from his fellows and consequently capable of intercourse with them. Naked I came into the world, naked I shall go out of it! And a very good thing too, for it reminds me that I am naked under my shirt, whatever its colour.

Endnotes

1. *Erasmus/Montaigne*: humanists, not religious figures, as were *Moses* and *Paul*; *Mt. Moriah*: Biblical site where Abraham was to sacrifice his son Isaac; *Elysian Fields*: in Greek mythology, Paradise, a happy land; *Lord, I disbelieve*: Forster's adaption of the words of a man witnessing Jesus' performance of a miracle in healing his son—"Lord, I believe . . ." (Mark 9:24).

2. In *The Divine Comedy*, masterpiece of Italian poet Dante Alighieri (1265–1321).

3. *Der Ring des Nibelungen* (1876), opera in four parts by German composer Richard Wagner based on medieval Scandinavian legends. Forster, writing on the eve of World War II, sees in the story certain lessons for his contemporaries.

4. English poet John Keats (1795–1823) wrote "I am certain of nothing but the holiness of the Heart's affection and the truth of imagination."

Questions for Reading and Analysis

1. Why, according to Forster, is democracy "less hateful than other contemporary forms of government"?

2. In your own words, define what Forster means by "force." How does force relate to civilization?

3. In what way does Forster believe in democracy? In what way does he believe in aristocracy? How do the two relate?

4. Considering that Forster wrote this essay in 1939, at the beginning of World War II, do you think his outlook on humankind is predominantly positive or negative? Justify your answer.

In A Jury of Her Peers, *which tells the story of a Midwestern farmwife accused of murdering her husband, Susan Glaspell (1882–1948) illuminates the differences in the way men and women perceive reality. First published in 1917, the story is based on Glaspell's 1916 play* Trifles.

A Jury of Her Peers

Susan Glaspell

When Martha Hale opened the storm-door and got a cut of the north wind, she ran back for her big woolen scarf. As she hurriedly wound that round her head her eye made a scandalized sweep of her kitchen. It was no ordinary thing that called her away—it was probably farther from ordinary than anything that had ever happened in Dickson County. But what her eye took in was that her kitchen was in no shape for leaving: her bread all ready for mixing, half the flour sifted and half unsifted.

She hated to see things half done; but she had been at that when the team from town stopped to get Mr. Hale, and then the sheriff came running in to say his wife wished Mrs. Hale would come too—adding, with a grin, that he guessed she was getting scary and wanted another woman along. So she had dropped everything right where it was.

"Martha!" now came her husband's impatient voice. "Don't keep folks waiting out here in the cold."

She again opened the storm-door, and this time joined the three men and the one woman waiting for her in the big two-seated buggy.

After she had the robes tucked around her she took another look at the woman who sat beside her on the back seat. She had met Mrs. Peters the year before at the county fair, and the thing she remembered about her was that she didn't seem like a sheriff's wife. She was small and thin and didn't have a strong voice. Mrs. Gorman, sheriff's wife before Gorman went out and Peters came in, had a voice that somehow seemed to be backing up the law with every word. But if Mrs. Peters didn't look like a sheriff's wife, Peters made it up in looking like a sheriff. He was to a dot the kind of man who could get himself elected sheriff—a heavy man with a big voice, who was particularly genial with the law-abiding, as if to make it plain that he knew the difference between criminals and noncriminals. And right there it came into Mrs. Hale's mind, with a stab, that this man who was so pleasant and lively with all of them was going to the Wrights' now as a sheriff.

"The country's not very pleasant this time of year," Mrs. Peters at last ventured, as if she felt they ought to be talking as well as the men.

Mrs. Hale scarcely finished her reply, for they had gone up a little hill and could see the Wright place now, and seeing it did not make her feel like talking. It looked very lonesome this cold March morning. It had always been a lonesome-looking place. It was down in a hollow, and the poplar trees around it were lonesome-looking trees. The men were looking at it and talking about What had happened. The county attorney was bending to one side of the buggy, and kept looking steadily at the place as they drew up to it.

"I'm glad you came with me," Mrs. Peters said nervously, as the two women were about to follow the men in through the kitchen door.

Even after she had her foot on the door-step, her hand on the knob, Martha Hale had a moment of feeling she could not cross that threshold. And the reason it seemed she couldn't cross it now was simply because she hadn't crossed it before. Time and time again it has been in her mind, "I ought to go over and see Minnie Foster"—she still thought of her as Minnie Foster, though for twenty years she had been Mrs. Wright. And then there was always something to do and Minnie Foster would go from her mind. But *now* she could come.

The men went over to the stove. The women stood close together by the door. Young Henderson, the county attorney, turned around and said, "Come up to the fire ladies."

Mrs. Peters took a step forward, then stopped. "I'm not—cold," she said.

And so the two women stood by the door, at first not even so much as looking around the kitchen.

The men talked for a minute about what a good thing it was, the sheriff had sent his deputy out that morning to make a fire for them, and then Sheriff Peters stepped back from the stove, unbuttoned his outer coat, and leaned his hands on the kitchen table in a way that seemed to mark the beginning of official business. "Now, Mr. Hale," he said in a sort of semi-official voice, "before we move things about, you tell Mr. Henderson just what it was you saw when you came here yesterday morning."

The county attorney was looking around the kitchen.

"By the way," he said, "has anything been moved?" He turned to the sheriff. "Are things just as you left them yesterday?"

Peters looked from cupboard to sink; from that to a small worn rocker a little to one side of the kitchen table.

"It's just the same."

"Somebody should have been left here yesterday," said the county attorney.

"Oh—yesterday," returned the sheriff, with a little gesture as of yesterday having been more than he could bear to think of. "When I had to send Frank to Morris Center for that man who went crazy—let me tell you, I had my hands full *yesterday*. I knew you could get back from Omaha by to-day, George, and as long as I went over everything here myself—"

"Well, Mr. Hale," said the county attorney, in a way of letting what was past and gone go, "tell just what happened when you came here yesterday morning."

Mrs. Hale, still leaning against the door, had that sinking feeling of the mother whose child is about to speak a piece. Lewis often wandered along and got things mixed up in a story. She hoped he would tell this straight and plain, and not say unnecessary things that would just make things harder for Minnie Foster. He didn't begin at once, and she noticed that he looked queer—as if standing in that kitchen and having to tell what he had seen there yesterday morning made him almost sick.

"Yes, Mr. Hale?" the county attorney reminded.

"Harry and I had started to town with a load of potatoes," Mrs. Hale's husband began.

Harry was Mrs. Hale's oldest boy. He wasn't with them now, for the very good reason that those potatoes never got to town yesterday and he was taking them this morning, so he hadn't been home when the sheriff stopped to say he wanted Mr. Hale to come over to the Wright place and tell the county attorney his story there, where he could point it all out. With all Mrs. Hale's other emotions came the fear that maybe Harry wasn't dressed warm enough—they hadn't any of them realized how that north wind did bite.

"We come along this road," Hale was going on, with a motion of his hand to the road over which they had just come, "and as we got in sight of the house I says to Harry, 'I'm goin' to see if I can't get John Wright to take a telephone.' You see," he explained to Henderson, "unless I can get somebody to go in with me they won't come out this branch road except for a price *I* can't pay. I'd spoke to Wright about it once before; but he put me off, saying folks talked too much anyway, and all he asked was peace and quiet—guess you know about how much he talked himself. But I thought maybe if I went to the house and talked about it before his wife, and said all the woman-folks liked the telephones, and that in this lonesome stretch of road it would be a good thing—well, I said to Harry that that was what I was going to say—though I said at the same that I didn't know as what his wife wanted made much difference to John—"

Now, there he was!—saying things he didn't need to say. Mrs. Hale tried to catch her husband's eye, but fortunately the county attorney interrupted with:

"Let's talk about that a little later, Mr. Hale. I do want to talk about that, but I'm anxious now to get along to just what happened when you got here."

When he began this time, it was very deliberately and carefully:

"I didn't see or hear anything. I knocked at the door. And still it was all quiet inside. I knew they must be up—it was past eight o'clock. So I knocked again, louder, and I thought I heard somebody say 'Come in.' I wasn't sure—I'm not sure yet. But I opened the door—this door," jerking a hand toward the door by which the two women stood, "and there, in that rocker"—pointing to it—"sat Mrs. Wright."

Everyone in the kitchen looked at the rocker. It came into Mrs. Hale's mind that that rocker didn't look in the least like Minnie Foster—the Minnie Foster of twenty years before. It was a dingy red, with wooden rungs up the back, and the middle rung was gone, and the chair sagged to one side.

"How did she—look?" the county attorney was inquiring.

"Well," said Hale, "she looked—queer."

"How do you mean—queer?"

As he asked it he took out a note-book and pencil. Mrs. Hale did not like the sight of that pencil. She kept her eye fixed on her husband, as if to keep him from saying unnecessary things that would go into that note-book and make trouble.

Hale did speak guardedly, as if the pencil had affected him too.

"Well, as if she didn't know what she was going to do next. And kind of—done up."

"How did she seem to feel about your coming?"

"Why, I don't think she minded—one way or other. She didn't pay much attention. I said, 'Ho' do, Mrs. Wright? It's cold, ain't it?' And she said: 'Is it?'—and went on pleatin' at her apron.

"Well, I was surprised. She didn't ask me to come up to the stove, or sit down, but just set there, not even lookin' at me. And so I said: 'I want to see John.'

"And then she—laughed. I guess you could call it a laugh.

"I thought of Harry and the team outside, so I said, a little sharp, 'Can I see John?' 'No,' says she—kinda dull like. 'Ain't he home?' says I. Then she looked at me. 'Yes,' says she, 'he's home.' 'Then why can't I see him?' I asked her, out of patience with her now. 'Cause he's dead,' says she, just as quiet and dull—and fell to pleatin' her apron. 'Dead?' says I, like you do when you can't take in what you've heard.

"She just nodded her head, not getting a bit excited, but rockin' back and forth.

"'Why—where is he?' says I, not knowing *what* to say.

"She just pointed upstairs—like this"—pointing to the room above.

"I got up, with the idea of going up there myself. By this time I—didn't know what to do. I walked from there to here; then I says: 'Why, what did he die of?'

"'He died of a rope around his neck,' says she; and just went on pleatin' at her apron."

Hale stopped speaking, and stood staring at the rocker, as if he were still seeing the woman who had sat there the morning before. Nobody spoke; it was as if every one were seeing the woman who had sat there the morning before.

"And what did you do then?" the county attorney at last broke the silence.

"I went out and called Harry. I thought I might—need help. I got Harry in, and we went upstairs." His voice fell almost to a whisper. "There he was—lying over the—"

"I think I'd rather have you go into that upstairs," the county attorney interrupted, "where you can point it all out. Just go on now with the rest of the story."

"Well, my first thought was to get that rope off. It looked—"

He stopped, his face twitching.

"But Harry, he went up to him, and he said, 'No, he's dead all right, and we'd better not touch anything.' So we went downstairs."

"She was still sitting that same way. 'Has anybody been notified?' I asked. 'No,' says she, unconcerned.

"'Who did this, Mrs. Wright?' said Harry. He said it business-like, and she stopped pleatin' at her apron. 'I don't know,' she says. 'You don't *know*?' says Harry. 'Weren't you sleepin' in the bed with him?' 'Yes,' says she, 'but I was on the inside.' 'Somebody slipped a rope round his neck and strangled him, and you didn't wake up?' says Harry. 'I didn't wake up,' she said after him.

"We may have looked as if we didn't see how that could be, for after a minute she said, 'I sleep sound.'

"Harry was going to ask her more questions, but I said maybe that weren't our business; maybe we ought to let her tell her story first to the coroner or the sheriff.

So Harry went fast as he could over to High Road—the River's place, where there's a telephone."

"And what did she do when she knew you had gone for the coroner?" The attorney got his pencil in his hand all ready for writing.

"She moved from that chair to this one over here"—Hale pointed to a small chair in the corner—"and just sat there with her hands held together and looking down. I got a feeling that I ought to make some conversation, so I said I had come in to see if John wanted to put in a telephone; and at that she started to laugh, and then she stopped and looked at me—scared."

At the sound of a moving pencil the man who was telling the story looked up.

"I dunno—maybe it wasn't scared," he hastened; "I wouldn't like to say it was. Soon Harry got back, and then Dr. Lloyd came, and you, Mr. Peters, and so I guess that's all I know that you don't."

He said that last with relief, and moved a little, as if relaxing. Every one moved a little. The county attorney walked toward the stair door.

"I guess we'll go upstairs first—then out to the barn and around there."

He paused and looked around the kitchen.

"You're convinced there was nothing important here?" he asked the sheriff. "Nothing that would—point to any motive?"

The sheriff too looked all around, as if to re-convince himself.

"Nothing here but kitchen things," he said, with a little laugh for the insignificance of kitchen things.

The county attorney was looking at the cupboard—a peculiar, ungainly structure, half closet and half cupboard, the upper part of it being built in the wall, and the lower part just the old-fashioned kitchen cupboard. As if its queerness attracted him, he got a chair and opened the upper part and looked in. After a moment he drew his hand away sticky.

"Here's a nice mess," he said resentfully.

The two women had drawn nearer, and now the sheriff's wife spoke.

"Oh—her fruit," she said, looking to Mrs. Hale for sympathetic understanding. She turned back to the county attorney and explained: "She worried about that when it turned so cold last night. She said the fire would go out and her jars might burst."

Mrs. Peters' husband broke into a laugh.

"Well, can you beat the woman! Held for murder, and worrying about her preserves!"

The young attorney set his lips.

"I guess before we're through with her she may have something more serious than preserves to worry about."

"Oh, well," said Mrs. Hale's husband, with good-natured superiority, "women are used to worrying over trifles."

The two women moved a little closer together. Neither of them spoke. The county attorney seemed suddenly to remember his manners—and think of his future.

"And yet," said he, with the gallantry of a young politician, "for all their worries, what would we do without the ladies?"

The women did not speak, did not unbend. He went to the sink and began washing his hands. He turned to wipe them on the roller towel—whirled it for a cleaner place.

"Dirty towels! Not much of a housekeeper, would you say ladies?"

He kicked his foot against some dirty pans under the sink.

"There's a great deal of work to be done on a farm," said Mrs. Hale stiffly.

"To be sure. And yet"—with a little bow to her—"I know there are some Dickson County farm-houses that do not have such roller towels." He gave it a pull to expose its full length again.

"Those towels get dirty awful quick. Men's hands aren't always as clean as they might be."

"Ah, loyal to your sex, I see," he laughed. He stopped and gave her a keen look. "But you and Mrs. Wright were neighbors. I suppose you were friends, too."

Martha Hale shook her head.

"I've seen little enough of her of late years. I've not been in this house—it's more than a year."

"And why was that? You didn't like her?"

"I liked her well enough," she replied with spirit. "Farmers' wives have their hands full, Mr. Henderson. And then"—She looked around the kitchen.

"Yes?" he encouraged.

"It never seemed a very cheerful place," said she, more to herself than to him.

"No," he agreed; "I don't think any one would call it cheerful. I shouldn't say she had the home-making instinct."

"Well, I don't know as Wright had either," she muttered.

"You mean they didn't get on very well?" he was quick to ask.

"No; I don't mean anything," she answered, with decision. As she turned a little away from him, she added: "But I don't think a place would be any the cheerfuler for John Wright's bein' in it."

"I'd like to talk to you about that a little later, Mrs. Hale," he said. "I'm anxious to get the lay of things upstairs now."

He moved toward the stair door, followed by the two men.

"I suppose anything Mrs. Peters does'll be all right?" the sheriff inquired. "She was to take in some clothes for her, you know—and a few little things. We left in such a hurry yesterday."

The county attorney looked at the two women whom they were leaving alone there among the kitchen things.

"Yes—Mrs. Peters," he said, his glance resting on the woman who was not Mrs. Peters, the big farmer woman who stood behind the sheriff's wife. "Of course Mrs. Peters is one of us," he said, in a manner of entrusting responsibility. "And keep your eye out, Mrs. Peters, for anything that might be of use. No telling; you women might come upon a clue to the motive—and that's the thing we need."

Mr. Hale rubbed his face after the fashion of a show man getting ready for a pleasantry.

"But would the women know a clue if they did come upon it?" he said; and, having delivered himself of this, he followed the others through the stair door.

The women stood motionless and silent, listening to the footsteps, first upon the stairs, and then in the room above them.

Then, as if releasing herself from something strange, Mrs. Hale began to arrange the dirty pans under the sink, which the county attorney's disdainful push of the foot had deranged.

"I'd hate to have men comin' into my kitchen," she said testily—"snoopin' round and criticizin'."

"Of course it's no more than their duty," said the sheriff's wife, in her manner of timid acquiescence.

"Duty's all right," replied Mrs. Hale bluffly; "but I guess that the deputy sheriff that come out to make the fire might have got a little of this on." She gave the roller towel a pull. "Wish I'd thought of that sooner! Seems mean to talk about her for not having things slicked up, when she had to come away in such a hurry."

She looked around the kitchen. Certainly it was not "slicked up." Her eye was held by a bucket of sugar on a low shelf. The cover was off the wooden bucket, and beside it was a paper bag—half full.

Mrs. Hale moved toward it.

"She was putting this in there," she said to herself—slowly.

She thought of the flour in her kitchen at home—half sifted, half not sifted. She had been interrupted and had left things half done. What had interrupted Minnie Foster? Why had that work been left half done? She made a move as if to finish it,—unfinished things always bothered her,—and then she glanced around and saw that Mrs. Peters was watching her—and she didn't want Mrs. Peters to get that feeling she had got of work begun and then—for some reason—not finished.

"It's a shame about her fruit," she said, and walked toward the cupboard that the county attorney had opened, and got on the chair, murmuring: "I wonder if it's all gone."

It was a sorry enough looking sight, but "Here's one that's all right," she said at last. She held it toward the light. "This is cherries, too." She looked again. "I declare I believe that's the only one."

With a sigh, she got down from the chair, went to the sink, and wiped off the bottle.

"She'll feel awful bad, after all her hard work in the hot weather. I remember the afternoon I put up my cherries last summer."

She set the bottle on the table, and, with another sigh, started to sit down in the rocker. But she did not sit down. Something kept her from sitting down in that chair. She straightened—stepped back, and, half turned away, stood looking at it, seeing the woman who sat there "pleatin' at her apron."

The thin voice of the sheriff's wife broke in upon her: "I must be getting those things from the front room closet." She opened the door into the other room, started in, stepped back. "You coming with me, Mrs. Hale?" she asked nervously. "You—you could help me get them."

They were soon back—the stark coldness of that shut-up room was not a thing to linger in.

"My!" said Mrs. Peters, dropping the things on the table and hurrying to the stove.

Mrs. Hale stood examining the clothes the woman who was being detained in town had said she wanted.

"Wright was close!" she exclaimed, holding up a shabby black skirt that bore the marks of much making over. "I think maybe that's why she kept so much to herself. I s'pose she felt she couldn't do her part; and then, you don't enjoy things when you feel shabby. She used to wear pretty clothes and be lively—when she was Minnie Foster, one of the town girls, singing in the choir. But that—oh, that was twenty years ago."

With a carefulness in which there was something tender, she folded the shabby clothes and piled them at one corner of the table. She looked at Mrs. Peters, and there was something in the other woman's look that irritated her.

"She don't care," she said to herself. "Much difference it makes to her whether Minnie Foster had pretty clothes when she was a girl."

Then she looked again, and she wasn't so sure; in fact, she hadn't at any time been perfectly sure about Mrs. Peters. She had that shrinking manner, and yet, her eyes looked as if they could see a long way into things.

"This all you was to take in?" asked Mrs. Hale.

"No," said the sheriff's wife; "she said she wanted an apron. Funny thing to want," she ventured in her nervous little way, "for there's not much to get you dirty in jail, goodness knows. But I suppose just to make her feel more natural. If you're used to wearing an apron—. She said they were in the bottom drawer of this cupboard. Yes—here they are. And then her little shawl that always hung on the stair door."

She took the small gray shawl from behind the door leading upstairs, and stood a minute looking at it.

Suddenly Mrs. Hale took a quick step toward the other woman.

"Mrs. Peters!"

"Yes, Mrs. Hale?"

"Do you think she—did it?"

A frightened look blurred the other things in Mrs. Peters' eyes.

"Oh, I don't know," she said, in a voice that seemed to shrink away from the subject.

"Well, I don't think she did," affirmed Mrs. Hale stoutly. "Asking for an apron, and her little shawl. Worryin' about her fruit."

"Mr. Peters says—" Footsteps were heard in the room above; she stopped, looked up, then went on in a lowered voice: "Mr. Peters says—it looks bad for her. Mr. Henderson is awful sarcastic in a speech, and he's going to make fun of her saying she didn't—wake up."

For a moment Mrs. Hale had no answer. Then, "Well, I guess John Wright didn't wake up—when they was slippin' that rope under his neck," she muttered.

"No, it's *strange*," breathed Mrs. Peters. "They think it was such a—funny way to kill a man."

She began to laugh; at sound of the laugh, abruptly stopped.

"That's just what Mr. Hale said," said Mrs. Hale, in a resolutely natural voice. "There was a gun in the house. He says that's what he can't understand."

"Mrs. Henderson said, coming out, that what was needed for the case was a motive. Something to show anger—or sudden feeling."

"Well, I don't see any signs of anger around here," said Mrs. Hale. "I don't—"

She stopped. It was as if her mind tripped on something. Her eye was caught by a dish-towel in the middle of the kitchen table. Slowly she moved toward the table. One half of it was wiped clean, the other half messy. Her eyes made a slow, almost unwilling turn to the bucket of sugar and the half empty bag beside it. Things begun—and not finished.

After a moment she stepped back, and said, in that manner of releasing herself: "Wonder how they're finding things upstairs? I hope she had it a little more red up there. You know,"—she paused, and feeling gathered,—"it seems kind of *sneaking*; locking her up in town and coming out here to get her own house to turn against her!"

"But, Mrs. Hale," said the sheriff's wife, "the law is the law."

"I s'pose 'tis," answered Mrs. Hale shortly.

She turned to the stove, saying something about that fire not being much to brag of. She worked with it a minute, and when she straightened up she said aggressively: "The law is the law—and a bad stove is a bad stove. How'd you like to cook on this?"—pointing with the poker to the broken lining. She opened the oven door and started to express her opinion of the oven; but she was swept into her own thoughts, thinking of what it would mean, year after year, to have that stove to wrestle with. The thought of Minnie Foster trying to bake in that oven—and the thought of never going over to see Minnie Foster—.

She was startled by hearing Mrs. Peters say: "A person gets discouraged—and loses heart."

The sheriff's wife had looked from the stove to the sink—to the pail of water which had been carried in from outside. The two women stood there silent, above them the footsteps of the men who were looking for evidence against the woman who had worked in that kitchen. That look of seeing into things, of seeing through a thing to something else, was in the eyes of the sheriff's wife now. When Mrs. Hale next spoke to her, it was gently:

"Better loosen up your things, Mrs. Peters. We'll not feel them when we go out."

Mrs. Peters went to the back of the room to hang up the fur tippet she was wearing. A moment later she exclaimed, "Why, she was piecing a quilt," and held up a large sewing basket piled high with quilt pieces.

Mrs. Hale spread some of the blocks on the table.

"It's a log-cabin pattern," she said, putting several of them together. "Pretty, isn't it?"

They were so engaged with the quilt that they did not hear the footsteps on the stairs. Just as the stair door opened Mrs. Hale was saying:

"Do you suppose she was going to quilt it or just knot it?"

The sheriff threw up his hands.

"They wonder whether she was going to quilt it or just knot it!"

There was a laugh for the ways of women, a warming of hands over the stove, and then the country attorney said briskly:

"Well, let's go right out to the barn and get that cleared up."

"I don't see as there's anything so strange," Mrs. Hale said resentfully, after the outside door had closed on the three men—"our taking up our time with little things while we're waiting for them to get the evidence. I don't see as it's anything to laugh about."

"Of course they've got awful important things on their minds," said the sheriff's wife apologetically.

They returned to an inspection of the blocks for the quilt. Mrs. Hale was looking at the fine, even sewing, and preoccupied with thoughts of the woman who had done that sewing, when she heard the sheriff's wife's voice say, in a queer tone:

"Why look at this one."

She turned to take the block held out to her.

"The sewing," said Mrs. Peters, in a troubled way. "All the rest of them have been so nice and even—but—this one. Why, it looks as if she didn't know what she was about!"

Their eyes met—something flashed to life, passed between them; then, as if with an effort, they seemed to pull away from each other. A moment Mrs. Hale sat there, her hands folded over that sewing which was so unlike all the rest of the sewing. Then she had pulled a knot and drawn the threads.

"Oh, what are you doing, Mrs. Hale?" asked the sheriff's wife, startled.

"Just pulling out a stitch or two that's not sewed very good," said Mrs. Hale mildly.

"I don't think we ought to touch things," Mrs. Peters said, a little helplessly.

"I'd just finish up this end," answered Mrs. Hale, still in that mild, matter-of-fact fashion.

She threaded the needle and started to replace the bad sewing with good. For a little while she sewed in silence. Then, in that thin, timid voice, she heard:

"Mrs. Hale!"

"Yes, Mrs. Peters?"

"What do you suppose she was so—nervous about?"

"Oh, I don't know," said Mrs. Hale, as if dismissing a thing not important enough to spend much time on. "I don't know as she was—nervous. I sew awful queer sometimes when I'm just tired."

She cut a thread, and out of the corner of her eye looked up at Mrs. Peters. The small, lean face of the sheriff's wife seemed to have tightened up. Her eyes had that look of peering into something. But the next moment she moved, and said in her thin, indecisive way:

"Well, I must get those clothes wrapped. They may be through sooner than we think. I wonder where I could find a piece of paper—and string."

"In that cupboard, maybe," suggested Mrs. Hale, after a glance around.

One piece of the crazy sewing remained unripped. Mrs. Peters' back turned, Martha Hale now scrutinized that piece, compared it with the dainty, accurate sewing of the other blocks. The difference was startling. Holding this block made her feel queer, as if the distracted thoughts of the woman who had perhaps turned to it to try and quiet herself were communicating themselves to her.

Mrs. Peters' voice roused her.

"Here's a bird-cage," she said. "Did she have a bird, Mrs. Hale?"

"Why, I don't know whether she did or not." She turned to look at the cage Mrs. Peters was holding up. "I've not been here in so long." She sighed. "There was a man round last year selling canaries cheap—but I don't know as she took one. Maybe she did. She used to sing real pretty herself."

Mrs. Peters looked round the kitchen.

"Seems kind of funny to think of a bird here." She half laughed—an attempt to put up a barrier. "But she must have had one—or why would she have a cage? I wonder what happened to it."

"I suppose maybe the cat got it," suggested Mrs. Hale, resuming her sewing.

"No; she didn't have a cat. She's got that feeling some people have about cats—being afraid of them. When they brought her to our house yesterday, my cat got in the room, and she was real upset and asked me to take it out."

"My sister Bessie was like that," laughed Mrs. Hale.

The sheriff's wife did not reply. The silence made Mrs. Hale turn round. Mrs. Peters was examining the bird-cage.

"Look at this door," she said slowly. "It's broke. One hinge has been pulled apart."

Mrs. Hale came nearer.

"Looks as if some one must have been—rough with it."

Again their eyes met—startled, questioning, apprehensive. For a moment neither spoke nor stirred. Then Mrs. Hale, turning away, said brusquely:

"If they're going to find any evidence, I wish they'd be about it. I don't like this place."

"But I'm awful glad you came with me, Mrs. Hale." Mrs. Peters put the bird-cage on the table and sat down. "It would be lonesome for me—sitting here alone."

"Yes, it would, wouldn't it?" agreed Mrs. Hale, a certain determined naturalness in her voice. She picked up the sewing, but now it dropped in her lap, and she murmured in a different voice: "But I tell you what I *do* wish, Mrs. Peters. I wish I had come over sometimes when she was here. I wish—I had."

"But of course you were awfully busy, Mrs. Hale. Your house—and your children."

"I could've come," retorted Mrs. Hale shortly. "I stayed away because it weren't cheerful—and that's why I ought to have come. I"—she looked around—"I've never liked this place. Maybe because it's down in a hollow and you don't see the road. I don't know what it is, but it's a lonesome place, and always was. I wish I had come over to see Minnie Foster sometimes. I can see now—" She did not put it into words.

"Well, you mustn't reproach yourself," counseled Mrs. Peters. "Somehow, we just don't see how it is with other folks till—something comes up."

"Not having children makes less work," mused Mrs. Hale, after a silence, "but it makes a quiet house—and Wright out to work all day—and no company when he did come in. Did you know John Wright, Mrs. Peters?"

"Not to know him. I've seen him in town. They say he was a good man."

"Yes—good," conceded John Wright's neighbor grimly. "He didn't drink, and kept his word as well as most, I guess, and paid his debts. But he was a hard man, Mrs. Peters. Just to pass the time of day with him—." She stopped, shivered a little. "Like a raw wind that gets to the bone." Her eye fell upon the cage on the table before her, and she added, almost bitterly: "I should think she would've wanted a bird!"

Suddenly she leaned forward, looking intently at the cage. "But what do you s'pose went wrong with it?"

"I don't know," returned Mrs. Peters; "unless it got sick and died."

But after she said it she reached over and swung the broken door. Both women watched it as if somehow held by it.

"You didn't know—her?" Mrs. Hale asked, a gentler note in her voice.

"Not till they brought her yesterday," said the sheriff's wife.

"She—come to think of it, she was kind of like a bird herself. Real sweet and pretty, but kind of timid and—fluttery. How—she—did—change."

That held her for a long time. Finally, as if struck with a happy thought and relieved to get back to everyday things, she exclaimed:

"Tell you what, Mrs. Peters, why don't you take the quilt in with you? It might take up her mind."

"Why, I think that's a real nice idea, Mrs. Hale," agreed the sheriff's wife, as if she too were glad to come into the atmosphere of simple kindness. "There couldn't possibly be any objection to that, could there? Now, just what will I take? I wonder if her patches are in here—and her things."

They turned to the sewing basket.

"Here's some red," said Mrs. Hale, bringing out a roll of cloth. Underneath that was a box. "Here, maybe her scissors are in here—and her things." She held it up. "What a pretty box! I'll warrant that was something she had a long time ago—when she was a girl."

She held it in her hand a moment; then, with a little sigh, opened it.

Instantly her hand went to her nose.

"Why—!"

Mrs. Peters drew nearer—then turned away.

"There's something wrapped up in this piece of silk," faltered Mrs. Hale.

"This isn't her scissors," said Mrs. Peters in a shrinking voice.

Her hand not steady, Mrs. Hale raised the piece of silk. "Oh, Mrs. Peters!" she cried. "It's—"

Mrs. Peters bent closer.

"It's the bird," she whispered.

"But, Mrs. Peters!" cried Mrs. Hale. "*Look* at it! Its neck—look at its neck! It's all—other side *to*."

She held the box away from her.

The sheriff's wife again bent closer.

"Somebody wrung its neck," said she, in a voice that was slow and deep.

And then again the eyes of the two women met—this time clung together in a look of dawning comprehension, of growing horror. Mrs. Peters looked from the dead bird to the broken door of the cage. Again their eyes met. And just then there was a sound at the outside door.

Mrs. Hale slipped the box under the quilt pieces in the basket, and sank into the chair before it. Mrs. Peters stood holding to the table. The county attorney and the sheriff came in from outside.

"Well, ladies," said the county attorney, as one turning from serious things to little pleasantries, "have you decided whether she was going to quilt it or knot it?"

"We think," began the sheriff's wife in a flurried voice, "that she was going to—knot it."

He was too preoccupied to notice the change that came in her voice on that last.

"Well, that's very interesting, I'm sure," he said tolerantly. He caught sight of the bird-cage. "Has the bird flown?"

"We think the cat got it," said Mrs. Hale in a voice curiously even.

He was walking up and down, as if thinking something out.

"Is there a cat?" he asked absently.

Mrs. Hale shot a look at the sheriff's wife.

"Well, not *now*," said Mrs. Peters. "They're superstitious, you know; they leave."

She sank into her chair.

The county attorney did not heed her. "No sign at all of any one having come in from the outside," he said to Peters, in the manner of continuing an interrupted conversation. "Their own rope. Now let's go upstairs again and go over it, piece by piece. It would have to have been some one who knew just the—"

The stair door closed behind them and their voices were lost.

The two women sat motionless, not looking at each other, but as if peering into something and at the same time holding back. When they spoke now it was as if they were afraid of what they were saying, but as if they could not help saying it.

"She liked the bird," said Martha Hale, low and slowly. "She was going to bury it in that pretty box."

"When I was a girl," said Mrs. Peters, under her breath, "my kitten—there was a boy who took a hatchet, and before my eyes—before I could get there—" She covered her face an instant. "If they hadn't held me back I would have"—she caught herself, looked upstairs where footsteps were heard, and finished weakly—"hurt him."

Then they sat without speaking or moving.

"I wonder how it would seem," Mrs. Hale at last began, as if feeling her way over strange ground— "never to have had any children around?" Her eyes made a slow sweep of the kitchen, as if seeing what that kitchen had meant through all the years. "No, Wright wouldn't have liked the bird," she said after that—"a thing that sang. She used to sing. He killed that too." Her voice tightened.

Mrs. Peters moved uneasily.

"Of course we don't know who killed the bird."

"I knew John Wright," was Mrs. Hale's answer.

"It was an awful thing was done in this house that night, Mrs. Hale," said the sheriff's wife. "Killing a man while he slept—slipping a thing round his neck that choked the life out of him."

Mrs. Hale's hand went out to the bird-cage.

"His neck. Choked the life out of him."

"We don't *know* who killed him," whispered Mrs. Peters wildly. "We don't *know*."

Mrs. Hale had not moved. "If there had been years and years of nothing, then a bird to sing to you, it would be awful—still—after the bird was still."

It was as if something within her not herself had spoken, and it found in Mrs. Peters something she did not know as herself.

"I know what stillness is," she said, in a queer, monotonous voice. "When we homesteaded in Dakota, and my first baby died—after he was two years old—and me with no other then—"

Mrs. Hale stirred.

"How soon do you suppose they'll be through looking for evidence?"

"I know what stillness is," repeated Mrs. Peters, in just that same way. Then she too pulled back. "The law has got to punish crime, Mrs. Hale," she said in her little tight way.

"I wish you'd seen Minnie Foster," was the answer, "when she wore a white dress with blue ribbons, and stood up there in the choir and sang."

The picture of that girl, the fact that she had lived neighbor to that girl for twenty years, and had let her die for lack of life, was suddenly more than she could bear.

"Oh, I *wish* I'd come over here once in a while!" she cried. "That was a crime! That was a crime! Who's going to punish that?"

"We mustn't take on," said Mrs. Peters, with a frightened look toward the stairs.

"I might 'a' *known* she needed help! I tell you, it's *queer*, Mrs. Peters. We live close together, and we live far apart. We all go through the same things—it's all just a different kind of the same thing! If it weren't—why do you and I *understand*? Why do we *know*—what we know this minute?"

She dashed her hand across her eyes. Then, seeing the jar of fruit on the table, she reached for it and choked out:

"If I was you I wouldn't tell her her fruit was gone! Tell her it ain't. Tell her it's all right—all of it. Here—take this in to prove it to her! She—she may never know whether it was broke or not."

She turned away.

Mrs. Peters reached out for the bottle of fruit as if she were glad to take it—as if touching a familiar thing, having something to do, could keep her from something else. She got up, looked about for something to wrap the fruit in, took a petticoat from the pile of clothes she had brought from the front room, and nervously started winding that round the bottle.

"My!" she began, in a high, false voice, "It's a good thing the men couldn't hear us! Getting all stirred up over a little thing like a—dead canary." She hurried over that. "As if that could have anything to do with—with—My, wouldn't they *laugh*?"

Footsteps were heard on the stairs.

"Maybe they would," muttered Mrs. Hale—"maybe they wouldn't."

"No, Peters," said the county attorney incisively, "it's all perfectly clear, except the reason for doing it. But you know juries when it comes to women. If there was some definite thing—something to show. Something to make a story about. A thing that would connect up with this clumsy way of doing it."

In a covert way Mrs. Hale looked at Mrs. Peters. Mrs. Peters was looking at her. Quickly they looked away from each other. The outer door opened and Mr. Hale came in.

"I've got the team round now," he said. "Pretty cold out there."

"I'm going to stay here awhile by myself," the county attorney suddenly announced. "You can send Frank out for me, can't you? He asked the sheriff. "I want to go over everything. I'm not satisfied we can't do better."

Again, for one brief moment, the two women's eyes found one another.

The sheriff came up to the table.

"Did you want to see what Mrs. Peters was going to take in?"

The county attorney picked up the apron. He laughed.

"Oh, I guess they're not very dangerous things the ladies have picked out."

Mrs. Hale's hand was on the sewing basket in which the box was concealed. She felt that she ought to take her hand off the basket. She did not seem able to. He picked up one of the quilt blocks which she had piled on to cover the box. Her eyes felt like fire. She had a feeling that if he took up the basket she would snatch it from him.

But he did not take it up. With another little laugh, he turned away, saying:

"No; Mrs. Peters doesn't need supervising. For that matter, a sheriff's wife is married to the law. Ever think of it that way, Mrs. Peters?"

Mrs. Peters was standing beside the table. Mrs. Hale shot a quick look up at her; but she could not see her face. Mrs. Peters had turned away. When she spoke, her voice was muffled.

"Not—just that way," she said.

"Married to the law!" chuckled Mrs. Peters' husband. He moved toward the door into the front room, and said to the county attorney:

"I just want you to come in here a minute, George. We ought to take a look at these windows."

"Oh—windows," said the county attorney scoffingly.

"We'll be right out, Mr. Hale," said the sheriff to the farmer, who was still waiting by the door.

Hale went to look after the horses. The sheriff followed the county attorney into the other room. Again—for one moment—the two women were alone in that kitchen.

Martha Hale sprang up, her hands tight together, looking at that other woman, with whom it rested. At first she could not see her eyes, for the sheriff's wife had not turned back, since she turned away at the suggestion of being married to the law. But now Mrs. Hale made her turn back. Her eyes made her turn back. Slowly, unwillingly, Mrs. Peters turned her head until her eyes met the eyes of the other woman. There was a moment when they held each other in a steady, burning look in which there was no evasion nor flinching. Then Martha Hale's eyes pointed the way to the basket in which was hidden the thing that would make certain the conviction of the other woman—that woman who was not there and yet who had been there with them all through the hour.

For a moment Mrs. Peters did not move. And then she did it. With a rush forward, she threw back the quilt pieces, got the box, tried to put it in her handbag. It was too big. Desperately she opened it, started to take the bird out. But there she broke—she could not touch the bird. She stood helpless, foolish.

There was a sound of a knob turning in the inner door. Martha Hale snatched the box from the sheriff's wife, and got it in the pocket of her big coat just as the sheriff and the county attorney came back into the kitchen.

"Well, Henry," said the county attorney facetiously, "at least we found out that she was not going to quilt it. She was going to—what is it you call it, ladies?"

Mrs. Hale's hand was against the pocket of her coat.

"We call it—knot it, Mr. Henderson."

Questions for Reading and Analysis

1. What attitude do the men in the story have toward the women and the work they do? How do the women react to this attitude? How does the men's attitude toward the women influence their decision to destroy the evidence?

2. Why did Minnie Wright kill her husband? Do you think she should get away with it?

3. Why do Mrs. Hale and Mrs. Peters decide to destroy the evidence they fear would have convicted Minnie? Do you think they make the right choice?

4. What role does the bird play in the story?

5. What is the significance of the story's title?

A longtime writer at the Boston Globe *and author of several collections of essays, Ellen Goodman (b. 1941) often addresses women's and family issues in her syndicated column. In the following piece, which appeared on September 24, 2000, she criticizes unethical advertising and takes particular aim at Nike for an ad aired during the 2000 Olympics that trivialized women's fear of violence.*

Sorry, Nike, I Just Don't Get That Ad

Ellen Goodman

I am sorry that the marketing moguls at Nike think I've lost my sense of humor. In the aftermath of a flap over their Olympic ads, it appears that the corporate honchos are looking down their noses at anyone who didn't "get it."

Let's go to the videotape. During the opening ceremonies and between assorted swimming and gymnastics competitions, NBC broke to an ad featuring a woman in a remote cabin. She is getting ready for a bath when a hockey-masked, chain saw-wielding Jason figure pops up in her mirror. He chases the screaming woman through the woods. (Are you laughing yet?)

Thirty seconds later, this woman, Olympic runner Suzy Favor Hamilton, gets away because she's in better shape than the would-be slasher. The moral: "Why sport? You'll live longer."

I can just imagine the Madison Avenue creative geniuses sitting around a table applauding this work. "Hip." "Edgy." "Postmodern." "Ironic." There are high fives all around.

But those of us who did not share the hip, edgy, postmodern, ironic sensibility of these sophisticated ad mongers were just plain horrified by the ad called "Horror." Within short order NBC had thousands of protests and pulled the ad on the network and its younger siblings MSNBC and CNBC.

Nike, on the other hand, remained unrepentant and promised to go on running the ad on ESPN. They even posted the patronizing remarks of the company's vice president, Mike Wilskey, on their Web page: "Our rule has always been to respect the intelligence of our consumer. . . . We know they get the joke."

As someone who didn't get the joke, I would be glad to explain to Mike why a slasher ad is as welcome as a fork in the eye of the Olympic family audience. This alleged satire of women's fear on a program about strengths didn't strike my funny bone. I'm sure it didn't make some girl tuned in to see Andrea Raducan break into giggles.

But I am most dismayed by the utter disconnect between the ad makers and the audience. If I may echo one reader's e-mail: What was Nike thinking?

This disconnect is at the heart of advertising violence to kids, a subject that has at last gotten our attention. But violence isn't the only unhealthy product being pushed.

This month, the Golden Marble Awards were bestowed on "the best advertising aimed at kids." Again, it was the creativity of the ads and not the value of the products or the ethics of the business that got the plaudits.

The common word of praise was "hip." But what were the winners selling? Foods like Hostess Twinkies and restaurants like McDonald's. The judges praised the Happy Meal toy campaign because it "required parents and children to keep coming back to McDonald's to get pieces of their toy."

Susan Linn, a Harvard Medical School psychologist who has clearly lost her sense of humor about child obesity, says, "You don't see ads for broccoli for children." Linn joined a band protesting the ceremony for "essentially rewarding creativity used to manipulate children for profit."

If you need any more proof of the disconnect between the business and the ethics of this marketing mania, the Government Accounting Office has a new study of advertising in one of the newer venues: schools.

Talk about a captive audience. If it isn't Channel One on school TV or Zap Me on school computers, it's Pepsi in the halls and Clairol ads on the book jackets. As Alex Molnar at the Center for the Analysis of Commercialism in Education says, "The start of the school year now resembles the release of a blockbuster movie with all the gimmicks aimed at children."

Overall, the amount of money spent marketing directly to kids—which is to say, around parents—has nearly doubled in seven years, to $12 billion. Molnar describes this "like the wind that blows off the ocean. It shapes and bends everything it blows against. It's shaping kids."

Our hip, ironic, postmodern friends at Nike are not overtly advertising to children (though teen-age males are an important part of their market), but even here, kids get the collateral damage. Only occasionally is a commercial so outrageous that all of us pay attention to the overwhelming ad-vironment.

"We have a de facto ministry of culture, and its capital is Madison Avenue," says Molnar. In this capital, the folks in "creative" can't tell the difference between selling shoes and selling horror.

Remember what the Nike veep said: "Our rule has always been to respect the intelligence of our consumer." Now that's funny.

Questions for Reading and Analysis

1. Is the point of Goodman's column an attack on Nike—or does she have a larger purpose?

2. Underline several words or phrases that reveal Goodman's attitude.

3. What does Goodman imply is the effect of tags like "hip," "ironic," and "postmodern"? What is the effect of her repetition of these words? Is it fair?

4. The Nike vice-president's response to criticism of the Nike ad is to say that Nike knows its customers "get the joke." Do you agree or disagree with his position?

Feminist Kay Leigh Hagan would readily count herself among the "bitches from hell," a term used by the abusive truck driver in the movie Thelma and Louise *"for women who in any way acknowledge or resist male violence." Since women are habitually the victims of male violence, she argues that they need to learn to defend themselves with martial arts and firearms. The essay is an excerpt from her book* Fugitive Information: Essays from a Feminist Hothead *(1993).*

Bitches from Hell:
The Politics of Self-Defense

Kay Leigh Hagan

I am answering a survey concerning women's experiences of male violence. Pencil in hand, ready to begin, I feel I am one of the lucky ones.

The statistics are familiar: every fifteen seconds, a woman is beaten; one of four women will be a victim of rape; four out of five murdered women are killed by men—between a half and a third are married to their murderers; 42 percent of all women employed by the federal government, a group the size of Denver, Colorado, have been sexually harassed.

I think I am lucky because only my father has hit me, no stranger-to-stranger rape, only dimly recalled incest, maybe a couple of date rapes, and many times I didn't want to but did it anyway. I've been followed, I had a persistent obscene caller for two years, I've seen numerous men jerking off in cars or in parks, and when I was twenty-five, an employer encouraged me to get drunk, then had sex with me. I've seen and heard men beating women, including my father and mother, and I've intervened in a few public incidents. But all in all, I consider myself lucky. So far, so good.

Do you feel at risk:

in an elevator with a strange man?

parking in a deserted lot?

climbing a stairwell?

hiking or biking alone?

staying alone in a motel?

taking public transportation alone?[1]

As far as I can tell, men's violence against women is part of the invisible obvious of everyday life. Invisible because it is accepted, for the most part goes unpunished, and is rarely even referred to in public or private discourse. (For instance, the national hate crimes bill passed recently did not include compiling incidents of male violence against women because "there would be too many of them.") Obvious because fear of men's violence laces our every decision. This fear does not have to be conscious to be effective. Most of us live in denial, and many women say they don't feel afraid, shaking their heads at the women who do. But ask if they walk alone at night or go to certain parts of the city unaccompanied or leave their windows open as they fall asleep, and you'll notice that the majority of women are aware, deep inside, that danger lurks just beyond the thin veil of their denial. The gender of that danger, you can be sure, is male.

In a recent survey of 4,450 respondents conducted by *Ms.* magazine,[2] three out of four women had experienced male violence; 83 percent knew at least one woman who had been raped, and only 7 percent of the respondents could say they had never experienced male violence and also say they did not know a rape victim. The implications of such numbers are staggering, and yet we do not stagger. We go on living our lives, enduring our own violent encounters with men as if we are the only women in the world who do. We are encouraged to write off male violence as the work of a few sick individuals. We are numbed by the numbers, and that is precisely the intention, to isolate and immobilize women. What else can we learn from these statistics?

The rules of grammar, one might think, are straightforward enough and unlikely to be twisted for political purposes, but propaganda is crafty, its purpose to manipulate and persuade through subtle, preferably undetectable means. In the case of statistics, consider what linguist Julia Penelope calls agent deletion: Take a common statistic, say, "Every four minutes, a woman is raped." What do you see? A woman, walking down the street perhaps, and suddenly—what? She *becomes* raped? Do you see the man jumping out from the shadow in that statement? No. You do not. With a grammatical sleight of hand, the agent is deleted, the man disappears, and you see only women, many of them, frequently and inexplicably raped. But change your focus and look again.

> *Every four minutes, a man rapes a woman.*

> *Every fifteen seconds, a man beats a woman.*

Suddenly men are in the picture. Lots of men. Men with something on their minds. Countless men raping, beating, and murdering women. (Refraining from such extremes, myriad others are leering at women, feeling up women on public transportation, telling sexist jokes, and otherwise sexually harassing women on the job or verbally demeaning them at home.) And *countless* would be the operative term here since my efforts to find statistics describing the numbers of men who commit violence against women, rather than the numbers of women who are victims of it, have been unsuccessful. If they were to be computed, these facts might sound something like, "One out of five men have raped at least one woman," or "Men commit twenty-one thousand acts of violence against women every week"— and thus a different picture would begin to emerge in public view. A fellow who works with male batterers suggested to me that the statistics are worded to focus on the victims instead of the perpetrators because this image, of so many violent and abusive men, is unbearable. (More so, I suppose, than so many dead and injured women.) The grammar of the statistics serves to distract us from the very image that might trigger our constructive and concerted outrage. With the agent deleted, we simply see women beaten, raped, and murdered. It just happens. A fact of life. The invisible obvious.

To look at the picture from another angle, we might turn to the natural world, to nonhuman creatures who rely on their instincts for survival. Some animals are natural enemies, such as owls and field mice, cats and birds, lions and gazelles. There are, we see, predators and prey. These are facts of life, and we can presume that such babies are taught early on which are predators and which are prey. Predators are avoided or fought: there is no in-between stance, no moral judgment, no plea for justice. Fight or flight. We can assume it is never suggested to gazelles that they cozy up to a lion or that field mice try reasoning with owls. You don't lobby for your rights with a natural enemy.

Of course, we are not talking about the so-called natural world, we are talking about civilized human beings, men and women. We are of the same species (or so we are taught), and thus it is painful to consider that one gender might be the natural enemy—the predator—of the other, although we can observe this phenomenon in a few other species. Could male violence against women be innate? Can it be that they cannot help themselves? If so, how would this knowledge change our attitude toward them? Would a biological predisposition somehow absolve them of responsibility (as if they take responsibility anyway)? However interesting it might be to speculate on reasons for this behavior, ultimately it is a moot point. The evidence is in. Men *act* like predators of women.

What activities would you do alone, at night?

go out for a walk

go jogging/running

drink at a bar

walk to a friend's house

see a movie

go grocery shopping

explore an unfamiliar neighborhood

speak with a stranger

I slip into my own denial like a familiar cardigan, pulling it close against fleeting chilly moments of awareness. I find such a moment in a journal entry, a decade old.

"July 1980. What to do about Rape Season? The summer heat, worst in thirty years, exacerbates my fear of attack. I sweat through the nights, recalling at random the recent stories of intruders who appear at the foot of the bed, having stolen in through an open window. My windows barred and shut, I finally admit that as the heat has little to do with the rape frequency, the bars on the window have little effect on my fear. One more story does it: She was walking to the grocery store three blocks from her house in my neighborhood. It was just dark, she saw a tall jogger approaching, and she stepped to the side of the walk to let him pass. As he came closer, she nodded and he nodded, and when he came even with her he stretched out his arm, took her by the neck, and as she screamed, he slit her throat. She dropped to the ground, found some long minutes later in a growing pool of blood. Everyone in the emergency room, the story goes, said he meant to kill her. She is not dead, but the new stitches reach from the hollow of her throat to her ear.

"All my rationalizations cannot explain away this knowledge: the violence is random, it is intentional, it is deadly, it is male. A new connection, a new frame of reference: questioning why the danger exists is a separate activity from protecting myself from the danger. Understanding why men taunt/rape/beat/kill women at random will not protect me from it. I know, finally, that I am never safe. I take action. I sign up for a workshop in self-defense.

"I will remember Marianna's voice, her presence, her strength, her warnings, her insistence in telling us we are strong, have the right to be strong, have the right to defend ourselves. Twenty-five women in a circle, telling each other why we are taking this course: I was beaten. I was attacked. I was abused as a child. I am being followed. I was raped. I am afraid to walk alone. I am tired of being afraid.

"Marianna teaches us to punch with our fists. I realize as I mold my hand to match hers and jab it into the padded bolster that I have never thrown a full blow. An entirely new sensation, the arm straight and true as an arrow, the fist landing squarely on target, the pad shuddering from the power of the impact. 'If you still think you are weak,' Marianna suggests, 'imagine what that much force would do to a face.' I fold my arms across my stomach and wince. It would hurt someone's face.

"Applying our new skills, we act out the familiar scenes: the parking deck, the bus stop, the walk from store to home. We create our nightmares, becoming the one with the gun, the one with the knife, we become the attacker, grabbing each other by the neck from behind. We learn to spin away, to yell from the gut, to punch, jab, kick, and throw. We learn to say, 'GET AWAY FROM ME. YOU HAVE NO RIGHT HERE.'

"I am stronger now because I know I can hurt someone who tries to hurt me. My body is not a handicap, some soft burden wrapped around a fierce core. I can defend my center if necessary. I know this now. By this awareness, this action, I transform my anger into protection. I cannot change the world of violence, but I can choose to change myself, and that act impacts my world."

Reading this entry ten years later, I am impressed with my clarity and commitment. Then I notice I have not pursued self-defense skills beyond that single weekend, preferring the comforts of denial to the disturbance of consciousness. I just want to live my life, do my work, and ignore the violence, the fear, and the anger.

Have you ever not done the following because you were afraid of violent consequences? (frequently, occasionally, never)

disagreed with spouse/lover

talked back to father

argued with an adult child

argued with boss

gotten drunk on a date

Of course, denial is at best a temporary solution. The violence continues, my anger increases, and like many women after seeing the film *Thelma and Louise*, I found myself harboring a secret longing for a gun. I envied their bold responses to men's disgusting behavior that left some guys cowering and another one dead. My philosophical and spiritual commitment to nonviolence was challenged by my joyful burst of shameless gratitude when Louise deftly put the insidious rapist away. Justice! How refreshing. Their bravado enlivened the outrage I keep bridled somewhere between my heart and my gut, and for the first time I wondered quite frankly why most women, myself included, don't carry guns. So I began to ask.

Over six months, I talked to women all over the country and solicited their opinions on women and guns. Their responses ranged from complete rejection of guns to a cool and practiced use of them. I found my own reactions telling: just as something about Thelma's chirpy armed robbery and Louise's resigned murder of the rapist thrilled me, "real-life" women who feel at ease with both the need for and the use of guns elicited from me a kind of shock. Women are not supposed to do this kind of thing, I hear in my mind.

Do you now carry (circle all that apply):

gun

knife

pocketknife or something sharp

mace

whistle

The young woman from Texas is matter-of-fact when I ask if she uses a gun. Certainly, she says. She learned to use a shotgun as a girl and keeps one in her rural home. Her work requires frequent road trips across desolate Texas plains, so she has a pistol for the car. And lately, she adds, she's been wanting to do some long-distance bicycling. "I might get a little Beretta," she says as if talking about a certain pair of shoes. "I wouldn't consider biking alone without a gun," she adds. I am staring, dumbstruck by her casual acceptance of weaponry. I ask how she came to feel this way. She looks at me straight on, her eyes narrow slightly, and she shrugs. "It's a war out there. Men against women. I'm not about to go around undefended. That would be stupid."

Many women who carry guns began doing so after experiences of being personally attacked, and many women who are against the use of guns suspect their feelings might change if they were attacked. The results of my random survey revealed a variety of reasons why women don't carry guns: they don't know how to use one and don't want to/don't feel they can learn; they fear a gun will be used against them by an assailant; they don't want to use "male" methods; they don't believe in the use of violence. This divergence among women seems to be related to shedding the veil of denial. Considering the prevalence of male violence against women, to remain unprepared does seem—in the words of the young Texas woman—stupid.

Stories from women who are prepared—by training in the use of guns, for instance—amazed me. Some of them were in law enforcement. Because the nature of their job removes the taboo from women using weapons, essentially "allowing" women to become proficient with guns, the power differential I am accustomed to between men and women is turned on its head. A national park ranger related this story:

"My first week on the job I did a felony car stop on a man who was running from the local police. I ordered him to get out of the car. He waited and then made a quick movement to his waistband. I had been aiming the shotgun in his general direction, and when he moved I put a shell in the chamber and waited to see if he pulled out a gun. The sound of the shotgun's action convinced him to get out of the car with his hands up and his pants wet! He told me later he was so scared that he couldn't keep from wetting his pants."

In another instance, a woman was pulled over on a rural road by a car with flashing lights, which she assumed was a policeman. When the uniformed man pushed her down on the front seat and began to rape her, she managed to pull out her gun from underneath the seat and shoot him. She then pushed him out on the highway, drove to the emergency room of the nearest hospital, and turned herself in. He was not, as it turned out, a policeman, but a serial rapist. She was his eighth known victim.

I must admit that the image in the first story of a man being that scared of a woman appeals to me, and the evidence in both stories that a woman can learn to use a gun is reassuring. Like many women, I imagine myself being hopelessly inept with such a device, despite the fact that I have demonstrated a high level of manual dexterity with other more complex tools. My assumption, that I could not learn to use a gun, was echoed with such frequency throughout my interviews with women that I suspect it is based not on experience or personal knowledge but stems instead from the propaganda that tells us what is appropriate behavior for women. Naming the prevalence of male violence is not tactful, self-defense is not ladylike, and retaliation is utterly monstrous.

The truck driver who repeatedly taunts Thelma and Louise with obscene gestures from the cab of his gleaming semi goes slightly mad when instead of shooting him they elect to blow up his precious truck. As the vehicle explodes in flames and the women drive off, he shakes his fist and calls them bitches from hell. This, I think, is the category men reserve for women who in any way acknowledge or resist male violence.

I could justify killing (1. yes, 2. no, 3. don't know)

someone trying to rape me

convicted serial killer

someone attempting murder

Adolf Hitler

Yet Audre Lorde has reminded us that we cannot dismantle the master's house using the master's tools. Many women responded to my query with similar feelings, saying they do not want to condone the use of violence. "To match an enemy, we become no better than he. You can only gain peace by being peaceful," said one woman. "I want 'claiming my power' to mean something very different from the male model," said another. In a group discussion during a women's music festival, a woman described her belief that resorting to violence obscures the connection to our unique female powers and is against our basic peaceful nature. By remaining true to ourselves, she suggested, our womanly ways will eventually overwhelm the culture of male violence we now endure, creating a society of peace, safety, and mutual respect.

All these principles are true enough, and certainly more noble than my occasional sordid fantasies of using cattle prods to herd violent men into re-education camps. As a feminist, I agree that the means are the ends. I am disturbed by the prospect of women taking up arms. I, too, dream of a world without violence. However, I cannot fail to notice that at the moment, we're apparently in a rather long and awkward transition period between patriarchal hell and that feminist utopia. The particular era to which we are consigned requires that we contend with the reality of male violence against women. In the face of this clear and present danger, I wonder once again, what's a principled gal to do?

What precautions do you take to stay safe?

walk in pairs whenever possible

have house keys at the ready

check car before getting in

always watch who is around

take self-defense classes

carry purse strapped to body so it won't be stolen

avoid wearing clothing that could restrict movement

never put telephone number on checks

The issue of self-defense caused even the women most fervently against the use of guns to waiver. Nearly every woman described encounters with violent men when she wished she'd had a gun, or said she was sure if she'd had one, she would have used it. Yet a minority of women I talked to have self-defense training of any sort. I ponder again why the obvious need for self-defense does not motivate more women to carry a weapon, practice a martial art, or otherwise learn to protect ourselves. In this strange jigsaw puzzle, there seems to be a missing piece.

The invisible obvious dawns on me slowly. One of the main symptoms of sustained oppression, I have learned from feminist theory, is the destruction of a sense of self. Characteristically, oppressed people exhibit low self-esteem, low self-worth, a lack of identity. As we absorb the oppressor's relentless messages about our inferiority, we come to believe them. Could it be that as women in a woman-hating society, we do not feel we have a self to defend? Such a belief would make "women's self-defense" an oxymoron. In a peculiar twist, agent deletion strikes again.

Self-defense is a pragmatic and necessary extension of self-love, self-respect, and self-determination. Self-defense does not contradict a commitment to nonviolence. While the form of self-defense is up to the individual woman, the need for self-defense is unquestionable. Carry Mace, learn akido, always wear shoes you can run in, stay alert—whatever you choose to do to protect yourself within the context of your own principled integrity, do it. Beyond the obvious need for self-protection, there is another, perhaps even more important, reason to take action.

Women deserve to live in safety and dignity. Male violence against women in any form is unacceptable. Our righteous outrage on behalf of our own precious selves must lead us first to take measures to insure our personal survival. To build a utopia, it helps to be alive.

Afterword

Deborah Brink, after reading this essay, created the Oath of the Bitches from Hell:

> *I pledge to raise Holy Hell*
> *For the sake of my Self and my Sisters.*
> *I will continue to take back my power,*
> *And take back the night,*
> *And no man will ever feel safe*
> *To harm any woman again.*

Endnotes

1. All survey questions taken from *Ms.* 1, 2 (1990).
2. For the survey itself, see *Ms.* 1, 2 (1990). For survey results, see *Ms.* 1, 5 (1991).

Questions for Reading and Analysis

1. In what way does the grammar used to convey statistics about violence towards women obscure the reality of male perpetrators?

2. Why, according to Hagan, is it necessary for every woman to become efficient at self-defense?

3. What is Hagan's answer to the question as to why so many women she talked to refused to carry guns?

4. How does Hagan reconcile the desire for peace with the necessity to arm herself?

5. What is Hagan's definition of a "bitch from hell"? Where does the term come from?

6. Hagan intersperses her discussion of violence against women with questions from a *Ms.* survey about the subject. What effect does she achieve by including these quotes?

As a lifelong journalist, Pete Hamill has the "inside track" on what makes the newspapers and why. In the following excerpt from his 1998 book, News Is a Verb, *Hamill argues that celebrity journalism, however popular, harms the integrity of journalists and newspapers and insults the readers' intelligence.*

News Is a Verb

Pete Hamill

Any visit to an American newsstand will illustrate the most widespread phenomenon of the times: The print media are runny with the virus of celebrity. The names and faces of movie actors, rock musicians, rappers, and fashion models adorn the covers of most magazines. If the subjects are not people who perform for a living, they are people whose celebrity is derived from notoriety. Depending upon the week or the year, Madonna competes with Joey Buttafuoco. Hugh Grant duels with Lorena Bobbitt. Eddie Murphy is cast beside the parents of JonBenet Ramsey. When accomplishment predates notoriety, the names are even bigger. Hey, folks, here's O. J. Simpson! And Marv Albert! And Frank Gifford! Big names, folks. Bigger than you insignificant schnooks! Bigger than God!

Newspapers are not immune to the celebrity virus. Depending upon the editors, they peddle a blander or coarser version of the same obsession with big names. True accomplishment is marginal to the recognition factor. There is seldom any attention paid to scientists, poets, educators, or archaeologists. Citizens who work hard, love their spouses and children, pay taxes, give to charities, and break no laws are never in a newspaper unless they die in some grisly murder. Even solid politicians, those who do the work of the people without ambitions for immense power, and do so without scandal, are ignored. The focus of most media attention, almost to the exclusion of all other subjects, are those big names.

Newspaper reporters and editors know that most of these people aren't worth six minutes of anybody's time. Privately, they sneer at them or shrug them off. But they and their publishers are convinced that the mass audience is demanding these stories, so they keep churning them out. They defend their choices by insisting they are only giving the people what they want. If they are right, the country is in terrible trouble. I think they're wrong.

Newspaper people have more reason than others to know that some of these big names are mere creatures of hype and self-promotion. After all, they take the calls that are soon eagerly converted into stories. One entire subgenre flows from the jowly megalomania of New York real estate operator Donald Trump. There are many real estate people of more solid achievement and greater power than Trump's, and certainly many more accomplished businessmen. But such men and women usually prefer to live outside the spotlight; like people who really have money or those with truly interesting sex lives, they don't brag about them. They don't invent their lives in cahoots with press agents; they live them.

But Trump flies to the spotlight, even demands it. His motto seems to be "I'm written about, therefore I exist." He personally telephones gossip columnists and reporters to present them with stories about the wonders of himself, his great love life, his brusque divorces. In the spirit of true collaboration, the newspapers quote "sources close to Trump" as their authority, a code known to other editors and reporters but not revealed to the readers. In a way, Trump has his own brilliance. He has a genius for self-inflation, for presenting an illusion of accomplishment that often becomes the accomplishment itself. A tiny solar system now revolves around Trump's own self-created persona: his ex-wives, Ivana Trump and Marla Maples Trump, followed by his poor teenage daughter, Ivanka Trump, who as I write is being hurled into the world of fashion models under the benevolent gaze of Daddy. This vulgar saga threatens to go on and on.

No offense against taste is beyond Trump and his journalistic collaborators. Months after the death of Diana Spencer in a car wreck in Paris, Trump was publishing another of his ghostwritten hardcover hymns to his own genius. He gave an interview to the *New York Daily News*, which was serializing this book, even though most editors knew it was a second-rate exercise in self-promotion. Trump knew exactly what the publishers of the *Daily News* wanted, and the next day's front page showed his face, his book, and a nauseating headline that screamed "I WISH I HAD DATED DI."

When I was editing the *Daily News*, I tried to control the virus of which Trump was the local symbol. Trump was not banned from the newspaper, but he did have to *do* something to appear in its pages. The "stories" slowed to a trickle, and one result was that we were beaten by the *New York Post* on the story of Trump's divorce. We had a rumor; they had Trump, speaking as a "source close to Trump." It was my responsibility and I chose not to run an unverified rumor. I was glad I made that choice. After I was canned, Trump "stories" came back in a fetid rush.

Trump is virtually a genre now. But another genre has been dominating the tabloids and other newspapers in the last year. I call it necrojournalism—the journalism of dead, or near-dead, celebrities. Princess Di was the greatest example of the genre. Certainly her death demanded extensive coverage. But after the known facts had been printed, the mysteries of the car crash defined, the paparazzi accused, and then the drunken limo driver, conveniently dead, arraigned in the public dock, the coverage kept on going. And it swiftly degenerated into a flood of mindless, sentimental custard. The funeral played live, the Elton John tune was thrown at us over and over and over again, the brother was hauled out and then her kids and then Prince Charles and the Queen and an endless parade of other royal unemployables. We didn't bury Franklin Roosevelt this way. The British didn't do this for Winston Churchill. Somewhere in the middle of this maudlin orgy, Mother Teresa, another celeb, died, but somehow she became a long footnote to the Princess Di story. Finally, this Olympics of emotion—some of it genuine and most of it fraudulent—was over. Most people scrubbed away at the grimy film of bathos; some must have been vaguely ashamed; others remained baffled by it all. But the stories kept coming. Long after the emotions were spent, necrojournalism was in full command.

Newspapers serialized books about Princess Di. There were stories about how "brave" her kids were. There were stories implying that Princess Di, all by herself, stopped the spread of land mines. There were stories claiming that she was planning to marry Dodi and stories denying that she was going to marry Dodi. There were stories wondering who the hell Dodi was. Still it kept coming: accounts of planned Princess Di movies and Princess Di postage stamps and Princess Di memorials in England. And *still* it wasn't over. At the end of the year, there were even *more* special supplements. The *Daily News* in New York ran a total of thirty-five pages on Princess Di in its final Sunday paper of the year.

Meanwhile, there seemed to be a collective judgment that death sells—or, rather, that the deaths of famous people will sell. More examples of necrojournalism filled the narrow space between Princess Di stories. We read page-one stories about Marilyn Monroe, dead for thirty-five years; John F. Kennedy, dead for thirty-four years; Jacqueline Onassis, dead for four years; Frank Sinatra, nearly dead (as contrary as ever, he refused to die); Marv Albert, whose career was dead; and of course, Trump, who was brain-dead. The great fear in certain newspaper city rooms was that Sinatra, Ronald Reagan, Bob Hope, Boris Yeltsin, and the Pope would all die on the same day. To match the space given to Princess Di, they'd need to add 160 pages in special supplements alone.

Please don't misunderstand. As a newspaperman and a reader, I'm not against celebrity journalism; it just must be *journalism*. The profiles that run in *Vanity Fair*, the *New Yorker*, *GQ*, *Esquire*, and *People* are journalism. For the most part, the reporters devote time to understanding the subjects of their portraits. They take nothing for granted and make no a priori assumptions; if they begin the reporting admiring the big name and come to despise him, they tell that story. If they start with contempt and finish with admiration, they tell that story, too. They begin by poring over all previous stories about the big name, looking for patterns, contradictions, flaws, and strengths. They understand that any interview granted by a celebrity is itself a kind of performance, not evidence of anything authentic. It is commerce, part of the selling of a movie, a TV show, or an album. The good reporters know that a transient fifteen-minute interview in a hotel room during a big name's promotional tour is not really an interview. It is time pried out of the big name's tight schedule, the reporter taking his turn between two other interviewers who are gnawing at the soggy mound of cheese Danish in an outer room. It can be the *beginning* of journalism; it is seldom the end.

Serious journalists don't usually engage in this empty ritual. They need to spend extended time with the subject, like a fly on the wall, seeing what the big name actually *does*, in contrast to what he *says* he does. They attempt to make a rounded character out of the big name by discovering the origins of his or her art or craft, the often complicated or tortuous route that was taken to fame. They interview numerous sources among the subject's friends and enemies, parents and siblings, fellow professionals and old teachers, children, ex-wives or former husbands, and discarded lovers. The point of all this work is not to dish dirt, but to make intelligent connections between the life and the art.

A good writer of celebrity profiles follows in a fine tradition. Lytton Strachey's *Eminent Victorians* should be the model for the form: The pieces are well researched, witty, intelligent, and add to our understanding not only of the human beings sitting for Strachey's pen but of the era to which they belonged. From St. Clair McKelway to Gay Talese, Lillian Ross to David Halberstam, Joseph Mitchell to Richard Ben Cramer, journalists have shown how varied, powerful, and humane the form can be, and how it can help us understand our own times—in some rare cases, ourselves.

Most of the finest writers of big-name profiles work in other forms of journalism; they have covered wars, or sports, or foreign affairs. Jimmy Breslin, for example, is one of the greatest of all newspaper columnists; he has also written superb profiles. David Remnick was a fine foreign correspondent for the *Washington Post*; he also gives us profiles in the *New Yorker* that always enlarge our understanding of the subjects. Such journalists are properly humble about what they are doing. Because they have had wide experience of the real world, they have a sense of proportion about the big names. They have no interest in being publicists but are not afraid to celebrate human beings who have added something valuable to the world. They are also uninterested in working as hangmen, and for the same reason: that sense of proportion. They know that no profile can ever go as deeply into the secret places of the human heart as great fiction can. People lie to themselves as well as to others. The journalist is always a prisoner of what he or she is told. The truth is always elusive. But a proper humility on the part of reporters doesn't prevent the making of fine portraits.

That level of celebrity journalism certainly belongs in newspapers, even if it requires a series of articles. The examination of individual celebrities can tell us something about celebrity itself and how it functions in the collective American imagination. It can help readers to understand what they are really looking at when they go to a play or a movie or park in front of a TV set. It can offer guides to young people who are trying to make their own lives. When the reporting and writing are themselves examples of quality, as solidly constructed and handsomely designed as a Mercedes, a subtler message is also conveyed: Quality matters, and this newspaper is a quality product.

Quality is not demonstrated when space is turned over to press agents or when press agents are allowed to dictate the limits of an interview. Quality is not served by publishing unsubstantiated rumors based on single sources. Quality is not honored when a "profile" is the result of one brief interview and a tour of the clips (there is, of course, plenty of room in a newspaper for the one-on-one interview, clearly labeled as such; but the level of the questions must be high, and the interviewer must listen to what is being said by the big name in order to keep moving the talk to a deeper level). Quality is not enforced when significant news stories are deleted, cut to the bone, or shoved into the back of the paper to make room for a photograph of some big name going shopping.

Every celebrity story should be subjected to the same standards applied to stories of crime or politics. Celebrities didn't surrender their constitutional or legal rights when they began to practice their various crafts. It's evidence of naïveté or ignorance to say, "Well, they wanted to be rich and famous, and the paparazzi are part of the price they pay." I've known dozens of actors and actresses over the course of a reasonably long life; virtually none of them had as their primary goal the acquisition of fame and money. Later, as agents and managers and flacks begin to surround them, often cutting them off from "normal" life, fame and money can become more important. But even then, most of them just want the chance to do better and better work. Successful movies help in that ambition because more parts become available to choose from; but they don't get those parts by getting photographed on a nude beach or at a theater opening with a girlfriend.

To qualify as news, celebrities must *do* something. Not only that, they must do something that is surprising, interesting, or new. Mr. Big Name browsing in the Gap among the piles of jeans is not news. If Mr. Big Name throws the former Mrs. Big Name under the Sixth Avenue bus, that is news. Ms. Big Name sitting with friends in a restaurant is not news. If Ms. Big Name takes a job as a salesclerk at Saks, that is news. The proper noun is not enough; there must be a verb.

It is absolutely valid for a newspaper to report on big names when they get arrested, divorced, trampled by crazed fans, run over by taxis, or killed. Those are verbs to respect. It might even be news when a big name is given a ticket for speeding on some highway at midnight; it is just not *important* news and can be run as a box in the back of the newspaper. But large or small, the stories must be journalism. The most popular celebrity genre is also the most dangerous: the big name in trouble. Newspapers must ensure that the stories are true, or as close to truth as the imperfect tools of reporting can make them. They must be multiply sourced, not completely dependent upon versions of the event presented by cops or prosecutors. These days, newspapers should be very wary of charges of a sexual nature. If a woman's name is shielded by law, the celebrity is particularly vulnerable; basic fairness demands that the charges—and the person making them—be scrutinized in the toughest possible way. One basic rule of journalism is: *Things ain't always what they seem to be.* Even more important, perhaps, is this one: *If you want it to be true, it usually isn't.*

To guard against destroying the reputation of a celebrity, and the credibility of the newspaper itself, editors must be more cautious than ever. Every editor would be wise to mount in the city room large photographs of Richard Jewell, the security guard convicted by the press of the bombing at the 1996 Olympics, and Michael Irvin and Erik Williams of the Dallas Cowboys, convicted in the press of sexually assaulting a young woman. Both stories, as first presented, turned out to be dead wrong. Jewell collected a bundle of money from media organizations as a result. Another maxim that all readers should remember: *In the first twenty-four hours of a big story, about half the facts are wrong.* And editors must also keep clearly in mind that charges are not investigations; investigations are not indictments; indictments are not convictions.

The celebrity virus has infected many people who are supposed to be more neutral. This is the age of the prosecutor, not the defense attorney. Thirty years ago, Perry Mason served as counsel for the defense in the American imagination. Now TV shows glorify the cops and the prosecutors. And real-life prosecutors, like real-life cops, watch these shows. They also look at television news. They read the newspapers. They see what editors believe is important. If a legal process can be transformed into a drama with a basic conflict, white hats up against black hats, they will make it into the newspapers. If they can assemble enough facts, no matter how circumstantial or spurious, to indict a big name, they will be famous. There will be a chance of cashing in the greatest of all American lotto tickets, the book deal (in the O. J. Simpson murder trial, the prosecutor, who lost, made a bigger score than the defense attorney, who won). Beyond that, they can run for higher office: In the world of celebrity, anything is possible.

Newspapers shouldn't be feeding this process. One of their roles in an era when fact keeps blending with or imitating fiction should be to separate myth from reality. And yet those myths are powerful. When I was a kid, I was as susceptible to the movie version of the newspaperman myth as any cop or prosecutor is to his or her own myth. At least once a year, I still watch the video of *Deadline U.S.A.*, with Humphrey Bogart as the tough, fearless editor of a dying (of course!) newspaper; it reminds me of the emotions and ambitions that drew me to the newspaper business in the first place. I know that there is a vast gap between a wonderful fiction and the practice of a difficult craft, but if we don't recognize the myths that drive us, we get in trouble. That recognition should make us all pause. Kenneth Starr, in his obsessive pursuit of Bill Clinton, should have wondered if he was becoming Inspector Javert of *Les Misérables*.

Still, the myths can be useful. One article of faith in the reporter's myth is that we must let the chips fall where they may. We are not fans. We can't write about big names as if we were looking for autographs. We can't take an active part in the process of turning prosecutors into big names in return for that curse of the reporting craft, *access*. It is better to lose a story than to become an unpaid flack for any public figure. When there are undisclosed factors in the relationships between reporters and the people they cover, the reader is being cheated. Eventually, the swindle becomes clear and credibility is a casualty.

Long-term credibility must always be considered when editors decide how to cover the professional activities of big names. The way a story is played, the space awarded to it, and the tone of the text are all messages to the readers. Just because the Spice Girls are the show-business phenomenon of the month, newspapers are not obliged to hand-deliver page after breathless page to the act's publicity machine. Let them buy ads. Certainly there is room in the features section to explain how the act was created and cast, to explain that it did not grow organically from shared friendships and love of music. Editors can ask reporters to make well-defined parallels to similarly concocted show-business acts, from the Monkees and Menudo to the silicone glories of *Baywatch*. They can underline the differences, too. It is legitimate to look at the Spice Girls as a triumph of marketing, not art. Psychologists can discuss the phenomenon, lyrics can be analyzed. But all must be within the broad context of hard reporting. Newspapers are not in the business of selling CDs; to do so in the guise of reporting news is a form of consumer fraud. To simply run pictures of five hot babes, with text that sounds like advertising copy, is a form of journalistic lip-synching.

The typical publisher's reply to such complaints would be a combination of three sentences: (1) "Lighten up"; (2) "Who does it hurt?" and (3) "The readers can't get enough of these chicks." But hard reporting doesn't have to be written with a heavy hand; telling the story of a show-business act doesn't have to sound like a report on the civil war in Rwanda. Lightness of touch is a great gift. But newspaper stories that are simpleminded, cheap, mindless, and trivial *can* be hurtful. They hurt the credibility of the newspaper. When publicity handouts are dressed up as stories and crowd out real reporting on education, politics, or the environment, hurt is done to the entire newspaper. It becomes thinner; its spine of substance is weakened; it looks as if it is pandering. And   we don't really know if such stories, done this way, *are* what the readers want. In a variety of polls, readers have said what they want: ongoing scrutiny of public officials; news about education, the environment, and their own communities. Everything else is of much less interest, including gossip and celebrity reporting. But if an editor cites these studies to a publisher, the publisher usually replies, "That's because they're ashamed to admit they like this stuff." In my experience, publishers have almost no direct contact with the readers and have no way of knowing whether such an assumption is true. But if it *were* true, then why waste money on expensive polls? The money could be better spent on hiring reporters. And if the publishers are right about what readers want, why is circulation at so many newspapers stagnant or in decline?

Again, one reason for reader indifference is content. Loading down a newspaper with trivialities at the expense of substance sends out a clear message: The reader is dumb, or at least a little simple. And as a simpleton, says the logic of the assumption, the reader has an endless appetite for shit. Publishers and editors who wouldn't consider for a minute the purchase of a third-rate car or a third-rate suit of clothes are too often engaged in making a third-rate product of their own and knowingly sending it out to the public. Sooner or later, the reader wises up. Sometimes sooner. Always later.

In any popular newspaper, there must be room for stories that are light or funny, about subjects that are less than earthshaking. In the same way, in a department store, there is room for toys and games, not just apparel and appliances. These stories can be done with high style. They can be sassy. They can make a city laugh. But they just have to be journalism. At their core, they too must have an interesting verb. There can't be different standards in different sections of the same newspaper. The reader doesn't finish with the news section and then accept that everything else is less than true. The readers want to believe that it's *all* true. It's just not all of the same importance. Put the Spice Girls on page three and the story of the cuts in library funds on page twenty-eight and you are making a statement about relative importance. You are also making a comment about those readers you so desperately want and for whom you have such utter contempt.

Questions for Reading and Analysis

1. What does Hamill mean by "celebrity virus"? Define the term in your own words.

2. How does Hamill define real journalism against what he calls "celebrity journalism"? What are the true journalist's responsibilities in reporting on a subject (even if the subject is a celebrity)? What does Hamill mean when he says that news "must be a verb"?

3. What evidence does he give to support his points about what good journalism should do? Do you find his evidence convincing?

4. Do you agree with Hamill's claim that celebrity journalism both diminishes the quality of a newspaper and shows contempt for its readers?

An expert on jazz, Hentoff turned towards education and free speech issues in the seventies and has received several awards for his writing in this field. The following essay, first published in the Progressive *in 1983, uses an impressive array of examples to demonstrate that censorship is practiced as freely by political liberals as by their conservative counterparts.*

When Nice People Burn Books

Nat Hentoff

It happened one splendid Sunday morning in a church. Not Jerry Falwell's[1] Baptist sanctuary in Lynchburg, Virginia, but rather the First Unitarian Church in Baltimore. On October 4, 1981, midway through the 11 A.M. service, pernicious ideas were burned at the altar.

As reported by Frank P. L. Somerville, religion editor of the *Baltimore Sun*, "Centuries of Jewish, Christian, Islamic, and Hindu writings were 'expurgated'—because of sections described as 'sexist.'

"Touched off by a candle and consumed in a pot on a table in front of the altar were slips of paper containing 'patriarchal' excerpts from Martin Luther, Thomas Aquinas, the Koran, St. Augustine, St. Ambrose, St. John Chrysostom, the Hindu Code of Manu V, an anonymous Chinese author, and the Old Testament."[2] Also hurled into the purifying fire were works by Kierkegaard and Karl Barth.[3]

The congregation was much exalted: "As the last flame died in the pot, and the organ pealed, there was applause," Somerville wrote.

I reported this news of the singed holy spirit to a group of American Civil Liberties Union members in California, and one woman was furious. At me.

"We did the same thing at our church two Sundays ago," she said. "And long past time, too. Don't you understand it's just *symbolic*?"

I told this ACLU member that when the school board in Drake, North Dakota, threw thirty-four copies of Kurt Vonnegut's *Slaughterhouse Five* into the furnace in 1973, it wasn't because the school was low on fuel. That burning was symbolic, too. Indeed, the two pyres—in North Dakota and in Baltimore—were witnessing to the same lack of faith in the free exchange of ideas.

What an inspiring homily for the children attending services at a liberated church: They now know that the way to handle ideas they don't like is to set them on fire.

The stirring ceremony in Baltimore is just one more illustration that the spirit of the First Amendment is not being savaged only by malign forces of the Right, whether private or governmental. Campaigns to purge school libraries, for example, have

199

been conducted by feminists as well as by Phyllis Schlafly.[4] Yet, most liberal watch-dogs of our freedom remain fixed on the Right as *the* enemy of free expression.

For a salubrious change, therefore, let us look at what is happening to freedom of speech and press in certain enclaves—some colleges, for instance—where the New Right has no clout at all. Does the pulse of the First Amendment beat more vigorously in these places than where the Yahoos[5] are?

Well, consider what happened when Eldridge Cleaver[6] came to Madison, Wisconsin, last October to savor the exhilarating openness of dialogue at the University of Wisconsin. Cleaver's soul is no longer on ice; it's throbbing instead with a religious conviction that is currently connected financially, and presumably theologically, to the Reverend Sun Myung Moon's Unification Church. In Madison, Cleaver never got to talk about his pilgrim's progress from the Black Panthers to the wondrously ecumenical Moonies. In the Humanities Building—*Humanities*—several hundred students and others outraged by Cleaver's apostasy shouted, stamped their feet, chanted "Sieg Heil," and otherwise prevented him from being heard.

After ninety minutes of the din, Cleaver wrote on the blackboard, "I regret that the totalitarians have deprived us of our constitutional rights to free assembly and free speech. Down with communism. Long live democracy."

And, raising a clenched fist while blowing kisses with his free hand, Cleaver left. Cleaver says he'll try to speak again, but he doesn't know when.

The University of Wisconsin administration, through Dean of Students Paul Ginsberg, deplored the behavior of the campus totalitarians of the Left, and there was a fiercely denunciatory editorial in the Madison *Capital Times*: "These people lack even the most primitive appreciation of the Bill of Rights."

It did occur to me, however, that if Eldridge Cleaver had not abandoned his secularist rage at the American Leviathan and had come to Madison as the still burning spear of black radicalism, the result might have been quite different if he had been shouted down that night by young apostles of the New Right. That would have made news around the country, and there would have been collectively signed letters to the *New York Review of Books* and *The Nation* warning of the prowling dangers to free speech in the land. But since Cleaver has long since taken up with bad companions, there is not much concern among those who used to raise bail for him as to whether he gets to speak freely or not.

A few years ago, William F. Buckley, Jr.,[7] invited to be commencement speaker at Vassar, was told by student groups that he not only would be shouted down if he came but might also suffer some contusions. All too few liberal members of the Vassar faculty tried to educate their students about the purpose of a university, and indeed a good many faculty members joined in the protests against Buckley's coming. He finally decided not to appear because, he told me, he didn't want to spoil the day for the parents. I saw no letters on behalf of Buckley's free-speech rights in any of the usual liberal forums for such concerns. After all, he had not only taken up with bad companions; he was an original bad companion.

During the current academic year, there were dismaying developments concerning freedom for bad ideas in the college press. The managing editor of *The Daily Lobo*, the University of New Mexico's student newspaper, claimed in an editorial that Scholastic Aptitude Test scores show minority students to be academically inferior. Rather than rebut his facile misinterpretation of what those scores actually show—that class, not race, affects the results—black students and their sympathizers invaded the newspaper's office.

The managing editor prudently resigned, but the protesters were not satisfied. They wanted the head of the editor. The brave Student Publications Board temporarily suspended her, although the chairman of the journalism department had claimed the suspension was a violation of her First Amendment rights. She was finally given her job back, pending a formal hearing, but she decided to quit. The uproar had not abated, and who knew what would happen at her formal hearing before the Student Publications Board?

When it was all over, the chairman of the journalism department observed that the confrontation had actually reinforced respect for First Amendment rights on the University of New Mexico campus because infuriated students now knew they couldn't successfully insist on the firing of an editor because of what had been published.

What about the resignations? Oh, they were free-will offerings.

I subscribe to most of the journalism reviews around the country, but I saw no offer of support to those two beleaguered student editors in New Mexico from professional journalists who invoke the First Amendment at almost any public opportunity.

Then there was a free-speech war at Kent State University, as summarized in the November 12, 1982, issue of *National On-Campus Report*. Five student groups at Kent State are vigorously attempting to get the editor of the student newspaper fired. They are: "gay students, black students, the undergraduate and graduate student governments, and a progressive student alliance."

Not a reactionary among them. Most are probably deeply concerned with the savaging of the free press in Chile, Uruguay, Guatemala, South Africa, and other such places.

What had this editor at Kent State done to win the enmity of so humanistic a grand alliance? He had written an editorial that said that a gay student group should not have access to student-fee money to sponsor a Hallowe'en dance. Ah, but how had he gone about making his point?

"In opening statements," says the *National On-Campus Report*, "he employed words like 'queer' and 'nigger' to show that prejudice against any group is undesirable." Just like Lenny Bruce.[8] Lenny, walking on stage in a club, peering into the audience, and asking, "Any spics here tonight? Any kikes? Any niggers?"

Do you think Lenny Bruce could get many college bookings today? Or write a column for a college newspaper?

In any case, the rest of the editorial went on to claim that the proper use of student fees was for educational, not social, activities. The editor was not singling out the Kent Gay/Lesbian Foundation. He was opposed to *any* student organization using those fees for dances.

Never mind. He had used impermissible words. Queer. Nigger. And those five influential cadres of students are after his head. The editor says that university officials have assured him, however, that he is protected at Kent State by the First Amendment. If that proves to be the case, those five student groups will surely move to terminate, if not defenestrate, those university officials.

It is difficult to be a disciple of James Madison on campus these days. Take the case of Phyllis Schlafly and Wabash College. The college is a small, well-regarded liberal arts institution in Crawfordsville, Indiana. In the spring of 1981, the college was riven with discord. Some fifty members of the ninety-odd faculty and staff wrote a stiff letter to the Wabash Lecture Series Committee, which had displayed the exceedingly poor taste to invite Schlafly to speak on campus the next year.

The faculty protesters complained that having the Sweetheart of the Right near the Wabash River would be "unfortunate and inappropriate." The dread Schlafly is "an ERA opponent . . . a far-right attorney who travels the country, being highly paid to tell women to stay at home fulfilling traditional roles while sending their sons off to war."

Furthermore, the authors wrote, "The point of view she represents is that of an ever-decreasing minority of American women and men, and is based in sexist mythology which promulgates beliefs inconsistent with those held by liberally educated persons, and this does not merit a forum at Wabash College under the sponsorship of our Lecture Series."

This is an intriguing document by people steeped in the traditions of academic freedom. One of the ways of deciding who gets invited to a campus is the speaker's popularity. If the speaker appeals only to a "decreasing minority of American women and men," she's not worth the fee. So much for Dorothy Day,[9] were she still with us.

And heaven forbid that anyone be invited whose beliefs are "inconsistent with those held by liberally educated persons." Mirror, mirror on the wall. . . .

But do not get the wrong idea about these protesting faculty members: "We subscribe," they emphasized, "to the principles of free speech and free association, of course."

All the same, "it does not enhance our image as an all-male college to endorse a well-known sexist by inviting her to speak on our Campus." If Phyllis Schlafly is invited nonetheless, "we intend not to participate in any of the activities surrounding Ms. Schlafly's visit and will urge others to do the same."

The moral of the story: If you don't like certain ideas, boycott them.

The lecture committee responded to the fifty deeply offended faculty members in a most unkind way. The committee told the signers that "William Buckley would endorse your petition. No institution of higher learning, he told us on a visit here, should allow to be heard on its campus any position that it regards as detrimental or 'untrue.'

"Apparently," the committee went on, "error is to be refuted not by rational persuasion, but by censorship."

Phyllis Schlafly did come to Wabash and she generated a great deal of discussion—most of it against her views—among members of the all-male student body. However, some of the wounded faculty took a long time to recover. One of them, a tenured professor, took aside at a social gathering the wife of a member of the lecture committee that had invited Schlafly. Both were in the same feminist group on campus.

The professor cleared her throat, and said to the other woman, "You are going to leave him, aren't you?"

"My husband? Why should I leave him?"

"Really, how can you stay married to someone who invited Phyllis Schlafly to this campus?"

And really, should such a man even be allowed visitation rights with the children?

Then there is the Ku Klux Klan. As Klan members have learned in recent months, both in Boston and in Washington, their First Amendment right peaceably to assemble—let alone actually to speak their minds—can only be exercised if they are prepared to be punched in the mouth. Klan members get the same reception that Martin Luther King, Jr,. and his associates used to receive in Bull Conner's Birmingham.

As all right-thinking people know, however, the First Amendment isn't just for anybody. That presumably is why the administration of the University of Cincinnati has refused this year to allow the KKK to appear on campus. Bill Wilkerson, the Imperial Wizard of the particular Klan faction that has been barred from the University of Cincinnati, says he's going to sue on First Amendment grounds.

Aside from the ACLU's, how many *amicus* briefs do you think the Imperial Wizard is likely to get from liberal organizations devoted to academic freedom?

The Klan also figures in a dismaying case from Vancouver, Washington. There, an all-white jury awarded $1,000 to a black high school student after he had charged the Battle Ground School District (including Prairie High School) with discrimination. One of the claims was that the school had discriminated against this young man by permitting white students to wear Ku Klux Klan costumes to a Hallowe'en assembly.

Symbolic speech, however, is like spoken or written speech. It is protected under the First Amendment. If the high school administration had originally forbidden the wearing of the Klan costumes to the Hallowe'en assembly, it would have spared itself that part of the black student's lawsuit, but it would have set a precedent for censoring symbolic speech which would have shrunken First Amendment protections at Prairie High School.

What should the criteria be for permissible costumes at a Hallowe'en assembly? None that injure the feelings of another student? So a Palestinian kid couldn't wear a PLO outfit. Or a Jewish kid couldn't come as Ariel Sharon,[10] festooned with maps. And watch out for the wise guy who comes dressed as that all-round pain-in-the-ass, Tom Paine.[11]

School administrators might say the best approach is to have no costumes at all. That way, there'll be no danger of disruption. But if there were real danger of physical confrontation in the school when a student wears a Klan costume, is the school so powerless that it can't prevent a fight? And indeed, what a compelling opportunity the costumes present to teach about the Klan, to ask those white kids who wore Klan costumes what they know of the history of the Klan. To get black and white kids *talking* about what the Klan represents, in history—and right now.

Such teaching is too late for Prairie High School. After that $1,000 award to the black student, the white kids who have been infected by Klan demonology will circulate their poison only among themselves, intensifying their sickness of spirit. There will be no more Klan costumes in that school, and so no more Klan costumes to stimulate class discussion.

By the way, in the trial, one offer of proof that the school district had been guilty of discrimination was a photograph of four white boys wearing Klan costumes to that Hallowe'en assembly. It's a rare picture. It was originally printed in the school yearbook but, with the lawsuit and all, the picture was cut out of each yearbook before it was distributed.

That's the thing about censorship, whether good liberals or bad companions engage in it. Censorship is like a greased pig. Hard to confine. You start trying to deal with offensive costumes and you wind up with a blank space in the yearbook. Isn't that just like the Klan? Causing decent people to do dumb things.

Endnotes

1. Minister and political activist identified with the Moral Majority.
2. Respected religious writers and works of the past.
3. Contemporary philosophers.
4. Activist opposed to views generally considered "feminist."
5. Brutish, uncivilized human characters in Book IV of Swift's eighteenth-century satire *Gullivers' Travels.*
6. Member of a radical group, jailed as a young man, and author of a book written in prison, titled *Soul on Ice.*
7. Outspoken conservative, editor of the *National Review.*
8. Comedian of biting humor popular in the 60s and early 70s.
9. Founder of the Catholic Workers Union and active feminist (1897–1980) who protested for women's suffrage.
10. Former Israeli Defense Minister held responsible for a massacre of Palestinian Christian refugees.
11. Supporter of the American and French Revolutions and author of *Common Sense.*

Questions for Reading and Analysis

1. What is Hentoff's main argument?
2. Hentoff develops his argument carefully, establishing the truth of his initial claim before moving on to his larger point. What is his initial claim and how does he support it?
3. How would Hentoff respond to those who, in the name of political correctness, would approve of censorship in certain cases?
4. Why does Hentoff reject the argument about burning the writing of others as a symbolic act?
5. How does Hentoff use irony throughout the essay?
6. Do you agree with Hentoff? How would you go about refuting his argument?

Thomas Jefferson (1743–1826), third President of the United States, drafted the Declaration of Independence in 1776, one of the few of his many accomplishments for which he claimed to want to be remembered. Jefferson's original draft blamed the British people directly for tolerating George III's tyranny in America and also included a strong anti-slavery statement although neither passage survived Congress's revisions. The Declaration of Independence serves as a classic example of deductive reasoning.

The Declaration of Independence

Thomas Jefferson

When in the course of human events, it becomes necessary for one people to dissolve the political bands which have connected them with another, and to assume among the powers of the earth, the separate and equal station to which the Laws of Nature and of Nature's God entitle them, a decent respect to the opinions of mankind requires that they should declare the causes which impel them to the separation.

We hold these truths to be self-evident, that all men are created equal, that they are endowed by their Creator with certain inalienable rights, that among these are life, liberty, and the pursuit of happiness. That to secure these rights, governments are instituted among men, deriving their just powers from the consent of the governed. That whenever any form of government becomes destructive of these ends, it is the right of the people to alter or to abolish it, and to institute new government, laying its foundation on such principles and organizing its powers in such form, as to them shall seem most likely to effect their safety and happiness. Prudence, indeed, will dictate that governments long established should not be changed for light and transient causes; and accordingly all experience hath shown, that mankind are more disposed to suffer, while evils are sufferable, than to right themselves by abolishing the forms to which they are accustomed. But when a long train of abuses and usurpations, pursuing invariably the same object, evinces a design to reduce them under absolute despotism, it is their right, it is their duty, to throw off such government, and to provide new guards for their future security. Such has been the patient sufferance of these Colonies; and such is now the necessity which constrains them to alter their former systems of government. The history of the present King of Great Britain is a history of repeated injuries and usurpations, all having in direct object the establishment of an absolute tyranny over these States. To prove this, let facts be submitted to a candid world.

He has refused his assent to laws, the most wholesome and necessary for the public good.

He has forbidden his Governors to pass laws of immediate and pressing importance, unless suspended in their operation till his assent should be obtained; and when so suspended, he has utterly neglected to attend to them.

He has refused to pass other laws for the accommodation of large districts of people, unless those people would relinquish the right of representation in the legislature, a right inestimable to them and formidable to tyrants only.

He has called together legislative bodies at places unusual, uncomfortable, and distant from the depository of their public records, for the sole purpose of fatiguing them into compliance with his measures.

He has dissolved representative houses repeatedly, for opposing with manly firmness his invasions on the rights of the people.

He has refused for a long time, after such dissolutions, to cause others to be elected; whereby the legislative powers, incapable of annihilation, have returned to the people at large for their exercise; the State remaining in the meantime exposed to all the dangers of invasion from without and convulsions within.

He has endeavoured to prevent the population of these States; for that purpose obstructing the laws for naturalization of foreigners; refusing to pass others to encourage their migration hither, and raising the conditions of new appropriations of lands.

He has obstructed the administration of justice, by refusing his assent to laws for establishing judiciary powers.

He has made judges dependent on his will alone, for the tenure of their offices, and the amount and payment of their salaries.

He has erected a multitude of new offices, and sent hither swarms of officers to harass our people, and eat out their substance.

He has kept among us, in times of peace, standing armies without the consent of our legislatures.

He has affected to render the military independent of and superior to the civil power.

He has combined with others to subject us to a jurisdiction foreign of our constitution, and unacknowledged by our laws; giving his assent to their acts of pretended legislation:

For quartering large bodies of armed troops among us:

For protecting them, by a mock trial, from punishment for any murders which they should commit on the inhabitants of these States:

For cutting off our trade with all parts of the world:

For imposing taxes on us without our consent:

For depriving us in many cases of the benefits of trial by jury:

For transporting us beyond seas to be tried for pretended offences:

For abolishing the free system of English laws in a neighboring Province, establishing therein an arbitrary government, and enlarging its boundaries so as to render it at once an example and fit instrument for introducing the same absolute rule into these Colonies:

For taking away our Charters, abolishing our most valuable laws, and altering fundamentally the forms of our governments:

For suspending our own legislatures, and declaring themselves invested with power to legislate for us in all cases whatsoever.

He has abdicated government here, by declaring us out of his protection, and waging war against us.

He has plundered our seas, ravaged our coasts, burnt our towns, and destroyed the lives of our people.

He is at this time transporting large armies of foreign mercenaries to complete the works of death, desolation, and tyranny, already begun with circumstances of cruelty and perfidy scarcely paralleled in the most barbarous ages, and totally unworthy the head of a civilized nation.

He has constrained our fellow citizens taken captive on the high seas to bear arms against their country, to become the executioners of their friends and brethren, or to fall themselves by their hands.

He has excited domestic insurrections among us, and has endeavored to bring on the inhabitants of our frontiers, the merciless Indian savages, whose known rule of warfare, is an undistinguished destruction of all ages, sexes and conditions.

In every stage of these oppressions we have petitioned for redress in the most humble terms: our repeated petitions have been answered only by repeated injury. A prince whose character is thus marked by every act which may define a tyrant is unfit to be the ruler of a free people.

Nor have we been wanting in attention to our British brethren. We have warned them from time to time of attempts by their legislature to extend an unwarrantable jurisdiction over us. We have reminded them of the circumstances of our emigration and settlement here. We have appealed to their native justice and magnanimity, and we have conjured them by the ties of our common kindred to disavow these usurpations, which would inevitably interrupt our connections and correspondence. They too have been deaf to the voice of justice and consanguinity. We must, therefore, acquiesce in the necessity which denounces our separation, and hold them, as we hold the rest of mankind, enemies in war, in peace friends.

We, therefore, the Representatives of the United States of America, in General Congress assembled, appealing to the Supreme Judge of the world for the rectitude of our intentions, do, in the name, and by authority of the good people of these Colonies, solemnly publish and declare, that these United Colonies are, and of right ought to be, Free and Independent States; that they are absolved from all allegiance to the British Crown, and that all political connection between them and the state of Great Britain, is and ought to be totally dissolved; and that as Free and Independent States, they have full power to levy war, conclude peace, contract alliances, establish commerce, and to do all other acts and things which Independent States may of right do. And for the support of this declaration, with a firm reliance on the protection of Divine Providence, we mutually pledge to each other our lives, our fortunes, and our sacred honor.

Questions for Reading and Analysis

1. Summarize the logical premises of The Declaration of Independence.

2. Within Jefferson's argument is a long section of inductive reasoning. What argument must he establish, using facts, before proceeding to his conclusion? Is the evidence adequate?

3. What do you think is the most important sentence in the Declaration?

A regular contributor to The New Yorker *and author of two books—*Typical American *(1991) and* Mona in the Promised Land *(1996), Gish Jen keeps coming back to the same question: What does it mean to be an American? The story "What Means Switch," first published in the* Atlantic Monthly *in 1990, examines the question from the point of view of a 13-year-old Chinese-American girl who befriends a Japanese classmate.*

What Means Switch

Gish Jen

There we are, nice Chinese family—father, mother, two born-here girls. Where should we live next? My parents slide the question back and forth like a cup of ginseng neither one wants to drink. Until finally it comes to them, what they really want is a milkshake (chocolate) and to go with it a house in Scarsdale. What else? The broker tries to hint: the neighborhood, she says. Moneyed. Many delis. Meaning rich and Jewish. But someone has sent my parents a list of the top ten schools nation-wide (based on the opinion of selected educators and others) and so *many-deli* or not we nestle into a Dutch colonial on the Bronx River Parkway. The road's windy where we are, very charming; drivers miss their turns, plow up our flower beds, then want to use our telephone. "Of course," my mom tells them, like it's no big deal, we can replant. We're the type to adjust. You know—the lady drivers weep, my mom gets out the Kleenex for them. We're a bit down the hill from the private plane set, in other words. Only in our dreams do our jacket zippers jam, what with all the lift tickets we have stapled to them, Killington on top of Sugarbush on top of Stowe, and we don't even know where the Virgin Islands are—although certain of us do know that virgins are like priests and nuns, which there were a lot more of in Yonkers, where we just moved from, than there are here.

This is my first understanding of class. In our old neighborhood everybody knew everything about virgins and non-virgins, not to say the technicalities of staying in between. Or almost everybody, I should say; in Yonkers I was the laugh-along type. Here I'm an expert.

"You mean the man . . . ?" Pig-tailed Barbara Gugelstein spits a mouthful of Coke back into her can. "That is *so* gross!"

Pretty soon I'm getting popular for a new girl. The only problem is Danielle Meyers, who wears blue mascara and has gone steady with two boys. "How do *you* know," she starts to ask, proceeding to edify us all with how she French-kissed one boyfriend and just regular kissed another. ("Because, you know, he had braces.") We hear about his rubber bands, how once one popped right into her mouth. I begin to realize I need to find somebody to kiss too. But how?

Luckily, I just about then happen to tell Barbara Gugelstein I know karate. I don't know why I tell her this. My sister Callie's the liar in the family; ask anybody. I'm the one who doesn't see why we should have to hold our heads up. But for some reason I tell Barbara Gugelstein I can make my hands like steel by thinking hard. "I'm not supposed to tell anyone," I say.

The way she backs away, blinking, I could be the burning bush.

"I can't do bricks," I say—a bit of expectation management. "But I can do your arm if you want." I set my hand in chop position.

"Uhh, it's okay," she says. "I know you can, I saw it on TV last night."

That's when I recall that I too saw it on TV last night—in fact, at her house. I rush on to tell her I know how to get pregnant with tea.

"With *tea?*"

"That's how they do it in China."

She agrees that China is an ancient and great civilization that ought to be known for more than spaghetti and gunpowder. I tell her I know Chinese. "*Be-yeh fa-foon,*" I say. "*Shee-veh. Ji nu.*" Meaning, "Stop acting crazy. Rice gruel. Soy sauce." She's impressed. At lunch the next day, Danielle Meyers and Amy Weinstein and Barbara's crush, Andy Kaplan, are all impressed too. Scarsdale is a liberal town, not like Yonkers, where the Whitman Road Gang used to throw crabapple mash at my sister Callie and me and tell us it would make our eyes stick shut. Here we're like permanent exchange students. In another ten years, there'll be so many Orientals we'll turn into Asians; a Japanese grocery will buy out that one deli too many. But for now, the mid-sixties, what with civil rights on TV, we're not so much accepted as embraced. Especially by the Jewish part of town—which, it turns out, is not all of town at all. That's just an idea people have, Callie says, and lots of them could take us or leave us same as the Christians, who are nice too; I shouldn't generalize. So let me not generalize except to say that pretty soon I've been to so many bar and bas mitzvahs, I can almost say myself whether the kid chants like an angel or like a train conductor, maybe they could use him on the commuter line. At seder I know to forget the bricks, get a good pile of that mortar. Also I know what is schmaltz. I know that I am a goy. This is not why people like me, though. People like me because I do not need to use deodorant, as I demonstrate in the locker room before and after gym. Also, I can explain to them, for example, what is tofu (*der-voo*, we say at home). Their mothers invite me to taste-test their Chinese cooking.

"Very authentic." I try to be reassuring. After all, they're nice people, I like them. "De-lish." I have seconds. On the question of what we eat, though, I have to admit, "Well, no, it's different than that." I have thirds. "What my mom makes is home style, it's not in the cookbooks."

Not in the cookbooks! Everyone's jealous. Meanwhile, the big deal at home is when we have turkey pot pie. My sister Callie's the one introduced them—Mrs. Wilder's, they come in this green-and-brown box—and when we have them, we both get suddenly interested in helping out in the kitchen. You know, we stand in front of the oven and help them bake. Twenty-five minutes. She and I have a deal, though, to keep it secret from school, as everybody else thinks they're gross. We think they're a big improvement over authentic Chinese home cooking. Oxtail soup—now that's gross. Stir-fried beef with tomatoes. One day I say, "You know Ma, I have never seen a stir-fried tomato in any Chinese restaurant we have ever been in, ever."

"In China," she says, real lofty, "we consider tomatoes are a delicacy."

"Ma," I say. "Tomatoes are *Italian*."

"No respect for elders." She wags her finger at me, but I can tell it's just to try and shame me into believing her. "I'm tell you, tomatoes *invented* in China."

"*Ma*."

"Is true. Like noodles. Invented in China."

"That's not what they said in *school*."

"In *China*," my mother counters, "we also eat tomatoes uncooked, like apple. And in summertime we slice them, and put some sugar on top."

"Are you sure?"

My mom says of course she's sure, and in the end I give in, even though she once told me that China was such a long time ago, a lot of things she can hardly remember. She said sometimes she has trouble remembering her characters, that sometimes she'll be writing a letter, just writing along, and all of a sudden she won't be sure if she should put four dots or three.

"So what do you do then?"

"Oh, I just make a little sloppy."

"You mean you *fudge*?"

She laughed then, but another time, when she was showing me how to write my name, and I said, just kidding, "Are you sure that's the right number of dots now?" she was hurt.

"I mean, of course you know," I said. "I mean, *oy*."

Meanwhile, what *I* know is that in the eighth grade, what people want to hear does not include how Chinese people eat sliced tomatoes with sugar on top. For a gross fact, it just isn't gross enough. On the other hand, the fact that somewhere in China somebody eats or has eaten or once ate living monkey brains—now that's conversation.

"They have these special tables," I say, "kind of like a giant collar. With a hole in the middle, for the monkey's neck. They put the monkey in the collar, and then they cut off the top of its head."

"Whadda they use for cutting?"

I think. "Scalpels."

"*Scalpels*?" says Andy Kaplan.

"Kaplan, don't be dense," Barbara Gugelstein says. "The Chinese *invented* scalpels."

Once a friend said to me, You know, everybody is valued for something. She explained how some people resented being valued for their looks; others resented being valued for their money. Wasn't it still better to be beautiful and rich than ugly and poor, though? You should be just glad, she said, that you have something people value. It's like having a special talent, like being good at ice-skating, or opera-singing. She said, You could probably make a career out of it.

Here's the irony: I am.

211

Anyway. I am ad-libbing my way through eighth grade, as I've described. Until one bloomy spring day, I come in late to homeroom, and to my chagrin discover there's a new kid in class.

Chinese.

So what should I do, pretend to have to go to the girls' room, like Barbara Gugelstein the day Andy Kaplan took his ID back? I sit down; I am so cool I remind myself of Paul Newman. First thing I realize, though, is that no one looking at me is thinking of Paul Newman. The notes fly:

"*I think he's cute.*"

"Who?" I write back. (I am still at an age, understand, when I believe a person can be saved by aplomb.)

"I don't think he talks English too good. Writes it either."

"Who?"

"They might have to put him behind a grade, so don't worry."

"He has a crush on you already, you could tell as soon as you walked in, he turned kind of orangeish."

I hope I'm not turning orangeish as I deal with my mail; I could use a secretary. The second round starts:

"What do you mean who? Don't be weird. Didn't you *see* him??? Straight back over your right shoulder!!!!"

I have to look; what else can I do? I think of certain tips I learned in Girl Scouts about poise. I cross my ankles. I hold a pen in my hand. I sit up as though I have a crown on my head. I swivel my head slowly, repeating to myself, *I could be Miss America.*

"Miss Mona Chang."

Horror raises its hoary head.

"Notes, please."

Mrs. Mandeville's policy is to read all notes aloud.

I try to consider what Miss America would do, and see myself, back straight, knees together, crying. Some inspiration. Cool Hand Luke, on the other hand, would, quick, eat the evidence. And why not? I should yawn as I stand up, and boom, the notes are gone. All that's left is to explain that it's an old Chinese reflex.

I shuffle up to the front of the room.

"One minute please," Mrs. Mandeville says.

I wait, noticing how large and plastic her mouth is.

She unfolds a piece of paper.

And I, Miss Mona Chang, who got almost straight A's her whole life except in math and conduct, am about to start crying in front of everyone.

I am delivered out of hot Egypt by the bell. General pandemonium. Mrs. Mandeville still has her hand clamped on my shoulder, though. And the next thing I know, I'm holding the new boy's schedule. He's standing next to me like a big blank piece of paper. "This is Sherman," Mrs. Mandeville says.

"Hello," I say.

"*Non how a,*" I say.

I'm glad Barbara Gugelstein isn't there to see my Chinese in action.

"*Ji nu,*" I say. "*Shee veh.*"

Later I find out that his mother asked if there were any other Orientals in our grade. She had him put in my class on purpose. For now, though, he looks at me as though I'm much stranger than anything else he's seen so far. Is this because he understands I'm saying "soy sauce rice gruel" to him or because he doesn't?

"Sher-man," he says finally.

I look at his schedule card. Sherman Matsumoto. What kind of name is that for a nice Chinese boy?

(Later on, people ask me how I can tell Chinese from Japanese. I shrug. You just kind of know, I say. *Oy!*)

Sherman's got the sort of looks I think of as prettyboy. Monsignor-black hair (not monk-brown like mine), bouncy. Crayola eyebrows, one with a round bald spot in the middle of it, like a golf hole. I don't know how anybody can think of him as orangeish; his skin looks white to me, with pink triangles hanging down the front of his cheeks like flags. Kind of delicate-looking, but the only truly uncool thing about him is that his spiral notebook has a picture of a kitty cat on it. A big white fluffy one, with a blue ribbon above each perky little ear. I get much opportunity to view this, as all the poor kid understands about life in junior high school is that he should follow me everywhere. It's embarrassing. On the other hand, he's obviously even more miserable than I am, so I try not to say anything. Give him a chance to adjust. We communicate by sign language, and by drawing pictures, which he's better at than I am; he puts in every last detail, even if it takes forever. I try to be patient.

A week of this. Finally I enlighten him. "You should get a new notebook."

His cheeks turn a shade of pink you mostly only see in hyacinths.

"Notebook." I point to his. I show him mine, which is psychedelic, with big purple and yellow stick-on flowers. I try to explain he should have one like this, only without the flowers. He nods enigmatically, and the next day brings me a notebook just like his, except that this cat sports pink bows instead of blue.

"Pret-ty," he says. "You."

He speaks English! I'm dumbfounded. Has he spoken it all this time? I consider: Pretty. You. What does that mean? Plus actually, he's said *plit-ty*, much as my parents would; I'm assuming he means pretty, but maybe he means pity. Pity. You.

"Jeez," I say finally.

"You are wel-come," he says.

I decorate the back of the notebook with stick-on flowers, and hold it so that these show when I walk through the halls. In class I mostly keep my book open, After all, the kid's so new; I think I really ought to have a heart. And for a livelong day nobody notices.

Then Barbara Gugelstein sidles up. "Matching notebooks, huh?"

I'm speechless.

"First comes love, then comes marriage, and then come chappies in a baby carriage."

"Barbara!"

"Get it?" she says. "Chinese Japs."

"Bar-*bra*," I say to get even.

"Just make sure he doesn't give you any *tea*," she says.

Are Sherman and I in love? Three days later, I hazard that we are. My thinking proceeds this way: I think he's cute, and I think he thinks I'm cute. On the other hand, we don't kiss and we don't exactly have fantastic conversations. Our talks *are* getting better, though. We started out, "This is a book." "Book." "This is a chair." "Chair." Advancing to, "What is this?" "This is a book." Now, for fun, he tests me.

"What is this?" he says.

"This is a book," I say, as if I'm the one who has to learn how to talk.

He claps. "Good!"

Meanwhile, people ask me all about him. I could be his press agent.

"No, he doesn't eat raw fish."

"No, his father wasn't a kamikaze pilot."

"No, he can't do karate."

"Are you sure?" somebody asks.

Indeed he doesn't know karate, but judo he does. I am hurt I'm not the one to find this out; the guys know from gym class. They line up to be flipped, he flips them all onto the floor, and after that he doesn't eat lunch at the girls' table with me anymore. I'm more or less glad. Meaning, when he was there, I never knew what to say. Now that he's gone, though, I seem to be stuck at the "This is a chair" level of conversation. Ancient Chinese eating habits have lost their cachet; all I get are more and more questions about me and Sherman. "I dunno," I'm saying all the time. *Are* we going out? We do stuff, it's true. For example, I take him to the department stores, explain to him who shops in Alexander's, who shops in Saks. I tell him my family's the type that shops in Alexander's. He says he's sorry. In Saks he gets lost; either that, or else I'm the lost one. (It's true I find him calmly waiting at the front door, hands behind his back, like a guard.) I take him to the candy store. I take him to the bagel store. Sherman is crazy about bagels. I explain to him that Lender's is gross, he should get his bagels from the bagel store. He says thank you.

"Are you going steady?" people want to know.

How can we go steady when he doesn't have an ID bracelet? On the other hand, he brings me more presents than I think any girl's ever gotten before. Oranges. Flowers. A little bag of bagels. But what do they mean? Do they mean thank you, I enjoyed our trip; do they mean I like you; do they mean I decided I liked the Lender's better even if they are gross, you can have these? Sometimes I think he's acting on his mother's instructions. Also I know at least a couple of the presents were supposed to go to our teachers. He told me that once and turned red. I figured it still might mean something that he didn't throw them out.

More and more now, we joke. Like, instead of "I'm thinking," he always says, "I'm sinking," which we both think is so funny, that all either one of us has to do is pretend to be drowning and the other one cracks up. And he tells me things—for example, that there are electric lights everywhere in Tokyo now.

"You mean you didn't have them before?"

"Everywhere now!" He's amazed too. "Since Olympics!"

"Olympics?"

"1960," he says proudly, and as proof, hums for me the Olympic theme song. "You know?"

"Sure," I say, and hum with him happily. We could be a picture on a UNICEF poster. The only problem is that I don't really understand what the Olympics have to do with the modernization of Japan, any more than I get this other story he tells me, about that hole in his left eyebrow, which is from some time his father accidentally hit him with a lit cigarette. When Sherman was a baby. His father was drunk, having been out carousing; his mother was very mad but didn't say anything, just cleaned the whole house. Then his father was so ashamed he bowed to ask her forgiveness.

"Your mother cleaned the house?"

Sherman nods solemnly.

"And your father *bowed*?" I find this more astounding than anything I ever thought to make up. "That is so weird," I tell him.

"Weird," he agrees. "This I no forget, forever. *Father* bow to *mother*!"

We shake our heads.

As for the things he asks me, they're not topics I ever discussed before. Do I like it here? Of course I like it here, I was born here, I say. Am I Jewish? Jewish! I laugh. *Oy!* Am I American? "Sure I'm American," I say. "Everybody who's born here is American, and also some people who convert from what they were before. You could become American." But he says no, he could never. "Sure you could," I say. "You only have to learn some rules and speeches."

"But I Japanese," he says.

"You could become American anyway," I say. "Like I *could* become Jewish, if I wanted to. I'd just have to switch, that's all."

"But you Catholic," he says.

I think maybe he doesn't get what means switch.

I introduce him to Mrs. Wilder's turkey pot pies. "Gross?" he asks. I say they are, but we like them anyway. "Don't tell anybody." He promises. We bake them, eat them. While we're eating, he's drawing me pictures.

"This American," he says, and he draws something that looks like John Wayne. "This Jewish," he says, and draws something that looks like the Wicked Witch of the West, only male.

"I don't think so," I say.

He's undeterred. "This Japanese," he says, and draws a fair rendition of himself. "This Chinese," he says, and draws what looks to be another fair rendition of himself.

"How can you tell them apart?"

"This way," he says, and he puts the picture of the Chinese so that it is looking at the pictures of the American and the Jew. The Japanese faces the wall. Then he draws another picture, of a Japanese flag, so that the Japanese has that to contemplate. "Chinese lost in department store," he says. "Japanese know how go." For fun, he then takes the Japanese flag and fastens it to the refrigerator door with magnets. "In school, in ceremony, we this way," he explains, and bows to the picture.

When my mother comes in, her face is so red that with the white wall behind her she looks a bit like the Japanese flag herself. Yet I get the feeling I better not say so. First she doesn't move. Then she snatches the flag off the refrigerator, so fast the magnets go flying. Two of them land on the stove. She crumples up the paper. She hisses at Sherman, "*This is the U.S. of A., do you hear me!*"

Sherman hears her.

"You call your mother right now, tell her come pick you up."

He understands perfectly. *I*, on the other hand, am stymied. How can two people who don't really speak English understand each other better than I can understand them? "But Ma," I say.

"Don't *Ma* me," she says.

Later on she explains that World War II was in China, too. "Hitler," I say. "Nazis. Volkswagens." I know the Japanese were on the wrong side, because they bombed Pearl Harbor. My mother explains about before that. The Napkin Massacre. "*Nan*king," she corrects me.

"Are you sure?" I say. "In school, they said the war was about putting the Jews in ovens."

"Also about ovens."

"About both?"

"Both."

"That's not what they said in school."

"*Just forget about school.*"

Forget about school? "I thought we moved here for the schools."

"We moved here," she says, "for your education."

Sometimes I have no idea what she's talking about.

"I like Sherman," I say after a while.

"He's nice boy," she agrees.

Meaning what? I would ask, except that my dad's just come home, which means it's time to start talking about whether we should build a brick wall across the front of the lawn. Recently a car made it almost into our living room, which was so scary, the driver fainted and an ambulance had to come. "We should have discussion," my dad said after that. And so for about a week, every night we do.

"Are you just friends, or more than just friends?" Barbara Gugelstein is giving me the cross-ex.

"Maybe," I say.

"Come on," she says, "I told you *everything* about me and Andy."

I actually *am* trying to tell Barbara everything about Sherman, but everything turns out to be nothing. Meaning, I can't locate the conversation in what I have to say. Sherman and I go places, we talk, one time my mother threw him out of the house because of World War II.

"I think we're just friends," I say.

"You think or you're sure?"

Now that I do less of the talking at lunch, I notice more what other people talk about—cheerleading, who likes who, this place in White Plains to get earrings. On none of these topics am I an expert. Of course, I'm still friends with Barbara Gugelstein, but I notice Danielle Meyers has spun away to other groups.

Barbara's analysis goes this way: To be popular, you have to have big boobs, a note from your mother that lets you use her Lord & Taylor credit card, and a boyfriend. On the other hand, what's so wrong with being unpopular? "We'll get them in the end," she says. It's what her dad tells her. "Like they'll turn out too dumb to do their own investing, and then they'll get killed in fees and then they'll have to move to towns where the schools stink. And my dad should know," she winds up. "He's a broker."

"I guess," I say.

But the next thing I know, I have a true crush on Sherman Matsumoto. *Mister Judo*, the guys call him now, with real respect; and the more they call him that, the more I don't care that he carries a notebook with a cat on it.

I sigh. "Sherman."

"I thought you were just friends," says Barbara Gugelstein.

"We were," I say mysteriously. This, I've noticed, is how Danielle Meyers talks; everything's secret, she only lets out so much, it's like she didn't grow up with everybody telling her she had to share.

And here's the funny thing: The more I intimate that Sherman and I are more than just friends, the more it seems we actually are. It's the old imagination giving reality a nudge. When I start to blush; he starts to blush; we reach a point where we can hardly talk at all.

"Well, there's first base with tongue, and first base without," I tell Barbara Gugelstein.

In fact, Sherman and I have brushed shoulders, which was equivalent to first base I was sure, maybe even second. I felt as though I'd turned into one huge shoulder; that's all I was, one huge shoulder. We not only didn't talk, we didn't breathe. But how can I tell Barbara Gugelstein that? So instead I say, "Well there's second base and second base."

Danielle Meyers is my friend again. She says, "I know exactly what you mean," just to make Barbara Gugelstein feel bad.

"Like *what* do I mean?" I say.

Danielle Meyers can't answer.

"You know what I think?" I tell Barbara the next day. "I think Danielle's giving us a line."

Barbara pulls thoughtfully on one of her pigtails.

If Sherman Matsumoto is never going to give me an ID to wear, he should at least get up the nerve to hold my hand. I don't think he sees this. I think of the story he told me about his parents, and in a synaptic firestorm realize we don't see the same things at all.

So one day, when we happen to brush shoulders again, I don't move away. He doesn't move away either. There we are. Like a pair of bleachers, pushed together but not quite matched up. After a while, I have to breathe, I can't help it. I breathe in such a way that our elbows start to touch too. We are in a crowd, waiting for a bus. I crane my neck to look at the sign that says where the bus is going; now our wrists are touching. Then it happens: He links his pinky around mine.

Is that holding hands? Later, in bed, I wonder all night. One finger, and not even the biggest one.

Sherman is leaving in a month. Already! I think, well, I suppose he will leave and we'll never even kiss. I guess that's all right. Just when I've resigned myself to it, though, we hold hands all five fingers. Once when we are at the bagel shop, then again in my parents' kitchen. Then, when we are at the playground, he kisses the back of my hand.

He does it again not too long after that, in White Plains.

I invest in a bottle of mouthwash.

Instead of moving on, though, he kisses the back of my hand again. And again. I try raising my hand, hoping he'll make the jump from my hand to my cheek. It's like trying to wheedle an inchworm out the window. You know, *This way, this way.*

All over the world, people have their own cultures. That's what we learned in social studies.

If we never kiss, I'm not going to take it personally.

It is the end of the school year. We've had parties. We've turned in our textbooks. Hooray! Outside the asphalt already steams if you spit on it. Sherman isn't leaving for another couple of days, though, and he comes to visit every morning, staying until the afternoon, when Callie comes home from her big-deal job as a bank teller. We drink Kool-Aid in the backyard and hold hands until they are sweaty and make smacking noises coming apart. He tells me how busy his parents are, getting ready for the move. His mother, particularly, is very tired. Mostly we are mournful.

The very last day we hold hands and do not let go. Our palms fill up with water like a blister. We do not care. We talk more than usual. How much airmail is to Japan, that kind of thing. Then suddenly he asks, will I marry him?

I'm only thirteen.

But when old? Sixteen?

If you come back to get me.

I come. Or you can come to Japan, be Japanese.

How can I be Japanese?

Like you become American. Switch.

He kisses me on the cheek, again and again and again.

His mother calls to say she's coming to get him. I cry. I tell him how I've saved every present he's ever given me—the ruler, the pencils, the bags from the bagels, all the flower petals. I even have the orange peels from the oranges.

All?

I put them in a jar.

I'd show him, except that we're not allowed to go upstairs to my room. Anyway, something about the orange peels seems to choke him up too. *Mister Judo,* but I've gotten him in a soft spot. We are going together to the bathroom to get some toilet paper to wipe our eyes when poor tired Mrs. Matsumoto, driving a shiny new station wagon, skids up onto our lawn.

"Very sorry!"

We race outside.

"Very sorry!"

Mrs. Matsumoto is so short that about all we can see of her is a green cotton sun hat, with a big brim. It's tied on. The brim is trembling.

I hope my mom's not going to start yelling about World War II.

"Is all right, no trouble," she says, materializing on the steps behind me and Sherman. She's propped the screen door wide open; when I turn I see she's waving. "No trouble, no trouble!"

"No trouble, no trouble!" I echo, twirling a few times with relief.

Mrs. Matsumoto keeps apologizing; my mom keeps insisting she shouldn't feel bad, it was only some grass and a small tree. Crossing the lawn, she insists Mrs. Matsumoto get out of the car, even though it means trampling some lilies-of-the-valley. She insists that Mrs. Matsumoto come in for a cup of tea. Then she will not talk about anything unless Mrs. Matsumoto sits down, and unless she lets my mom prepare her a small snack. The coming in and the tea and the sitting down are settled pretty quickly, but they negotiate ferociously over the small snack, which Mrs. Matsumoto will not eat unless she can call Mr. Matsumoto. She makes the mistake of linking Mr. Matsumoto with a reparation of some sort, which my mom will not hear of.

"Please!"

"No no no no."

Back and forth it goes: "No no no no." "No no no no." "No no no no." What kind of conversation is that? I look at Sherman, who shrugs. Finally Mr. Matsumoto calls on his own, wondering where his wife is. He comes over in a taxi. He's a heavy-browed businessman, friendly but brisk—not at all a type you could imagine bowing to a lady with a taste for tie-on sun hats. My mom invites him in as if it's an idea she just this moment thought of. And would he maybe have some tea and a small snack?

Sherman and I sneak back outside for another farewell, by the side of the house, behind the forsythia bushes. We hold hands. He kisses me on the cheek again, and then—just when I think he's finally going to kiss me on the lips—he kisses me on the neck.

Is this first base?

He does it more. Up and down, up and down. First it tickles, and then it doesn't. He has his eyes closed. I close my eyes too. He's hugging me. Up and down. Then down.

He's at my collarbone.

Still at my collarbone. Now his hand's on my ribs. So much for first base. More ribs. The idea of second base would probably make me nervous if he weren't on his way back to Japan and if I really thought we were going to get there. As it is, though, I'm not in much danger of wrecking my life on the shoals of passion; his unmoving hand feels more like a growth than a boyfriend. He has his whole face pressed to my neck skin so I can't tell his mouth from his nose. I think he may be licking me.

From indoors, a burst of adult laughter. My eyelids flutter. I start to try and wiggle such that his hand will maybe budge upward.

Do I mean for my top blouse button to come accidentally undone?

He clenches his jaw, and when he opens his eyes, they're fixed on that button like it's a gnat that's been bothering him for far too long. He mutters in Japanese. If later in life he were to describe this as a pivotal moment in his youth, I would not be surprised. Holding the material as far from my body as possible, he buttons the button. Somehow we've landed up too close to the bushes.

What to tell Barbara Gugelstein? She says, "Tell me what were his last words. He must have said something last."

"I don't want to talk about it."

"Maybe he said, Good-bye?" she suggests. "Sayonara?" She means well.

"I don't want to talk about it."

"Aw, come on, I told you everything about—"

I say, "Because it's private, excuse me."

She stops, squints at me as though at a far-off face she's trying to make out. Then she nods and very lightly places her hand on my forearm.

The forsythia seemed to be stabbing us in the eyes. Sherman said, more or less, *You will need to study how to switch.*

And I said, *I think you should switch. The way you do everything is weird.*

And he said, *You just want to tell everything to your friends. You just want to have boyfriend to become popular.*

Then he flipped me. Two swift moves, and I went sprawling through the air, a flailing confusion of soft human parts such as had no idea where the ground was.

It is the fall, and I am in high school, and still he hasn't written, so finally I write him.

I still have all your gifts, I write. *I don't talk so much as I used to. Although I am not exactly a mouse either. I don't care about being popular anymore. I swear. Are you happy to be back in Japan? I know I ruined everything. I was just trying to be entertaining. I miss you with all my heart, and hope I didn't ruin everything.*

He writes back, *You will never be Japanese.*

I throw all the orange peels out that day. Some of them, it turns out, were moldy anyway. I tell my mother I want to move to Chinatown.

"Chinatown!" she says.

I don't know why I suggested it.

"What's the matter?" she says. "Still boy-crazy? That Sherman?"

"No."

"Too much homework?"

I don't answer.

"Forget about school."

Later she tells me if I don't like school, I don't have to go every day. Some days I can stay home.

"Stay home?" In Yonkers, Callie and I used to stay home all the time, but that was because the schools there were *waste of time.*

"No good for a girl be too smart anyway."

For a long time I think about Sherman. But after a while I don't think about him so much as I just keep seeing myself flipped onto the ground, lying there shocked as the Matsumotos get ready to leave. My head has hit a rock; my brain aches as though it's been shoved to some new place in my skull. Otherwise I am okay. I see the forsythia, all those whippy branches, and can't believe how many leaves there are on a bush—every one green and perky and durably itself. And past them, real sky. I try to remember about why the sky's blue, even though this one's gone the kind of indescribable gray you associate with the insides of old shoes. I smell grass. Probably I have grass stains all over my back. I hear my mother calling through the back door, "Mon-a! Everyone leaving now," and "Not coming to say good-bye?" I hear Mr. and Mrs. Matsumoto bowing as they leave—or at least I hear the embarrassment in my mother's voice as they bow. I hear their car start. I hear Mrs. Matsumoto directing Mr. Matsumoto how to back off the lawn so as not to rip any more of it up. I feel the back of my head for blood—just a little. I hear their chug-chug grow fainter and fainter, until it has faded into the whuzz-whuzz of all the other cars. I hear my mom singing, "*Mon-a! Mon-a!*" until my dad comes home. Doors open and shut. I see myself standing up, brushing myself off so I'll have less explaining to do if she comes out to look for me. Grass stains—just like I thought. I see myself walking around the house, going over to have a look at our churned-up yard. It looks pretty sad, two big brown tracks, right through the irises and the lilies-of-the-valley, and that was a new dogwood we'd just planted. Lying there like that. I hear myself thinking about my father, having to go dig it up all over again. Adjusting. I think how we probably ought to put up that brick wall. And sure enough, when I go inside, no one's thinking about me, or that little bit of blood at the back of my head, or the grass stains. That's what they're talking about—that wall. Again. My mom doesn't think it'll do any good, but my dad thinks we should give it a try. Should we or shouldn't we? How high? How thick? What will the neighbors say? I plop myself down on a hard chair. And all I can think is, we are the only complete family that has to worry about this. If I could, I'd switch everything to be different. But since I can't, I might as well sit here at the table for a while, discussing what I know how to discuss. I nod and listen to the rest.

Questions for Reading and Analysis

1. What is Mona Chang's relationship with her Chinese heritage as she ad-libs her way through eighth grade?

2. In what way is Sherman different from Mona? Why would she be attracted to him? Is he attracted to her?

3. Before he leaves, Sherman tells Mona that she should marry him and become Japanese. However, he answers her first letter by telling her: "You will never be Japanese." What has changed his mind?

4. How does the title relate to the rest of the story?

5. What does Gish Jen accomplish by letting 13-year-old Mona tell her own story? How would the story have been different with a more omniscient third-person narrator?

*O*n a vacation in the Bahamas, poet-writer June Jordan contem-
plates the ways in which everything—from having her hotel room
cleaned to reading a novel to ordering lunch—is informed by her consciousness of race, gender, and class. Flying home, she thinks about the
connection made by two of her students, women from very different
worlds, when one reaches out to the other, a victim of domestic abuse,
and says, "I want to be your friend." This essay comes from Jordan's
On Call: Political Essays, *published in 1985.*

Report from the Bahamas

1982

June Jordan

I am staying in a hotel that calls itself The Sheraton British Colonial. One of the
photographs advertising the place displays a middle-aged Black man in a waiter's
tuxedo, smiling. What intrigues me most about the picture is just this: while the
Black man bears a tray full of "colorful" drinks above his left shoulder, both of his
feet, shoes and trouserlegs, up to ten inches above his ankles, stand in the also
"colorful" Caribbean salt water. He is so delighted to serve you he will wade into
the water to bring you Banana Daiquiris while you float! More precisely, he will
wade into the water, fully clothed, oblivious to the ruin of his shoes, his trousers,
his health, and he will do it with a smile.

I am in the Bahamas. On the phone in my room, a spinning complement of
plastic pages offers handy index clues such as CAR RENTAL and CASINOS. A
message from the Ministry of Tourism appears among these travellers tips. Opening
with a paragraph of "WELCOME," the message then proceeds to "A PAGE OF
HISTORY," which reads as follows:

> New World History begins on the same day that modern Bahamian
> history begins—October 12, 1492. That's when Columbus stepped
> ashore—British influence came first with the Eleutherian Adven-
> turers of 1647—After the Revolutions, American Loyalists fled
> from the newly independent states and settled in the Bahamas. Con-
> federate blockade-runners used the island as a haven during the
> War between the States, and after the War, a number of Southerners
> moved to the Bahamas. . .

There it is again. Something proclaims itself a legitimate history and all it does is
track white Mr. Columbus to the British Eleutherians through the Confederate
Southerners as they barge into New World surf, land on New World turf, and

nobody saying one word about the Bahamian people, the Black peoples, to whom the only thing new in their island world was this weird succession of crude intruders and its colonial consequences.

This is my consciousness of race as I unpack my bathing suit in the Sheraton British Colonial. Neither this hotel nor the British nor the long ago Italians nor the white Delta airline pilots belong here, of course. And every time I look at the photograph of that fool standing in the water with his shoes on I'm about to have a West Indian fit, even though I know he's no fool; he's a middle-aged Black man who needs a job and this is his job—pretending himself a servile ancillary to the pleasures of the rich. (Compared to his options in life, I am a rich woman. Compared to most of the Black Americans arriving for this Easter weekend on a three nights four days' deal of bargain rates, the middle-aged waiter is a poor Black man.)

We will jostle along with the other (white) visitors and join them in the tee shirt shops or, laughing together, learn ruthless rules of negotiation as we, Black Americans as well as white, argue down the price of handwoven goods at the nearby straw market while the merchants, frequently toothless Black women seated on the concrete in their only presentable dress, humble themselves to our careless games:

"Yes? You like it? Eight dollar."

"Five."

"I give it to you. Seven."

And so it continues, this weird succession of crude intruders that, now, includes me and my brothers and my sisters from the North.

This is my consciousness of class as I try to decide how much money I can spend on Bahamian gifts for my family back in Brooklyn. No matter that these other Black women incessantly weave words and flowers into the straw hats and bags piled beside them on the burning dusty street. No matter that these other Black women must work their sense of beauty into these things that we will take away as cheaply as we dare, or they will do without food.

We are not white, after all. The budget is limited. And we are harmlessly killing time between the poolside rum punch and "The Native Show on the Patio" that will play tonight outside the hotel restaurant.

This is my consciousness of race and class and gender identity as I notice the fixed relations between these other Black women and myself. They sell and I buy or I don't. They risk not eating. I risk going broke on my first vacation afternoon.

We are not particularly women anymore; we are parties to a transaction designed to set us against each other.

"Olive" is the name of the Black woman who cleans my hotel room. On my way to the beach I am wondering what "Olive" would say if I told her why I chose The Sheraton British Colonial; if I told her I wanted to swim. I wanted to sleep. I did not want to be harassed by the middle-aged waiter, or his nephew. I did not want to be raped by anybody (white or Black) at all and I calculated that my safety as a Black woman alone would best be assured by a multinational hotel corporation. In my experience, the big guys take customer complaints more seriously than the little ones. I would suppose that's one reason why they're big; they don't like to lose money anymore than I like to be bothered when I'm trying to read a goddamned book underneath a palm tree I paid $264 to get next to. A Black woman seeking refuge in a multinational corporation may seem like a contradiction to some, but there you are. In this case it's a coincidence of entirely different self-interests: Sheraton/cash = June Jordan's short run safety.

Anyway, I'm pretty sure "Olive" would look at me as though I came from someplace as far away as Brooklyn. Then she'd probably allow herself one indignant query before righteously removing her vacuum cleaner from my room; "and why in the first place you come down you without your husband?"

I cannot imagine how I would begin to answer her.

My "rights" and my "freedom" and my "desire" and a slew of other New World values; what would they sound like to this Black woman described on the card atop my hotel bureau as "Olive the Maid"? "Olive" is older than I am and I may smoke a cigarette while she changes the sheets on my bed. Whose rights? Whose freedom? Whose desire?

And why should she give a shit about mine unless I do something, for real, about hers?

It happens that the book that I finished reading under a palm tree earlier today was the novel, *The Bread Givers*, by Anzia Yezierska. Definitely autobiographical, Yezierska lays out the difficulties of being both female and "a person" inside a traditional Jewish family at the start of the 20th century. That any Jewish woman became anything more than the abused servant of her father or her husband is really an improbable piece of news. Yet Yezierska managed such an unlikely outcome for her own life. In *The Bread Givers*, the heroine also manages an important, although partial, escape from traditional Jewish female destiny. And in the unpardonable, despotic father, the Talmudic scholar of that Jewish family, did I not see my own and hate him twice, again? When the heroine, the young Jewish child, wanders the streets with a filthy pail she borrows to sell herring in order to raise the ghetto rent and when she cries, "Nothing was before me but the hunger in our house, and no bread for the next meal if I didn't sell the herring. No longer like a fire engine, but like a houseful of hungry mouths my heart cried, 'herring-herring! Two cents apiece!'" Who would doubt the ease, the sisterhood of conversation possible between that white girl and the Black women selling straw bags on the streets of paradise because they do not want to die? And is it not obvious that the wife of that Talmudic scholar and "Olive," who cleans my room here at the hotel, have more in common than I can claim with either of them?

This is my consciousness of race and class and gender identity as I collect wet towels, sunglasses, wristwatch, and head towards a shower.

I am thinking about the boy who loaned this novel to me. He's white and he's Jewish and he's pursuing an independent study project with me, at the State University where I teach whether or not I feel like it, where I teach without stint because, like the waiter, I am no fool. It's my job and either I work or I do without everything you need money to buy. The boy loaned me the novel because he thought I'd be interested to know how a Jewish-American writer used English so that the syntax, and therefore the cultural habits of mind expressed by the Yiddish language, could survive translation. He did this because he wanted to create another connection between us on the basis of language, between his knowledge/his love of Yiddish and my knowledge/my love of Black English.

He has been right about the forceful survival of the Yiddish. And I had become excited by this further evidence of the written voice of spoken language protected from the monodrone of "standard" English, and so we had grown closer on this account. But then our talk shifted to student affairs more generally, and I had learned that this student does not care one way or the other about currently jeopardized Federal Student Loan Programs because, as he explained it to me, they do not affect him. He does not need financial help outside his own family. My own son, however, is Black. And I am the only family help available to him and that means, if Reagan succeeds in eliminating Federal programs to aid minority students, he will have to forget about furthering his studies, or he or I or both of us will have to hit the numbers pretty big. For these reasons of difference, the student and I had moved away from each other, even while we continued to talk.

My consciousness turned to race, again, and class.

Sitting in the same chair as the boy, several weeks ago, a graduate student came to discuss her grade. I praised the excellence of her final paper; indeed it had seemed to me an extraordinary pulling together of recent left brain/right brain research with the themes of transcendental poetry.

She told me that, for her part, she'd completed her reading of my political essays. "You are so lucky!" she exclaimed.

"What do you mean by that?"

"You have a cause. You have a purpose to your life."

I looked carefully at this white woman; what was she really saying to me?

"What do you mean?" I repeated.

"Poverty. Police violence. Discrimination in general."

(Jesus Christ, I thought: Is that her idea of lucky?)

"And how about you?" I asked.

"Me?"

"Yeah, you. Don't you have a cause?"

"Me? I'm just a middle aged woman: a housewife and a mother. I'm a nobody."

For a while, I made no response.

First of all, speaking of race and class and gender in one breath, what she said meant that those lucky preoccupations of mine, from police violence to nuclear wipe-out, were not shared. They were mine and not hers. But here she sat, friendly as an old stuffed animal, beaming good will or more "luck" in my direction.

In the second place, what this white woman said to me meant that she did not believe she was "a person" precisely because she had fulfilled the traditional female functions revered by the father of that Jewish immigrant, Anzia Yezierska. And the woman in front of me was not a Jew. That was not the connection. The link was strictly female. Nevertheless, how should that woman and I, another female connect, beyond this bizarre exchange?

If she believed me lucky to have regular hurdles of discrimination then why shouldn't I insist that she's lucky to be a middle class white Wasp female who lives in such well-sanctioned and normative comfort that she even has the luxury to deny the power of the privileges that paralyze her life?

If she deserts me and "my cause" where we differ, if, for example, she abandons me to "my" problems of race, then why should I support her in "her" problems of housewifely oblivion?

Recollection of this peculiar moment brings me to the shower in the bathroom cleaned by "Olive." She reminds me of the usual Women's Studies curriculum because it has nothing to do with her or her job: you won't find "Olive" listed anywhere on the reading list. You will likewise seldom hear of Anzia Yezierska. But yes, you will find, from Florence Nightingale to Adrienne Rich, a white procession of independently well-to-do women writers. (Gertrude Stein/Virginia Woolf/Hilda Doolittle are standard names among the "essential" women writers.)

In other words, most of the women of the world—Black and First World and white who work because we must—most of the women of the world persist far from the heart of the usual Women's Studies syllabus.

Similarly, the typical Black History course will slide by the majority experience it pretends to represent. For example, Mary McLeod Bethune will scarcely receive as much attention as Nat Turner, even though Black women who bravely and efficiently provided for the education of Black people hugely outnumber those few Black men who led successful or doomed rebellions against slavery. In fact, Mary McLeod Bethune may not receive even honorable mention because Black History too often apes those ridiculous white history courses which produce such dangerous gibberish as The Sheraton British Colonial "history" of the Bahamas. Both Black and white history courses exclude from their central consideration those people who neither killed nor conquered anyone as the means to new identity, those people who took care of every one of the people who wanted to become "a person," those people who still take care of the life at issue: the ones who wash and who feed and who teach and who diligently decorate straw hats and bags with all of their historically unrequired gentle love: the women.

> *Oh the old rugged cross*
> *on a hill far away*
> *Well I cherish the old rugged cross*

It's Good Friday in the Bahamas. Seventy-eight degrees in the shade. Except for Sheraton territory, everything's closed.

It so happens that for truly secular reasons I've been fasting for three days. My hunger has now reached nearly violent proportions. In the hotel sandwich shop, the Black woman handling the counter complains about the tourists; why isn't the shop closed and why don't the tourists stop eating for once in their lives. I'm famished and I order chicken salad and cottage cheese and lettuce and tomato and a hard boiled egg and a hot cross bun and apple juice.

She eyes me with disgust.

To be sure, the timing of my stomach offends her serious religious practices. Neither one of us apologizes to the other. She seasons the chicken salad to the peppery max while I listen to the loud radio gospel she plays to console herself. It's a country Black version of "The Old Rugged Cross."

As I heave much chicken into my mouth tears start. It's not the pepper. I am, after all, a West Indian daughter. It's the Good Friday music that dominates the humid atmosphere.

> *Well I cherish the old rugged cross*

And I am back, faster than a 747, in Brooklyn, in the home of my parents where we are wondering, as we do every year, if the sky will darken until Christ has been buried in the tomb. The sky should darken if God is in His heavens. And then, around 3 p.m., at the conclusion of our mournful church service at the neighborhood St. Phillips, and even while we dumbly stare at the black cloth covering the gold altar and the slender unlit candles, the sun should return through the high gothic windows and vindicate our waiting faith that the Lord will rise again, on Easter.

How I used to bow my head at the very name of Jesus: ecstatic to abase myself in deference to His majesty.

My mouth is full of salad. I can't seem to eat quickly enough. I can't think how I should lessen the offense of my appetite. The other Black woman on the premises, the one who disapprovingly prepared this very tasty break from my fast, makes no remark. She is no fool. This is a job that she needs. I suppose she notices that at least I included a hot cross bun among my edibles. That's something in my favor. I decide that's enough.

I am suddenly eager to walk off the food. Up a fairly steep hill I walk without hurrying. Through the pastel desolation of the little town, the road brings me to a confectionery pink and white plantation house. At the gates, an unnecessarily large statue of Christopher Columbus faces me down, or tries to. His hand is fisted to one hip. I look back at him, laugh without deference, and turn left.

It's time to pack it up. Catch my plane. I scan the hotel room for things not to forget. There's that white report card on the bureau.

"Dear Guests:" it says, under the name "Olive." I am your maid for the day. Please rate me: Excellent. Good. Average. Poor. Thank you."

I tuck this memento from the British Colonial Sheraton into my notebook. How would "Olive" rate *me*? What would it mean for us to seem "good" to each other? What would that rating require?

But I am hastening to leave. Neither turtle soup nor kidney pie nor any conch shell delight shall delay my departure. I have rested, here, in the Bahamas, and I'm ready to return to my usual job, my usual work. But the skin on my body has changed and so has my mind. On the Delta flight home I realize I am burning up, indeed.

So far as I can see, the usual race and class concepts of connection, or gender assumptions of unity, do not apply very well. I doubt that they ever did. Otherwise why would Black folks forever bemoan our lack of solidarity when the deal turns real. And if unity on the basis of sexual oppression is something natural, then why do we women, the majority people on the planet, still have a problem?

The plane's ready for takeoff. I fasten my seatbelt and let the tumult inside my head run free. Yes: race and class and gender remain as real as the weather. But what they must mean about the contact between two individuals is less obvious and, like the weather, not predictable.

And when these factors of race and class and gender absolutely collapse is whenever you try to use them as automatic concepts of connection. They may serve well as indicators of commonly felt conflict, but as elements of connection they seem about as reliable as precipitation probability for the day after the night before the day.

It occurs to me that much organizational grief could be avoided if people understood that partnership in misery does not necessarily provide for partnership for change: *When we get the monsters off our backs all of us may want to run in very different directions.*

And not only that: even though both "Olive" and "I" live inside a conflict neither one of us created, and even though both of us therefore hurt inside that conflict, I may be one of the monsters she needs to eliminate from her universe and, in a sense, she may be one of the monsters in mine.

I am reaching for the words to describe the difference between a common identity that has been imposed and the individual identity any one of us will choose, once she gains that chance.

That difference is the one that keeps us stupid in the face of new, specific information about somebody else with whom we are supposed to have a connection because a third party, hostile to both of us, has worked it so that the two of us, like it or not, share a common enemy. *What happens beyond the idea of that enemy and beyond the consequences of that enemy?*

I am saying that the ultimate connection cannot be the enemy. The ultimate connection must be the need that we find between us. It is not only who you are, in other words, but what we can do for each other that will determine the connection.

I am flying back to my job. I have been teaching contemporary women's poetry this semester. One quandary I have set myself to explore with my students is the one of taking responsibility without power. We had been wrestling ideas to the floor for several sessions when a young Black woman, a South African, asked me for help, after class.

Sokutu told me she was "in a trance" and that she'd been unable to eat for two weeks.

"What's going on?" I asked her, even as my eyes startled at her trembling and emaciated appearance.

"My husband. He drinks all the time. He beats me up. I go to the hospital. I can't eat. I don't know what/anything."

In my office, she described her situation. I did not dare to let her sense my fear and horror. She was dragging about, hour by hour, in dread. Her husband, a young Black South African, was drinking himself into more and more deadly violence against her.

Sokutu told me how she could keep nothing down. She weighed 90 lbs. at the outside, as she spoke to me. She'd already been hospitalized as a result of her husband's battering rage.

I knew both of them because I had organized a campus group to aid the liberation struggles of Southern Africa.

Nausea rose in my throat. What about this presumable connection: this husband and this wife fled from that homeland of hatred against them, and now what? He was destroying himself. If not stopped, he would certainly murder his wife.

She needed a doctor, right away. It was a medical emergency. She needed protection. It was a security crisis. She needed refuge for battered wives and personal therapy and legal counsel. She needed a friend.

I got on the phone and called every number in the campus directory that I could imagine might prove helpful. Nothing worked. There were no institutional resources designed to meet her enormous, multifaceted, and ordinary woman's need.

I called various students. I asked the Chairperson of the English Department for advice. I asked everyone for help.

Finally, another one of my students, Cathy, a young Irish woman active in campus IRA activities, responded. She asked for further details. I gave them to her.

"Her husband," Cathy told me, "is an alcoholic. You have to understand about alcoholics. It's not the same as anything else. And it's a disease you can't treat any old way."

I listened, fearfully. Did this mean there was nothing we could do?

"That's not what I'm saying," she said. "But you have to keep the alcoholic part of the thing central in everybody's mind, otherwise her husband will kill her. Or he'll kill himself."

She spoke calmly, I felt there was nothing to do but to assume she knew what she was talking about.

"Will you come with me?" I asked her, after a silence. "Will you come with me and help us figure out what to do next?"

Cathy said she would but that she felt shy: Sokutu comes from South Africa. What would she think about Cathy?

"I don't know," I said. "But let's go."

We left to find a dormitory room for the young battered wife.

It was late, now, and dark outside.

On Cathy's VW that I followed behind with my own car, was the sticker that reads BOBBY SANDS FREE AT LAST. My eyes blurred as I read and reread the words. This was another connection: Bobby Sands and Martin Luther King Jr. and who would believe it? I would not have believed it; I grew up terrorized by Irish kids who introduced me to the word "nigga."

And here I was following an Irish woman to the room of a Black South African. We were going to that room to try to save a life together.

When we reached the little room, we found ourselves awkward and large. Sokutu attempted to treat us with utmost courtesy, as though we were honored guests. She seemed surprised by Cathy, but mostly Sokutu was flushed with relief and joy because we were there, with her.

I did not know how we should ever terminate her heartfelt courtesies and address, directly, the reason for our visit: her starvation and her extreme physical danger.

Finally, Cathy sat on the floor and reached out her hands to Sokutu.

"I'm here," she said quietly, "Because June has told me what has happened to you. And I know what it is. Your husband is an alcoholic. He has a disease. I know what it is. My father was an alcoholic. He killed himself. He almost killed my mother. I want to be your friend."

"Oh," was the only small sound that escaped from Sokutu's mouth. And then she embraced the other student. And then everything changed and I watched all of this happen so I know that this happened: this connection.

And after we called the police and exchanged phone numbers and plans were made for the night and for the next morning, the young South African woman walked down the dormitory hallway, saying goodbye and saying thank you to us.

I walked behind them, the young Irish woman and the young South African, and I saw them walking as sisters walk, hugging each other, and whispering and sure of each other and I felt how it was not who they were but what they both know and what they were both preparing to do about what they know that was going to make them both free at last.

And I look out the windows of the plane and I see clouds that will not kill me and I know that someday soon other clouds may erupt to kill us all.

And I tell the stewardess No thanks to the cocktails she offers me. But I look about the cabin at the hundred strangers drinking as they fly and I think even here and even now I must make the connection real between me and these strangers everywhere before those other clouds unify this ragged bunch of us, too late.

Questions for Reading and Analysis

1. How do the ad for the hotel in which Jordan is staying and the written "history" she discovers in the guest services index in her hotel room introduce the issues at the core of her essay?

2. List several incidents which seem to make Jordan uncomfortable during her stay in the Bahamas.

3. Jordan recognizes a contradiction in her choice of the Sheraton British Colonial. Why does she decide to stay there anyway?

4. Is Jordan optimistic about the possibilities of overcoming barriers of race, class, and gender? Explain.

5. Several times during the essay, Jordan begins paragraphs with the words, "This is my consciousness of [race, gender, class, identity] . . . ." What is the effect of the repetition?

6. How do you interpret Jordan's final paragraph?

Martin Luther King, Jr. (1929–1968), a Baptist minister at the forefront of the Civil Rights movement, advocated non-violent forms of protest and peaceful resistance to racial inequality. In 1964, he became the youngest recipient of the Nobel Peace Prize; in 1968, an assassin's bullet silenced him. King's Letter from Birmingham Jail, *written while he was jailed briefly in April 1963, is a response to a* Letter from Eight White Clergymen *(follows here) urging King to discourage "unwise and untimely" demonstrations. King's letter is a careful exercise in deductive reasoning.*

Letter from Birmingham Jail

Martin Luther King, Jr.

MY DEAR FELLOW CLERGYMEN:

While confined here in the Birmingham city jail, I came across your recent statement calling my present activities "unwise and untimely." Seldom do I pause to answer criticism of my work and ideas. If I sought to answer all the criticisms that cross my desk, my secretaries would have little time for anything other than such correspondence in the course of the day, and I would have no time for constructive work. But since I feel that you are men of genuine good will and that your criticisms are sincerely set forth, I want to try to answer your statement in what I hope will be patient and reasonable terms.

I think I should indicate why I am here in Birmingham, since you have been influenced by the view which argues against "outsiders coming in." I have the honor of serving as president of the Southern Christian Leadership Conference, an organization operating in every southern state, with headquarters in Atlanta, Georgia. We have some eighty-five affiliated organizations across the South, and one of them is the Alabama Christian Movement for Human Rights. Frequently we share staff, educational, and financial resources with our affiliates. Several months ago the affiliate here in Birmingham asked us to be on call to engage in a nonviolent direct-action program if such were deemed necessary. We readily consented, and when the hour came we lived up to our promise. So I, along with several members of my staff, am here because I was invited here. I am here because I have organizational ties here.

But more basically, I am in Birmingham because injustice is here. Just as the prophets of the eighth century B.C. left their villages and carried their "thus saith the Lord" far beyond the boundaries of their home towns, and just as the Apostle Paul left his village of Tarsus and carried the gospel of Jesus Christ to the far corners of the Greco-Roman world, so am I compelled to carry the gospel of freedom beyond my own home town. Like Paul, I must constantly respond to the Macedonian call for aid.

Moreover, I am cognizant of the interrelatedness of all communities and states. I cannot sit idly by in Atlanta and not be concerned about what happens in Birmingham. Injustice anywhere is a threat to justice everywhere. We are caught in an inescapable network of mutuality, tied in a single garment of destiny. Whatever affects one directly, affects all indirectly. Never again can we afford to live with the narrow, provincial "outside agitator" idea. Anyone who lives inside the United States can never be considered an outsider anywhere within its bounds.

You deplore the demonstrations taking place in Birmingham. But your statement, I am sorry to say, fails to express a similar concern for the conditions that brought about the demonstrations. I am sure that none of you would want to rest content with the superficial kind of social analysis that deals merely with effects and does not grapple with underlying causes. It is unfortunate that demonstrations are taking place in Birmingham, but it is even more unfortunate that the city's white power structure left the Negro community with no alternative.

In any nonviolent campaign there are four basic steps: collection of the facts to determine whether injustices exist; negotiation; self-purification; and direct action. We have gone through all these steps in Birmingham. There can be no gainsaying the fact that racial injustice engulfs this community. Birmingham is probably the most thoroughly segregated city in the United States. Its ugly record of brutality is widely known. Negroes have experienced grossly unjust treatment in the courts. There have been more unsolved bombings of Negro homes and churches in Birmingham than in any other city in the nation. These are the hard, brutal facts of the case. On the basis of these conditions, Negro leaders sought to negotiate with the city fathers. But the latter consistently refused to engage in good-faith negotiation.

Then, last September, came the opportunity to talk with leaders of Birmingham's economic community. In the course of the negotiations, certain promises were made by the merchants—for example, to remove the stores' humiliating racial signs. On the basis of these promises, the Reverend Fred Shuttlesworth and the leaders of the Alabama Christian Movement for Human Rights agreed to a moratorium on all demonstrations. As the weeks and months went by, we realized that we were the victims of a broken promise. A few signs, briefly removed, returned; the others remained.

As in so many past experiences, our hopes had been blasted, and the shadow of deep disappointment settled upon us. We had no alternative except to prepare for direct action, whereby we would present our very bodies as a means of laying our case before the conscience of the local and the national community. Mindful of the difficulties involved, we decided to undertake a process of self-purification. We began a series of workshops on nonviolence, and we repeatedly asked ourselves: "Are you able to accept blows without retaliating?" "Are you able to endure the ordeal of jail?" We decided to schedule our direct-action program for the Easter season, realizing that except for Christmas, this is the main shopping period of the year. Knowing that a strong economic-withdrawal program would be the by-product of direct action, we felt that this would be the best time to bring pressure to bear on the merchants for the needed change.

Then it occurred to us that Birmingham's mayoral election was coming up in March, and we speedily decided to postpone action until after election day. When we discovered that the Commissioner of Public Safety, Eugene "Bull" Connor, had piled up enough votes to be in the run-off, we decided again to postpone action until the day after the run-off so that the demonstrations could not be used to cloud the issues. Like many others, we wanted to see Mr. Connor defeated, and to this end we endured postponement after postponement. Having aided in this community need, we felt that our direct-action program could be delayed no longer.

You may well ask: "Why direct action? Why sit-ins, marches, and so forth? Isn't negotiation a better path?" You are quite right in calling for negotiation. Indeed, this is the very purpose of direct action. Nonviolent direct action seeks to create such a crisis and foster such a tension that a community which has constantly refused to negotiate is forced to confront the issue. It seeks so to dramatize the issue that it can no longer be ignored. My citing the creation of tension as part of the work of the nonviolent-resister may sound rather shocking. But I must confess that I am not afraid of the word "tension." I have earnestly opposed violent tension, but there is a type of constructive, nonviolent tension which is necessary for growth. Just as Socrates felt that it was necessary to create a tension in the mind so that individuals could rise from the bondage of myths and half-truths to the unfettered realm of creative analysis and objective appraisal, so must we see the need for nonviolent gadflies to create the kind of tension in society that will help men rise from the dark depths of prejudice and racism to the majestic heights of understanding and brotherhood.

The purpose of our direct-action program is to create a situation so crisis-packed that it will inevitably open the door to negotiation. I therefore concur with you in your call for negotiation. Too long has our beloved Southland been bogged down in a tragic effort to live in monologue rather than dialogue.

One of the basic points in your statement is that the action that I and my associates have taken in Birmingham is untimely. Some have asked: "Why didn't you give the new city administration time to act?" The only answer that I can give to this query is that the new Birmingham administration must be prodded about as much as the outgoing one, before it will act. We are sadly mistaken if we feel that the election of Albert Boutwell as mayor will bring the millennium to Birmingham. While Mr. Boutwell is a much more gentle person than Mr. Connor, they are both segregationists, dedicated to maintenance of the status quo. I have hoped that Mr. Boutwell will be reasonable enough to see the futility of massive resistance to desegregation. But he will not see this without pressure from devotees of civil rights. My friends, I must say to you that we have not made a single gain in civil rights without determined legal and nonviolent pressure. Lamentably, it is an historical fact that privileged groups seldom give up their privileges voluntarily. Individuals may see the moral light and voluntarily give up their unjust posture; but, as Reinhold Niebuhr[2] has reminded us, groups tend to be more immoral than individuals.

We know through painful experience that freedom is never voluntarily given by the oppressor; it must be demanded by the oppressed. Frankly, I have yet to engage in a direct-action campaign that was "well timed" in the view of those who have not suffered unduly from the disease of segregation. For years now I have heard the word "Wait!" It rings in the ear of every Negro with piercing familiarity.

This "Wait" has almost always meant "Never." We must come to see, with one of our distinguished jurists, that "justice too long delayed is justice denied."

We have waited for more than 340 years for our constitutional and God-given rights. The nations of Asia and Africa are moving with jet-like speed toward gaining political independence, but we still creep at horse-and-buggy pace toward gaining a cup of coffee at a lunch counter. Perhaps it is easy for those who have never felt the stinging darts of segregation to say, "Wait." But when you have seen vicious mobs lynch your mothers and fathers at will and drown your sisters and brothers at whim; when you have seen hate-filled policemen curse, kick, and even kill your black brothers and sisters; when you see the vast majority of your twenty million Negro brothers smothering in an airtight cage of poverty in the midst of an affluent society; when you suddenly find your tongue twisted and your speech stammering as you seek to explain to your six-year-old daughter why she can't go to the public amusement park that has just been advertised on television, and see tears welling up in her eyes when she is told that Funtown is closed to colored children, and see ominous clouds of inferiority beginning to form in her little mental sky, and see her beginning to distort her personality by developing an unconscious bitterness toward white people; when you have to concoct an answer for a five-year-old son who is asking, "Daddy, why do white people treat colored people so mean?"; when you take a cross-country drive and find it necessary to sleep night after night in the uncomfortable corners of your automobile because no motel will accept you; when you are humiliated day in and day out by nagging signs reading "white" and "colored"; when your first name becomes "nigger," your middle name becomes "boy" (however old you are) and your last name becomes "John," and your wife and mother are never given the respected title "Mrs."; when you are harried by day and haunted by night by the fact that you are a Negro, living constantly at tiptoe stance, never quite knowing what to expect next, and are plagued with inner fears and outer resentments; when you are forever fighting a degenerating sense of "nobod-iness"—then you will understand why we find it difficult to wait. There comes a time when the cup of endurance runs over, and men are no longer willing to be plunged into the abyss of despair. I hope, sirs, you can understand our legitimate and unavoidable impatience.

You express a great deal of anxiety over our willingness to break laws. This is certainly a legitimate concern. Since we so diligently urge people to obey the Supreme Court's decision of 1954 outlawing segregation in the public schools, at first glance it may seem rather paradoxical for us consciously to break laws. One may well ask: "How can you advocate breaking some laws and obeying others?" The answer lies in the fact that there are two types of laws: just and unjust. I would be the first to advocate obeying just laws. One has not only a legal but a moral responsibility to obey just laws. Conversely, one has a moral responsibility to dis-obey unjust laws. I would agree with St. Augustine[3] that "an unjust law is no law at all."

Now, what is the difference between the two? How does one determine whether a law is just or unjust? A just law is a man-made code that squares with the moral law or the law of God. An unjust law is a code that is out of harmony with the moral law. To put it in the terms of St. Thomas Aquinas:[4] An unjust law is a human law that is not rooted in eternal law and natural law. Any law that uplifts human personality is just. Any law that degrades human personality is unjust. All segregation statutes are unjust because segregation distorts the soul and damages the personality. It gives the segregator a false sense of superiority and the segregated a false sense of inferiority. Segregation, to use the terminology of the Jewish philosopher Martin Buber,[5] substitutes an "I-it" relationship for an "I-thou" relationship and ends up relegating persons to the status of things. Hence segregation is not only politically, economically, and sociologically unsound, it is morally wrong and sinful. Paul Tillich[6] has said that sin is separation. Is not segregation an existential expression of man's tragic separation, his awful estrangement, his terrible sinfulness? Thus it is that I can urge men to obey the 1954 decision of the Supreme Court, for it is morally right; and I can urge them to disobey segregation ordinances, for they are morally wrong.

Let us consider a more concrete example of just and unjust laws. An unjust law is a code that a numerical or power majority group compels a minority group to obey but does not make binding on itself. This is *difference* made legal. By the same token, a just law is a code that a majority compels a minority to follow and that it is willing to follow itself. This is *sameness* made legal.

Let me give another explanation. A law is unjust if it is inflicted on a minority that, as a result of being denied the right to vote, had no part in enacting or devising the law. Who can say that the legislature of Alabama which set up that state's segregation laws was democratically elected? Throughout Alabama all sorts of devious methods are used to prevent Negroes from becoming registered voters, and there are some counties in which, even though Negroes constitute a majority of the population, not a single Negro is registered. Can any law enacted under such circumstances be considered democratically structured?

Sometimes a law is just on its face and unjust in it's application. For instance, I have been arrested on a charge of parading without a permit. Now, there is nothing wrong in having an ordinance which requires a permit for a parade. But such an ordinance becomes unjust when it is used to maintain segregation and to deny citizens the First-Amendment privilege of peaceful assembly and protest.

I hope you are able to see the distinction I am trying to point out. In no sense do I advocate evading or defying the law, as would the rabid segregationist. That would lead to anarchy. One who breaks an unjust law must do so openly, lovingly, and with a willingness to accept the penalty. I submit that an individual who breaks a law that conscience tells him is unjust, and who willingly accepts the penalty of imprisonment in order to arouse the conscience of the community over its injustice, is in reality expressing the highest respect for law.

Of course, there is nothing new about this kind of civil disobedience. It was evidenced sublimely in the refusal of Shadrach, Meshach, and Abednego to obey the laws of Nebuchadnezzar,[7] on the ground that a higher moral law was at stake. It was practiced superbly by the early Christians, who were willing to face hungry lions and the excruciating pain of chopping blocks rather than submit to certain unjust laws of the Roman Empire. To a degree, academic freedom is a reality today because Socrates practiced civil disobedience.[8] In our own nation, the Boston Tea Party represented a massive act of civil disobedience.

We should never forget that everything Adolf Hitler did in Germany was "legal" and everything the Hungarian freedom fighters[9] did in Hungary was "illegal." It was "illegal" to aid and comfort a Jew in Hitler's Germany. Even so, I am sure that, had I lived in Germany at the time, I would have aided and comforted my Jewish brothers. If today I lived in a Communist country where certain principles dear to the Christian faith are suppressed, I would openly advocate disobeying that country's anti-religious laws.

I must make two honest confessions to you, my Christian and Jewish brothers. First, I must confess that over the past few years I have been gravely disappointed with the white moderate. I have almost reached the regrettable conclusion that the Negro's great stumbling block in his stride toward freedom is not the White Citizen's Counciler or the Ku Klux Klanner, but the white moderate, who is more devoted to "order" than to justice; who prefers a negative peace which is the absence of tension to a positive peace which is the presence of justice; who constantly say, "I agree with you in the goal you seek, but I cannot agree with your methods of direct action"; who paternalistically believes he can set the timetable for another man's freedom; who lives by a mythical concept of time and who constantly advises the Negro to wait for a "more convenient season." Shallow understanding from people of good will is more frustrating than absolute misunderstanding from people of ill will. Lukewarm acceptance is much more bewildering than outright rejection.

I had hoped that the white moderate would understand that law and order exist for the purpose of establishing justice and that when they fail in this purpose they become the dangerously structured dams that block the flow of social progress. I had hoped that the white moderate would understand that the present tension in the South is a necessary phase of the transition from an obnoxious negative peace, in which the Negro passively accepted his unjust plight, to a substantive and positive peace, in which all men will respect the dignity and worth of human personality. Actually, we who engage in nonviolent direct action are not the creators of tension. We merely bring to the surface the hidden tension that is already alive. We bring it out in the open, where it can be seen and dealt with. Like a boil that can never be cured so long as it is covered up but must be opened with all its ugliness to the natural medicines of air and light, injustice must be exposed, with all the tension its exposure creates, to the light of human conscience and the air of national opinion, before it can be cured.

In your statement you assert that our actions, even though peaceful, must be condemned because they precipitate violence. But is this a logical assertion? Isn't this like condemning a robbed man because his possession of money precipitated the evil act of robbery? Isn't this like condemning Socrates because his unswerving commitment to truth and his philosophical inquiries precipitated the act by the misguided populace in which they made him drink hemlock? Isn't this like condemning Jesus because his unique God-consciousness and never-ceasing devotion to God's will precipitated the evil act of crucifixion? We must come to see that, as the federal courts have consistently affirmed, it is wrong to urge an individual to cease his efforts to gain his basic constitutional rights because the quest may precipitate violence. Society must protect the robbed and punish the robber.

I had also hoped that the white moderate would reject the myth concerning time in relation to the struggle for freedom. I have just received a letter from a white brother in Texas. He writes: "All Christians know that the colored people will receive equal rights eventually, but it is possible that you are in too great a religious hurry. It has taken Christianity almost two thousand years to accomplish what it has. The teachings of Christ take time to come to earth." Such an attitude stems from a tragic misconception of time, from the strangely irrational notion that there is something in the very flow of time that will inevitably cure all ills. Actually, time itself is neutral; it can be used either destructively or constructively. More and more I feel that the people of ill will have used time much more effectively that have the people of good will. We will have to repent in this generation not merely for the hateful words and actions of the bad people, but for the appalling silence of the good people. Human progress never rolls in on wheels of inevitability; it comes through the tireless efforts of men willing to be co-workers with God, and without this hard work, time itself becomes an ally of the forces of social stagnation. We must use time creatively, in the knowledge that the time is always ripe to do right. Now is the time to make real the promise of democracy and transform our pending national elegy into a creative psalm of brotherhood. Now is the time to lift our national policy from the quicksand of racial injustice to the solid rock of human dignity.

You speak of our activity in Birmingham as extreme. At first I was rather disappointed that fellow clergymen would see my nonviolent efforts as those of an extremist. I began thinking about the fact that I stand in the middle of two opposing forces in the Negro community. One is a force of complacency, made up in part of Negroes who, as a result of long years of oppression, are so drained of self-respect and a sense of "somebodiness" that they have adjusted to segregation; and in part of a few middle-class Negroes who, because of a degree of academic and economic security and because in some ways they profit by segregation, have become insensitive to the problems of the masses. The other force is one of bitterness and hatred, and it comes perilously close to advocating violence. It is expressed in the various black nationalist groups that are springing up across the nation, the largest and best-known being Elijah Muhammad's Muslim movement.[10] Nourished by the Negro's frustration over the continued existence of racial discrimination, this movement is made up of people who have lost faith in America, who have absolutely repudiated Christianity, and who have concluded that the white man is an incorrigible "devil."

I have tried to stand between these two forces, saying that we need emulate neither the "do-nothingism" of the complacent nor the hatred and despair of the black nationalist. For there is the more excellent way of love and nonviolent protest. I am grateful to God that, through the influence of the Negro church, the way of nonviolence became an integral part of our struggle.

If this philosophy had not emerged, by now many streets of the South would, I am convinced, be flowing with blood. And I am further convinced that if our white brothers dismiss as "rabblerousers" and "outside agitators" those of us who employ nonviolent direct action, and if they refuse to support our nonviolent efforts, millions of Negroes will, out of frustration and despair, seek solace and security in black-nationalist ideologies—a development that would inevitably lead to a frightening racial nightmare.

Oppressed people cannot remain oppressed forever. The yearning for freedom eventually manifests itself, and that is what has happened to the American Negro.

Something within has reminded him of his birthright of freedom, and something without has reminded him that it can be gained. Consciously or unconsciously, he has been caught up by the *Zeitgeist*,[11] and with his black brothers of Africa and his brown and yellow brothers of Asia, South America, and the Caribbean, the United States Negro is moving with a sense of great urgency toward the promised land of racial justice. If one recognizes this vital urge that has engulfed the Negro community, one should readily understand why public demonstrations are taking place. The Negro has many pent-up resentments and latent frustrations, and he must release them. So let him march; let him make prayer pilgrimages to the city hall; let him go on freedom rides—and try to understand why he must do so. If his repressed emotions are not released in nonviolent ways, they will seek expression through violence; this is not a threat but a fact of history. So I have not said to my people, "Get rid of your discontent." Rather, I have tried to say that this normal and healthy discontent can be channeled into the creative outlet of nonviolent direct action. And now this approach is being termed extremist.

But though I was initially disappointed at being categorized as an extremist, as I continued to think about the matter I gradually gained a measure of satisfaction from the label. Was not Jesus an extremist for love: "Love your enemies, bless them that curse you, do good to them that hate you, and pray for them which despite-fully use you, and persecute you." Was not Amos an extremist for justice: "Let justice roll down like waters and righteousness like an ever-flowing stream." Was not Paul an extremist for the Christian gospel: "I bear in my body the marks of the Lord Jesus." Was not Martin Luther an extremist: "Here I stand; I cannot do otherwise, so help me God." And John Bunyan:[12] "I will stay in jail to the end of my days before I make a butchery of my conscience." And Abraham Lincoln: "This nation cannot survive half slave and half free." And Thomas Jefferson: "We hold these truths to be self-evident, that all men are created equal. . . ." So the question is not whether we will be extremists, but what kind of extremists we will be. Will we be extremists for hate or for love? Will we be extremists for the preservation of injustice or for the extension of justice? In that dramatic scene on Calvary's hill three men were crucified. We must never forget that all three were crucified for the same crime—the crime of extremism. Two were extremists for immorality, and thus fell below their environment. The other, Jesus Christ, was an extremist for love, truth, and goodness, and thereby rose above his environment. Perhaps the South, the nation, and the world are in dire need of creative extremists.

I had hoped that the white moderate would see this need. Perhaps I was too optimistic; perhaps I expected too much. I suppose I should have realized that few members of the oppressor race can understand the deep groans and passionate yearnings of the oppressed race, and still fewer have the vision to see that injustice must be rooted out by strong, persistent, and determined action. I am thankful, however, that some of our white brothers in the South have grasped the meaning of this social revolution and committed themselves to it. They are still all too few in quantity, but they are big in quality. Some—such as Ralph McGill, Lillian Smith, Harry Golden, James McBride Dabbs, Ann Braden, and Sarah Patton Boyle— have written about our struggle in eloquent and prophetic terms. Others have marched with us down nameless streets of the South. They have languished in filthy, roach-infested jails, suffering the abuse and brutality of policemen who view them as "dirty nigger-lovers." Unlike so many of their moderate brothers and sisters, they have recognized the urgency of the moment and sensed the need for powerful "action" antidotes to combat the disease of segregation.

Let me take note of my other major disappointment. I have been so greatly disappointed with the white church and its leadership. Of course, there are some notable exceptions. I am not unmindful of the fact that each of you has taken some significant stands on this issue. I commend you, Reverend Stallings, for your Christian stand on this past Sunday, in welcoming Negroes to your worship service on a non-segregated basis. I commend the Catholic leaders of this state for integrating Spring Hill College several years ago.

But despite these notable exceptions, I must honestly reiterate that I have been disappointed with the church. I do not say this as one of those negative critics who can always find something wrong with the church. I say this as a minister of the gospel, who loves the church; who was nurtured in its bosom; who has been sustained by its spiritual blessings and who will remain true to it as long as the cord of life shall lengthen.

When I was suddenly catapulted into the leadership of the bus protest in Montgomery, Alabama, a few years ago,[13] I felt we would be supported by the white church. I felt that the white ministers, priests, and rabbis of the South would be among our strongest allies. Instead, some have been outright opponents, refusing to understand the freedom movement and misrepresenting its leaders; all too many others have been more cautious than courageous and have remained silent behind the anesthetizing security of stained glass windows.

In spite of my shattered dreams, I came to Birmingham with the hope that the white religious leadership of this community would see the justice of our cause and, with deep moral concern, would serve as the channel through which our just grievances could reach the power structure. I had hoped that each of you would understand. But again I have been disappointed.

I have heard numerous southern religious leaders admonish their worshipers to comply with a desegregation decision because it is the law, but I have longed to hear white ministers declare: "Follow this decree because integration is morally right and because the Negro is your brother." In the midst of blatant injustices inflicted upon the Negro, I have watched white churchmen stand on the sideline and mouth pious irrelevancies and sanctimonious trivialities. In the midst of a mighty struggle to rid our nation of racial and economic injustice, I have heard many ministers say: "Those are social issues, with which the gospel has no real concern." And I have watched many churches commit themselves to a completely otherworldly religion which makes a strange, un-Biblical distinction between body and soul, between the sacred and the secular.

I have traveled the length and breadth of Alabama, Mississippi, and all the other southern states. On sweltering summer days and crisp autumn mornings I have looked at the South's beautiful churches with their lofty spires pointing heavenward. I have beheld the impressive outlines of her massive religious-education buildings. Over and over I have found myself asking: "What kind of people worship here? Who is their God? Where were their voices when the lips of Governor Barnett dripped with words of interposition and nullification? Where were they when Governor Wallace gave a clarion call for defiance and hatred?[14] Where were their voices of support when bruised and weary Negro men and women decided to rise from the dark dungeons of complacency to the bright hills of creative protest?"

Yes, these questions are still in my mind. In deep disappointment I have wept over the laxity of the church. But be assured that my tears have been tears of love. There can be no deep disappointment where there is not deep love. Yes, I love the church. How could I do otherwise? I am in the rather unique position of being the son, the grandson, and the great-grandson of preachers. Yes, I see the church as the body of Christ. But, oh! How we have blemished and scarred that body through social neglect and through fear of being nonconformists.

There was a time when the church was very powerful—in the time when the early Christians rejoiced at being deemed worthy to suffer for what they believed. In those days the church was not merely a thermometer that recorded the ideas and principles of popular opinion; it was a thermostat that transformed the mores of society. Whenever the early Christians entered a town, the people in power became disturbed and immediately sought to convict the Christians for being "disturbers of the peace" and "outside agitators." But the Christians pressed on, in the conviction that they were "a colony of heaven," called to obey God rather than man. Small in number, they were big in commitment. They were too God-intoxicated to be "astronomically intimidated." By their effort and example they brought an end to such ancient evils as infanticide and gladiatorial contests.

Things are different now. So often the contemporary church is a weak, ineffectual voice with an uncertain sound. So often it is an arch-defender of the status quo. Far from being disturbed by the presence of the church, the power structure of the average community is consoled by the church's silent—and often even vocal—sanction of things as they are.

But the judgment of God is upon the church as never before. If today's church does not recapture the sacrificial spirit of the early church, it will lose its authenticity, forfeit the loyalty of millions, and be dismissed as an irrelevant social club with no meaning for the twentieth century. Every day I meet young people whose disappointment with the church has turned into outright disgust.

Perhaps I have once again been too optimistic. Is organized religion too inextricably bound to the status quo to save our nation and the world? Perhaps I must turn my faith to the inner spiritual church, the church within the church, as the true *ekklesia*[15] and the hope of the world. But again I am thankful to God that some noble souls from the ranks of organized religion have broken loose from the paralyzing chains of conformity and joined us as active partners in the struggle for freedom. They have left their secure congregations and walked the streets of Albany, Georgia, with us. They have gone down the highways of the South on tortuous rides for freedom. Yes, they have gone to jail with us. Some have been dismissed from their churches, have lost the support of their bishops and fellow ministers. But they have acted in the faith that right defeated is stronger than evil triumphant. Their witness has been the spiritual salt that has preserved the true meaning of the gospel in these troubled times. They have carved a tunnel of hope though the dark mountain of disappointment.

I hope the church as a whole will meet the challenge of this decisive hour. But even if the church does not come to the aid of justice, I have no despair about the future. I have no fear about the outcome of our struggle in Birmingham, even if our motives are at present misunderstood. We will reach the goal of freedom in Birmingham and all over the nation, because the goal of America is freedom. Abused and scorned though we may be, our destiny is tied up with America's destiny. Before the pilgrims landed at Plymouth, we were here. Before the pen of Jefferson etched the majestic words of the Declaration of Independence across the pages of history, we were here. For more than two centuries our forebears labored in this country without wages; they made cotton king; they built the homes of their masters while suffering gross injustice and shameful humiliation—and yet out of a bottomless vitality they continued to thrive and develop. If the inexpressible cruelties of slavery could not stop us, the opposition we now face will surely fail. We will win our freedom because the sacred heritage of our nation and the eternal will of God are embodied in our echoing demands.

Before closing I feel impelled to mention one other point in your statement that has troubled me profoundly. You warmly commended the Birmingham police force for keeping "order" and "preventing violence." I doubt that you would have so warmly commended the police force if you had seen its dogs sinking their teeth into unarmed, nonviolent Negroes. I doubt that you would so quickly commend the policemen if you were to observe their ugly and inhumane treatment of Negroes here in the city jail; if you were to watch them push and curse old Negro women and young Negro girls; if you were to see them slap and kick old Negro men and young boys; if you were to observe them, as they did on two occasions, refuse to give us food because we wanted to sing our grace together. I cannot join you in your praise of the Birmingham police department.

It is true that the police have exercised a degree of discipline in handling the demonstrators. In this sense they have conducted themselves rather "nonviolently" in public. But for what purpose? To preserve the evil system of segregation. Over the past few years I have consistently preached that nonviolence demands that the means we use must be as pure as the ends we seek. I have tried to make clear that it is wrong to use immoral means to attain moral ends. But now I must affirm that it is just as wrong, or perhaps even more so, to use moral means to preserve immoral ends. Perhaps Mr. Connor and his policemen have been rather nonviolent in public, as was Chief Pritchett in Albany, Georgia, but they have used the moral means of nonviolence to maintain the immoral end of racial injustice. As T. S. Eliot has said: "The last temptation is the greatest treason: To do the right deed for the wrong reason."[16]

I wish you had commended the Negro sit-inners and demonstrators of Birmingham for their sublime courage, their willingness to suffer, and their amazing discipline in the midst of great provocation. One day the South will recognize its real heroes. They will be the James Merediths,[17] with the noble sense of purpose that enables them to face jeering and hostile mobs, and with the agonizing loneliness that characterizes the life of the pioneer. They will be old, oppressed, battered Negro women, symbolized in a seventy-two-year-old woman in Montgomery, Alabama, who rose up with a sense of dignity and with her people decided not to ride segregated buses, and who responded with ungrammatical profundity to one who inquired about her weariness: "My feets is tired, but my soul is at rest." They will be the young high school and college students, the young ministers of the gospel and a host of their elders, courageously and nonviolently sitting in at lunch counters and willingly going to jail for conscience' sake. One day the South will know that when these disinherited children of God sat down at lunch counters, they were in reality standing up for what is best in the American dream and for the most sacred values in our Judaeo-Christian heritage, thereby bringing our nation back to those great wells of democracy which were dug deep by the founding fathers in their formulation of the Constitution and the Declaration of Independence.

Never before have I written so long a letter. I'm afraid it is much too long to take your precious time. I can assure you that it would have been much shorter if I had been writing from a comfortable desk, but what else can one do when he is alone in a narrow jail cell, other than write long letters, think long thoughts, and pray long prayers?

If I have said anything in this letter that overstates the truth and indicates an unreasonable impatience, I beg you to forgive me. If I have said anything that understates the truth and indicates my having a patience that allows me to settle for anything less than brotherhood, I beg God to forgive me.

I hope this letter finds you strong in the faith. I also hope that circumstances will soon make it possible for me to meet each of you, not as an integrationist or a civil-rights leader but as a fellow clergyman and a Christian brother. Let us all hope that the dark clouds of racial prejudice will soon pass away and the deep fog of misunderstanding will be lifted from our fear-drenched communities, and in some not too distant tomorrow the radiant stars of love and brotherhood will shine over our great nation with all their scintillating beauty.

Yours for the cause of Peace and Brotherhood,
Martin Luther King, Jr.

Letter from Eight White Clergymen[18]

A Call for Unity

April 12, 1963

We the undersigned clergymen are among those who, in January, issued "An Appeal for Law and Order and Common Sense," in dealing with racial problems in Alabama. We expressed understanding that honest convictions in racial matters could properly be pursued in the courts, but urged that decisions of those courts should in the meantime be peacefully obeyed.

Since that time there had been some evidence of increased forebearance and a willingness to face facts. Responsible citizens have undertaken to work on various problems which cause racial friction and unrest. In Birmingham, recent public events have given indication that we all have opportunity for a new constructive and realistic approach to racial problems.

However, we are now confronted by a series of demonstrations by some of our Negro citizens, directed and led in part by outsiders. We recognize the natural impatience of people who feel that their hopes are slow in being realized. But we are convinced that these demonstrations are unwise and untimely.

We agree rather with certain local Negro leadership which has called for honest and open negotiation of racial issues in our area. And we believe this kind of facing of issues can best be accomplished by citizens of our own metropolitan area, white and Negro, meeting with their knowledge and experience of the local situation. All of us need to face that responsibility and find proper channels for its accomplishment.

Just as we formerly pointed out that "hatred and violence have no sanction in our religious and political traditions," we also point out that such actions as incite to hatred and violence, however technically peaceful those actions may be, have not contributed to the resolution of our local problems. We do not believe that these days of new hope are days when extreme measures are justified in Birmingham.

We commend the community as a whole, and the local news media and law enforcement officials in particular, on the calm manner in which these demonstrations have been handled. We urge the public to continue to show restraint should the demonstrations continue, and the law enforcement officials to remain calm and continue to protect our city from violence.

We further strongly urge our own Negro community to withdraw support from these demonstrations, and to unite locally in working peacefully for a better Birmingham. When rights are consistently denied, a cause should be pressed in the courts and in negotiations among local leaders, and not in the streets. We appeal to both our white and Negro citizenry to observe the principles of law and order and common sense.

C. C. J. Carpenter, D.D., L.L.D., Bishop of Alabama; Joseph A. Durick, D.D., Auxiliary Bishop, Diocese of Mobile-Birmingham; Rabbi Milton L. Grafman, Temple Emanu-El, Birmingham, Alabama; Bishop Paul Hardin, Bishop of the Alabama-West Florida Conference of the Methodist Church; Bishop Nolan B. Harmon, Bishop of the North Alabama Conference of the Methodist Church; George M. Murray, D.D., L.L.D., Bishop Coadjutor, Episcopal Diocese of Alabama; Edward V. Ramage, Moderator, Synod of the Alabama Presbyterian Church in the United States; Earl Stallings, Pastor, First Baptist Church, Birmingham.

Endnotes

1. This response to a published statement by eight fellow clergymen from Alabama (Bishop C. C. J. Carpenter, Bishop Joseph A. Durick, Rabbi Milton L. Grafman, Bishop Paul Hardin, Bishop Nolan B. Harmon, the Reverend George M. Murray, the Reverend Edward V. Ramage and the Reverend Earl Stallings) was composed under somewhat constricting circumstances. Begun on the margins of the newspaper in which the statement appeared while I was in jail, the letter was continued on scraps of writing paper supplied by a friendly Negro trusty, and concluded on a pad my attorneys were eventually permitted to leave me. Although the text remains in substance unaltered, I have indulged in the author's prerogative of polishing it for publication [King's note].

2. American Protestant theologian (1892–1971).

3. Early Christian church father (354–430).

4. Christian philosopher and theologian (1225–1274).

5. German-born Israeli (1878–1965).

6. German-born American Protestant theologian (1886–1965).

7. Daniel 3.

8. The ancient Greek philosopher Socrates was tried by the Athenians for corrupting their youth through his skeptical, questioning manner of teaching. He refused to change his ways and was condemned to death.

9. In the anti-Communist revolution of 1956, which was quickly put down by the Russian army.

10. Elijah Muhammed (1897–1975), succeeded to the leadership of the Nation of Islam in 1934.

11. The spirit of the times.

12. English preacher and author (1628–1688); Amos was an Old Testament prophet; Paul a New Testament apostle; Luther (1483–1546), German Protestant reformer.

13. Began in December 1955, when Rosa Parks refused to move to the Negro section of a bus.

14. George Wallace (1919–), governor of Alabama, opposed admission of several black students to the University of Alabama. Ross Barnett (1898–1988), governor of Mississippi, opposed James Meredith's admission to the University of Mississippi.

15. The Greek New Testament word for the early Christian church.

16. Eliot (1888–1965), American-born English poet, in *Murder in the Cathedral*.

17. Meredith was the first black to enroll at the University of Mississippi.

18. This account is drawn from Lee E. Bains, Jr., "Birmingham, 1963: Confrontation over Civil Rights," in *Birmingham, Alabama, 1956–1963: The Black Struggle for Civil Rights*, ed. David J. Garrow (Brooklyn: Carlson, 1989), pp. 175–183.

Questions for Reading and Analysis

1. Read the "Letter from Eight White Clergymen," the document to which King responds in his "Letter From Birmingham Jail." Make a list of the arguments the eight white clergymen make against Civil Rights demonstrations in Birmingham. Then show, in some detail, how King refutes these arguments.

2. What arguments does King make in addition to his refutations of the eight white clergymen's accusations?

3. Most of paragraph 14 consists of a single sentence. What rhetorical effect does King gain from employing this technique?

4. In what ways does King's writing style reflect his training as a preacher and clergyman?

5. Who is King's audience? In what way does he anticipate the values of his audience and present his ideas in a way so as not to alienate them?

6. Do you agree with King's statement that "one has the moral responsibility to disobey unjust laws"? Can you think of modem-day examples of unjust laws?

Paul Kingsnorth, an environmental campaigner, first published his article in The Ecologist *in 2000, warning his audience about the medical (and, consequently, economic) problems global warming has in store for the human race.*

Human Health on the Line

Paul Kingsnorth

"Climate Change is likely to have wide-ranging and mostly adverse impacts on human health, with significant loss of life." Thus, the 2,000 scientists of the IPCC condemn future generations to the sort of battle against deadly diseases which the wonder drugs and scientific miracles of the twentieth century were supposed to have banished forever.

Of the many scientists who have projected, predicted and warned of the likely health effects of climate change, almost all agree on the basics: they will be widespread and unpredictable, they are likely to be severe, and many, many people across the world will die as a result.

The likely health effects are best divided into two categories: direct and indirect. Direct effects will result from direct exposure to the weather extremes that climate change will cause, for example: heat-stroke, hypothermia and deaths or injuries resulting from tidal waves, floods, hurricanes etc. Indirect effects will result from subsequent changes in environment and ecosystems—for example: the spread of vector-borne diseases into new areas, nutrition problems resulting from crop failure, diseases spread by algal blooms in warming seas, and even the mental health problems which may result from social and political dislocation.

Direct Effects

We are already seeing examples of some of the more obvious direct effects of climate change on human health. Just a few examples give some idea of the scale of the problem. In 1996, North Koreans were reduced to eating leaves and grass, following flash floods that destroyed their crops. Many suffered from malnutrition. That same year, 60 people in Spain died after a flash flood in the Pyrenees. In 1997, the worst rains in 30 years destroyed half of all Bolivia's crops, with hunger resulting, and a November typhoon in Vietnam resulted in 2,500 dead or missing. In 1998, heat-waves in India and the mid-USA killed over 4,000 people. Hurricane Mitch in Central America killed or injured an estimated 11,000. The Indonesian forest fires, started by man and exacerbated by warmer and drier-than-average weather caused a massive increase in respiratory illnesses; crops were drowned in several countries, and fisheries failed, leading to an increase in hunger. Almost every one of these events was record-setting or breaking, and there are hundreds more such examples that could be quoted.

Predictions for the future point to more—much more—of the same, on a wider scale. The latest predictions from the UK's Hadley Centre, published in 1998 and based on an updated computer model, predict that at least 170 million people will be living in areas which are "extremely stressed" through lack of water in the next century, with death and severe illness the likely result. The Hadley Centre also predicts that 18 per cent more of the African population will suffer from hunger and malnutrition due to climate change than at present, and that, globally, over 20 million extra people each year will be at risk of flooding.[1]

One health problem that is likely to become much more widespread in the 21st century is that known by scientists as "thermal stress"—in everyday language, the effects of getting too hot or too cold, particularly during ever-more-frequent heat-waves and extreme winters. Detailed studies of the effects of extreme weather on mortality rates have been conducted in many countries and, unsurprisingly, report a close correlation, particularly amongst children, the elderly and the infirm. Deaths from stroke, various cardiovascular illnesses, heat-stroke, hypothermia and influenza, in particular, are much more common during extremes of weather: and this applies to "developed" as well as "developing" countries. [2]

Indirect Effects

A recent issue of *New Scientist* magazine reported that "human disease is emerging as one of the most sensitive, and distressing, indicators of climate change."[3] It is accepted by virtually all climate scientists that the likely increase in, and spread of, potentially fatal diseases is likely to be the single most dangerous threat that climate change poses to human health. If many of the direr predictions are right, the flowering of diseases as the climate changes is very likely to negate the benefits of twentieth-century medical advances, and see the rebirth of diseases currently assumed to be "conquered."

A major threat will come from an increase of so-called "vector-borne" diseases—those spread by pests, insects and other small creatures, such as snails. Dr. Paul Epstein, of the Harvard Medical School, who has produced numerous studies and reports on this subject, believes that the spread of these diseases could be even more serious than currently feared.

"Pests" such as rodents, insects and weeds, points out Epstein, are "opportunists": they reproduce rapidly, have huge broods and wide appetites, and can quickly overrun an ecosystem if left to themselves. In a healthy ecosystem, there will be enough predators—lizards, birds and bats to eat the mosquitoes: owls and snakes to eat the rodents, etc.—to keep pest populations under control. However, the effect of global climate change will be to destabilise ecosystems across the globe, and disrupt predator-prey relationships. The result, in many places, is likely to be a vast increase in disease-carrying pests.[4]

Epstein recently produced a study showing that, in many parts of the world, climatic disruption is already causing rodent-borne diseases to spread—and in some cases actually causing new diseases to emerge. In the early 1990s in the USA, for example, a combination of prolonged drought—which killed predators such as coyotes, snakes and owls—followed by heavy rains, precipitated a ten-fold increase in the rodent population (rodents thrive in and around water, even if it is contaminated). This plague of rodents led to the emergence of a new disease—Hantavirus Pulmonary Syndrome—which was apparently transmitted to humans via the rodents' droppings. Similar hantaviruses have also emerged, in similar climatic conditions, in several European nations, particularly Yugoslavia, while other rodent-borne diseases, like leptospirosis and vital haemorrhagic fevers, have spread across Latin America.[5]

While localised and regional climatic changes are likely to lead to an increase in vector-borne diseases, the average global rise in temperature will also exacerbate the same trend. Many disease-carrying insects—most obviously the malarial mosquito—thrive in warm conditions; as the world warms, they will begin to find more places in which they can breed. A 1996 report from the London School of Hygiene and Tropical Medicine illustrated this point clearly when it calculated that, of ten of the world's most dangerous vector-borne diseases (malaria, schistosomiasis, dengue fever, lymphatic filariasis, sleeping sickness, Guinea worm, leishmaniasis, river blindness, Chagas' disease and yellow fever), all but one were likely to increase, or in some way change their range as a result of climate change.[6]

Malaria is the world's most prevalent mosquito-borne disease: two million people die from it every year.[7] But it is likely to get worse. One scientist has called malaria "an old disease with the potential of re-emerging as a new disease, especially in association with climate change,"[8] and virtually all experts seem to agree that one effect of climate change will be to increase the range of the malarial mosquito. The IPCC predicts that malaria will spread from affecting 45 per cent of the population, as it does today, to affecting 60 per cent by the latter half of the next century—of the order of 50–80 million additional annual cases.[9] The Hadley Centre's 1998 study predicted a significant spread in the mosquito's range, largely as a result of the warming of previously temperate areas—including parts of Europe and North America. Malaria is also likely to spread to high altitude areas, such as the Andes, as their average temperature rises.[10]

Again, it seems that in some places this is already beginning: malaria has already begun to affect the previously mosquito-free African highlands,[11] and upland rural areas of Papua New Guinea.[12] Urban centres are beginning to suffer as well: many central African cities are experiencing urban malaria for the first time,[13] and two recent cases in New York City were traced to local mosquitoes.[14] Furthermore Paul Epstein, in studying cases of malaria linked to the recent El Nino, has found that large and deadly outbreaks across Asia were one result of climatic upheavals there.[15]

Other vector-borne diseases are likely to become more common—and hence more deadly—too. Again, the spread is already beginning. Mosquito-borne yellow fever has recently invaded Ethiopia, and dengue fever, spreading through the Americas, has already reached Texas. Recent floods in north-east Kenya caused Rift Valley Fever, a cattle disease, to jump the species barrier and kill hundreds of people.[16] In 1994, the pneumonic plague resurfaced in India, during a summer in which temperatures reached as high as 124 degrees Fahrenheit.[17] We should expect more of the same as the thermometers of many nations are thrown out of kilter by man-made climate change.

And it is not just vector-borne diseases that are likely to take advantage of the changing climate. Other infectious killers are likely to enjoy a resurgence too, particularly diseases associated with water supply and sanitation. A 1996 WHO report laid out the threat starkly: "climate change could have a major impact on water resources and sanitation by reducing water supply. This could in turn reduce the water available for drinking and washing, and lower the efficiency of local sewerage systems, leading to increased concentration of pathogenic organisms in raw water supplies."[18]

This was the situation in 1991, when Peru was devastated by a cholera epidemic (which quickly spread across Latin America, killing over 5,000 people in eighteen months) linked with the warmer waters of El Nino. "Of course," wrote Karen Schmidt, in the *New Scientist*, "it is really global warming that is involved."[19] Cholera, often assumed to be largely a disease of the past, may well become common again in the 21st century, as global warming bites. Paul Epstein's pioneering work has also pointed out a hidden threat in this area, too: not only is cholera associated with poor sanitation and polluted inland waters, but it can also be harboured in marine plankton. Epstein believes that this was the original cause of the 1991 epidemic in Latin America.[20]

Apart from cholera, other water-borne and water-related diseases are also likely to increase and spread too, for the same reasons: typhoid, hepatitis A, diarrhoeal diseases (major killers of young children in "developing" countries), scabies, trachoma and schistosomiasis, to name but a few.[21] But water-and-climate-change-caused diseases are linked in another way, too: the ocean itself could become, and may even already be becoming, a new vector for fatal diseases.

In January this year, the *New York Times* reported that previously unknown bacteria, fungi and viruses are beginning to bloom in the oceans as they warm, killing coral and fish, and threatening human health. Joan B. Rose, from the University of South Florida, reported that human viruses were spreading into the warming seas from the 1.8 million septic tanks along the Florida coast. "Many people are becoming infected with viruses picked up while swimming, windsurfing or bathing in infected waters," she confirmed. James W. Porter, from the University of Georgia, believes that this unprecedented problem is linked to a rise of 1.8 degrees Celsius in ocean temperature which climate change has already caused in the area.[22]

Paul Epstein has studied the relationship between climate change, ocean pollution and disease, too, and has produced equally worrying conclusions. His suggestion that cholera can be transmitted by marine plankton has already been mentioned, but he has also postulated that coastal algal blooms already being seen in many of the world's seas—as a direct result of the warming of the water—are also transmitters of disease, often via fish and shellfish. In the summer of 1992, for example, after a long warm period, blooms known as Alexandrium tamarense developed in the seas around Newfoundland, infecting shellfish with a disease known as Paralytic Shellfish Poisoning (PSP) which was transmitted to humans who ate the shellfish. Similar PSP incidents have since occurred in waters around the east coast of the USA, Canada and the UK. Toxic "brown tides" have poisoned scallops and eels, and numerous other episodes of fish intended for human consumption being poisoned by algal blooms have been catalogued by Epstein.[23]

One obvious, but often overlooked, consequence of the health problems which climate change is preparing to visit on us, is the financial cost of dealing with the problem. Economists and industrialists who insist that taking any action to combat climate change will threaten the world's economies might like to consider the economic costs of doing nothing. In terms of human health, some of those costs are already being borne: Epstein reports that the 1991 cholera epidemic cost Peru over $1 billion, while airline and hotel industries lost between $2 billion and $5 billion from the 1994 Indian plague. Cruise boats are already avoiding islands in the Indian Ocean plagued by dengue fever—and are threatening the area's $12 billion tourist industry in the process.[24]

This short article has only scratched the surface of this issue. It has not even begun to address some of the threats that are more difficult to predict, such as the potential diseases of the mind which could stem from the chaos caused by a changing climate—what psychiatrists call the "psychosocial" problems associated with economic collapse, institutional breakup and social upheaval.[25] Hundreds of papers, millions of words and many laboratories and books have been dedicated to predicting the likely effects of climate change on human health. But the simple fact is that many of those effects are likely to catch us unawares. In medical terms, it is more than likely that, as Paul Epstein succinctly puts it, we are "vastly underestimating the true costs of 'business-as-usual'; and underestimating the benefits to society as a whole of using the resources we have inherited efficiently."[26]

Endnotes

1. *Climate Change and Its Impacts.* Met Office/DETR, November 1998.

2. McMichael, A.; Haines, A.; Slooff, R.; Kovats, S. (Eds.), *Climate Change and Human Health*, WHO, 1996, Ch. 4.

3. Pearce, F. "Health Crisis," *New Scientist.* 19 December–2 January 1999, p. 33.

4. Epstein, P. "Health Consequences of Climate Change," unpublished manuscript, 1998.

5. Ibid.

6. McMichael, A., quoted in Martens, P., "Health and Climate Change," *Earthscan*, 1998, p. 29.

7. Op. cit. 2, p. 78.

8. Colwell, R., "Global Climate and Infectious Disease: The Cholera Paradigm," *Science.* Vol. 274. 20 Dec. 1996. pp. 2025–2031.

9. *Climate Change 1995: IPCC Second Assessment Report* (summary), UNEP/WMO, 1995, p. 36

10. Op. cit. 2.

11. Op. cit. 3.

12. Op. cit. 4.

13. Op. cit. 4.

14. Op. cit, 6.

15. Op. cit. 4.

16. Op. cit. 3.

17. Op, cit. 4.

18. Op. cit. 2, p.96.

19. Schmidt, K., "Testing the Waters," *New Scientist*. 15 November 1997, p. 46.

20. Op. cit. 4.

21. Op. cit. 2, p. 97,

22. "As Oceans Warm, Problems from Viruses and Bacteria Mount," *New York Times*. 24 January 1999.

23. Epstein, P., "Emergent Stressors and Public Health Implications in Large Marine Ecosystems: An Overview," US EPA, 1996.

24. Op. cit. 4.

25. Op. cit, 4, p. 139.

26. Op. cit. 4.

Questions for Reading and Analysis

1. What is Kingsnorth's major point? What does Kingsnorth hope readers will know and/or do after reading his piece?

2. Kingsnorth uses a variety of sources to back up his argument, and he documents them carefully. What is the effect of this technique on the reader?

3. Consider Kingsnorth's intended audience, readers of *The Ecologist*. In what ways does he cater to this particular audience?

In "Kids in the Mall," *an excerpt from his 1985 book,* The Malling of America, *William Kowinski investigates the possible dangers of teenagers' over-exposure to shopping malls.*

Kids in the Mall:
Growing Up Controlled

William Severini Kowinski

Butch heaved himself up and loomed over the group. "Like it was different for me," he piped. "My folks used to drop me off at the shopping mall every morning and leave me all day. It was like a big free babysitter, you know? One night they never came back for me. Maybe they moved away. Maybe there's some kind of a Bureau of Missing Parents I could check with."

Richard Peck
Secrets of the Shopping Mall,
a novel for teenagers

From his sister at Swarthmore, I'd heard about a kid in Florida whose mother picked him up after school every day, drove him straight to the mall, and left him there until it closed—all at his insistence. I'd heard about a boy in Washington who, when his family moved from one suburb to another, pedaled his bicycle five miles every day to get back to his old mall, where he once belonged.

These stories aren't unusual. The mall is a common experience for the majority of American youth: they have probably been going there all their lives. Some ran within their first large open space, saw their first fountain, bought their first toy, and read their first book in a mall. They may have smoked their first cigarette or first joint, or turned them down, had their first kiss or lost their virginity in the mall parking lot. Teenagers in America now spend more time in the mall than anywhere else but home and school. Mostly it is their choice, but some of that mall time is put in as the result of two-paycheck and single-parent households, and the lack of other viable alternatives. But are these kids being harmed by the mall?

I wondered first of all what difference it makes for adolescents to experience so many important moments in the mall. They are, after all, at play in the fields of its little world and they learn its ways: they adapt to it and make it adapt to them. It's here that these kids get their street sense, only it's mall sense. They are learning the ways of a large-scale, artificial environment; its subtleties and flexibilities, its particular pleasures and resonances, and the attitudes it fosters.

252

The presence of so many teenagers for so much time was not something mall developers planned on. In fact, it came as a big surprise. But kids became a fact of mall life very easily, and the International Council of Shopping Centers found it necessary to commission a study, which they published along with a guide to mall managers on how to handle the teenage incursion.

The study found that "teenagers in suburban centers are bored and come to the shopping centers mainly as a place to go. Teenagers in suburban centers spent more time fighting, drinking, littering, and walking than did their urban counterparts, but presented fewer overall problems." The report observed that "adolescents congregated in groups of two to four and predominantly at locations selected by them rather than management." This probably had something to do with the decision to install game arcades, which allow management to channel these restless adolescents into naturally contained areas away from major traffic points of adult shoppers.

The guide concluded that mall management should tolerate and even encourage the teenage presence because, in the words of the report, "The vast majority support the same set of values as does shopping center management." *The same set of values* means simply that mall kids are already preprogrammed to be consumers and that the mall can put the finishing touches to them as hard-core, lifelong shoppers just like everybody else. That, after all, is what the mall is about. So it shouldn't be surprising that in spending a lot of time there, adolescents find little that challenges the assumption that the goal of life is to make money and buy products, or that just about everything else in life is to be used to serve those ends.

Growing up in a high-consumption society already adds inestimable pressure to kids' lives. Clothes consciousness has invaded the grade schools, and popularity is linked with having the best, newest clothes in the currently acceptable styles. Even what they read has been affected. "Miss [Nancy] Drew wasn't obsessed with her wardrobe," noted the *Wall Street Journal*. "But today the mystery in teen fiction for girls is what outfit the heroine will wear next." Shopping has become a survival skill and there is certainly no better place to learn it than the mall, where its importance is powerfully reinforced and certainly never questioned.

The mall as a university of suburban materialism, where Valley Girls and Boys from coast to coast are educated in consumption, has its other lessons in this era of change in family life and sexual mores and their economic and social ramifications. The plethora of products in the mall, plus the pressure on teens to buy them, may contribute to the phenomenon that psychologist David Elkind calls "the hurried child": kids who are exposed to too much of the adult world too quickly and must respond with a sophistication that belies their still-tender emotional development. Certainly the adult products marketed for children—form-fitting designer jeans, sexy tops for preteen girls—add to the social pressure to look like an adult, along with the home-grown need to understand adult finances (why mothers must work) and adult emotions (when parents divorce).

Kids spend so much time at the mall partly because their parents allow it and even encourage it. The mall is safe, doesn't seem to harbor any unsavory activities, and there is adult supervision; it is, after all, a controlled environment. So the temptation, especially for working parents, is to let the mall be their baby-sitter. At least the kids aren't watching TV. But the mall's role as a surrogate mother may be more extensive and more profound.

Karen Lansky, a writer living in Los Angeles, has looked into the subject, and she told me some of her conclusions about the effects on its teenaged denizens of the mall's controlled and controlling environment. "Structure is the dominant idea, since true 'mall rats' lack just that in their home lives," she said, "and adolescents about to make the big leap into growing up crave more structure than our modern society cares to acknowledge." Karen pointed out some of the elements malls supply that kids used to get from their families, like warmth (Strawberry Shortcake dolls and similar cute and cuddly merchandise), old-fashioned mothering ("We do it all for you," the fast-food slogan), and even home cooking (the "homemade" treats at the food court).

The problem in all this, as Karen Lansky sees it, is that while families nurture children by encouraging growth through the assumption of responsibility and then by letting them rest in the bosom of the family from the rigors of growing up, the mall as a structural mother encourages passivity and consumption, as long as the kid doesn't make trouble. Therefore all they learn about becoming adults is how to act and how to consume.

Kids are in the mall not only in the passive role of shoppers—they also work there, especially as fast-food outlets infiltrate the mall's enclosure. There they learn how to hold a job and take responsibility, but still within the same value context. When *CBS Reports* went to Oak Park Mall in suburban Kansas City, Kansas, to tape part of their hour-long consideration of malls, "After the Dream Comes True," they interviewed a teenaged girl who worked in a fast-food outlet there. In a sequence that didn't make the final program, she described the major goal of her present life, which was to perfect the curl on top of the ice-cream cones that were her store's specialty. If she could do that, she would be moved from the lowly soft-drink dispenser to the more prestigious ice-cream division, the curl on top of the status ladder at her restaurant. These are the achievements that are important at the mall.

Other benefits of such jobs may also be overrated, according to Laurence D. Steinberg of the University of California at Irvine's social ecology department, who did a study on teenage employment. Their jobs, he found, are generally simple, mindlessly repetitive and boring. They don't really learn anything, and the jobs don't lead anywhere. Teenagers also work primarily with other teenagers; even their supervisors are often just a little older than they are. "Kids need to spend time with adults," Steinberg told me. "Although they get benefits from peer relationships, without parents and other adults it's one-side socialization. They hang out with each other, have age-segregated jobs, and watch TV."

Perhaps much of this is not so terrible or even so terribly different. Now that they have so much more to contend with in their lives, adolescents probably need more time to spend with other adolescents without adult impositions, just to sort things out. Though it is more concentrated in the mall (and therefore perhaps a clearer target), the value system there is really the dominant one of the whole society. Attitudes about curiosity, initiative, self-expression, empathy, and disinterested learning aren't necessarily made in the mall; they are mirrored there, perhaps a bit more intensely—as through a glass brightly.

Besides, the mall is not without its educational opportunities. There are bookstores, where there is at least a short shelf of classics at great prices, and other books from which it is possible to learn more than how to do sit-ups. There are tools, from hammers to VCRs, and products, from clothes to records, that can help the young find and express themselves. There are older people with stories, and places to be alone or to talk one-on-one with a kindred spirit. And there is always the passing show.

The mall itself may very well be an education about the future. I was struck with the realization, as early as my first forays into Greengate, that the mall is only one of a number of enclosed and controlled environments that are part of the lives of today's young. The mall is just an extension, say, of those large suburban schools—only there's Karmelkorn instead of chem lab, the ice rink instead of the gym: It's high school without the impertinence of classes.

Growing up, moving from home to school to the mall—from enclosure to enclosure, transported in cars—is a curiously continuous process, without much in the way of contrast or contact with unenclosed reality. Places must tend to blur into one another. But whatever differences and dangers there are in this, the skills these adolescents are learning may turn out to be useful in their later lives. For we seem to be moving inexorably into an age of preplanned and regulated environments, and this is the world they will inherit.

Still, it might be better if they had more of a choice. One teenaged girl confessed to *CBS Reports* that she sometimes felt she was missing something by hanging out at the mall so much. "But I'm here," she said, "and this is what I have."

Questions for Reading and Analysis

1. What central question prompts Kowinski's close look at mall culture?

2. In what ways do mall rats "support the same set of values" as the mall management? Why does the study commissioned by International Council of Shopping Centers recommend that teenagers not be discouraged from hanging out at the mall?

3. In what ways do malls replace families in the mall rats' lives? Are there advantages to this development?

4. Where is his thesis? Why doesn't he state it in the beginning? (What does he put in his introduction, though, as a hint to the reader about his thesis?)

5. Is Kowinski's point that malls are just an extension of the various "enclosed and controlled environments" teenagers grow up in (home, school) scary? Does the prospect of moving "into an age of preplanned and regulated environments" scare you?

Jonathan Kozol taught in a Boston inner-city school before becoming a leading proponent of public education reform. He has since written extensively on the subject. The following article, which argues that the illiterate are the most invisible and politically powerless group in America, is a chapter from his 1985 work Illiterate America.

The Disenfranchised: Silent and Unseen

Jonathan Kozol

Im 33 now and finly made a go. But the walls are up agent. and this time I don't think I can go around them. What Im I to do. I still have some engeny left. But running out. Im afraide to run out. I don't know if I can settle for noting.

—*letter to the author, 1983*

It is difficult for most Americans to place full credence in the facts described above.

If we did, we would be forced to choose between enormous guilt and efficacious action. The willingness of decent people to withhold belief or to anaesthetize their capability for credence represents the hardest problem that we need to overcome in dealing with the dangers that we know in abstract ways but somehow cannot concretize in ways that force us to take action.

One reason for the nation's incredulity, of course, is the deceptive impact of the U.S. census figures. Until recent years, these figures have been taken as authoritative indices of national reality. While it has been recognized for decades that the nonwhite population has been underrepresented in the census, it may be that it is not black people but illiterate adults who represent, in categorical terms, the largest sector of invisible Americans. Many blacks and other minorities decline, for fear of government intrusion, to respond to written forms. Illiterates do not "decline"; they cannot read the forms at all.

This, however, is not the only explanation. Illiterates find it painful to identify themselves. In a print society, enormous stigma is attached to the adult nonreader. Early in the game we see the evolution of a whole line of defensive strategies against discovery by others. "Lying low" and watching out for "traps" become a pattern of existence.

An illiterate young man, nineteen years of age, sits beside me in a restaurant and quietly surveys the menu. After a long time he looks at the waitress, hesitates as if uncertain of his preference, then tells her: "Well, I guess I'll have a hamburger—with fries." When she asks what he would like to drink, he pauses again, then states with some conviction: "Well, I guess I'd like a Coke."

It took me several months, although I was this young man's neighbor, to discover that he could not read a word. He had learned to order those three items which he felt assured of finding in all restaurants. He had had a lot of hamburgers and french fries in nineteen years.

Peter had been victimized initially by some incredibly incompetent officials in the Boston schools. He could not look for backup to his family. His father could not read. His mother had died when he was very young. This was a one-parent family which, unlike the stereotype that is accepted as the norm, was headed not by an unmarried woman, but by an undereducated and religious man. But Peter had been victimized a final time by some of those (myself included) who were living in his neighborhood and who ought to have perceived that he was literally frozen in the presence of the written word.

Being ingenious and sophisticated far beyond his years, he was able to disguise his fear of words to a degree that totally deceived me. I might never have identified his inability to read if it had not been for an entirely social happenstance. One day, driving by the ocean north of Boston, I stopped to take him to a seafood restaurant in Gloucester. He broke into a sweat, began to tremble, and then asked if we could leave. He asked me, suddenly, if we could go to Howard Johnson's.

This, I discovered, was the one escape hatch he had managed to contrive. Howard Johnson's, unattractive as it may appear in contrast to a lobster restaurant beside the sea, provided Peter with his only opportunity for culinary options. Here, because of the array of color photographs attached in celluloid containers to each item on the menu, he was able to branch out a bit and treat himself to ice cream sodas and fried clams. Howard Johnson's, knowingly or not, has held for many years a captive clientele of many millions of illiterate adults.

Today, the other fast-food chains provide the pictures too. Certain corporations, going even further in the wish to give employment to illiterate teenagers, now are speaking of a plan to make use of cash registers whose keys are marked with product symbols in the place of numbers. The illiterate employee merely needs to punch the key that shows "two burgers" or one "Whopper." It is a good device for giving jobs to print (and numerate) nonreaders. Obviating errors and perhaps some personal embarrassment, it pacifies the anguish of illiterates but it does not give them motivation to escape the trap which leaves them powerless to find more interesting employment. Illiterates, in this way, come to be both captive customers and captive counter workers for such corporations.

An illiterate cattle farmer in Vermont describes the strategies that he employs to hide his inability to read. "You have to be careful," he explains, "not to get into situations where it would leak out . . . . You always try to act intelligent . . . If somebody gives you something to read, you make believe you read it."

Sooner or later, the strategies run out. A man who has been able to obtain a good job in a laboratory testing dairy products for impurities survives by memorizing crystals and their various reactions. Offered promotion, he is told that he will be obliged to take a brief exam. He brings home books that have been given to him by his boss for preparation. Knowing the examination is a written one, he loses heart. He never shows up at this job again. His boss perhaps will spend some hours wondering why.

Husbands and wives can sometimes cover for each other. Illiterates may bring home applications, written forms of various kinds, and ask their spouse or children to fill in the answers. When this stratagem no longer works (when they are asked, for instance, to check out a voucher or a bill of lading on the job) the game is up, the worker disappears.

Once we get to know someone like Peter, we can understand the courage that it takes for an illiterate adult to break down the defenses and to ask for help. Our government's refusal to provide an answer for the millions who have found the nerve to ask seems all the more heartbreaking for this reason. One hundred forty thousand men and women in the State of Illinois alone have asked for literacy help from local agencies which have been forced to turn them down for lack of federal funds. They have been consigned to waiting lists. How many of these people, having asked and been refused, will find the courage to apply for help again?

On the streets of New York City or Chicago, one out of every three or four adults we pass is a nonreader. Unlike the stranger who does not speak English, or whose skin is brown or black, the person who is illiterate can "pass." By virtue of those strategies that guard them from humiliation, illiterates have also managed to remain unseen.

Political impotence may represent an even larger obstacle to recognition than the fear of personal humiliation.

Others who have been victimized at least are able to form lobbies, organize agendas, issue press releases, write to politicians, and, if they do not receive responsive answers, form a voting bloc to drive those politicians out of office. Illiterates have no access to such methods of political redress.

We are told in school that, when we have a problem or complaint, we should write a letter "to our representative at City Hall" or to an elected politician in the nation's capitol. Politicians do not answer letters that illiterates can't write. The leverage of political negotiation that we take for granted and assign such hopeful designations as "the Jeffersonian ideal" is denied the man or woman who cannot participate in print society. Neither the press release nor the handwritten flier that can draw a crowd into a protest meeting at a local church lies within the reach of the nonreader. Victims exist, but not constituencies. Democracy is posited on efficacious actions that require print initiative. Even the most highly motivated persons, if they do not read and write, cannot lobby for their own essential needs. They can speak (and now and then a journalist may hear) but genuine autonomy is far beyond them.

Illiterates may carry picket signs but cannot write them and, in any case, can seldom read them. Even the rock-bottom levels of political communication—the spray paint and graffiti that adorn the walls of subways and deserted buildings in impoverished neighborhoods—are instruments of discourse which are far beyond the range of the illiterate American. Walking in a ghetto neighborhood or in a poor white area of Boston, we see the sprawl of giant letters that decry the plight of black, Hispanic, women, gay, or other persecuted groups. We read no cogent outcries from illiterates.

The forfeiture of self-created lobbies is perhaps the major reason for political inaction. Those who might speak, however, on behalf of the illiterate—neighborhood organizers, for example, or the multitude of private literacy groups—tend to default on an apparent obligation. For this, there seems to be at least one obvious explanation.

Community leaders—black leaders in particular—have been reluctant to direct the focus of attention to the crisis of adult illiteracy within the lowest economic levels of the population. Their reticence is based upon misguided fear. In pointing to the 44 percent of black adults who cannot read or write at levels needed for participation in American society, they are afraid that they may offer ammunition to those racist and reactionary persons who are often eager to attribute failure to innate inadequacy or who, while they refrain from stating this, will nonetheless believe it. Naming the victim should not be equated with the age-old inclination to place blame upon the victim. Indeed, it tends to work the other way around. Refusal to name a victim and, still more, to offer details as to how that victimization is perpetuated and passed on is a fairly certain guarantee that people in pain will not be seen and that their victimization will not be addressed. Well-intentioned white allies of black political groups are even more susceptible to this mistake than most black leaders.*

Sensible organizers understand that silence on this subject is a no-win strategy. If people are injured, injury must be described. If they have not been injured—as the silence of some partisans dogmatically implies—then they have no claim upon compassion and no right to seek corrective measures. Blaming this victim is *vindictive*. Naming the victim is the first step in a struggle to remove the chains.

If understandable, this hesitation on the part of many leaders is politically unsound. They lose the massive voting bloc which otherwise might double and, in certain urban areas, quadruple their constituencies. Black citizens, illiterate or not, may vote in overwhelming numbers for black candidates. When, as in some recent mayoral elections and in the campaign of Jesse Jackson in the presidential primaries of 1984, the options are a single black and one or more white candidates, the voting power of black people is self-evident. But when, in the more common situation, the choices are among a number of white candidates of widely differing positions (or, for that matter, a number of black candidates of widely differing degrees of merit), a black electorate which is substantially excluded from print access cannot make discerning or autonomous decisions. A physically attractive demagogue who knows the way to key his language to immediate and short-term interests of poor people may win himself a large part of the vote from those for whom his long-term bias and his past performance ought to constitute a solemn admonition.

Illiterate voters, cut off from the most effective means of repossession of the past, denied the right to learn from recent history because they are denied all access to the written record of the candidate (or to the editorial reminders of that record which most newspapers supply), are locked into the present and enslaved by the encapsulated moment which is symbolized by the sixty-second newsclip on TV or the thirty-second paid advertisement that candidates employ in order to exploit the well-organized amnesia of Americans.

Illiterate Americans, denied almost all contact with the print-recorded past, cannot effectively address the present nor anticipate the future. They cannot learn from Santayana's warning. They have never heard of Santayana.

Exclusion from the printed word renders one third of America the ideal supine population for the "total state" that Auden feared and Orwell prophesied: undefended against doublespeak, unarmed against the orchestrated domination of their minds. Choice demands reflection and decision. Readers of the press at least can stand back and react; they can also find dissenting sources of opinion. The speed and power of electric media allow no time for qualified reflection. The TV viewer, whether literate or not, is temporarily a passive object: a receptacle for someone else's views. While all of us have proven vulnerable to this effect, it is the illiterate who has been rendered most susceptible to that entire domination which depends upon denial of the full continuum of time and its causations.

There is some danger of implicit overstatement here. Illiterate people do not represent a single body of undifferentiated human beings. Most illiterates do not remain all day in front of the TV, silent and entranced, to "drink it in." Many, moreover, draw upon their own experience to discount or refute nine-tenths of what they see before them on TV. Others can draw on oral history, the stories they hear, the anecdotes they have been told by parents or by older friends. Injustice itself is a profound instructor. Intuitive recognition of a fraud—a politician or a product—can empower many people to resist the absoluteness of control which television otherwise might exercise upon their wishes or convictions.

Nonetheless, it is the truth that many illiterates, deeply depressed and socially withdrawn, do not venture far from home and, out of the sheer longing for escape and for the simulation of "communication," do become for hours and weeks the passive addicts of the worst of what is offered on TV. Their lives and even eating schedules have been parceled out to match the thirty-minute packages of cultural domestication and the sixty-second units of purported information which present the news in isolation from the history that shaped it or the future that it threatens to extinguish.

Many of these people would not choose to undermine or to refute a form of entertainment which has come to take a permanent place within their home—their one fast-talking friend. Many more have been so long and indoctrinated to indict themselves, and not society, for their impoverished and illiterate condition that there is no chance of taking lessons from injustice. They cannot denounce what seems to them to be the normal world of those who have the "know-how" to enjoy it. Nor can they profit from the learnings of an older family member who is frequently too weary and depressed to speak at length about a lifetime (or a recent history) which he or she may not desire to remember and may have been led to view not as a blessing to pass on but as a curse to be denied or wished away.

For people like these (and there are many millions, I believe) the following is true: They live in a truncated present tense. The future seems hopeless. The past remains unknown. The amputated present tense, encapsulated by the TV moment, seems to constitute the end and the beginning of cognition.

Many black children, when they speak about their lives, do not seem to differentiate between the present, past and future. "I be doing good today." "Last year I be with my family in Alabama." "Someday I be somebody important." In the year that I began to teach, knowing little about sociology and less about linguistics, I perceived this first as inability, then as unwillingness, to conjugate. I summarized my explanation of the matter in somewhat these terms: People who are robbed of history, whether by slavery or by the inability to read, do not have much reason to distinguish between past and present. Those who have been robbed of opportunity to shape a future different from the ones their parents and grandparents knew do not have much reason to distinguish between now and never.

I was equally perplexed by something else about the patterns of my students' speech. Even the continuous present tense that seemed to me to be the common usage of these kids was not expressed in a present indicative but in a form that seemed to hold subjunctive implications. The children did not say: "I am." They said: "I be." This too appeared to me to carry metaphoric meaning. Existence itself, I felt, had been grammatically reduced to a subjunctive possibility.

Now it turns out that all of this is true except the starting point, which is entirely incorrect and which derives from my lack of awareness of some basic points of history and speech. Many scholars I have studied since have made it clear that nonwhite children "conjugate" as well as anybody else, that what I heard was not exactly what the children really said, that I was missing out on words as well as intonations that conveyed a sense of tense and mode to anyone (all of their friends, for instance) who shared in a knowledge of the language which they chose to use and one that had a logic and consistency that I could not perceive. It is not "a failure to differentiate" which is at stake. The differentiation was effected, rather, by a different body of linguistic rules.

Metaphors have a curious way of living beyond the point at which the evidence from which they grew has been discarded. It is now quite obvious to me that nonwhite children, whatever the thefts they have incurred, distinguish very well between past and present. No matter how grim the future may appear, they also distinguish clearly between "now" and "never." The fact that they can do so, and persist in doing so, may be regarded as a tribute to their courage and indomitable refusal to accede before appalling odds. The metaphor, born of my first encounter with their pain and with a world I did not understand, remains to haunt me.

Whatever the language children use, the fact that matters here may be established in a few words: Illiterate adults have been substantially excluded from political effectiveness by lack of access to the written word. Political impotence, in turn, diminishes the visibility of those in greatest verbal subjugation and makes it all the harder for the rest of us to recognize the full dimensions of their need.

It is argued by some cynical observers that elected leaders are politically astute to follow policies which keep out of the voting booth those who, reinforced by substantive decision-making data, could not quite so easily be led to vote for those who do not serve their needs. I suspect that such observers have attributed a little too much shrewdness and a great deal too much keen farsightedness to those whose actions seem more often motivated by a nineteenth century myopia than by a sinister anticipation of the future.

Enlightened politicians, if they wish to win at once political success and more credibility, soon may demonstrate the acumen of picking up an issue which can hardly fail to better their position. Few of the votes of those who have been viewed for so long as expendable are likely to be cast for politicians who have done their best to cut off aid to programs that have given even fleeting glints of hope to those who cannot read and write.

This is the point at which to take a second look at the miscalculations of the census.

For one hundred years, starting in 1840, the census posed the question of the population's literacy level in its ten-year compilations. The government removed this question from its survey in the 1940 census. The reason, according to a U.S. Census Bureau publication, was a general conviction that "most people [by this time] could read and write . . . "

In 1970, pressured by the military, the Bureau of Census agreed to reinstate the literacy question. Even then, instead of posing questions about actual skills, the census simply asked adults how many years of school they had attended. More than 5 percent of those the census reached replied that they had had less than a 5th grade education. For no known reason, the government assumed that four-fifths of these people probably could read and, on this dangerous assumption, it was publicly announced that 99 percent of all American adults could read and write. These are the figures which the U.S. government passed on to the United Nations for the purposes of worldwide compilations and comparisons.

The numbers in the 1980 census improved a bit on those of 1970. This time it was found that 99.5 percent of all American adults could read and write.

It will help us to assess the value of the U.S. census figures if we understand the methods used in 1980. First, as we have seen, the census mailed out printed forms and based most of its calculations upon written answers in response to questions about grade-completion levels. A second source of information was provided by a subdivision of the Bureau of the Census known as "Current Population Surveys." This information, based on only a small sample, was obtained by telephone interviews or home visits. In all cases the person was asked how many years of school he (she) had completed. If the answer was less than five, the person was asked if he or she could read. This was the full extent of the investigation.

It is self-evident that this is a process guaranteed to give a worthless data base. First, it is apparent that illiterates will not have much success in giving written answers to a printed questionnaire. The census believed that someone in the home or neighborhood—a child or a relative perhaps—could read enough to interview those who could not and that that person would complete the forms. This belief runs counter both to demographics and to the demands of human dignity. Illiterate people tend to live in neighborhoods of high illiteracy. In the home itself, it is repeatedly the case that mother, father, grandparent, and child are illiterate. Parents, moreover, try very hard to hide their lack of competence from their children and indeed, as we have seen, develop complicated masking skills precisely to defend themselves against humiliation. The first assumption of the Census Bureau, therefore, must be viewed as fatuous at worst, naive at best.

Illiterates, being the poorest of our citizens, are far less likely to have telephones than others in the population. Those who do are likely to experience repeated cutoffs for nonpayment. Anyone who organizes in a poverty community takes it as a rule of thumb that mail and telephone contacts are the worst of ways to find out anything about the population. Experienced organizers also understand quite well that doorway interviews are almost certain to be unsuccessful if the occupant does not know or trust the person who is knocking at the door. Decades of well-justified distrust have led poor men and women to regard the stranger with his questionnaire and clipboard as the agent of a system which appears infrequently and almost never for a purpose which does not portend substantial danger. Bill collector, welfare worker, court investigator, census taker, or encyclopedia salesman—all will be received with the same reticence and stealth. If the census taker should elicit any facts at all, there is a good chance that they will be facts contrived to fence him out, not enlighten him as to the actualities of anyone's existence.

In the case of illiterates, moreover, living already with the stigma of a disability that is regarded as an indication of inherent deficit, there is an even stronger inclination to refuse collaboration with the government's investigator. Many will profess a competence which they do not possess.

Finally, there is a problem with the question that the census seeks to pose. The fact that someone has attended school through fifth grade cannot be accepted as an indication that that person reads at a fifth grade level. People who are doing well in school are likely to continue. Those who drop out are almost always people who already find themselves two years or more behind the class and see no realistic hope of catching up. With the sole exception of those children who (as in the migrant streams) drop out of school because their families need another pair of hands to add a tiny increment of income, those who leave schools in elementary years are those who have already failed—or who have *been* failed by the system. The census, therefore, in asking people how long they have sat it out in public school, is engaging in a bit of foolishness which cannot easily be justified by ignorance or generosity. At best, by asking questions keyed not to attainment but to acquisition of grade numbers the Bureau of the Census might be learning something vague about the numbers of adults who read at any point from first to third grade level. As we have seen, however, even this much information is unlikely to be gleaned by methods flawed so badly and so stubbornly maintained.

A census, of course, may have more than one purpose in a modern nation. Certain information is desired for enlightened national self-interest. Other forms of information are required for the purposes of international prestige. Literacy statistics are one of the universal indices of national well-being. The first statistics listed in the "nation profiles" that are used for international comparisons include illiteracy, infant mortality, per capita income, life expectancy. It can be argued, from the point of view of chauvinistic pride, that it is in the short-term interest of an unwise nation to report the lowest possible statistics for illiterates. In a curious respect, therefore, the motives of the Census Bureau coincide with those of the distrustful or humiliated adult who is frightened to concede a problem that is viewed as evidence of human failing. A calamitous collusion is the obvious result: The nation wants to guard its pride. The illiterate needs to salve self-respect. The former wants to hide its secret from the world; the latter wants to hide it from the nation. It is easy to understand, in light of all of the above, why a nation within which 60 million people cannot even read the 1980 census should offer census figures to UNESCO that announce our status as a land of universal literacy.

In the preface to a 1969 edition of *The Other America*, Michael Harrington pointed to "the famous census undercount" of 1960. "Almost six million Americans, mainly black adults living in Northern cities, were not enumerated. Their lives were so marginal—no permanent address, no mail, no phone number, no regular job—that they did not even achieve the dignity of being a statistic."

The same may be said in 1985 for the much larger number—not 6 million this time, but some tens of millions—who do not exist within the inventories of the Bureau of the Census. The census tabulations would be less alarming if at least the nation's scholars would agree to disavow them. Instead, too many scholars take these figures with a certain skepticism but proceed to rescue them from condemnation by allowing that they hold at least one particle of truth. Their resolution of the conflict works somewhat like this: They interpret the census as an accurate indication that there are "no absolute nonreaders" in the nation. They then go on to indicate that—on a higher level, and by using definitions more appropriate to a developed nation—we are doing much less than we can. The second of these two points is correct. The first one is not.

The census itself, though unintentionally, suggests that 5 percent (over 8 million adults) read at a third grade level or below. If we make some rough adjustments for the recent immigrants and the undocumented residents, but especially for all those the census taker doesn't reach and those who claim that they can read to get the census taker off their back, we can bet that well above 10 million adult residents of the United States are absolute or nearly absolute illiterates. The government, as we have seen, has now conceded an enormous crisis constituted by the "functionally illiterate" in our society; but it has attempted to convey the somewhat reassuring thought that none of these people are "nonreaders" in the sense that word would hold for Third World nations. In all likelihood, almost one third of those defined as "functional" nonreaders would be judged illiterate by any standard and in any social system.

It was Michael Harrington who spoke of "an underdeveloped nation" living within the borders of America. This is an accurate description. There is a Third World hidden in the First World: because its occupants must live surrounded by the constant, visible, and unavoidable reminders of the comforts and the opportunities of which they denied, their suffering may very well be greater than that which is undergone by those who live with none of those reminders in a nation where illiterate existence is accepted as the norm.

Even for those who read at fifth or sixth grade levels in this nation, the suffering, by reason of the visible rewards identified with verbal and with arithmetic competence around them, must be very, very great. "The American poor," wrote Michael Harrington, "are not poor in Hong Kong or in the sixteenth century; they are poor here and now in the United States. They are disposed in terms of what the rest of the nation enjoys, in terms of what the society could provide if it had the will. They live on the fringe, the margin . . . They are internal exiles."

We know enough by now to treat the census figures with the skepticism and the indignation they deserve. History will not be generous with those who have compounded suffering by arrogant concealment. Sooner or later, the world will find us out. Neither our reputation nor our capability for self-correction can fail to suffer deeply from the propagation of these lies.

Endnote

* For an important exception, see description of the black-run organization "*Assault on Illiteracy.*"

Questions for Reading and Analysis

1. According to Kozol, what are some of the reasons we cannot trust census figures?

2. What common motive does Kozol ascribe to both illiterate adults and the Census Bureau?

3. How does illiteracy render one invisible?

4. What does Kozol suggest about politicians' treatment of the problem of illiteracy?

In the August 2000 Harper's, Lewis H. Lapham argues that politicians merely pay lip service in their campaign speeches about education reform because neither they nor those who run our national economy are at all interested in a population who is literate and capable of critical analysis.

School Bells

Lewis H. Lapham

Education is a companion which no misfortune can depress, no crime can destroy, no enemy can alienate, no despotism can enslave. At home a friend, abroad an introduction, in solitude a solace, and in society an ornament. . . . Without it, what is man? A splendid slave, a reasoning savage.

—Joseph Addison

Between the winter primary campaigns and the summer nominating conventions the two principal candidates for president discovered—much to their dismay and seasonable surprise—"the crisis of literacy" in the nation's public schools. The opinion polls were showing 76 percent of the respondents more concerned about the shambles of American education than about any other problem on the political agenda, and for nearly three months on any evening's news broadcast if Al Gore wasn't to be found seated on a tiny classroom chair in North Carolina or Ohio, George Bush was to be seen reading *The Very Hungry Caterpillar* to kindergarten children in California or Wisconsin.

The photo op was always smiling, the lesson invariably grim. The boys and girls weren't learning how to read, didn't know the difference between an aardvark and an anarchist, couldn't count to twenty or point to California on a map. The time had come to do something "bold" and "innovative," maybe even something "revolutionary," about the rising flood of ignorance that threatened to spill over the sandbags of the American dream. Unless everybody began to pay attention to the instructions on the blackboard, the United States could lose it all—the cruise missiles and the stock options, the ball game and the farm.

The news was bad but not unfamiliar. For the last twenty years the communiqués from the nation's classrooms have resembled the casualty reports from a lost war. Ever since the early hours of the Reagan Administration, anxious committees have been publishing statements about the dwindling supplies of verbal aptitude and mathematical comprehension, about the urgent need for more money and better teachers, about next semester's redesign of special programs for the poor, the foolish, the outnumbered, and the inept.

The expressions of alarm I take to be a matter of pious ritual, like a murmuring of prayers or the beating of ornamental gongs. If as a nation we wished to improve the performance of the schools, I assume that we could do so. Certainly we possess the necessary resources. We are an energetic people, rich in money and intelligence, capable of making high-performance automobiles and venture-capital funds, and if our intentions were anything other than ceremonial, I don't doubt that we could bring the schools to the standard of efficiency required of a well-run amusement park. Over the last twenty years we have added $10 trillion to the sum of the national wealth, cloned monkeys, reconfigured the weather, multiplied (by factors too large to calculate) the reach and value of the Internet.

Why, then, do the public schools continue to decay while at the same time the voices of the proctors poking through the wreckage continue to rise to the pitch of lamentations for the dead? Possibly because the condition of the public schools is neither an accident nor a mistake. The schools as presently constituted serve the interests of a society content to define education as a means of indoctrination and a way of teaching people to know their place. We have one set of schools for the children of the elite, another for children less fortunately born, and why disrupt the seating arrangement with a noisy shuffling of chairs? Serious reform of the public schools would beg too many questions about racial prejudice, the class system, the division of the nation's spoils. A too well-educated public might prove more trouble than it's worth, and so we mask our tacit approval of an intellectually inferior result with the declarations of a morally superior purpose. The sweet words come easy and cheap, and, if often enough repeated, they gain the weight of hard decision and accomplished fact.

On their tours of the country's schoolrooms, candidates Bush and Gore produced lists of brisk suggestion, stressing the principle of "accountability" (on the part of teachers as well as students and state legislatures), underlining the importance of frequent quizzes, recommending additions to the cafeteria, improvements for the gym. They might as well have been scattering flowers or dispensing incense. That they had little intention of doing anything else could be inferred from the amounts of money they pledged for the projects of reclamation. Bush offered $13.5 billion over five years; Gore proposed $115 billion over ten years—both negligible sums when compared with the price of an aircraft carrier or the annual cost of the milk subsidy. The federal government provides only 7 percent of the funding allocated to the nation's public schools, and when the candidates talked about making "major investments" they were speaking the language of diplomatic protocol. The American public school was a setting as foreign to their experience as the breadfruit market in Zanzibar, and here they were with the native children and the local dignitaries, posing for pictures and admiring the handicrafts. They could have mentioned any number—$250 billion in three years, $500 billion in six—and nobody would have questioned it. Nor would anybody have expected them to make good the promise or send the check. It was enough that they dropped by the story corner, greeted the geography teacher, and remembered the dates of the Civil War.

If either presidential candidate were to make the mistake of exposing the educational system to the rigors of "revolutionary change," who would thank him for his trouble? Not the politicians, who depend for their safety in office upon an uninformed electorate, apathetic and disinclined to vote, unable to remember its history or name its civil rights. Not the marketers of the gross domestic product, who depend upon the eager and uncritical consumption of junk merchandise in every available color and size. Not the ringmasters of the national media circus, who play to the lowest common denominators of credulous applause. Not the sellers of sexual fantasy, the proprietors of gambling casinos, the composers of financial fraud, the dealers in cosmetics and New Age religion. The consumer society rests on the great economic truth proclaimed by P. T. Barnum (the one about a sucker being born every minute), and the country's reserves of ignorance constitute a natural resource as precious as the Mississippi River or the long-lost herds of buffalo. As a nation, we now spend upward of a trillion dollars a year on liquor, pornography, and drugs, and the Cold War against the American intellect yields a higher rate of return than the old arrangement with the Russians. Unless obliged to make a campaign or a commencement speech, who in his right mind would want to kill the geese that lay the golden eggs?

The question sometimes occurs to me when I attend one of those conferences addressed to the sorrows of American education and convened under rubrics along the lines of "Investing in Human Capital: Leadership for the Challenges of the Twenty-first Century." After the keynote speech—usually a requiem for the 70 million functional illiterates in the country unable to read the Constitution or a complicated menu, sometimes a sermon about the high school girl in Oklahoma who thought the Holocaust was a Jewish holiday—the participants adjourn to workshops where they complain about the failure of the schools to deliver "high-quality product to the infrastructure." They seldom discuss the powers of the human intellect or imagination. Construing education as a commodity and the graduating classes as an assembly-line product (like peeled potatoes or empty aluminum cans), they talk about the manufacture of contented computer operators who can process insurance forms and change Italian lire into French francs or British pounds. As often as not it turns out that somebody in the crowd owns a company that leaflets the schools with films, textbooks, and computer software (a.k.a. "curriculum materials") touting the wonders of its consumer goods. Revlon offers a lesson in self-esteem that investigates the differences between good and bad hair days; the Campbell Soup Company once handed out the "slotted-spoon test," which asked the students to compare the texture of Campbell's Prego with a competitor's Ragú. The students who failed to find Prego the thicker of the two sauces failed the lesson in "the scientific method."

A similar bias shapes the strategies of Channel One, the for-profit distributor of educational services that provides impoverished school districts with computers, television sets, and access to the Internet. The schools in turn deliver a captive audience of 12 million students obliged to watch, every day, ten minutes of news programming and two minutes of commercial advertising. ZapMe!, another company that supplies educational paraphernalia, requires a million students in forty-five states to spend four hours a day in front of a computer screen that flashes commercial messages in the lower left-hand corner while they do their studies or browse the Internet. Three times a year they must bring their parents a marketing packet that installs the same software in their computers at home.

The United States is the only country in the civilized world that grants the commercial interests unfettered access to the minds of its children, and it should come as no surprise that the reading skills of American students improve during their primary-school years and then rapidly decline. Once inducted into a sixth- or seventh-grade classroom, they make less progress than their peers in Britain, France, Germany, or Spain. The instruction in the uses of the Internet prepares the class for the art of shopping, not for the art of reading.

The official mourners at the bier of American public education never fail to say something sad about "abbreviated attention spans" and the "diminished capacity to think," and apparently it never occurs to them that both those habits of mind sustain the profits of the credit-card industry and the banks.

Nor does it occur to them that if much of what passes for education in the United States deadens the desire for learning, the achievement is deliberate. High schools in large cities possess many of the same attributes as minimum-security prisons—metal detectors in the corridors, zero tolerance for rowdy behavior, the principal a warden and the faculty familiar with the syllabus of concealed weapons. Defined as day-care centers for the restless poor, the schools regulate the supply of unskilled labor, holding adolescents off the market until they have been hobbled by the rope of debt and injected with the virus of unbridled appetite for goods and services they can't afford to buy. The double bind instills the attitudes of passivity and apprehension, which in turn induce the fear of authority and the habits of obedience. An active intelligence tends to ask too many rude questions—of doctors and politicians, of the loan officer at the mortgage company or the nice man at the police station—and the schools do what they can to hold it for ransom and keep it at bay. A recent study conducted by the U.S. Department of Education found one third of the country's teachers lacking a thorough knowledge of the subject in which they gave instruction; textbooks that satisfy the requirements of ideological doctrine in lieu of literary expression inoculate the class against the danger of reading. To learn to read is to learn to think, possibly to discover the strength and freedom of one's own mind. Not a discovery that the consumer society wishes too many of its customers to make. Few pleasures equal the joy of the mind when it's being put to creative use, but the commercial markets have an interest in promoting the line of costly synthetics, and against the powers of the individual imagination they offer prescription drugs and prerecorded dreams.

Every now and then a hint of what's afoot shows up in the television advertisements selling the miracle of a cell phone or a retirement investment fund, and I can still remember seeing (last year or maybe the year before) a Merrill Lynch commercial that put the proposition about as plainly as it can be put.

The cautionary tale opens on the stage of a grammar school auditorium. It is prize day, and the principal on the podium is handing out a scroll—"For the best science report, Neil Gallagher and his team for 'Twenty-four Hours in the Life of a Trout.'" Gallagher is a fat kid, a nerd aged nine or ten; his teammates, a black boy and two white girls, stand and smile. Close-up shots of other kids, all nerds, applauding wildly. Gallagher shuffles off the stage, and the principal welcomes a very pretty girl, white and rosy-cheeked, a picture-perfect eleven-year-old wearing a charming necklace and an elegant dress.

"And finally, this year's winner, Robin Van Ness and the Merrill Lynch team, for their report 'Investment Strategies for Today's BioTechnology Market.'"

Robin smiles as winsomely as a beauty queen, and the surprised kids in the first five rows turn around in their seats to see four handsome adults standing in the back of the auditorium—except for the principal, the only other adults present. The Merrill Lynch team. Way cool, very smooth. The team (two white men, a black man, a white woman in an Armani suit) glows with parental happiness and pride. Expressions of amazement on the faces of the kids, who have seen a great light. Wonderful day for Robin. Wonderful day for American education. Loud applause, students rising to their feet, and in luminous print on the top of the visual, the words, "Now everyone can access the thinking of the world's most honored research team." The Merrill Lynch logo fills the screen, the voice-over (feminine and soft), saying, "ml dot-com: the smartest place to invest online."

End of lesson, boys and girls, and nothing more to learn. Why fool around with penniless trout when the swell people at Merrill Lynch can make you rich enough to buy a river in Montana? Why go to the trouble of learning how to read when you can grow up to be president of the United States without knowing how to write a grammatical sentence?

Candidates Bush and Gore voiced their alarm about the failure of American education in such feeble, made-for-hire prose that they refuted their own message about "the crisis of literacy." What crisis? If the language of politics becomes the stuff of sound bites, and if the electorate doesn't object to the secession of the confederacy of the rich from the union of the poor, asks for little else except the comfort of being constantly amused, believes the fairy tales about the invincible missile shield, who can say that illiteracy is not a consummation devoutly to be wished.

Questions for Reading and Analysis

1. In the first section of his essay, Lapham describes the political candidates' "expressions of alarm" at the state of our school system as "a matter of a pious ritual, like a murmuring of prayers or the beating of ornamental gongs." What do you think he means by this? How does he back up his claim?

2. What stand does Lapham take on public education? Where in the text is his thesis stated or implied?

3. The last section of the essay contains a long description of a Merril Lynch commercial. What does the writer accomplish with this expanded example at the end of his essay?

4. Do you think Lapham draws a faithful picture of the state of the American (public) school system? Why or why not?

*P*ublished in Newsweek *in May 2000, Rita Lazzaroni's article ques-tions the definition of "art" and what constitutes the value of a piece of art.*

Did a Car Hit It— Or Maybe a Train?

Rita Lazzaroni

On a family outing several years ago, I drove past an office park where a bright red tubular sculpture leaned in front of a building. "What's that?" asked my then 4-year-old daughter, intrigued enough to remove her thumb from her mouth.

"A sculpture," I answered. "An artist imagined it, shaped it out of steel and painted it."

"Did a car hit it?" my daughter asked. "No," I replied.

"Then maybe a train?"

At that moment I thought of the Hans Christian Andersen tale "The Emperor's New Clothes," the story of a monarch tricked into buying exquisite, invisible gar-ments that he wears in a parade, until a boy declares him stark naked.

Since that car ride, I've found myself wondering why adults don't view art work with the honest, critical eyes of a child. Could it be that the grownups on review boards who approve public projects don't want to appear unsophisticated? So they commission and give accolades to artworks and buildings that any child (or anyone listening to his inner child) would readily say look ugly.

Just because an artist or architect is famous doesn't mean we should applaud everything he or she creates. I see this happening everywhere, from superstar archi-tect Frank Gehry's new $46 million medical research center in Cincinnati (a building that I think could win the "Ugliest Building in the United States" award) to the public library in the Connecticut town where I live.

With much fanfare, our library board hired an esteemed New York architec-tural firm to design the river front building. The result? A dreary, flat-roofed, red-brick building with no windows overlooking the water.

While the library earned respect for its wealth of resources, it also earned itself a nickname. I first heard it when I informed my editor that I was on my way there to do some research. "Oh, you mean you're going to the 'Russian Fish Factory'?" she said.

Today, only 15 years after it was built, our library has a totally new look. The board hired a lesser-known architectural firm to enlarge the structure. While the firm was at it, it added a pitched roof and huge bay windows to take advantage of the magnificent river view. No one calls it the Fish Factory any more.

Just before he left office, our mayor accepted on the town's behalf a rusty sculpture he was told was made by a famous artist. After seeing this "generous gift," many townspeople agreed that the couple who donated the sculpture got the better deal—a sizable tax write-off and the removal of this metal monstrosity from their lawn.

Within weeks of being placed amid picnic tables in a downtown park, this sculpture was spray-painted with the words UGLY, VERY UGLY by an outraged passerby. The culprit was no teenage graffiti artist. He was a local house painter who confessed that he just flipped when he saw it. The sculpture was moved to a safer spot in front of our renovated library, in direct view of police headquarters.

Now I don't condone defacing art, nor do I believe that art should be pretty and safe. Art should lift you, provoke you and transport you, but it should also be honest. The intentions of artists whose work aspires to shock, like the controversial "Sensation" exhibit at the Brooklyn Museum of Art, are as transparent as those garments worn by the emperor. Just as transparent are the intentions of architects who design attention-grabbing buildings with no consideration for the needs of their inhabitants.

I recall my first visits to SoHo galleries and performance-art shows. Talk about artistic insecurity. I'd speed-read the arcane gallery notes, desperate for guidance: tell me what I'm looking at, please, before someone sees I'm clueless.

I quickly learned art-speak lingo, as I had learned to decipher "medicalese" as a health-and-science TV news producer. Dressing safely in black, I mingled at openings, nodding my head and regurgitating buzzwords like "artistic sensibility," "spacial," "organic."

It's this privy language of the art world that keeps people unfamiliar with the jargon from challenging its concepts. Added to this is the reality that most people don't want to be taken for rubes. It's much safer to praise a work by a famous architect or artist than to risk ridicule by criticizing it.

That's why, all around us, ugly buildings continue to be erected without question and paintings of no artistic merit draw crowds. Perhaps if we offered a few seats on review boards to kindergartners, we grown-ups might begin to judge art more critically. We'd hear questions like, "Did a car hit it?" before a sculpture is plunked on the town green. Before millions are spent transforming blueprints into buildings. Before the emperor struts out naked into the parade.

Questions for Reading and Analysis

1. Lazzaroni starts with an anecdote about her 4-year-old daughter. What does her daughter's reaction to a sculpture tell her about art? How does she define art?

2. What is her thesis, the most important point she wants her reader to get?

3. How does Lazzaroni use Hans Christian Andersen's tale of the emperor's new clothes in her essay? What does she accomplish by her allusion to this fairy tale?

4. Do you think she is right in saying that the "privy language of the art world . . . keeps people unfamiliar with the jargon from challenging its concepts"? Do you think that art should be judged not exclusively by those "in the know" but by those who know nothing about it (children or adults "listening to their inner child")?

5. What are the implications of letting the public decide what kind of art should be displayed in public places and galleries?

*A moralist and professor of medieval and Renaissance English lit-
erature at Cambridge, C.S. Lewis delivered "The Inner Ring" as
the 1944 Memorial Lecture at King's College at the University of
London. Rejecting Freud's conviction that sexual desire motivates all
human action, Lewis argues that humans are to a great extent motivated by their desire to belong to the "Inner Ring," a "secret society"
in every hierarchy that makes membership attractive because it exists
only to exclude others.*

The Inner Ring

C. S. Lewis

May I read you a few lines from Tolstoi's *War and Peace?*

> *When Boris entered the room, Prince Andrey was listening to an old
> general, wearing his decorations, who was reporting something to
> Prince Andrey, with an expression of soldierly servility on his purple
> face. "Alright. Please wait!" he said to the general, speaking in Russian
> with the French accent which he used when he spoke with contempt.
> The moment he noticed Boris he stopped listening to the general who
> trotted imploringly after him and begged to be heard, while Prince
> Andrey turned to Boris with a cheerful smile and a nod of the head.
> Boris now clearly understood—what he had already guessed—that
> side by side with the system of discipline and subordination which
> were laid down in the Army Regulations, there existed a different and
> a more real system—the system which compelled a tightly laced gen-
> eral with a purple face to wait respectfully for his turn while a mere
> captain like Prince Andrey chatted with a mere second lieutenant like
> Boris. Boris decided at once that he would be guided not by the offi-
> cial system but by this other unwritten system.[1]*

When you invite a middle-aged moralist to address you, I suppose I must conclude, however unlikely the conclusion seems, that you have a taste for middle-aged
moralizing. I shall do my best to gratify it. I shall in fact give you advice about the
world in which you are going to live. I do not mean by this that I am going to
attempt to talk on what are called current affairs. You probably know quite as
much about them as I do. I am not going to tell you—except in a form so general
that you will hardly recognize it—what part you ought to play in post-war reconstruction. It is not, in fact, very likely that any of you will be able, in the next ten
years, to make any direct contribution to the peace or prosperity of Europe. You

will be busy finding jobs, getting married, acquiring facts. I am going to do something more old-fashioned than you perhaps expected. I am going to give advice. I am going to issue warnings. Advice and warnings about things which are so perennial that no one calls them "current affairs."

And of course everyone knows what a middle-aged moralist of my type warns his juniors against. He warns them against the World, the Flesh, and the Devil. But one of this trio will be enough to deal with today. The Devil, I shall leave strictly alone. The association between him and me in the public mind has already gone quite as deep as I wish: in some quarters it has already reached the level of confusion, if not of identification. I begin to realize the truth of the old proverb that he who sups with that formidable host needs a long spoon. As for the Flesh, you must be very abnormal young people if you do not know quite as much about it as I do. But on the World I think I have something to say.

In the passage I have just read from Tolstoi, the young second lieutenant Boris Dubretskoi discovers that there exist in the army two different systems or hierarchies. The one is printed in some little red book and anyone can easily read it up. It also remains constant. A general is always superior to a colonel and a colonel to a captain. The other is not printed anywhere. Nor is it even a formally organized secret society with officers and rules which you would be told after you had been admitted. You are never formally and explicitly admitted by anyone. You discover gradually, in almost indefinable ways, that it exists and that you are outside it; and then later, perhaps, that you are inside it. There are what correspond to passwords, but they too are spontaneous and informal. A particular slang, the use of particular nicknames, an allusive manner of conversation, are the marks. But it is not constant. It is not easy, even at a given moment, to say who is inside and who is outside. Some people are obviously in and some are obviously out, but there are always several on the border-line. And if you come back to the same Divisional Headquarters, or Brigade Headquarters, or the same regiment or even the same company, after six weeks' absence, you may find this second hierarchy quite altered. There are no formal admissions or expulsions. People think they are in it after they have in fact been pushed out of it, or before they have been allowed in: this provides great amusement for those who are really inside. It has no fixed name. The only certain rule is that the insiders and outsiders call it by different names. From inside it may be designated, in simple cases, by mere enumeration: it may be called "You and Tony and me." When it is very secure and comparatively stable in membership it calls itself "we." When it has to be suddenly expanded to meet a particular emergency it calls itself "All the sensible people at this place." From outside, if you have despaired of getting into it, you call it "That gang" or "They" or "So-and-so and his set" or "the Caucus" or "the Inner Ring." If you are a candidate for admission you probably don't call it anything. To discuss it with the other outsiders would make you feel outside yourself. And to mention it in talking to the man who is inside, and who may help you if this present conversation goes well, would be madness.

Badly as I may have described it, I hope you will all have recognized the thing I am describing. Not, of course, that you have been in the Russian Army or perhaps in any army. But you have met the phenomenon of an Inner Ring. You discovered one in your house at school before the end of the first term. And when you had climbed up to somewhere near it by the end of your second year, perhaps you discovered that within the Ring there was a Ring yet more inner, which in its turn was the fringe of the great school Ring to which the house Rings were only satellites. It is even possible that the School Ring was almost in touch with a Masters' Ring. You were beginning, in fact, to pierce through the skins of the onion. And here, too, at your university—shall I be wrong in assuming that at this very moment, invisible to me, there are several rings—independent systems or concentric rings—present in this room? And I can assure you that in whatever hospital, inn of court, diocese, school, business, or college you arrive after going down, you will find the Rings—what Tolstoi calls the second or unwritten systems.

All this is rather obvious. I wonder whether you will say the same of my next step, which is this. I believe that in all men's lives at certain periods, and in many men's lives at all periods between infancy and extreme old age, one of the most dominant elements is the desire to be inside the local Ring and the terror of being left outside. This desire, in one of its forms, has indeed had ample justice done to it in literature. I mean, in the form of snobbery. Victorian fiction is full of characters who are hag-ridden by the desire to get inside that particular Ring which is, or was, called Society. But it must be clearly understood that "Society," in that sense of the word, is merely one of a hundred Rings and snobbery therefore only one form of the longing to be inside. People who believe themselves to be free, and indeed are free, from snobbery, and who read satires on snobbery with tranquil superiority, may be devoured by the desire in another form. It may be the very intensity of their desire to enter some quite different Ring which renders them immune from the allurements of high life. An invitation from a duchess would be very cold comfort to a man smarting under the sense of exclusion from some artistic or communist côterie. Poor man—it is not large, lighted rooms, or champagne, or even scandals about peers and Cabinet Ministers that he wants: it is the sacred little attic or studio, the heads bent together, the fog of tobacco smoke, and the delicious knowledge that we—we four or five all huddled beside this stove—are the people who *know*. Often the desire conceals itself so well that we hardly recognize the pleasures of fruition. Men tell not only their wives but themselves that it is a hardship to stay late at the office or the school on some bit of important extra work which they have been let in for because they and So-and-so and the two others are the only people left in the place who really know how things are run. But it is not quite true. It is a terrible bore, of course, when old Fatty Smithson draws you aside and whispers "Look here, we've got to get you in on this examination somehow" or "Charles and I saw at once that you've got to be on this committee." A terrible bore . . . ah, but how much more terrible if you were left out! It is tiring and unhealthy to lose your Saturday afternoons: but to have them free because you don't matter, that is much worse.

Freud would say, no doubt, that the whole thing is a subterfuge of the sexual impulse. I wonder whether the shoe is not sometimes on the other foot, I wonder whether, in ages of promiscuity, many a virginity has not been lost less in obedience to Venus than in obedience to the lure of the caucus. For of course, when promiscuity is the fashion, the chaste are outsiders. They are ignorant of something that other people know. They are uninitiated. And as for lighter matters, the number who first smoked or first got drunk for a similar reason is probably very large.

I must now make a distinction. I am not going to say that the existence of Inner Rings is an evil. It is certainly unavoidable. There must be confidential discussions: and it is not only not a bad thing, it is (in itself) a good thing, that personal friendship should grow up between those who work together. And it is perhaps impossible that the official hierarchy of any organization should quite coincide with its actual workings. If the wisest and most energetic people invariably held the highest posts, it might coincide; since they often do not, there must be people in high positions who are really deadweights and people in lower positions who are more important than their rank and seniority would lead you to suppose. In that way the second, unwritten system is bound to grow up. It is necessary; and perhaps it is not a necessary evil. But the desire which draws us into Inner Rings is another matter. A thing may be morally neutral and yet the desire for that thing may be dangerous. As Byron has said:

> *Sweet is a legacy, and passing sweet*
> *The unexpected death of some old lady.*

The painless death of a pious relative at an advanced age is not an evil. But an earnest desire for her death on the part of her heirs is not reckoned a proper feeling, and the law frowns on even the gentlest attempt to expedite her departure. Let Inner Rings be an unavoidable and even an innocent feature of life, though certainly not a beautiful one: but what of our longing to enter them, our anguish when we are excluded, and the kind of pleasure we feel when we get in?

I have no right to make assumptions about the degree to which any of you may already be compromised. I must not assume that you have ever first neglected, and finally shaken off, friends whom you really loved and who might have lasted you a lifetime, in order to court the friendship of those who appeared to you more important, more esoteric. I must not ask whether you have ever derived actual pleasure from the loneliness and humiliation of the outsiders after you yourself were in: whether you have talked to fellow members of the Ring in the presence of outsiders simply in order that the outsiders might envy; whether the means whereby, in your days of probation, you propitiated the Inner Ring, were always wholly admirable. I will ask only one question—and it is, of course, a rhetorical question which expects no answer. In the whole of your life as you now remember it, has the desire to be on the right side of that invisible line ever prompted you to any act or word on which, in the cold small hours of a wakeful night, you can look back with satisfaction? If so, your case is more fortunate than most.

But I said I was going to give advice, and advice should deal with the future, not the past. I have hinted at the past only to awake you to what I believe to be the real nature of human life. I don't believe that the economic motive and the erotic motive account for everything that goes on in what we moralists call the World. Even if you add Ambition I think the picture is still incomplete. The lust for the esoteric, the longing to be inside, take many forms which are not easily recognizable as Ambition. We hope, no doubt, for tangible profits from every Inner Ring we penetrate: power, money, liberty to break rules, avoidance of routine duties, evasion of discipline. But all these would not satisfy us if we did not get in addition the delicious sense of secret intimacy. It is no doubt a great convenience to know that we need fear no official reprimands from our official senior because he is old Percy, a fellow-member of our Ring. But we don't value the intimacy only for the sake of convenience; quite equally we value the convenience as a proof of the intimacy.

My main purpose in this address is simply to convince you that this desire is one of the great permanent mainsprings of human action. It is one of the factors which go to make up the world as we know it—this whole pell-mell of struggle, competition, confusion, graft, disappointment, and advertisement, and if it is one of the permanent mainsprings then you may be quite sure of this. Unless you take measures to prevent it, this desire is going to be one of the chief motives of your life, from the first day on which you enter your profession until the day when you are too old to care. That will be the natural thing—the life that will come to you of its own accord. Any other kind of life, if you lead it, will be the result of conscious and continuous effort. If you do nothing about it, if you drift with the stream, you will in fact be an "inner ringer." I don't say you'll be a successful one; that's as may be. But whether by pining and moping outside Rings that you can never enter, or by passing triumphantly further and further in—one way or the other you will be that kind of man.

I have already made it fairly clear that I think it better for you not to be that kind of man. But you may have an open mind on the question. I will therefore suggest two reasons for thinking as I do.

It would be polite and charitable, and in view of your age reasonable too, to suppose that none of you is yet a scoundrel. On the other hand, by the mere law of averages (I am saying nothing against free will) it is almost certain that at least two or three of you before you die will have become something very like scoundrels. There must be in this room the makings of at least that number of unscrupulous, treacherous, ruthless egotists. The choice is still before you: and I hope you will not take my hard words about your possible future characters as a token of disrespect to your present characters. And the prophecy I make is this. To nine out of ten of you the choice which could lead to scoundrelism will come, when it does come, in no very dramatic colors. Obviously bad men, obviously threatening or bribing, will almost certainly not appear. Over a drink or a cup of coffee, disguised as a triviality and sandwiched between two jokes, from the lips of a man, or woman, whom you have recently been getting to know rather better and whom you hope to know better still—just at the moment when you are most anxious not to appear crude, or naïf, or a prig—the hint will come. It will be the hint of something which is not quite in accordance with the technical rules of fair play: something which the public, the ignorant, romantic public, would never understand: something which even the outsiders, in your own profession are apt to make a fuss about: but something, says your new friend, which "we"—and at the word "we" you try not to blush for mere pleasure—something "we always do." And you will be drawn in, if you are drawn in, not by desire for gain or ease, but simply because at that moment, when the cup was so near your lips, you cannot bear to be thrust back again into the cold outer world. It would be so terrible to see the other man's face—that genial, confidential, delightfully sophisticated face—turn suddenly cold and contemptuous, to know that you had been tried for the Inner Ring and rejected. And then, if you are drawn in, next week it will be something a little further from the rules, and next year something further still, but all in the jolliest, friendliest spirit. It may end in a crash, a scandal, and penal servitude: it may end in millions, a peerage and giving the prizes at your old school. But you will be a scoundrel.

That is my first reason. Of all the passions the passion for the Inner Ring is most skillful in making a man who is not yet a very bad man do very bad things.

My second reason is this. The torture allotted to the Danaids in the classical underworld, that of attempting to fill sieves with water, is the symbol not of one vice but of all vices. It is the very mark of a perverse desire that it seeks what is not to be had. The desire to be inside the invisible line illustrates this rule. As long as you are governed by that desire you will never get what you want. You are trying to peel an onion: if you succeed there will be nothing left. Until you conquer the fear of being an outsider, an outsider you will remain.

This is surely very clear when you come to think of it. If you want to be made free of a certain circle for some wholesome reason—if, say, you want to join a musical society because you really like music—then there is a possibility of satisfaction. You may find yourself playing in a quartet and you may enjoy it. But if all you want is to be in the know, your pleasure will be short-lived. The circle cannot have from within the charm it had from outside. By the very act of admitting you it has lost its magic. Once the first novelty is worn off the members of this circle will be no more interesting than your old friends. Why should they be? You were not looking for virtue or kindness or loyalty or humor or learning or wit or any of the things that can be really enjoyed. You merely wanted to be "in." And that is a pleasure that cannot last. As soon as your new associates have been staled to you by custom, you will be looking for another Ring. The rainbow's end will still be ahead of you. The old Ring will now be only the drab background for your endeavor to enter the new one.

And you will always find them hard to enter, for a reason you very well know. You yourself, once you are in, want to make it hard for the next entrant, just as those who are already in made it hard for you. Naturally. In any wholesome group of people which holds together for a good purpose, the exclusions are in a sense accidental. Three or four people who are together for the sake of some piece of work exclude others because there is work only for so many or because the others can't in fact do it. Your little musical group limits its numbers because the rooms they meet in are only so big. But your genuine Inner Ring exists for exclusion. There'd be no fun if there were no outsiders. The invisible line would have no meaning unless most people were on the wrong side of it. Exclusion is no accident: it is the essence.

The quest of the Inner Ring will break your hearts unless you break it. But if you break it, a surprising result will follow. If in your working hours you make the work your end, you will presently find yourself all unawares inside the only circle in your profession that really matters. You will be one of the sound craftsmen, and other sound craftsmen will know it. This group of craftsmen will by no means coincide with the inner Ring or the Important People or the People in the Know. It will not shape that professional policy or work up that professional influence which fights for the profession as a whole against the public: nor will it lead to those periodic scandals and crises which the Inner Ring produces. But it will do those things which that profession exists to do and will in the long run be responsible for all the respect which that profession in fact enjoys and which the speeches and advertisements cannot maintain. And if in your spare time you consort simply with the people you like, you will again find that you have come unawares to a real inside: that you are indeed snug and safe at the center of something which, seen from without, would look exactly like an Inner Ring. But the difference is that its secrecy is accidental, and its exclusiveness a by-product, and no one was led thither by the lure of the esoteric: for it is only four or five people who like one another meeting to do things that they like. This is friendship. Aristotle placed it among the virtues. It causes perhaps half of all the happiness in the world, and no Inner Ring can ever have it.

We are told in Scripture that those who ask get. That is true, in senses I can't now explore. But in another sense there is much truth in the schoolboy's principle "them as asks shan't have." To a young person, just entering on adult life, the world seems full of "insides," full of delightful intimacies and confidentialities, and he desires to enter them. But if he follows that desire he will reach no "inside" that is worth reaching. The true road lies in quite another direction. It is like the house in *Alice Through the Looking Glass*.[2]

Endnotes

1. Part III, chapter 9. [author's note]
2. Lewis Carroll's Alice imagines that the mirror over her mantel is actually a window through which she sees another room in another house.

Questions for Reading and Analysis

1. In your own words, describe the concept of the "Inner Ring." Where, according to Lewis, do Inner Rings exist?

2. How does Lewis support his claim that Inner Rings are not necessarily evil but the desire to belong to them is?

3. What advice does Lewis give his audience about how to free themselves from the allure of the Inner Ring?

4. Lewis wrote "The Inner Ring" as a commencement speech at King's College. In what way does he tailor his remarks to his audience, a class of graduating seniors?

Much of Nancy Mairs's writing is informed by her struggle with multiple sclerosis. Candid and philosophical, she considers her losses—and gains—in "On Being a Cripple," first published in Plaintext *(1986).*

On Being a Cripple

Nancy Mairs

To escape is nothing. Not to escape is nothing.

—Louise Bogan

The other day I was thinking of writing an essay on being a cripple. I was thinking hard in one of the stalls of the women's room in my office building, as I was shoving my shirt into my jeans and tugging up my zipper. Preoccupied, I flushed, picked up my book bag, took my cane down from the hook, and unlatched the door. So many movements unbalanced me, and as I pulled the door open I fell over backward, landing fully clothed on the toilet seat with my legs splayed in front of me: the old beetle-on-its-back routine. Saturday afternoon, the building deserted, I was free to laugh aloud as I wriggled back to my feet, my voice bouncing off the yellowish tiles from all directions. Had anyone been there with me, I'd have been still and faint and hot with chagrin. I decided that it was high time to write the essay.

First, the matter of semantics. I am a cripple. I choose this word to name me. I choose from among several possibilities, the most common of which are "handicapped" and "disabled." I made the choice a number of years ago, without thinking, unaware of my motives for doing so. Even now, I'm not sure what those motives are, but I recognize that they are complex and not entirely flattering. People—crippled or not—wince at the word "cripple," as they do not at "handicapped" or "disabled." Perhaps I want them to wince. I want them to see me as a tough customer, one to whom the fates/gods/viruses have not been kind, but who can face the brutal truth of her existence squarely. As a cripple, I swagger.

But, to be fair to myself, a certain amount of honesty underlies my choice. "Cripple" seems to me a clean word, straightforward and precise. It has an honorable history, having made its first appearance in the Lindisfarne Gospel[1] in the tenth century. As a lover of words, I like the accuracy with which it describes my condition: I have lost the full use of my limbs. "Disabled," by contrast, suggests any incapacity, physical or mental. And I certainly don't like "handicapped," which implies that I have deliberately been put at a disadvantage, by whom I can't imagine (my God is not a Handicapper General), in order to equalize chances in the great race of life. These words seem to me to be moving away from my condition, to be widening the gap between word and reality. Most remote is the recently coined euphemism "differently abled," which partakes of the same semantic hopefulness that transformed countries from "undeveloped" to "underdeveloped," then to "less developed," and finally to "developing" nations. People have continued to starve in those countries during the shift. Some realities do not obey the dictates of language.

Mine is one of them. Whatever you call me, I remain crippled. But I don't care what you call me, so long as it isn't "differently abled," which strikes me as pure verbal garbage designed, by its ability to describe anyone, to describe no one. I subscribe to George Orwell's thesis that "the slovenliness of our language makes it easier for us to have foolish thoughts."[2] And I refuse to participate in the degeneration of the language to the extent that I deny that I have lost anything in the course of this calamitous disease; I refuse to pretend that the only differences between you and me are the various ordinary ones that distinguish any one person from another. But call me "disabled" or "handicapped" if you like. I have long since grown accustomed to them; and if they are vague, at least they hint at the truth. Moreover, I use them myself. Society is no readier to accept crippled-ness than to accept death, war, sex, sweat, or wrinkles. I would never refer to another person as a cripple. It is the word I use to name only myself.

I haven't always been crippled, a fact for which I am soundly grateful. To be whole of limb is, I know from experience, infinitely more pleasant and useful than to be crippled; and if that knowledge leaves one open to bitterness at my loss, the physical soundness I once enjoyed (though I did not enjoy it half enough) is well worth the occasional stab of regret. Though never any good at sports, I was a normally active child and young adult. I climbed trees, played hopscotch, jumped rope, skated, swam, rode my bicycle, sailed. I despised team sports, spending some of the wretchedest afternoons of my life, sweaty and humiliated, behind a field-hockey stick and under a basketball hoop. I tramped alone for miles along the bridle paths that webbed the woods behind the house I grew up in. I swayed through countless dim hours in the arms of one man or another under the scattered shot of light from mirrored balls, and gyrated through countless more as Tab Hunter and Johnny Mathis[3] gave way to the Rolling Stones, Creedence Clearwater Revival, Cream. I walked down the aisle. I pushed baby carriages, changed tires in the rain, marched for peace.

When I was twenty-eight I started to trip and drop things. What at first seemed my natural clumsiness soon became too pronounced to shrug off. I consulted a neurologist, who told me that I had a brain tumor. A battery of tests, increasingly disagreeable, revealed no tumor. About a year and a half later I developed a blurred spot in one eye. I had, at last, the episodes "disseminated in space and time" requisite for a diagnosis: multiple sclerosis. I have never been sorry for the doctor's initial misdiagnosis, however. For almost a week, until the negative results of the tests were in, I thought that I was going to die right away. Every day for the past nearly ten years, then, has been a kind of gift. I accept all gifts.

Multiple sclerosis is a chronic degenerative disease of the central nervous system, in which the myelin that sheathes the nerves is somehow eaten away and scar tissue forms in its place, interrupting the nerves' signals. During its course, which is unpredictable and uncontrollable, one may lose vision, hearing, speech, the ability to walk, control of bladder and/or bowels, strength in any or all extremities, sensitivity to touch, vibration, and/or pain, potency, coordination of movements—the list of possibilities is lengthy and, yes, horrifying. One may also lose one's sense of humor. That's the easiest to lose and the hardest to survive without.

In the past ten years, I have sustained some of these losses. Characteristic of MS are sudden attacks, called exacerbations, followed by remissions, and these I have not had. Instead, my disease has been slowly progressive. My left leg is now so weak that I walk with the aid of a brace and a cane; and for distances I use an Amigo, a variation on the electric wheelchair that looks rather like an electrified kiddie car. I no longer have much use of my left hand. Now my right side is weakening as well. I still have the blurred spot in my right eye. Overall, though, I've been lucky so far. My world has, of necessity, been circumscribed by my losses, but the terrain left me has been ample enough for me to continue many of the activities that absorb me: writing, teaching, raising children and cats and plants and snakes, reading, speaking publicly about MS and depression, even playing bridge with people patient and honorable enough to let me scatter cards every which way without sneaking a peek.

Lest I begin to sound like Pollyanna, however, let me say that I don't like having MS. I hate it. My life holds realities—harsh ones, some of them—that no right-minded human being ought to accept without grumbling. One of them is fatigue. I know of no one with MS who does not complain of bone-weariness; in a disease that presents an astonishing variety of symptoms, fatigue seems to be a common factor. I wake up in the morning feeling the way most people do at the end of a bad day, and I take it from there. As a result, I spent a lot of time *in extremis*[4] and, impatient with limitation, I tend to ignore my fatigue until my body breaks down in some way and forces rest. Then I miss picnics, dinner parties, poetry readings, the brief visits of old friends from out of town. The offspring of a puritanical tradition of exceptional venerability, I cannot view these lapses without shame. My life often seems a series of small failures to do as I ought.

I lead, on the whole, an ordinary life, probably rather like the one I would have led had I not had MS. I am lucky that my predilections were already solitary, sedentary, and bookish—unlike the world-famous French cellist I have read about,[5] or the young woman I talked with one long afternoon who wanted only to be a jockey. I had just begun graduate school when I found out something was wrong with me, and I have remained, interminably, a graduate student. Perhaps I would not have if I'd thought I had the stamina to return to a full-time job as a technical editor; but I've enjoyed my studies.

In addition to studying, I teach writing courses. I also teach medical students how to give neurological examinations. I pick up freelance editing jobs here and there. I have raised a foster son and sent him into the world, where he has made me two grandbabies, and I am still escorting my daughter and son through adolescence. I go to Mass every Saturday. I am a superb, if messy, cook. I am also an enthusiastic laundress, capable of sorting a hamper full of clothes into five subtly differentiated piles, but a terrible housekeeper. I can do italic writing and, in an emergency, bathe an oil-soaked cat. I play a fiendish game of Scrabble. When I have the time and the money, I like to sit on my front steps with my husband, drinking Amaretto and smoking a cigar, as we imagine our counterparts in

Leningrad and make sure that the sun gets down once more behind the sharp childish scrawl of the Tucson Mountains.

This lively plenty has its bleak complement, of course, in all the things I can no longer do. I will never run again, except in dreams, and one day I may have to write that I will never walk again. I like to go camping, but I can't follow George and the children along the trails that wander out of a campsite through the desert or into the mountains. In fact, even on the level I've learned never to check the weather or try to hold a coherent conversation: I need all my attention for my wayward feet. Of late, I have begun to catch myself wondering how people can propel themselves without canes. With only one usable hand, I have to select my clothing with care not so much for style as for ease of ingress and egress, and even so, dressing can be laborious. I can no longer do fine stitchery, pick up babies, play the piano, braid my hair. I am immobilized by acute attacks of depression, which may or may not be physiologically related to MS but are certainly its logical concomitant.

These two elements, the plenty and the privation, are never pure, nor are the delight and wretchedness that accompany them. Almost every pickle that I get into as a result of my weakness and clumsiness—and I get into plenty—is funny as well as maddening and sometimes painful. I recall one May afternoon when a friend and I were going out for a drink after finishing up at school. As we were climbing into opposite sides of my car, chatting, I tripped and fell, flat and hard, onto the asphalt parking lot, my abrupt departure interrupting him in mid-sentence. "Where'd you go?" he called as he came around the back of the car to find me hauling myself up by the door frame. "Are you all right?" Yes, I told him, I was fine, just a bit rattly, and we drove off to find a shady patio and some beer. When I got home an hour or so later, my daughter greeted me with "What have you done to yourself?" I looked down. One elbow of my white turtleneck with the green froggies, one knee of my white trousers, one white kneesock were bloodsoaked. We peeled off the clothes and inspected the damage, which was nasty enough but not alarming. That part wasn't funny: The abrasions took a long time to heal, and one got a little infected. Even so, when I think of my friend talking earnestly, suddenly, to the hot thin air while I dropped from his view as though through a trap door, I find the image as silly as something from a Marx Brothers movie.

I may find it easier than other cripples to amuse myself because I live propped by the acceptance and the assistance and, sometimes, the amusement of those around me. Grocery clerks tear my checks out of my checkbook for me, and sales clerks find chairs to put into dressing rooms when I want to try on clothes. The people I work with make sure I teach at times when I am least likely to be fatigued, in places I can get to, with the materials I need. My students, with one anonymous exception (in an end-of-the-semester evaluation), have been unperturbed by my disability. Some even like it. One was immensely cheered by the information that I paint my own fingernails; she decided, she told me, that if I could go to such trouble over fine details, she could keep on writing essays. I suppose I became some sort of bright-fingered muse. She wrote good essays, too.

The most important struts in the framework of my existence, of course, are my husband and children. Dismayingly few marriages survive the MS test, and why should they? Most twenty-two- and nineteen-year-olds, like George and me, can vow in clear conscience, after a childhood of chicken pox and summer colds, to keep one another in sickness and in health so long as they both shall live. Not many are equipped for catastrophe: the dismay, the depression, the extra work, the boredom that a degenerative disease can insinuate into a relationship. And our society, with its emphasis on fun and its association of fun with physical performance, offers little encouragement for a whole spouse to stay with a crippled partner. Children experience similar stresses when faced with a crippled parent, and they are more helpless, since parents and children can't usually get divorced. They hate, of course, to be different from their peers, and the child whose mother is tacking down the aisle of a school auditorium packed with proud parents like a Cape Cod dinghy in a stiff breeze jolly well stands out in a crowd. Deprived of legal divorce, the child can at least deny the mother's disability, even her existence, forgetting to tell her about recitals and PTA meetings, refusing to accompany her to stores or church or the movies, never inviting friends to the house. Many do.

But I've been limping along for ten years now, and so far George and the children are still at my left elbow, holding tight. Anne and Matthew vacuum floors and dust furniture and haul trash and rake up dog droppings and button my cuffs and bake lasagna and Toll House cookies with just enough grumbling so I know that they don't have brain fever. And far from hiding me, they're forever dragging me by racks of fancy clothes or through teeming school corridors, or welcoming gaggles of friends while I'm wandering through the house in Anne's filmy pink baby-doll pajamas. George generally calls before he brings someone home, but he does just as many dumb thankless chores as the children. And they all yell at me, laugh at some of my jokes, write me funny letters when we're apart—in short, treat me as an ordinary human being for whom they have some use. I think they like me. Unless they're faking. . . .

Faking. There's the rub. Tugging at the fringes of my consciousness always is the terror that people are kind to me only because I'm a cripple. My mother almost shattered me once, with that instinct mothers have—blind, I think, in this case, but unerring nonetheless—for striking blows along the fault-lines of their children's hearts, by telling me, in an attack on my selfishness, "We all have to make allowances for you, of course, because of the way you are." From the distance of a couple of years, I have to admit that I haven't any idea just what she meant, and I'm not sure that she knew either. She was awfully angry. But at the time, as the words thudded home, I felt my worst fear, suddenly realized. I could bear being called selfish: I am. But I couldn't bear the corroboration that those around me were doing in fact what I'd always suspected them of doing, professing fondness while silently putting up with me because of the way I am. A cripple. I've been a little cracked ever since.

Along with this fear that people are secretly accepting shoddy goods comes a relentless pressure to please—to prove myself worth the burdens I impose, I guess, or to build a substantial account of goodwill against which I may write drafts in times of need. Part of the pressure arises from social expectations. In our society, anyone who deviates from the norm had better find some way to compensate. Like fat people, who are expected to be jolly, cripples must bear their lot meekly and cheerfully. A grumpy cripple isn't playing by the rules. And much of the pressure is self-generated. Early on I vowed that, if I had to have MS, by God I was going to do it well. This is a class act, ladies and gentlemen. No tears, no recriminations, no faint-heartedness.

One way and another, then, I wind up feeling like Tiny Tim,[6] peering over the edge of the table at the Christmas goose, waving my crutch, piping down God's blessing on us all. Only sometimes I don't want to play Tiny Tim. I'd rather be Caliban,[7] a most scurvy monster. Fortunately, at home no one much cares whether I'm a good cripple or a bad cripple as long as I make vichyssoise with fair regularity. One evening several years ago, Anne was reading at the dining-room table while I cooked dinner. As I opened a can of tomatoes, the can slipped in my left hand and juice spattered me and the counter with bloody spots. Fatigued and infuriated, I bellowed, "I'm so sick of being crippled!" Anne glanced at me over the top of her book. "There now," she said, "do you feel better?" "Yes," I said, "yes, I do." She went back to her reading. I felt better. That's about all the attention my scurviness ever gets.

Because I hate being crippled, I sometimes hate myself for being a cripple. Over the years I have come to expect—even accept—attacks of violent self-loathing. Luckily, in general our society no longer connects deformity and disease directly with evil (though a charismatic once told me that I have MS because a devil is in me) and so I'm allowed to move largely at will, even among small children. But I'm not sure that this revision of attitude has been particularly helpful. Physical imperfection, even freed of moral disapprobation, still defies and violates the ideal, especially for women, whose confinement in their bodies as objects of desire is far from over. Each age, of course, has its ideal, and I doubt that ours is any better or worse than any other. Today's ideal woman, who lives on the glossy pages of dozens of magazines, seems to be between the ages of eighteen and twenty-five; her hair has body, her teeth flash white, her breath smells minty, her underarms are dry; she has a career but is still a fabulous cook, especially of meals that take less than twenty minutes to prepare; she does not ordinarily appear to have a husband or children; she is trim and deeply tanned; she jogs, swims, plays tennis, rides a bicycle, sails, but does not bowl; she travels widely, even to out-of-the-way places like Finland and Samoa, always in the company of the ideal man, who possesses a nearly identical set of characteristics. There are a few exceptions. Though usually white and often blonde, she may be black, Hispanic, Asian, or Native American, so long as she is unusually sleek. She may be old, provided she is selling a laxative or is Lauren Bacall. If she is selling a detergent, she may be married and have a flock of strikingly messy children. But she is never a cripple.

Like many women I know, I have always had an uneasy relationship with my body. I was not a popular child, largely, I think now, because I was peculiar: intelligent, intense, moody, shy, given to unexpected actions and inexplicable notions and emotions. But as I entered adolescence, I believed myself unpopular because I was homely: my breasts too flat, my mouth too wide, my hips too narrow, my clothing never quite right in fit or style. I was not, in fact, particularly ugly, old photographs inform me, though I was well off the ideal; but I carried this sense of self-alienation with me into adulthood, where it regenerated in response to the depredations of MS. Even with my brace I walk with a limp so pronounced that, seeing myself on the videotape of a television program on the disabled, I couldn't believe that anything but an inchworm could make progress humping along like that. My shoulders droop and my pelvis thrusts forward as I try to balance myself upright, throwing my frame into a bony S. As a result of contractures, one shoulder is higher than the other and I carry one arm bent in front of me, the fingers curled into a claw. My left arm and leg have wasted into pipe-stems, and I try always to keep them covered. When I think about how my body must look to others, especially to men, to whom I have been trained to display myself, I feel ludicrous, even loathsome.

At my age, however, I don't spend much time thinking about my appearance. The burning egocentricity of adolescence, which assures one that all the world is looking all the time, has passed, thank God, and I'm generally too caught up in what I'm doing to step back, as I used to, and watch myself as though upon a stage. I'm also too old to believe in the accuracy of self-image. I know that I'm not a hideous crone, that in fact, when I'm rested, well dressed, and well made up, I look fine. The self-loathing I feel is neither physically nor intellectually substantial. What I hate is not me but a disease.

I am not a disease.

And a disease is not—at least not singlehandedly—going to determine who I am, though at first it seemed to be going to. Adjusting to a chronic incurable illness, I have moved through a process similar to that outlined by Elizabeth Kübler-Ross in *On Death and Dying*. The major difference—and it is far more significant than most people recognize—is that I can't be sure of the outcome, as the terminally ill cancer patient can. Research studies indicate that, with proper medical care, I may achieve a "normal" life span. And in our society, with its vision of death as the ultimate evil, worse even than decrepitude, the response to such news is, "Oh well, at least you're not going to *die*." Are there worse things than dying? I think that there may be.

I think of two women I know, both with MS, both enough older than I to have served me as models. One took to her bed several years ago and has been there ever since. Although she can sit in a high-backed wheelchair, because she is incontinent she refuses to go out at all, even though incontinence pants, which are readily available at any pharmacy, could protect her from embarrassment. Instead, she stays at home and insists that her husband, a small quiet man, a retired civil servant, stay there with her except for a quick weekly foray to the supermarket. The other woman, whose illness was diagnosed when she was eighteen, a nursing student engaged to a young doctor, finished her training, married her doctor, accompanied him to Germany when he was in the service, bore three sons and a daughter, now grown and gone. When she can, she travels with her husband; she plays bridge, embroiders, swims regularly; she works, like me, as a symptomatic-patient instructor of medical students in neurology. Guess which woman I hope to be.

At the beginning, I thought about having MS almost incessantly. And because of the unpredictable course of the disease, my thoughts were always terrified. Each night I'd get into bed wondering whether I'd get out again the next morning, whether I'd be able to see, to speak, to hold a pen between my fingers. Knowing that the day might come when I'd be physically incapable of killing myself, I thought perhaps I ought to do so right away, while I still had the strength. Gradually I came to understand that the Nancy who might one day lie inert under a bedsheet, arms and legs paralyzed, unable to feed or bathe herself, unable to reach out for a gun, a bottle of pills, was not the Nancy I was at present, and that I could not presume to make decisions for that future Nancy, who might well not want in the least to die. Now the only provision I've made for the future Nancy is that when the time comes—and it is likely to come in the form of pneumonia, friend to the weak and the old—I am not to be treated with machines and medications. If she is unable to communicate by then, I hope she will be satisfied with these terms.

Thinking all the time about having MS grew tiresome and intrusive, especially in the large and tragic mode in which I was accustomed to considering my plight. Months and even years went by without catastrophe (at least without one related to MS), and really I was awfully busy, what with George and children and snakes and students and poems, and I hadn't the time, let alone the inclination, to devote myself to being a disease. Too, the richer my life became, the funnier it seemed, as though there were some connection between largesse and laughter, and so my tragic stance began to waver until, even with the aid of a brace and a cane, I couldn't hold it for very long at a time.

After several years I was satisfied with my adjustment. I had suffered my grief and fury and terror, I thought, but now I was at ease with my lot. Then one summer day I set out with George and the children across the desert for a vacation in California. Part way to Yuma I became aware that my right leg felt funny. "I think I've had an exacerbation," I told George. "What shall we do?" he asked. "I think we'd better get the hell to California," I said, "because I don't know whether I'll ever make it again." So we went on to San Diego and then to Orange, up the Pacific Coast Highway to Santa Cruz, across to Yosemite, down to Sequoia and Joshua Tree, and so back over the desert to home. It was a fine two-week trip, filled with friends and fair weather, and I wouldn't have missed it for the world, though I did in fact make it back to California two years later. Nor would there have been any point in missing it, since in MS, once the symptoms have appeared, the neurological damage has been done, and there's no way to predict or prevent that damage.

The incident spoiled my self-satisfaction, however. It renewed my grief and fury and terror, and I learned that one never finishes adjusting to MS. I don't know now why I thought one would. One does not, after all, finish adjusting to life, and MS is simply a fact of my life—not my favorite fact, of course—but as ordinary as my nose and my tropical fish and my yellow Mazda station wagon. It may at any time get worse, but no amount of worry or anticipation can prepare me for a new loss. My life is a lesson in losses. I learn one at a time.

And I had best be patient in the learning, since I'll have to do it like it or not. As any rock fan knows, you can't always get what you want. Particularly when you have MS. You can't, for example, get cured. In recent years researchers and the organizations that fund research have started to pay MS some attention even though it isn't fatal; perhaps they have begun to see that life is something other than a quantitative phenomenon, that one may be very much alive for a very long time in a life that isn't worth living. The researchers have made some progress toward understanding the mechanism of the disease: It may well be an autoimmune reaction triggered by a slow-acting virus. But they are nowhere near its prevention, control, or cure. And most of us want to be cured. Some, unable to accept incurability, grasp at one treatment after another, no matter how bizarre: megavitamin therapy, gluten-free diet, injections of cobra venom, hypothermal suits, lymphocytopharesis, hyperbaric chambers. Many treatments are probably harmless enough, but none are curative.

The absence of a cure often makes MS patients bitter toward their doctors. Doctors are, after all, the priests of modern society, the new shamans, whose business is to heal, and many an MS patient roves from one to another, searching for the "good" doctor who will make him well. Doctors too think of themselves as healers, and for this reason many have trouble dealing with MS patients, whose disease in its intransigence defeats their aims and mocks their skills. Too few doctors, it is true, treat their patients as whole human beings, but the reverse is also true. I have always tried to be gentle with my doctors, who often have more at stake in terms of ego than I do. I may be frustrated, maddened, depressed by the incurability of my disease, but I am not diminished by it, and they are. When I push myself up from my seat in the waiting room and stumble toward them, I incarnate the limitation of their powers. The least I can do is refuse to press on their tenderest spots.

This gentleness is part of the reason that I'm not sorry to be a cripple. I didn't have it before. Perhaps I'd have developed it anyway—how could I know such a thing?—and I wish I had more of it, but I'm glad of what I have. It has opened and enriched my life enormously, this sense that my frailty and need must be mirrored in others, that in searching for and shaping a stable core in a life wrenched by change and loss, change and loss, I must recognize the same process, under individual conditions, in the lives around me. I do not deprecate such knowledge, however I've come by it.

All the same, if a cure were found, would I take it? In a minute. I may be a cripple, but I'm only occasionally a loony and never a saint. Anyway, in my brand of theology God doesn't give bonus points for a limp. I'd take a cure; I just don't need one. A friend who also has MS startled me once by asking, "Do you ever say to yourself, 'Why me, Lord?'" "No, Michael, I don't," I told him, "because whenever I try, the only response I can think of is 'Why not?'" If I could make a cosmic deal, who would I put in my place? What in my life would I give up in exchange for sound limbs and a thrilling rush of energy? No one. Nothing. I might as well do the job myself. Now that I'm getting the hang of it.

Endnotes

1. Illustrated manuscript of the New Testament done by Irish monks; English commentaries were added in the tenth century.

2. A quotation from "Politics and the English Language" (see p. 216), by Orwell (1903–1950), British essayist and novelist, famous for his political satires.

3. American singer (b. 1935), popular in the 1950s and 1960s and well known for his love ballads. Tab Hunter (b. 1931), American actor and singer popular in the 1960s.

4. Latin for "in the last straits"—here it means "at the limits of endurance."

5. Jacqueline du Pre (1945–1987), a great cellist whose career was ended by MS.

6. A crippled, frail young boy saved by Scrooge's eventual generosity in Charles Dickens's novel A *Christmas Carol*.

7. The monstrous son of the witch Sycorax in Shakespeare's play *The Tempest*.

Questions for Reading and Analysis

1. Why does Nancy Mairs choose to describe herself as a "cripple"? How does her choice of terms tally with the advocates of political correctness? Is she aware of the political implications of her choice of terms?

2. In paragraph 13, Mairs talks about her life as the "plenty and the privation." Give examples from the essay for each of these two aspects.

3. If you had to pick one sentence from the essay to sum up its main point, which sentence would it be? Explain your choice.

4. The Louise Bogan quote Mairs chooses as the epigraph for her essay ("To escape is nothing. Not to escape is nothing.") is a paradox, a statement that looks like a contradiction but that, upon closer inspection, reveals an underlying truth. In what way does Mairs's essay explain and illustrate this paradox?

5. What does this essay teach readers about the lives of people with disabilities? Does it offer a new perspective?

Thomas Gale Moore, an economist, argues that global warming, despite the concerns of the scientific community, "would probably benefit most Americans." His argument concentrates largely on the economic effects of global warming; he claims that the issue is not to try and prevent inevitable climate changes but "to promote growth and prosperity so that people will have the resources to deal with the normal set of natural disasters."

Happiness Is a Warm Planet

Thomas Gale Moore

President Clinton convened a conference on global warming yesterday, as the White House agonizes over its posture at the forthcoming talks in Kyoto, Japan, on a worldwide global warming treaty. Mr. Clinton is eager to please his environmentalist supporters, but industry, labor and members of the Senate have told the administration that this treaty would wreck the economy, cost millions of jobs and provoke a flight of investment to more hospitable climes.

A crucial point gets lost in the debate: Global warming, if it were to occur, would probably *benefit* most Americans.

If mankind had to choose between a warmer or a cooler climate, we would certainly choose the former: Humans, nearly all other animals and most plants would be better off with higher temperatures. The climate models suggest, and so far the record confirms, that under global warming nighttime winter temperatures would rise the most, and daytime summer temperatures the least. Most Americans prefer a warmer climate to a colder one—and that preference is justified. More people die of the cold than of the heat; more die in the winter than the summer. Statistical evidence suggests that the climate predicted for the end of the next century might reduce U.S. deaths by about 40,000 annually.

In addition, less snow and ice would reduce transportation delays and accidents. A warmer winter would cut heating costs, more than offsetting any increase in air conditioning expenses in the summer. Manufacturing, mining and most services would be unaffected. Longer growing seasons, more rainfall and higher concentrations of carbon dioxide would benefit plant growth. Already there is evidence that trees and other plants are growing more vigorously. Although some locales may become too dry, too wet or too warm, on the whole mankind should benefit from an upward tick in the thermometer.

What about the economic effects? In the pessimistic view of the Intergovernmental Panel on Climate Change, the costs of global warming might be as high as 1.5 percent of the U.S. gross domestic product by the end of the next century. The cost of reducing carbon dioxide emissions, however, would be much higher. William

Cline of the Institute for International Economics has calculated that the cost of cutting emissions by one-third from current levels by 2040 would be 3.5 percent of worldwide GDP. The IPCC also reviewed various estimates of losses from stabilizing emissions at 1990 levels, a more modest objective, and concluded that the cost to the U.S. economy would be at least 1.5 percent of GDP by 2050, with the burden continuing to increase thereafter.

The forecast cost of warming is for the end of the next century, not the middle. Adjusting for the time difference, the cost to the U.S. from a warmer climate at mid-century, according to the IPCC, would be at most 0.75 percent of GDP, meaning that the costs of holding carbon dioxide to 1990 levels would be twice the gain from preventing any climate change. But the benefit-cost calculus is even worse. The administration is planning to exempt Third World nations, such as China, India and Brazil, from the requirements of the treaty. Under such a scheme, Americans would pay a huge price for virtually no benefit.

And even if the developing countries agreed to return emissions to 1990 levels, greenhouse gas concentrations would not be stabilized. Since for many decades more carbon dioxide would be added to the atmosphere than removed through natural processes, the buildup would only slow; consequently temperatures would continue to go up. Instead of saving the full 0.75 percent of GDP by keeping emissions at 1990 levels, we would be saving much less.

It is true that whatever dangers global warming may pose, they will be most pronounced in the developing world. It is much easier for rich countries to adapt to any long-term shift in weather than it is for poor countries, which tend to be much more dependent on agriculture. Poor countries lack the resources to aid their flora and fauna in adapting, and many of their farmers earn too little to survive a shift to new conditions. But the best insurance for these poor countries is an increase in their wealth, which would diminish their dependence on agriculture and make it easier for them to adjust to changes in weather, including increases in precipitation and possible flooding or higher sea level. Subjecting Americans to high taxes and onerous regulations will help neither them—we could buy less from them—nor us.

The optimal way to deal with potential climate change is not to embark on a futile attempt to prevent it, but to promote growth and prosperity so that people will have the resources to deal with the normal set of natural disasters. Based on the evidence, including historical records, global warming is likely to be good for most of mankind. The additional carbon, rain and warmth should promote the plant growth necessary to sustain an expanding world population. Global change is inevitable; warmer is better; richer is healthier.

Questions for Reading and Analysis

1. What arguments does Moore bring in to support his thesis?

2. Moore, an economist, first published his piece in *The Wall Street Journal*. What kind of audience is he writing for? How does his piece show that he is very much aware of his particular audience?

3. What is your reaction to his last sentence: "Global change is inevitable; warmer is better; richer is healthier." Is this is an effective way to end his argument?

4. Should Moore consider other issues besides money when discussing global warming?

In the following excerpt from her 1987 book A Restricted Country, *writer Joan Nestle looks back on a family vacation to Arizona, to an area of "restricted country," the beauty of which she admired, the ugliness of which she could not understand. The discrimination against Jews startles her, begins to shape her awareness of difference—but she realizes, too, in her mother's discomfort at the Jewish dude ranch, that one can be an exile among one's own.*

A Restricted Country

Joan Nestle

1.

When the plane landed on the blazing tar strip, I knew Arizona was a new world. My mother and brother stared with me out at the mountain-fringed field of blue. The Nestles three on their first vacation together had crossed the Mississippi and entered the shining new land of the American West. The desert air hit us with its startling clarity: this was not the intimate heat of New York, the heat that penetrated flesh and transformed itself into our sweat and earned our curses. We walked through it, like the others, and stood waiting for the station wagon to pick us up.

I should have known from the skeptical look on my mother's face that we were in for trouble, but I chalked it up to the fact that she had never traveled further west than New Jersey. My brother's new job at American Airlines had made this trip possible: the company compensated for low wages by offering its employees special cut-rate vacation packages, and many of his fellow workers had recommended this one-week stay at Shining Star Guest Ranch as the best bargain. From the moment he had told us of the possibility, to the time we were standing in front of the Tucson Airport, I could not believe the trip was really going to happen. I had dreamed horses all my sixteen years, played wild stallion in the Bronx vacant lots that were my childhood fields, had read every book about wild horses, mustangs, rangy colts that I could find, and through all the splintering agonies of my family I galloped on plains that were smooth and never-ending. For my brother, who had seldom been with my mother and me, this trip was both a reunion and an offering. After years of turmoil, mistakes, and rage, he was giving us the spoils of his manhood. He lay this vacation at the feet of our fatherless family as if it were a long-awaited homecoming gift. For my mother, it was a simple thing: her week's vacation from the office, her first trip in over twenty years.

We finally spotted the deep-purple station wagon that bore the ranch's name and hurried to it. A large man in a cowboy hat asked if we were the Nestle family, looked at us intently, and then fell silent as he loaded our suitcases into the wagon. We rode though the outskirts of Tucson and continued into the desert. The man never said another word to us, and feeling the strangeness of the desert, we too fell silent. Cacti rose around us, twisted strong creatures that, like the untouching heat, seemed only to tolerate the temporary intrusion of roads into their world. I felt the desert clumps of tufted grass under my feet. I was already moving my horse's haunches, for now it was only a sheet of glass that separated me from Annie Oakley. Dusk came suddenly and the heat fled.

We pulled into the ranch, and another man poked his head into the front window and stared at the three of us. "Do you want fish or meat for dinner?" were his only words. My mother answered that it made no difference, meat would be fine. Everything was still in the blue-black night as we were shown our rooms and then led to the dining room. The room was long, low-roofed with heavy beams; a fireplace glowed at one end. All the other guests were seated at the same table, ladling out huge portions of food from communal platters. We were seated at the long last table, a far distance from the rest, near the large stone fireplace. As our places were being set, the waitress placed a small white card near each of our plates. I picked up mine and read, *Because this guest ranch is run like a family, we are restricted to members of the Gentile faith only.* I could now envision the chain of events that our arrival had set in motion. The man who peered in at us must have realized we were Jewish, rushed in to tell his boss, who pulled out the appropriate cards to be served with our dinner. My brother and I sat stunned; My mother said we would talk to the manager after dinner.

As I tried to eat, the voices of the other guests caught in my throat. I had grown up with the language of New York's garment district. I knew the word *goy*, but this was my introduction to *Gentiles*. We can't stay here, my mother said. My brother kept saying he was sorry, he didn't know. How could his coworkers recommend this place? How could American Airlines have a working agreement with such a place? When we finished eating, my mother asked to speak to the manager. She and my brother were led to his office. I stayed outside in what seemed to be a reading room. I paced the room, looking at the books lining the wall. Finally, I found what I knew had to be there: a finely bound volume of *Mein Kampf*. For one moment it wasn't 1956 but another time, a time of flaming torches and forced marches. It wasn't just my Jewishness that I learned at that moment: it was also the stunning reality of exclusion unto death. It was the history lesson of those judged not to be human, and I knew our number was legion and so were our dyings.

Huddled in the privacy of our room, my mother and brother told me what the manager had said. Since it was-off season, he was willing to compromise. If we told no one that we were Jewish, if we left and entered through the back door, and if we ate our meals by ourselves, we could stay. We looked at each other. Here was an offer to the Nestles to pass as Gentiles. To eat and walk in shame.

We waited until the morning to tell the manager our decision. I stayed in our room while my mother and brother went in for breakfast. In a strange twist of feeling, my anger had turned to shyness. I thought of the priest I had noticed sitting at the table the night before, and I could not bear the thought of making him see we were human. I could not bear the challenge to his geniality that we would represent. After breakfast, the three of us entered the manager's office to tell him we would not stay under his conditions.

I stared at the man as my mother spoke for us, looking for his embarrassment, waiting for the moment when he would say this was all a joke. His answer was that he was sure we would not want to stay some place we were not wanted, but there was a Jewish Dude ranch several miles away. Perhaps the owners would consider allowing us to stay there for the same price. He made the call for us, saying, "By mistake some of your people came here." The voice on the other end agreed to take us. Once again we were ushered into the station wagon and driven to a parking lot in downtown Tucson. We sat on the curb waiting for the new station wagon to pick us up. The men walking by wore big brown belts with turquoise stones embedded in the leather, pointed boots, and wide-brimmed hats. The sun shone with that same impersonal heat, and the shimmering mountains were still waiting for us in the distance.

2.

When the station wagon pulled into our new destination, we were greeted by a small circle of elderly guests who welcomed us with hugs and low-voiced comments to my mother about "the *kinder*." After the novelty of our sad mistake wore off, the three of us were left to our own devices. As the youngest person at the ranch, I was indulged in my unladylike ways. Riding clothes were lent to me, and my desire to smell as much like a horse as possible was humorously accepted. My brother spent his time playing tennis and dating a young woman who cleaned the rooms. As soon as it grew dark, they would take off for the nearest town. My mother, however, had a harder time in our Jewish haven. All the other guests were retired, wealthy married couples who moved with ease in this sunlit world. While they were sympathetic to my mother, a woman alone raising two kids, they were also embarrassed by her. She dressed wrong and did not know how to enjoy herself.

My mother was a dedicated gin and poker player. Shortly after our arrival she tried to join the nightly card game, but here, under the Arizona sun, the stakes had multiplied beyond her resources. I watched her as she approached the table of cigar-smoking men. She sat for one round, growing smaller in her seat while the pile of chips grew bigger and bigger in the center of the table. She was a working-class gambler who played with her week's salary while these men played with their retired riches. Her Seventh Avenue bravado could not cover her cards. For the first time in my life, I saw my mother defeated by the people she said she despised. She could not fight the combination of a strange country, high fashion, pity, money, and physical pride.

One afternoon I noticed a crowd of guests gesturing and laughing at something in the center of the riding ring. I pushed through and saw it was my mother. Dressed in her checked polyester suit, she sat on top of a large brown gelding attempting to move it. She rocked back and forth in the saddle as if she were on a rocking horse, or making love, while voices cried out to her, "Come on, Regina, kick him. You can do it." The intimate spectacle of my mother's awkwardness, the one-sided laughter, and the desperate look on her face pushed me back from the railing. These people were my people; they had been kind to me. But something terrible was going on here. We were Jewish, but we were different.

Toward evening, at the end of our stay, I went in search of my mother. I looked by the pool, in the lounge, and everywhere else the other guests habitually gathered, but I could not find her. I wandered to the far end of the ranch and saw her in the distance. She was sitting on a child's swing, trailing one leg in the dust. A small round woman whose belly bulged in her too-tight, too-cheap pants. Her head was lowered, and the air shimmered around her as if loneliness had turned to heat. Where was Seventh Avenue, the coffee shops, the crowded subways, the city which covered her aloneness because she had work to do there. Arizona was not for Regina Nestle, not this resort with its well-married ladies. While I scrambled over this new brown earth, my mother sat in the desert, a silent exile.

3.

Bill, the tired, aging cowboy who ran the corral, was my date for the evening. Elliot was with Mary, a woman in her twenties who worked at the ranch. We had been to see a movie and were now parked behind the ranch house. Bill kissed me as we twisted around in the front seat. His bony hand pushed into my crotch while his tongue opened my mouth. I pushed his hand away, sure of what I wanted and of what I did not. I did not want his fingers in me, but I did want to see his cheek against my breast. My brother and Mary gave up their squirming in the back seat and left the two of us alone. Bill was respectful. One word from me was enough to get him to stop his attempts at penetration. "Lay in my arms," I told him. He slipped his long legs through the open window at one end of the front seat and leaned back into my arms. His lips pulled at my nipples. We sat that way for a long time as the Arizona sky grew darker and darker. Right before he fell asleep, he said, "Best thing that's happened to me in twenty years." I knew this did not have very much to do with me, but a lot to do with my sixteen-year-old breasts. I sat there holding him for what seemed like hours, afraid to move because I did not want to wake him, when suddenly he jerked in his sleep and knocked into the steering wheel, setting off the horn. The desert stillness was split by its harsh alarm, and I knew my idyll was coming to an end.

One by one, the lights came on in the guest cottages. My brother was the first to reach the car, his pajamas shining white in the moonlight. "I'm alright, I'm alright," I whispered, as I maneuvered my body away from Bill's. I wanted to escape before the other guests came pouring out, to save Bill from having to explain what we were doing. He would be held responsible for breaking the boundaries between guests and workers, between young girls and old men, and I would never be able to convince them that I knew exactly what I was doing, that tenderness was my joy that night, that I danced in the moonlight knowing my body could be a home in the freezing desert air.

4.

I spent most of my time around the horses, following Bill on his daily chores. He eventually gave me his chaps to wear because I was constantly riding into the cholla plants, and ending up with their needles sticking into my thighs. My horse for the week was not the sleek stallion I had dreamed of, but a fat wide-backed white mare that was safe. Ruby and I were always on the tail end of the rides, but I did not care: the Bronx streets had disappeared, and I could bend over and talk to my steed while I stroked her powerful neck.

Each day we rode up into the mountains, the same mountains that had looked so distant from the airport. Our party was usually Elliot and myself, and Bill and Elizabeth. Elizabeth was a small muscular woman in her fifties whose husband was dying of Parkinson's disease. She had made my riding possible by lending me a pair of boots. Each morning her husband, a large burly man who walked in tiny trembling steps, would stand in the doorway of their cottage and slowly raise his hand to wave good-bye. Elizabeth loved him deeply, and each morning I saw the grief on her face. She would ride her horse like a demon far up into the mountains, leaving the rest of us behind. As the week passed, I slowly realized that she and Bill were lovers. I saw the tenderness between them as if it were an invisible rope that kept them both from falling off the rocky hills. Like two aging warriors, both grey and lean, they fought off sadness with sharp, quick actions. We would ride up into the mountain clefts, find a grassy spot to stretch out on in the afternoon sun, and silently be glad for each other's company. I never spoke or intruded on their moments together. I just watched and learned from their sad, tough, erotic connection all I could bear about illness and love and sexuality. On the way home, stumbling down the stony trails, I would ride as close as I could to these two silent adults.

Then it was our last ride together. We had come down from the mountains on a different path. We found a dirt road, smooth enough for cars, and I started to see real estate signs announcing that this area was the most restricted country in Arizona. I pushed my horse closer to Elizabeth and Bill and asked, "What does *restricted* mean?"

"No Jews allowed," Elizabeth answered. I looked around again in wonder at this land we were moving through. The distant hills had become known, and I loved this earth so different from my own. I silently rode beside my two older friends, wanting to be protected by their gentle toughness and not understanding how the beauty of the land could be owned by ugliness.

Questions for Reading and Analysis

1. What word in the cards placed near the Nestles' plates do the proprietors of the Shining Star Guest Ranch manipulate to accommodate their own prejudices? In doing so, what do they suggest?

2. For what reason(s), is Nestle's mother exiled, even at the Jewish dude ranch?

3. List several of the restrictions or barriers Nestle examines in her essay.

4. List the various awakenings Nestle experiences.

George Orwell (1903–1950), for whom writing was a means of addressing injustice, is best known for his novels Animal Farm *and* 1984, *but he was also a prolific essayist.* A Hanging, *informed by his experience as a policeman in Burma, examines the inhumanity of which humans are capable. The classic* Politics and the English Language *illustrates an abiding Orwellian truth—the moral-political responsibility of language.*

A Hanging

George Orwell

It was in Burma, a sodden morning of the rains. A sickly light, like yellow tinfoil, was slanting over the high walls into the jail yard. We were waiting outside the condemned cells, a row of sheds fronted with double bars, like small animal cages. Each cell measured about ten feet by ten and was quite bare within except for a plank bed and a pot for drinking water. In some of them brown silent men were squatting at the inner bars, with their blankets draped round them. These were the condemned men, due to be hanged within the next week or two.

One prisoner had been brought out of his cell. He was a Hindu, a puny wisp of a man, with a shaven head and vague liquid eyes. He had a thick sprouting moustache, absurdly too big for his body, rather like the moustache of a comic man on the films. Six tall Indian warders were guarding him and getting him ready for the gallows. Two of them stood by with rifles and fixed bayonets, while the others handcuffed him, passed a chain through his handcuffs and fixed it to their belts, and lashed his arms tight to his sides. They crowded very close about him, with their hands always on him in a careful, caressing grip, as though all the while feeling him to make sure he was there. It was like men handling a fish which is still alive and may jump back into the water. But he stood quite unresisting, yielding his arms limply to the ropes, as though he hardly noticed what was happening.

Eight o'clock struck and a bugle call, desolately thin in the wet air, floated from the distant barracks. The superintendent of the jail, who was standing apart from the rest of us, moodily prodding the gravel with his stick, raised his head at the sound. He was an army doctor, with a grey toothbrush moustache and a gruff voice. "For God's sake, hurry up, Francis," he said irritably. "The man ought to have been dead by this time. Aren't you ready yet?"

Francis, the head jailer, a fat Dravidian in a white drill suit and gold spectacles, waved his black hand. "Yes sir, yes sir," he bubbled. "All is satisfactorily prepared. The hangman is waiting. We shall proceed."

"Well, quick march, then. The prisoners can't get their breakfast till this job's over."

We set out for the gallows. Two warders marched on either side of the prisoner, with their rifles at the slope; two others marched close against him, gripping him by arm and shoulder, as though at once pushing and supporting him. The rest of us, magistrates and the like, followed behind. Suddenly, when we had gone ten yards, the procession stopped short without any order or warning. A dreadful thing had happened—a dog, come goodness knows whence, had appeared in the yard. It came bounding among us with a loud volley of barks, and leapt round us wagging its whole body, wild with glee at finding so many human beings together. It was a large woolly dog, half Airedale, half pariah. For a moment it pranced round us, and then, before anyone could stop it, it had made a dash for the prisoner and, jumping up, tried to lick his face. Everybody stood aghast, too taken aback even to grab the dog.

"Who let that bloody brute in here?" said the superintendent angrily. "Catch it, someone!"

A warder, detached from the escort, charged clumsily after the dog, but it danced and gamboled just out of his reach, taking everything as part of the game. A young Eurasian jailer picked up a handful of gravel and tried to stone the dog away, but it dodged the stones and came after us again. Its yaps echoed from the jail walls. The prisoner, in the grasp of the two warders, looked on incuriously, as though this was another formality of the hanging. It was several minutes before someone managed to catch the dog. Then we put my handkerchief through its collar and moved off once more, with the dog still straining and whimpering.

It was about forty yards to the gallows. I watched the bare brown back of the prisoner marching in front of me. He walked clumsily with his bound arms, but quite steadily, with that bobbing gait of the Indian who never straightens his knees. At each step his muscles slid neatly into place, the lock of hair on his scalp danced up and down, his feet printed themselves on the wet gravel. And once, in spite of the men who gripped him by each shoulder, he stepped lightly aside to avoid a puddle on the path.

It is curious, but till that moment I had never realized what it means to destroy a healthy, conscious man. When I saw the prisoner step aside to avoid the puddle I saw the mystery, the unspeakable wrongness, of cutting a life short when it is in full tide. This man was not dying, he was alive just as we are alive. All the organs of his body were working—bowels digesting food, skin renewing itself, nails growing, tissues forming—all toiling away in solemn foolery. His nails would still be growing when he stood on the drop, when he was falling through the air with a tenth-of-a-second to live. His eyes saw the yellow gravel and the gray walls, and his brain still remembered, foresaw, reasoned—reasoned even about puddles. He and we were a party of men walking together, seeing, hearing, feeling, understanding the same world; and in two minutes, with a sudden snap, one of us would be gone—one mind less, one world less.

The gallows stood in a small yard, separate from the main grounds of the prison, and overgrown with tall prickly weeds. It was a brick erection like three sides of a shed, with planking on top, and above that two beams and a crossbar with the rope dangling. The hangman, a gray-haired convict in the white uniform of the prison, was waiting beside his machine. He greeted us with a servile crouch as we entered. At a word from Francis the two warders, gripping the prisoner more closely than ever, half led half pushed him to the gallows and helped him clumsily up the ladder. Then the hangman climbed up and fixed the rope round the prisoner's neck.

We stood waiting, five yards away. The warders had formed in a rough circle round the gallows. And then, when the noose was fixed, the prisoner began crying out to his god. It was a high, reiterated cry of "Ram! Ram! Ram! Ram!" not urgent and fearful like a prayer or cry for help, but steady, rhythmical, almost like the tolling of a bell. The dog answered the sound with a whine. The hangman, still standing on the gallows, produced a small cotton bag like a flour bag and drew it down over the prisoner's face. But the sound, muffled by the cloth, still persisted, over and over again: "Ram! Ram! Ram! Ram! Ram!"

The hangman climbed down and stood ready, holding the lever. Minutes seemed to pass. The steady, muffled crying from the prisoner went on and on, "Ram! Ram! Ram!" never faltering for an instant. The superintendent, his head on his chest, was slowly poking the ground with his stick; perhaps he was counting the cries, allowing the prisoner a fixed number—fifty, perhaps, or a hundred. Everyone had changed color. The Indians had gone gray like bad coffee, and one or two of the bayonets were wavering. We looked at the lashed, hooded man on the drop, and listened to his cries—each cry another second of life; the same thought was in all our minds; oh, kill him quickly, get it over, stop that abominable noise!

Suddenly the superintendent made up his mind. Throwing up his head he made a swift motion with his stick. "Chalo!" he shouted almost fiercely.

There was a clanking noise, and then dead silence. The prisoner had vanished, and the rope was twisting on itself. I let go of the dog, and it galloped immediately to the back of the gallows; but when it got there it stopped short, barked, and then retreated into a corner of the yard, where it stood among the weeds, looking timorously out at us. We went round the gallows to inspect the prisoner's body. He was dangling with his toes pointed straight downwards, very slowly revolving, as dead as a stone.

The superintendent reached out with his stick and poked the bare brown body; it oscillated slightly. "*He's* all right," said the superintendent. He backed out from under the gallows, and blew out a deep breath. The moody look had gone out of his face quite suddenly. He glanced at his wristwatch. "Eight minutes past eight. Well, that's all for this morning, thank God."

The warders unfixed bayonets and marched away. The dog, sobered and conscious of having misbehaved itself, slipped after them. We walked out of the gallows yard, past the condemned cells with their waiting prisoners, into the big central yard of the prison. The convicts, under the command of warders armed with lathis, were already receiving their breakfast. They squatted in long rows, each man holding a tin pannikin, while two warders with buckets marched around ladling out rice; it seemed quite a homely, jolly scene, after the hanging. An enormous relief had come upon us now that the job was done. One felt an impulse to sing, to break into a run, to snigger. All at once everyone began chattering gaily.

The Eurasian boy walking beside me nodded toward the way we had come, with a knowing smile: "Do you know, sir, our friend [he meant the dead man] when he heard his appeal had been dismissed, he pissed on the floor of his cell. From fright. Kindly take one of my cigarettes, sir. Do you not admire my new silver case, sir? From the boxwalah, two rupees eight annas. Classy European style."

Several people laughed—at what, nobody seemed certain.

Francis was walking by the superintendent, talking garrulously: "Well, sir, all hass passed off with the utmost satisfactoriness. It was all finished—flick! like that. It iss not always so—oah, no! I have known cases where the doctor was obliged to go beneath the gallows and pull the prissoner's legs to ensure decease. Most disagreeable!"

"Wriggling about, eh? That's bad," said the superintendent.

"Ach, sir, it is worse when they become refractory! One man, I recall, clung to the bars of hiss cage when we went to take him out. You will scarcely credit, sir, that it took six warders to dislodge him, three pulling at each leg. We reasoned with him. 'My dear fellow,' we said, 'think of all the pain and trouble you are causing to us!' But no, he would not listen! Ach, he was very troublesome!"

I found that I was laughing quite loudly. Everyone was laughing. Even the superintendent grinned in a tolerant way. "You'd better all come out and have a drink," he said quite genially. "I've got a bottle of whisky in the car. We could do with it."

We went through the big double gates of the prison into the road. "Pulling at his legs!" exclaimed a Burmese magistrate suddenly, and burst into a loud chuckling. We all began laughing again. At that moment Francis' anecdote seemed extraordinarily funny. We all had a drink together, native and European alike, quite amicably. The dead man was a hundred yards away.

Questions for Reading and Analysis

1. What is Orwell's persuasive purpose? What aspect of the essay suggests such a purpose?

2. What is the significance of Orwell's lengthy description of the dog?

3. What is the effect of the final paragraph? Why does Orwell end the essay with such an image? Does it advance his persuasive intent?

Politics and the English Language

George Orwell

Most people who bother with the matter at all would admit that the English language is in a bad way, but it is generally assumed that we cannot by conscious action do anything about it. Our civilization is decadent and our language—so the argument runs—must inevitably share in the general collapse. It follows that any struggle against the abuse of language is a sentimental archaism, like preferring candles to electric light or hansom cabs to aeroplanes. Underneath this lies the half-conscious belief that language is a natural growth and not an instrument which we shape for our own purposes.

Now, it is clear that the decline of a language must ultimately have political and economic causes: it is not due simply to the bad influence of this or that individual writer. But an effect can become a cause, reinforcing the original cause and producing the same effect in an intensified form, and so on indefinitely. A man may take to drink because he feels himself to be a failure, and then fail all the more completely because he drinks. It is rather the same thing that is happening to the English language. It becomes ugly and inaccurate because our thoughts are foolish, but the slovenliness of our language makes it easier for us to have foolish thoughts. The point is that the process is reversible. Modern English, especially written English, is full of bad habits which spread by imitation and which can be avoided if one is willing to take the necessary trouble. If one gets rid of these habits one can think more clearly, and to think clearly is a necessary first step towards political regeneration: so that the fight against bad English is not frivolous and is not the exclusive concern of professional writers. I will come back to this presently, and I hope that by that time the meaning of what I have said here will have become clearer. Meanwhile, here are five specimens of the English language as it is now habitually written.

These five passages have not been picked out because they are especially bad—I could have quoted far worse if I had chosen—but because they illustrate various of the mental vices from which we now suffer. They are a little below the average, but are fairly representative samples. I number them so that I can refer to them when necessary:

> *(1) I am not, indeed, sure whether it is not true to say that the Milton who once seemed not unlike a seventeenth-century Shelley had not become, out of an experience ever more bitter in each year, more alien [sic] to the founder of that Jesuit sect which nothing could induce him to tolerate.*
>
> *Professor Harold Laski (Essay in* Freedom of Expression*)*

(2) Above all, we cannot play ducks and drakes with a native battery of idioms which prescribes such egregious collocations of vocables as the Basic put up with for tolerate or put at a loss for bewilder.

Professor Lancelot Hogben (Interglossa)

(3) On the one side we have the free personality: by definition it is not neurotic, for it has neither conflict nor dream. Its desires, such as they are, are transparent, for they are just what institutional approval keeps in the forefront of consciousness; another institutional pattern would alter their number and intensity; there is little in them that is natural, irreducible, or culturally dangerous. But on the other side, the social bond itself is nothing but the mutual reflection of these self-secure integrities. Recall the definition of love. Is not this the very picture of a small academic? Where is there a place in this hall of mirrors for either personality or fraternity?

Essay on psychology in Politics *(New York)*

(4) All the "best people" from the gentlemen's clubs, and all the frantic fascist captains, united in common hatred of Socialism and bestial horror of the rising tide of the mass revolutionary movement, have turned to acts of provocation, to foul incendi-arism, to medieval legends of poisoned wells, to legalize their own destruction of proletarian organizations, and rouse the agitated petty-bourgeoisie to chauvinistic fervour on behalf of the fight against the revolutionary way out of the crisis.

Communist pamphlet

(5) If a new spirit is to be infused into this old country, there is one thorny and contentious reform which must be tackled, and that is the humanization and galvanization of the B.B.C. Timidity here will bespeak cancer and atrophy of the soul. The heart of Britain may be sound and of strong beat, for instance, but the British lion's roar at present is like that of Bottom in Shakespeare's Midsummer Night's Dream—as gentle as any sucking dove. A virile new Britain cannot continue indefinitely to be traduced in the eyes or rather ears, of the world by the effete languors of Langham Place, brazenly masquerading as "standard English." When the Voice of Britain is heard at nine o'clock, better far and infinitely less ludicrous to hear aitches honestly dropped than the present priggish, inflated, inhibited, school-ma'amish arch braying of blameless bashful mewing maidens!

Letter in Tribune

Each of these passages has faults of its own, but, quite apart from avoidable ugliness, two qualities are common to all of them. The first is staleness of imagery; the other is lack of precision. The writer either has a meaning and can-not express it, or he inadvertently says something else, or he is almost indifferent as to whether his words mean anything or not. This mixture of vagueness and sheer incompetence is the most marked characteristic of modern English prose, and especially of any kind of political writing. As soon as certain topics are raised, the concrete melts into the abstract and on one seems able to think of turns of speech that are not hackneyed: prose consists less and less of *words* chosen for the sake of their meaning, and more and more of *phrases* tacked together like the sections of a prefabricated henhouse. I list below, with notes and examples, various of the tricks by means of which the work of prose-construction is habitually dodged:

Dying Metaphors

A newly invented metaphor assists thought by evoking a visual image, while on the other hand a metaphor which is technically "dead" (e.g. *iron resolution*) has in effect reverted to being an ordinary word and can generally be used without loss of vividness. But in between these two classes there is a huge dump of worn-out metaphors which have lost all evocative power and are merely used because they save people the trouble of inventing phrases for themselves. Examples are: *Ring the changes on, take up the cudgels for, toe the line, ride roughshod over, stand shoulder to shoulder with, play into the hands of, no axe to grind, grist to the mill, fishing in troubled waters, on the order of the day, Achilles' heel, swan song, hotbed.* Many of these are used without knowledge of their meaning (what is a "rift," for instance?), and incompatible metaphors are frequently mixed, a sure sign that the writer is not interested in what he is saying. Some metaphors now current have been twisted out of their original meaning without those who use them even being aware of the fact. For example, *toe the line* is sometimes written *tow the line*. Another example is the *hammer and the anvil*, now always used with the implication that the anvil gets the worst of it. In real life it is always the anvil that breaks the hammer, never the other way about: a writer who stopped to think what he was saying would be aware of this, and would avoid perverting the original phrase.

Operators or Verbal False Limbs

These save the trouble of picking out appropriate verbs and nouns, and at the same time pad each sentence with extra syllables which give it an appearance of symmetry. Characteristic phrases are: *render inoperative, militate against, make contact with, be subjected to, give rise to, give grounds for, have the effect of, play a leading part (role) in, make itself felt, take effect, exhibit a tendency to, serve the purpose of, etc., etc.* The keynote is the elimination of simple verbs. Instead of being a single word, such as *break, stop, spoil, mend, kill*, a verb becomes a *phrase*, made up of a noun or adjective tacked on to some general-purposes verb such as *prove, serve, form, play, render*. In addition, the passive voice is wherever possible used in preference to the active, and noun constructions are used instead of gerunds (*by examination of* instead of *by examining*). The range of verbs is further cut down by means of the *-ize* and *de-* formations, and the banal statements are given an appearance of profundity by means of the *not un-* formation. Simple conjunctions and prepositions are replaced by such phrases as *with respect to, having regard to, the fact that, by dint of, in view of, in the interests of, on the hypothesis* *that;* and the ends of sentences are saved from anticlimax by such resounding commonplaces as *greatly to be desired, cannot be left out of account, a development to be expected in the near future, deserving of serious consideration, brought to a satisfactory conclusion,* and so on and so forth.

Pretentious Diction

Words like *phenomenon, element, individual* (as noun), *objective, categorical, effective, virtual, basic, primary, promote, constitute, exhibit, exploit, utilize, eliminate, liquidate,* are used to dress up simple statements and give an air of scientific impartiality to biased judgments. Adjectives like *epoch-making, epic, historic, unforgettable, trimphant, age-old, inevitable, inexorable, veritable,* are used to dignify the sordid processes of international politics, while writing that aims at glorifying war usually takes on an archaic color, its characteristic words being: *realm, throne, chariot, mailed fist, trident, sword, shield, buckler, banner, jackboot, clarion.* Foreign words and expressions such as *cul de sac, ancien régime, deus ex machina, mutatis mutandis, status quo, gleichschaltung, weltanschauung,* are used to give an air of culture and elegance. Except for the useful abbreviations *i.e., e.g.,* and *etc.,* there is no real need for any of the hundreds of foreign phrases now current in English. Bad writers, and especially scientific, political and sociological writers, are nearly always haunted by the notion that Latin or Greek words are grander than Saxon ones, and unnecessary words like *expedite, ameliorate, predict, extraneous, deracinated, clandestine, subaqueous* and hundreds of others constantly gain ground from their Anglo-Saxon opposite numbers.[1] The jargon peculiar to Marxist writing (*hyena, hangman, cannibal, petty bourgeois, these gentry, lacquey, flunkey, mad dog, White Guard,* etc.) consists largely of words and phrases translated from Russian, German or French; but the normal way of coining a new word is to use a Latin or Greek root with the appropriate affix and, where necessary, the *-ize* formation. It is often easier to make up words of this kind (*deregionalize, impermissible, extramarital, nonfragmentary* and so forth) than to think up the English words that will cover one's meaning. The result, in general, is an increase in slovenliness and vagueness.

Meaningless Words

In certain kinds of writing, particularly in art criticism and literary criticism, it is normal to come across long passages which are almost completely lacking in meaning.[2] Words like *romantic, plastic, values, human, dead, sentimental, natural, vitality,* as used in art criticism, are strictly meaningless, in the sense that they not only do not point to any discoverable object, but are hardly ever expected to do so by the reader. When one critic writes, "The outstanding feature of Mr. X's work is its living quality," while another writes, "The immediately striking thing about Mr. X's work is its peculiar deadness," the reader accepts this as a simple difference of opinion. If words like *black* and *white* were involved, instead of the jargon words *dead* and *living,* he would see at once that language was being used in an improper way. Many political words are similarly abused. The word *Fascism* has now no meaning except in so far as it signifies "something not desirable." The words *democracy, socialism, freedom, patriotic, realistic, justice,* have each of them several different meanings which cannot be reconciled with one another. In the case of a word like *democracy,* not only is there no agreed definition, but the attempt to make one is resisted from all sides. It is almost universally felt that when we call a country democratic we are praising it: consequently the defenders of every kind of régime claim that it is a democracy, and fear that they might have to stop using the word if it were tied down to any one meaning. Words of this kind are often used in a consciously dishonest way. That is, the person who uses them has his own private definition, but allows his hearer to think he means something quite different. Statements like *Marshal Pétain was a true patriot, The Soviet Press is the freest in the world, The Catholic Church is opposed to persecution,* are almost always made with intent to deceive. Other words used in variable meanings, in most cases more or less dishonestly, are: *class, totalitarian, science, progressive, reactionary, bourgeois, equality.*

Now that I have made this catalogue of swindles and perversions, let me give another example of the kind of writing that they lead to. This time it must of its nature be an imaginary one. I am going to translate a passage of good English into modern English of the worst sort. Here is a well-known verse from *Ecclesiastes:*

> *I returned and saw under the sun, that the race is not to the swift, nor the battle to the strong, neither yet bread to the wise, nor yet riches to men of understanding, nor yet favour to men of skill; but time and chance happeneth to them all.*

Here it is in modern English:

> *Objective consideration of contemporary phenomena compels the conclusion that success or failure in competitive activities exhibits no tendency to be commensurate with innate capacity, but that a considerable element of the unpredictable must invariably be taken into account.*

This is a parody, but not a very gross one. Exhibit (3), above, for instance, contains several patches of the same kind of English. It will be seen that I have not made a full translation. The beginning and ending of the sentence follow the original meaning fairly closely, but in the middle the concrete illustrations—race, battle, bread—dissolve into the vague phrase "success or failure in competitive activities." This had to be so, because no modern writer of the kind I am discussing—no one capable of using phrases like "objective consideration of contemporary phenomena"—would ever tabulate his thoughts in that precise and detailed way. The whole tendency of modern prose is away from concreteness. Now analyse these two sentences a little more closely. The first contains forty-nine words but only sixty syllables, and all its words are those of everyday life. The second contains thirty-eight words of ninety syllables: eighteen of its words are from Latin roots, and one from Greek. The first sentence contains six vivid images, and only one phrase ("time and chance") that could be called vague. The second contains not a single fresh, arresting phrase, and in spite of its ninety syllables it gives only a shortened version of the meaning contained in the first. Yet without a doubt it is the second kind of sentence that is gaining ground in modern English. I do not want to exaggerate. This kind of writing is not yet universal, and outcrops of simplicity will occur here and there in the worst-written page. Still, if you or I were told to write a few lines on the uncertainty of human fortunes, we should probably come much nearer to my imaginary sentence than to the one from *Ecclesiastes*.

As I have tried to show, modern writing at its worst does not consist in picking out words for the sake of their meaning and inventing images in order to make the meaning clearer. It consists in gumming together long strips of words which have already been set in order by someone else, and making the results presentable by sheer humbug. The attraction of this way of writing is that it is easy. It is easier—even quicker, once you have the habit—to say *In my opinion it is not an unjustifiable assumption that* than to say I *think*. If you use ready-made phrases, you not only don't have to hunt about for words; you also don't have to bother with the rhythms of your sentences, since these phrases are generally so arranged as to be more or less euphonious. When you are composing in a hurry—when you are dictating to a stenographer, for instance, or making a public speech—it is natural to fall into a pretentious, Latinized style. Tags like *a consideration which we should do well to bear in mind* or *a conclusion to which all of us would readily assent* will save many a sentence from coming down with a bump. By using stale metaphors, similes and idioms, you save much mental effort, at the cost of leaving your meaning vague, not only for your reader but for yourself. This is the significance of mixed metaphors. The sole aim of a metaphor is to call up a visual image. When these images clash—as in *The Fascist octopus has sung its swan song, the jackboot is thrown into the melting pot*—it can be taken as certain that the writer is not seeing a mental image of the objects he is naming; in other words he is not really thinking. Look again at the examples I gave at the beginning of this essay. Professor Laski (1) uses five negatives in fifty-three words. One of these is superfluous, making nonsense of the whole passage, and in addition there is the slip *alien* for *akin*, making further nonsense, and several avoidable pieces of clumsiness which increase the general vagueness. Professor Hogben (2) plays ducks and drakes with a battery which is able to write prescriptions, and, while disapproving of the everyday phrase *put up with*, is unwilling to look *egregious* up in the dictionary and see what it means. (3), if one takes an uncharitable attitude towards it, is simply meaningless: probably one could work out its intended meaning by reading the whole of the article in which it occurs. In (4), the writer knows more or less what he wants to say, but an accumulation of stale phrases chokes him like tea leaves blocking a sink. In (5), words and meaning have almost parted company. People who write in this manner usually have a general emotional meaning—they dislike one thing and want to express solidarity with another—but they are not interested in the detail of what they are saying. A scrupulous writer, in every sentence that he writes, will ask himself at least four questions, thus: What am I trying to say? What words will express it? What image or idiom will make it clear? Is this image fresh enough to have an effect? And he will probably ask himself two more: Could I put it more shortly? Have I said anything that is avoidably ugly? But you are not obliged to go to all this trouble. You can shirk it by simply throwing your mind open and letting the ready-made phrases come crowding in. They will construct your sentences for you—even think your thoughts for you, to a certain extent—and at need they will perform the important service of partially concealing your meaning even from yourself. It is at this point that the special connection between politics and the debasement of language becomes clear.

In our time it is broadly true that political writing is bad writing. Where it is not true, it will generally be found that the writer is some kind of rebel, expressing his private opinions and not a "party line." Orthodoxy, of whatever colour, seems to demand a lifeless, imitative style. The political dialects to be found in pamphlets, leading articles, manifestos, White Papers and the speeches of under-secretaries do, of course, vary from party to party, but they are all alike in that one almost never finds in them a fresh, vivid, home-made turn of speech. When one watches some tired hack on the platform mechanically repeating the familiar phrases—*bestial atrocities, iron heel, bloodstained tyranny, free peoples of the world, stand shoulder to shoulder*—one often has a curious feeling that one is not watching a live human being but some kind of dummy: a feeling which suddenly becomes stronger at moments when the light catches the speaker's spectacles and turns them into blank discs which seem to have no eyes behind them. And this is not altogether fanciful. A speaker who uses that kind of phraseology has gone some distance towards turning himself into a machine. The appropriate noises are coming out of his larynx, but his brain is not involved as it would be if he were choosing his words for himself. If the speech he is making is one that he is accustomed to make over and over again, he may be almost unconscious of what he is saying, as one is when one utters the responses in church. And this reduced state of consciousness, if not indispensable, is at any rate favourable to political conformity.

In our time, political speech and writing are largely the defence of the indefensible. Things like the continuance of British rule in India, the Russian purges and deportations, the dropping of the atom bombs on Japan, can indeed be defended, but only by arguments which are too brutal for most people to face, and which do not square with the professed aims of political parties. Thus political language has to consist largely of euphemism, question-begging and sheer cloudy vagueness. Defenceless villages are bombarded from the air, the inhabitants driven out into the countryside, the cattle machine-gunned, the huts set on fire with incendiary bullets: this is called *pacification*. Millions of peasants are robbed of their farms and sent trudging along the roads with no more than they can carry: this is called *transfer of population* or *rectification of frontiers*. People are imprisoned for years without trial, or shot in the back of the neck or sent to die of scurvy in Arctic lumber camps: this is called *elimination of unreliable elements*. Such phraseology is needed if one wants to name things without calling up mental pictures of them. Consider for instance some comfortable English professor defending Russian totalitarianism. He cannot say outright, "I believe in killing off your opponents when you can get good results by doing so." Probably, therefore, he will say something like this:

"While freely conceding that the Soviet régime exhibits certain features which the humanitarian may be inclined to deplore, we must, I think, agree that a certain curtailment of the right to political opposition is an unavoidable concomitant of transitional periods, and that the rigors which the Russian people have been called upon to undergo have been amply justified in the sphere of concrete achievement."

The inflated style is itself a kind of euphemism. A mass of Latin words falls upon the facts like soft snow, blurring the outlines and covering up all the details.

The great enemy of clear language is insincerity. When there is a gap between one's real and one's declared aims, one turns as it were instinctively to long words and exhausted idioms, like a cuttlefish squirting out ink. In our age there is no such thing as "keeping out of politics." All issues are political issues, and politics itself is a mass of lies, evasions, folly, hatred and schizophrenia. When the general atmosphere is bad, language must suffer. I should expect to find—this is a guess which I have not sufficient knowledge to verify—that the German, Russian and Italian languages have all deteriorated in the last ten or fifteen years, as a result of dictatorship.

But if thought corrupts language, language can also corrupt thought. A bad usage can spread by tradition and imitation, even among people who should and do know better. The debased language that I have been discussing is in some ways very convenient. Phrases like *a not unjustifiable assumption, leaves much to be desired, would serve no good purpose, a consideration which we should do well to bear in mind,* are a continuous temptation, a packet of aspirins always at one's elbow. Look back through this essay, and for certain you will find that I have again and again committed the very faults I am protesting against. By this morning's post I have received a pamphlet dealing with conditions in Germany. The author tells me that he "felt impelled" to write it. I open it at random, and here is almost the first sentence that I see: "[The Allies] have an opportunity not only of achieving a radical transformation of Germany's social and political structure in such a way as to avoid a nationalistic reaction in Germany itself, but at the same time of laying the foundations of a co-operative and unified Europe." You see, he "feels impelled" to write—feels, presumably, that he has something new to say—and yet his words, like cavalry horses answering the bugle, group themselves automatically into the familiar dreary pattern. This invasion of one's mind by ready-made phrases (*lay the foundations, achieve a radical transformation*) can only be prevented if one is constantly on guard against them, and every such phrase anaesthetizes a portion of one's brain.

I said earlier that the decadence of our language is probably curable. Those who deny this would argue, if they produced an argument at all, that language merely reflects existing social conditions, and that we cannot influence its development by any direct tinkering with words and constructions. So far as the general tone or spirit of a language goes, this may be true, but it is not true in detail. Silly words and expressions have often disappeared, not through any evolutionary process but owing to the conscious action of a minority. Two recent examples were *explore every avenue* and *leave no stone unturned,* which were killed by the jeers of a few journalists. There is a long list of fly-blown metaphors which could similarly be got rid of if enough people would interest themselves in the job; and it should also be possible to laugh the *not un-* formation out of existence,[3] to re-duce the amount of Latin and Greek in the average sentence, to drive out foreign phrases and strayed scientific words, and, in general, to make pretentiousness unfashionable. But all these are minor points. The defence of the English language implies more than this, and perhaps it is best to start by saying what it does *not* imply.

To begin with, it has nothing to do with archaism, with the salvaging of obsolete words and turns of speech, or with the setting up of a "standard English" which must never be departed from. On the contrary, it is especially concerned with the scrapping of every word or idiom which has outworn its usefulness. It has nothing to do with correct grammar and syntax, which are of no importance so long as one makes one's meaning clear, or with the avoidance of Americanisms, or with having what is called a "good prose style." On the other hand it is not concerned with fake simplicity and the attempt to make written English colloquial. Nor does it even imply in every case preferring the Saxon word to the Latin one, though it does imply using the fewest and shortest words that will cover one's meaning. What is above all needed is to let the meaning choose the word, and not the other way about. In prose, the worst thing one can do with words is to surrender to them. When you think of a concrete object, you think wordlessly, and then, if you want to describe the thing you have been visualizing you probably hunt about till you find the exact words that seem to fit. When you think of something abstract you are more inclined to use words from the start, and unless you make a conscious effort to prevent it, the existing dialect will come rushing in and do the job for you, at the expense of blurring or even changing your meaning. Probably it is better to put off using words as long as possible and get one's meaning as clear as one can through pictures or sensations. Afterwards one can choose—not simply *accept*—the phrases that will best cover the meaning, and then switch round and decide what impression one's words are likely to make on another person. This last effort of the mind cuts out all stale or mixed images, all prefabricated phrases, needless repetitions, and humbug and vagueness generally. But one can often be in doubt about the effect of a word or a phrase, and one needs rules that one can rely on when instinct fails. I think the following rules will cover most cases:

(i)   Never use a metaphor, simile, or other figure of speech which you are used to seeing in print.

(ii) Never use a long word where a short one will do.

(iii) If it is possible to cut a word out, always cut it out.

(iv) Never use the passive where you can use the active.

(v)   Never use a foreign phrase, a scientific word or a jargon word if you can think of an everyday English equivalent.

(vi) Break any of these rules sooner than say anything outright barbarous.

These rules sound elementary, and so they are, but they demand a deep change of attitude in anyone who has grown used to writing in the style now fashionable. One could keep all of them and still write bad English, but one could not write the kind of stuff that I quoted in those five specimens at the beginning of this article.

I have not here been considering the literary use of language, but merely language as an instrument for expressing and not for concealing or preventing thought. Stuart Chase and others have come near to claiming that all abstract words are meaningless, and have used this as a pretext for advocating a kind of political quietism. Since you don't know what Fascism is, how can you struggle against Fascism? One need not swallow such absurdities as this, but one ought to recognize that the present political chaos is connected with the decay of language, and that one can probably bring about some improvement by starting at the verbal end. If you simplify your English, you are freed from the worst follies of orthodoxy. You cannot speak any of the necessary dialects, and when you make a stupid remark its stupidity will be obvious, even to yourself. Political language—and with variations this is true of all political parties, from Conservatives to Anarchists—is designed to make lies sound truthful and murder respectable, and to give an appearance of solidity to pure wind. One cannot change this all in a moment, but one can at least change one's own habits, and from time to time one can even, if one jeers loudly enough, send some worn-out and useless phrase—some *jackboot, Achilles' heel, hotbed, melting pot, acid test, veritable inferno* or other lump of verbal refuse—into the dustbin where it belongs.

Endnotes

1. An interesting illustration of this is the way in which the English flower names which were in use till very recently are being ousted by Greek ones, *snapdragon* becoming *antirrhinum*, *forget-me-not* becoming *myosotis*, etc. It is hard to see any practical reason for this change of fashion: it is probably due to an instinctive turning-away from the more homely word and a vague feeling that the Greek word is scientific [Orwell's note].

2. Example: "Comfort's catholicity of perception and image, strangely Whitman-esque in range, almost the exact opposite in aesthetic compulsion, continues to evoke that trembling atmospheric accumulative hinting at a cruel, an inexorably serene time-lessness. . . . Wrey Gardiner scores by aiming at simple bull's-eyes with precision. Only they are not so simple, and through this contented sadness runs more than the surface bittersweet of resignation" (*Poetry Quarterly*)[Orwell's note].

3. One can cure oneself of the *not un-* formation by memorizing this sentence: *A not unblack dog was chasing a not unsmall rabbit across a not ungreen field* [Orwell's note].

Questions for Reading and Analysis

1. Orwell establishes the purpose of his argument early in the essay. What is it?

2. Are the examples Orwell uses effective?

3. Can you pull a single sentence from the essay that summarizes Orwell's main point?

4. Orwell's essay was originally published in 1946. Are his points relevant today? Can you cite recent examples of "political language" of the sort Orwell describes?

Plato's allegory of the cave is a classic argument about the nature of truth and our perception of it and the duty of the philosopher to enlighten others. According to Plato, most humans are incapable of understanding the ideal world, of which the real world is only a vague reflection. Like prisoners in a cave with their backs to the light, they mistake dancing shadows on the wall before them for reality. Those that escape the cave and see the light of truth, he argues, have a moral duty to return to teach the unenlightened.

The Allegory of the Cave

Plato

And now, I said, let me show in a figure how far our nature is enlightened or unenlightened;—Behold! human beings living in an underground den, which has a mouth open towards the light and reaching all along the den; here they have been from their childhood, and have their legs and necks chained so that they cannot move, and can only see before them, being prevented by the chains from turning round their heads. Above and behind them a fire is blazing at a distance, and between the fire and the prisoners there is a raised way; and you will see, if you look, a low wall built along the way, like the screen which marionette players have in front of them, over which they show the puppets.

I see.

And do you see, I said, men passing along the wall carrying all sorts of vessels, and statues and figures of animals made of wood and stone and various materials, which appear over the wall? Some of them are talking, others silent.

You have shown me a strange image, and they are strange prisoners.

Like ourselves, I replied; and they see only their own shadows, or the shadows of one another, which the fire throws on the opposite wall of the cave?

True, he said; how could they see anything but the shadows if they were never allowed to move their heads?

And of the objects which are being carried in like manner they would only see the shadows?

Yes, he said.

And if they were able to converse with one another, would they not suppose that they were naming what was actually before them?

Very true.

And suppose further that the prison had an echo which came from the other side, would they not be sure to fancy when one of the passers-by spoke that the voice which they heard came from the passing shadow?

No question, he replied.

To them, I said, the truth would be literally nothing but the shadows of the images.

That is certain.

And now look again, and see what will naturally follow if the prisoners are released and disabused of their error. At first, when any of them is liberated and compelled suddenly to stand up and turn his neck round and walk and look towards the light, he will suffer sharp pains; the glare will distress him, and he will be unable to see the realities of which in his former state he had seen the shadows; and then conceive some one saying to him, that what he saw before was an illusion, but that now, when he is approaching nearer to being and his eye is turned towards more real existence, he has a clearer vision—what will be his reply? And you may further imagine that his instructor is pointing to the objects as they pass and requiring him to name them,—will he not be perplexed? Will he not fancy that the shadows which he formerly saw are truer than the objects which are now shown to him?

Far truer.

And if he is compelled to look straight at the light, will he not have a pain in his eyes which will make him turn away to take refuge in the objects of vision which he can see, and which he will conceive to be in reality clearer than the things which are now being shown to him?

True, he said.

And suppose once more, that he is reluctantly dragged up a steep and rugged ascent, and held fast until he is forced into the presence of the sun himself, is he not likely to be pained and irritated? When he approaches the light his eyes will be dazzled, and he will not be able to see anything at all of what are now called realities.

Not all in a moment, he said.

He will require to grow accustomed to the sight of the upper world. And first he will see the shadows best, next the reflections of men and other objects in the water, and then the objects themselves; then he will gaze upon the light of the moon and the stars and the spangled heaven; and he will see the sky and the stars by night better than the sun or the light of the sun by day?

Certainly.

Last of all he will be able to see the sun, and not mere reflections of him in the water, but he will see him in his own proper place, and not in another; and he will contemplate him as he is.

Certainly.

He will then proceed to argue that this is he who gives the season and the years, and is the guardian of all that is in the visible world, and in a certain way the cause of all things which he and his fellows have been accustomed to behold?

Clearly, he said, he would first see the sun and then reason about him.

And when he remembered his old habitation, and the wisdom of the den and his fellow prisoners, do you not suppose that he would felicitate himself on the change, and pity them?

Certainly, he would.

And if they were in the habit of conferring honors among themselves on those who were quickest to observe the passing shadows and to remark which of them went before, and which followed after, and which were together; and who were therefore best able to draw conclusions as to the future, do you think that he would care for such honors and glories, or envy the possessors of them? Would he not say with Homer,

Better to be the poor servant of a poor master,

and to endure anything, rather than think as they do and live after their manner?

Yes, he said, I think that he would rather suffer anything than entertain these false notions and live in this miserable manner.

Imagine once more, I said, such an one coming suddenly out of the sun to be replaced in his old situation; would he not be certain to have his eyes full of darkness?

To be sure, he said.

And if there were a contest, and he had to compete in measuring the shadows with the prisoners who had never moved out of the den, while his sight was still weak, and before his eyes had become steady (and the time which would be needed to acquire this new habit of sight might be very considerable), would he not be ridiculous? Men would say of him that up he went and down he came without his eyes; and that it was better not even to think of ascending; and if any one tried to loose another and lead him up to the light, let them only catch the offender, and they would put him to death.

No question, he said.

The entire allegory, I said, you may now append, dear Glaucon, to the previous argument; the prison house is the world of sight, the light of the fire is the sun, and you will not misapprehend me if you interpret the journey upwards to be the ascent of the soul into the intellectual world according to my poor belief, which, at your desire, I have expressed—whether rightly or wrongly God knows. But, whether true or false, my opinion is that in the world of knowledge the idea of good appears last of all, and is seen only with an effort; and, when seen, is also inferred to be the universal author of all things beautiful and right, parent of light and of the lord of light in this visible world, and the immediate source of reason and truth in the intellectual; and that this is the power upon which he who would act rationally either in public or private life must have his eye fixed.

I agree, he said, as far as I am able to understand you.

Moreover, I said, you must not wonder that those who attain to this beatific vision are unwilling to descend to human affairs; for their souls are ever hastening into the upper world where they desire to dwell; which desire of theirs is very natural, if our allegory may be trusted.

Yes, very natural.

And is there anything surprising in one who passes from divine contemplations to the evil state of man, misbehaving himself in a ridiculous manner; if, while his eyes are blinking and before he has become accustomed to the surrounding darkness, he is compelled to fight in courts of law, or in other places, about the images or the shadows of images of justice, and is endeavouring to meet the conceptions of those who have never yet seen absolute justice?

Anything but surprising, he replied.

Anyone who has common sense will remember that the bewilderments of the eyes are of two kinds, and arise from two causes, either from coming out of the light or from going into the light, which is true of the mind's eye, quite as much as of the bodily eye; and he who remembers this when he sees anyone whose vision is perplexed and weak, will not be too ready to laugh; he will first ask whether that soul of man has come out of the brighter life, and is unable to see because unaccustomed to the dark, or having turned from darkness to the day is dazzled by excess of light. And he will count the one happy in his condition and state of being, and he will pity the other; or, if he have a mind to laugh at the soul which comes from below into the light, there will be more reason in this than in the laugh which greets him who returns from above out of the light into the den.

That, he said, is a very just distinction.

But then, if I am right, certain professors of education must be wrong when they say that they can put a knowledge into the soul which was not there before, like sight into blind eyes.

They undoubtedly say this, he replied.

Whereas, our argument shows that the power and capacity of learning exists in the soul already; and that just as the eye was unable to turn from darkness to light without the whole body, so too the instrument of knowledge can only by the movement of the whole soul be turned from the world of becoming into that of being, and learn by degrees to endure the sight of being, and of the brightest and best of being, or in other words, of the good.

Very true.

And must there not be some art which will effect conversion in the easiest and quickest manner; not implanting the faculty of sight, for that exists already, but has been turned in the wrong direction, and is looking away from the truth?

Yes, he said, such an art may be presumed.

And whereas the other so-called virtues of the soul seem to be akin to bodily qualities, for even when they are not originally innate they can be implanted later by habit and exercise, the virtue of wisdom more than anything else contains a divine element which always remains, and by this conversion is rendered useful and profitable; or, on the other hand, hurtful and useless. Did you never observe the narrow intelligence flashing from the keen eye of a clever rogue—how eager he is, how clearly his paltry soul sees the way to his end; he is the reverse of blind, but his keen eyesight is forced into the service of evil, and he is mischievous in proportion to his cleverness?

Very true, he said.

But what if there had been a circumcision of such natures in the days of their youth; and they had been severed from those sensual pleasures, such as eating and drinking, which, like leaden weights, were attached to them at their birth, and which drag them down and turn the vision of their souls upon the things that are below—if, I say, they had been released from these impediments and turned in the opposite direction, the very same faculty in them would have seen the truth as keenly as they see what their eyes are turned to now.

Very likely.

Yes, I said; and there is another thing which is likely, or rather a necessary inference from what has preceded, that neither the uneducated and uninformed of the truth, nor yet those who never make an end of their education, will be able ministers of State; not the former, because they have no single aim of duty which is the rule of all their actions, private as well as public; nor the latter, because they will not act at all except upon compulsion, fancying that they are already dwelling apart in the islands of the blessed.

Very true, he replied.

Then, I said, the business of us who are founders of the State will be to compel the best minds to attain that knowledge which we have already shown to be the greatest of all—they must continue to ascend until they arrive at the good; but when they have ascended and seen enough we must not allow them to do as they do now.

What do you mean?

I mean that they remain in the upper world: but this must not be allowed; they must be made to descend again among the prisoners in the den, and partake of their labours and honours, whether they are worth having or not.

But is not this unjust? he said; ought we to give them a worse life, when they have a better?

You have again forgotten, my friend, I said, the intention of the legislator, who did not aim at making any one class in the State happy above the rest; the happiness was to be in the whole State, and he held the citizens together by persuasion and necessity, making them benefactors of the State, and therefore benefactors of one another; to this end he created them, not to please themselves, but to be his instruments in binding up the State.

True, he said, I had forgotten.

Observe, Glaucon, that there will be no injustice in compelling our philosophers to have a care and providence of others; we shall explain to them that in other States, men of their class are not obliged to share in the toils of politics: and this is reasonable, for they grow up at their own sweet will, and the government would rather not have them. Being self-taught, they cannot be expected to show any gratitude for a culture which they have never received. But we have brought you into the world to be rulers of the hive, kings of yourselves and of the other citizens, and have educated you far better and more perfectly than they have been educated, and you are better able to share in the double duty. Wherefore each of you, when his turn comes, must go down to the general underground abode, and get the habit of seeing in the dark. When you have acquired the habit, you will see ten thousand times better than the inhabitants of the den, and you will know what the several images are, and what they represent, because you have seen the beautiful and just and good in their truth. And thus our State, which is also yours, will be a reality, and not a dream only, and will be administered in a spirit unlike that of other States, in which men fight with one another about shadows only and are distracted in the struggle for power, which in their eyes is a great good. Whereas the truth is that the State in which the rulers are most reluctant to govern is always the best and most quietly governed, and the State in which they are most eager, the worst.

Quite true, he replied.

And will our pupils, when they hear this, refuse to take their turn at the toils of State, when they are allowed to spend the greater part of their time with one another in the heavenly light?

Impossible, he answered; for they are just men, and the commands which we impose upon them are just; there can be no doubt that every one of them will take office as a stern necessity, and not after the fashion of our present rulers of State.

Yes, my friend, I said; and there lies the point. You must contrive for your future rulers another and a better life than that of a ruler, and then you may have a well-ordered State; for only in the State which offers this, will they rule who are truly rich, not in silver and gold, but in virtue and wisdom, which are the true blessings of life. Whereas if they go to the administration of public affairs, poor and hungering after their own private advantage, thinking that hence they are to snatch the chief good, order there can never be; for they will be fighting about office, and the civil and domestic broils which thus arise will be the ruin of the rulers themselves and of the whole State.

Most true, he replied.

And the only life which looks down upon the life of political ambition is that of true philosophy. Do you know of any other?

Indeed, I do not, he said.

Questions for Reading and Analysis

1. In your own words, describe the situation in the cave. In what way are the "prisoners" deceived in what they think is the truth?

2. How does the experience of the light change a person? How are those who return to the cave different from those who never left? What conflicts arise from this difference?

3. Why does Plato insist that the "philosophers" (those who have "seen the light") return to the cave even though life would be much more pleasant for them if they didn't? What ethical and civic values does this insistence reveal about Plato?

4. Plato's allegory is written in the form of a Socratic dialogue, named after Socrates, Plato's teacher. In what way is the Socratic dialogue different from a lecture? Is the method more effective? Why?

5. Plato maintains a person who has enjoyed the rewards of higher education is often ridiculed by those who have been deprived of it: "Men would say of him that up he went and down he came without his eyes; and that it was better not even to think of ascending; and if any one tried to loose another and lead him up to the light, let them only catch the offender, and they would put him to death." Plato might have been thinking of his teacher Socrates, who was sentenced to death for this very reason. Are things different in our day and age? Does our society show the proper respect towards those who have "seen the light," accepting their teachings willingly?

"My father, you see, was a lawn dissident," states Michael Pollan, a man who "could not see much point in cranking up the Toro more than once a month or so." Reflecting on the contempt his father got from his lawn-abiding neighbors, Pollan concludes that our love for uniform, closely cropped lawns reflects "our skewed relationship to the land." He proposes gardening—the "search for some middle ground between culture and nature"—as an alternative to tedious (and unnatural) lawn maintenance.

Why Mow?
The Case Against Lawns

Michael Pollan

Anyone new to the experience of owning a lawn, as I am, soon figures out that there is more at stake here than a patch of grass. A lawn immediately establishes a certain relationship with one's neighbors and, by extension, the larger American landscape. Mowing the lawn, I realized the first time I gazed into my neighbor's yard and imagined him gazing back into mine, is a civic responsibility.

For no lawn is an island, at least in America. Starting at my front stoop, this scruffy green carpet tumbles down a hill and leaps across a one-lane road into my neighbor's yard. From there it skips over some wooded patches and stone walls before finding its way across a dozen other unfenced properties that lead down into the Housatonic Valley, there to begin its march south to the metropolitan area. Once below Danbury, the lawn—now purged of weeds and meticulously coiffed—races up and down the suburban lanes, heedless of property lines. It then heads west, crossing the New York border; moving now at a more stately pace, it strolls beneath the maples of Scarsdale, unfurls across a dozen golf courses, and wraps itself around the pale blue pools of Bronxville before pressing on toward the Hudson. New Jersey next is covered, an emerald postage stamp laid down front and back of ten thousand split levels, before the broadening green river divides in two.

One tributary pushes south, and does not pause until it has colonized the thin, sandy soils of Florida. The other dilates and spreads west, easily overtaking the Midwest's vast grid before running up against the inhospitable western states. But neither flinty soil nor obdurate climate will impede the lawn's march to the Pacific: it vaults the Rockies and, abetted by a monumental irrigation network, proceeds to green great stretches of western desert.

Nowhere in the world are lawns as prized as in America. In little more than a century, we've rolled a green mantle of grass across the continent, with scarcely a thought to the local conditions or expense. America has more than fifty thousand square *miles* of lawn under cultivation, on which we spend an estimated $30 billion a year—this according to the Lawn Institute, a Pleasant Hill, Tennessee, outfit devoted to publicizing the benefits of turf to Americans (surely a case of preaching to the converted).

Like the interstate highway system, like fast-food chains, like television, the lawn has served to unify the American landscape; it is what makes the suburbs of Cleveland and Tucson, the streets of Eugene and Tampa, look more alike than not. According to Ann Leighton, the late historian of gardens, America has made essentially one important contribution to world garden design: the custom of "uniting the front lawns of however many houses there may be on both sides of the street to present an untroubled aspect of expansive green to the passer-by." France has its formal, geometric gardens, England its picturesque parks, and America this unbounded democratic river of manicured lawn along which we array our houses.

It is not easy to stand in the way of such a powerful current. Since we have traditionally eschewed fences and hedges in America (looking on these as Old World vestiges), the suburban vista can be marred by the negligence—or dissent—of a single property owner. This is why lawn care is regarded as such an important civic responsibility in the suburbs, and why the majority will not tolerate the laggard. I learned this at an early age, growing up in a cookie-cutter subdivision in Farmingdale, Long Island.

My father, you see, was a lawn dissident. Whether owing to laziness or contempt for his neighbors I was never sure, but he could not see much point in cranking up the Toro more than once a month or so. The grass on our quarter-acre plot towered over the crew-cut lawns on either side of us and soon disturbed the peace of the entire neighborhood.

That subtle yet unmistakable frontier, where the closely shaved lawn rubs up against a shaggy one, is a scar on the face of suburbia, an intolerable hint of trouble in paradise. The scar shows up in *The Great Gatsby*, when Nick Carraway rents the house next to Gatsby's and fails to maintain his lawn according to West Egg standards. The rift between the two lawns so troubles Gatsby that he dispatches his gardener to mow Nick's grass and thereby erase it.

Our neighbors in Farmingdale displayed somewhat less class. "Lawn mower on the fritz?" they'd ask. "Want to borrow mine?" But the more heavily they leaned on my father, the more recalcitrant he became, until one summer—probably 1959, or 1960—he let the lawn go altogether. The grass plants grew tall enough to flower and set seed; the lawn rippled in the breeze like a flag. There was beauty here, I'm sure, but it was not visible in this context. Stuck in the middle of a row of tract houses on Long Island, our lawn said *turpitude* rather than *meadow*, even though strictly speaking that is what it had become.

That summer I felt the hot breath of the majority's tyranny for the first time. No one said anything now, but you could hear it all the same: *Mow your lawn or get out.* Certain neighbors let it be known to my parents that I was not to play with their children. Cars would slow down as they drove by. Probably some of the drivers were merely curious: they saw the unmowed lawn and wondered if someone had left in a hurry, or perhaps died. But others drove by in a manner that was unmistakably expressive, slowing down as they drew near and then hitting the gas angrily as they passed—pithy driving, the sort of move that is second nature to a Klansman.

We got the message by other media, too. Our next-door neighbor, a mild engineer who was my father's last remaining friend in the development, was charged with the unpleasant task of conveying the sense of the community to my father. It was early on a summer evening that he came to deliver his message.

I don't remember it all (I was only four or five at the time), but I can imagine him taking a highball glass from my mother, squeaking out what he had been told to say about the threat to property values, and then waiting for my father—who next to him was a bear—to respond.

My father's reply could not have been more eloquent. Without a word he strode out to the garage and cranked up the rusty old Toro for the first time since fall; it's a miracle the thing started. He pushed it out to the curb and then started back across the lawn to the house, but not in a straight line: he swerved right, then left, then right again. He had cut an *S* in the high grass. Then he made an *M*, and finally a *P*. These are his initials, and as soon as he finished writing them he wheeled the lawn mower back to the garage, never to start it up again.

I wasn't prepared to take such a hard line on my new lawn, at least not right off. So I bought a lawn mower, a Toro, and started mowing. Four hours every Saturday. At first I tried for a kind of Zen approach, clearing my mind of everything but the task at hand, immersing myself in the lawn-mowing here-and-now. I liked the idea that my weekly sessions with the grass would acquaint me with the minutest details of my yard. I soon knew by heart the exact location of every stump and stone, the tunnel route of each resident mole, the address of every anthill. I noticed that where rain collected white clover flourished, that it was on the drier rises that crabgrass thrived. After a few weekends I had a map of the lawn in my head as precise and comprehensive as the mental map one has of the back of one's hand.

The finished product pleased me too, the fine scent and the sense of order restored that a new-cut lawn exhales. My house abuts woods on two sides, and mowing the lawn is, in both a real and metaphorical sense, how I keep the forest at bay and preserve my place in this landscape. Much as we've come to distrust it, the urge to dominate nature is a deeply human one, and lawn mowing answers to it. I thought of the lawn mower as civilization's knife and my lawn as the hospitable plane it carved out of the wilderness. My lawn was a part of nature made fit for human habitation.

So perhaps the allure of lawns is in the genes. The sociobiologists think so: they've gone so far as to propose a "Savanna Syndrome" to explain our fondness for grass. Encoded in our DNA is a preference for an open grassy landscape resembling the short-grass savannas of Africa on which we evolved and spent our first few million years. This is said to explain why we have remade the wooded landscapes of Europe and North America in the image of East Africa.

Such theories go some way toward explaining the widespread appeal of grass, but they don't really account for the American Lawn. They don't, for instance, account for the keen interest Jay Gatsby takes in Nick Carraway's lawn, or the scandal my father's lawn sparked in Farmingdale. Or the fact that, in America, we have taken down our fences and hedges in order to combine our lawns. And they don't even begin to account for the unmistakable odor of virtue that hovers in this country over a scrupulously maintained lawn.

If any individual can be said to have invented the American lawn, it is Frederick Law Olmsted. In 1868, he received a commission to design Riverside, outside Chicago, one of the first planned suburban communities in America. Olmsted's design stipulated that each house be set back thirty feet from the road and it proscribed walls. He was reacting against the "high deadwalls" of England, which he felt made a row of homes there seem "as of a series of private madhouses." In Riverside, each owner would maintain one or two trees and a lawn that would flow seamlessly into his neighbors', creating the impression that all lived together in a single park.

Olmsted was part of a generation of American landscape designer-reformers who set out at midcentury to beautify the American landscape. That it needed beautification may seem surprising to us today, assuming as we do that the history of the landscape is a story of decline, but few at the time thought otherwise. William Cobbett, visiting from England, was struck at the "out-of-door slovenliness" of, American homesteads. Each farmer, he wrote, was content with his "shell of boards, while all around him is as barren as the sea beach . . . though there is no English shrub, or flower, which will not grow and flourish here."

The land looked as if it had been shaped and cleared in a great hurry—as indeed it had: the landscape largely denuded of trees, makeshift fences outlining badly plowed fields, tree stumps everywhere one looked. As Cobbett and many other nineteenth-century visitors noted, hardly anyone practiced ornamental gardening; the typical yard was "landscaped" in the style southerners would come to call "white trash"—a few chickens, some busted farm equipment, mud and weeds, an unkempt patch of vegetables.

This might do for farmers, but for the growing number of middle-class city people moving to the "borderland" in the years following the Civil War, something more respectable was called for. In 1870, Frank J. Scott, seeking to make Olmsted's ideas accessible to the middle class, published the first volume ever devoted to "suburban home embellishment": *The Art of Beautifying Suburban Home Grounds,* a book that probably did more than any other to determine the look of the suburban landscape in America. Like so many reformers of his time, Scott was nothing if not sure of himself: "A smooth, closely shaven surface of grass is by far the most essential element of beauty on the grounds of a suburban house."

Americans like Olmsted and Scott did not invent the lawn; lawns had been popular in England since Tudor times. But in England, lawns were usually found only on estates; the Americans democratized them, cutting the vast manorial greenswards into quarter-acre slices everyone could afford. Also, the English never considered the lawn an end in itself: it served as a setting for lawn games and as a backdrop for flower beds and trees. Scott subordinated all other elements of the landscape to the lawn; flowers were permissible, but only on the periphery of the grass: "Let your lawn be your home's velvet robe, and your flowers its not too promiscuous decoration."

But Scott's most radical departure from Old World practice was to dwell on the individual's responsibility to his neighbors. "It is unchristian," he declared, "to hedge from the sight of others the beauties of nature which it has been our good fortune to create or secure." One's lawn, Scott held, should contribute to the collective landscape. "The beauty obtained by throwing front grounds open together, is of that excellent quality which enriches all who take part in the exchange, and makes no man poorer." Like Olmsted before him, Scott sought to elevate an unassuming patch of turfgrass into an institution of democracy.

With our open-faced front lawns we declare our like-mindedness to our neighbors—and our distance from the English, who surround their yards with "inhospitable brick wall, topped with broken bottles," to thwart the envious gaze of the lower orders. The American lawn is an egalitarian concept, implying that there is no reason to hide behind fence or hedge since we all occupy the same middle class. We are all property owners here, the lawn announces, and that suggests its other purpose: to provide a suitably grand stage for the proud display of one's own house. Noting that our yards were organized "to capture the admiration of the street," one garden writer in 1921 attributed the popularity of open lawns to our "infantile instinct to cry 'hello!' to the passer-by, to lift up our possessions to his gaze."

Of course the democratic front yard has its darker, more coercive side, as my family learned in Farmingdale. In specifying the "plain style" of an unembellished lawn for American front yards, the midcentury designer-reformers were, like Puritan ministers, laying down rigid conventions governing our relationship to the land, our observance of which would henceforth be taken as an index of our character. And just as the Puritans would not tolerate any individual who sought to establish his or her own backchannel relationship with the divinity, the members of the Suburban utopia do not tolerate the homeowner who establishes a relationship with the land that is not mediated by the group's conventions.

The parallel is not as farfetched as it might sound, when you recall that nature in America has often been regarded as divine. Think of nature as Spirit, the collective suburban lawn as the Church, and lawn mowing as a kind of sacrament. You begin to see why ornamental gardening would take so long to catch on in America, and why my father might seem an antinomian in the eyes of his neighbors. Like Hester Prynne, he claimed not to need their consecration for his actions; perhaps his initials in the front lawn were a kind of Emerald Letter.

Possibly because it is this common land, rather than race or tribe, that makes us all Americans, we have developed a deep distrust of individualistic approaches to the landscape. The land is too important to our identity as Americans to simply allow everyone to have his own way with it. And once we decide that the land should serve as a vehicle of consensus, rather than an arena of self-expression, the American lawn—collective, national, ritualized, and plain—begins to look inevitable.

After my first season of lawn mowing, the Zen approach began to wear thin. I had taken up flower and vegetable gardening, and soon came to resent the four hours that lawn demanded of me each week. I tired of the endless circuit, pushing the howling mower back and forth across the vast page of my yard, recopying the same green sentences over and over: "I am a conscientious homeowner. I share your middle-class values." Lawn care was gardening aimed at capturing "the admiration of the street," a ritual of consensus I did not have my heart in. I began to entertain idle fantasies of rebellion: Why couldn't I plant a hedge along the road, remove my property from the national stream of greensward and do something else with it?

The third spring I planted fruit trees in the front lawn, apple, peach, cherry, and plum, hoping these would relieve the monotony and begin to make the lawn productive. Behind the house, I put in a perennial border. I built three raised beds out of old Chestnut barnboards and planted two dozen different vegetable varieties. Hard work though it was, removing the grass from the site of my new beds proved a keen pleasure. First I outlined the beds with string. Then I made an incision in the lawn with the sharp edge of a spade. Starting at one end, I pried the sod from the soil and slowly rolled it up like a carpet. The grass made a tearing sound as I broke its grip on the earth. I felt a little like a pioneer subduing the forest with his ax; I daydreamed of scalping the entire yard. But I didn't do it—I continued to observe front-yard conventions, mowing assiduously and locating all my new garden beds in the back yard.

The more serious about gardening I became, the more dubious lawns seemed. The problem for me was not, as it was for my father, the relation to my neighbors that a lawn implied; it was the lawn's relationship to nature. For however democratic a lawn may be with respect to one's neighbors, with respect to nature it is authoritarian. Under the mower's brutal indiscriminate rotor, the landscape is subdued, homogenized, dominated utterly. I became convinced that lawn care had about as much to do with gardening as floor waxing or road paving. Gardening was a subtle process of give and take with the landscape, a search for some middle ground between culture and nature. A lawn was nature under culture's boot.

Mowing the lawn, I felt that I was battling the earth rather than working it; each week it sent forth a green army and each week I beat it back with my infernal machine. Unlike every other plant in my garden, the grasses were anonymous, massified, deprived of any change or development whatsoever, not to mention any semblance of self-determination. I ruled a totalitarian landscape.

Hot, monotonous hours behind the mower gave rise to existential speculations. I spent part of one afternoon trying to decide who, in the absurdist drama of lawn mowing, was Sisyphus. Me? A case could certainly be made. Or was it the grass, pushing up through the soil every week, one layer of cells at a time, only to be cut down and then, perversely, encouraged (with fertilizer, lime, etc.) to start the whole doomed process over again? Another day it occurred to me that time as we know it doesn't exist in the lawn, since grass never dies or is allowed to flower and set seed. Lawns are nature purged of sex and death. No wonder Americans like them so much.

And just where *was* my lawn, anyway? The answer's not as obvious as it seems. Gardening, I had come to appreciate, is a painstaking exploration of place; everything that happens in my garden—the thriving and dying of particular plants, the maraudings of various insects and other pests—teaches me to know this patch of land intimately, its geology and microclimate, the particular ecology of its local weeds and animals and insects. My garden prospers to the extent I grasp these particularities and adapt to them.

Lawns work on the opposite principle. They depend for their success on the *overcoming* of local conditions. Like Jefferson superimposing one great grid over the infinitely various topography of the Northwest territory, we superimpose our lawns on the land. And since the geography and climate of much of this country is poorly suited to turf grasses (none of which are native), this can't be accomplished without the tools of twentieth-century industrial civilization—its chemical fertilizers, pesticides, herbicides, and machinery. For we won't settle for the lawn that will grow here; we want the one that grows *there,* that dense springy supergreen and weed-free carpet, that Platonic ideal of a lawn we glimpse in the Chem-Lawn commercials, the magazine spreads, the kitschy sitcom yards, the sublime links and pristine diamonds. Our lawns exist less here than there; they drink from the national stream of images, lift our gaze from the real places we live and fix it on unreal places elsewhere. Lawns are a form of television.

Need I point out that such an approach to "nature" is not likely to be environmentally sound? Lately we have begun to recognize that we are poisoning ourselves with our lawns, which receive, on average, more pesticide and herbicide per acre than just about any crop grown in this country. Suits fly against the national lawn-care companies, and interest is kindled in "organic" methods of lawn care. But the problem is larger than this. Lawns, I am convinced, are a symptom of, and a metaphor for, our skewed relationship to the land. They teach us that, with the help of petrochemicals and technology, we can bend nature to our will. Lawns stoke our hubris with regard to the land.

What is the alternative? To turn them into gardens. I'm not suggesting that there is no place for lawns *in* these gardens or that gardens by themselves will right our relationship to the land, but the habits of thought they foster can take us some way in that direction.

Gardening, as compared to lawn care, tutors us in nature's ways, fostering an ethic of give and take with respect to the land. Gardens instruct us in the particularities of place. They lessen our dependence on distant sources of energy, technology, food, and, for that matter, interest.

For if lawn mowing feels like copying the same sentence over and over, gardening is like writing out new ones, an infinitely variable process of invention and discovery. Gardens also teach the necessary if rather un-American lesson that nature and culture can be compromised, that there might be some middle ground between the lawn and the forest—between those who would complete the conquest of the planet in the name of progress and those who believe it's time we abdicated our rule and left the earth in the care of its more innocent species. The garden suggests there might be a place where we can meet nature halfway.

Probably you will want to know if I have begun to practice what I'm preaching. Well, I have not ripped out my lawn entirely. But each spring larger and larger tracts of it give way to garden. Last year I took a half acre and planted a meadow of black-eyed Susans and oxeye daisies. In return for a single annual scything, I am rewarded with a field of flowers from May until frost.

The lawn is shrinking, and I've hired a neighborhood kid to mow what's left of it. Any Saturday that Bon Jovi, Twisted Sister, or Van Halen isn't playing the Hartford Civic Center, this large blond teenaged being is apt to show up with a forty-eight-inch John Deere mower that shears the lawn in less than an hour. It's $30 a week, but he's freed me from my dark musings about the lawn and so given me more time in the garden.

Out in front, along the road where my lawn overlooks my neighbors', and in turn the rest of the country's, I have made my most radical move. I built a split rail fence and have begun to plant a hedge along it—a rough one made up of forsythia, lilac, bittersweet, and bridal wreath. As soon as this hedge grows tall and thick, my secession from the national lawn will be complete.

Anything then is possible. I *could* let it all revert to meadow, or even forest, except that I don't go in for that sort of self-effacement. I could put in a pumpkin patch, a lily pond, or maybe an apple orchard. And I could even leave an area of grass. But even if I did, this would be a very different lawn from the one I have now. For one thing, it would have a frame, which means it could accommodate plants more subtle and various than the screaming marigolds, fierce red salvias, and musclebound rhododendrons that people usually throw into the ring against a big unfenced lawn. Walled off from the neighbors, no longer a tributary of the national stream, my lawn would now form a distinct and private space—become part of a garden rather than a substitute for one.

Yes, there might well be a place for a small lawn in my new garden. But I think I'll wait until the hedge fills in before I make a decision. It's a private matter, and I'm trying to keep politics out of it.

Questions for Reading and Analysis

1. What does Pollan mean when he says that Americans have "democratized" lawns? How does the history of lawn care he gives illustrate this point?

2. In what way do people's attitudes towards their lawns (and their neighbors') reflect the Puritan attitudes of colonial America?

3. Pollan claims that lawns "are a symptom of, and a metaphor for, our skewed relationship to the land." What does he mean by this?

4. Point out where Pollan uses humor in his essay. What purpose do the humorous elements serve?

First published in 1990, Robert Pool's essay investigates the diffi-culties scientists encounter when their research gets mixed up with political policy issues. For those scientists who will not escape the double bind of being analysts and advocates, Pool suggests that they "learn to understand policy-making better," to learn how to deal with the press, pay close attention to who funds their research, and integrate public interests into their research.

Struggling to Do Science for Society

Robert Pool

Last fall, an editorial in the *Detroit News* slammed meteorologist Stephen Schneider for contributing to "the debasement of American environmental science into cheap political theater." Schneider's offense, it seems, was to step outside his role as a scientist and publicly advocate a response to the global climate change that many researchers predict will take place in the next century.

The opinion piece, one of thousands generated by the debate over global warming, shows how hot it can get for scientists involved in a public policy issue. So far, relatively few researchers have found themselves embroiled in such topics—the entire climate modeling community, for example, consists of just a few hundred scientists—but that's likely to change. Genetic engineering and the use of fetal tissue, nuclear wastes, chemicals in the environment, and low frequency electro-magnetic fields—these are just a few of the policy areas where science will be called upon to make a key contribution in the 1990s.

And that raises some significant questions. What role should individual scien-tists play in policy debates? How can science be used to help policy-makers arrive at the best solutions? There are no easy answers.

The vast majority of scientists simply go about the business of research, arguing with their peers through journals and at meetings, and helping define a consensus that can serve as a basis for policy debates. But some researchers, either by choice or just by being in the wrong place at the wrong time, make it into the public eye.

Jim Hansen, for instance. Hansen is the meteorologist at NASA's Goddard Institute for Space Studies who ignited the current concern about global warning in 1988 when he told a congressional committee he was 99% certain the world is getting warmer and that the greenhouse effect is probably the reason. But as Hansen tells it, he wasn't trying to spark a controversy at all. "I feel I was only trying to report an accurate description of our scientific research," he says.

To use a religious metaphor, Hansen is a "witness "—someone who believes he has information so important that he cannot keep silent. "A couple of weeks before the 1988 testimony, I weighed the costs of being wrong versus the costs of not talking," he says; the costs of not talking seemed much heavier. "That testimony has been criticized a lot since then, but when I look back I feel as strongly as ever that my points were correct." He continues to tell Congress, the media, and the public his scientific conclusions about global warming.

If Hansen is a witness, Schneider, who works at the National Center for Atmospheric Research, is more of a preacher. "A human being has an obligation to make the world a better place," he says, so he has injected himself into the greenhouse policy debate, arguing that the consequences of global climate change could be so ruinous that steps to prevent it should be taken now. "I am an advocate for what I see to be the urgent need to 'buy insurance,'" he says. To make the case effectively, he paints explicit—some say sensationalistic—pictures of what could happen to the world if the average global temperature rose several degrees.

Should other scientists follow Schneider's example? "Everyone has the right to become an advocate," says Granger Morgan, head of the Department of Engineering and Public Policy at Carnegie-Mellon University. "But you really want to choose one role or the other—advocate or analyst. The two-roles don't mix very well." A scientist who lobbies strongly for one side in a debate risks losing his objectivity.

Schneider himself recognizes the conflict and speaks of the "double ethical bind" that pulls him in opposite directions. As a scientist he must be cautious, giving all the caveats and not pushing his data too far. As an advocate, however, he must be bold and effective. In a widely quoted interview in *Discover,* he explained: "To [reduce the risk of global warming], we need to get some broad-based support, to capture the public's imagination. That, of course, means getting loads of media coverage. So we have to offer up scary scenarios, make simplified, dramatic statements, and make little mention of any doubts that we might have. . . . Each of us has to decide what the right balance is between being effective and being honest. I hope that means being both."

The double bind of effective action versus scientific objectivity is not the only problem created by the decision to become an advocate. Although one's scientific peers may recognize the difference between the roles of scientist and advocate, the media and the public may not be so sophisticated—with the result that carefully nuanced positions disappear. "I always tell the media there are two Stephen Schneiders," Schneider says, but he admits the distinction is often lost. When the evening news devotes only 15 seconds to a scientist-advocate's views, the result is inevitably a blurring of the line between science and advocacy.

Whether a scientist decides to be an advocate, a witness, or simply a researcher who stays out of the spotlight, he or she will find that once a topic becomes a public policy issue, it is no longer science as usual.

Funding decisions, for instance, take on a whole new complexion when research conclusions will affect policy. By their nature, funding agencies like results that buoy their own programs and dislike results that undermine them. In 1981, Hansen lost his Department of Energy funding after a front-page story in the *New York Times* reported his conclusion that the world was getting warmer and that the warming was consistent with the greenhouse effect. The energy department, Hansen says, "saw these climate concerns as being environmentalists blocking economic and industrial progress without sufficient basis, and felt that if they supported the research it would only give more publicity to these concerns." In short, indications that carbon dioxide emissions might have to be limited was not a message the DOE wanted to hear. Eventually, the Environmental Protection Agency began supporting Hansen's work.

Even if solid, unbiased research does get funded, the science behind an issue frequently does not take center stage. Many other factors enter into policy-making, particularly when the scientific evidence is not definitive. This was the case, for instance, in determining the acid rain portion of the current Clean Air Act, says economist Robert Hahn, who helped draft part of the bill while on the Council of Economic Advisers. "Once it became a salient political issue, then science no longer played a major role," Hahn says. The act calls for a reduction of 10 million tons in sulfur dioxide emissions, but there was "very little serious analysis about what that number will buy us." Instead, 10 million tons was a convenient number that had been circulating for a while, and no one was willing to even consider 6 million or 8 million tons, which would have been cheaper and might have done just as much to clean up acid rain. "Politically it was a line drawn in the sand that would have been very difficult to cross," Hahn says.

And once a policy becomes law, the science often fades even further into the background. "Regulations sometimes take on a life of their own," notes presidential science adviser Allan Bromley. "Even after the scientific basis is gone, the regulation lives on." The current Environmental Protection Agency regulations on asbestos removal may be one of the most egregious examples of this. Taxpayers will pay about $5 billion this year to remove asbestos from schools and other buildings, and the final bill could run from $50 billion to $150 billion. But a study published earlier this year in *Science* (19 January, p. 294) reported that more than 90% of the asbestos actually poses no health risk. The EPA regulations ignore the distinction between different types of asbestos, some of which are dangerous and others relatively benign.

"The information in the article in *Science* is at least 10 years old as far as people in the field know it," says Ann Wylie, a geologist at the University of Maryland. But federal regulators were more concerned with the letter of the law than with the spirit, she says, and refused to accept the findings that some asbestos was relatively safe.

Do these problems mean that scientists should opt out of the arena of policy altogether? Surely that conclusion is too draconian. Perhaps the answer is that scientists should learn to understand policy-making better, so that they can at least anticipate the pitfalls. People who study policy-making have a few suggestions along those lines.

For starters, funding, for research into issues with policy implications should come from several sources. If the support comes from sources with different missions, no single point of view is likely to dominate the research. With such funding, scientists will be in a better position to provide the factual base needed to base decisions on.

But Morgan of Carnegie-Mellon argues that providing this base is something scientists do not do very well. "It's hard to get the scientific community to work on policy issues when it has its own research agenda set," he says. The questions that are most interesting scientifically may not be the questions that are important to setting policy. If science is to guide policy and not just provoke it, researchers may have to redirect some of their efforts.

The key, Morgan says, is directing the research so as to narrow down the uncertainties, the unknown quantities that make it impossible to set sound policy. By working with economists and policy experts, researchers can determine which of the uncertainties are most relevant and concentrate on them. Policy-makers debating a response to global warming, for instance, might find it more valuable to know how different strategies will affect the pace of global warming, as opposed to knowing what the total rise in temperature is likely to be. In that case, researchers could focus their efforts on understanding the dynamics of the process instead of the equilibrium states.

Besides providing the scientific context to understand a problem, scientists should analyze suggested remedies, says Richard Lindzen at the Massachusetts Institute of Technology. For instance, EPA regulations aimed at curbing urban ozone pollution by cutting hydrocarbon emissions from automobiles may not work, says Gregory McRae of Carnegie-Mellon's chemical engineering department. Computer simulations show that the key to cutting ozone in such places as Los Angeles is actually reducing the amount of nitrogen oxides, McRae says.

In the case of global warming, concern over rising levels of carbon dioxide and other greenhouse gases has led some to call for a 20% reduction in carbon dioxide emissions by 2000, which is likely to be a very expensive step for the industrial nations. But there has been little discussion about the effects of such a policy, Lindzen says. According to the models that predict that a doubling of carbon dioxide will cause a 4[degrees]C rise in global temperature by 2100, cutting carbon dioxide emissions by 20% would make a difference of less than half a degree, he says. Is it worth the cost? That's a question that must be debated, but often the argument doesn't get so far.

Clearly, there is a whole new set of considerations for a researcher whose work has consequences for public policy, even though his basic role—getting answers—is unchanged. To do that job effectively, a scientist in a policy-sensitive field must decide how he should interact with the press, pay particular attention to where his funding is coming from, consider angling his research in directions of general interest, and prepare himself for the possibility that much careful work could be ignored when push comes to shove in the political process. It's a lot to ask, but some scientists do find they are compensated by the feeling that they made a difference in the world.

Questions for Reading and Analysis

1. How does Pool distinguish between "analysts" and "advocates" in the scientific community? What examples does he give to illustrate these concepts?

2. Explain what Pool means by the "double ethical bind" that pulls scientists in opposite directions?

3. In what way does public exposure change the research process?

4. The article was first published in *Science*. In what way does Pool cater to his intended audience?

5. Do you think Pool's solution to encourage scientists to pay more attention to the process of public policy making is a good one? Or do you think it hampers the scientists' freedom to pursue their research for the sake of knowledge?

*N*eil Postman, a professor of communications at New York University, published Television News Narcosis *five years before his critically acclaimed* Amusing Ourselves to Death *(1985), a critical analysis of how television has shaped our culture. In both works he maintains that "news shows" are aptly named because they turn actual events into entertainment, thus depriving them of their link to reality and robbing them of their potential to motivate the viewers to act on what they have seen. TV turns us into passive consumers of useless information, Postman argues.*

Television News Narcosis

Neil Postman

In the quest to understand the effects of media, it is always useful to regard the names of media formats with circumspection. What are called newspapers, for example, do not consist mostly of news, adult movies appear to be puerile fantasies, and talk radio features a succession of thirty-second temper tantrums. Of course, the media will use such words as fit their fancy, but we are not required on that account to allow *their* words to become *ours*.

But sometimes a medium's format will be aptly named by its masters, even if unconsciously. And then we may not only take them at their word but we may also use their word as an entry point for analysis. I refer here in particular to what is called on television a news show. A show implies an entertainment, a world of artifice and fantasy carefully staged to produce a particular series of effects so that the audience is left laughing or crying or stupefied. This is exactly the business of a news show, and it is puffery to claim, as producers do when they accept their Emmy Awards, that the purpose of such shows is to make the public knowledgeable.

In the first place, events of serious and urgent public interest such as the taking of hostages in Iran are already known by the audience, through radio, newspapers, TV bulletins and word of mouth, before the audience settles in for its evening show. In the second place, whatever else one may say for or against TV news shows, it is clear that the audience can do practically nothing about the things it is shown or told. If knowledge is power, if the function of information is to modify or provide direction to action, then it is almost precisely true that TV news shows give nearly no information and even less knowledge. Except of course through their commercials. One can be told about Bounty, Braniff and Burger King, and then do something in relation to them.

But beyond this, there is in fact very little that the public comes "to know" from these shows, if "to know" implies, at the very least, to remember. Inquiries into what people remember about the "news" as depicted on TV consistently reveal that they remember almost nothing. Sometimes this is so after a mere thirty minutes have elapsed from the show's end. In some instances, people forget the "news" they have been shown or told while the show is still in progress.

This is not a case of stupidity. Everything on a TV news show is arranged so that it is unnecessary, undesirable and, in any event, very difficult to attend to the sense of what is depicted. After all, if it is commonplace for people to eat a chicken sandwich while watching a mother collapsing from grief over a dead child, in what sense can we say that news shows make people knowledgeable?

To understand what manner of thing a TV news show is—that is, any of the late news shows as seen in New York, Chicago or San Francisco—we must look carefully at its structure. For example, all such shows begin and end with music; there is also music at every break for a commercial. What is its purpose? The same as in a theater or film: to excite the emotions of the audience, to create tension, to build expectations. But there is an important functional difference between, say, film music and TV news music in that in a film the music is varied according to the particular emotion the content calls for. There is frightening music, happy music, romantic music and the like. On TV news shows, the same music is played whether the lead story is the invasion of Afghanistan or the adoption of a municipal budget or a Super Bowl victory. By using the same music each night, in the same spots, as an accompaniment to a *different* set of events, TV news shows contribute toward the development of their leitmotif: that there are no important differences between one day and another, that the same emotions that were called for yesterday are called for today, and that in any case the events of the day are meaningless.

This theme is developed through diverse means, including beauty, tempo and discontinuity. Of beauty not much needs to be said beyond observing that TV news readers are almost all young and attractive—perhaps the handsomest class of people in America. Television, naturally enough, is biased toward compelling visual imagery, and in almost all cases the charms of a human face take precedence over the capabilities of a human voice. It is not essential that a TV news reader grasp the meaning of what is being reported; many of them cannot even produce an appropriate facial display to go along with the words they are speaking. And some have even given up trying. What is essential is that the audience like looking at their faces. To put it bluntly, as far as TV is concerned, in the entire United States there is not one 60-year-old woman capable of being a news reader. Audiences, it would appear, are not captivated by their faces. It is the teller, not what is told, that matters here.

It is also believed that audiences are captivated by variety and repelled by complexity, which is why, during a typical thirty-minute show, there will be between fifteen and twenty "stories." Discounting time for commercials, promos for stories to come, and news readers' banter, this works out to an average of sixty seconds a story. On a recent CBS show (February 4, 11:00 P.M.), it went like this: 264 seconds for a story about bribery of public officials; thirty-seven seconds for a related story about Senator Larry Pressler; forty seconds about Iran; twenty-two seconds about Aeroflot; twenty-eight seconds about a massacre in Afghanistan; twenty-five seconds about Muhammad Ali; fifty-three seconds about a New Mexico prison rebellion; 160 seconds about protests against the film *Cruising*; eighteen seconds about the owners of Studio 54; eighteen seconds about Suzanne Somers; sixteen seconds about the Rockettes; 174 seconds for an "in-depth" study of depression (Part I); twenty-two seconds about Lake Placid; 166 seconds for the St. John's-Louisville basketball game; 120 seconds for the weather; 100 seconds for a film review.

This way of defining the "news" achieves two interesting effects. First, it makes it difficult to think about an event, and second, it makes it difficult to feel about an event. By thinking, I mean having the time and motivation to ask oneself: What is the meaning of such an event? What is its history? What are the reasons for it? How does it fit into what I know about the world? By feeling, I mean the normal human responses to murder, rape, fire, bribery and general mayhem. During a recent survey I conducted, I was able to identify only one story to which audiences responded with a recollectable feeling of disgust or horror: the burning to death of a "demon-possessed" baby by its mother. I believe there is some significance in the fact that news shows will frequently include thirty to forty-five seconds of "feeling" responses by "the man and woman in the street," as if to remind the audience that it is *supposed* to feel something about a particular story. I take this to be an expression of guilt on the part of the producers who know full well that their shows leave little room for such reaction. On the February 4 CBS show, no reactions were asked for about the massacre in Afghanistan or the New Mexico prison riot. However, thirty-five seconds were given up over to "on the street" reactions to bribery charges against Senator Harrison Williams of New Jersey. The people allowed to comment said they felt terrible.

The point is, of course, that all events on TV come completely devoid of historical continuity or any other context, and in such fragmented and rapid succession that they wash over our minds in an undifferentiated stream. This is television as narcosis, dulling to both sense and sensibility. To be sure, the music, the promos ("Coming up next, a riot in a New Mexico prison . . .") and the news readers' interactions ("What's happening in New Jersey, Jane?") create an air of excitement, of tension to be resolved. But it is entirely ersatz, for what is presented is so compressed and hurried—another story always fidgeting offstage, half mad with anxiety to do its thirty-seven seconds—that one can scarcely retain in one's mind the connection between the promise of excitement and its resolution; that is to say, the excitement of a TV news show is largely a function of tempo, not substance. It is excitement about the movement of information, not its meaning.

But if it is difficult to think and feel about the news, this must not be taken to mean that the audience is not expected to have a feeling, or at least an attitude, about the world. That attitude, as I have said, is that all events, having no precedent causes or subsequent consequences, are without value and therefore meaningless. It must be kept in mind here that TV news shows are terrifyingly surrealistic, discontinuous to the point where almost nothing has anything to do with anything else. What, for example, is the connection between Aeroflot and Suzanne Somers? Between Studio 54 and Iran? Between *Cruising* and a massacre in Afghanistan? Bribed officials and the Rockettes? Will any of these stories be followed up? Were they there yesterday? Why is Iran worth forty seconds and the St. John's game 120? How is it determined that Suzanne Somers should get less time than Muhammad Ali? And what in the end is the relationship of the commercials to the other stories? There were, on the February 4 show, twenty-one commercials, occupying close to ten minutes. Three commercials preceded the bribery story, four commercials preceded the New Mexico prison riot, three preceded the special report (Part I) on depression. As you can well imagine, the commercials were cheerful, filled with the promise of satisfaction, security and, in two cases, erotic pleasure.

Given such juxtapositions, what is a person to make of the world? How is one to measure the importance of events? What principles of human conduct are displayed, and according to what scheme of moral order are they valued? To any such questions, the TV news show has this invariable reply: There is no sense of proportion to be discerned in the world. Events are entirely idiosyncratic; history is irrelevant; there is no rational basis for valuing one thing over another.

Indeed, one cannot even find in this world-view a sense of contradiction. Otherwise, we would not be shown four commercials celebrating the affluence of America, followed by the despair and degradation of prisoners in a New Mexico jail. One would have expected the news reader at least to wink, but he took no notice of what he was saying.

What it all adds up to is that a TV news show is a form of absurdist literature which nightly instructs us on how we shall see the day. Here is your window on the world, we are told. It will reveal to you the fevered discontinuities of modern times. You need not think more about them, feel much about them, or even remember the details. There is nothing you can do about this. No need to be depressed. Pan Am will fly you to Hawaii for $60 down, the rest to be paid later.

Questions for Reading and Analysis

1. According to Postman, why is "news show" an appropriate term for television news programs?

2. What does the unvarying music that introduces every news show suggest about the events presented on the news?

3. When news shows present a large variety of short clips about different unrelated events, what consequences does this arrangement of information have on the viewer?

4. What is the thesis of Postman's essay? Where in the essay does he clearly state or imply it?

5. Explain the significance of the title.

*R*aphael, a social scientist, presents the results of many interviews
with poor, working women, demonstrating that, in the journey
from welfare to work, many have had to surmount one problem not
anticipated by service agencies and policy makers in the zeal for welfare reform—abuse by male partners.

Keeping Women Poor

How Domestic Violence Prevents Women From Leaving Welfare and Entering the World of Work

Jody Raphael

*Evelyn, a former heroin addict, needs methadone in order to func-
tion. Because she is on a waiting list for a free methadone maintenance clinic, her intimate partner pays for the drug. Evelyn enrolled
in a literacy program, but as she got closer to getting her GED (high
school equivalency), her partner began to feel threatened by her
progress and her plans to get a job. When she refused to quit the program at his insistence, he simply stopped buying her methadone.
Evelyn was forced to drop out of the literacy program in order to
maintain her physical well-being.*

Sabotage? Yes. Domestic violence? Yes. Within the past few years, program
providers working with low-income girls and women have come to realize
that domestic violence is a major welfare-to-work barrier. Threatened by the
independence of their partners, some men use threats of violence, violence itself,
and sabotage like that in Evelyn's case to keep their partners from education,
training, and employment. Providers have also noted that the effects of past violence serve as major barriers to work, including depression and anxiety, as well as
the more full-blown symptoms of post-traumatic stress disorder (PTSD).

Some current and past victims of domestic violence receiving welfare will have
difficulty when the violence prevents them from complying with their states' new
work requirements within the context of new transitional welfare systems. It
appears likely that because some victims will not be able to enter the labor market,
they will lose their welfare benefits and, as a result, will remain locked in the arms
of their abusers. Still others may try to work or participate in job-training programs but will return home to be faced with violence and sabotage. In this era of
welfare reform, therefore, it is important for all practitioners working with low-

income women and their children to understand better the role that domestic violence plays in making and keeping women and children poor.

This chapter explores the patterns of violence and abuse that sabotage women's welfare-to-work journeys. I summarize my own research consisting of interviews in programs throughout the country (Raphael, 1995, 1996; Raphael & Tolman, 1997) and corroborated by a research study in New York City (Kenney & Brown, 1996) all of which reveal consistent patterns of violence and sabotage during the welfare-to-work transition. Next, I explain what new research can tell us about the extent of the problem within state welfare caseloads. Last, I outline the policy and service responses that are necessary for meeting the needs of domestic violence victims on welfare.

Patterns of Sabotage and Abuse
In-Home Sabotage

Interviews with welfare-to-work program participants and staff reveal consistent and multiple instances of male sabotage of women's welfare-to-work efforts. Although the variety of methods and devices used by these men to keep women at home and out of the workplace are startling, even more astonishing is the consistency of these practices throughout the country:

> Women's partners surreptitiously turn off the alarm clocks set by the women to make sure they would be on time for job interviews (Raphael, 1996).

> Partners cut off the women's hair because they believe, correctly, that the women would be too embarrassed to return to work (Raphael, 1996).

> Partners inflict visible injuries such as black eyes and cigarette burns, hoping the women will not return to the training program out of embarrassment and will be expelled for nonattendance or unexplained absences. "My father would inflict black eyes, bruises all over my mother's body, and knock her teeth out. My mom couldn't go to work and was ashamed to be around any of her friends because of the way she looked," explains one welfare participant (Raphael, 1996, p. 6)

> Women's partners hide or destroy books or tear up completed homework assignments (Raphael, 1996).

> Men hide or destroy their partners' clothing, including winter coats, so that they are unable to leave the home to take a GED test or to complete an important job interview. "My abuser stole all my clothes," explains one woman. "All my work uniforms. I worked in hotels and they all had the same blue uniforms. So all my uniforms, all my dress clothes. I couldn't even go to a job interview because all I had was a pair of jeans. I couldn't go anywhere decent until I finally got help" (Raphael & Tolman, 1997, p. 12).

> Men sabotage their partners' forms of transportation. "They don't want you to better yourself. It was my first semester at college and he started working on my car and making it to where my car wouldn't

run so I couldn't get to school, because he knew that if I got to school, that I would better myself and that I wouldn't need him. You know, that I could survive without him and support myself. And that was a threat to him," explained another (Raphael & Tolman, 1997, p. 12).

Partners promise to provide needed child care so that the women can attend a special career event, such as a job fair or an interview, but fail to show up or arrive inebriated when needed (Raphael, 1996).

Partners harass the women at their place of employment so that they are fired or are forced to quit. The men come around uninvited, refuse to leave, or harass the women with numerous telephone calls. "He called them and told them that I was to quit and I was to quit right then. And he made a horrible scene. My employer can't have things like that going on, you know," explained one welfare participant (Raphael & Tolman, 1997, p. 10). Another woman was forced by her abuser to quit the job she had obtained at a local school. "He kept accusing me of having an affair with the school bus driver," she stated, and because of the physical and mental abuse, she quit the job (personal interview, January 27, 1997).

The most common form of male sabotage uncovered in the Taylor Institute's research is the practice of getting into fights and inflicting violence the night or morning before key events such as a GED test or a job interview. One woman's partner instigated a major argument and inflicted severe physical abuse the night before the final examination in her licensed practical nursing course. Sleep-deprived and profoundly depressed by the renewed onset of the abuse, she failed the test and was unable to continued in the program (Raphael, 1996).

A case manager at a literacy program gives two examples of this kind of sabotage:

The abuser argues with my client before school every day. She can't concentrate. I have to talk to her every morning to calm her down and focus her. I have another client who is close to getting her GED. He broke her right arm (she's right-handed). As soon as it healed he broke it again and she was in a cast again. You have to call it sabotage—its not just anger. Women have to recognize it for what it is. (Raphael & Tolman, 1997, p. 12)

Writes Karen Brown, formerly with the City Works Program at Bronx Community College (Bronx, New York):

Often students will get into altercations with their partners before such crucial events, causing them either to miss the event altogether or arrive in such an agitated state that their performance in compromised. After this became a pattern I personally began to suspect that it was not a coincidence that these events were occurring right before the important job-related event that was important for the student. (Raphael, 1996, p.6)

Another job placement counselor reports:

We sent one participant our for a job interview, but she did not show up. When we called to follow up with her, she told us that her partner had proceeded to drive her to the interview. He was not quite happy that she was going to be working or even trying to get out and find employment for herself. They started arguing and one thing led to another and he started hitting her. So by the time she did get out there she was beaten up. He drove her half-way back and let her out, and she had to hitchhike the rest of the way home. She has now obtained a job but comes home and gets beaten. She feels that she cannot abandon him. He is a recovering addict who tells her that she is the only person that he has. She is a victim of both physical abuse and emotional blackmail. (Raphael & Tolman, 1997, p. 12)

Threats of death and suicide are the ultimate weapon of sabotage. The Worcester Family Research Project, for example, found that, in 26.4% of its homeless AFDC sample and 18.1% of its housed AFDC sample, the male partner threatened to kill himself (Raphael & Tolman, 1997). The following true story is, unfortunately, typical of what can happen when a battered women decides to leave an abusive relationship. The welfare department worker explains:

After five years together, my client told her abuser she was leaving. In the presence of the woman and her two children, ages three and two, he threatened to kill her and her unborn child by sticking a gun into her womb. Then, turning the gun on himself, he took his own life in front of them. My client had a miscarriage and is now in therapy. She is extremely angry for allowing herself to be in the situation and feeling guilty and responsible for what happened at the same time. (Raphael & Tolman, 1997, p. 12)

Leaving the Violence: Harassment and Stalking

Unfortunately, leaving a violent relationship is often not the end of the violence, but rather marks the beginning of an escalation of domestic violence. Crime statistics bear out the fact that it is more dangerous for the woman and her family after she has left the abuser than before. Although divorced and separated women make up only 10% of all women in the United States, they account for 75% of all battered women and report being battered 14 times as often as women still living with their partners (U.S. Department of Justice, 1991).

One literacy program participant described the time when her ex-partner met her coming out of her literacy program, grabbed her by the hair, threw her into the car, and kidnapped her by force for a 48-hour period. "I am determined to get my GED. The only way I won't get it is if he kidnaps me and takes me. He's done it before" (Raphael, 1996, p. 8).

Stalking seriously interferes with the participants' ability to perform at job training or on the job. Explained one victim, who had left her abuser and moved in with a supportive uncle, "I was constantly aggravated. I couldn't function. I couldn't sit, I couldn't think, I was always wondering, if I walk out of this building, is he going to be outside? I finally had enough courage to lock him up" (Raphael, 1996, p. 9).

A former welfare participant reported that she had been applying for jobs, unsuccessfully, over a 2-year period. Eventually, she noticed that she was being trailed by a particular van. When the license plate was checked, she discovered that it was a surveillance company hired by her former boyfriend. She discovered that he would then call the potential employer and say whatever it would take to make certain she would not be hired. Only when she was able to halt this behavior was she able to land a job (Raphael, 1996, p. 9).

Participants report that their former partners trump up police charges or child abuse charges against them, requiring them to attend numerous court appearances, resulting in job losses (Raphael, 1996). Enrolled in a training program after she separated from her abuser, one welfare participant explained that he called the Department of Family Services to complain that she was abusing her daughter:

> I made an appointment to meet the worker so he could come investigate us for 8:00 Monday morning because I had to get to school. And that Sunday he came and we had a horrible assault situation. I'm pressing charges at 4:00 in the morning at the police station, and before that I had to take my daughter to my mother's house because I don't want her to go to the police station. I didn't even have time to go to the emergency room until the next afternoon because I had to meet the worker at 8:00 in the morning and then go to school. This abuse causes me to miss school all the time and I couldn't tell all these people, so I had to come up with reasons as to why. And now I think, I can't believe that I was assaulted and was actually grateful that it was just my body and not my face, I didn't have any bruises. With the police station, the 8:00 thing and then school, I couldn't even go to the emergency room. (Raphael & Tolman, 1997, p. 10)

Harassment at the job site is a particularly common form of abuse. Because the women have left their relationships, a worksite may be the only place where such abuse can take place. If women keep their jobs, they risk being shadowed by their abusers as they leave work, which results in their new whereabouts being discovered and in further violence.

Some survivors of domestic violence report that their abusers try to get back at them by threatening to kidnap their children. Leaving children in child care centers can be problematic for these survivors. "I was always scared that he would go get my children from their day care and schools and things like that, so there was that kind of stress too," explains one former battered woman (Raphael & Tolman, 1997, p. 8).

Karen's case epitomizes how domestic violence continues to plague past victims and to interfere with their employment. Karen had evicted her abusive partner, who was seriously addicted to drugs, and obtained a part-time job supplemented by a small welfare grant. Her order of protection was not enough to prevent him from coming by her apartment in a public housing project one evening, after which he beat her up, broke her arm, and took the money she had laid aside for the rent at the first of the month. Because no shelter space was available in Chicago, the next day she was taken to a hotel room in the western suburbs in a program operated by a suburban domestic violence program. The hotel now housing Karen and her children is so far away that Karen is not able to get to work. Her coworkers are desperately trying to find a shelter bed for Karen that is on a bus line to her job. Karen's abuser has threatened to kill her, so a return to her apartment is not feasible.

The Ongoing Effects of Domestic Violence

Welfare-to-work programs report that the physical and mental effects of past violence serve as major barriers to labor market participation. Some victims suffer from depression or persistent anxiety that seriously affects their ability to seek and hold employment. Others may suffer from the more serious symptoms of PTSD, which involves reliving or reexperiencing the trauma, the numbing of responses, or increased arousal, demonstrated by an inability to sleep, focus, or concentrate (Herman, 1992).

A letter I recently received from a domestic violence survivor provides a complete picture of how past violence can continue to play a current role:

> *I was a tenured professor on a research grant in Italy when I met my ex-husband. Within a few months, my productivity suffered significantly due to emotional turmoil, lack of sleep, and the demands he made upon the flexibility of my writing schedule. . . . When I returned to full-time teaching and took on the responsibility of department chair . . . he made things difficult for me professionally by such antics as abusing me all night before important meetings, making me late for meetings, and intimidating me about conversing with male colleagues in my department. . . . Once he made me miss a meeting by closing the garage door before I was able to pull the car out and then threatening me with a can of gasoline until I turned the car off and talked to him for another hour. . . . I returned to work the next academic year, overriding my inner wisdom, due to fear of having no income and started to deteriorate physically and psychologically. By December I was having suicidal ideation; by March, I was in bed every waking hour . . . due to environmental and food allergies, psychotropic drug reactions, and the exhaustion of being in a constant state of hyperarousal. By May I was able to support my claim for disability on the SSI program. (Raphael & Tolman, 1997, p.4)*

Memories of domestic violence can also continue to reoccur, often with paralyzing results. Explained one domestic violence survivor:

> *The last Valentine's Day we were together my husband had raped me. This Valentine's Day the memory came up and hit me over the head. I was almost catatonic—it was just left-over trauma. It's really difficult to put your life together again because there's so much pressure just to survive, to provide food and clothing for your child. If you try to do that and don't deal with the psychological issues at the same time, it's self-defeating. Someday that stuff will catch up with you. . . .*

> *Leaving—it's not just walking out one day and okay, that's the end of it. . . . I've been out of the relationship three years, and I'm just starting to deal with the trauma. It's difficult for me to trust anybody. I assume if anybody promises to do something, they'll probably back out of it. Even normal day-to-day interaction with people is exhausting. There's no way you can rebuild your life in two years. (Raphael & Tolman, 1997, p.4)*

Thoughts of suicide can be a common response to domestic violence. According to one job counselor, when one of her program participants, a survivor of domestic violence, was confronted with the pressure of going on job interviews as part of a welfare-department mandated job search, she locked herself in the program's bathroom and attempted to slit her wrists. Later, with the assistance of inpatient and outpatient therapy and medication, she was able to hold down two part-time cashier jobs and leave welfare (Raphael & Tolman, 1997).

Another welfare-to-work participant, a survivor of domestic violence enrolled in a junior college paralegal training program, now takes three psychotropic medications. The bruising and jarring of her brain, along with eye injuries, cause frequent and intolerable headaches. She needs to develop the organizational skills necessary for successful school completion. Because of her abuse, she was never able to plan her life:

> *Any minute or hour of any given day, I could be dead. I saw no importance to it. My life was fear, insecurity, confusion, uncertainty, worry, pain, and many days of wishing I was dead, since death was the final escape. . . . I still encounter physical and mental barriers and I always will. (Raphael, 1996, p. 3)*

Other survivors report problems completing tasks at work because of the traumatic effects of domestic violence. Explains one,

> *I have trouble at work as a result of past domestic violence. I have a communications defect. I don't feel I am educated enough to get my points across. I am always writing my points down. I worry that I am always missing something. I am always watching for an attack so I am on guard all the time and I am not really listening. I am always needing to ask for clarification and that angers people on the job. (Raphael & Tolman, 1997, p. 10)*

Explains another,

> *They tell me I wouldn't make decisions on the job without somebody okaying. I could not make a decision on my own. That's the biggest drawback that I've had, learning how to make decisions and feeling comfortable with what I can do. (Raphael & Tolman, 1997, p. 8)*

Determining the Extent of the Problem

Until recently, researchers have depended on data from welfare-to-work programs to estimate the extent of the problem of domestic violence within welfare caseloads.

Now, results from four recent in-depth studies, each involving fairly large samples, provide a more accurate answer to the question of the extent of current and past domestic violence among women receiving welfare. All of these studies were published in reports in 1996 and 1997:

1. The Passaic County Study of AFDC Recipients in a Welfare-to-Work Program, *a sample of 846 women on AFDC in a mandatory pre-employment training program between December 1995 and January 1997 (Curcio, 1997).*

    14.6% of the sample reported current physical abuse by an intimate partner and 25% verbal or emotional abuse, with 57.3% of the entire sample reporting physical abuse sometime during their adulthood.

    12.9% of the entire sample, and 39.7% of those current abuse victims, reported that their partners actively prevent their participation in education and training.

2. In Harm's Way? Domestic Violence, AFDC Receipt, and Welfare Reform in Massachusetts, *a random sample of 734 women in the current state caseload, surveyed between January and June 1996 by the University of Massachusetts, Boston. This study is the first scientific sampling of one state's entire AFDC caseload that measured both current and past prevalence of domestic violence (Allard, Colten, Albelda, & Cosenza, 1997).*

    19.5% of the sample reported current physical violence at the hands of an intimate partner, with 64% experiencing intimate partner violence ever in life as an adult.

    This study supports the contention that perpetrators of violence interfere with women's attempts to comply with welfare work requirements. Abused women in the sample were 10 times more likely than their never-abused counterparts to have current partners who would not like them going to school or work (15.5% vs. 1.6%).

3. The Worcester Family Research Project, *a 5-year study of 436 homeless and housed women, most of whom received AFDC, in Worcester, Massachusetts, conducted by the Better Homes Fund between August 1992 and July 1995 (Bassuk et al., 1996).*

    The study found that, of the entire sample of homeless and housed women, 61% had been severely physically assaulted by intimate male partners as adults and that nearly one third (32%) had experienced severe violence from their current or most recent partners. Over one third (34%) had been threatened with death by their intimate partners.

    This research also showed current high prevalences of mental health problems and PTSD within the entire welfare sample at levels two to three times that in the general female population. Because of the high percentages of battered women in the sample, it is likely that some victims were suffering from these effects of trauma.

4. The Effects of Violence on Women's Employment, *a random survey of 824 women in one low-income neighborhood of Chicago, conducted by the Joint Center for Poverty Research at Northwestern University between September 1994 and May 1995 (Lloyd, 1996).*

> *Although rates of domestic violence were high for the entire neigh-*
> *borhood sample (11.8%), AFDC recipients experienced 3 times the*
> *amount of physical violence as their non-AFDC neighborhood coun-*
> *terparts within the last year (31.3%) and 2.4 times the amount of*
> *severe physical aggression within the last year (19.5% vs. 8.1%).*

These four studies clearly demonstrate that domestic violence is a factor in a high percentage of welfare recipients' lives. Current domestic violence victims represent 14.6% to 32% of these welfare samples, and approximately 60% of the samples are composed of past victims of domestic violence (Raphael & Tolman, 1997). The patterns of sabotage described by the qualitative research are corroborated by this new research. High percentages of abused women in the Massachusetts caseload survey reported arguments about child support (30%), visitation (23%), and child custody (14.7%), and police visits to their homes (36%), as well as interference from their intimate partners with education, training, and work (Allard et al., 1997). In the Passaic County study, three times as many currently abused women as nonabused women stated that their intimate partners actively tried to prevent them from obtaining education or training (39.7% vs. 12.9% for the entire sample) (Curcio, 1997).

Policy and Service Delivery Implications

This new research does not provide definitive answers necessary to frame effective policy and service delivery responses. For this, we need to know more about the abusive men in these women's lives. It is important to understand better why some men are so threatened by the employment of their partners. In the context of current welfare policies, some men who are themselves uneducated, unemployed, or underemployed may feel abandoned by governmental programs; this feeling may increase their need to control and dominate their partners. It is not known whether, in addition to criminal justice sanctions, interventions geared to helping men develop themselves in the labor market could be useful in eliminating domestic violence.

Nor does the research assist us in determining what strategies will be able to help battered women on welfare become economically self-sufficient. As is apparent from the wide variety of methods by which abusive men sabotage their partners' efforts to become economically independent, it is essential that service providers and policymakers not overgeneralize about battered women. For many battered women, work is the only way they can permanently escape violence.

Rather than an exemption from work, they need better supports and assistance to enter the workforce and to maintain employment. Some battered women will be able to comply with welfare requirements if well-structured welfare-to-work programs are available to them. Many dealing with abusive partners may be successful only if they have increased safety planning and domestic violence services. Others, because of the severity of the threat, the likelihood of escalation of violence, or the traumatic effects of the violence, will need short-term or long-term waivers of welfare work requirements.

As a result, welfare policy at the state level must be flexible enough to ensure that each battered woman receives the services she needs in order to take the appropriate pathway toward work that does not further endanger herself or her children. This policy result is in no way precluded by the new federal welfare legislation.

Each community, however, must develop a network of needed services for battered women and their children. Without these services, all the good assessment and sensitive welfare policy in the world will not meet the needs of battered women on welfare. Battered women need a variety of services, including counseling and safety planning; legal services; emergency housing; vocational counseling; literacy and job training; mental health services; and alcohol and drug treatment. Specialized support for battered women can also be structured effectively within the context of welfare-to-work and job-training programs. In serving battered women within the welfare system, it is important that these efforts be coordinated with agencies serving abused women in the community. Partnerships with battered women's advocates who have experience and expertise in serving domestic violence victims are crucial.

Given the prevalence of domestic violence within welfare caseloads, it is incumbent upon every helping professional and every welfare department worker to become trained in domestic violence. Because of the pervasiveness of the problem among low-income girls and women, all agencies serving low-income populations must be specially trained in domestic violence and its assessment.

It is now time for service providers and policymakers to become more aware of the role that domestic violence plays in keeping low-income girls and women trapped in poverty. Because domestic violence is a hidden secret, one rarely shared with others, those in the helping professions cannot assume that domestic violence is not present if it is not mentioned by their clients. It is time to connect what we know about domestic violence with antipoverty efforts. Not only does the failure to take domestic violence into account cause conventional antipoverty interventions to fail, but it also can make life even more difficult and dangerous for girls and women. We must all learn to feel more comfortable with talking about domestic violence and helping girls and women eliminate it from their lives.

References

Allard, M. A., Colten, M. E., Albelda, R., & Cosenza, C. (1997). *In harm's way? Domestic violence, AFDC receipt, and welfare reform in Massachusetts.* Boston: University of Massachusetts, McCormack Institute, Center for Survey Research.

Bassuk, E., Weinreb, L., Buckner, J., Browne, A., Salomon, A., & Bassuk, S. (1996). The characteristics and needs of sheltered homeless and low-income housed mothers. *Journal of the American Medical Association, 276*(8), 640–646.

Curcio, W. (1997). *The Passaic County study of AFDC recipients in a welfare-to-work program: A preliminary analysis.* Paterson, NJ: Passaic County Board of Social Services.

Herman, J. (1992). *Trauma and recovery.* New York: Basic Books.

Kenney, C., & Brown, K. (1996). *Report from the front lines: The impact of violence on poor women.* New York: NOW Legal Defense and Education Fund.

Lloyd, S. (1996). *The effects of violence on women's employment.* Evanston, IL: North-western University, Joint Center for Poverty Research and Institute for Policy Research.

Raphael, J. (1995). *Domestic violence: Telling the untold welfare-to-work story.* Chicago: Taylor Institute.

Raphael, J. (1996). *Prisoners of abuse: Domestic violence and welfare receipt.* Chicago: Taylor Institute.

Raphael J., & Tolman, R. (1997). *Trapped by poverty/Trapped by abuse: New evidence documenting the relationship between domestic violence and welfare.* Chicago: Taylor Institute and the University of Michigan Research Development Center on Poverty, Risk, and Mental Health.

U.S. Department of Justice. (1991). *Female victims of violent crimes 5.* Washington, DC: Government Printing Office.

Questions for Reading and Analysis

1. What is Raphael's main argument?

2. In what specific ways does domestic violence impede participation in the labor force?

3. What kind of evidence does Raphael use in this piece? Is it effective?

Richard Rodriguez (b. 1944), essayist and journalist, writes often about issues of identity and assimilation. In "Complexion," from his 1982 autobiography Hunger of Memory: The Education of Richard Rodriguez, *he writes of his youthful self-consciousness about his dark complexion and his identity as a Mexican-American.*

Complexion

Richard Rodriguez

Complexion. My first conscious experience of sexual excitement concerns my complexion. One summer weekend, when I was around seven years old, I was at a public swimming pool with the whole family. I remember sitting on the damp pavement next to the pool and seeing my mother, in the spectators' bleachers, holding my younger sister on her lap. My mother, I noticed, was watching my father as he stood on a diving board, waving to her. I watched her wave back. Then saw her radiant, bashful, astonishing smile. In that second I sensed that my mother and father had a relationship I knew nothing about. A nervous excitement encircled my stomach as I saw my mother's eyes follow my father's figure curving into the water. A second or two later, he emerged. I heard him call out. Smiling, his voice sounded, buoyant, calling me to swim to him. But turning to see him, I caught my mother's eye. I heard her shout over to me. In Spanish she called through the crowd: "Put a towel on over your shoulders." In public, she didn't want to say why. I knew.

That incident anticipates the shame and sexual inferiority I was to feel in later years because of my dark complexion. I was to grow up an ugly child. Or one who thought himself ugly. *(Feo.)* One night when I was eleven or twelve years old, I locked myself in the bathroom and carefully regarded my reflection in the mirror over the sink. Without any pleasure I studied my skin. I turned on the faucet. (In my mind I heard the swirling voices of aunts, and even my mother's voice, whispering incessantly about lemon juice solutions and dark, *feo* children.) With a bar of soap, I fashioned a thick ball of lather. I began soaping my arms. I took my father's straight razor out of the medicine cabinet. Slowly, with steady deliberateness, I put the blade against my flesh, pressed it as close as I could without cutting, and moved it up and down across my skin to see if I could get out, somehow lessen, the dark. All I succeeded in doing, however, was in shaving my arms bare of their hair. For as I noted with disappointment, the dark would not come out. It remained. Trapped. Deep in the cells of my skin.

Throughout adolescence I felt myself mysteriously marked. Nothing else about my appearance would concern me so much as the fact that my complexion was dark. My mother would say how sorry she was that there was not money enough to get braces to straighten my teeth. But I never bothered about my teeth. In three-way mirrors at department stores, I'd see my profile dramatically defined by a long nose, but it was really only the color of my skin that caught my attention.

I wasn't afraid that I would become a menial laborer because of my skin. Nor did my complexion make me feel especially vulnerable to racial abuse. (I didn't really consider my dark skin to be a racial characteristic. I would have been only too happy to look as Mexican as my light-skinned older brother.) Simply, I judged myself ugly. And, since the women in my family had been the ones who discussed it in such worried tones, I felt my dark skin made me unattractive to women.

Thirteen years old. Fourteen. In a grammar school art class, when the assignment was to draw a self-portrait, I tried and tried but could not bring myself to shade in the face on the paper to anything like my actual tone. With disgust then I would come face to face with myself in mirrors. With disappointment I located myself in class photographs—my dark face undefined by the camera which had clearly described the white faces of classmates. Or I'd see my dark wrist against my long-sleeved white shirt.

I grew divorced from my body. Insecure, overweight, listless. On hot summer days when my rubber-soled shoes soaked up the heat from the sidewalk, I kept my head down. Or walked in the shade. My mother didn't need anymore to tell me to watch out for the sun. I denied myself a sensational life. The normal, extra-ordinary, animal excitement of feeling my body alive—riding shirtless on a bicycle in the warm wind created by furious self-propelled motion—the sensations that first had excited in me a sense of my maleness, I denied. I was too ashamed of my body. I wanted to forget that I had a body because I had a brown body. I was grateful that none of my classmates ever mentioned the fact.

I continued to see the *braceros*, those men I resembled in one way and in another way, didn't resemble at all. On the watery horizon of a Valley afternoon, I'd see them. And though I feared looking like them, it was with silent envy that I regarded them still. I envied them their physical lives, their freedom to violate the taboo of the sun. Closer to home I would notice the shirtless construction workers, the roofers, the sweating men tarring the street in front of the house. And I'd see the Mexican gardeners. I was unwilling to admit the attraction of their lives. I tried to deny it by looking away. But what was denied became strongly desired.

In high school physical education classes, I withdrew, in the regular company of five or six classmates, to a distant corner of a football field where we smoked and talked. Our company was composed of bodies too short or too tall, all grace-less and all—except mine—pale. Our conversation was usually witty. (In fact we were intelligent.) If we referred to the athletic contests around us, it was with sarcasm. With savage scorn I'd refer to the "animals" playing football or baseball. It would have been important for me to have joined them. Or for me to have taken off my shirt, to have let the sun burn dark on my skin, and to have run barefoot on the warm wet grass. It would have been very important. Too important. It would have been too telling a gesture—to admit the desire for sensation, the body, my body.

Fifteen, sixteen. I was a teenager shy in the presence of girls. Never dated. Barely could talk to a girl without stammering. In high school I went to several dances, but I never managed to ask a girl to dance. So I stopped going. I cannot remember high school years now with the parade of typical images: bright drive-ins or gliding blue shadows of a Junior Prom. At home most weekend nights, I would pass evenings reading. Like those hidden, precocious adolescents who have no real-life sexual experiences, I read a great deal of romantic fiction. "You won't find it in your books," my brother would playfully taunt me as he prepared to go to a party by freezing the crest of the wave in his hair with sticky pomade. Through my reading, however, I developed a fabulous and sophisticated sexual imagination. At seventeen, I may not have known how to engage a girl in small talk, but I had read *Lady Chatterley's Lover*.

It annoyed me to hear my father's teasing: that I would never know what "real work" is; that my hands were so soft. I think I knew it was his way of admitting pleasure and pride in my academic success. But I didn't smile. My mother said she was glad her children were getting their educations and would not be pushed around like *los pobres*. I heard the remark ironically as a reminder of my separation from *los braceros*. At such times I suspected that education was making me effeminate. The odd thing, however, was that I did not judge my classmates so harshly. Nor did I consider my male teachers in high school effeminate. It was only myself I judged against some shadowy, mythical Mexican laborer—dark like me, yet very different.

Language was crucial. I knew that I had violated the ideal of the *macho* by becoming such a dedicated student of language and literature. *Machismo* was a word never exactly defined by the persons who used it. (It was best described in the "proper" behavior of men.) Women at home, nevertheless, would repeat the Old Mexican dictum that a man should be *feo, fuerte, y formal*. "The three F's," my mother called them, smiling slyly. *Feo* I took to mean not literally ugly so much as ruggedly handsome. (When my mother and her sisters spent a loud, laughing afternoon determining ideal male good looks, they finally settled on the actor Gilbert Roland, who was neither too pretty nor ugly but had looks "like a man.") *Fuerte*, "strong," seemed to mean not physical strength as much as inner strength, character. A dependable man is *fuerte*. *Fuerte* for that reason was a characteristic subsumed by the last of the three qualities, and the one I most often considered—*formal*. To be *formal* is to be steady. A man of responsibility, a good provider. Someone *formal* is also constant. A person to be relied upon in adversity. A sober man, a man of high seriousness.

I learned a great deal about being *formal* just by listening to the way my father and other male relatives of his generation spoke. A man was not silent necessarily. Nor was he limited in the tones he could sound. For example, he could tell a long, involved, humorous story and laugh at his own humor with high-pitched giggling. But a man was not talkative the way a woman could be. It was permitted a woman to be gossipy and chatty. (When one heard many voices in a room, it was usually women who were talking.) Men spoke much less rapidly. And often men spoke in monologues. (When one voice sounded in a crowded room, it was most often a man's voice one heard.) More important than any of this was the fact that a man never verbally revealed his emotions. Men did not speak about their unease in moments of crisis or danger. It was the woman who worried aloud when her husband got laid off from work. At times of illness or death in the family, a man was usually quiet, even silent. Women spoke up to voice prayers. In distress, women always sounded quick ejaculations to God or the Virgin; women prayed in clearly audible voices at a wake held in a funeral parlor. And on the subject of love, a woman was verbally expansive. She spoke of her yearning and delight. A married man, if he spoke publicly about love, usually did so with playful, mischievous irony. Younger, unmarried men more often were quiet. (The *macho* is a silent suitor. *Formal.*)

At home I was quiet, so perhaps I seemed *formal* to my relations and other Spanish-speaking visitors to the house. But outside the house—my God!—I talked. Particularly in class or alone with my teachers, I chattered. (Talking seemed to make teachers think I was bright.) I often was proud of my way with words. Though, on other occasions, for example, when I would hear my mother busily speaking to women, it would occur to me that my attachment to words made me like her. Her son. Not *formal* like my father. At such times I even suspected that my nostalgia for sounds—the noisy, intimate Spanish sounds of my past—was nothing more than effeminate yearning.

High school English teachers encouraged me to describe very personal feelings in words. Poems and short stories I wrote, expressing sorrow and loneliness, were awarded high grades. In my bedroom were books by poets and novelists— books that I loved—in which male writers published feelings the men in my family never revealed or acknowledged in words. And it seemed to me that there was something unmanly about my attachment to literature. Even today, when so much about the myth of the *macho* no longer concerns me, I cannot altogether evade such notions. Writing these pages, admitting my embarrassment or my guilt, admitting my sexual anxieties and my physical insecurity, I have not been able to forget that I am not being *formal.*

So be it.

1982

Questions for Reading and Analysis

1. What is Rodriguez's thesis?

2. What is the meaning of *formal* as used by Rodriguez's mother? How does his recognition that he lacks this attribute of the ideal male make him feel?

3. What do the final three words of the essay convey about Rodriguez's development? Compare the attitude revealed here to his adolescent consciousness of himself.

4. Besides the obvious one, what other meanings does the title suggest?

W riter and second-generation feminist Katie Roiphe's article
caused quite a stir among readers of the New York Times Magazine after its October 1997 publication. Citing recent celebrity cases
of adultery and other evidence from popular culture, she argues that
the double standard for adultery has been reversed: In the past, society
tended to excuse infidelity in men and punish it in women. Today, a
cheating husband is simply "a pig," while a cheating wife may be a
heroine in pursuit of liberation and romantic self-fulfillment.

Adultery's Double Standard

Katie Roiphe

T he story of the world's most public dysfunctional marriage is over. Even
before Diana's death transformed her into a full-fledged saint, her marital
troubles, like her bulimia, lent her an air of vulnerability that somehow
made us love her more. Both Charles and Diana had affairs. Yet while hers seemed
justified, his seemed comic or disgusting or unmanly, depending on how you looked
at it. Very few people were willing to see Charles as the hero of a tragic love story.
His obvious devotion to Camilla Parker-Bowles didn't count in his favor at all.

As the royal scandals revealed, we've grown much more tolerant of adultery,
at least when it comes to women. Women's magazines practically recommend it to
their readers as a fun and healthy activity, like buying a new shade of lipstick or
vacationing in the Caribbean. In *Elle* we read that "an affair can be a sexual
recharging, an escape from a worn-out relationship, a way into something better."
Harper's Bazaar breathlessly tells us about women whose "marriages are improved
by their affairs. Because they get their fill of rapture elsewhere, these wives are not
apt to complain or nag or find fault with their husbands." *Glamour* announces that
"women are cheating, and not feeling guilty." But we seem to have a double standard for this sort of thing: if a woman has an adulterous affair, she is, according
to *Harper's Bazaar*, "asserting her femininity," but if a man does it, he's a pig.

Though there were sordid elements to Diana's relationship with the car
salesman who called her Squidgy on the phone, it somehow didn't feel sordid the
way Charles's story did, or Dick Morris's, or Frank Gifford's, or Michael Kennedy's.
These men came off as sheepish and pathetic, whereas Diana just seemed victimized. And Diana is not the only woman in the news whose affairs generated an out-
pouring of public sympathy. Kelly Flinn, the 26-year-old fighter pilot who stole an
enlisted woman's husband, emerged, even to the Republican Senate majority leader,
Trent Lott, as "badly abused." *Time* headlined its story "Tale Full of Passion and
Lies," and for a few weeks, Lieutenant Flinn was the radiant heroine of a romance
novel in the news, a woman who, in her own words, "fell deeply in love with a man

351

who led me down the path of self-destruction." But imagine if Clinton had said he was "deeply in love" with Gennifer Flowers, or Gary Hart "deeply in love" with Donna Rice, or Michael Kennedy "deeply in love" with the baby sitter.

The grand-passion defense just doesn't work for a man, as Charles's experience proved. We think of men shopping for lingerie with their secretaries out of a casual lust and women sipping chardonnay with their lovers out of a deep, poetic unhappiness. When a man cheats, we assume it's all about a new naked body, but when a woman does it, we assume it's for love. No matter how sophisticated we are, it's almost impossible to get away from this primitive perception of how men and women conduct their emotional lives. Eleanor Alter, a prominent New York divorce lawyer, says of her 30 years' worth of clients: "Women are more likely to use the word love to justify adultery to themselves. You have to be in love. Otherwise you're a whore."

Because the stereotypes of carnal men and sensitive women are so ingrained, because we have trouble thinking of women being as sleazy as men, or men being as needy as women, we have created a heightened romantic vocabulary to talk about female adultery. Take the public scandal of Kimba Wood. Headlines about the Love Judge notwithstanding, Wood emerged as a glamorous figure. Her affair with Frank Richardson was, according to *The Daily News*, "a blossoming romance against the backdrop of intimate dinners at the restaurant Lutèce." *Newsday* described her as a tragic heroine "whose long, dark hair frames her face and who looks strangely pale after her time in sunny Italy."

If reporters seem to drape women's affairs in the purple prose of a Harlequin romance, the rest of us tend to do the same thing. In *Vogue*, one woman tells us that after she slept with a man who was not her husband, "every staple item of life appeared transformed, transubstantiated even, newly lit, radiant."

The shimmering air of romance that surrounds the modern adulteress is nowhere more visible than in the phenomenally popular novel and movie *The Bridges of Madison County*. The story of a bored housewife who has a four-day affair with a roving photographer and free spirit is very distinctly not a tragedy. Only through an affair is Francesca Johnson, wife and mother of two, really alive. Millions of women seem to identify with the story's romantic fatalism, with the scenario of being swept away by a passion that cannot be controlled.

Glamour reports that the phrases "It was meant to be" and "We were made for each other" crop up in hundreds of letters from readers. The language of dime-store romance novels allows women to surrender responsibility, to think of their experience in the passive voice, as if destiny itself planned their trysts and lied to their husbands. Of course, the perfume and passion of romance novels have been around for a long time. The new ingredient is feminism, which has added intellectual heft and political respectability to affairs, provided they are carried on by women. An extramarital fling offers a rebellion against cookie dough and car pools. It offers what is euphemistically called freedom. While most of us still interpret male infidelity as a threat to the family, female infidelity has become a titillating form of self-expression.

The double standard that so many of us have in our heads goes back to the 70s and early 80s, when it began to seem as if a woman's pursuit of orgasms was progress but a man's leaving his family for a 22-year-old tootsie was patriarchal oppression. Think of the landmark stories of the period. When the husband cheats on his pregnant wife in Nora Ephron's *Heartburn*, he is the scum of the earth, but when Isadora Wing cheats on her husband in Erica Jong's *Fear of Flying*, it's hailed as an erotic triumph worldwide.

A book on the liberating potential of adultery, Dalma Heyn's *Erotic Silence of the American Wife*, was published a few years ago. Though it may seem as if there's nothing this country needs more than a little erotic silence, this book was taken very seriously by the feminist establishment. It declares that adultery is "a revolutionary way for women to rise above the conventional" and calls on women to shatter this "rigid institutional cage . . . which imprisoned their sexual selves." According to this popular volume, sneaking off to a hotel with your lover is a blow for the cause. It's as political as voting. And there is definitely something seductive about this point of view, at least for women.

Still, it's hard not to wonder about the politics at work. Would Gloria Steinem have given a glowing endorsement to a book that advised men to cheat on their wives? This hypocrisy about male and female sexuality is so acceptable, so much a part of our culture, that we barely notice it. It's as if the historical oppression of women justifies all sorts of bad behavior and self-indulgence and a whole new double standard.

Though in the current cultural climate it's easier to assume that men are villains and women romantics, the truth is more elusive. Raoul Felder, another prominent divorce lawyer, says after 39 years of watching people who have committed adultery: "Women are motivated by the same forces as men—loneliness, hostility, boredom, the need to feel younger and attractive, the need to be worshiped."

There are those who justify our new double standard by pointing out that men have traditionally gotten away with sleeping around while women have traditionally been shamed and condemned. But if adultery was ever perceived as a sign of roguish male virility in this country, it isn't anymore. Whispers of John F. Kennedy's affairs during his Presidency only added to his charisma, to the incandescent mist of Kennedyness that surrounded him. Michael Kennedy just seems sleazy. The men caught in adulterous affairs today apologize and repent and hang their heads like chastened marionettes. Some of them manage to maintain their status, while others see their careers suffer (like the general who was passed over for Chairman of the Joint Chiefs of Staff for an affair he had when he and his wife were separated). But they are all humiliated. They are the punch lines of a thousand jokes across the nation. Lady columnists barely conceal their desire to see them fall, to see their reputations destroyed as completely and irreversibly as those of adulterous heroines like Anna Karenina, Emma Bovary and Hester Prynne were in 19th-century literature.

With glowing reports in women's magazines on the healthiness of adultery, and the candlelight romance of *The Bridges of Madison County*, the days of the 19th-century adulteress's suffering seem far away. Or maybe we're just looking for our tragic heroines in the wrong places. Think of poor Charles, amid the global scorn of the tabloids and the public, who may have to give up his crown for his adulterous passion.

Prince Charles is our Emma Bovary.

Questions for Reading and Analysis

1. According to Roiphe, how do many women defend their adulterous affairs?

2. How does Roiphe connect the new double standard with traditional stereotypes about men and women?

3. What does Roiphe mean when she says: "Prince Charles is our Emma Bovary"? (Flaubert's novel *Madame Bovary* was published in 1856.)

4. Do you agree with Roiphe that the media treats male and female adultery differently?

First published in Psychology Today *in 1996, Theodore Roszak's article investigates the psychological causes of environmental destruction, claiming that blaming people for destroying the planet is not going to make them stop. Instead, he argues that we need to integrate our connection to the natural environment into our definition of sanity, because once "our culture is out of balance with nature, everything about our lives is affected; family, workplace, school, community—all take on a crazy shape."*

The Nature of Serenity

Theodore Roszak

I recently attended a meeting of the International Rivers Network, a San Francisco-area environmental group. The featured speaker was Dan Beard, head of the U.S. Bureau of Reclamation. After detailing the ways in which big dams have devastated natural watersheds and riverine cultures, he ended with an appeal: "Somehow we have got to convince people that projects like this are crazy." There was applause all around.

"Crazy" . . . In the presence of environmental horrors, the word leaps to mind. Depleting the ozone is "crazy," killing off the rhinos is "crazy," destroying rain forests is "crazy." Our gut feeling is immediate, the judgment made with vehemence. "Crazy" is a word freighted with strong emotion.

Inflicting irreversible damage on the biosphere might seem to be the most obvious kind of craziness. But when we turn to the psychiatric literature of the modern Western world, we find no such category as ecological madness.

The American Psychiatric Association lists more than 300 mental diseases in its *Diagnostic and Statistical Manual*. Among the largest of *DSM* categories is sex. In mapping sexual dysfunction, therapists have been absolutely inspired. We have sexual aversion disorder, female sexual arousal disorder, hypoactive sexual desire disorder (male and female), gender identity disorder, transient stress-related cross-dressing behavior, androgen insensitivity syndrome, fetishism, transvestic fetishism, transvestic fetishism with gender dysphoria, voyeurism, frotteurism, pedophilia (six varieties), and paraphiliac telephone scatologia.

Granted, the *DSM* bears about the same relationship to psychology as a building code bears to architecture. It is nonetheless revealing that the volume contains only one listing remotely connected to nature: seasonal affective disorder, a depressive mood swing occasioned by seasonal changes. Even here, nature comes in second: If the mood swing reflects seasonal unemployment, economics takes precedence as a cause.

Psychotherapists have exhaustively analyzed every form of dysfunctional family and social relations, but "dysfunctional environmental relations" does not exist even as a concept. Since its beginning, mainstream Western psychology has limited the definition of mental health to the interpersonal context of an urban industrial society: marriage, family, work, school, community. All that lies beyond the citified psyche has seemed of no human relevance—or perhaps too frightening to think about. "Nature," Freud dismally concluded, "is eternally remote. She destroys us—coldly, cruelly, relentlessly." Whatever else has been revised and rejected in Freud's theories, this tragic sense of estrangement from nature continues to haunt psychology, making the natural world seem remote and hostile.

Now all is changing. In the past 10 years, a growing number of psychologists have begun to place their theory and practice in an ecological context. Already ecopsychology has yielded insights of great value.

For one thing, it has called into question the standard strategy of scaring, shaming, and blaming that environmentalists have used in addressing the public since Rachel Carson wrote *Silent Spring*. There is evidence this approach does more harm than good—especially if, as ecopsychologists suggest, some environmentally destructive behavior bears the earmarks of addiction.

Take consumption habits. In ecopsychology workshops, people frequently admit their need to shop is "crazy." Why do they buy what they do not need? A common answer is: "I shop when I'm depressed. I go to the mall to be among happy people." Buying things is strictly secondary—and in fact does little to relieve the depression.

Some ecopsychologists believe that, as with compulsive gamblers, the depression that drives people to consume stems not from greed but from a sense of emptiness. This void usually traces back to childhood experiences of inadequacy and rejection; it may have much to do with the typically middle-class need for competitive success. The insecurity born of that drive may grow into a hunger for acquisition that cannot be satisfied even when people have consumed so much that they themselves recognize they are behaving irrationally.

If the addiction diagnosis of overconsumption is accurate, then guilt-tripping the public is worse than futile. Faced with scolding, addicts often resort to denial— or hostility. That makes them prey for antienvironmentalist groups like the Wise Use Movement, which then persuade an aggravated public to stop paying attention to "grieving greenies" and "ecofascists" who demand too much change too quickly.

As every therapist knows, addictive behavior cannot be cured by shame, because addicts are already deeply ashamed. Something affirmative and environmentally benign must be found to fill the inner void. Some ecopsychologists believe the joy and solace of the natural world can itself provide that emotional sustenance. Some, therefore, use wilderness, restoration projects, or gardens as a new "outdoor office."

"Nature heals" is one of the oldest therapeutic dicta. Ecopsychologists are finding new ways to apply that ancient insight. Over a century ago, Emerson lamented that "few adult persons can see nature." If they could, they would know that "in the woods, we return to reason and faith. There I feel that nothing can befall me in life, no disgrace or calamity . . . which nature cannot repair."

Why have therapists made so little of this obvious resource? When highly stressed people are asked to visualize a soothing scene, nobody imagines a freeway or a shopping mall. Rather, images of wilderness, forest, seascape, and starry skies invariably emerge. In taking such experiences seriously, ecopsychologists are broadening the context of mental health to include the natural environment. They are hastening the day when calling our bad environmental habits "crazy" will be more than a rhetorical outburst. The word will have behind it the full weight of considered professional consensus.

This, in turn, could be of enormous value in opening people to our spiritual, as well as physical, dependence upon nature. The time may not be far off when environmental policymakers will have something more emotionally engaging to work with than the Endangered Species Act. They will be able to defend the beauties and biodiversity of nature by invoking an environmentally based definition of mental health. We might then see an assault upon endangered species or old-growth forest as an assault upon the sanity of a community, upon children, or upon our species as a whole.

In devastating the natural environment, we may be undermining a basic requirement of sanity: our sense of moral reciprocity with the nonhuman environment. Yet ecopsychology also offers hope. As ecocidal as our behavior may have become, our bond with the planet endures; something within us voices a warning.

Ecopsychologists have begun to detect in people evidence of an unspoken grieving for the great environmental losses the world is suffering. Sometimes, indeed, clients themselves demand to have that sense of loss taken seriously in their therapy. In a letter to *Ecopsychology Newsletter*, one reader reports how she confessed her anxiety for our environmental condition to her psychiatrist. "I felt depressed that things had gotten so bad I could no longer drink tap water safely." Her therapist, all too typically, dismissed her feelings as an "obsession with the environment." That judgment eventually drove the client to seek help elsewhere and finally toward a commitment to the environmental movement.

Denying the relevance of nature to our deepest emotional needs is still the rule in mainstream therapy, as in the culture generally. It is apt to remain so until psychologists expand our paradigm of the self to include the natural habitat—as was always the case in indigenous cultures, whose methods of healing troubled souls included the trees and rivers, the sun and stars.

At a conference titled "Psychology As If the Whole Earth Mattered," at Harvard's Center for Psychology and Social Change, psychologists concluded that "if the self is expanded to include the natural world, behavior leading to destruction of this world will be experienced as self-destruction."

Such an intimate connection with the earth means taking our evolutionary heritage seriously and putting it in an ecological framework. Ecopsychology reinforces insights from naturalists like E. O. Wilson, who suggests that we possess "an innately emotional affiliation with all living organisms"—biophilia—that inclines us toward fostering biodiversity.

If our culture is out of balance with nature, everything about our lives is affected; family, workplace, school, community—all take on a crazy shape. For this reason, ecopsychology does not seek to create new categories of pathology, but to show how our ecological disconnection plays into all ensuing ones. For example, the *DSM* defines "separation anxiety disorder" as "excessive anxiety concerning separation from home and from those to whom the individual is attached." But no separation is more pervasive in this Age of Anxiety than our disconnection from the natural world.

Freud coined the term reality principle to designate that objective order of things to which the healthy psyche must adapt if it is to qualify as "sane." Writing in a preecological era, he failed to include the biosphere. Ecopsychology is seeking to rectify that failure by expanding the definition of sanity to embrace the love for the living planet that is reborn in every child.

Questions for Reading and Analysis

1. What does Roszak's consultation of the American Psychiatric Association's *Diagnostic and Statistical Manual* reveal about the standard definition of mental illness? What is conspicuously absent from the ranks of certified psychological disorders?

2. How does Roszak link consumption addiction and the environmental destruction?

3. What evidence does Roszak give to support his claim that "in devastating the natural environment, we may be undermining a basic requirement of sanity"?

4. By publishing his article in *Psychology Today*, Roszak aimed his article at a certain type of audience. Who are his readers and how does the presentation of his argument take his audience into consideration?

*P*olitical theorist and Harvard professor of government Michael J.
Sandel examines affirmative action policies from the point of view
of honor. Looking at the case of a handicapped cheerleader, university admission policies, and working-class opposition to welfare programs, Sandel concludes that very few people understand how honor,
the reward for certain social practices and virtues, "is relative to social
institutions, whose purposes are open to argument and revision." His
essay was first published in The New Republic, December 1996.

Honor and Resentment

Michael J. Sandel

The politics of the ancients was about virtue and honor, but we moderns are
concerned with fairness and rights. There is some truth in this familiar adage,
but only to a point. On the surface, our political debates make little mention of honor, a seemingly quaint concern best suited to a status-ridden world of
chivalry and duels. Not far beneath the surface, however, some of our fiercest
debates about fairness and rights reflect deep disagreement about the proper basis
of social esteem.

Consider the fuss over Callie Smartt, a 15-year-old cheerleader at a high school
in West Texas. Last year she was a popular freshman cheerleader, despite the fact that
she has cerebral palsy and moves about in a wheelchair. As Sue Anne Pressley reported
recently in *The Washington Post*, "She had plenty of school spirit to go around. . . .
The fans seemed to delight in her. The football players said they loved to see her dazzling smile." But at the end of the season, Callie was kicked off the squad.

Earlier this fall, she was relegated to the status of honorary cheerleader; now, even
that position is being abolished. At the urging of some other cheerleaders and their
parents, school officials have told Callie that, to make the squad next year, she will
have to try out like anyone else, in a rigorous routine involving splits and tumbles.

The head cheerleader's father opposes Callie's participation. He claims he is only
concerned for Callie's safety. If a player comes flying off the field, he worries, "the
cheerleader girls who aren't handicapped could move out of the way a little faster."
But Callie has never been hurt cheerleading. Her mother suspects the opposition
may be motivated by resentment of the acclaim Callie has received.

But what kind of resentment might motivate the head cheerleader's father? It
cannot be fear that Callie's inclusion deprives his daughter of a place; she is already
on the team. Nor is it the simple envy he might feel toward a girl who outshines his
daughter at tumbles and splits, which Callie, of course, does not. The resentment
more likely reflects the conviction that Callie is being accorded an honor she does
not deserve, in a way that mocks the pride he takes in his daughter's cheerleading

prowess. If great cheerleading is something that can be done from a wheelchair, then what becomes of the honor accorded those who excel at tumbles and splits? Indignation at misplaced honor is a moral sentiment that figures prominently in our politics, complicating and sometimes inflaming arguments about fairness and rights.

Should Callie be allowed to continue on the team? Some would answer by invoking the right of nondiscrimination: provided she can perform well in the role, Callie should not be excluded from cheerleading simply because, through no fault of her own, she lacks the physical ability to perform gymnastic routines. But the nondiscrimination argument begs the question at the heart of the controversy: What does it mean to perform well in the role of cheerleader? This question, in turn, is about the virtues and excellences that the practice of cheerleading honors and rewards. The case for Callie is that, by roaring up and down the sidelines in her wheelchair, waving her pom-poms and motivating the team, she does well what cheerleaders are supposed to do: inspire school spirit.

But if Callie should be a cheerleader because she displays, despite her disability, the virtues appropriate to her role, her claim does pose a certain threat to the honor accorded the other cheerleaders. The gymnastic skills they display no longer appear essential to excellence in cheerleading, only one way among others of rousing the crowd. Ungenerous though he was, the father of the head cheerleader correctly grasped what was at stake. A social practice once taken as fixed in its purpose and in the honors it bestowed was now, thanks to Callie, redefined.

Disputes about the allocation of honor underlie other controversies about fairness and rights. Consider, for example, the debate over affirmative action in university admissions. Here too, some try to resolve the question by invoking a general argument against discrimination. Advocates of affirmative action argue it is necessary to remedy the effects of discrimination, while opponents maintain that taking race into account amounts to reverse discrimination. Again the nondiscrimination argument begs a crucial question. All admissions policies discriminate on some ground or other. The real issue is, what kind of discrimination is appropriate to the purposes universities serve? This question is contested, not only because it decides how educational opportunities are distributed but also because it determines what virtues universities define as worthy of honor.

If the sole purpose of a university were to promote scholarly excellence and intellectual virtues, then it should admit the students most likely to contribute to these ends. But if another mission of a university is to cultivate leadership for a pluralistic society, then it should seek students likely to advance civic purposes as well as intellectual ones. In a recent court case challenging its affirmative action program, the University of Texas Law School invoked its civic purpose arguing that its minority admissions program had helped equip black and Mexican-American graduates to serve in the Texas legislature, on the federal bench and even in the president's Cabinet.

Some critics of affirmative action resent the idea that universities should honor qualities other than intellectual ones, for to do so implies that standard meritocratic virtues lack a privileged moral place. If race and ethnicity can be relevant to university admissions, then what becomes of the proud parent's conviction that his daughter is worthy of admission by virtue of her grades and test scores alone? Like the father's pride in his cheerleader daughter's tumbles and splits, it would have to be qualified by the recognition that honor is relative to social institutions, whose purposes are open to argument and revision.

Perhaps the most potent instance of the politics of honor plays itself out in debates about work. One reason many working-class voters despise welfare is not that they begrudge the money it costs but that they resent the message it conveys about what is worthy of honor and reward. Liberals who defend welfare in terms of fairness and rights often miss this point. More than an incentive to elicit effort and skills in socially useful ways, income is a measure of the things we prize. For many who "work hard and play by the rules," rewarding those who stay at home mocks the effort they expend and the pride they take in the work they do. Their resentment against welfare is not a reason to abandon the needy. But it does suggest that liberals need to articulate more convincingly the notions of virtue and honor that underlie their arguments for fairness and rights.

Questions for Reading and Analysis

1. Why, according to Sandel, does the head cheerleader's father insist on Callie Smartt's being kicked off the cheerleading squad? What is at stake for him to make such a fuss?

2. "A social practice once taken as fixed in its purpose and in the honor it bestowed was now, thanks to Callie, redefined." What do you think Sandel means by this statement? How does it explain what happened in the Callie Smartt case?

3. What is Sandel's thesis? Where in the essay does he state it?

4. Sandel acknowledges that universities might "honor qualities other than intellectual ones" when they decide who gets admitted. What criteria other than academic performance can you think of that could determine a student's college admission? Do you think universities should use any criteria other than academic performance? Why or why not?

*A*n award-winning writer of fiction and non-fiction, Scott Russell
*Sanders is, by his own admission, more interested in the way
people live together than in the lives of individuals. His essay "The
Common Life," published in his 1995 collection* Writing from the
Center, *bears witness to his interest. In it he argues that in taking care
of our families, our neighborhoods, our communities, and the land on
which we all live lies our hope for survival and social redemption.*

The Common Life

Scott Russell Sanders

One delicious afternoon while my daughter Eva was home from college for
spring vacation, she invited two neighbor girls to help her make bread.
The girls are sisters, five-year-old Alexandra and ten-year-old Rachel, both
frolicky, with eager dark eyes and shining faces.

They live just down the street from us here in Bloomington, Indiana, and whenever they see me pass by, on bicycle or on foot, they ask about Eva, whom they adore.

I was in the yard that afternoon mulching flower beds with compost, and I
could hear the girls chattering as Eva led them up the sidewalk to our door. I had
plenty of others chores to do in the yard, where every living thing was urgent with
April. But how could I stay outside, when so much beauty and laughter and spunk
were gathered in the kitchen?

I kept looking in on the cooks, until Eva finally asked, "Daddy, you wouldn't
like to knead some dough, would you?"

"I'd love to," I said. "You sure there's room for me?"

"There's room," Eva replied, "but you'll have to wash in the basement."

Hands washed, I took my place at the counter beside Rachel and Alexandra,
who perched on a stool I had made for Eva when she was a toddler. Eva had still
needed that stool when she learned to make bread on this counter; and my son, now
six feet tall, had balanced there as well for his own first lessons in cooking. I never
needed the stool, but I needed the same teacher—my wife Ruth, a woman with eloquent fingers.

Our kitchen is small; Ruth and I share that cramped space by moving in a kind
of dance we have been practicing for years. When we bump one another, it is usually for the pleasure of bumping. But Eva and the girls and I jostled like birds too
numerous for a nest. We spattered flour everywhere. We told stories. We joked. All
the while I bobbed on a current of bliss, delighting in the feel of live dough beneath
my fingers, the smell of yeast, the piping of child-voices so much like the birdsong
cascading through our open windows, the prospect of whole-wheat loaves hot
from the oven.

An artist might paint this kitchen scene in pastels for a poster, with a tender motto below, as evidence that all is right with the world. All is manifestly *not* right with the world. The world, most of us would agree, is a mess: rife with murder and mayhem, abuse of land, extinction of species, lying and theft and greed. There are days when I can see nothing but a spectacle of cruelty and waste, and the weight of dismay pins me to my chair. On such days I need a boost merely to get up, uncurl my fists, and go about my work. The needed strength may come from family, from neighbors, from a friend's greeting in the mail, from the forked leaves of lark-spur breaking ground, from rainstorms and music and wind, from the lines of a handmade table or the lines in a well-worn book, from the taste of an apple or the brash trill of finches in our backyard trees. Strength also comes to me from memories of times when I have felt a deep and complex joy, a sense of being exactly where I should be and doing exactly what I should do, as I felt on that bread-making afternoon.

I wish to reflect on the sources of that joy, that sense of being utterly in place, because I suspect they are the sources of all that I find authentic in my life. So much in life seems to me unauthentic, I cannot afford to let the genuine passages slip by without considering what makes them ring true. It is as though I spend my days wandering about, chasing false scents, lost, and then occasionally, for a few ticks of the heart, I stumble onto the path. While making bread with my daughter and her two young friends, I was on the path. So I recall that time now as a way of keeping company with Eva, who has gone back to college, but also as a way of discovering in our common life a reservoir of power and hope.

What is so powerful, so encouraging, in that kitchen scene? To begin with, I love my three fellow cooks; I relish every tilt of their heads and turn of their voices. In their presence I feel more alive and alert, as if the rust had been knocked off my nerves. The armor of self dissolves, ego relaxes its grip, and I am simply there, on the breeze of the moment.

Rachel and Alexandra belong to the Abed family, with whom we often share food and talk and festivities. We turn to the Abeds for advice, for starts of plants, for cheer, and they likewise turn to us. Not long ago they received troubling news that may force them to move away, and we have been sharing in their distress. So the Abed girls brought into our kitchen a history of neighborliness, a history all the more valuable because it might soon come to an end.

The girls also brought a readiness to learn what Eva had to teach. Eva, as I mentioned, had learned from Ruth how to make bread, and Ruth had learned from a Canadian friend, and our friend had learned from her grandmother. As Rachel and Alexandra shoved their hands into the dough, I could imagine the rope of knowledge stretching back and back through generations, to folks who ground their grain with stones and did their baking in wood stoves or fireplaces or in pits of glowing coals.

If you have made yeast bread, you know how at first the dough clings to your fingers, and then gradually, as you knead in more flour, it begins to pull away and take on a life of its own, becoming at last as resilient as a plump belly. If you have not made yeast bread, no amount of hearing or reading about it will give you that knowledge, because you have to learn through your body, through fingers and wrists and aching forearms, through shoulders and backs. Much of what we know comes to us that way, passed on from person to person, age after age, surviving in muscle and bone. I learned from my mother how to transplant a seedling, how to sew on a button; I learned from my father how to saw a board square, how to curry a horse, how to change the oil in a car. The pleasure I take in sawing or currying, in planting or sewing, even in changing oil, like my pleasure in making bread, is bound up with the affection I feel for my teachers and the respect I feel for the long, slow accumulation of knowledge that informs our simplest acts.

Those simple acts come down to us because they serve real needs. You plant a tree or sweep a floor or rock a baby without asking the point of your labors. You patch the roof to stop a leak, patch a sweater to keep from having to throw it out. You pluck the banjo because it tickles your ears and rouses Grandpa to dance. None of us can live entirely by such meaningful acts; our jobs, if nothing else, often push us through empty motions. But unless at least some of what we do has a transparent purpose, answering not merely to duty or fashion but to actual needs, then the heart has gone out of our work. What art could be more plainly valuable than cooking? The reason for baking bread is as palpable as your tongue. After our loaves were finished, Eva and I delivered two of them to the Abeds, who showed in their faces a perfect understanding of the good of bread.

When I compare the dough to a plump belly, I hear the sexual overtones, of course. By making the comparison, I do not wish to say, with Freud, that every sensual act is a surrogate for sex; on the contrary, I believe sex comes closer to being a stand-in, rather brazen and obvious, like a ham actor pretending to be the whole show, when it is only one player in the drama of our sensual life. That life flows through us constantly, so long as we do not shut ourselves off. The sound of birds and the smell of April dirt and the brush of wind through the open door were all ingredients in the bread we baked.

Before baking, the yeast was alive, dozing in the refrigerator. Scooped out of its jar, stirred into warm water, fed on sugar, it soon bubbled out gas to leaven the loaves. You have to make sure the water for the yeast, like milk for a baby, is neither too hot nor too cold, and so, as for a baby's bottle, I test the temperature on my wrist. The flour, too, had been alive not long before as wheat thriving in sun and rain. Our nourishment is borrowed life. You need not be a Christian to feel, in a bite of bread, a sense of communion with the energy that courses through all things. The lump in your mouth is a chunk of earth; there is nothing else to eat. In our house we say grace before meals, to remind ourselves of that gift and that dependence.

The elements of my kitchen scene—loving company, neighborliness, inherited knowledge and good work, shared purpose, sensual delight, and union with the creation—sum up for me what is vital in community. Here is the spring of hope I have been led to by my trail of bread. In our common life we may find the strength not merely to carry on in face of the world's bad news, but to resist cruelty and waste. I speak of it as common because it is ordinary, because we make it together, because it binds us through time to the rest of humanity and through our bodies to the rest of nature. By honoring this common life, nurturing it, carrying it steadily in mind, we might renew our households and neighborhoods and cities, and in doing so might redeem ourselves from the bleakness of private lives spent in frenzied pursuit of sensation and wealth.

Ever since the eclipse of our native cultures, the dominant American view has been more nearly the opposite: that we should cultivate the self rather than the community; that we should look to the individual as the source of hope and the center of value, while expecting hindrance and harm from society.

What other view could have emerged from our history? The first Europeans to reach America were daredevils and treasure seekers, as were most of those who mapped the interior. Many colonists were renegades of one stripe or another, some of them religious nonconformists, some political rebels, more than a few of them fugitives from the law. The trappers, hunters, traders, and freebooters who pushed the frontier westward seldom recognized any authority beyond the reach of their own hands. Coast to coast, our land has been settled and our cities have been filled by generations of immigrants more intent on leaving behind old tyrannies than on seeking new social bonds.

Our government was forged in rebellion against alien control. Our economy was founded on the sanctity of private property, and thus our corporations have taken on a sacred immunity through being defined under the law as persons. Our criminal justice system is so careful to protect the rights of individuals that it may require years to convict a bank robber who killed a bystander in front of a crowd, or a bank official who left a trail of embezzlement as wide as the Mississippi.

Our religion has been marked by an evangelical Protestantism that emphasizes personal salvation rather than social redemption. To "Get Right with God," as signs along the roads here in the Midwest gravely recommend, does not mean to reconcile your fellow citizens to the divine order, but to make a separate peace, to look after the eternal future of your own singular soul. True, we have a remarkable history of communal experiments, most of them religiously inspired—from Plymouth Colony, through the Shaker villages, Robert Owen's New Harmony, the settlements at Oneida, Amana, and countless other places, to the communes in our own day. But these are generally known to us, if they are known at all, as utopian failures.

For much of the present century, Americans have been fighting various forms of collectivism—senile empires during World War I, then Nazism, communism, and now fundamentalist theocracies—and these wars, the shouting kind as well as the shooting kind, have only strengthened our commitment to individualism. We have understood freedom for the most part negatively rather than positively, as release from constraints rather than as the condition for making a decent life in common. Hands off, we say; give me elbow room; good fences make good neighbors; my home is my castle; don't tread on me. I'm looking out for number one, we say; I'm doing my own thing. We have a Bill of Rights, which protects each of us from a bullying society, but no Bill of Responsibilities, which would oblige us to answer the needs of others.

Even where America's founding documents clearly address the public good, they have often been turned to private ends. Consider just one notorious example, the Second Amendment to the Constitution:

> *As well regulated Militia, being necessary to the security of a free State, the right of the people to keep and bear Arms, shall not be infringed.*

It would be difficult to say more plainly that arms are to be kept for the sake of a militia, and a militia is to be kept for defense of the country. In our day, a reasonable person might judge that the Pentagon deploys quite enough weapons, without requiring any supplement from household arsenals. Yet this lucid passage has been construed to justify a domestic arms race, until we now have in America more gun shops than gas stations, we have nearly as many handguns as hands, and we have concentrated enough firepower in the average city to carry on a war—which is roughly what, in some cities, is going on. Thus, by reading the Second Amendment through the lens of our obsessive individualism, we have turned a provision for public safety into a guarantee of public danger.

Observe how zealously we have carved up our cities and paved our land and polluted our air and burned up most of the earth's petroleum within a single generation—all for the sake of the automobile, a symbol of personal autonomy even more potent than the gun. There is a contemptuous ring to the word "mass" in mass transportation, as if the only alternative to private cars were cattle cars. Motorcycles and snowmobiles and three-wheelers fill our public lands with the din of engines and tear up the terrain, yet any effort to restrict their use is denounced as an infringement of individual rights. Millions of motorists exercise those rights by hurling the husks of their pleasures onto the roadside, boxes and bottles and bags. Ravines and ditches in my part of the country are crammed with rusty cars and refrigerators, burst couches and stricken TVs, which their former owners would not bother to haul to the dump. Meanwhile, advertisers sell us everything from jeeps to jeans as tokens of freedom, and we are so infatuated with the sovereign self that we fall for the spiel, as if by purchasing one of a million identical products we could distinguish ourselves from the herd.

The cult of the individual shows up everywhere in American lore, which celebrates drifters, rebels, and loners, while pitying or reviling the pillars of the community. The backwoods explorer like Daniel Boone, the riverboat rowdy like Mike Fink, the lumberjack, the prospector, the rambler and gambler, the daring crook like Jesse James and the resourceful killer like Billy the Kid, along with countless lonesome cowboys, all wander, unattached, through the great spaces of our imagination. When society begins to close in, making demands and asking questions, our heroes hit the road. Like Huckleberry Finn, they are forever lighting out for the Territory, where nobody will tell them what to do. Huck Finn ran away from what he called civilization in order to leave behind the wickedness of slavery, and who can blame him, but he was also running away from church and school and neighbors, from aunts who made him wash before meals, from girls who cramped his style, from chores, from gossip, from the whole nuisance of living alongside other people.

In our literature, when community enters at all, it is likely to appear as a conspiracy against the free soul of a hero or heroine. Recall how restless Natty Bumppo becomes whenever Cooper drags him in from the woods to a settlement. Remember how strenuously Emerson preaches against conforming to society and in favor of self-reliance, how earnestly Hawthorne warns us about the tyranny of those Puritan villages. Think of Thoreau running errands in Concord, rushing in the front door of a house and out the back, then home to his cabin in the woods, never pausing, lest he be caught in the snares of the town. Think of the revulsion Edna Pontellier feels toward the Creole society of New Orleans in Kate Chopin's *The Awakening*.

Think of Willa Cather's or Toni Morrison's or James Baldwin's high-spirited women and men who can only thrive by fleeing their home communities. Think of Spoon River, Winesburg, Gopher Prairie, Zenith, all those oppressive fictional places, the backward hamlets and stifling suburbs and heartless cities that are fit only for drones and drudges and mindless Babbitts.

In *The Invasion of the Body Snatchers*, a film from my childhood that still disturbs my dreams, an alien life form takes over one person after another in a small town, merging them into a single creature with a single will, until just one free-thinking individual remains, and even he is clearly doomed. Along with dozens of other invasion tales, the film was a warning against communism, I suppose, but it was also a caution against the perils of belonging, of losing your one sweet self in the group, and thus it projected a fear as old as America.

Of course you can find American books and films that speak as passionately for the virtues of our life together as for the virtues of our lives apart. To mention only a few novels from the past decade, I think of Gloria Naylor's *Mama Day*, Wendell Berry's *A Place on Earth*, Ursula Le Guin's *Always Coming Home*, and Ernest Gaines's *A Gathering of Old Men*. But they represent a minority opinion. The majority opinion fills bestseller lists and cinema screens and billboards with isolated, alienated, rebellious figures who are too potent or sensitive for membership in any group.

I have been shaped by this history, and I, too, am uneasy about groups, especially large ones, above all those that are glued together by hatred, those that use a color of skin or a cut of clothes for admission tickets, and those that wrap themselves in scriptures or flags. I have felt a chill from blundering into company where I was not wanted. I have known women and men who were scorned because they refused to fit the molds their neighbors had prepared for them. I have seen Klansmen parading in white hoods, their crosses burning on front lawns. I have seen a gang work its way through a subway car, picking on the old, the young, the weak. Through film I have watched the Nuremberg rallies, watched policemen bashing demonstrators in Chicago, missiles parading in Red Square, tanks crushing dissidents in Tiananmen Square. Like everyone born since World War II, I have grown up on television images of atrocities carried out, at home and abroad, with the blessing of governments or revolutionary armies or charismatic thugs.

In valuing community, therefore, I do not mean to approve of any and every association of people. Humans are drawn together by a variety of motives, some of them worthy, some of them ugly. Anyone who has spent recess on a school playground knows the terror of mob rule. Anyone who has lived through a war knows that mobs may pretend to speak for an entire nation. I recently saw, for the first time in a long while, a bumper sticker that recalled for me the angriest days of the Vietnam War: AMERICA—LOVE IT OR LEAVE IT. What loving America seemed to mean, for those who brandished that slogan back around 1970, was the approval of everything the government said or the army did in our name. "All those who seek to destroy the liberty of a democratic nation ought to know," Alexis de Tocqueville observed in *Democracy in America*, "that war is the surest and the shortest means to accomplish it." As a conscientious objector, with a sister who studied near my home in Ohio on a campus where National Guardsmen killed several protesters, I felt the force of despotism in that slogan.

Rather than give in to despotism, some of my friends went to jail and others into exile. My wife and I considered staying in England, where we had been studying for several years and where I had been offered a job. But instead we chose to come home, here to the Midwest where we had grown up, to work for change. In our idealism, we might have rephrased that bumper sticker to read: AMERICA—LOVE IT AND REDEEM IT. For us, loving America had little to do with politicians and even less with soldiers, but very much to do with what I have been calling the common life: useful work, ordinary sights, family, neighbors, ancestors, our fellow creatures, and the rivers and woods and fields that make up our mutual home.

During the more than twenty years since returning to America, I have had some of the idealism knocked out of me, but I still believe that loving your country or city or neighborhood may require you to resist, to call for change, to speak on behalf of what you believe in, especially if what you believe in has been neglected.

What we have too often neglected, in our revulsion against tyranny and our worship of the individual, is the common good. The results of that neglect are visible in the decay of our cities, the despoiling of our land, the fouling of our rivers and air, the haphazard commercial sprawl along our highways, the gluttonous feeding at the public trough, the mortgaging of our children's and grandchildren's future through our refusal to pay for current consumption. Only a people addicted to private pleasure would allow themselves to be defined as consumers—rather than conservers or restorers—of the earth's abundance.

In spite of the comforting assurances, from Adam Smith onward, that the unfettered pursuit of private wealth should result in unlimited public good, we all know that to be mostly a lie. If we needed reminders of how great that lie is, we could look at the savings and loan industry, where billions of dollars were stolen from small investors by rich managers who yearned to be richer; we could look at the Pentagon, where contracts are routinely encrusted with graft, or at Wall Street, where millionaires finagle to become billionaires through insider trading; we could look at our national forests, where logging companies buy timber for less than the cost to taxpayers of harvesting it; or we could look at our suburbs, where palaces multiply, while downtown more and more people are sleeping in cardboard boxes. Wealth does not precipitate like dew from the air; it comes out of the earth and from the labor of many hands. When a few hands hold onto great wealth, using it only for personal ease and display, that is a betrayal of the common life, the sole source of riches.

Fortunately, while our tradition is heavily tilted in favor of private life, we also inherit a tradition of caring for the community. Although Tocqueville found much to fear and quite a bit to despise in this raw democracy, he praised Americans for having "carried to the highest perfection the art of pursuing in common the object of their common desires." Writing of what he had seen in the 1830s, Tocqueville judged Americans to be avaricious, self-serving, and aggressive; but he was also amazed by our eagerness to form clubs, to raise barns or town halls, to join together in one cause or another: "in no country in the world, do the citizens make such exertions for the common weal. I know of no people who have established schools so numerous and efficacious, places of public worship better suited to the wants of the inhabitants, or roads kept in better repair."

Today we might revise his estimate of our schools or roads, but we can still see all around us the fruits of that concern for the common weal—the libraries, museums, courthouses, hospitals, orphanages, universities, parks, on and on. Born as most of us are into places where such amenities already exist, we may take them for granted; but they would not be there for us to use had our forebears not cooperated in building them. No matter where we live, our home places have also benefited from the Granges and unions, the volunteer fire brigades, the art guilds and garden clubs, the charities, food kitchens, homeless shelters, soccer and baseball teams, the Scouts and 4-H, the Girls and Boys Clubs, the Lions and Elks and Rotarians, the countless gatherings of people who saw a need and responded to it.

This history of local care hardly ever makes it into our literature, for it is less glamorous than rebellion, yet it is a crucial part of our heritage. Any of us could cite examples of people who dug in and joined with others to make our home places better places. Women and men who invest themselves in their communities, fighting for good schools or green spaces, paying attention to where they are, seem to me as worthy of celebration as those adventurous loners who keep drifting on, prospecting for pleasure.

A few days after our breadmaking, Eva and I went to a concert in Bloomington's newly opened arts center. The old limestone building had once been the town hall, then a fire station and jail, then for several years an abandoned shell. Volunteers bought the building from the city for a dollar, then renovated it with materials, labor, and money donated by local people. Now we have a handsome facility that is in constant use for pottery classes, theater productions, puppet shows, art exhibits, poetry readings, and every manner of musical event.

The music Eva and I heard was *Hymnody of Earth*, for hammer dulcimer, percussion, and children's choir. Composed by our next-door neighbor, Malcolm Dalglish, and featuring lyrics by our Ohio Valley neighbor, Wendell Berry, it was performed that night by Malcolm, percussionist Glen Velez, and the Bloomington Youth Chorus. As I sat there with Eva in a sellout crowd—about a third of whom I knew by name, another third by face—I listened to music that had been elaborated within earshot of my house, and I heard my friend play his instrument, and I watched those children's faces shining with the colors of the human spectrum, and I felt the restored building clasping us all like the cupped hands of our community. I knew once more that I was in the right place, a place created and filled and inspired by our lives together.

A woman who recently moved from Los Angeles to Bloomington told me that she would not be able to stay here long, because she was already beginning to recognize people in the grocery stores, on the sidewalks, in the library. Being surrounded by familiar faces made her nervous, after years in a city where she could range about anonymously. Every traveler knows the sense of liberation that comes from journeying to a place where nobody expects anything of you. Everyone who has gone to college knows the exhilaration of slipping away from the watchful eyes of Mom and Dad. We all need seasons of withdrawal from responsibility. But if we make a career of being unaccountable, we have lost something essential to our humanity, and we may well become a burden or a threat to those around us. A community can support a number of people who are just passing through, or who care about no one's needs but their own; the greater the proportion of such people, however, the more vulnerable the community, until eventually it breaks down. That is true on any scale, from a household to a planet.

The words *community, communion,* and *communicate* all derive from *common,* and the two syllables of *common* grow from separate roots, the first meaning "together" or "next to," the second having to do with barter or exchange. Embodied in that word is a sense of our shared life as one of giving and receiving—music, touch, ideas, recipes, stories, medicine, tools, the whole range of artifacts and talents. After twenty-five years with Ruth, that is how I have come to understand marriage, as a constant exchange of labor and love. We do not calculate who gives how much; if we had to, the marriage would be in trouble. Looking outward from this community of two, I see my life embedded in ever larger exchanges—those of family and friendship, neighborhood and city, countryside and country—and on every scale there is giving and receiving, calling and answering.

Many people shy away from community out of a fear that it may become suffocating, confining, even vicious; and of course it may, if it grows rigid or exclusive. A healthy community is dynamic, stirred up by the energies of those who already belong, open to new members and fresh influences, kept in motion by the constant bartering of gifts. It is fashionable just now to speak of this open quality as "tolerance," but that word sounds too grudging to me—as though, to avoid strife, we must grit our teeth and ignore whatever is strange to us. The community I desire is not grudging; it is exuberant, joyful, grounded in affection, pleasure, and mutual aid. Such a community arises not from duty or money but from the free interchange of people who share a place, share work and food, sorrows and hope. Taking part in the common life means dwelling in a web of relationships, the many threads tugging at you while also holding you upright.

I have told elsewhere the story of a man who lived in the Ohio township where I grew up, a builder who refused to join the volunteer fire department. Why should he join, when his house was brick, properly wired, fitted out with new appliances? Well, one day that house caught fire. The wife dialed the emergency number, the siren wailed, and pretty soon the volunteer firemen, my father among them, showed up with the pumper truck. But they held back on the hoses, asking the builder if he still saw no reason to join, and the builder said he could see a pretty good reason to join right there and then, and the volunteers let the water loose.

I have also told before the story of a family from that township whose house burned down. The fire had been started accidentally by the father, who came home drunk and fell asleep smoking on the couch. While the place was still ablaze, the man took off, abandoning his wife and several young children. The local people sheltered the family, then built them a new house. This was a poor township. But nobody thought to call in the government or apply to a foundation. These were neighbors in a fix, and so you helped them, just as you would harvest corn for an ailing farmer or pull a flailing child from the creek or put your arm around a weeping friend.

I am not harking back to some idyllic past, like the one embalmed in the *Saturday Evening Post* covers by Norman Rockwell or the prints of Currier and Ives. The past was never golden. As a people, we still need to unlearn some of the bad habits formed during the long period of settlement. One good habit we might reclaim, however, is that of looking after those who live nearby. For much of our history, neighbors have kept one another going, kept one another sane. Still today, in town and country, in apartment buildings and barrios, even in suburban estates, you are certain to lead a narrower life without the steady presence of neighbors. It is neither quaint nor sentimental to advocate neighborliness; it is far more sentimental to suggest that we can do without such mutual aid.

Even Emerson, preaching self-reliance, knew the necessity of neighbors. He lived in a village, gave and received help, and delivered his essays as lectures for fellow citizens whom he hoped to sway. He could have left his ideas in his journals, where they first took shape, but he knew those ideas would only have effect when they were shared. I like to think he would have agreed with the Lakota shaman, Black Elk, that "a man who has a vision is not able to use the power of it until after he has performed the vision on earth for the people to see." If you visit Emerson's house in Concord, you will find leather buckets hanging near the door, for he belonged to the village fire brigade, and even in the seclusion of his study, in the depths of thought, he kept his ears open for the alarm bell.

We should not have to wait until our houses are burning before we see the wisdom of facing our local needs by joining in common work. We should not have to wait until gunfire breaks out in our schools, rashes break out on our skin, dead fish float in our streams, or beggars sleep on our streets before we act on behalf of the community. On a crowded planet, we had better learn how to live well together, or we will live miserably apart.

In cultural politics these days there is much talk of diversity and difference. This is all to the good, insofar as it encourages us to welcome the many distinctive traditions and visions that have flowed into America from around the world. But if, while respecting how we differ, we do not also recognize how much we have in common, we will have climbed out of the melting pot into the fire. Every day's newspaper brings word of people suffering and dying in the name of one distinction or another. We have never been slow to notice differences—of accent, race, dress, habits. If we merely change how those differences are valued, celebrating what had formerly been despised or despising what had been celebrated, we continue to define ourselves and one another in the old divisive ways.

Ethnic labels are especially dangerous, for, while we pin them on as badges of pride, we may have difficulty taking them off when others decide to use them as targets. The larger the group identified by a label, the less likely it is to be a genuine community. Haste or laziness may lead us to speak of blacks and whites, of Christians and Muslims and Jews, of Armenians and Mexicans, yet the common life transcends such categories. Sharing a national anthem, a religion, or a skin color may be grounds for holding rallies or waging war, but community is more intimate than nationality, more subtle than race or creed, arising not from abstract qualities but from the daily give-and-take among particular people in a particular place.

It is also dangerous to separate a concern for human diversity from a concern for natural diversity. Since Europeans arrived in North America, we have been drawing recklessly on beaver and bison, trees and topsoil, petroleum, coal, iron and copper ore, clean air and water. Many of the achievements on which we pride ourselves are the result not of our supposed virtues but of this plundered bounty. We do not have another continent to use up; unless we learn to inhabit this one more conservingly, we will see our lives, as well as the land, swiftly degraded. There is no contradiction between caring for our fellow human beings and caring for the rest of nature; on the contrary, only by attending to the health of the land can we measure our true needs or secure a lasting home.

Just before Eva was to leave again for college, she and I went for a hike in a nature preserve along Clear Creek, near Bloomington, to look at the hepatica and bloodroot and listen to the spring-high water. At the edge of the preserve, a wooden sign declared that the riding of horses was prohibited. The trail had been freshly gouged by horseshoes and was eroding badly. Trash snagged in the roots of sycamores along the stream. Much of the soil and its cover of wildflowers had washed from the slopes where people scrambled up to picnic on the limestone bluff. Some of the cans they had left behind glinted among white stars of trillium.

I wondered what it would take to persuade the riders to get down off their horses and go on foot. What would it take to discourage people from dumping their worn-out washing machines in ditches? What would convince farmers to quit spraying poisons on their fields, suburbanites to quit spraying poisons on their lawns? What power in heaven or earth could stop loggers from seeing every tree as lumber, stop developers from seeing every acre of land as real estate, stop oil-company executives from seeing our last few scraps of wilderness as pay dirt waiting to be drilled? What would it take to persuade all of us to eat what we need, rather than what we can hold; to buy what we need, rather than what we can afford; to draw our pleasure from inexhaustible springs?

Signs will not work that change of mind, for in a battle of signs the billboards always win. Police cannot enforce it. Tongue lashings and sermons and earnest essays will not do it, nor will laws alone bring it about. The framers of the Constitution may have assumed that we did not need a Bill of Responsibilities because religion and reason and the benign impulses of our nature would lead us to care for one another and for our home. At the end of a bloody century, on the eve of a new millennium that threatens to be still bloodier, few of us now feel much confidence in those redeeming influences. Only a powerful ethic might restrain us, retrain us, restore us. Our survival is at stake, yet worrying about our survival alone is too selfish a motive to carry us as far as we need to go. Nothing short of reimagining where we are and what we are will be radical enough to transform how we live.

Aldo Leopold gave us the beginnings of this new ethic nearly half a century ago, in *A Sand Country Almanac*, where he described the land itself as a community made up of rock, water, soil, plants, and animals—including Homo sapiens, the only species clever enough to ignore, for a short while, the conditions of membership. "We abuse land because we see it as a commodity belonging to us," Leopold wrote. "When we see land as a community to which we belong, we may begin to use it with love and respect." To use our places with love and respect demands from us the same generosity and restraint that we show in our dealings with a wife or husband, a child or parent, a neighbor, a stranger in trouble.

Once again this spring, the seventy-seventh of her life, my mother put out lint from her clothes dryer for the birds to use in building their nests. "I know how hard it is to make a home from scratch," she says, "I've done it often enough myself." That is not anthropomorphism; it is fellow feeling, the root of all kindness.

Doctors the world over study the same physiology, for we are one species, woven together by strands of DNA that stretch back to the beginnings of life. There is, in fact, only one life, one pulse animating the dust. Sycamores and snakes, grasshoppers and grass, hawks and humans all spring from the same source and all return to it. We need to make of this common life not merely a metaphor, although we live by metaphors, and not merely a story, although we live by stories; we need to make the common life a fact of the heart. That awareness, that concern, that love needs to go as deep in us as the feeling we have when a child dashes into the street and we hear a squeal of brakes, or when a piece of our home ground goes under concrete, or when a cat purrs against our palms or rain sends shivers through our bones or a smile floats back to us from another face.

With our own population booming, with frogs singing in the April ponds, with mushrooms cracking the pavement, life may seem the most ordinary of forces, like hunger or gravity; it may seem cheap, since we see it wasted every day. But in truth life is expensive, life is extraordinary, having required five billion years of struggle and luck on one stony, watery planet to reach its present precarious state. And so far as we have been able to discover from peering out into the great black spaces, the life that is common to all creatures here on earth is exceedingly uncommon, perhaps unique, in the universe. How, grasping that, can we remain unchanged?

It may be that we will not change, that nothing can restrain us, that we are incapable of reimagining our relations to one another or our place in creation. So many alarm bells are ringing, we may be tempted to stuff our ears with cotton. Better that we should keep ears and eyes open, take courage as well as joy from our common life, and work for what we love. What I love is curled about a loaf of bread, a family, a musical neighbor, a building salvaged for art, a town of familiar faces, a creek and a limestone bluff and a sky full of birds. Those may seem like frail threads to hold anyone in place while history heaves us about, and yet, when they are braided together, I find them to be amazingly strong.

Questions for Reading and Analysis

1. How does Sanders support his claim that American history has traditionally favored the individual over the community?

2. "What we have too often neglected, in our revulsion against tyranny and our worship of the individual," says Sanders, "is the common good." In your own words, describe the kind of community Sanders has in mind.

3. How does Sanders expand his argument about human communities to environmental concerns? What connections does he draw between caring for fellow humans and caring for the land we live on?

4. Comment on the significance of Sanders's title. In what way does his essay explore the different meanings of "common"?

5. Sanders abandons the American doctrine of individualism in favor of the virtues of neighborliness and the "small" life. Do you agree with his argument that our redemption as a society lies in shifting our focus to the "common" rather than the extraordinary life?

Even though Dorothy Sayers is best known for her mystery novels featuring amateur detective Lord Peter Wimsey, she was a prolific and witty writer of essays; of her several essay collections, Unpopular Opinions *(1946) remains a classic. When she wrote "Living to Work" for a radio broadcast during World War II, the BBC suppressed it because her opinions on why people work seemed too political—and too radical to have come from a woman's pen.*

Living to Work

Dorothy L. Sayers

When I look at the world—not particularly at the world at war, but at our Western civilization generally—I find myself dividing people into two main groups according to the way they think about work. And I feel sure that the new world after the war will be satisfactory or not according to the view we are all prepared to take about the work of the world. So let us look for a moment at these two groups of people.

One group—probably the larger and certainly the more discontented—look upon work as a hateful necessity, whose only use is to make money for them, so that they can escape from work and do something else. They feel that only when the day's labor is over can they really begin to live and be themselves. The other group—smaller nowadays, but on the whole far happier—look on their work as an opportunity for enjoyment and self-fulfillment. They only want to make money so that they may be free to devote themselves more single-mindedly to their work. Their work and their life are one thing; if they were to be cut off from their work, they would feel that they were cut off from life. You will realize that we have here a really fundamental difference of outlook, which is bound to influence all schemes about work, leisure and wages.

Now the first group—that of the work-haters—is not made up solely of people doing very hard, uninteresting and ill-paid work. It includes a great many well-off people who do practically no work at all. The rich man who lives idly on his income, the man who gambles or speculates in the hope of getting money without working for it, the woman who marries for the mere sake of being comfortably established for life—all these people look on money in the same way: as something that saves them from the curse of work. Except that they have had better luck, their outlook is exactly the same as that of the sweated factory hand whose daily work is one long round of soul-and-body-destroying toil. For all of them, work is something hateful, only to be endured because it makes money; and money is desirable because it represents a way of escape from work. The only difference is that the rich have already made their escape, and the poor have not.

The second group is equally mixed. It includes the artists, scholars and scientists—the people really devoured with the passion for making and discovering things. It includes also the rapidly-diminishing band of old-fashioned craftsmen, taking a real pride and pleasure in turning out a good job of work. It includes also—and this is very important—those skilled mechanics and engineers who are genuinely in love with the complicated beauty of the machines they use and look after. Then there are those professional people in whom we recognize a clear, spiritual vocation—a call to what is sometimes very hard and exacting work—those doctors, nurses, priests, actors, teachers, whose work is something more to them than a mere means of livelihood; seamen who, for all they may grumble at the hardships of the sea, return to it again and again and are restless and unhappy on dry land; farmers and farm-workers who devotedly serve the land and the beasts they tend; airmen; explorers; and those comparatively rare women to whom the nurture of children is not merely a natural function but also a full-time and absorbing intellectual and emotional interest. A very mixed bag, you will notice, and not exclusively confined to the "possessing classics,"[1] or even to those who, individually or collectively, "own the means of production."

But we must also admit that, of late, the second group of workers has become more and more infected with the outlook of the first group. Agriculture—especially in those countries where farming is prosperous—has been directed, not to serving the land, but to bleeding it white in the interests of moneymaking. Certain members of the medical profession—as you may read in Dr. Cronin's book, *The Citadel*—are less interested in preserving their patients' health than in exploiting their weaknesses for profit. Some writers openly admit that their sole aim is the manufacture of best-sellers. And if we are inclined to exclaim indignantly that this kind of conduct is bad for the work, bad for the individual, and bad for the community, we must also confess that we ourselves—the ordinary public—have been only too ready to acquiesce in these commercial standards, not only in trade and manufacture, but in the professions and public services as well.

For us, a "successful" author is one whose sales run into millions; any other standard of criticism is dismissed as "highbrow." We judge the skill of a physician or surgeon, not by his hospital record, but by whether or not he has many wealthy patients and an address in Harley Street.[2] The announcement that a new film has cost many thousands of pounds to make convinces us that it must be a good film; though very often these excessive production costs are evidence of nothing more than graft, incompetence and bad organization in the studios. Also, it is useless to pretend that we do not admire and encourage the vices of the idle rich so long as our cinemas are crowded with young men and women gaping at film-stars in plutocratic surroundings and imbecile situations and wishing with all their hearts that they too could live like the heroes and heroines of these witless million-dollar screen stories. Just as it is idle to demand selfless devotion to duty in public servants, so long as we respect roguery in business, or so long as we say, with an admiring chuckle, about some fellow citizen who has pulled off some shady deal with our local borough authorities, that "Old So-and-so is hot stuff, and anybody would have to get up early to find any flies on *him*."

We have *all* become accustomed to rate the value of work by a purely money standard. The people who still cling to the old idea that work should be served and enjoyed for its own sake are diminishing and—what is worse—are being steadily pushed out of the control of public affairs and out of contact with the public. We find them odd and alien—and a subservient journalism (which we encourage by buying and reading it) persuades us to consider them absurd and contemptible. It is only in times of emergency and national disaster that we realize how much we depend upon the man who puts the integrity of his job before money, before success, before self—before all those standards by which we have come to assess the value of work.

Consequently, in planning out our post-war economic paradise, we are apt to concentrate exclusively on questions of hours, wages and conditions, and to neglect the really fundamental question whether, in fact, we want work to be something in which a man can enjoy the exercise of his full natural powers; or merely a disagreeable task, with its hours as short as possible and its returns as high as possible, so that the worker may be released as quickly as possible to enjoy his life in his leisure. Mind, I do not say for a moment that hours, wages and conditions ought not to be dealt with; but we shall deal with them along different lines, according as we believe it right and natural that men should work to live or live to work.

At this point, many of you will be thinking: "Before we can do anything about this, we must get rid of the capitalist system." But the much-abused "system" is precisely the system that arises when we think of work in terms of money-returns. The capitalist is faithfully carrying to its logical conclusion the opinion that work is an evil, that individual liberty means liberty to emancipate one's self from work, and that whatever pays best is right. And I see no chance of getting rid of "the system," or of the people who thrive on it, so long as in our hearts we accept the standards of that system, envy the very vices we condemn, build up with one hand what we pull down with the other, and treat with ridicule and neglect the people who acknowledge a less commercial—if you like, a more religious—conception of what work ought to be.

But now we are faced with a big difficulty. Suppose we decide that we want work to provide our natural fulfillment and satisfaction, how are we to manage this in an age of industrial machinery? You will have noticed that all the workers in my second group possess three privileges. (1) Their work provides opportunity for individual initiative. (2) It is of a kind that, however laborious it may be in detail, allows them to view with satisfaction the final results of their labor. (3) It is of a kind that fits in with the natural rhythm of the human mind and body, since it involves periods of swift, exacting energy, followed by periods of repose and recuperation, and does not bind the worker to the monotonous, relentless, deadly pace of an inhuman machine.

The factory hand has none of these advantages. He is not required to show initiative, but only to perform one unimaginative operation over and over again. He usually sees no step in the process of manufacture except that one operation, and so can take no interest in watching the thing he is making grow to its final perfection; often, indeed, it is some useless thing that only exists to create profits and wages, and which no worker could admire or desire for its own sake. Thirdly, it is the pace that kills—the subjection of the human frame to the unresting, unchanging, automatic movement of the machine. The other day, a journalist was talking to some miners. He says: "With one voice they told me that they think the machines are becoming monsters, draining their life-blood, and how they longed for the old days when they worked longer shifts, but with their hands, and the process of procuring the coal was less exhausting."

This last statement is very interesting, since it shows that the regulation of hours and wages cannot by itself do away with the difficulty about certain kinds of work. The economic solution will not solve this problem, because it is not really an economic problem at all, but a problem about human nature and the nature of work.

Some people are so greatly depressed by these considerations that they can see no way out of the difficulty except to do away with machines altogether, as things evil in themselves and destructive of all good living. But this is a counsel of despair. For one thing, it is not a practical proposition in the present state of things. Also, this suggestion takes no account of the real delight and satisfaction that the machines are capable of giving. It throws on the scrap-heap the skill and creative enthusiasm of the designer, the engineer's pride in his craft, the flying man's ecstasy in being air-borne, all the positive achievements of mechanical invention, and all those products—and they are many—which are actually *better* made by machinery than by hand. To renounce the machines means, at this time of day, to renounce the world and to retire to a kind of hermitage of the spirit. But society cannot be exclusively made of saints and solitaries; the average good citizen, like the average Christian, has to live *in* the world; his task is not to run away from the machines but to learn to use them so that they work in harmony with human nature instead of injuring or oppressing it.

Now, I will not attempt, in the last few minutes of a short broadcast, to produce a cut-and-dried scheme for taming machinery to the service of man. I will only say that I believe it can be done, and (since my opinion would not carry very much weight) that there are many people, with personal experience of factory conditions, who have already worked out practical proposals for doing it. But it can only be done if we ourselves—all of us—know what we want and are united in wanting the same thing; if we are all prepared to revise our ideas about what work ought to be, and about what we mean by "having a good time."

For there is one fact we must face. Victory is the only possible condition upon which we can look forward to a "good time" of any kind; but victory will not leave us in a position where we can just relax all effort and enjoy ourselves in leisure and prosperity. We shall be living in a confused, exhausted and impoverished world, and there will be a great deal of work to do. Our best chance of having a good time will be to arrange our ideas, and our society, in such a way that everybody will have an opportunity to work hard and find happiness in doing *well* the work that will so desperately need to be done.

Endnotes

1. "possessing classics": almost certainly a misprint for "possessing classes," a term imported from Marxist thought.
2. Harley Street: the traditional address of London's most prosperous physicians.

Questions for Reading and Analysis

1. What, according to Sayers, characterizes the two different attitudes toward work she describes in her essay?

2. In what way is the second group becoming "more and more infected with the first"? What is the cause of this development?

3. Sayer's essay was written over fifty years ago. Do you think the tendencies she describes hold true today?

Investigating English terms that refer to women, Muriel Schulz demonstrates how almost every term describing women has deteriorated into a pejorative term, often associated with prostitution. Words describing men, for the most part, have escaped such pejoration. The article was first published in 1975.

The Semantic Derogation
of Woman

Muriel R. Schulz

The question of whether or not language affects the thought and culture of the people who use it remains to be answered. Even if we were to agree that it does, we would have difficulty calculating the extent to which the language we use influences our society. There is no doubt, on the other hand, that a language reflects the thoughts, attitudes, and culture of the people who make it and use it. A rich vocabulary on a given subject reveals an area of concern of the society whose language is being studied. The choice between positive and negative terms for any given concept (as, for example, in the choice between *freedom fighter* and *terrorist*) reveals the presence or absence of prejudicial feelings toward the subject. The presence of taboo reveals underlying fears and superstitions of a society. The occurrence of euphemism *(passed away)* or dysphemism *(croaked)* reveals areas which the society finds distasteful or alarming. To this extent, at least, analysis of a language tells us a great deal about the interests, achievements, obsessions, hopes, fears, and prejudices of the people who created the language.

Who are the people who created English? Largely men—at least until the present generation. Stuart Flexner (1960: xii) points out that it is mostly males who create and use slang, and he explains why. A woman's life has been largely restricted to the home and family, while men have lived in a larger world, belonged to many sub-groups, and had acquaintances who belonged to many other sub-groups. That men are the primary creators and users of the English language generally follows from the primary role they have traditionally played in English-speaking cultures. They have created our art, literature, science, philosophy, and education, as well as the language which describes and manipulates these areas of culture.

An analysis of the language used by men to discuss and describe women reveals something about male attitudes, fears, and prejudices concerning the female sex. Again and again in the history of the language, one finds that a perfectly innocent term designating a girl or woman may begin with totally neutral or even positive connotations, but that gradually it acquires negative implications, at first perhaps only slightly disparaging, but after a period of time becoming abusive and ending as a sexual slur.

That disparagement gravitates more toward terms for women than for men is evident from some matched pairs designating males and females. Compare, for example, the connotations of *bachelor* with those of *spinster* or *old maid*. Or compare the innocuousness of *warlock* with the insinuations of *witch*. *Geezer* "an eccentric, queer old man"[1] and *codger* "a mildly derogatory, affectionate term for an old man" carry little of the opprobrium of such corresponding terms for old women as *trot, hen, heifer, war horse, crone, hag, beldam,* and *frump.* Furthermore, if terms designating men are used to denote a woman, there is usually no affront. On the other hand, use a term generally applied to women to designate a man, and you have probably delivered an insult. You may call a woman a *bachelor* without implying abuse, but if you call a man a *spinster* or an *old maid*, you are saying that he is "a prim, nervous person who frets over inconsequential details." If you speak of a woman as being a *warlock*, you may be corrected; if you say a man is a *witch*, he is presumed to have a vile temper. Or call a woman an *old man* and you have simply made an error of identification. Call a man an *old woman* or a *granny* and you have insulted him.

The term used to denote a semantic change whereby a word acquires debased or obscene reference is *pejoration*, and its opposite is *amelioration*. It is the purpose of this paper to study the pejoration of terms designating women in English and to trace the pattern whereby virtually every originally neutral word for women has at some point in its existence acquired debased connotations or obscene reference, or both.

The mildest form of debasement is a democratic leveling, whereby a word once reserved for persons in high places is generalized to refer to people in all levels of society. Even this mild form of derogation is more likely to occur with titles of women than with titles of men. *Lord*, for example, is still reserved as a title for deities and certain Englishmen, but any woman may call herself a *lady*. Only a few are entitled to be called *Baronet* and only a few wish to be called *Dame*, since as a general term, *dame* is opprobrious. Although *governor* degenerated briefly in nineteenth-century Cockney slang, the term still refers to men who "exercise a sovereign authority in a colony, territory, or state." A *governess*, on the other hand, is chiefly "a nursemaid," operating in a realm much diminished from that of Queen Elizabeth I, who was acknowledged to be "the supreme majesty and governess of all persons" *(OED)*. We might conceivably, and without affront, call the Queen's Equerry a *courtier*, but would we dare refer to her lady-in-waiting as a *courtesan*? *Sir*, and *Master* seem to have come down through time as titles of courtesy without taint. However, *Madam, Miss,* and *Mistress* have all derogated, becoming euphemisms respectively for "a mistress of a brothel," "a prostitute," and "a woman with whom a man habitually fornicates."

The latter titles illustrate the most frequent course followed by pejorated terms designating women. In their downhill slide, they slip past respectable women and settle upon prostitutes and mistresses. When *abbey, academy,* and *nunnery* became euphemisms for "brothel," *abbess* acquired the meaning "keeper of a brothel," *academician,* "a harlot," and *nun,* "a courtesan." (Here, at last, one male title also pejorated. *Abbot* at the same time, came to mean "the husband, or preferred male of a brothel keeper.") Although technically *queen* has withstood pejoration in English (*princess* has not), a thinly veiled homonym has existed side-by-side with it since Anglo-Saxon times. The *queen* is "the consort of the king" or "a female sovereign," whereas *quean* means "prostitute." Spelling has kept the two terms apart visually (both derived from the same Old English root, *cwen* "woman"), but as homonyms they have long provided writers with material for puns. Thus, in *Piers Plowman* (IX, 46) we are told that in the grave one cannot tell "a knight from a knave, or a quean from a queen," and Byron calls Catherine the Great "the Queen of queans" (*Don Juan*, Canto 6, stanza xcvi).

Female kinship terms have also been subject to a kind of derogation which leaves the corresponding male terms untouched. *Wife* was used as a euphemism for "a mistress" in the fifteenth century, as was *squaw*, in America during the Second World War. *Niece* has been used as a euphemism for "a priest's illegitimate daughter or concubine," and surely Humbert Humbert was not the first man to hide his mistress behind the locution, *daughter*. Browning uses *cousin* as an evasive term for Lucrezia's lover in "Andrea del Sarto" (1.200). As a term for a woman, it was cant for "a strumpet or trull" in the nineteenth century. And *aunt* was generalized first to mean "an old woman" and then "a bawd or a prostitute." It is the latter meaning which Shakespeare draws upon in the lines: "Summer songs for me and my aunts/As we lie tumbling in the hay" (*Winter's Tale*, IV, 3, 11-12). Even *mother* was used as a term for "a bawd" and *sister* as a term for "a disguised whore" in the seventeenth century.

Terms for domestics are also more subject to pejoration if they denote females. *Hussy* derives from Old English *huswif* "housewife" and at one time meant simply "the female head of the house." Its degeneration was gradual. It declined in reference to mean "a rustic, rude woman;" then it was used as an opprobrious epithet for women in general; and finally it referred to "a lewd, brazen woman or a prostitute." In their original employment, a *laundress* made beds, a *needlewoman* came in to sew, a *spinster* tended the spinning wheel, and a *nurse* cared for the sick. But all apparently acquired secondary duties in some households, because all became euphemisms for "a mistress" or "a prostitute" at some time during their existence.

One generally looks in vain for the operation of a similar pejoration of terms referring to men. *King, prince, father, brother, uncle, nephew, footman, yeoman,* or *squire,* for example, have failed to undergo the derogation found in the history of their corresponding feminine designations. Words indicating the station, relationship, or occupation of men have remained untainted over the years. Those identifying women have repeatedly suffered the indignity of degeneration, many of them becoming sexually abusive. It is clearly not the women themselves who have coined and used these terms as epithets for each other. One sees today that it is men who describe and discuss women in sexual terms and insult them with sexual slurs, and the wealth of derogatory terms for women reveals something of their hostility.

If the derogation of terms denoting women marks out an area of our culture found contemptible by men, the terms they use as endearments should tell us who or what they esteem. Strangely enough, in English the endearments men use for women have been just as susceptible to pejoration as have the terms identifying the supposedly beloved object itself.[2] *Dolly, Kitty, Biddy, Gill* (or *Jill*), and *Polly* all began as pet names derived from nicknames. All underwent derogation and eventually acquired the meaning of "a slattern," "a mistress," or "a prostitute." *Jug* and *Pug*, both originally terms of endearment, degenerated to apply contemptuously to "a mistress or a whore." *Mopsy*, a term of endearment still found in Beatrix Potter's *Peter Rabbit*, for centuries also meant "a slatternly, untidy woman." *Mouse* began as a playful endearment, but came to mean "a harlot, especially one arrested for brawling or assault." Even *sweetheart* meant "one loved illicitly" in the seventeenth century, although it has ameliorated since. Duncan MacDougald (1961: 594) describes the course all of these endearments seem to have followed:

> *"Tart," referring to a small pie or pastry, was first applied to a young woman as a term of endearment, next to young women who were sexually desirable, then to women who were careless in their morals, and finally—more recently—to women of the street.*

If endearments for young girls have undergone pejoration, so have terms denoting girls and young women. *Doll* "a small-scale figure of a human being" referred first to "a young woman with a pretty babyish face," then became an insulting epithet for women generally, and finally acquired the meaning of "a paramour." *Minx* originally meant "a pert, young girl," and this meaning exists today, despite its pejoration to "a lewd or wanton woman; a harlot." *Nymph* and *nymphet* both referred to beautiful young girls, or women. *Nymph* became a euphemism in such phrases as "nymph of the pave" and "nymph of darkness," while *nymphet* acquired the derogated meaning of "a sexually precocious girl; a loose young woman." *Peach* is an enduring metaphor for "a luscious, attractive girl or woman," but around 1900 it, too, degenerated to mean a "promiscuous woman." *Broad* was originally used with no offensive connotations for "a young woman or a girl" (Wentworth and Flexner 1960), but it acquired the suggestion of "a promiscuous woman" or "a prostitute." *Floozie*, first "an attractive but uncultivated girl," pejorated to mean "an undisciplined, promiscuous, flirtatious young woman; cynical, calculating." *Girl*, itself, has a long history of specialization and pejoration. It meant originally "a child of either sex"; then it was specialized to mean "a female child"; later it meant a serving girl or maidservant"; and eventually it acquired the meanings "a prostitute," "a mistress," or "the female sex—or that part of it given to unchastity." Today *girl* has ameliorated (but *girlie* has sexual undertones), and we can call a female child, a *sweetheart*, or even a woman a *girl* without insult (although the emcee who jollies along the middle-aged "girls" in the audience is plainly talking down to them).

That emcee has a problem, though. There just aren't many terms in English for middle-aged or older women,[3] and those which have occurred have inevitably taken on unpleasant connotations. Even a relatively innocuous term like *dowager* is stigmatized. *Beldam* is worse. Formed by combining the English usage of *dam* "mother" with *bel* indicating the relationship of a grandparent, it simply meant "grandmother" in its earliest usage. It was later generalized to refer to any "woman of advanced age," and, as so frequently happens with words indicating "old woman," it pejorated to signify "a loathsome old woman; a hag." *Hag*, itself, originally meant simply "a witch" and was later generalized as a derisive term for "an ugly old woman," often with the implication of viciousness or maliciousness. Julia

Stanley (1973) records it as a synonym for "a prostitute." *Bat* followed the opposite course. Originally a metaphor for "prostitute" (a "night bird"), it has become a generalized form of abuse meaning simply "an unpleasant woman, unattractive." It still bears the taint of its earlier metaphoric use, however, and is banned on TV as an epithet for a woman (Wentworth and Flexner 1960). *Bag* meant "a middle-aged or elderly slattern" or "a pregnant woman" before it came to mean "a slatternly prostitute" or "a part-time prostitute" in the late nineteenth century. In the US it has ameliorated slightly and refers (still derisively) to "an unattractive, ugly girl; an old shrew."

To be fat and sloppy is just as unforgivable in a woman as is being old, and the language has many terms designating such a person (are there any designating slovenly men?)—terms which have undergone pejoration and acquired sexual overtones at one time or another.[4] A *cow* "a clumsy, obese, coarse, or otherwise unpleasant person" became specialized to refer chiefly to women and then acquired the additional sense of "a degraded woman" and eventually "a prostitute." *Drab* (also occurring as *drap*) originally referred to "a dirty, untidy woman," but was further pejorated to refer to "a harlot or prostitute." Both *slut* and *slattern* were first used to designate "a person, especially a woman, who is negligent of his appearance. Both acquired the more derogatory meaning "a woman of loose character or a prostitute," and both are currently polysemantic, meaning concurrently "a sloppy woman" or "a prostitute." *Trollop*, another word for "an unkempt woman," extended to mean "a loose woman," and eventually "a hedge whore." *Mab*, first "a slattern" and then "a woman of loose character" seems to have withstood the third logical step of degeneration in England. In the US, however, it is used as an epithet for "a prostitute" as well.

Horse metaphors used to denote women have also undergone sexual derogation. *Harridan*, "a worn-out horse" seems to have originally been used as a metaphor for "a gaunt woman," then "a disagreeable old woman," and later "a decayed strumpet" or "a half-whore, half-bawd." A *jade* was originally "a broken-down, vicious or worthless horse," or else such a man, as is illustrated in the lines from *The Taming of the Shrew*: "Gremio: What! This gentleman will outtalk us all./ Lucentio: Sir. Give him head. I know he'll prove a jade" (1, 2, 249). It became a contemptuous epithet for women, however, and was eventually another synonym for "whore." A *hackney* (or *hack*) was first "a common riding horse, often available for hire." Its meaning was extended to encompass, with derogatory connotations, anyone who hires himself out (hence *hack writer*), but when used for women it acquired sexual overtones as a metaphor for "a woman who hires out as a prostitute" or for "a bawd." A *tit* referred either to "a small horse" or "a small girl," but degenerated to mean "a harlot." There is in all of these horse metaphors, perhaps, the sense of a woman as being a *mount*, a term used indifferently for "a wife" or "a mistress" in the nineteenth century.[5]

All these terms originated as positive designations for women and gradually degenerated to become negative in the milder instances and abusive in the extremes. A degeneration of endearments into insulting terms for men has not occurred. Words denoting boys and young men have failed to undergo the pejoration so common with terms for women. *Boy, youth, stripling, lad, fellow, puppy,* and *whelp*, for example, have been spared denigration. As for terms for slovenly, obese, or elderly men, the language has managed with very few of them. A similar sexual difference is evident in terms which originated as words denoting either sex. Often, when they began to undergo pejoration, they specialized to refer solely to women in derogatory terms. Later they frequently underwent further degeneration and became sexual terms of abuse. *Whore* is a well-known example of the process. Latin *carus* "dear" is a derivative of the same Indo-European root. It was probably at one time a polite term (Bloomfield 1933: 401). Originally it seems to have referred to "a lover of either sex," but eventually it specialized to refer solely to women. Later it degenerated to meaning "a prostitute," and it became a term occurring only in "coarse, abusive speech" *(OED)*. A *harlot* was originally "a fellow of either sex," referring more to men than women in Middle English and characterizing them as "riffraff." It degenerated further and Shakespeare's *harlot King (Winter's Tale* II, 3, 4) was characterized as "lewd." However, after Elizabethan times the word was specialized for women only, meaning first "a disreputable woman" and later, specifically, "a prostitute." *Bawd*, similarly, originally referred to a "go-between or panderer of either sex," but after 1700 it was used only for women, either as "a keeper of a brothel" or "a prostitute."

Wench, "a child of either sex," had sufficient prestige to appear in *Piers Plowman* in the phrase *Goddes Wench* "the Virgin Mary" (1. 336). Later it was specialized to refer to "a rustic or working woman." As do so many terms referring to rustics, male or female (compare *villain, boor, peasant, churl,* for example), the term degenerated. Then it acquired sexual undertones, coming to refer first to "a lewd woman" and finally to "a wanton." *Wench* has been rehabilitated and has lost its stigma. Today it can be used to refer to a woman without suggesting wantonness. Another term which specialized to refer to women, then degenerated to the point of abusiveness, and later ameliorated is *cat*. Originally it was a term of contempt for "any human being who scratches like a cat." Later it was specialized to refer to "a spiteful, backbiting woman" (a usage which survives). For a period it meant "a prostitute," but this sexual taint was lost in the nineteenth century, and only the less denigrating (but still pejorative) sense of "spiteful woman" remains.

A comparison of the metaphors *cat* and *dog* illustrates the difference evident in many terms designating male and female humans. The term for the female is more likely to become pejorative, more likely to acquire sexual suggestions, and less likely to be transferable to a male. *Cat* originally meant "any spiteful person," but specialized to refer only to women. It remains an abusive term for women. *Dog* is only "sometimes used contemptuously for males." More frequently it is used "in half-serious chiding" (Farmer and Henley 1965) as in *He's a sly dog,* or to mean "a gay, jovial, gallant fellow" *(OED)*, as in *Oh, you're a clever dog!* However, *dog* has recently been transferred to women, and it occurs in totally negative contexts, meaning either "a woman inferior in looks, character, or accomplishments" or "a prostitute." Or compare the use of *bitch*. It is an abusive term when applied to a woman, meaning either "a malicious, spiteful, domineering woman" or "a lewd or immoral woman." When applied to a man it is "less opprobrious and somewhat whimsical—like the modern use of *dog*" *(OED)*. *Pig*, applied contemptuously to men, means "a person who in some way behaves like a pig." When applied to a woman, it means "a woman who has sloppy morals." *Sow* is not transferable to men. It is an abusive metaphor for "a fat, slovenly woman," which in the US has acquired the additional sense of "a promiscuous young woman or a prostitute."

Robin Lakoff (1973) has pointed out that metaphors and labels are likely to have wide reference when applied to men, whereas metaphors for women are likely to be narrower and to include sexual reference. She uses as an example the term *professional*. If you say that a man is a *professional*, you suggest that he is a member of one of the respected professions. If you call a woman a *professional*, you imply that she follows "the oldest profession." In a similar way, if you call a man a *tramp* you simply communicate that he is "a drifter." Call a woman a *tramp* and you imply that she is "a prostitute." Historically, terms like *game, natural, jay, plover,* and *Jude* have meant merely "simpleton or dupe" when applied to men, but "loose woman or prostitute" when applied to women. A male *pirate* is "one who infringes on the rights of others or commits robbery on the high seas," whereas a female *pirate* is "an adultress who chases other women's men."[6]

What is the cause of the degeneration of terms designating women? Stephen Ullman (1967: 231–2) suggests three origins for pejoration: association with a contaminating concept euphemism, and prejudice. As for the first possibility, there is some evidence that contamination is a factor. Men tend to think of women in sexual terms whatever the context, and consequently any term denoting women carries sexual suggestiveness to the male speaker. The subtle operation of this kind of contamination is seen in the fortunes of such words as *female, lady,* and *woman*. *Woman* was avoided in the last century, probably as a Victorian sexual taboo, since it had acquired the meaning "paramour or mistress" or the sense of intercourse with women when used in plural, as in *Wine, Women, and Song*. It was replaced by *female*, but this term also came to be considered degrading and indelicate. Freyer (1963: 69) tells that "When the Vassar Female College was founded in 1861, Mrs Sarah Josepha Hale, editor of *Godey's Lady's Book,* spent six years in securing the removal of the offending adjective from the college sign." The *OED* recorded *female* as a synonym "avoided by writers," and the *Third* identifies it as a disparaging term when used for women. It was replaced in the nineteenth century by *lady*, which Mencken (1963: 350) called "the English euphemism-of-all-work." *Lady* also vulgarized, however, and by the time Mencken wrote, it was already being replaced by *woman*, newly rehabilitated. Even so neutral a term as *person*, when it was used as a substitute for *woman*, suffered contamination which Greenough and Kittredge found amusing (1901: 326):

> It has been *more or less employed as a substitute for* woman *by those who did not wish to countenance the vulgar abuse of* lady *and yet shrank from giving offense. The result has been to give a comically slighting connotation to one of the most innocent words imaginable.*

Despite this repeated contamination of terms designating women, we cannot accept the belief that there is a quality inherent in the concept of *woman* which taints any word associated with it. Indeed, the facts argue against this interpretation. Women are generally acknowledged to be—for whatever reasons—the more continent of the two sexes, the least promiscuous, and the more monogamous. Nevertheless, the largest category of words designating humans in sexual terms are those for women—especially for loose women. I have located roughly a thousand words and phrases describing women in sexually derogatory ways.[7] There is nothing approaching this multitude for describing men. Farmer and Henley (1965), for example, have over 500 terms (in English alone) which are synonyms for *prostitute*. They have only sixty-five synonyms for *whoremonger*.

As for the second possibility, one must acknowledge that many terms for "women of the night" have arisen from euphemism—a reluctance to name the profession outright. The majority of terms, however, are dysphemistic, not euphemistic. For example, the bulk of terms cited by Farmer and Henley (1965) as synonyms for prostitute are clearly derogatory: *broadtail, carrion, cleaver, cocktail, flagger, guttersnipe, mutton, moonlighter, omnibus, pinchprick, tail trader, tickletail, twofer,* and *underwear* are just a few.

The third possibility—prejudice—is the most likely source for pejorative terms for women. They illustrate what Gordon Allport calls (1954: 179) "the labels of primary potency" with which an in-group stereotypes an out-group. Certain symbols, identifying a member of an out-group, blind the prejudiced speaker to any qualities the minority person may have which contradict the stereotype.

> *Most people are unaware of this basic law of language—that every label applied to a given person refers properly only to one aspect of his nature. You may correctly say that a certain person is* human, *a* philanthropist, *a* Chinese, *a* physician, *an* athlete. *A given person may be all of these but the chances are that* Chinese *stands out in your mind as the symbol of primary potency. Yet neither this nor any other classificatory label can refer to the whole of a man's nature.*

Anti-feminism, he points out, contains the two basic ingredients of prejudice: denigration and gross overgeneralization (p. 34).

Derogatory terms for women illustrate both qualities which Allport attributes to prejudice. And what is the source or cause of the prejudice? Several writers have suggested that it is fear, based on a supposed threat to the power of the male. Fry (1972: 131) says of male humor: "In man's jokes about sex can be found an answer as to why man is willing to forego to a large extent the satisfactions of a reality and equality relationship with his fellow mortal, woman. Part of this answer has to do with the question of control or power." He theorizes that power becomes a question because the male is biologically inferior to the female in several respects. Girls mature earlier than boys physically, sexually, and intellectually. Boys are biologically frailer in their first years of life than girls. At the other end of their life span, they also prove to be weaker. More men have heart attacks, gout, lung cancer, diabetes, and other degenerative diseases than women. Finally, they deteriorate biologically and die earlier than women. Fry (1972: 133) continues: "The jokes men tell about the relationships between the sexes—especially the frankly sexual jokes—reveal awareness and concern, even anxiety, about the general presence of these biologic disadvantages and frailties."[8] Grotjahn (1972:53) concurs that anxiety prompts man's hostility, but he believes the source is fear of sexual inadequacy. A woman knows the truth about his potency; he cannot lie to her. Yet her own performance remains a secret, a mystery to him. Thus, man's fear of woman is basically sexual, which is perhaps the reason why so many of the derogatory terms for women take on sexual connotations.

I began with the acknowledgement that we cannot tell the extent to which any language influences the people who use it. This is certainly true for most of what we call *language*. However, words which are highly charged with emotion, taboo, or distaste do not only reflect the culture which uses them. They teach and perpetuate the attitudes which created them. To make the name of God taboo is to perpetuate the mystery, power, and awesomeness of the divine. To surround a concept with euphemisms, as Americans have done with the idea of death, is to render the reality of the concept virtually invisible. And to brand a class of persons as obscene is to taint them to the users of the language. As Mariana Birnbaum (1971: 248) points out, prejudicial language "always mirror[s] generalized tabloid thinking which contains prejudices and thus perpetuates discrimination." This circularity in itself is justification for bringing such linguistic denigration of women to a conscious level. The semantic change discussed here, by which terms designating women routinely undergo pejoration, both reflects and perpetuates derogatory attitudes towards women. They should be abjured.

Endnotes

1. Citations are based upon, but are not necessarily direct quotations from, the *Oxford English Dictionary*, cited henceforth as *(OED)*, *Webster's Third International (Third)*, the *Dictionary of American Slang* (Wentworth and Flexner 1960), *Slang and its Analogues* (Farmer and Henley 1965), *A Dictionary of Slang and Unconventional English* (Partridge 1961), and the *American Thesaurus of Slang* (Berrey and Van den Bark 1952). Sources are only indicated if the source is other than one of the above, or if the citation contains unusual information.

2. Endearments and terms for young women have undergone a similar pejoration in other languages, as well. Thass-Thienemann (1967: 336) cites *Metze* and *Dirne* from German, *fille* or *fille de joie* from French, *hêtaira* and *pallakis* or *pallakê* from Greek, and *puttana* from Italian as endearments which degenerated and became sexual slurs.

3. There are few terms for old people of either sex in English, "senior citizen" being our current favorite euphemism. However, the few terms available to denote old men (*elder, oldster, codger, geezer, duffer*) are, as was mentioned above, less vituperative than are those denoting women.

4. C. S. Lewis (1961), in discussing four-letter words, makes a point which is perhaps applicable to the tendency these words have to acquire sexual implications. He argues, with evidence from Sheffield and Montaigne, that four-letter words are not used in order to provoke desire. In fact, they have little to do with sexual arousal. They arc used rather to express force and vituperation.

5. Several bird names originating as metaphors for young girls have also become abusive epithets for them. *Columbine, quail, flapper, bird, chicken, hen,* and in the US *seagull* all began affectionately but acquired the meaning "a prostitute."

6. Several terms which originally applied to thieves, beggars, and their female accomplices have specialized and pejorated as terms for women: *Badger, doxy, moll* (from *Mary*), *mollisher,* and *bulker,* for example. *Blowse* reversed the process. Denoting first "a prostitute," and then "a beggar's trull," it finally ameliorated slightly to

mean "a slattern or a shrew." Other terms which originally designated either sex but came to refer only to women with the sense of "a prostitute" are *filth, morsel* (perhaps with the present sense of *piece*), *canary, rig*, and *rep*. The reverse has happened in a strange way with *fagot* (or *faggot*). It was first a term of abuse for women (sixteenth to nineteenth centuries) or a term for "a dummy soldier." Today it has transferred as an abusive term for "a male homosexual." Not all the terms specializing to women acquired sexual implications. *Potato* "ugly face," *prig, prude, termagant*, and *vixen* were all used in a general sense first and only later narrowed to refer specifically to women.

7. I have restricted myself in this paper to terms which have undergone the process of pejoration or amelioration—terms which have not always been abusive. The majority of derogatory words for women, of course, were coined as dysphemisms and are, hence, outside the scope of my study. In Farmer and Henley (1965), the chief entry containing synonyms for "prostitute" is *tart*, while for "whoremonger" it is *mutton-monger*. There are, in addition to the English synonyms, over 200 French phrases used to refer to women in a derogatory and sexual way, and another extended listing occurs under the entry *barrack-hack*. Stanley (1973) lists 200, and I found another 100, culled chiefly from Fryer (1963), Sagarin (1962), Berrey and Van den Bark (1952), Partridge (1961), and Wentworth and Flexner (1960).

8. Bettelheim and Janowitz (1950: 54–5) also cite anxiety as the source of prejudice. They argue that the prejudiced person "seeks relief through prejudice, which serves to reduce anxiety because prejudice facilitates the discharge of hostility, and if hostility is discharged anxiety is reduced. Prejudice reduces anxiety because it suggests to the person that he is better than others, hence does not need to feel so anxious."

References

Allport, Gordon W. (1954) *The Nature of Prejudice*, Cambridge, Mass.: Addison-Wesley.

Berrey Lester V. and Van den Bark, Melvin (1952) *The American Thesaurus of Slang*, New York: Thomas Y. Crowell.

Bettelheim, Bruno and Janowitz, Morris (1950) *Dynamics of Prejudice*, New York: Harper & Row.

Birnbaum, Mariana D. (1971) "On the language of prejudice," *Western Folklore* 30: 247–68.

Bloomfield, Leonard (1933) *Language*, New York: Henry Holt.

Farmer, J. S. and Henley, W. E. (1965) *Slang and its Analogues*, repr. of 7 vols. publ. 1890–1904, New York: Kraus Reprint Corp.

Flexner, Stuart, (1960) "Preface' to Harold Wentworth and Stuart Flexner (eds) *Dictionary of American Slang*, New York: Thomas Y. Crowell.

Fry, William P. (1972) "Psychodynamics of sexual humor: man's view of sex," *Medical Aspects of Human Sexuality* 6: 128–34.

Fryer, Peter (1963) *Mrs. Grundy: Studies in English Prudery*, London: Dennis Dobson.

Gove, Philip (ed.) (1971) *Webster's Third New International Dictionary*, Springfield, Mass.: G. & C. Merriam.

Greenough, James Bradstreet and Kittredge, George Lyman (1901) *Words and Their Ways in English Speech*, New York: Macmillan.

Grotjahn, Martin (1972) "Sexuality and humor. Don't laugh!," *Psychology Today* 6: 51–53.

Lakoff, Robin (1973) "Language and woman's place," *Language in Society* 2: 45–80.

Lewis, C. S . (1961) "Four-letter words," *Critical Quarterly* 3: 118–22.

MacDougald, Duncan, Jr (1961) "Language and sex," in Albert Ellis and Albert Abarbanel (eds) *The Encyclopedia of Sexual Behavior*, London: Hawthorne Books, vol. II.

Mencken, H. L. (1963) *The American Language. The Fourth Edition and the Two Supplements*, abridged and ed. by Raven I. McDavid, Jr, New York: Knopf.

Oxford English Dictionary (1933) Oxford: Clarendon Press.

Partridge, Eric (ed.) (1961) *A Dictionary of Slang and Unconventional English*, 5th ed., New York: Macmillan.

Sagarin, Edward (1962) *The Anatomy of Dirty Words*, New York: Lyle Stuart.

Stanley, Julia (1973) "The metaphors some people live by," unpublished mimeo.

Thass-Thienemann, Theodore (1967) *The Subconscious Language*, New York: Washington Square Press.

Ullman, Stephen (1967) *Semantics. An Introduction to the Science of Meaning*, New York: Barnes & Noble.

Wentworth, Harold and Flexner, Stuart Berg (eds) (1960) *Dictionary of American Slang*, New York: Thomas Y. Crowell.

Questions for Reading and Analysis

1. Schulz claims in the introduction to her essay that "language reflects the thoughts, attitudes, and culture of the people who make it and use it." What does she mean by this?

2. According to Schulz, what has happened to most terms referring to women in the history of the English language? List a couple of examples that you find particularly interesting.

3. What, for Schulz, is the most likely reason that there are so many derogatory words for women? What does this abundance say about men?

4. Advocates of political correctness have long tried to substitute "neutral" terms for words that have become tainted ("Italian American" for the derogatory "wop," for instance). Is this a good way to eliminate cultural, racial, and sexual prejudices?

*D*avid Sedaris's autobiographical 1994 essay "Diary of a Smoker"
is dedicated to his mother, Sharon, who died of lung cancer. Nevertheless, Sedaris rallies against any attempt by the public to curb the
right of smokers to light up.

Diary of a Smoker

David Sedaris

I rode my bike to the boat pond in Central Park, where I bought myself a cup of
coffee and sat down on a bench to read. I lit a cigarette and was enjoying myself
when the woman seated twelve feet away, on the other side of the bench, began
waving her hands before her face. I thought she was fighting off a bee.

She fussed at the air and called out, "Excuse me, do you mind if we make this
a no-smoking bench?"

I don't know where to begin with a statement like that. "Do you mind if *we*
make this a no-smoking bench?" There is no "we." Our votes automatically cancel
one another out. What she meant was, "Do you mind if *I* make this a no-smoking
bench?" I could understand it if we were in an elevator or locked together in the
trunk of a car, but this was outdoors. Who did she think she was? This woman was
wearing a pair of sandals, which are always a sure sign of trouble. They looked like
the sort of shoes Moses might have worn while he chiseled regulations onto stone
tablets. I looked at her sandals and at her rapidly moving arms and I crushed my
cigarette. I acted like it was no problem and then I stared at the pages of my book,
hating her and Moses—the two of them.

The trouble with aggressive nonsmokers is that they feel they are doing you a
favor by not allowing you to smoke. They seem to think that one day you'll look
back and thank them for those precious fifteen seconds they just added to your life.
What they don't understand is that those are just fifteen more seconds you can
spend hating their guts and plotting revenge.

My school insurance expires in a few weeks so I made an appointment for a
checkup. It's the only thing they'll pay for as all my other complaints have been dismissed as "Cosmetic."

If you want a kidney transplant it's covered but if you desperately need a hair
transplant it's "Cosmetic." You tell me.

I stood around the examining room for twenty minutes, afraid to poke around
as, every so often, a nurse or some confused patient would open the door and
wander into the room. And it's bad enough to be caught in your underpants but
even worse to be caught in your underpants scratching out a valium prescription
on someone else's pad.

When the doctor finally came he looked over my chart and said, "Hey, we have almost the exact same birthday. I'm one day younger than you!"

That did wonders for my morale. It never occurred to me that my doctor could be younger than me. Never entered my mind.

He started in by asking a few preliminary questions then said, "Do you smoke?"

"Only cigarettes and pot," I answered.

He gave me a look. "*Only* cigarettes and pot? Only?"

"Not crack," I said. "Never touch the stuff. Cigars either. Terrible habit, nasty."

I was at work, defrosting someone's freezer, when I heard the EPA's report on secondhand smoke. It was on the radio and they reported it over and over again. It struck me the same way that previous EPA reports must have struck auto manufacturers and the owners of chemical plants: as reactionary and unfair. The report accuses smokers, especially smoking parents, of criminal recklessness, as if these were people who kept loaded pistols lying on the coffee table, crowded alongside straight razors and mugs of benzene.

Over Christmas we looked through boxes of family pictures and played a game we call "Find Mom, find Mom's cigarettes." There's one in every picture. We've got photos of her pregnant, leaning toward a lit match, and others of her posing with her newborn babies, the smoke forming a halo above our heads. These pictures gave us a warm feeling.

She smoked in the bathtub, where we'd find her drowned butts lined up in a neat row beside the shampoo bottle. She smoked through meals, and often used her half-empty plate as an ashtray. Mom's theory was that if you cooked the meal and did the dishes, you were allowed to use your plate however you liked. It made sense to us.

Even after she was diagnosed with lung cancer she continued to smoke, although less often. On her final trip to the hospital, sick with pneumonia, she told my father she'd left something at home and had him turn the car around. And there, standing at the kitchen counter, she entertained what she knew to be her last cigarette. I hope that she enjoyed it.

It never occurred to any of us that Mom might quit smoking. Picturing her without a cigarette was like trying to imagine her on water skis. Each of us is left to choose our own quality of life and take pleasure where we find it, with the understanding that, like Mom used to say, "Sooner or later, something's going to get you."

Something got me the moment I returned home from work and Hugh delivered his interpretation of the EPA report. He told me that I am no longer allowed to smoke in any room that he currently occupies. Our apartment is small—four tiny rooms.

I told him that seeing as I pay half the rent, I should be allowed to smoke half the time we're in the same room. He agreed, on the condition that every time I light a cigarette, all the windows must be open.

It's cold outside.

Questions for Reading and Analysis

1. What is Sedaris's thesis? Does his evidence clearly support his thesis?

2. Does Sedaris violate the rules of rational discourse in some parts of his essay? Where?

3. Is Sedaris's story of his mother's lung cancer and her final statement ("Sooner or later, something's going to get you.") convincing evidence against limiting the rights of smokers?

4. Do you find the compromise Sedaris and his roommate reach at the end of the essay a good solution to the problem of smokers and nonsmokers living together? Why or why not?

Earl Shorris, a contributing editor of Harper's Magazine, *has authored books on a variety of subjects. The following essay describes a university-level course in humanities that he and other volunteers taught at a community center in a poor neighborhood in lower Manhattan. His hypothesis for the course was that a liberal education would improve the students' quality of life—and his experiment, he says, proved him right. Shorris's article followed one by Mark Edmundson (see page 74) in the September 1997 issue of* Harper's.

On the Uses of Liberal Education: As a Weapon in the Hands of the Restless Poor

Earl Shorris

Next month I will publish a book about poverty in America, but not the book I intended. The world took me by surprise—not once, but again and again. The poor themselves led me in directions I could not have imagined, especially the one that came out of a conversation in a maximum-security prison for women that is set, incongruously, in a lush Westchester suburb fifty miles north of New York City.

I had been working on the book for about three years when I went to the Bedford Hill Correctional Facility for the first time. The staff and inmates had developed a program to deal with family violence, and I wanted to see how their ideas fit with what I had learned about poverty.

Numerous forces—hunger, isolation, illness, landlords, police, abuse, neighbors, drugs, criminals, and racism, among many others—exert themselves on the poor at all times and enclose them, making up a "surround of force" from which, it seems, they cannot escape. I had come to understand that this was what kept the poor from being political and that the absence of politics in their lives was what kept them poor. I don't mean "political" in the sense of voting in an election but in the way Thucydides used the word: to mean activity with other people at every level, from the family to the neighborhood to the broader community to the city-state.

By the time I got to Bedford Hills, I had listened to more than six hundred people, some of them over the course of two or three years. Although my method is that of the *bricoleur,* the tinkerer who assembles a thesis of the bric-a-brac he finds in the world, I did not think there would be any more surprises. But I had not counted on what Viniece Walker was to say.

It is considered bad form in prison to speak of a person's crime, and I will follow that precise etiquette here. I can tell you that Viniece Walker came to Bedford Hills when she was twenty years old, a high school dropout who read at the level of a college sophomore, a graduate of crackhouses, the streets of Harlem, and a long alliance with a brutal man. On the surface Viniece has remained as tough as she was on the street. She speaks bluntly, and even though she is HIV positive and the virus has progressed during her time in prison, she still swaggers as she walks down the long prison corridors. While in prison, Niecie, as she is known to her friends, completed her high school requirements and began to pursue a college degree (psychology is the only major offered at Bedford Hills, but Niece also took a special interest in philosophy). She became a counselor to women with a history of family violence and a comforter to those with AIDS.

Only the deaths of other women cause her to stumble in the midst of her swaggering step, to spend days alone with the remorse that drives her to seek redemption. She goes through life as if she had been imagined by Dostoevsky, but even more complex than his fictions, alive, a person, a fair-skinned and freckled African-American woman, and in prison. It was she who responded to my sudden question, "Why do you think people are poor?"

We had never met before. The conversation around us focused on the abuse of women. Niecie's eyes were perfectly opaque—hostile, prison eyes. Her mouth was set in the beginning of a sneer.

"You got to begin with the children," she said, speaking rapidly, clipping out the street sounds as they came into her speech.

She paused long enough to let the change of direction take effect, then resumed the rapid, rhythmless speech. "You've got to teach the moral life of downtown to the children. And the way you do that, Earl, is by taking them downtown to plays, museums, concerts, lectures, where they can learn the moral life of downtown."

I smiled at her, misunderstanding, thinking I was indulging her. "And then they won't be poor anymore?"

She read every nuance of my response, and answered angrily, "And they won't be poor *no more*."

"What you mean is—"

"What I mean is what I said—a moral alternative to the street."

She didn't speak of jobs or money. In that, she was like the others I had listened to. No one had spoken of jobs or money. But how could the "moral life of downtown" lead anyone out from the surround of force? How could a museum push poverty away? Who can dress in statues or eat the past? And what of the political life? Had Niecie skipped a step or failed to take a step? The way out of poverty was politics, not the "moral life of downtown." But to enter the public world, to practice the political life, the poor had first to learn to reflect. That was what Niecie meant by the "moral life of downtown." She did not make the error of divorcing ethics from politics. Niecie had simply said, in a kind of shorthand, that no one could step out of the panicking circumstance of poverty directly into the public world.

Although she did not say so, I was sure that when she spoke of the "moral life of downtown" she meant something that had happened to her. With no job and no money, a prisoner, she had undergone a radical transformation. She had followed the same path that led to the invention of politics in ancient Greece. She had learned to reflect. In further conversation it became clear that when she spoke of "the moral life of downtown" she meant the humanities, the study of human constructs and concerns, which has been the source of reflection for the secular world since the Greeks first stepped back from nature to experience wonder at what they beheld. If the political life was the way out of poverty, the humanities provided an entrance to reflection and the political life. The poor did not need anyone to release them; an escape route existed. But to open this avenue to reflection and politics a major distinction between the preparation for the life of the rich and the life of the poor had to be eliminated.

Once Niecie had challenged me with her theory, the comforts of tinkering came to an end; I could no longer make an homage to the happenstance world and rest. To test Niecie's theory, students, faculty, and facilities were required. Quantitative measures would have to be developed; anecdotal information would also be useful. And the ethics of the experiment had to be considered: I resolved to do no harm. There was no need for the course to have a "sink or swim" character; it could aim to keep as many afloat as possible.

When the idea for an experimental course became clear in my mind, I discussed it with Dr. Jaime Inclán, director of the Roberto Clemente Family Guidance Center in lower Manhattan, a facility that provides counseling to poor people, mainly Latinos, in their own language and in their own community. Dr. Inclán offered the center's conference room for a classroom. We would put the three metal tables end to end to approximate the boat-shaped tables used in discussion sections at the University of Chicago of the Hutchins era,[1] which I used as a model for the course. A card table in the back of the room would hold a coffeemaker and a few cookies. The setting was not elegant, but it would do. And the front wall was covered by a floor-to-ceiling blackboard.

Now the course lacked only students and teachers. With no funds and a budget that grew every time a new idea for the course crossed my mind, I would have to ask the faculty to donate its time and effort. Moreover, when Hutchins said, "The best education for the best is the best education for us all," he meant it: he insisted that full professors teach discussion sections in the college. If the Clemente Course in the Humanities was to follow the same pattern, it would require a faculty with the knowledge and prestige that students might encounter in their first year at Harvard, Yale, Princeton, or Chicago.

I turned first to the novelist Charles Simons. He had been assistant editor of *The New York Times Book Review* and had taught at Columbia University. He volunteered to teach poetry, beginning with simple poems, Housman, and ending with Latin poetry. Grace Glueck, who writes art news and criticism for the *New York Times*, planned a course that began with cave paintings and ended in the late twentieth century. Timothy Koranda, who did his graduate work at MIT, had published journal articles on mathematical logic, but he had been away from his field for some years and looked forward to getting back to it. I planned to teach the American history course through documents, beginning with the Magna Carta, moving on to the second of Locke's *Two Treatises of Government*, the Declaration of Independence, and so on through the documents of the Civil War. I would also teach the political philosophy class.

Since I was a naïf in this endeavor, it did not immediately occur to me that recruiting students would present a problem. I didn't know how many I needed. All I had were criteria for selection:

Age: 18–35

Household income: Less than 150 percent of the Census Bureau's Official Poverty Threshold (though this was to change slightly).

Educational level: Ability to read a tabloid newspaper.

Educational goals: An expression of intent to complete the course.

Dr. Inclán arranged a meeting of community activists who could help recruit students. Lynette Lauretig of The Door, a program that provides medical and educational services to adolescents, and Angel Roman of the Grand Street Settlement, which offers work and training and GED programs, were both willing to give us access to prospective students. They also pointed out some practical considerations. The course had to provide bus and subway tokens, because fares ranged between three and six dollars per class per student, and the students could not afford sixty or even thirty dollars a month for transportation. We also had to offer dinner or a snack, because the classes were to be held from 6:00 to 7:30 P.M.

The first recruiting session came only a few days later. Nancy Mamis-King, associate executive director of the Neighborhood Youth & Family Services program in the South Bronx, had identified some Clemente Course candidates and had assembled about twenty of her clients and their supervisors in a circle of chairs in a conference room. Everyone in the room was black or Latino, with the exception of one social worker and me.

After I explained the idea of the course, the white social worker was the first to ask a question: "Are you going to teach African history?"

"No. We'll be teaching a section on American history, based on documents, as I said. We want to teach the ideas of history so that—"

"You have to teach African history."

"This is America, so we'll teach American history. If we were in Africa, I would teach African history, and if we were in China, I would teach Chinese history."

"You're indoctrinating people in Western culture."

I tried to get beyond her. "We'll study African art," I said, "as it affects art in America. We'll study American history and literature; you can't do that without studying African-American culture, because culturally all Americans are black as well as white, Native American, Asian, and so on." It was no use; not one of them applied for admission to the course.

A few days later Lynette Lauretig arranged a meeting with some of her staff at The Door. We disagreed about the course. They thought it should be taught at a much lower level. Although I could not change their views, they agreed to assemble a group of Door members who might be interested in the humanities.

On an early evening that same week, about twenty prospective students were scheduled to meet in a classroom at The Door. Most of them came late. Those who arrived first slumped in their chairs, staring at the floor or greeting me with sullen glances. A few ate candy or what appeared to be the remnants of a meal. The students were mostly black and Latino, one was Asian, and five were white; two of the whites were immigrants who had severe problems with English. When I introduced myself, several of the students would not shake my hand, two or three refused even to look at me, one girl giggled, and the last person to volunteer his name, a young man dressed in a Tommy Hilfiger sweatshirt and wearing a cap turned sideways, drawled, "Henry Jones, but they call me Sleepy, because I got these sleepy eyes—"

"In our class, we'll call you Mr. Jones."

He smiled and slid down in his chair so that his back was parallel to the floor.

Before I finished attempting to shake hands with the prospective students, a waiflike Asian girl with her mouth half-full of cake said, "Can we get on with it? I'm bored."

I liked the group immediately.

Having failed in the South Bronx, I resolved to approach these prospective students differently. "You've been cheated," I said. "Rich people learn the humanities; you didn't. The humanities are a foundation for getting along in the world, for thinking, for learning to reflect on the world instead of just reacting to whatever force is turned against you. I think the humanities are one of the ways to become political, and I don't mean political in the sense of voting in an election but in the broad sense." I told them Thucydides' definition of politics.

"Rich people know politics in that sense. They know how to negotiate instead of using force. They know how to use politics to get along, to get power. It doesn't mean that rich people are good and poor people are bad. It simply means that rich people know a more effective method for living in this society.

"Do all rich people, or people who are in the middle, know the humanities? Not a chance. But some do. And it helps. It helps to live better and enjoy life more. Will the humanities make you rich? Yes. Absolutely. But not in terms of money. In terms of life.

"Rich people learn the humanities in private schools and expensive universities. And that's one of the ways in which they learn the political life. I think that is the real difference between the haves and have-nots in this country. If you want real power, legitimate power, the kind that comes from the people and belongs to the people, you must understand politics. The humanities will help.

"Here's how it works: We'll pay your subway fare; take care of your children, if you have them; give you a snack or a sandwich; provide you with books and any other materials you need. But we'll make you think harder, use your mind more fully, than you ever have before. You'll have to read and think about the same kinds of ideas you would encounter in a first-year course at Harvard or Yale or Oxford.

"You'll have to come to class in the snow and rain and the cold and the dark. No one will coddle you, no one will slow down for you. There will be tests to take, papers to write. And I can't promise you anything but a certificate of completion at the end of the course. I'll be talking to colleges about giving credit for the course, but I can't promise anything. If you come to the Clemente Course, you must do it because you want to study the humanities, because you want a certain kind of life, a richness of mind and spirit. That's all I offer you: philosophy, poetry, art history, logic, rhetoric, and American history.

"Your teachers will all be people of accomplishment in their fields," I said, and I spoke a little about each teacher. "That's the course. October through May, with a two-week break at Christmas. It is generally accepted in America that the liberal arts and the humanities in particular belong to the elites. I think you're the elites."

The young Asian woman said, "What are you getting out of this?"

"This is a demonstration project. I'm writing a book. This will be proof, I hope, of my idea about the humanities. Whether it succeeds or fails will be up to the teachers and you."

All but one of the prospective students applied for admission to the course.

I repeated the new presentation at the Grand Street Settlement and at other places around the city. There were about fifty candidates for the thirty positions in the course. Personal interviews began in early September.

Meanwhile, almost all of my attempts to raise money had failed. Only the novelist Starling Lawrence, who is also editor in chief of W. W. Norton, which had contracted to publish the book; the publishing house itself; and a small, private family foundation supported the experiment. We were far short of our budgeted expenses, but my wife, Sylvia, and I agreed that the cost was still very low, and we decided to go ahead.

Of the fifty prospective students who showed up at the Clemente Center for personal interviews, a few were too rich (a postal supervisor's son, a fellow who claimed his father owned a factory in Nigeria that employed sixty people) and more than a few could not read. Two home-care workers from Local 1199 could not arrange their hours to enable them to take the course. Some of the applicants were too young: a thirteen-year-old and two who had just turned sixteen.

Lucia Medina, a woman with five children who told me that she often answered the door at the single-room occupancy hotel where she lived with a butcher knife in her hand, was the oldest person accepted into the course. Carmen Quiñones, a recovering addict who had spent time in prison, was the next eldest. Both were in their early thirties.

The interviews went on for days.

Abel Lomas[2] shared an apartment and worked part-time wrapping packages at Macy's. His father had abandoned the family when Abel was born. His mother was murdered by his stepfather when Abel was thirteen. With no one to turn to and no place to stay, he lived on the streets, first in Florida, then back in New York City. He used the tiny stipend from his mother's Social Security to keep himself alive.

After the recruiting session at The Door, I drove up Sixth Avenue from Canal Street with Abel, and we talked about ethics. He had a street tough's delivery, spitting out his ideas in crudely formed sentences of four, five, eight words, strings of blunt declarations, with never a dependent clause to qualify his thoughts. He did not clear his throat with badinage, as timidity teaches us to do, nor did he waste his breath with tact.

"What do you think about drugs?" he asked, the strangely breathless delivery further coarsened by his Dominican accent. "My cousin is a dealer."

"I've seen a lot of people hurt by drugs."

"Your family has nothing to eat. You sell drugs. What's worse? Let your family starve or sell drugs?"

"Starvation and drug addiction are both bad, aren't they?"

"Yes," he said, not "yeah" or "uh-huh" but a precise, almost formal "yes."

"So it's a question of the worse of two evils? How shall we decide?"

The question came up near Thirty-fourth Street, where Sixth Avenue remains hellishly traffic-jammed well into the night. Horns honked, people flooded into the street against the light. Buses and trucks and taxicabs threatened their way from one lane to the next where the overcrowded avenue crosses the equally crowded Broadway. As we passed Herald Square and made our way north again, I said, "There are a couple of ways to look at it. One comes from Immanuel Kant, who said that you should not do anything unless you want it to become a universal law; that is, unless you think it's what everybody should do. So Kant wouldn't agree to selling drugs *or* letting your family starve."

Again he answered with a formal "Yes."

"There's another way to look at it, which is to ask what is the greatest good for the greatest number: in this case, keeping your family from starvation or keeping tens, perhaps hundreds of people from losing their lives to drugs. So which is the greatest good for the greatest number?"

"That's what I think," he said.

"What?"

"You shouldn't sell drugs. You can always get food to eat. Welfare. Something."

"You're a Kantian."

"Yes."

"You know who Kant is?"

"I think so."

We arrived at Seventy-seventh Street, where he got out of the car to catch the subway before I turned east. As he opened the car door and the light came on, the almost military neatness of him struck me. He had the newly cropped hair of a cadet. His clothes were clean, without a wrinkle. He was an orphan, a street kid, an immaculate urchin. Within a few weeks he would be nineteen years old, the Social Security payments would end, and he would have to move into a shelter.

Some of those who came for interviews were too poor. I did not think that was possible when we began, and I would like not to believe it now, but it was true. There is a point at which level of forces that surround the poor can become insurmountable, when there is no time or energy left to be anything but poor. Most often I could not recruit such people for the course; when I did, they soon dropped out.

Over the days of interviewing, a class slowly assembled. I could not then imagine who would last the year and who would not. One young woman submitted a neatly typed essay that said, "I was homeless once, then I lived for some time in a shelter. Right now, I have got my own space granted by the Partnership for the Homeless. Right now, I am living alone, with very limited means. Financially I am overwhelmed by debts. I cannot afford all the food I need . . ."

A brother and sister, refugees from Tashkent, lived with their parents in the farthest reaches of Queens, far beyond the end of the subway line. They had no money, and they had been refused admission by every school to which they had applied. I had not intended to accept immigrants or people who had difficulty with the English language, but I took them into the class.

I also took four who had been in prison, three who were homeless, three who were pregnant, one who lived in a drugged dream-state in which she was abused, and one whom I had known for a long time and who was dying of AIDS. As I listened to them, I wondered how the course would affect them. They had no public life, no place; they lived within the surround of force, moving as fast as they could, driven by necessity, without a moment to reflect. Why should they care about fourteenth-century Italian painting or truth tables or the death of Socrates?

Between the end of recruiting and the orientation session that would open the course, I made a visit to Bedford Hills to talk with Niecie Walker. It was hot, and the drive up from the city had been unpleasant. I didn't yet know Niecie very well. She didn't trust me, and I didn't know what to make of her. While we talked, she held a huge white pill in her hand. "For AIDS," she said.

"Are you sick?"

"My T-cell count is down. But that's neither here nor there. Tell me about the course, Earl. What are you going to teach?"

"Moral philosophy."

"And what does that include?"

She had turned the visit into an interrogation. I didn't mind. At the end of the conversation I would be going out into "the free world"; if she wanted our meeting to be an interrogation, I was not about to argue. I said, "We'll begin with Plato: the *Apology*, a little of the *Crito*, a few pages of the *Phaedo* so that they'll know what happened to Socrates. Then we'll read Aristotle's *Nicomachean Ethics*. I also want them to read Thucydides, particularly Pericles' Funeral Oration in order to make the connection between ethics and politics, to lead them in the direction I hope the course will take them. Then we'll end with *Antigone*, but read as moral and political philosophy as well as drama."

"There's something missing," she said, leaning back in her chair taking on an air of superiority.

The drive had been long, the day was hot, the air in the room was dead and damp. "Oh, yeah," I said, "and what's that?"

"Plato's Allegory of the Cave. How can you teach philosophy to poor people without the Allegory of the Cave? The ghetto is the cave. Education is the light. Poor people can understand that."

At the beginning of the orientation at the Clemente Center a week later, each teacher spoke for a minute or two. Dr. Inclán and his research assistant, Patricia Vargas, administered the questionnaire he had devised to measure, as best he could, the role of force and the amount of reflection in the lives of the students. I explained that each class was going to be videotaped as another way of documenting the project. Then I gave out the first assignment: "In preparation for our next meeting, I would like you to read a brief selection from Plato's *Republic*: the Allegory of the Cave."

I tried to guess how many students would return for the first class. I hoped for twenty, expected fifteen, and feared ten. Sylvia, who had agreed to share the administrative tasks of the course, and I prepared coffee and cookies for twenty-five. We had a plastic container filled with subway tokens. Thanks to Starling Lawrence, we had thirty copies of Bernard Knox's *Norton Book of Classical Literature*, which contained all of the texts for the philosophy section except the *Republic* and the *Nicomachean Ethics*.

At six o'clock there were only ten students seated around the long table, but by six-fifteen the number had doubled, and a few minutes later two more straggled in out of the dusk. I had written a time line on the blackboard, showing them the temporal progress of thinking—from the role of myth in Neolithic societies to *The Gilgamesh Epic* and forward to the Old Testament, Confucius, the Greeks, the New Testament, the Koran, the *Epic of Son-Jara*, and ending with Nahuatl and Maya poems, which took us up to the contact between Europe and America, where the history course began. The time line served as context and geography as well as history: no race, no major culture was ignored. "Let's agree," I told them, "that we are all human, whatever our origins. And now let's go into Plato's cave."

I told them that there would be no lectures in the philosophy section of the course; we would use the Socratic method, which is called maieutic dialogue. "'Maieutic' comes from the Greek word for midwifery. I'll take the role of midwife in our dialogue. Now what do I mean by that? What does a midwife do?"

It was the beginning of a love affair, the first moment of their infatuation with Socrates. Later, Abel Lomas would characterize that moment in his no-nonsense fashion, saying that it was the first time anyone ever paid attention to their opinions.

Grace Glueck began the art history class in a darkened room lit with slides of Lascaux caves and next turned the students' attention to Egypt, arranging for them to visit the Metropolitan Museum of Art to see the Temple of Dendur and the Egyptian Galleries. They arrived at the museum on a Friday evening. Darlene Codd brought her two-year-old-son. Pearl Lau was late, as usual. One of the students, who had told me how much he was looking forward to the museum visit, didn't show up, which surprised me. Later I learned that he had been arrested for jumping a turnstile in a subway station on his way to the museum and was being held in a prison cell under the Brooklyn criminal courthouse. In the Temple of Dendur, Samantha Smoot asked questions of Felicia Blum, a museum lecturer. Samantha was the student who had burst out with the news, in one of the first sessions of the course, that people in her neighborhood believed it "wasn't no use goin' to school, because the white man wouldn't let you up no matter what." But in a hall where the statuary was of half-human, half-animal female figures, it was Samantha who asked what the glyphs meant, encouraging Felicia Blum to read them aloud, to translate them into English. Toward the end of evening, Grace led the students out of the halls of antiquities into the Rockefeller Wing, where she told them of the connections of culture and art in Mali, Benin, and the Pacific Islands. When the students had collected their coats and stood together near the entrance to the museum, preparing to leave, Samantha stood apart, a tall, slim young woman, dressed in a deerstalker cap and a dark blue peacoat. She made an exaggerated farewell wave at us and returned to Egypt—her ancient mirror.

Charles Simmons began the poetry class with poems as puzzles and laughs. His plan was to surprise the class, and he did. At first he read the poems aloud to them, interrupting himself with footnotes to bring them along. He showed them poems of love and of seduction, and satiric commentaries on those poems by later poets. "Let us read," the students demanded, but Charles refused. He tantalized them with the opportunity to read poems aloud. A tug-of-war began between him and the students, and the standoff was ended not by Charles directly but by Hector Anderson. When Charles asked if anyone in the class wrote poetry, Hector raised his hand.

401

"Can you recite one of your poems for us?" Charles said.

Until that moment, Hector had never volunteered a comment, though he had spoken well and intelligently when asked. He preferred to slouch in his chair, dressed in full camouflage gear, wearing a nylon stocking over his hair and eating slices of fresh cantaloupe or honeydew melon.

In response to Charles's question, Hector slid up to a sitting position. "If you turn that camera off," he said. "I don't want anybody using my lyrics." When he was sure the red light of the video camera was off, Hector stood and recited verse after verse of a poem that belonged somewhere in the triangle formed by Ginsberg's *Howl*, the Book of Lamentations, and hip-hop. When Charles and the students finished applauding, they asked Hector to say the poem again, and he did. Later Charles told me, "That kid is the real thing." Hector's discomfort with Sylvia and me turned to ease. He came to our house for a small Christmas party and at other times. We talked on the telephone about a scholarship program and about what steps he should take next in his education. I came to know his parents. As a student, he began quietly, almost secretly, to surpass many of his classmates.

Timothy Koranda was the most professorial of the professors. He arrived precisely on time, wearing a hat of many styles—part fedora, part Borsalino, part Stetson, and at least one-half World War I campaign hat. He taught logic during class hours, filling the blackboard from floor to ceiling, wall to wall, drawing the intersections of sets here and truth tables there and a great square of oppositions in the middle of it all. After class, he walked with students to the subway, chatting about Zen or logic or Heisenberg.

On one of the coldest nights of the winter, he introduced the students to logic problems stated in ordinary language that they could solve by reducing the phrases to symbols. He passed out copies of a problem, two pages long, then wrote out some of the key phrases on the blackboard. "Take this home with you," he said, "and at our next meeting we shall see who has solved it. I shall also attempt to find the answer."

By the time he finished writing out the key phrases, however, David Iskhakov raised his hand. Although they listened attentively, neither David nor his sister Susana spoke often in class. She was shy, and he was embarrassed at his inability to speak perfect English.

"May I go to blackboard?" David said. "And will see if I have found correct answer to zis problem."

Together Tim and David erased the blackboard, then David began covering it with signs and symbols. "If first man is earning this money, and second man is closer to this town . . .," he said, carefully laying out the conditions. After five minutes or so, he said, "And the answer is: B will get first to Cleveland!"

Samantha Smoot shouted, "That's not the answer. The mistake you made is in the first part there, where it says who earns more money."

Tim folded his arms across his chest, happy. "I shall let you all take the problem home," he said.

When Sylvia and I left the Clemente Center that night, a knot of students was gathered outside, huddled against the wind. Snow had begun to fall, a slippery powder on the gray ice that covered all but a narrow space down the center of the sidewalk. Samantha and David stood in the middle of the group, still arguing over the answer to the problem. I leaned in for a moment to catch the character of the argument. It was even more polite than it had been in the classroom, because now they governed themselves.

One Saturday morning in January, David Howell telephoned me at my home. "Mr. Shores," he said, Anglicizing my name, as many of the students did.

"Mr. Howell," I responded, recognizing his voice.

"How you doin', Mr. Shores?"

"I'm fine. How are you?"

"I had a little problem at work."

Uh-oh, I thought, bad news was coming. David is a big man, generally good-humored but with a quick temper. According to his mother, he had a history of violent behavior. In the classroom he had been one of the best students, a steady man, twenty-four years old, who always did the reading assignments and who often made interesting connections between the humanities and daily life. "What happened?"

"Mr. Shores, there's a woman at my job, she said some things to me and I said some things to her. And she told my supervisor I had said things to her, and he called me in about it. She's forty years old and she don't have no social life, and I have a good social life, and she's jealous of me."

"And then what happened?" The tone of his voice and the timing of the call did not portend good news.

"Mr. Shores, she made me so mad, I wanted to smack her up against the wall. I tried to talk to some friends to calm myself down a little, but nobody was around."

"And what did you do?" I asked, fearing this was his one telephone call from the city jail.

"Mr. Shores, I asked myself, 'What would Socrates do?'"

David Howell had reasoned that his co-worker's envy was not his problem after all, and he had dropped his rage.

One evening, in the American history section, I was telling the students about Gordon Wood's ideas in *The Radicalism of the American Revolution*. We were talking about the revolt by some intellectuals against classical learning at the turn of the eighteenth century, including Benjamin Franklin's late-life change of heart, when Henry Jones raised his hand.

"If the Founders loved the humanities so much, how come they treated the natives so badly?"

I didn't know how to answer this question. There were confounding explanations to offer about changing attitudes toward Native Americans, vaguely useful references to views of Rousseau and James Fenimore Cooper. For a moment I wondered if I should tell them about Heidegger's Nazi past. Then I saw Abel Lomas's raised hand at the far end of the table. "Mr. Lomas," I said.

Abel said, "That's what Aristotle means by incontinence, when you know what's morally right but you don't do it, because you're overcome by your passions."

The other students nodded. They were all inheritors of wounds caused by the incontinence of educated men; now they had an ally in Aristotle, who had given them a way to analyze the actions of their antagonists.

Those who appreciate ancient history understand the radical character of the humanities. They know that politics did not begin in a perfect world but in a society even more flawed than ours: one that embraced slavery, denied the rights of women, practiced a form of homosexuality that verged on pedophilia, and endured the intrigues and corruption of its leaders. The genius of that society originated in man's re-creation of himself through the recognition of his humanness as expressed in art, literature, rhetoric, philosophy, and the unique notion of freedom. At that moment, the isolation of the private life ended and politics began.

The winners in the game of modern society, and even those whose fortune falls in the middle, have other means to power: they are included at birth. They know this. And they know exactly what to do to protect their place in the economic and social hierarchy. As Allan Bloom, author of the nationally best-selling tract in defense of elitism, *The Closing of the American Mind*, put it, they direct the study of the humanities exclusively at those young people who "have been raised in comfort and with the expectation of ever increasing comfort."

In the last meeting before graduation, the Clemente students answered the same set of questions they'd answered at orientation. Between October and May, students had fallen to AIDS, pregnancy, job opportunities, pernicious anemia, clinical depression, a schizophrenic child, and other forces, but of the thirty students admitted to the course, sixteen had completed it, and fourteen had earned credit from Bard College. Dr. Inclán found that the students' self-esteem and their abilities to divine and solve problems had significantly increased; their use of verbal aggression as a tactic for resolving conflicts had significantly decreased. And they all had notably more appreciation for the concepts of benevolence, spirituality, universalism, and collectivism.

It cost about $2,000 for a student to attend the Clemente Course. Compared with unemployment, welfare, or prison, the humanities are a bargain. But coming into possession of the faculty of reflection and the skills of politics leads to a choice for the poor—and whatever they choose, they will be dangerous: they may use politics to get along in a society based on the game, to escape from the surround of force into a gentler life, to behave as citizens, and nothing more; or they may choose to oppose the game itself. No one can predict the effect of politics, although we all would like to think that wisdom goes our way. That is why the poor are so often mobilized and so rarely politicized. The possibility that they will adopt a moral view other than that of their mentors can never be discounted. And who wants to run that risk?

On the night of the first Clemente Course graduation, the students and their families filled the eighty-five chairs we crammed into the conference room where classes had been held. Robert Martin, associate dean of Bard College, read the graduates' names. David Dinkins, the former mayor of New York City, handed out the diplomas. There were speeches and presentations. The students gave me a plaque on which they had misspelled my name. I offered a few words about each student, congratulated them, and said finally, "This is what I wish for you: May you never be more active than when you are doing nothing . . ." I saw their smiles of recognition at the words of Cato, which I had written on the blackboard early in the course. They could recall again too the moment when we had come to the denouement of Aristotle's brilliantly constructed thriller, the *Nicomachean Ethics*— the idea that in the contemplative life man was most like God. One or two, perhaps more of the students, closed their eyes. In the momentary stillness of the room it was possible to think.

The Clemente Course in the Humanities ended a second year in June 1997. Twenty-eight new students had enrolled; fourteen graduated. Another version of the course will begin this fall in Yucatán, Mexico, using classical Maya literature in Maya.

On May 14, 1997, Viniece Walker came up for parole for the second time. She had served more than ten years of her sentence, and she had been the best of prisoners. In a version of the Clemente Course held at the prison, she had been my teaching assistant. After a brief hearing, her request for parole was denied. She will serve two more years before the parole board will reconsider her case.

A year after graduation, ten of the first sixteen Clemente Course graduates were attending four-year colleges or going to nursing school; four of them had received full scholarships to Bard College. The other graduates were attending community college or working full-time. Except for one: she had been fired from her job in a fast-food restaurant for trying to start a union.

Endnotes

1. Under the guidance of Robert Maynard Hutchins (1929–1951), the University of Chicago required year-long courses in the humanities, social sciences and natural sciences for the Bachelor of Arts degree. Hutchins developed the curriculum with the help of Mortimer Adler, among others; the Hutchins courses later influenced Adler's Great Books program.

2. Not his real name.

Questions for Reading and Analysis

1. How does Viniece Walker's remark inspire Shorris's educational experiment? What is the hypothesis he sets out to prove? What conclusions does he draw about his experiment? Does he think it was successful?

2. After failing in the South Bronx, Shorris gives a second speech to another group of prospective students. What does this speech reveal about his attitudes towards education?

3. What parallels does Viniece Walker draw between Shorris's course and Plato's "Allegory of the Cave"? Is there evidence that the education the students get is a way out of the "cave"?

4. In what way does the format Shorris chooses for his essay resemble a scientific experiment report? In what ways is it different? What effect does he achieve by organizing his essay the way he does?

In this short piece, Jane Slaughter muses about the immediate assumptions of friends and associates when someone has a black eye, reactions that are "an indication of just where relations between the sexes lie in 1987, twenty years after the second wave of feminism began."

A Beaut of a Shiner

Jane Slaughter

I have had a black eye for a week now; it's fading and I'm sorry to see it go. People are fascinated by shiners in a way other injuries can't match: Did you ever hear anyone call a broken arm or a bloody nose "a beaut"? Maybe it's got something to do with the pretty colors—mine started out with a pale green under the brow and dark purple for eyeliner and evolved into shades of lavender and magenta.

But that's not the main fascination. When a woman has a black eye, it is assumed that her husband or lover is responsible. I have two disinterested witnesses to the fact that I got mine by walking into a street sign at the corner of Michigan Avenue and Florida in southwest Detroit. So why are you all smirking and saying, "Oh, *sure*"? Okay, so my witnesses have left the country, and I neglected to get affidavits. I didn't know I was going to need them.

I'm reasonably confident that wife-beating is less common among the people I see regularly than it is in the general population. My friends of both sexes call themselves feminists; the women aren't financially dependent on their men. All of them think a poke in the eye is politically incorrect. And yet the most common reaction of my friends and co-workers to the state of my face is—no comment.

Someone you know walks in with a black eye and you don't say anything? If your male buddy shows up with a shiner, don't you ask what happened?

One girlfriend admitted, after I raised the subject, "I didn't want to say anything. I thought, 'Peter wouldn't hit her, would he?' But I didn't want to embarrass you so I kept my mouth shut." A male friend said, "I wanted to ask you, but there were too many people around." Another girlfriend said, "I figured if you wanted me to know how you got it, you'd tell me."

Offhand, I can think of three ways to acquire a black eye: a fight with a friend, a fight with a stranger, or an incident of klutz. Detroit is not a low-crime town, and I have been known to be a klutz, but all the kidding I got presumed the first option. "You can come up with a better story than *that*," was all I heard. And I hadn't even claimed to have bumped into a door.

A friend who works in an axle plant tells me that if I worked there, there's no way on earth I could convince my fellow workers that my old man hadn't knocked me around. The ragging would be nonstop, and its gist would be, "You must have really messed up this time." Nobody would be outraged. A shiner would be "kind of normal."

The universal assumption and my resulting defensiveness were so strong that sometimes I believed I really did have a guilty secret. (Notice that *I* would be the guilty one here.) When I repeated the tale of me and the street sign to those who did ask, I found it hard to make eye-contact; an embarrassed grin would steal across my face. If I elaborated, I felt like the lady who doth protest too much.

At the dentist and the oral surgeon, it was worse. The female assistants refrained from comment. And the surgeon, his eyes sliding away, reassured me, "I'm sure it wasn't your fault, whatever happened."

I believe the joking is our way of dealing with our culture's preoccupation with sex, violence, and the combination thereof. If you haven't been battered, you can make a joke of it and avoid admitting how nasty it is in real life.

Women explain innocent cuts and bruises with a catch-phrase: "My other lover's been beating me." Men and women both use language that disguises brutality and makes it sound almost playful. "Knock her around, give her a poke."

When I told one friend how people had been reacting to my black eye, she thought it was preposterous. "But you'd be the last person to let that happen to you," she said.

Well, thank you. But the unfunny truth is that it can happen to any woman once.

Meanwhile, my sweetheart says *his* feelings are hurt—that our friends would think for a moment that he hit me.

But he knew it would happen. His first thought, as I bounced off the street sign, was, "Now the rumors are going to fly." Just as my first words were, "Now your reputation is shot."

I'm convinced that people's reactions and assumptions are independent of the two individuals involved and are, instead, an indication of just where relations between the sexes lie in 1987, twenty years after the second wave of feminism began.

But I'm still defensive. Come to Detroit and I'll show you that bent street sign. I just hope Mayor Young hasn't gotten around to fixing it.

Questions for Reading and Analysis

1. How do the reactions (or non-reactions) to Slaughter's black eye make her feel?

2. Why, according to Slaughter, do people make jokes about women's bruises?

3. Do you agree with Slaughter's assertion that our universal response to a woman's black eye is the result of a lack of progress in the relations between the sexes?

A prolific author of fiction and non-fiction, Jane Smiley argues in this 1995 piece that mandatory chores do not teach children anything besides a negative attitude towards work.

The Case Against Chores

Jane Smiley

I've lived in the upper Midwest for twenty-one years now, and I'm here to tell you that the pressure to put your children to work is unrelenting. So far I've squirmed out from under it, and my daughters have led a life of almost tropical idleness, much to their benefit. My son, however, may not be so lucky. His father was himself raised in Iowa and put to work at an early age, and you never know when, in spite of all my husband's best intentions, that early training might kick in.

Although "chores" are so sacred in my neck of the woods that almost no one ever discusses their purpose, I have over the years gleaned some of the reasons parents give for assigning them. I'm not impressed. Mostly the reasons have to do with developing good work habits or, in the absence of good work habits, at least habits of working. No such thing as a free lunch, any job worth doing is worth doing right, work before play, all of that. According to this reasoning, the world is full of jobs that no one wants to do. If we divide them up and get them over with, then we can go on to pastimes we like. If we do them "right," then we won't have to do them again. Lots of times, though, in a family, that *we* doesn't operate. The operative word is *you*. The practical result of almost every child-labor scheme that I've witnessed is the child doing the dirty work and the parent getting the fun: Mom cooks and Sis does the dishes; the parents plan and plant the garden, the kids weed it. To me, what this teaches the child is the lesson of alienated labor: not to love the work but to get it over with; not to feel pride in one's contribution but to feel resentment at the waste of one's time.

Another goal of chores: the child contributes to the work of maintaining the family. According to this rationale, the child comes to understand what it takes to have a family, and to feel that he or she is an important, even indispensable member of it. But come on. Would you really want to feel loved primarily because you're the one who gets the floors mopped? Wouldn't you rather feel that your family's love simply exists all around you, no matter what your contribution? And don't the parents love their children anyway, whether the children vacuum or not? Why lie about it just to get the housework done? Let's be frank about the other half of the equation too. In this day and age, it doesn't take much work at all to manage a household, at least in the middle class—maybe four hours a week to clean the house and another four to throw the laundry into the washing machine, move it to the dryer, and fold it. Is it really a good idea to set the sort of example my former neighbors used to set, of mopping the floor every two days, cleaning the toilets every week, vacuuming every day, dusting, dusting, dusting? Didn't they have anything better to do than serve their house?

Let me confess that I wasn't expected to lift a finger when I was growing up. Even when my mother had a full-time job, she cleaned up after me, as did my grandmother. Later there was a housekeeper. I would leave my room in a mess when I headed off for school and find it miraculously neat when I returned. Once in a while I vacuumed, just because I liked the pattern the Hoover made on the carpet. I did learn to run water in my cereal bowl before setting it in the sink.

Where I discovered work was at the stable, and, in fact, there is no housework like horsework. You've got to clean the horses' stalls, feed them, groom them, tack them up, wrap their legs, exercise them, turn them out, and catch them. You've got to clip them and shave them. You have to sweep the aisle, clean your tack and your boots, carry bales of hay and buckets of water. Minimal horsekeeping, rising just to the level of humaneness, requires many more hours than making a few beds, and horsework turned out to be a good preparation for the real work of adulthood, which is rearing children. It was a good preparation not only because it was similar in many ways but also because my desire to do it, and to do a good job of it, grew out of my love of and interest in my horse. I can't say that cleaning out her bucket when she manured in it was an actual joy, but I knew she wasn't going to do it herself. I saw the purpose of my labor, and I wasn't alienated from it.

Probably to the surprise of some of those who knew me as a child, I have turned out to be gainfully employed. I remember when I was in seventh grade, one of my teachers said to me, strongly disapproving, "The trouble with you is you only do what you want to do!" That continues to be the trouble with me, except that over the years I have wanted to do more and more.

My husband worked hard as a child, out-Iowa-ing the Iowans, if such a thing is possible. His dad had him mixing cement with a stick when he was five, pushing wheelbarrows not long after. It's a long sad tale on the order of two miles to school and both ways uphill. The result is, he's a great worker, much better than I am, but all the while he's doing it he wishes he weren't. He thinks of it as work; he's torn between doing a good job and longing not to be doing it at all. Later, when he's out on the golf course, where he really wants to be, he feels a little guilty, knowing there's work that should have been done before he gave in and took advantage of the beautiful day.

Good work is not the work we assign children but the work they want to do, whether it's reading in bed (where would I be today if my parents had rousted me out and put me to scrubbing floors?) or cleaning their rooms or practicing the flute or making roasted potatoes with rosemary and Parmesan for the family dinner. It's good for a teenager to suddenly decide that the bathtub is so disgusting she'd better clean it herself. I admit that for the parent, this can involve years of waiting. But if she doesn't want to wait, she can always spend her time dusting.

Questions for Reading and Analysis

1. Why, according to popular opinion, are "chores" a good thing? Why, according to Smiley, are they not?

2. How does Smiley distinguish between (meaningful) "work" and "chores"?

3. How does Smiley use personal examples to illustrate her points? Does she convince her readers with this technique?

In "Black Men and Public Space," published in the New York Times in 1987, Brent Staples (b. 1951) describes a phenomenon encountered by many black men: the fear they inspire in others in public places. Recounting numerous tales of people avoiding him, of car doors being locked at his approach, of near arrests for merely entering office buildings, Staples testifies to the "alienation that comes of being ever the suspect." In his 1997 editorial "Turning People into Product," Staples points out the connection between the successful cloning of Dolly the sheep and the warnings issued by writers from Mary Shelley to Philip K. Dick against the manufacturing of "synthetic human life."

Black Men and Public Space

Brent Staples

My first victim was a woman—white, well dressed, probably in her early twenties. I came upon her late one evening on a deserted street in Hyde Park, a relatively affluent neighborhood in an otherwise mean, impoverished section of Chicago. As I swung onto the avenue behind her, there seemed to be a discreet, uninflammatory distance between us. Not so. She cast back a worried glance. To her, the youngish black man—a broad six feet two inches with a beard and billowing hair, both hands shoved into the pockets of a bulky military jacket—seemed menacingly close. After a few more quick glimpses, she picked up her pace and was soon running in earnest. Within seconds she disappeared into a cross street.

That was more than a decade ago. I was twenty-two years old, a graduate student newly arrived at the University of Chicago. It was in the echo of that terrified woman's footfalls that I first began to know the unwieldy inheritance I'd come into—the ability to alter public space in ugly ways. It was clear that she thought herself the quarry of a mugger, a rapist, or worse. Suffering a bout of insomnia, however, I was stalking sleep, not defenseless wayfarers. As a softy who is scarcely able to take a knife to a raw chicken—let alone hold it to a person's throat—I was surprised, embarrassed, and dismayed all at once. Her flight made me feel like an accomplice in tyranny. It also made it clear that I was indistinguishable from the muggers who occasionally seeped into the area from the surrounding ghetto. That first encounter, and those that followed, signified that a vast, unnerving gulf lay between nighttime pedestrians—particularly women—and me. And I soon gathered that being perceived as dangerous is a hazard in itself. I only needed to turn a corner into a dicey situation, or crowd some frightened, armed person in a foyer somewhere, or make an errant move after being pulled over by a policeman. Where fear and weapons meet—and they often do in urban America—there is always the possibility of death.

In that first year, my first away from my hometown, I was to become thoroughly familiar with the language of fear. At dark, shadowy intersections, I could cross in front of a car stopped at a traffic light and elicit the *thunk, thunk, thunk, thunk* of the driver—black, white, male, or female—hammering down the door locks. On less traveled streets after dark, I grew accustomed to but never comfortable with people who crossed to the other side of the street rather than pass me. Then there were the standard unpleasantries with policemen, doormen, bouncers, cabdrivers, and others whose business it is to screen out troublesome individuals *before* there is any nastiness.

I moved to New York nearly two years ago and I have remained an avid night walker. In central Manhattan, the near-constant crowd cover minimizes tense one-on-one street encounters. Elsewhere—visiting friends in SoHo, for example, where sidewalks are narrow and tightly spaced buildings shut out the sky—things can get very taut indeed.

After dark, on the warrenlike streets of Brooklyn where I live, I often see women who fear the worst from me. They seem to have set their faces on neutral, and with their purse straps strung across their chests bandolier-style, they forge ahead as though bracing themselves against being tackled. I understand, of course, that the danger they perceive is not a hallucination. Women are particularly vulnerable to street violence, and young black males are drastically overrepresented among the perpetrators of that violence. Yet these truths are no solace against the kind of alienation that comes of being ever the suspect, a fearsome entity with whom pedestrians avoid making eye contact.

It is not altogether clear to me how I reached the ripe old age of twenty-two without being conscious of the lethality nighttime pedestrians attributed to me. Perhaps it was because in Chester, Pennsylvania, the small, angry industrial town where I came of age in the 1960s, I was scarcely noticeable against a backdrop of gang warfare, street knifings, and murders. I grew up one of the good boys, had perhaps a half-dozen fistfights. In retrospect, my shyness of combat has clear sources.

As a boy, I saw countless tough guys locked away; I have since buried several, too. They were babies, really—a teenage cousin, a brother of twenty-two, a childhood friend in his mid-twenties—all gone down in episodes of bravado played out in the streets. I came to doubt the virtues of intimidation early on. I chose, perhaps unconsciously, to remain a shadow—timid, but a survivor.

The fearsomeness mistakenly attributed to me in public places often has a perilous flavor. The most frightening of these confusions occurred in the late 1970s and early 1980s, when I worked as a journalist in Chicago. One day, rushing into the office of a magazine I was writing for with a deadline story in hand, I was mistaken for a burglar. The office manager called security and, with an ad hoc[1] posse, pursued me through the labyrinthine halls, nearly to my editor's door. I had no way of proving who I was. I could only move briskly toward the company of someone who knew me.

Another time I was on assignment for a local paper and killing time before an interview. I entered a jewelry store on the city's affluent Near North Side. The proprietor excused herself and returned with an enormous red Doberman pinscher straining at the end of a leash. She stood, the dog extended toward me, silent to my questions, her eyes bulging nearly out of her head. I took a cursory look around, nodded, and bade her good night.

Relatively speaking, however, I never fared as badly as another black male journalist. He went to nearby Waukegan, Illinios, a couple of summers ago to work on a story about a murderer who was born there. Mistaking the reporter for the killer, police officers hauled him from his car at gunpoint and but for his press credentials would probably have tried to book him. Such episodes are not uncommon. Black men trade tales like this all the time.

Over the years, I learned to smother the rage I felt at so often being taken for a criminal. Not to do so would surely have led to madness. I now take precautions to make myself less threatening. I move about with care, particularly late in the evening. I give a wide berth to nervous people on subway platforms during the wee hours, particularly when I have exchanged business clothes for jeans. If I happen to be entering a building behind some people who appear skittish, I may walk by, letting them clear the lobby before I return, so as not to seem to be following them. I have been calm and extremely congenial on those rare occasions when I've been pulled over by the police.

And on late-evening constitutionals I employ what has proved to be an excellent tension-reducing measure: I whistle melodies from Beethoven and Vivaldi and the more popular classical composers. Even steely New Yorkers hunching toward nighttime destinations seem to relax, and occasionally they even join in the tune. Virtually everybody seems to sense that a mugger wouldn't be warbling bright, sunny selections from Vivaldi's *Four Seasons*.[2] It is my equivalent of the cowbell that hikers wear when they know they are in bear country.

Endnotes

1. For a particular purpose.
2. Work by composer Antonio Vivaldi (c. 1675–1741), celebrating the seasons.

Questions for Reading and Analysis

1. What is the effect of Staples's opening sentence? How might your response to it support Staples's thesis?

2. How effective are Staples's examples?

3. Staples acknowledges the reasons that he is able to "alter public space." Are they justified, in his view?

4. How does he solve the problem?

5. Consider the last line of the essay. How does Staples alter the relationship of victim and aggressor?

Turning People into Product

Brent Staples

The disclosure that scientists had cloned several sheep—including a handsome ewe named Dolly—surprised much of the world but not those who follow these things closely. Embryologists feigned surprise, but those who had already experimented with human embryos must surely have expected this. The science-fiction writers, meanwhile, took the news of the cloning completely in stride. They have long assumed that synthetic life would one day be common.

Where the scientists and futurists part company is on their reading of the consequences. The scientists see cloning as a beneficent tool to be used in fighting diseases, infertility and animal extinction. Writers like Ray Bradbury, Ursula K. Le Guin, William Gibson and the most visionary futurist of them all, Philip K. Dick, would probably disagree. When cloning and related technologies become commonplace, Mr. Dick writes, a moral and spiritual crisis is sure to follow.

The first stop in this story line is Mary Shelly's novel *Frankenstein*, published in 1818, which tells the now-familiar tale of the medical student who stitches together a body and brings it to life. Far from Hollywood's box-headed idiot, Mary Shelley's beast is bright, articulate and deeply anguished by his unnatural origin and appearance. Driven mad by grief and anger, he finally murders the good doctor himself.

No one explored the agonies of synthetic creatures more obsessively than Mr. Dick—the author, among 50 other books, of *Do Androids Dream of Electric Sheep?* from which came the cult film *Blade Runner*. The sheep in Mr. Dick's title sprang instantly to mind when Scottish embryologists trotted out the ewe they had created using DNA from an adult animal.

Mr. Dick envisioned a world where in vitro fertilization and cloning are old hat, and have long since given way to the wholesale manufacture of synthetic human life. Ethical considerations evaporate as corporations do a brisk business producing and selling concubines, performers and mercenaries. Like orphans who yearn to know their pasts, the synthetics suffer anguish, self-doubt and rage. *Blade Runner*'s action centers on a bounty hunter who makes a living killing escaped "replicants" but develops doubts once he falls in love with one. The point, of course, is that synthetic humans would be easy prey for humanity's worst instincts.

Cloning is still devilishly difficult—it took 300 tries to get Dolly—and a long way from mass production. But even in its infancy, reproductive science is already afflicted by the ugly forces that Mr. Dick forecasts in his novels—commercialism and even industrial espionage. The University of California is currently embroiled in a scandal in which a doctor is accused of implanting stolen embryos in infertile patients. The doctor is also accused of giving a fellow scientist stolen embryos.

The Federal Government, which could have controlled research through targeted funding, has steered clear of the field since the early 1970's, leaving researchers to grapple with the marketplace. For obvious reasons the market is intensely interested in the product, and Congressional attempts to tighten regulations will merely drive researchers further underground. Like Mary Shelley's young Frankenstein, scientists may already be working in secrecy, hot for the big score.

News of Dolly's arrival scared a lot of people. If the futurists are right, the widespread sense of dread will be justified.

Questions for Reading and Analysis

1. How does Staples connect the news of the successful cloning of Dolly the sheep and the works of writers like Mary Shelley and Philip K. Dick?

2. Staples uses two novels/movies to draw an analogy between the fears of futurists of the past and current developments in genetic engineering. Is this technique convincing? Why or why not?

3. Should we do everything possible to advance our knowledge of nature, without considering moral and ethical issues? Or do you think scientists should stop pursuing their inquiries once they get to a certain point? Where would that point be?

In the guise of a kindly social reformer, Jonathan Swift (1667–1734) proposes to solve the problem of poverty and oppression in Ireland by putting Irish children up for sale and subsequent consumption by their English landlords. Swift's biting irony hinges on the use of flawless reasoning to support an outrageous thesis, which has made A Modest Proposal a model for satirical writing since its first publication in 1729.

A Modest Proposal

For Preventing the Children of Poor People in Ireland from Being a Burden to Their Parents or Country, and for Making Them Beneficial to the Public

Jonathan Swift

It is a melancholy object to those who walk through this great town[1] or travel in the country, when they see the streets, the roads, and cabin doors, crowded with beggars of the female-sex, followed by three, four, or six children, all in rags and importuning every passenger for an alms. These mothers, instead of being able to work for their honest livelihood, are forced to employ all their time in strolling to beg sustenance for their helpless infants, who, as they grow up, either turn thieves for want of work, or leave their dear native country to fight for the Pretender in Spain, or sell themselves to the Barbadoes.[2]

I think it is agreed by all parties that this prodigious number of children in the arms, or on the backs, or at the heels of their mothers, and frequently of their fathers, is in the present deplorable state of the kingdom a very great additional grievance; and therefore whoever could find out a fair, cheap, and easy method of making these children sound, useful members of the commonwealth would deserve so well of the public as to have his statue set up for a preserver of the nation.

But my intention is very far from being confined to provide only for the children of professed beggars; it is of a much greater extent, and shall take in the whole number of infants at a certain age who are born of parents in effect as little able to support them as those who demand our charity in the streets.

As to my own part, having turned my thoughts for many years upon this important subject, and maturely weighed the several schemes of other projectors,[3] I have always found them grossly mistaken in their computation. It is true, a child just dropped from its dam may be supported by her milk for a solar year, with little other nourishment; at most not above the value of two shillings,[4] which the mother may certainly get, or the value in scraps, by her lawful occupation of begging; and it is exactly at one year old that I propose to provide for them in such a manner as instead of being a charge upon their parents or the parish, or wanting food and raiment for the rest of their lives, they shall on the contrary contribute to the feeding, and partly to the clothing, of many thousands.

There is likewise another great advantage in my scheme, that it will prevent those voluntary abortions, and that horrid practice of women murdering their bastard children, alas, too frequent among us, sacrificing the poor innocent babes, I doubt, more to avoid the expense than the shame, which would move tears and pity in the most savage and inhuman breast.

The number of souls in this kingdom being usually reckoned one million and a half, of these I calculate there may be about two hundred thousand couples whose wives are breeders; from which number I subtract thirty thousand couples who are able to maintain their own children, although I apprehend there cannot be so many under the present distresses of the kingdom; but this being granted, there will remain a hundred and seventy thousand breeders. I again subtract fifty thousand for those women who miscarry, or whose children die by accident or disease within the year. There only remain an hundred and twenty thousand children of poor parents annually born. The question therefore is, how this number shall be reared and provided for, which, as I have already said, under the present situation of affairs, is utterly impossible by all the methods hitherto proposed. For we can neither employ them in handicraft or agriculture; we neither build houses (I mean in the country) nor cultivate land. They can very seldom pick up a livelihood by stealing till they arrive at six years old, except where they are of towardly parts;[5] although I confess they learn the rudiments much earlier, during which time they can however be looked upon only as probationers, as I have been informed by a principal gentleman in the county of Cavan, who protested to me that he never knew above one or two instances under the age of six, even in a part of the kingdom so renowned for the quickest proficiency in that art.

I am assured by our merchants that a boy or a girl before twelve years old is no salable commodity; and even when they come to this age they will not yield above three pounds, or three pounds and half a crown[6] at most on the Exchange; which cannot turn to account either to the parents or the kingdom, the charge of nutriment and rags having been at least four times that value.

I shall now therefore humbly propose my own thoughts, which I hope will not be liable to the least objection.

I have been assured by a very knowing American of my acquaintance in London, that a young healthy child well nursed is at a year old a most delicious, nourishing, and wholesome food, whether stewed, roasted, baked, or boiled; and I make no doubt that it will equally serve in a fricassee or ragout.

I do therefore humbly offer it to public consideration that of the hundred and twenty thousand children, already computed, twenty thousand may be reserved for breed, whereof only one fourth part to be males, which is more than we allow to sheep, black cattle, or swine; and my reason is that these children are seldom fruits of marriage, a circumstance not much regarded by our savages, therefore one male will be sufficient to serve four females. That the remaining hundred thousand may at a year old be offered in sale to the persons of quality and fortune through the kingdom, always advising the mother to let them suck plentifully in the last month, so as to render them plump and fat for a good table. A child will make two dishes at an entertainment for friends; and when the family dines alone, the fore or hind quarter will make a reasonable dish, and seasoned with a little pepper or salt will be very good boiled on the fourth day, especially in winter.

I have reckoned upon a medium that a child just born will weigh twelve pounds, and in a solar year if tolerably nursed increaseth to twenty-eight pounds.

I grant this food will be somewhat dear, and therefore very proper for landlords, who, as they have already devoured most of the parents, seem to have the best title to the children.

Infant's flesh will be in season throughout the year, but more plentiful in March, and a little before and after. For we are told by a grave author, an eminent French physician,[7] that fish being a prolific diet, there are more children born in Roman Catholic countries about nine months after Lent than at any other season; therefore, reckoning a year after Lent, the markets will be more glutted than usual, because the number of popish infants is at least three to one in this kingdom; and therefore it will have one other collateral advantage, by lessening the number of Papists among us.[8]

I have already computed the charge of nursing a beggar's child (in which list I reckon all cottagers, laborers, and four fifths of the farmers) to be about two shillings per annum, rags included; and I believe no gentleman would repine to give ten shillings for the carcass of a good fat child, which, as I have said, will make four dishes of excellent nutritive meat, when he hath only some particular friend or his own family to dine with him. Thus the squire will learn to be a good landlord, and grow popular among the tenants; the mother will have eight shillings net profit, and be fit for work till she produces another child.

Those who are more thrifty (as I must confess the times require) may flay the carcass; the skin of which artificially[9] dressed will make admirable gloves for ladies, and summer boots for fine gentlemen.

As to our city of Dublin, shambles[10] may be appointed for this purpose in the most convenient parts of it, and butchers we may be assured will not be wanting; although I rather recommend buying the children alive, and dressing them hot from the knife as we do roasting pigs.

A very worthy person, a true lover of his country, and whose virtues I highly esteem, was lately pleased in discoursing on this matter to offer a refinement upon my scheme. He said that many gentlemen of this kingdom, having of late destroyed their deer, he conceived that the want of venison might be well supplied by the bodies of young lads and maidens, not exceeding fourteen years of age nor under twelve, so great a number of both sexes in every county being now ready to starve for want of work and service; and these to be disposed of by their parents, if alive, or otherwise by their nearest relations. But with due deference to so excellent a friend and so deserving a patriot, I cannot be altogether in his sentiments; for as to the males, my American acquaintance assured me from frequent experience that their flesh was generally tough and lean, like that of our schoolboys, by continual exercise, and their taste disagreeable; and to fatten them would not answer the charge. Then as to the females, it would, I think with humble submission, be a loss to the public, because they soon would become breeders themselves: and besides, it is not improbable that some scrupulous people might be apt to censure such a practice (although indeed very unjustly) as a little bordering upon cruelty; which, I confess, hath always been with me the strongest objection against any project, how well soever intended.

But in order to justify my friend, he confessed that this expedient was put into his head by the famous Psalmanazar, a native of the island Formosa,[11] who came from thence to London above twenty years ago, and in conversation told my friend that in his country when any young person happened to be put to death, the executioner sold the carcass to persons of quality as a prime dainty; and that in his time the body of a plump girl of fifteen, who was crucified for an attempt to poison the emperor, was sold to his Imperial Majesty's prime minister of state, and other great mandarins of the court, in joints from the gibbet, at four hundred crowns. Neither indeed can I deny that if the same use were made of several plump young girls in this town, who without one single groat[12] to their fortunes cannot stir abroad without a chair,[13] and appear at the playhouse and assemblies in foreign fineries which they never will pay for, the kingdom would not be the worse.

Some persons of a desponding spirit are in great concern about that vast number of poor people who are aged, diseased, or maimed, and I have been desired to employ my thoughts what course may be taken to ease the nation of so grievous an encumbrance. But I am not in the least pain upon that matter, because it is very well known that they are every day dying and rotting by cold and famine, and filth and vermin, as fast as can be reasonably expected. And as to the younger laborers, they are now in almost as hopeful a condition. They cannot get work, and consequently pine away for want of nourishment to a degree that if at any time they are accidentally hired to common labor, they have not strength to perform it; and thus the country and themselves are happily delivered from the evils to come.

I have too long digressed, and therefore shall return to my subject. I think the advantages by the proposal which I have made are obvious and many, as well as of the highest importance.

For first, as I have already observed, it would greatly lessen the number of Papists, with whom we are yearly overrun, being the principal breeders of the nation as well as our most dangerous enemies; and who stay at home on purpose to deliver the kingdom to the Pretender, hoping to take their advantage by the absence of so many good Protestants, who have chosen rather to leave their country than to stay at home and pay tithes against their conscience to an Episcopal curate.

Secondly, the poorer tenants will have something valuable of their own, which by law may be made liable to distress,[14] and help to pay their landlord's rent, their corn and cattle being already seized and money a thing unknown.

Thirdly, whereas the maintenance of an hundred thousand children, from two years old and upwards, cannot be computed at less than ten shillings a piece per annum, the nation's stock will be thereby increased fifty thousand pounds per annum, besides the profit of a new dish introduced to the tables of all gentlemen of fortune in the kingdom who have any refinement in taste. And the money will circulate among ourselves, the goods being entirely of our own growth and manufacture.

Fourthly, the constant breeders, besides the gain of eight shillings sterling per annum by the sale of their children, will be rid of the charge of maintaining them after the first year.

Fifthly, this food would likewise bring great custom to taverns, where the vintners will certainly be so prudent as to procure the best receipts for dressing it to perfection, and consequently have their houses frequented by all the fine gentlemen, who justly value themselves upon their knowledge in good eating; and a skillful cook, who understands how to oblige his guests, will contrive to make it as expensive as they please.

Sixthly, this would be a great inducement to marriage, which all wise nations have either encouraged by rewards or enforced by laws and penalties. It would increase the care and tenderness of mothers toward their children, when they were sure of a settlement for life to the poor babes, provided in some sort by the public, to their annual profit instead of expense. We should see an honest emulation among the married women, which of them could bring the fattest child to the market. Men would become as fond of their wives during the time of their pregnancy as they are now of their mares in foal, their cows in calf, or sows when they are ready to farrow; nor offer to beat or kick them (as is too frequent a practice) for fear of a miscarriage.

Many other advantages might be enumerated. For instance, the addition of some thousand carcasses in our exportation of barreled beef, the propagation of swine's flesh, and improvement in the art of making good bacon, so much wanted among us by the great destruction of pigs, too frequent at our tables, which are no way comparable in taste or magnificence to a well-grown, fat, yearling child, which roasted whole will make a considerable figure at a lord mayor's feast or any other public entertainment. But this and many others I omit, being studious of brevity.

Supposing that one thousand families in this city would be constant customers for infants' flesh, besides others who might have it at merry meetings, particularly weddings and christenings, I compute that Dublin would take off annually about twenty thousand carcasses, and the rest of the kingdom (where probably they will be sold somewhat cheaper) the remaining eighty thousand.

I can think of not one objection that will possibly be raised against this proposal, unless it should be urged that the number of people will be thereby much lessened in the kingdom. This I freely own, and it was indeed one principal design in offering it to the world. I desire the reader will observe, that I calculate my remedy for this one individual kingdom of Ireland and for no other that ever was, is, or I think ever can be upon earth. Therefore let no man talk to me of other expedients: of taxing our absentees at five shillings a pound: of using neither clothes nor household furniture except what is of our own growth and manufacture: of utterly rejecting the materials and instruments that promote foreign luxury: of curing the expensiveness of pride, vanity, idleness, and gaming in our women: of introducing a vein of parsimony, prudence, and temperance: of learning to love our country, in the want of which we differ even from Laplanders and the inhabitants of Topinamboo[15]: of quitting our animosities and factions, nor acting any longer like the Jews, who were murdering one another at the very moment their city was taken: of being a little cautious not to sell our country and conscience for nothing: of teaching landlords to have at least one degree of mercy toward their tenants: lastly, of putting a spirit of honesty, industry, and skill into our shop-keepers; who, if a resolution could now be taken to buy only our native goods, would immediately unite to cheat and exact upon us in the price, the measure, and the goodness, nor could ever yet be brought to make one fair proposal of just dealing, though often and earnestly invited to it.[16]

Therefore I repeat, let no man talk to me of these and the like expedients, till he hath at least some glimpse of hope that there will ever be some hearty and sincere attempt to put them in practice.

But as to myself, having been wearied out for many years with offering vain, idle, visionary thoughts, and at length utterly despairing of success, I fortunately fell upon this proposal, which, as it is wholly new, so it hath something solid and real, of no expense and little trouble, full in our own power, and whereby we can incur no danger in disobliging England. For this kind of commodity will not bear exportation, the flesh being of too tender a consistence to admit a long continuance in salt, although perhaps I could name a country[17] which would be glad to eat up our whole nation without it.

After all, I am not so violently bent upon my own opinion as to reject any offer proposed by wise men, which shall be found equally innocent, cheap, easy, and effectual. But before something of that kind shall be advanced in contradiction to my scheme, and offering a better, I desire the author or authors will be pleased maturely to consider two points. First, as things now stand, how they will be able to find food and raiment for an hundred thousand useless mouths and backs. And secondly, there being a round million of creatures in human figure throughout this kingdom, whose sole subsistence put into a common stock would leave them in debt two millions of pounds sterling, adding those who are beggars by profession to the bulk of farmers, cottagers, and laborers, with their wives and children who are beggars in effect; I desire those politicians who dislike my overture, and may perhaps be so bold to attempt an answer, that they will first ask the parents of these mortals whether they would not at this day think it a great happiness to have been sold for food at a year old in the manner I prescribe, and thereby have avoided such a perpetual scene of misfortunes as they have since gone through by the oppression of landlords, the impossibility of paying rent without money or trade, the want of common sustenance, with neither house nor clothes to cover them from the inclemencies of the weather, and the most inevitable prospect of entailing the like or greater miseries upon their breed forever.

I profess, in the sincerity of my heart, that I have not the least personal interest in endeavoring to promote this necessary work, having no other motive than the public good of my country, by advancing our trade, providing for infants, relieving the poor, and giving some pleasure to the rich. I have no children by which I can propose to get a single penny; the youngest being nine years old, and my wife past childbearing.

Endnotes

1. Dublin.
2. Many poor Irish sought to escape poverty by emigrating to the Barbadoes and other western English colonies, paying for transport by binding themselves to work

for a landowner there for a period of years. The Pretender, claimant to the English throne, was barred from succession after his father, King James II, was deposed in a Protestant revolution; thereafter, many Irish Catholics joined the Pretender in his exile in France and Spain, and in his unsuccessful attempts at counterrevolution.

3. People with projects; schemers.

4. A shilling used to be worth about twenty-five cents.

5. Promising abilities.

6. A pound was twenty shillings; a crown, five shillings.

7. The comic writer François Rabelais (1483–1553).

8. The speaker is addressing Protestant Anglo-Irish, who were the chief landowners and administrators, and his views of Catholicism in Ireland and abroad echo theirs.

9. Skillfully.

10. Slaughterhouses.

11. Actually a Frenchman, George Psalmanazar had passed himself off as from Formosa (now Taiwan) and had written a fictitious book about his "homeland," with descriptions of human sacrifice and cannibalism.

12. An English coin worth about four pennies.

13. A sedan chair.

14. Seizure for the payment of debts.

15. A district in Brazil.

16. Swift himself had made these proposals seriously in various previous works.

17. England.

Questions for Reading and Analysis

1. Satirical essays—essays that often argue the opposite of what an author believes—are often written by a "persona," a mask or character the author assumes to write the piece. Describe the persona the author has adopted for this essay.

2. How do you know Swift is not serious about his proposal? How does Swift signal to his readers that he does not share his persona's views?

3. What actual social circumstances does Swift touch upon in his essay? Where do you find social criticism in the mask of satire?

Originally published in the Washington Post *in 1990, Tannen's piece on the different ways in which men and women approach and understand communication has become a contemporary classic. A sociolinguist, Tannen bridges the gap between scholarship and popular reading in her books on gender and communication.*

Sex, Lies, and Conversation

Deborah Tannen

I was addressing a small gathering in a suburban Virginia living room—a women's group that had invited men to join them. Throughout the evening, one man had been particularly talkative, frequently offering ideas and anecdotes, while his wife sat silently beside him on the couch. Toward the end of the evening, I commented that women frequently complain that their husbands don't talk to them. This man quickly concurred. He gestured toward his wife and said, "She's the talker in our family." The room burst into laughter; the man looked puzzled and hurt. "It's true," he explained. "When I come home from work I have nothing to say. If she didn't keep the conversation going, we'd spend the whole evening in silence."

This episode crystallizes the irony that although American men tend to talk more than women in public situations, they often talk less at home. And this pattern is wreaking havoc with marriage.

The pattern was observed by political scientist Andrew Hacker in the late '70s. Sociologist Catherine Kohler Riessman reports in her new book *Divorce Talk* that most of the women she interviewed—but only a few of the men—gave lack of communication as the reason for their divorces. Given the current divorce rate of nearly 50 percent, that amounts to millions of cases in the United States every year—a virtual epidemic of failed conversation.

In my own research, complaints from women about their husbands most often focused not on tangible inequities such as having given up the chance for a career to accompany a husband to his, or doing far more than their share of daily life-support work like cleaning, cooking, social arrangements and errands. Instead, they focused on communication: "He doesn't listen to me," "He doesn't talk to me." I found, as Hacker observed years before, that most wives want their husbands to be, first and foremost, conversational partners, but few husbands share this expectation of their wives.

In short, the image that best represents the current crisis is the stereotypical cartoon scene of a man sitting at the breakfast table with a newspaper held up in front of his face, while a woman glares at the back of it, wanting to talk.

Linguistic Battle of the Sexes

How can women and men have such different impressions of communication in marriage? Why the widespread imbalance in their interests and expectations?

In the April [1990] issue of *American Psychologist*, Stanford University's Eleanor Maccoby reports the results of her own and others' research showing that children's development is most influenced by the social structure of peer interactions. Boys and girls tend to play with children of their own gender, and their sex-separate groups have different organizational structures and interactive norms.

I believe these systematic differences in childhood socialization make talk between women and men like cross-cultural communication, heir to all the attraction and pitfalls of that enticing but difficult enterprise. My research on men's and women's conversations uncovered patterns similar to those described for children's groups.

For women, as for girls, intimacy is the fabric of relationships, and talk is the thread from which it is woven. Little girls create and maintain friendships by exchanging secrets; similarly, women regard conversation as the cornerstone of friendship. So a woman expects her husband to be a new and improved version of a best friend. What is important is not the individual subjects that are discussed but the sense of closeness, of a life shared, that emerges when people tell their thoughts, feelings, and impressions.

Bonds between boys can be as intense as girls', but they are based less on talking, more on doing things together. Since they don't assume talk is the cement that binds a relationship, men don't know what kind of talk women want, and they don't miss it when it isn't there.

Boys' groups are larger, more inclusive, and more hierarchical, so boys must struggle to avoid the subordinate position in the group. This may play a role in women's complaints that men don't listen to them. Some men really don't like to listen, because being the listener makes them feel one-down, like a child listening to adults or an employee to a boss.

But often when women tell men, "You aren't listening," and the men protest, "I am," the men are right. The impression of not listening results from misalignments in the mechanics of conversation. The misalignment begins as soon as a man and a woman take physical positions. This became clear when I studied videotapes made by psychologist Bruce Dorval of children and adults talking to their same-sex best friends. I found that at every age, the girls and women faced each other directly, their eyes anchored on each other's faces. At every age, the boys and men sat at angles to each other and looked elsewhere in the room, periodically glancing at each other. They were obviously attuned to each other, often mirroring each other's movements. But the tendency of men to face away can give women the impression they aren't listening even when they are. A young woman in college was frustrated: Whenever she told her boyfriend she wanted to talk to him, he would lie down on the floor, close his eyes, and put his arm over his face. This signaled to her, "He's taking a nap." But he insisted he was listening extra hard. Normally, he looks around the room, so he is easily distracted. Lying down and covering his eyes helped him concentrate on what she was saying.

Analogous to the physical alignment that women and men take in conversation is their topical alignment. The girls in my study tended to talk at length about one topic, but the boys tended to jump from topic to topic. The second-grade girls exchanged stories about people they knew. The second-grade boys teased, told jokes, noticed things in the room and talked about finding games to play. The sixth-grade girls talked about problems with a mutual friend. The sixth grade boys talked about fifty-five different topics, none of which extended over more than a few turns.

Listening to Body Language

Switching topics is another habit that gives women the impression men aren't listening, especially if they switch to a topic about themselves. But the evidence of the tenth-grade boys in my study indicates otherwise. The tenth-grade boys sprawled across their chairs with bodies parallel and eyes straight ahead, rarely looking at each other. They looked as if they were riding in a car, staring out the windshield. But they were talking about their feelings. One boy was upset because a girl had told him he had a drinking problem, and the other was feeling alienated from all his friends.

Now, when a girl told a friend about a problem, the friend responded by asking probing questions and expressing agreement and understanding. But the boys dismissed each other's problems. Todd assured Richard that his drinking was "no big problem" because "sometimes you're funny when you're off your butt." And when Todd said he felt left out, Richard responded, "Why should you? You know more people than me."

Women perceive such responses as belittling and unsupportive. But the boys seemed satisfied with them. Whereas women reassure each other by implying, "You shouldn't feel bad because I've had similar experiences," men do so by implying, "You shouldn't feel bad because your problems aren't so bad."

There are even simpler reasons for women's impression that men don't listen. Linguist Lynette Hirschman found that women make more listener-noise, such as "mhm," "uhuh," and "yeah," to show "I'm with you." Men, she found, more often give silent attention. Women who expect a stream of listener-noise interpret silent attention as no attention at all.

Women's conversational habits are as frustrating to men as men's are to women. Men who expect silent attention interpret a stream of listener-noise as overreaction or impatience. Also, when women talk to each other in a close, comfortable setting, they often overlap, finish each other's sentences and anticipate what the other is about to say. This practice, which I call "participatory listenership," is often perceived by men as interruption, intrusion, and lack of attention.

A parallel difference caused a man to complain about his wife, "She just wants to talk about her own point of view. If I show her another view, she gets mad at me." When most women talk to each other, they assume a conversationalist's job is to express agreement and support. But many men see their conversational duty as pointing out the other side of an argument. This is heard as disloyalty by women, and refusal to offer the requisite support. It is not that women don't want to see other points of view, but that they prefer them phrased as suggestions and inquiries rather than as direct challenges.

In his book *Fighting for Life*, Walter Ong points out that men use "agonistic" or warlike, oppositional formats to do almost anything; thus discussion becomes debate, and conversation competitive sport. In contrast, women see conversation as a ritual means of establishing rapport. If Jane tells a problem and June says she has a similar one, they walk away feeling closer to each other. But this attempt at establishing rapport can backfire when used with men. Men take too literally women's ritual "troubles talk," just as women mistake men's ritual challenges for real attack.

The Sounds of Silence

These differences begin to clarify why women and men have such different expectations about communication in marriage. For women, talk creates intimacy. Marriage is an orgy of closeness: you can tell your feelings and thoughts, and still be loved. Their greatest fear is being pushed away. But men live in a hierarchical world, where talk maintains independence and status. They are on guard to protect themselves from being put down and pushed around.

This explains the paradox of the talkative man who said of his silent wife, "She's the talker." In the public setting of a guest lecture, he felt challenged to show his intelligence and display his understanding of the lecture. But at home, where he has nothing to prove and no one to defend against, he is free to remain silent. For his wife, being home means she is free from the worry that something she says might offend someone, or spark disagreement, or appear to be showing off; at home she is free to talk.

The communication problems that endanger marriage can't be fixed by mechanical engineering. They require a new conceptual framework about the role of talk in human relationships. Many of the psychological explanations that have become second nature may not be helpful, because they tend to blame either women (for not being assertive enough) or men (for not being in touch with their feelings). A sociolinguistic approach by which male-female conversation is seen as cross-cultural communication allows us to understand the problem and forge solutions without blaming either party.

Once the problem is understood, improvement comes naturally, as it did to the young woman and her boyfriend who seemed to go to sleep when she wanted to talk. Previously, she had accused him of not listening, and he had refused to change his behavior, since that would be admitting fault. But then she learned about and explained to him the differences in women's and men's habitual ways of aligning themselves in conversation. The next time she told him she wanted to talk, he began, as usual, by lying down and covering his eyes. When the familiar negative reaction bubbled up, she reassured herself that he really was listening. But then he sat up and looked at her. Thrilled, she asked why. He said, "You like me to look at you when we talk, so I'll try to do it." Once he saw their differences as cross-cultural rather than right and wrong, he independently altered his behavior.

Women who feel abandoned and deprived when their husbands won't listen to or report daily news may be happy to discover their husbands trying to adapt once they understand the place of small talk in women's relationships. But if their husbands don't adapt, the women may still be comforted that for men, this is not a failure of intimacy. Accepting the difference, the wives may look to their friends or family for that kind of talk. And husbands who can't provide it shouldn't feel their wives have made unreasonable demands. Some couples will still decide to divorce, but at least their decisions will be based on realistic expectations.

In these times of resurgent ethnic conflicts, the world desperately needs cross-cultural understanding. Like charity, successful cross-cultural communication should begin at home.

Questions for Reading and Analysis

1. What, according to Tannen, is the most frequent complaint women make of their husbands?

2. How does Tannen explain the communicative difference between men and women with regard to the socialization they go through when they are children and young adolescents?

3. What do women expect of their listeners? What do men expect of theirs? Where is the conflict that many married couples encounter in this regard?

4. A sociolinguist by trade, Tannen wrote her article for the readers of the *Washington Post*. In what way does she adapt her writing style to her audience?

A scientist and National Book Award-winning writer, Lewis Thomas is best known for his essays in which he discusses the humanistic implications of modern science and technology. In "Crickets, Bats, Cats, & Chaos," first published in 1992, Thomas argues that humans, despite their evolutionary superiority, share basic characteristics with lower animals and that this connection obliges us to take care of nature rather than destroy it.

Crickets, Bats, Cats, & Chaos

Lewis Thomas

I am not sure where to classify the mind of my cat Jeoffry. He is a small Abyssinian cat, a creature of elegance, grace, and poise, a piece of moving sculpture, and a total mystery. We named him Jeoffry after the eighteenth-century cat celebrated by the unpredictable poet Christopher Smart in a poem titled "Jubilate Agno," one section of which begins, "For I will consider my cat Jeoffry." The following lines are selected more or less at random:

> *For he counteracts the powers of darkness by his electrical skin and glaring eyes.*
>
> *For he counteracts the Devil, who is death, by brisking about the life . . .*
>
> *For he is of the tribe of Tiger . . .*
>
> *For he purrs in thankfulness, when God tells him he's a good Cat . . .*
>
> *For he is an instrument for the children to learn benevolence upon . . .*
>
> *For he is a mixture of gravity and waggery . . .*
>
> *For there is nothing sweeter than his peace when at rest.*
>
> *For there is nothing brisker than his life when in motion.*

I have not the slightest notion what goes on in the mind of my cat Jeoffry, beyond the conviction that it is a genuine mind, with genuine thoughts and a strong tendency to chaos, but in all other respects a mind totally unlike mine. I have a hunch, based on long moments of observing him stretched on the rug in sunlight, that his mind has more periods of geometric order, and a better facility for switching itself almost, but not quite, entirely off, and accordingly an easier access to pure pleasure. Just as he is able to hear sounds that I cannot hear, and smell important things of which I am unaware, and suddenly leap like a crazed gymnast from chair to chair, upstairs and downstairs through the house, flawless in every movement and searching for something he never finds, he has periods of meditation on matters I know nothing about.

While thinking about what nonhumans think is, in most biological quarters, an outlandish question, even an impermissible one, to which the quick and easy answer is nothing, or almost nothing, or certainly nothing like *thought* as we use the word, I still think about it. For while none of them may have real thoughts, foresee the future, regret the past, or be self-aware, most of us up here at the peak of evolution cannot manage the awareness of our own awareness, a state of mind only achieved when the mind succeeds in emptying itself of all other information and switches off all messages, interior and exterior. This is the state of mind for which the Chinese Taoists long ago used a term meaning, literally, no-knowledge. With no-knowledge, it is said, you get a different look at the world, an illumination.

Falling short of this, as I do, and dispossessed of anything I could call illumination, it has become my lesser satisfaction to learn secondhand whatever I can, and then to think, firsthand, about the behavior of other kinds of animals.

I think of crickets, for instance, and the thought of their unique, very small thoughts—principally about mating and bats—but also about the state of cricket society. The cricket seems to me an eminently suitable animal for sorting out some of the emotional issues bound to arise in any consideration of animal awareness. Nobody, so far as I know, not even an eighteenth-century minor poet, could imagine any connection between events in the mind of a cricket and those in the mind of a human. If there was ever a creature in nature meriting the dismissive description of a living machine, mindless and thoughtless, the cricket qualifies. So in talking about what crickets are up to when they communicate with each other, as they unmistakably do, by species-unique runs and rhythms of chirps and trills, there can be no question of *anthropomorphization*, that most awful of all terms for the deepest error a modern biologist can fall into.

If you reduce the temperature of a male cricket, the rate of his emission of chirping signals is correspondingly reduced. Indeed, some of the earlier naturalists used the technical term "thermometer crickets" because of the observation that you can make a close guess at the air temperature in a field by counting the rate of chirps of familiar crickets.

This is curious, but there is a much more curious thing going on when the weather changes. The female crickets in the same field, genetically coded to respond specifically to the chirp rhythm of their species, adjust their recognition mechanism to the same temperature change and the same new, slower rate of chirps. That is, as John Doherty and Ronald Hoy wrote on observing the phenomenon, "warm females responded best to the songs of warm males, and cold females responded best to the songs of cold males." The same phenomenon, known as temperature coupling, has been encountered in grasshoppers and tree frogs, and also in fireflies with their flash communication system. The receiving mind of the female cricket, if you are willing to call it that, adjusts itself immediately to match the sending mind of the male. This has always struck me as one of the neatest examples of animals adjusting to a change in their environment.

But I started thinking about crickets with something quite different in mind, namely bats. It has long been known that bats feed voraciously on the nocturnal flights of crickets and moths, which they detect on the wing by their fantastically accurate ultrasound mechanism. What should have been guessed at, considering the ingenuity of nature, is that certain cricket species, green lacewings, and certain moths have ears that can detect the ultrasound emissions of a bat, and can analyze the distance and direction from which the ultrasound is coming. These insects can employ two separate and quite distinct defensive maneuvers for evading the bat's keen sonar.

The first is simply swerving away. This is useful behavior when the bat signal is coming from a safe distance, twenty to thirty meters away. At this range the insect can detect the bat, but the bat is too far off to receive the bounced ultrasound back to its own ears. So the cricket or moth needs to do nothing more, at least for the moment, than swing out of earshot.

But when the bat is nearby, three meters or less, the insect is in immediate and mortal danger, for now the bat's sonar provides an accurate localization. It is too late for swerving or veering; because of its superior speed the bat can easily track such simple evasions. What to do? The answer has been provided by Kenneth Roeder, who designed a marvelous laboratory model for field studies, including instruments to imitate the intensity and direction of bat signals.

The answer, for a cricket or moth or lacewing who hears a bat homing in close by, is *chaos*. Instead of swerving away, the insect launches into wild, totally erratic, random flight patterns, as unpredictable as possible. This kind of response tends to confuse the bat and results in escape for the insect frequently enough to have been selected by evolution as the final, stereotyped, "last-chance" response to the threat. It has the look of a very smart move, whether thought out or not.

So chaos is part of the useful, everyday mental equipment of a cricket or a moth, and that, I submit, is something new to think about. I don't wish to push the matter beyond its possible significance, but it seems to me to justify a modest nudge. The long debate over the problem of animal awareness is not touched by the observation, but it does bring up the opposite side of that argument, the opposite of anthropomorphization. It is this: Leaving aside the deep question as to whether the lower animals have anything going on in their mind that we might accept as conscious thought, are there important events occurring in our human minds that are matched by habits of the animal mind?

Surely chaos is a capacious area of common ground. I am convinced that my own mind spends much of its waking hours, not to mention its sleeping time, in a state of chaos directly analogous to that of the cricket hearing the sound of the nearby bat. But there is a big difference. My chaos is not induced by a bat; it is not suddenly switched on in order to facilitate escape; it is not an evasive tactic set off by any new danger. It is, I think, the normal state of affairs, and not just for my brain in particular but for human brains in general. The chaos that is my natural state of being is rather like the concept of chaos that has emerged in higher mathematical circles in recent years.

As I understand it, and I am quick to say that I understand it only quite superficially, chaos occurs when any complex, dynamic system is perturbed by a small uncertainty in one or another of its subunits. The inevitable result is an amplification of the disturbance and then the spread of unpredictable, random behavior throughout the whole system. It is the total unpredictability and randomness that makes the word "chaos" applicable as a technical term, but it is not true that the behavior of the system becomes disorderly. Indeed, as James P. Crutchfield and his associates have written, "There is order in chaos: underlying chaotic behavior there are elegant geometric forms that create randomness in the same way as a card dealer shuffles a deck of cards or a blender mixes cake batter." The random behavior of a turbulent stream of water, or of the weather, or of Brownian movement, or of the central nervous system of a cricket in flight from a bat, are all determined by the same mathematical rules. Behavior of this sort has been encountered in computer models of large cities: When a small change was made in one small part of the city model, the amplification of the change resulted in enormous upheavals, none of them predictable, in the municipal behavior at remote sites in the models.

A moth or a cricket has a small enough nervous system to *seem* predictable and orderly most of the time. There are not all that many neurons, and the circuitry contains what seem to be mostly simple reflex pathways. Laboratory experiments suggest that in a normal day, one thing—the sound of a bat at a safe distance, say—leads to another, predictable thing—a swerving off to one side in flight. It is only when something immensely new and important happens—the bat sound at three meters away—that the system is thrown into chaos.

I suggest that the difference with us is that chaos is the norm. Predictable, small-scale, orderly, cause-and-effect sequences are hard to come by and don't last long when they do turn up. Something else almost always turns up at the same time, and then another sequential thought intervenes alongside, and there come turbulence and chaos again. When we are lucky, and the system operates at its random best, something astonishing may suddenly turn up, beyond predicting or imagining. Events like these we recognize as good ideas.

My cat Jeoffry's brain is vastly larger and more commodious than that of a cricket, but I wonder if it is qualitatively all that different. The cricket lives with his two great ideas in mind, mating and predators, and his world is a world of particular, specified sounds. He is a tiny machine, I suppose, depending on what you mean by "machine," but it is his occasional moments of randomness and unpredictability that entitle him to be called aware. In order to achieve that feat of wild chaotic flight, and thus escape, he has to make use, literally, of his brain. When Int 1, an auditory interneuron, is activated by the sound of a bat closing in, the message is transmitted by an axon connected straight to the insect's brain, and it is here, and only here, that the swerving is generated. This I consider to be a thought, a very small thought, but still a thought. Without knowing what to count as a thought, I figure that Jeoffry, with his kind of brain, has a trillion thoughts of about the same size in any waking moment. As for me, and my sort of brain, I can't think where to begin.

We like to think of our minds as containing trains of thought, or streams of consciousness, as though they were orderly arrangements of linear events, one notion leading in a cause-and-effect way to the next notion. Logic is the way to go; we set a high price on logic, unlike E. M. Forster's elderly lady in *Aspects of the Novel*, who, when accused of being illogical, replied, "Logic? Good gracious! What rubbish! How can I tell what I think till I see what I say?"

But with regard to our own awareness of nature, I believe we've lost sight of, lost track of, lost touch with, and to some measurable degree lost respect for, the chaotic and natural in recent years—and during the very period of history when we humans have been learning more about the detailed workings of nature than in all our previous millennia. The more we learn, the more we seem to distance ourselves from the rest of life, as though we were separate creatures, so different from other occupants of the biosphere as to have arrived from another galaxy. We seek too much to explain, we assert a duty to run the place, to dominate the planet, to govern its life, but at the same time we ourselves seem to be less a part of it than ever before.

We leave it whenever we can, we crowd ourselves from open green countrysides onto the concrete surfaces of massive cities, as far removed from the earth as we can get, staring at it from behind insulated glass, or by way of half-hour television clips.

At the same time, we talk a great game of concern. We shout at each other in high virtue, now more than ever before, about the befoulment of our nest and about whom to blame. We have mechanized our lives so extensively that most of us live with the illusion that our only connection with nature is the nagging fear that it may one day turn on us and do us in. Polluting our farmlands and streams, even the seas, worries us because of what it may be doing to the food and water supplies necessary for human beings. Raising the level of CO^2, methane, and hydrofluorocarbons in the atmosphere troubles us because of the projected effects of climate upheaval on human habitats. These anxieties do not extend, really, to nature at large. They are not the result of any new awareness.

Nature itself, that vast incomprehensible meditative being, has come to mean for most of us nothing much more than odd walks in the nearby woods, or flowers in the rooftop garden, or the soap opera stories of the last giant panda or whooping crane, or curiosities like the northward approach, from Florida, of the Asiatic flying cockroach.

I will begin to feel better about us, and about our future, when we finally start learning about some of the things that are still mystifications. Start with the events in the mind of a cricket, I'd say, and then go on from there. Comprehend my cat Jeoffry and we'll be on our way. Nowhere near home, but off and dancing, getting within a few millennia of understanding why the music of Bach is what it is, ready at last for open outer space. Give us time, I'd say, the kind of endless time we mean when we talk about the real world.

Questions for Reading and Analysis

1. Explain the connection Thomas establishes between order and chaos. What does he mean when he says "there is order in chaos"?

2. How do cats, crickets and humans compare with regard to chaos?

3. What do you think is Thomas's thesis? What is the main idea he tries to communicate to his reader?

4. Thomas starts his essay with a description of his cat, Jeoffry, and a poem about its 18th century namesake. What is the purpose of such a seemingly "unscientific" opening for a piece analyzing a very sophisticated scientific topic?

5. Thomas implies that because human minds share some of their basic properties with those of lower animals, we cannot regard ourselves as existing outside of nature and exploit it for our short-sighted goals. Do you agree?

*O*riginally published in 1849, anonymously, the most famous essay
by Henry David Thoreau (1817–1862), though largely ignored
during his time, had considerable influence upon the work of two
20th century giants—Mahatma Gandhi and Martin Luther King, Jr.
A classic anti-government argument, the work also provides a glimpse
into the anti-social, inherently rebellious, but rigidly principled nature
of one of a handful of American philosophers.

Civil Disobedience[1]

Henry David Thoreau

I heartily accept the motto, "That government is best which governs least";[2] and
I should like to see it acted up to more rapidly and systematically. Carried out,
it finally amounts to this, which also I believe—"That government is best which
governs not at all"; and when men are prepared for it, that will be the kind of government which they will have. Government is at best but an expedient; but most
governments are usually, and all governments are sometimes, inexpedient. The
objections which have been brought against a standing army, and they are many
and weighty, and deserve to prevail, may also at last be brought against a standing
government. The standing army is only an arm of the standing government. The
government itself, which is only the mode which the people have chosen to execute their will, is equally liable to be abused and perverted before the people can
act through it. Witness the present Mexican war,[3] the work of comparatively a
few individuals using the standing government as their tool; for in the outset, the
people would not have consented to this measure.

This American government—what is it but a tradition, though a recent one,
endeavoring to transmit itself unimpaired to posterity, but each instant losing some
of its integrity? It has not the vitality and force of a single living man; for a single
man can bend it to his will. It is a sort of wooden gun to the people themselves.
But it is not the less necessary for this; for the people must have some complicated
machinery or other, and hear its din, to satisfy that idea of government which they
have. Governments show thus how successfully men can be imposed on, even
impose on themselves, for their own advantage. It is excellent, we must all allow.
Yet this government never of itself furthered any enterprise, but by the alacrity
with which it got out of its way. *It* does not keep the country free. *It* does not settle
the West. *It* does not educate. The character inherent in the American people has
done all that has been accomplished; and it would have done somewhat more, if
the government had not sometimes got in its way. For government is an expedient
by which men would fain succeed in letting one another alone; and, as has been
said, when it is most expedient, the governed are most let alone by it. Trade and

commerce, if they were not made of India-rubber, would never manage to bounce over the obstacles which legislators are continually putting in their way; and if one were to judge these men wholly by the effects of their actions and not partly by their intentions, they would deserve to be classed and punished with those mischievous persons who put obstructions on the railroads.

But, to speak practically and as a citizen, unlike those who call themselves no-government men, I ask for, not at once no government, but *at once* a better government. Let every man make known what kind of government would command his respect, and that will be one step toward obtaining it.

After all, the practical reason why, when the power is once in the hands of the people, a majority are permitted, and for a long period continue, to rule is not because they are most likely to be in the right, nor because this seems fairest to the minority, but because they are physically the strongest. But a government in which the majority rule in all cases cannot be based on justice, even as far as men understand it. Can there not be a government in which the majorities do not virtually decide right and wrong, but conscience?—in which majorities decide only those questions to which the rule of expediency is applicable? Must the citizen ever for a moment, or in the least degree, resign his conscience to the legislator? Why has every man a conscience, then? I think that we should be men first, and subjects afterward. It is not desirable to cultivate a respect for the law, so much as for the right. The only obligation which I have a right to assume is to do at any time what I think right. It is truly enough said that a corporation has no conscience; but a corporation of conscientious men is a corporation *with* a conscience. Law never made men a whit more just; and, by means of their respect for it, even the well-disposed are daily made the agents of injustice. A common and natural result of an undue respect for the law is, that you may see a file of soldiers, colonel, captain, corporal, privates, powder-monkeys,[4] and all, marching in admirable order over hill and dale to the wars, against their wills, ay, against their common sense and consciences, which makes it very steep marching indeed, and produces a palpitation of the heart. They have no doubt that it is a damnable business in which they are concerned; they are all peaceably inclined. Now, what are they? Men at all? or small movable forts and magazines, at the service of some unscrupulous man in power? Visit the Navy-Yard,[5] and behold a marine, such a man as an American government can make, or such as it can make a man with its black arts—a mere shadow and reminiscence of humanity, a man laid out alive and standing, and already, as one may say, buried under arms with funeral accompaniments, though it may be,—

> "Not a drum was heard, not a funeral note,
> As his corse[6] to the rampart we hurried;
> Not a soldier discharged his farewell shot
> O'er the grave where our hero we buried."[7]

The mass of men serve the state thus, not as men mainly, but as machines, with their bodies. They are the standing army, and the militia, jailers, constables, *posse comitatus*,[8] etc. In most cases there is no free exercise whatever of the judgement or of the moral sense; but they put themselves on a level with wood and earth and stones; and wooden men can perhaps be manufactured that will serve the purpose as well. Such command no more respect than men of straw or a lump of dirt. They have the same sort of worth only as horses and dogs. Yet such as these even are commonly esteemed good citizens. Others—as most legislators, politicians, lawyers, ministers, and office-holders—serve the state chiefly with their heads; and, as they rarely make any moral distinctions, they are as likely to serve the devil, without *intending* it, as God. A very few—as heroes, patriots, martyrs, reformers in the great sense, and *men*—serve the state with their consciences also, and so necessarily resist it for the most part; and they are commonly treated as enemies by it. A wise man will only be useful as a man, and will not submit to be "clay," and "stop a hole to keep the wind away,"[9] but leave that office to his dust at least:—

> *"I am too high-born to be propertied,*
> *To be a secondary at control,*
> *Or useful serving-man and instrument*
> *To any sovereign state throughout the world."*[10]

He who gives himself entirely to his fellow-men appears to them useless and selfish; but he who gives himself partially to them is pronounced a benefactor and philanthropist.

How does it become a man to behave toward this American government to-day? I answer, that he cannot without disgrace be associated with it. I cannot for an instant recognize that political organization as *my* government which is the *slave's* government also.

All men recognize the right of revolution; that is, the right to refuse allegiance to, and to resist, the government, when its tyranny or its inefficiency are great and unendurable. But almost all say that such is not the case now. But such was the case, they think, in the Revolution of '75.[11] If one were to tell me that this was a bad government because it taxed certain foreign commodities brought to its ports, it is most probable that I should not make an ado about it, for I can do without them. All machines have their friction; and possibly this does enough good to counterbalance the evil. At any rate, it is a great evil to make a stir about it. But when the friction comes to have its machine, and oppression and robbery are organized, I say, let us not have such a machine any longer. In other words, when a sixth of the population of a nation which has undertaken to be the refuge of liberty are slaves, and a whole country[12] is unjustly overrun and conquered by a foreign army, and subjected to military law, I think that it is not too soon for honest men to rebel and revolutionize. What makes this duty the more urgent is that fact that the country so overrun is not our own, but ours is the invading army.

Paley,[13] a common authority with many on moral questions, in his chapter on the "Duty of Submission to Civil Government," resolves all civil obligation into expediency; and he proceeds to say that "so long as the interest of the whole society requires it, that is, so long as the established government cannot be resisted or changed without public inconveniency, it is the will of God . . . that the established government be obeyed,—and no longer. This principle being admitted, the justice of every particular case of resistance is reduced to a computation of the quantity of the danger and grievance on the one side, and of the probability and expense of redressing it on the other." Of this, he says, every man shall judge for himself. But

Paley appears never to have contemplated those cases to which the rule of expediency does not apply, in which a people, as well as an individual, must do justice, cost what it may. If I have unjustly wrested a plank from a drowning man, I must restore it to him though I drown myself. This, according to Paley, would be inconvenient. But he that would save his life, in such a case, shall lose it.[14] This people must cease to hold slaves, and to make war on Mexico, though it cost them their existence as a people.

In their practice, nations agree with Paley; but does any one think that Massachusetts does exactly what is right in the present crisis?

> *"A drab of state, a cloth-o'-silver slut,*
> *To have her train borne up, and her soul trail in the dirt."*[15]

Practically speaking, the opponents to a reform in Massachusetts are not a hundred thousand politicians at the South, but a hundred thousand merchants and farmers here, who are more interested in commerce and agriculture than they are in humanity, and are not prepared to do justice to the slave and to Mexico, *cost what it may*. I quarrel not with far-off foes, but with those who, near at home, cooperate with, and do the bidding of, those far away, and without whom the latter would be harmless. We are accustomed to say, that the mass of men are unprepared; but improvement is slow, because the few are not materially wiser or better than the many. It is not so important that many should be good as you, as that there be some absolute goodness somewhere; for that will leaven the whole lump.[16] There are thousands who are *in opinion* opposed to slavery and to the war, who yet in effect do nothing to put an end to them; who, esteeming themselves children of Washington and Franklin, sit down with their hands in their pockets, and say that they know not what to do, and do nothing; who even postpone the question of freedom to the question of free trade, and quietly read the prices-current along with the latest advices[17] from Mexico, after dinner, and, it may be, fall asleep over them both. What is the price-current of an honest man and patriot today? They hesitate, and they regret, and sometimes they petition; but they do nothing in earnest and with effect. They will wait, well disposed, for other to remedy the evil, that they may no longer have it to regret. At most, they give up only a cheap vote, and a feeble countenance and God-speed, to the right, as it goes by them. There are nine hundred and ninety-nine patrons of virtue to one virtuous man. But it is easier to deal with the real possessor of a thing than with the temporary guardian of it.

All voting is a sort of gaming, like checkers or backgammon, with a slight moral tinge to it, a playing with right and wrong, with moral questions; and betting naturally accompanies it. The character of the voters is not staked. I cast my vote, perchance, as I think right; but I am not vitally concerned that that right should prevail. I am willing to leave it to the majority. Its obligation, therefore, never exceeds that of expediency. Even voting *for the right* is *doing* nothing for it. It is only expressing to men feebly your desire that it should prevail. A wise man will not leave the right to the mercy of chance, nor wish it to prevail through the power of the majority. There is but little virtue in the action of masses of men. When the majority shall at length vote for the abolition of slavery, it will be because they are indifferent to slavery, or because there is but little slavery left to be abolished by their vote. *They* will then be the only slaves. Only *his* vote can hasten the abolition of slavery who asserts his own freedom by his vote.

I hear of a convention to be held at Baltimore,[18] or elsewhere, for the selection of a candidate for the Presidency, made up chiefly of editors, and men who are politicians by profession; but I think, what is it to any independent, intelligent, and respectable man what decision they may come to? Shall we not have the advantage of his wisdom and honesty, nevertheless? Can we not count upon some independent votes? Are there not many individuals in the country who do not attend conventions? But no: I find that the respectable man, so called, has immediately drifted from his position, and despairs of his country, when his country has more reason to despair of him. He forthwith adopts one of the candidates thus selected as the only *available* one, thus proving that he is himself *available* for any purposes of the demagogue. His vote is of no more worth than that of any unprincipled foreigner or hireling native, who may have been bought. O for a man who is a *man*, and, and as my neighbor says, has a bone in his back which you cannot pass your hand through! Our statistics are at fault: the population has been returned too large. How many *men* are there to a square thousand miles in this country? Hardly one. Does not America offer any inducement for men to settle here? The American has dwindled into an Odd Fellow,[19]—one who may be known by the development of his organ of gregariousness,[20] and a manifest lack of intellect and cheerful self-reliance; whose first and chief concern, on coming into the world, is to see that the almshouses are in good repair; and, before yet he has lawfully donned the virile garb,[21] to collect a fund to the support of the widows and orphans that may be; who, in short, ventures to live only by the aid of the Mutual Insurance company, which has promised to bury him decently.

It is not a man's duty, as a matter of course, to devote himself to the eradication of any, even the most enormous, wrong; he may still properly have other concerns to engage him; but it is his duty, at least, to wash his hands of it, and, if he gives it no thought longer, not to give it practically his support. If I devote myself to other pursuits and contemplations, I must first see, at least, that I do not pursue them sitting upon another man's shoulders. I must get off him first, that he may pursue his contemplations too. See what gross inconsistency is tolerated. I have heard some of my townsmen say, "I should like to have them order me out to help put down an insurrection of the slaves, or to march to Mexico—see if I would go"; and yet these very men have each, directly by their allegiance, and so indirectly, at least, by their money, furnished a substitute. The soldier is applauded who refuses to serve in an unjust war by those who do not refuse to sustain the unjust government which makes the war; is applauded by those whose own act and authority he disregards and sets at naught; as if the state were penitent to that degree that it hired one to scourge it while it sinned, but not to that degree that it left off sinning for a moment. Thus, under the name of Order and Civil Government, we are all made at last to pay homage to and support our own meanness. After the first blush of sin comes its indifference; and from immoral it becomes, as it were, *un*moral, and not quite unnecessary to that life which we have made.

The broadest and most prevalent error requires the most disinterested virtue to sustain it. The slight reproach to which the virtue of patriotism is commonly liable, the noble are most likely to incur. Those who, while they disapprove of the character and measures of a government, yield to it their allegiance and support are undoubtedly its most conscientious supporters, and so frequently the most serious obstacles to reform. Some[22] are petitioning the State to dissolve the Union, to disregard the requisitions of the President.[23] Why do they not dissolve it themselves—the union between themselves and the State—and refuse to pay their quota into its treasury? Do not they stand in the same relation to the State that the State does to the Union? And have not the same reasons prevented the State from resisting the Union which have prevented them from resisting the State?

How can a man be satisfied to entertain and opinion merely, and enjoy *it*? Is there any enjoyment in it, if his opinion is that he is aggrieved? If you are cheated out of a single dollar by your neighbor, you do not rest satisfied with knowing that you are cheated, or with saying that you are cheated, or even with petitioning him to pay you your due; but you take effectual steps at once to obtain the full amount, and see that you are never cheated again. Action from principle, the perception and performance of right, changes things and relations; it is essentially revolutionary, and does not consist wholly with anything which was. It not only divides States and churches, it divides families; ay, it divides the *individual*, separating the diabolical in him from the divine.

Unjust laws exist: shall we be content to obey them, or shall we endeavor to amend them, and obey them until we have succeeded, or shall we transgress them at once? Men generally, under such a government as this, think that they ought to wait until they have persuaded the majority to alter them. They think that, if they should resist, the remedy would be worse than the evil. But it is the fault of the government itself that the remedy *is* worse than the evil. *It* makes it worse. Why is it not more apt to anticipate and provide for reform? Why does it not cherish its wise minority? Why does it cry and resist before it is hurt? Why does it not encourage its citizens to be on the alert to point out its faults, and do better than it would have them? Why does it always crucify Christ and excommunicate Copernicus and Luther,[24] and pronounce Washington and Franklin rebels?

One would think, that a deliberate and practical denial of its authority was the only offense never contemplated by government; else, why has it not assigned its definite, its suitable and proportionate, penalty? If a man who has no property refuses but once to earn nine shillings[25] for the State, he is put in prison for a period unlimited by any law that I know, and determined only by the discretion of those who placed him there; but if he should steal ninety times nine shillings from the State, he is soon permitted to go at large again.

If the injustice is part of the necessary friction of the machine of government, let it go, let it go: perchance it will wear smooth—certainly the machine will wear out. If the injustice has a spring, or a pulley, or a rope, or a crank, exclusively for itself, then perhaps you may consider whether the remedy will not be worse than the evil; but if it is of such a nature that it requires you to be the agent of injustice to another, then I say, break the law. Let your life be a counter-friction[26] to stop the machine. What I have to do is to see, at any rate, that I do not lend myself to the wrong which I condemn.

As for adopting the ways which the State has provided for remedying the evil, I know not of such ways. They take too much time, and a man's life will be gone. I have other affairs to attend to. I came into this world, not chiefly to make this a good place to live in, but to live in it, be it good or bad. A man has not everything to do, but *something*; and because he cannot do *everything*, it is not necessary that he should do *something* wrong. It is not my business to be petitioning the Governor or the Legislature any more than it is theirs to petition me; and if they should not hear my petition, what should I do then? But in this case the State has provided no way: its very Constitution is the evil. This may seem to be harsh and stubborn and unconcilliatory; but it is to treat with the utmost kindness and consideration the only spirit that can appreciate or deserves it. So is all change for the better, like birth and death, which convulse the body.

I do not hesitate to say, that those who call themselves Abolitionists should at once effectually withdraw their support, both in person and property, from the government of Massachusetts, and not wait till they constitute a majority of one, before they suffer the right to prevail through them. I think that it is enough if they have God on their side, without waiting for that other one. Moreover, any man more right than his neighbors constitutes a majority of one already.

I meet this American government, or its representative, the State government, directly, and face to face, once a year—no more—in the person of its tax-gatherer; this is the only mode in which a man situated as I am necessarily meets it; and it then says distinctly, Recognize me; and the simplest, the most effectual, and, in the present posture of affairs, the indispensablest mode of treating with it on this head, of expressing your little satisfaction with and love for it, is to deny it then. My civil neighbor, the tax-gatherer, is the very man I have to deal with—for it is, after all, with men and not with parchment that I quarrel—and he has voluntarily chosen to be an agent of the government. How shall he ever know well what he is and does as an officer of the government, or as a man, until he is obliged to consider whether he shall treat me, his neighbor, for whom he has respect, as a neighbor and well-disposed man, or as a maniac and disturber of the peace, and see if he can get over this obstruction to his neighborliness without a ruder and more impetuous thought or speech corresponding with his action. I know this well, that if one thousand, if one hundred, if ten men whom I could name—if ten *honest* men only—ay, if *one* HONEST man, in this State of Massachusetts, *ceasing to hold slaves*, were actually to withdraw from this co-partnership, and be locked up in the county jail therefor, it would be the abolition of slavery in America. For it matters not how small the beginning may seem to be: what is once well done is done forever. But we love better to talk about it: that we say is our mission. Reform keeps many scores of newspapers in its service, but not one man. If my esteemed neighbor, the State's ambassador,[27] who will devote his days to the settlement of the question of human rights in the Council Chamber, instead of being threatened with the prisons of Carolina, were to sit down the prisoner of Massachusetts, that State which is so anxious to foist the sin of slavery upon her sister—though at present she can discover only an act of inhospitality to be the ground of a quarrel with her—the Legislature would not wholly waive the subject the following winter.

Under a government which imprisons any unjustly, the true place for a just man is also a prison. The proper place today, the only place which Massachusetts has provided for her freer and less desponding spirits, is in her prisons, to be put out and locked out of the State by her own act, as they have already put themselves out by their principles. It is there that the fugitive slave, and the Mexican prisoner on parole, and the Indian come to plead the wrongs of his race should find them; on that separate, but more free and honorable ground, where the State places those who are not *with* her, but *against* her—the only house in a slave State in which a free man can abide with honor. If any think that their influence would be lost there, and their voices no longer afflict the ear of the State, that they would not be as an enemy within its walls, they do not know by how much truth is stronger than error, nor how much more eloquently and effectively he can combat injustice who has experienced a little in his own person. Cast your whole vote, not a strip of paper merely, but your whole influence. A minority is powerless while it conforms to the majority; it is not even a minority then; but it is irresistible when it clogs by its whole weight. If the alternative is to keep all just men in prison, or give up war and slavery, the State will not hesitate which to choose. If a thousand men were not to pay their tax bills this year, that would not be a violent and bloody measure, as it would be to pay them, and enable the State to commit violence and shed innocent blood. This is, in fact, the definition of a peaceable revolution, if any such is possible. If the tax-gatherer, or any other public officer, asks me, as one has done, "But what shall I do?" my answer is, "If you really wish to do anything, resign his office." When the subject has refused allegiance, and the officer has resigned his office, then the revolution is accomplished. But even suppose blood should flow. Is there not a sort of blood shed when the conscience is wounded? Through this wound a man's real manhood and immortality flow out, and he bleeds to an everlasting death. I see this blood flowing now.

I have contemplated the imprisonment of the offender, rather than the seizure of his goods—though both will serve the same purpose—because they who assert the purest right, and consequently are most dangerous to a corrupt State, commonly have not spent much time in accumulating property. To such the State renders comparatively small service, and a slight tax is wont to appear exorbitant, particularly if they are obliged to earn it by special labor with their hands. If there were one who lived wholly without the use of money, the State itself would hesitate to demand it of him. But the rich man—not to make any invidious comparison—is always sold to the institution which makes him rich. Absolutely speaking, the more money, the less virtue; for money comes between a man and his objects, and obtains them for him; it was certainly no great virtue to obtain it. It puts to rest many questions which he would otherwise be taxed to answer; while the only new question which it puts is the hard but superfluous one, how to spend it. Thus his moral ground is taken from under his feet. The opportunities of living are diminished in proportion as what are called the "means" are increased. The best thing a man can do for his culture when he is rich is to endeavor to carry out those schemes which he entertained when he was poor. Christ answered the Herodians according to their condition. "Show me the tribute-money," said he—and one took a penny out of his pocket—if you use money which has the image of Caesar on it, and which he has made current and valuable, that is, *if you are men of the State*, and gladly enjoy the advantages of Caesar's government, then pay him back some of his own when he demands it. "Render therefore to Caesar that which is Caesar's, and to God those things which are God's"[28]—leaving them no wiser than before as to which was which; for they did not wish to know.

When I converse with the freest of my neighbors, I perceive that, whatever they may say about the magnitude and seriousness of the question, and their regard for the public tranquillity, the long and the short of the matter is, that they cannot spare the protection of the existing government, and they dread the consequences to their property and families of disobedience to it. For my own part, I should not like to think that I ever rely on the protection of the State. But, if I deny the authority of the State when it presents its tax-bill, it will soon take and waste all my property, and so harass me and my children without end. This is hard. This makes it impossible for a man to live honestly, and at the same time comfortably, in outward respects. It will not be worth the while to accumulate property; that would be sure to go again. You must hire[29] or squat somewhere, and raise but a small crop, and eat that soon. You must live within yourself, and depend upon yourself always tucked up and ready for a start, and not have many affairs. A man may grow rich in Turkey even, if he will be in all respects a good subject of the Turkish government. Confucius[30] said: "If a state is governed by the principles of reason, poverty and misery are subjects of shame; if a state is not governed by the principles of reason, riches and honors are the subjects of shame." No: until I want the protection of Massachusetts to be extended to me in some distant Southern port, where my liberty is endangered, or until I am bent solely on building up an estate at home by peaceful enterprise, I can afford to refuse allegiance to Massachusetts, and her right to my property and life. It costs me less in every sense to incur the penalty of disobedience to the State than it would to obey. I should feel as if I were worth less in that case.

Some years ago, the State met me in behalf of the Church, and commanded me to pay a certain sum toward the support of a clergyman whose preaching my father attended, but never I myself.[31] "Pay," it said, "or be locked up in the jail." I declined to pay. But, unfortunately, another man saw fit to pay it. I did not see why the schoolmaster should be taxed to support the priest, and not the priest the schoolmaster; for I was not the State's schoolmaster, but I supported myself by voluntary subscription. I did not see why the lyceum[32] should not present its tax bill, and have the State to back its demand, as well as the Church. However, at the request of the selectmen,[33] I condescended to make some such statement as this in writing:— "Know all men by these presents, that I, Henry Thoreau, do not wish to be regarded as a member of any incorporated society which I have not joined." This I gave to the town clerk; and he has it. The State, having thus learned that I did not wish to be regarded as a member of that church, has never made a like demand of me since; though it said that it must adhere to its original presumption that time. If I had known how to name them, I should then have signed off in detail from all the societies which I never signed on to; but I did not know where to find a complete list.

I have paid no poll tax for six years. I was put into a jail once on this account, for one night;[34] and, as I stood considering the walls of solid stone, two or three feet thick, the door of wood and iron, a foot thick, and the iron grating which strained the light, I could not help being struck with the foolishness of that institution which treated me as if I were mere flesh and blood and bones, to be locked up. I wondered that it should have concluded at length that this was the best use it could put me to, and had never thought to avail itself of my services in some way. I saw that, if there was a wall of stone between me and my townsmen, there was a still more difficult one to climb or break through before they could get to be as free as I was. I did not for a moment feel confined, and the walls seemed a great waste of stone and mortar. I felt as if I alone of all my townsmen had paid my tax. They plainly did not know how to treat me, but behaved like persons who are underbred. In every threat and in every compliment there was a blunder; for they thought that my chief desire was to stand the other side of that stone wall. I could not but smile to see how industriously they locked the door on my meditations, which followed them out again without let or hindrance, and *they* were really all that was dangerous. As they could not reach me, they had resolved to punish my body; just as boys, if they cannot come at some person against whom they have a spite, will abuse his dog. I saw that the State was half-witted, that it was timid as a lone woman with her silver spoons, and that it did not know its friends from its foes, and I lost all my remaining respect for it, and pitied it.

Thus the state never intentionally confronts a man's sense, intellectual or moral, but only his body, his senses. It is not armed with superior with or honesty, but with superior physical strength. I was not born to be forced. I will breathe after my own fashion. Let us see who is the strongest. What force has a multitude? They only can force me who obey a higher law than I. They force me to become like themselves. I do not hear of *men* being *forced* to live this way or that by masses of men. What sort of life were that to live? When I meet a government which says to me, "Your money our your life," why should I be in haste to give it my money? It may be in a great strait, and not know what to do: I cannot help that. It must help itself; do as I do. It is not worth the while to snivel about it. I am not responsible for the successful working of the machinery of society. I am not the son of the engineer. I perceive that, when an acorn and a chestnut fall side by side, the one does not remain inert to make way for the other, but both obey their own laws, and spring and grow and flourish as best they can, till one, perchance, overshadows and destroys the other. If a plant cannot live according to its nature, it dies; and so a man.

The night in prison was novel and interesting enough. The prisoners in their shirt-sleeves were enjoying a chat and the evening air in the doorway, when I entered. But the jailer[35] said, "Come, boys, it is time to lock up;" and so they dispersed, and I heard the sound of their steps returning into the hollow apartments.[36] My roommate was introduced to me by the jailer as "a first-rate fellow and a clever[37] man." When the door was locked, he showed me where to hang my hat, and how he managed matters there. The rooms were whitewashed once a month; and this one, at least, was the whitest, most simply furnished, and probably the neatest apartment in the town. He naturally wanted to know where I came from, and what brought me there; and, when I had told him, I asked him in my turn how he came there, presuming him to be an honest man, of course; and, as the world goes, I believe he was. "Why," said he, "they accuse me of burning a barn; but I never did it." As near as I could discover, he had probably gone to bed in a barn when drunk, and smoked his pipe there; and so a barn was burnt. He had the reputation of being a clever man, had been there some three months waiting for his trial to come on, and would have to wait as much longer; but he was quite domesticated and contented, since he got his board for nothing, and thought that he was well treated.

He occupied one window, and I the other; and I saw that if one stayed there long, his principal business would be to look out the window. I had soon read all the tracts that were left there, and examined where former prisoners had broken out, and where a grate had been sawed off, and heard the history of the various occupants of that room; for I found that even here there was a history and a gossip which never circulated beyond the walls of the jail. Probably this is the only house in town where verses are composed, which are afterward printed in a circular form, but not published. I was shown quite a long list of verses which were composed by some young men who had been detected in an attempt to escape, who avenged themselves by singing them.

I pumped my fellow-prisoner as dry as I could, for fear I should never see him again; but at length he showed me which was my bed, and left me to blow out the lamp.

It was like traveling into a far country, such as I had never expected to behold, to lie there for one night. It seemed to me that I never had heard the town clock strike before, nor the evening sounds of the village; for we slept with the windows open, which were inside the grating. It was to see my native village in the light of the Middle Ages, and our Concord was turned into a Rhine stream, and visions of knights and castles passed before me. They were the voices of old burghers that I heard in the streets. I was an involuntary spectator and auditor of whatever was done and said in the kitchen of the adjacent village inn—a wholly new and rare experience to me. It was a closer view of my native town. I was fairly inside of it. I never had seen its institutions before. This is one of its peculiar institutions; for it is a shire town.[38] I began to comprehend what its inhabitants were about.

In the morning, our breakfasts were put through the hole in the door, in small oblong-square tin pans, made to fit, and holding a pint of chocolate, with brown bread, and an iron spoon. When they called for the vessels again, I was green enough to return what bread I had left; but my comrade seized it, and said that I should lay that up for lunch or dinner. Soon after he was let out to work at haying in a neighboring field, whither he went every day, and would not be back till noon; so he bade me good-day, saying that he doubted if he should see me again.

When I came out of prison—for some one[39] interfered, and paid that tax—I did not perceive that great changes had taken place on the common, such as he observed who went in a youth and emerged a tottering and gray-headed man; and yet a change had to my eyes come over the scene—the town, and State, and country, greater than any that mere time could effect. I saw yet more distinctly the State in which I lived. I saw to what extent the people among whom I lived could be trusted as good neighbors and friends; that their friendship was for summer weather only; that they did not greatly propose to do right; that they were a distinct race from me by their prejudices and superstitions, as the Chinamen and Malays are; that in their sacrifices to humanity they ran no risks, not even to their property; that after all they were not so noble but they treated the thief as he had treated them, and hoped, by a certain outward observance and a few prayers, and by walking in a particular straight though useless path from time to time, to save their souls. This may be to judge my neighbors harshly; for I believe that many of them are not aware that they have such an institution as the jail in their village.

It was formerly the custom in our village, when a poor debtor came out of jail, for his acquaintances to salute him, looking through their fingers, which were crossed to represent the grating of the jail window, "How do ye do?" My neighbors did not thus salute me, but first looked at me, and then at one another, as if I had returned from a long journey. I was put into jail as I was going to the shoemaker's to get a shoe which was mended. When I was let out the next morning, I proceeded to finish my errand, and, having put on my mended shoe, joined a huckleberry party, who were impatient to put themselves under my conduct; and in half an hour—for the horse was soon tackled,[40]—was in the midst of a huckleberry field, on one of our highest hills, two miles off, and then the State was nowhere to be seen.

This is the whole history of "My Prisons."[41]

I have never declined paying the highway tax, because I am as desirous of being a good neighbor as I am of being a bad subject; and as for supporting schools, I am doing my part to educate my fellow countrymen now. It is for no particular item in the tax bill that I refuse to pay it. I simply wish to refuse allegiance to the State, to withdraw and stand aloof from it effectually. I do not care to trace the course of my dollar, if I could, till it buys a man or a musket to shoot one with—the dollar is innocent—but I am concerned to trace the effects of my allegiance. In fact, I quietly declare war with the State, after my fashion, though I will still make what use and get what advantages of her I can, as is usual in such cases.

If others pay the tax which is demanded of me, from a sympathy with the State, they do but what they have already done in their own case, or rather they abet injustice to a greater extent than the State requires. If they pay the tax from a mistaken interest in the individual taxed, to save his property, or prevent his going to jail, it is because they have not considered wisely how far they let their private feelings interfere with the public good.

This, then, is my position at present. But one cannot be too much on his guard in such a case, lest his actions be biased by obstinacy or an undue regard for the opinions of men. Let him see that he does only what belongs to himself and to the hour.

I think sometimes, Why, this people mean well, they are only ignorant; they would do better if they knew how: why give your neighbors this pain to treat you as they are not inclined to? But I think again, This is no reason why I should do as they do, or permit others to suffer much greater pain of a different kind. Again, I sometimes say to myself, When many millions of men, without heat, without ill will, without personal feeling of any kind, demand of you a few shillings only, without the possibility, such is their constitution, of retracting or altering their present demand, and without the possibility, on your side, of appeal to any other millions, why expose yourself to this overwhelming brute force? You do not resist cold and hunger, the winds and the waves, thus obstinately; you quietly submit to a thousand similar necessities. You do not put your head into the fire. But just in proportion as I regard this as not wholly a brute force, but partly a human force, and consider that I have relations to those millions as to so many millions of men, and not of mere brute or inanimate things, I see that appeal is possible, first and instantaneously, from them to the Maker of them, and, secondly, from them to themselves. But if I put my head deliberately into the fire, there is no appeal to fire or to the Maker of fire, and I have only myself to blame. If I could convince myself that I have any right to be satisfied with men as they are, and to treat them accordingly, and not according, in some respects, to my requisitions and expectations of what they and I ought to be, then, like a good Mussulman[42] and fatalist, I should endeavor to be satisfied with things as they are, and say it is the will of God. And, above all, there is this difference between resisting this and a purely brute or natural force, that I can resist this with some effect; but I cannot expect, like Orpheus,[43] to change the nature of the rocks and trees and beasts.

I do not wish to quarrel with any man or nation. I do not wish to split hairs, to make fine distinctions, or set myself up as better than my neighbors. I seek rather, I may say, even an excuse for conforming to the laws of the land. I am but too ready to conform to them. Indeed, I have reason to suspect myself on this head;[44] and each year, as the tax-gatherer comes round, I find myself disposed to review the acts and position of the general and State governments, and the spirit of the people to discover a pretext for conformity.

> "We must affect our country as our parents,
> And if at any time we alienate
> Out love or industry from doing it honor,
> We must respect effects and teach the soul
> Matter of conscience and religion,
> And not desire of rule or benefit."[45]

I believe that the State will soon be able to take all my work of this sort out of my hands, and then I shall be no better a patriot than my fellow-countrymen. Seen from a lower point of view, the Constitution, with all its faults, is very good; the law and the courts are very respectable; even this State and this American government are, in many respects, very admirable, and rare things, to be thankful for, such as a great many have described them; but seen from a point of view a little higher, they are what I have described them; seen from a higher still, and the highest, who shall say what they are, or that they are worth looking at or thinking of at all?

However, the government does not concern me much, and I shall bestow the fewest possible thoughts on it. It is not many moments that I live under a government, even in this world. If a man is thought-free, fancy-free, imagination-free, that which *is not* never for a long time appearing *to be* to him, unwise rulers or reformers cannot fatally interrupt him.

I know that most men think differently from myself; but those whose lives are by profession devoted to the study of these or kindred subjects content me as little as any. Statesmen and legislators, standing so completely within the institution, never distinctly and nakedly behold it. They speak of moving society, but have no resting-place without it. They may be men of a certain experience and discrimination, and have no doubt invented ingenious and even useful systems, for which we sincerely thank them; but all their wit and usefulness lie within certain not very wide limits. They are wont to forget that the world is not governed by policy and expediency. Webster[46] never goes behind government, and so cannot speak with authority about it. His words are wisdom to those legislators who contemplate no essential reform in the existing government; but for thinkers, and those who legislate for all time, he never once glances at the subject. I know of those whose serene and wise speculations on this theme would soon reveal the limits of his mind's range and hospitality. Yet, compared with the cheap professions of most reformers, and the still cheaper wisdom and eloquence of politicians in general, his are almost the only sensible and valuable words, and we thank Heaven for him. Comparatively, he is always strong, original, and, above all, practical. Still, his quality is not wisdom, but prudence. The lawyer's truth is not Truth, but consistency or a consistent expediency. Truth is always in harmony with herself, and is not concerned chiefly to reveal the justice that may consist with wrong-doing. He well deserves to be called, as he has been called, the Defender of the Constitution. There are really no blows to be given by him but defensive ones. He is not a leader, but a follower. His leaders are the men of '87.[47] "I have never made an effort," he says, "and never propose to make an effort; I have never countenanced an effort, and never mean to countenance an effort, to disturb the arrangement as originally made, by which various the States came into the Union." Still thinking of the sanction which the Constitution gives to slavery, he says, "Because it was part of the original compact—let it stand." Notwithstanding his special acuteness and ability, he is unable to take a fact out of its merely political relations, and behold it as it lies absolutely to be disposed of by the intellect—what, for instance, it behooves a man to do here in American today with regard to slavery—but ventures, or is driven, to make some such desperate answer to the following, while professing to speak absolutely, and as a private man—from which what new and singular code of social duties might be inferred? "The manner," says he, "in which the governments of those States where slavery exists are to regulate it, is for their own consideration, under the responsibility to their constituents, to the general laws of propriety, humanity, and justice, and to God. Associations formed elsewhere, springing from a feeling of humanity, or any other cause, have nothing whatever to do with it. They have never received any encouragement from me and they never will."

They who know of no purer sources of truth, who have traced up its stream no higher, stand, and wisely stand, by the Bible and the Constitution, and drink at it there with reverence and humility; but they who behold where it comes trickling into this lake or that pool, gird up their loins once more, and continue their pilgrimage toward its fountainhead.

No man with a genius for legislation has appeared in America. They are rare in the history of the world. There are orators, politicians, and eloquent men, by the thousand; but the speaker has not yet opened his mouth to speak who is capable of settling the much-vexed questions of the day. We love eloquence for its own sake, and not for any truth which it may utter, or any heroism it may inspire. Our legislators have not yet learned the comparative value of free trade and of freedom, of union, and of rectitude, to a nation. They have no genius or talent for comparatively humble questions of taxation and finance, commerce and manufactures and agriculture. If we were left solely to the wordy wit of legislators in Congress for our guidance, uncorrected by the seasonable experience and the effectual complaints of the people, America would not long retain her rank among the nations. For eighteen hundred years, though perchance I have no right to say it, the New Testament has been written; yet where is the legislator who has wisdom and practical talent enough to avail himself of the light which it sheds on the science of legislation?

The authority of government, even such as I am willing to submit to—for I will cheerfully obey those who know and can do better than I, and in many things even those who neither know nor can do so well—is still an impure one: to be strictly just, it must have the sanction and consent of the governed. It can have no pure right over my person and property but what I concede to it. The progress from an absolute to a limited monarchy, from a limited monarchy to a democracy, is a progress toward a true respect for the individual. Even the Chinese philosopher[48] was wise enough to regard the individual as the basis of the empire. Is a democracy, such as we know it, the last improvement possible in government? Is it not possible to take a step further towards recognizing and organizing the rights of man? There will never be a really free and enlightened State until the State comes to recognize the individual as a higher and independent power, from which all its own power and authority are derived, and treats him accordingly. I please myself with imagining a State at last which can afford to be just to all men, and to treat the individual with respect as a neighbor; which even would not think it inconsistent with its own repose if a few were to live aloof from it, not meddling with it, nor embraced by it, who fulfilled all the duties of neighbors and fellow men. A State which bore this kind of fruit, and suffered it to drop off as fast as it ripened, would prepare the way for a still more perfect and glorious State, which also I have imagined, but not yet anywhere seen.

Endnotes

1. First published as "Resistance to Civil Government," in a short-lived periodical, *Aesthetic Papers* (May 14, 1849), edited by the transcendentalist Elizabeth Peabody, Hawthorne's sister-in-law. Under its present title the essay was first published posthumously in *A Yankee in Canada* (1866).

2. The idea expressed in the motto was a common one at the time. In his *First Inaugural Address* (1801), Jefferson advocated a government that would leave men "free to regulate their own pursuits." In *Politics* (1841) Emerson had written "The less government we have the better." Thoreau derived his motto from the words on the masthead of the *United States Magazine and Democratic Review*, a New York monthly.

3. Thoreau wrote "Civil Disobedience" at the time of the Mexican War (1846–1848), a war which many New Englanders saw as a strategem to aid the spread of Southern slavery. The essay was first presented as a lecture at the Concord Lyceum on January 26, 1848, under the title "The Rights and Duties of the Individual in Relation to Government."

4. Boys who carried gunpowder to cannon.

5. Presumably a reference to the United States Navy Yard in Boston, Massachusetts.

6. Corpse.

7. From "The Burial of Sir John Moore at Corunna" (1817), by Charles Wolfe (1791–1823), Irish poet.

8. Citizens authorized to help keep the peace—a sheriff's "posse."

9. "Imperious Caesar, dead and turn'd to clay, / Might stop a hole to keep the wind away." *Hamlet*, Act V, Scene i, lines 236–237.

10. *King John*, Act V, Scene ii, lines 79–82.

11. The American Revolution (1775–1783).

12. Mexico.

13. William Paley (1743–1805), English theologian, author of *Principles of Moral and Political Philosophy* (1785), which Thoreau quotes.

14. Jesus said, "Whosoever will save his life shall lose it: but whosoever will lose his life for my sake, the same shall save it." Luke 9:24.

15. Cyril Tourneur (1575?–1626), *The Revenger's Tragedy* (1607), Act IV, Scene iv, lines 70–72.

16. "Know ye not that a little leaven leaveneth the whole lump?" I Corinthians 5:6.

17. News.

18. The Democratic Convention of 1848.

19. The Independent Order of Odd Fellows (established 1819), a benevolent and mutual aid society that still exists.

20. Phrenological terminology meaning one whose head shape indicates that he loves company.

21. I.e., before he has become a man. Upon reaching manhood, Roman boys were permitted to wear the *toga virilis* (the adult male's outer garment of white wool).

22. Radical Massachusetts abolitionists who feared that the Mexican War would lead to the creation of new slave states.

23. President James K. Polk's call for money and troops to fight Mexico.

24. Nicolaus Copernicus, Polish astronomer (1473–1543) threatened with excommunication from the church for asserting that the Earth was not the center of the universe. Martin Luther (1483–1546), German monk and founder of Protestantism.

25. I.e., tax money totaling nine shillings ($1.50), which Thoreau refused to pay. Although there was no U.S. coin named "shilling," the term was used through the nineteenth century, especially in New England, to reckon sums at the rate of six shillings to the dollar.

26. A device, like an automobile brake, that applies friction to slow or stop a moving part.

27. Samuel Hoar (1778–1856), Massachusetts senator and Thoreau's neighbor at Concord, was sent to South Carolina in 1844 to protest the seizure of black seamen on Massachusetts ships in South Carolina ports. He was driven from South Carolina by threats and legal action.

28. Matthew 22:16–22.

29. Rent.

30. Chinese philosopher (c. 551–479 B.C.). The quotation is from *The Analects*, chapter VIII, book 13.

31. In nineteenth-century Massachusetts, church assessments were collected by town governments. Because Thoreau's parents were church members, Thoreau was listed on the church "tax" rolls and thus received bills (beginning in 1838) from the town treasurer.

32. The Concord Lyceum, a voluntary educational society, sponsored an annual lecture series.

33. Town officials.

34. Thoreau was jailed July 23 or 24, 1846. Bronson Alcott had been arrested on the same charge three years before. Both Alcott and Thoreau refused to pay the poll tax (a general tax on all males between twenty and seventy) as a protest against Massachusetts' legal recognition of Southern slavery.

35. Thoreau's personal friend Sam Staples.

36. Jail cells.

37. I.e., honest.

38. A town where county (shire) offices, courts, and jails are located.

39. Probably Thoreau's Aunt Maria Thoreau.

40. Harnessed.

41. The title of a volume (1832) recounting the prison experiences of Silvio Pellico (1788–1854), Italian revolutionary patriot.

42. Muslim.

43. In Greek legend, the music of Orpheus "charmed" gods, beasts, and even inanimate objects.

44. Point.

45. Adapted from *The Battle of Alcazar* (1594), Act II, Scene ii, lines 425–430, a drama by George Peele (1558?–1597?).

46. Daniel Webster (1782–1852), Massachusetts senator and famous orator who angered abolitionists by supporting the Fugitive Slave Law, which assisted in the return of escaped slaves.

47. Those who drafted the Constitution in 1787.

48. "These extracts have been inserted since the lecture was read."—Thoreau's note. He quotes from speeches by Webster in 1845 and 1848.

49. Confucius.

Questions for Reading and Analysis

1. How does Thoreau justify not paying his taxes with which he does not agree?

2. What does Thoreau mean when he writes, "The mass of men serve the state . . . not as men mainly, but as machines, with their bodies"?

3. What is Thoreau's attitude toward government?

4. How does Thoreau view his night in jail?

5. Do you agree with Thoreau's view?

A nalyzing a study conduced by psychologist Terrie Moffitt, Nancy
Updike argues that we need to look at domestic violence "without
preconceived ideas about gender, violence, and relationships." Her
essay appeared in the May/June 1999 issue of Mother Jones.

Hitting the Wall

Nancy Updike

A surprising fact has turned up in the grimly familiar world of domestic violence: Women report using violence in their relationships more often than
men. This is not a crack by some antifeminist cad; the information will
soon be published by the Justice Department in a report summarizing the results
of in-depth, face-to-face interviews with a representative sample of 860 men and
women whom researchers have been following since birth. Conducted in New
Zealand by Terrie Moffitt, a University of Wisconsin psychology professor, the
study supports data published in 1980 indicating that wives hit their husbands at
least as often as husbands hit their wives.

When the 1980 study was released, it was so controversial that some of the
researchers received death threats. Advocates for battered women were outraged
because the data seemed to suggest that the risk of injury from domestic violence
is as high for men as it is for women, which isn't true. Whether or not women are
violent themselves, they are much more likely to be severely injured or killed by
domestic violence, so activists dismissed the findings as meaningless.

But Moffitt's research emerges in a very different context—namely, that of a
movement that is older, wiser, and ready to begin making sense of uncomfortable
truths. Twenty years ago, "domestic violence" meant men hitting women. Period.
That was the only way to understand it or to talk about it. But today, after decades
of research and activism predicated on that assumption, the number of women
killed each year in domestic violence incidents remains distressingly high: a sobering
1,326 in 1996, compared with 1,600 two decades earlier. In light of the persis-
tence of domestic violence, researchers are beginning to consider a broader range
of data, including the possible significance of women's violence. This willingness
to pay attention to what was once considered reactionary nonsense signals a fundamental conceptual shift in how domestic violence is being studied.

Violence in the home has never been easy to research. Even the way we measure it reflects the kind of murky data that has plagued the field. For instance, one
could argue that the number of fatalities resulting from domestic violence is not the
best measure of the problem, as not all acts of brutality end in death. It is, however, one of the few reliable statistics in a field where concrete numbers are difficult to come by. Many nonlethal domestic violence incidents go unreported or are

categorized as something else—aggravated assault, simple assault—when they are reported. But another reason we haven't been able to effectively measure domestic violence is that we don't understand it, and, because we don't understand it, we haven't been able to stop it. Money and ideology are at the heart of the problem.

For years, domestic violence research was underfunded and conducted piece-meal, sometimes by researchers with more zeal for the cause of battered women than training in research methodology. The results were often ideology-driven "statistics," such as the notorious (and false) claim that more men beat their wives on Super Bowl Sunday, which dramatized the cause of domestic violence victims but further confused an already intricate issue. In 1994, Congress asked the National Research Council, an independent Washington, D.C., think tank, to evaluate the state of knowledge about domestic abuse. The NRC report concluded that "this field of research is characterized by the absence of clear conceptual models, large-scale databases, longitudinal research, and reliable instrumentation."

Moffitt is part of a new wave of domestic violence researchers who are bringing expertise from other areas of study, and her work is symbolic of the way scientists are changing their conception of the roots of domestic violence.

"[She] is taking domestic violence out of its standard intellectual confines and putting it into a much larger context, that of violence in general," says Daniel Nagin, a crime researcher and the Theresa and H. John Heinz III Professor of Public Policy at Carnegie Mellon University.

Moffitt is a developmental psychologist who has spent most of her career studying juvenile delinquency, which was the original focus of her research. She started inter-viewing her subjects about violence in their relationships after 20 years of research into other, seemingly unrelated aspects of their lives: sex and drug-use habits, crim-inal activities, social networks and family ties, and signs of mental illness.

"I had looked at other studies of juvenile delinquency," Moffitt says, "and saw that people in their 20s were dropping out of street crime, and I wondered, 'Are all of these miraculous recoveries where they're just reforming and giving up crime? Or are they getting out of their parents' home and moving in with a girlfriend and finding victims who are more easily accessible?' So I decided we'd better not just ask them about street violence, but also about violence within the home, with a partner."

What she found was that the women in her study who were in violent rela-tionships were more like their partners, in many ways, than they were like the other women in the study. Both the victims and the aggressors in violent relation-ships, Moffitt found, were more likely to be unemployed and less educated than couples in nonviolent relationships. Moffitt also found that "female perpetrators of partner violence differed from nonviolent women with respect to factors that could not be solely the result of being in a violent relationship." Her research dis-putes a long-held belief about the nature of domestic violence: If a woman hits, it's only in response to her partner's attacks. The study suggests that some women may simply be prone to violence—by nature or circumstance—just as some men may be.

Moffitt's findings don't change the fact that women are much more at risk in domestic violence, but they do suggest new ways to search for the origins of violence in the home. And once we know which early experiences can lead to domestic violence, we can start to find ways to intervene before the problem begins.

Prevention is a controversial goal, however, because it often calls for changes in the behavior of the victim as well as the batterer, and for decades activists have been promoting the seemingly opposite view. And even though it is possible to talk about prevention without blaming victims or excusing abusers, the issue is a mine-field of preconceived ideas about gender, violence, and relationships, and new approaches may seem too scary to contemplate.

In domestic violence research, it seems, the meaning of any new data is pre-determined by ideological agendas set a long time ago, and the fear that new infor-mation can be misinterpreted can lead to a rejection of the information itself. In preparing this column, I called a well-known women's research organization and asked scientists there about new FBI statistics indicating a substantial recent increase in violent crime committed by girls ages 12 to 18. The media contact told me the organization had decided not to collect any information about those statistics and that it didn't think it was a fruitful area of research, because girls are still much more likely to be victims of violence than perpetrators.

It's impossible to know yet whether such numbers are useful, whether they're a statistical blip or a trend, or whether the girls committing violent crimes now are more likely to end up in violent relationships. But to ignore them on principle—as activists and researchers ignored the data about women's violence years ago—is to give up on determining the roots of violence, which seem to be much more complicated than whether a person is born with a Y chromosome.

What's clear is that women's and girls' violence is not meaningless, either for researchers or for the women themselves. It turns out that teenage girls who commit violent crimes "are two times more likely than juvenile male offenders to become victims themselves in the course of the offending incident," according to an FBI report. I'd like to hear more about that, please, not less. Moffitt's findings about women's violence and the FBI statistics are invitations to further research—not in spite of the fact that so many women are being beaten and killed every year, but because of it.

Questions for Reading and Analysis

1. What is the most important point Updike wants to get across to her readers? Where does she state this point?

2. Updike claims that "money and ideology are at the heart of the problem" of researching domestic violence objectively. What does she mean by this? How does she back up this statement?

3. In what way is Terrie Moffit's study an important milestone in domestic violence research?

4. What is the most important point that Moffit's study suggests?

5. Does Moffit's study *deny* violence against women? How does it relate to what you have heard and read about (male) aggression against women?

A lice Walker (b. 1944) is perhaps best known for her novel The
Color Purple. *She has written extensively, in fiction and non-
fiction, on issues concerning black women, especially the ways in
which they preserve their heritage through art. Her short story
"Everyday Use" treats the theme of heritage as it describes the struggle
of two sisters over an heirloom quilt.*

Everyday Use

Alice Walker

for your grandmamma

I will wait for her in the yard that Maggie and I made so clean and wavy yesterday
afternoon. A yard like this is more comfortable than most people know. It is not
just a yard. It is like an extended living room. When the hard clay is swept clean
as a floor and the fine sand around the edges lined with tiny, irregular grooves,
anyone can come and sit and look up into the elm tree and wait for the breezes that
never come inside the house.

Maggie will be nervous until after her sister goes: she will stand hopelessly in
corners, homely and ashamed of the burn scars down her arms and legs, eyeing her
sister with a mixture of envy and awe. She thinks her sister has held life always in
the palm of one hand, that "no" is a word the world never learned to say to her.

You've no doubt seen those TV shows where the child who has "made it" is
confronted, as a surprise, by her own mother and father, tottering in weakly from
backstage. (A pleasant surprise, of course: What would they do if parent and child
came on the show only to curse out and insult each other?) On TV mother and child
embrace and smile into each other's faces. Sometimes the mother and father weep,
the child wraps them in her arms and leans across the table to tell how she would
not have made it without their help. I have seen these programs.

Sometimes I dream a dream in which Dee and I are suddenly brought together
on a TV program of this sort. Out of a dark and soft-seated limousine I am ushered into a bright room filled with many people. There I meet a smiling, gray,
sporty man like Johnny Carson who shakes my hand and tells me what a fine girl
I have. Then we are on the stage and Dee is embracing me with tears in her eyes.
She pins on my dress a large orchid, even though she has told me once that she
thinks orchids are tacky flowers.

In real life I am a large, big-boned woman with rough, man-working hands.
In the winter I wear flannel nightgowns to bed and overalls during the day. I can
kill and clean a hog as mercilessly as a man. My fat keeps me hot in zero weather.

I can work outside all day, breaking ice to get water for washing; I can eat pork liver cooked over the open fire minutes after it comes steaming from the hog. One winter I knocked a bull calf straight in the brain between the eyes with a sledge hammer and had the meat hung up to chill before nightfall. But of course all this does not show on television. I am the way my daughter would want me to be: a hundred pounds lighter, my skin like an uncooked barley pancake. My hair glistens in the hot bright lights. Johnny Carson has much to do to keep up with my quick and witty tongue.

But that is a mistake. I know even before I wake up. Who ever knew a Johnson with a quick tongue? Who can even imagine me looking a strange white man in the eye? It seems to me I have talked to them always with one foot raised in flight, with my head turned in whichever way is farthest from them. Dee, though. She would always look anyone in the eye. Hesitation was no part of her nature.

"How do I look, Mama?" Maggie says, showing just enough of her thin body enveloped in pink skirt and red blouse for me to know she's there, almost hidden by the door.

"Come out into the yard," I say.

Have you ever seen a lame animal, perhaps a dog run over by some careless person rich enough to own a car, sidle up to someone who is ignorant enough to be kind to them? That is the way my Maggie walks. She has been like this, chin on chest, eyes on ground, feet in shuffle, ever since the fire that burned the other house to the ground.

Dee is lighter than Maggie, with nicer hair and a fuller figure. She's a woman now, though sometimes I forget. How long ago was it that the other house burned? Ten, twelve years? Sometimes I can still hear the flames and feel Maggie's arms sticking to me, her hair smoking and her dress falling off her in little black papery flakes. Her eyes seemed stretched open, blazed upon by the flames reflected in them. And Dee. I see her standing off under the sweet gum tree she used to dig gum out of; a look of concentration on her face as she watched the last dingy gray board of the house fall in toward the red-hot brick chimney. Why don't you do a dance around the ashes? I'd wanted to ask her. She had hated the house that much.

I used to think she hated Maggie, too. But that was before we raised the money, the church and me, to send her to Augusta to school. She used to read to us without pity; forcing words, lies, and other folks' habits, whole lives upon us two, sitting trapped and ignorant underneath her voice. She washed us in a river of make-believe, burned us with a lot of knowledge we didn't necessarily need to know. Pressed us to her with the serious way she read, to shove us away at just the moment, like dimwits, we seemed about to understand.

Dee wanted nice things. A yellow organdy dress to wear to her graduation from high school; black pumps to match a green suit she'd made from an old suit somebody gave me. She was determined to stare down any disaster in her efforts. Her eyelids would not flicker for minutes at a time. Often I fought off the temptation to shake her. At sixteen she had a style of her own: and knew what style was.

I never had an education myself. After second grade the school was closed down. Don't ask me why: in 1927 colored asked fewer questions than they do now. Sometimes Maggie reads to me. She stumbles along good naturedly but can't see well. She knows she is not bright. Like good looks and money, quickness passed her by. She will marry John Thomas (who has mossy teeth in an earnest face) and then I'll be free to sit here and I guess just sing church songs to myself. Although I was never a good singer. Never could carry a tune. I was always better at a man's job. I used to love to milk till I was hooked[1] in the side in '49. Cows are soothing and slow and don't bother you, unless you try to milk them the wrong way.

I have deliberately turned my back on the house. It is three rooms, just like the one that burned, except the roof is tin; they don't make shingle roofs any more. There are no real windows, just some holes cut in the sides, like the portholes in a ship, but not round and not square, with rawhide holding the shutters up on the outside. This house is in a pasture, too, like the other one. No doubt when Dee sees it she will want to tear it down. She wrote me once that no matter where we "choose" to live, she will manage to come see us. But she will never bring her friends. Maggie and I thought about this and Maggie asked me, "Mama, when did Dee ever *have* any friends?"

She had a few. Furtive boys in pink shirts hanging about on washday after school. Nervous girls who never laughed. Impressed with her they worshiped the well-turned phrase, the cute shape, the scalding humor that erupted like bubbles in lye. She read to them.

When she was courting Jimmy T she didn't have much time to pay to us, but turned all her faultfinding power on him. He *flew* to marry a cheap city girl from a family of ignorant flashy people. She hardly had time to recompose herself.

When she comes I will meet—but there they are!

Maggie attempts to make a dash for the house, in her shuffling way, but I stay her with my hand. "Come back here," I say. And she stops and tries to dig a well in the sand with her toe.

It is hard to see them clearly through the strong sun. But even the first glimpse of leg out of the car tells me it is Dee. Her feet were always neat-looking, as if God himself had shaped them with a certain style. From the other side of the car comes a short, stocky man. Hair is all over his head a foot long and hanging from his chin like a kinky mule tail. I hear Maggie suck in her breath. "Uhnnnh," is what it sounds like. Like when you see the wriggling end of a snake just in front of your foot on the road. "Uhnnnh."

Dee next. A dress down to the ground, in this hot weather. A dress so loud it hurts my eyes. There are yellows and oranges enough to throw back the light of the sun. I feel my whole face warming from the heat waves it throws out. Earrings gold, too, and hanging down to her shoulders. Bracelets dangling and making noises when she moves her arm up to shake the folds of the dress out of her armpits. The dress is loose and flows, and as she walks closer, I like it. I hear Maggie go "Uhnnnh" again. It is her sister's hair. It stands straight up like the wool on a sheep. It is black as night and around the edges are two long pigtails that rope about like small lizards disappearing behind her ears.

"Wa-su-zo-Tean-o!" she says, coming on in that gliding way the dress makes her move. The short stocky fellow with the hair to his navel is all grinning and he follows up with "Asalamalakim,[2] my mother and sister!" He moves to hug Maggie

457

but she falls back, right up against the back of my chair. I feel her trembling there and when I look up I see the perspiration falling off her chin.

"Don't get up," says Dee. Since I am stout it takes something of a push. You can see me trying to move a second or two before I make it. She turns, showing white heels through her sandals, and goes back to the car. Out she peeks next with a Polaroid. She stoops down quickly and lines up picture after picture of me sitting there in front of the house with Maggie cowering behind me. She never takes a shot without making sure the house is included. When a cow comes nibbling around the edge of the yard she snaps it and me and Maggie *and* the house. Then she puts the Polaroid in the back seat of the car, and comes up and kisses me on the forehead.

Meanwhile Asalamalakim is going through motions with Maggie's hand. Maggie's hand is as limp as a fish, and probably as cold, despite the sweat, and she keeps trying to pull it back. It looks like Asalamalakim wants to shake hands but wants to do it fancy. Or maybe he don't know how people shake hands. Anyhow, he soon gives up on Maggie.

"Well," I say. "Dee."

"No, Mama," she says. "Not 'Dee,' Wangero Leewanika Kemanjo!"

"What happened to 'Dee'?" I wanted to know.

"She's dead," Wangero said. "I couldn't bear it any longer, being named after the people who oppress me."

"You know as well as me you was named after your aunt Dicie," I said. Dicie is my sister. She named Dee. We called her "Big Dee" after Dee was born.

"But who was *she* named after?" asked Wangero.

"I guess after Grandma Dee," I said.

"And who was she named after?" asked Wangero.

"Her mother," I said, and saw Wangero was getting tired. "That's about as far back as I can trace it," I said. Though, in fact, I probably could have carried it back beyond the Civil War through the branches.

"Well," said Asalamalakim, "there you are."

"Uhnnnh," I heard Maggie say.

"There I was not," I said, "before 'Dicie' cropped up in our family, so why should I try to trace it that far back?"

He just stood there grinning, looking down on me like somebody inspecting a Model A car. Every once in a while he and Wangero sent eye signals over my head.

"How do you pronounce this name?" I asked.

"You don't have to call me by it if you don't want to," said Wangero.

"Why shouldn't I?" I asked. "If that's what you want us to call you, we'll call you."

"I know it might sound awkward at first," said Wangero.

"I'll get used to it," I said. "Ream it out again."

Well, soon we got the name out of the way. Asalamalakim had a name twice as long and three times as hard. After I tripped over it two or three times he told me to just call him Hakim-a-barber. I wanted to ask him was he a barber, but I didn't really think he was, so I didn't ask.

"You must belong to those beef-cattle peoples down the road," I said. They said "Asalamalakim" when they met you, too, but they didn't shake hands. Always too busy: feeding the cattle, fixing the fences, putting up salt-lick shelters, throwing down hay. When the white folks poisoned some of the herd the men stayed up all night with rifles in their hands. I walked a mile and a half just to see the sight.

Hakim-a-barber said, "I accept some of their doctrines, but farming and raising cattle is not my style." (They didn't tell me, and I didn't ask, whether Wangero (Dee) had really gone and married him.)

We sat down to eat and right away he said he didn't eat collards and pork was unclean. Wangero, though, went on through the chitlins and corn bread, the greens and everything else. She talked a blue streak over the sweet potatoes. Everything delighted her. Even the fact that we still used the benches her daddy made for the table when we couldn't afford to buy chairs.

"Oh, Mama!" she cried. Then turned to Hakim-a-barber. "I never knew how lovely these benches are. You can feel the rump prints," she said, running her hands underneath her and along the bench. Then she gave a sigh and her hand closed over Grandma Dee's butter dish. "That's it!" she said. "I knew there was something I wanted to ask you if I could have." She jumped up from the table and went over in the corner where the churn stood, the milk in it clabber by now. She looked at the churn and looked at it.

"This churn top is what I need," she said. "Didn't Uncle Buddy whittle it out of a tree you all used to have?"

"Yes," I said.

"Uh huh," she said happily. "And I want the dasher, too."

"Uncle Buddy whittle that, too"? asked the barber.

Dee (Wangero) looked up at me.

"Aunt Dee's first husband whittled the dash," said Maggie so low you almost couldn't hear her. "His name was Henry, but they called him Stash."

"Maggie's brain is like an elephant's," Wangero said, laughing. "I can use the churn top as a centerpiece for the alcove table," she said, sliding a plate over the churn, "and I'll think of something artistic to do with the dasher."

When she finished wrapping the dasher the handle stuck out. I took it for a moment in my hands. You didn't even have to look close to see where hands pushing the dasher up and down to make butter had left a kind of sink in the wood. In fact, there were a lot of small sinks; you could see where thumbs and fingers had sunk into the wood. It was beautiful light yellow wood, from a tree that grew in the yard where Big Dee and Stash had lived.

After dinner Dee (Wangero) went to the trunk at the foot of my bed and started rifling through it. Maggie hung back in the kitchen over the dishpan. Out came Wangero with two quilts. They had been pieced by Grandma Dee and then Big Dee and me had hung them on the quilt frames on the front porch and quilted them. One was in the Lone Star pattern. The other was Walk Around the Mountain. In both of them were scraps of dresses Grandma Dee had worn fifty and more years ago. Bits and pieces of Grandpa Jarrell's Paisley shirts. And one teeny faded blue piece, about the size of a penny matchbox, that was from Great Grandpa Ezra's uniform that he wore in the Civil War.

"Mama," Wangero said sweet as a bird. "Can I have these old quilts?"

I heard something fall in the kitchen, and a minute later the kitchen door slammed.

"Why don't you take one or two of the others?" I asked. "These old things was just done by me and Big Dee from some tops your grandma pieced before she died."

"No," said Wangero. "I don't want those. They are stitched around the borders by machine."

"That'll make them last better," I said.

"That's not the point," said Wangero. "These are all pieces of dresses Grandma used to wear. She did all this stitching by hand. Imagine!" She held the quilts securely in her arms, stroking them.

"Some of the pieces, like those lavender ones, come from old clothes her mother handed down to her," I said, moving up to touch the quilts. Dee (Wangero) moved back just enough so that I couldn't reach the quilts. They already belonged to her.

"Imagine!" she breathed again, clutching them closely to her bosom.

"The truth is," I said, "I promised to give them quilts to Maggie, for when she marries John Thomas."

She gasped like a bee had stung her.

"Maggie can't appreciate these quilts!" she said. "She'd probably be backward enough to put them to everyday use."

"I reckon she would," I said. "God knows I've been saving 'em for long enough with nobody using 'em. I hope she will!" I didn't want to bring up how I had offered Dee (Wangero) a quilt when she went away to college. Then she had told me they were old-fashioned, out of style.

"But they're *priceless!*" She was saying now, furiously; for she has a temper. "Maggie would put them on the bed and in five years they'd be in rags. Less than that!"

"She can always make some more," I said. "Maggie knows how to quilt."

Dee (Wangero) looked at me with hatred. "You just will not understand. The point is these quilts, *these* quilts!"

"Well," I said, stumped. "What would *you* do with them?"

"Hang them," she said. As if that was the only thing you *could* do with quilts.

Maggie by now was standing in the door. I could almost hear the sound her feet made as they scraped over each other.

"She can have them, Mama," she said, like somebody used to never winning anything, or having anything reserved for her. "I can 'member Grandma Dee without the quilts."

I looked at her hard. She had filled her bottom lip with checkerberry snuff and it gave her face a kind of dopey, hangdog look. It was Grandma Dee and Big Dee who taught her how to quilt herself. She stood there with her scarred hands hidden in the folds of her skirt. She looked at her sister with something like fear but she wasn't mad at her. This was Maggie's portion. This was the way she knew God to work.

When I looked at her like that something hit me in the top of my head and ran down to the soles of my feet. Just like when I'm in church and the spirit of God touches me and I get happy and shout. I did something I never had done before: hugged Maggie to me, then dragged her into the room, snatched the quilts out of Miss Wangero's hands and dumped them into Maggie's lap. Maggie just sat there on my bed with her mouth open.

"Take one or two of the others," I said to Dee.

But she turned without a word and went to Hakim-a-barber.

"You just don't understand," she said, as Maggie and I came out to the car.

"What don't I understand?" I wanted to know.

"Your heritage," she said. And then she turned to Maggie, kissed her, and said, "You ought to try to make something of yourself, too, Maggie. It's really a new day for us. But from the way you and Mama still live you'd never know it."

She put on some sunglasses that hid everything above the tip of her nose and her chin.

Maggie smiled; maybe at the sunglasses, but a real smile, not scared. After we watched the car dust settle I asked Maggie to bring me a dip of snuff. And then the two of us sat there just enjoying, until it was time to go in the house and go to bed.

Endnotes

1. i.e., by the horn of the cow being milked.

2. Phonetic rendering of a Muslim greeting. "Wa-su-zo-Tean-o" is a similar rendering of an African dialect salutation.

Questions for Reading and Analysis

1. What is the mother's relationship with Dee? What is her relationship with Maggie?

2. What was Dee's attitude toward her family and the traditions of this family before she went to college? Do you think Dee has changed fundamentally since she left to go to school?

3. What does Dee see in the quilt? What does Maggie see in it? In what way do the two sisters represent different attitudes toward heritage and cultural traditions?

4. The mother decides in the end that Maggie is to have the quilt to put to "everyday use." Do you think she made the right decision? Why or why not?

A professor of Afro-American Studies and Religion at Harvard, Cornel West pays tribute to Malcolm X and his concept of "psychic conversion [that] holds that blacks must no longer view themselves through white lenses." However, he argues that black rage should not be directed exclusively at the white oppressors but against "any form of racism, patriarchy, homophobia, or economic injustice that impedes the opportunities of people to live lives of dignity and decency." The essay comes from his highly acclaimed Race Matters *(1993).*

Malcolm X and Black Rage

Cornel West

You don't stick a knife in a man's back nine inches and then pull it out six inches and say you're making progress.

—Malcolm X

No matter how much respect, no matter how much recognition, whites show towards me, as far as I'm concerned, as long as it is not shown to every one of our people in this country, it doesn't exist for me.

—Malcolm X

Malcolm X articulated Black rage in a manner unprecedented in American history. His style of communicating this rage bespoke a boiling urgency and an audacious sincerity; the substance of what he said highlighted the chronic refusal of most Americans to acknowledge the sheer absurdity that confronts human beings of African descent in this country—the incessant assaults on Black intelligence, beauty, character, and possibility. His profound commitment to affirm Black humanity at any cost and his tremendous courage to accent the hypocrisy of American society made Malcolm X the prophet of Black rage—then and now.

Malcolm X was the prophet of Black rage primarily because of his great love for Black people. His love was neither abstract nor ephemeral. Rather, it represented a concrete connection with a degraded and devalued people in need of *psychic conversion*. This connection is why Malcolm X's articulation of Black rage was not directed first and foremost at white America. Malcolm spoke love to Black people; he believed the love that motivated Black rage had to be felt by Black people in order for the rage to take on institutional forms. This love would produce a psychic conversion in Black people in that they would affirm themselves as human beings, no longer viewing their bodies, minds, and souls through white lenses, but believing themselves capable of taking control of their own destinies.

In American society—especially during Malcolm X's life in the 1950s and early '60s—such a psychic conversion could easily result in death. A proud, self-affirming Black person who truly believed in the capacity of Black people to throw off the yoke of white racist oppression and control their own destiny usually ended up as one of those strange fruit that Southern trees bore, about which the great Billie Holiday poignantly sang. So when Malcolm X articulated Black rage, he knew he also had to exemplify in his own life the courage and sacrifice that any truly self-loving Black person needs in order to confront the frightening consequences of being self-loving in American society. In other words, Malcolm X crystallized sharply the relation of Black affirmation of self, Black desire for freedom, Black rage against American society, and the likelihood of early Black death. Black psychic conversion—the decolonization of the mind, body, and soul that strips white supremacist lies of their authority, legitimacy, and efficacy—begins with a bold and defiant rejection of Black degradation and is sustained by urgent efforts to expand those spaces wherein Black humanity is affirmed; it often ends with early death owing to both white contempt for such a subversive sensibility and, among those captive to Black self-contempt and self-doubt, a Black disbelief.

Malcolm X's notion of psychic conversion holds that Black people must no longer view themselves through white lenses. His claim is that Black people will never value themselves as long as they subscribe to a standard of valuation that devalues them. For example, Michael Jackson may rightly wish to be viewed as a person, not a color (neither black nor white), but his facial revisions reveal a self-measurement based on a white yardstick. Despite the fact that Jackson is one of the greatest entertainers who has ever lived, he still views himself, at least in part, through white aesthetic lenses that devalue some of his African characteristics. Needless to say, Michael Jackson's example is but the more honest and visible instance of a rather pervasive self-loathing among many wealthy and professional-class Black people. Malcolm X's call for psychic conversion often strikes horror into this privileged group because so much of who they are and what they do is evaluated in terms of their wealth, status, and prestige in American society. On the other hand, this group often understands Malcolm X's claim more than others precisely because they have lived so intimately in a white world in which the devaluation of Black people is so often taken for granted or unconsciously assumed. It is no accident that the Black middle class has always had an ambivalent relation to Malcolm X—an open rejection of his militant strategy of wholesale defiance of American society and a secret embrace of his bold truth-telling about the depths of racism in American society. One rarely encounters a picture of Malcolm X (as one does Martin Luther King, Jr.) in the office of a Black professional, but there is no doubt that he dangles as the skeleton in the closet lodged in the racial memory of most Black professionals.

In short, Malcolm X's notion of psychic conversion is an implicit critique of W. E. B. Du Bois's idea of "double-consciousness." From Malcolm X's viewpoint, double-consciousness pertains more to those Black people who live "betwixt and between" the Black and white worlds—traversing and crisscrossing these worlds yet never settled in either. Hence, they crave peer acceptance in both, receive genuine approval from neither, yet persist in viewing themselves through the lenses of the dominant white society. For Malcolm X, this "double-consciousness" is less a description of the Black mode of being in America than a particular kind of colonized mind-set of a special group in Black America. Psychic conversion calls for not simply a rejection of the white lenses through which one sees oneself but, more specifically, a refusal to measure one's humanity by appealing to any white supremacist standard. Du Bois's double-consciousness seems to lock Black people into the quest for white approval and disappointment due mainly to white racist assessment, whereas Malcolm X suggests that this tragic syndrome can be broken. But how?

Malcolm X does not put forward a direct answer to this question. First, his well-known distinction between "house negroes" (who love and protect the white master) and "field negroes" (who hate and resist the white master) suggests that the masses of Black people are more likely to acquire decolonized sensibilities and hence less likely to be "co-opted" by the white status quo. Yet this rhetorical device, though insightful in highlighting different perspectives among Black people, fails as a persuasive description of the behavior of "well-to-do" Black folk and "poor" Black folk. In other words, there are numerous instances of "field negroes" with "house negro" mentalities and "house negroes" with "field negro" mentalities. Malcolm X's often-quoted distinction rightly highlights the propensity among highly assimilated black professionals to put "whiteness" (in all its various forms) on a pedestal, but it also tends to depict "poor" Black people's notions and enactments of "blackness" in an uncritical manner. Hence his implicit critique of Du Bois's idea of double-consciousness contains some truth yet offers an inadequate alternative.

Second, Malcolm X's Black nationalist viewpoint claims that the only legitimate response to white supremacist ideology and practice is Black self-love and Black self-determination free of the tension generated by double-consciousness. This claim is both subtle and problematic. It is subtle in that every Black Freedom Movement is predicated on an affirmation of African humanity and a quest for Black control over the destinies of Black people. Yet not every form of Black self-love affirms African humanity. Furthermore, not every project of Black self-determination consists of a serious quest for Black control over the destinies of Black people. Malcolm's claim tends to assume that Black nationalisms have a monopoly on Black self-love and Black self-determination. This fallacious assumption confuses the issues highlighted by Black nationalisms with the various ways in which Black nationalists and others understand these issues.

For example, the grand legacy of Marcus Garvey forces us never to forget that Black self-love and Black self-respect sit at the center of any possible Black Freedom Movement. Yet this does not mean that we must talk about Black self-love and Black self-respect in the way in which Garvey did, that is, on an imperial model in which Black armies and navies signify Black power. Similarly, the tradition of Elijah Muhammad compels us to acknowledge the centrality of Black self-regard and Black self-esteem, yet that does not entail an acceptance of how Elijah Muhammad talked about achieving this aim—by playing a game of Black supremacy that awakens us from our captivity to white supremacy. My point here is that a focus on the issues rightly targeted by Black nationalists and an openness to the insights of Black nationalists does not necessarily result in an acceptance of Black nationalist ideology. Malcolm X tended to make such an unwarranted move.

Malcolm X's notion of psychic conversion is based on the idea of Black spaces in American society in which Black community, humanity, love, care, concern, and support flourish. He sees this Black coming-together as the offspring of the recognition of a boiling Black rage. Facilitating this coming-together is where Malcolm X's project really falters. The fundamental challenge is: How can the boiling Black rage be contained and channeled in the Black spaces such that destructive and self-destructive consequences are abated? The greatness of Malcolm X is, in part, that he raises this question with a sharpness and urgency never before posed in Black America. Unfortunately, in his short life he never had a chance to grapple with it or solve it in idea and deed. Instead, until 1964, he adopted Elijah Muhammad's response to this challenge and castigated Martin Luther King, Jr.'s response to it.

In contrast to Malcolm X, Elijah Muhammad and Martin Luther King, Jr., understood one fundamental truth about Black rage: It must neither be ignored nor ignited. Both leaders, in their own ways, knew how to work with Black rage in a constructive manner, shape it through moral discipline, channel it into political organization, and guide it by charismatic leadership. Malcolm X could articulate Black rage much better than Elijah Muhammad or Martin Luther King, Jr.—but for most of his public life he tended to ignite Black rage and harness it for the Nation of Islam. Hence Malcolm's grappling with how to understand Black rage and what to do with it was subordinate to Elijah Muhammad's project of Black separate spaces for Black community, humanity, love, care, concern, and support. Malcolm X, however, did have two psychic conversions—the first was to the Nation of Islam, but the second, in 1964, was to orthodox Islam that rejected any form of racial supremacy.

The project of Black separatism—to which Malcolm X was beholden for most of his life after his first psychic conversion—suffered from deep intellectual and organizational problems. Unlike Malcolm X's notion of psychic conversion, Elijah Muhammad's idea of religious conversion was predicated on an obsession with white supremacy. The basic aim of Black Muslim theology—with its distinct Black supremacist account of the origins of white people—was to counter white supremacy. Yet this preoccupation with white supremacy still allowed white people to serve as the principal point of reference. That which fundamentally motivates one still dictates the terms of what one thinks and does—so the motivation of a Black supremacist doctrine reveals how obsessed one is with white supremacy. This is understandable in a white racist society—but it is crippling for a despised people struggling for freedom, in that one's eyes should be on the prize, not the perpetuator of one's oppression. In short, Elijah Muhammad's project remained captive to the supremacy game—a game mastered by the white racists he opposed and imitated with his *Black* supremacy doctrine.

Malcolm X's notion of psychic conversion can be understood and used such that it does not necessarily *entail* Black supremacy; it simply rejects Black captivity to white supremacist ideology and practice. Hence, as the major Black Muslim spokesperson, he had many sympathizers, though few of them actually became Muslim members. Why did Malcolm X permit his notion of psychic conversion to serve the Black supremacist claims of the Nation of Islam—claims that undermine much of the best of his call for psychic conversion? Malcolm X remained a devoted follower of Elijah Muhammad until 1964 partly because he believed the other major constructive channels of Black rage in America—the Black church and Black music—were less effective in producing and sustaining psychic conversion than the Nation of Islam. He knew that the electoral political system could never address the existential dimension of Black rage—hence he, like Elijah, shunned it. Malcolm X also recognized, as do too few Black leaders today, that the Black encounter with the absurd in racist American society yields a profound spiritual need for human affirmation and recognition. Hence the centrality of religion and music—those most spiritual of human activities—in Black life.

Yet, for Malcolm, much of Black religion and Black music had directed Black rage away from white racism and toward another world of heaven and sentimental romance. Needless to say, Malcolm's conception of Black Christianity as a white man's religion of pie-in-the-sky and Black music as soupy "I Love You B-a-b-y" romance is wrong. While it's true that most—but not all—of the Black music of Malcolm's day shunned Black rage, the case of the church-based Civil Rights movement would seem to counter his charge that Black Christianity serves as a sedative to put people to sleep rather than to ignite them to action. Like Elijah Muhammad (and unlike Malcolm X), Martin Luther King, Jr., concluded that Black rage was so destructive and self-destructive that without a moral theology and political organization, it would wreak havoc on Black America. His project of nonviolent resistance to white racism was an attempt to channel Black rage in political directions that preserved Black dignity and changed American society. But his despair at the sight of Watts in 1965 or Detroit and Newark in 1967 left him more and more pessimistic about the moral channeling of Black rage in America. To King, it looked as if cycles of chaos and destruction loomed on the horizon if these moral channels were ineffective or unappealing to the coming generation. For Malcolm, however, the Civil Rights movement was not militant enough. It failed to speak clearly and directly to and about Black rage.

Malcolm X also seems to have had almost no intellectual interest in dealing with what is distinctive about the Black church and Black music: *their cultural hybrid character in which the complex mixture of African, European, and Amerindian elements are constitutive of something that is new and Black in the modern world.* Like most Black nationalists, Malcolm X feared the culturally hybrid character of Black life. This fear resulted in the dependence on Manichean (black-and-white or male/female) channels for the direction of Black rage—forms characterized by charismatic leaders, patriarchal structures, and dogmatic pronouncements. The Manichean theology kept the white world at bay even as it heralded dominant white notions such as racial supremacy per se or the nation-state per se. The authoritarian arrangements imposed a top-down disciplined corps of devoted followers who contained their rage in an atmosphere of cultural repression (regulation of clothing worn, books and records consumed, sexual desire, etc.) and paternalistic protection of women.

The complex relation of cultural hybridity and critical sensibility (or jazz and democracy) evident here raises interesting questions. If Malcolm X feared cultural hybridity, to what degree or in what sense was he a serious democrat? Did he believe that the cure to the egregious ills of a racist American "democracy" was more democracy that included Black people? Did his relative silence regarding the monarchies he visited in the Middle East bespeak a downplaying of the role of democratic practices in empowering oppressed peoples? Was his fear of cultural hybridity partly rooted in his own reluctance to come to terms with his own personal hybridity, for example, his "redness," light skin, close white friends, and so on?

Malcolm X's fear of cultural hybridity rested on two political claims: that cultural hybridity downplayed the vicious character of white supremacy and that it so intimately linked the destinies of Black and white people that the possibility of Black freedom was unimaginable. Malcolm's fundamental focus on the varieties, subtleties, and cruelties of white racism made him suspicious of any discourse about cultural hybridity. Those figures who were most eloquent and illuminating about Black cultural hybridity in the 1950s and early '60s, such as Ralph Ellison and Albert Murray, were, in fact, political integrationists. Their position seemed to pass over too quickly the physical terror and psychic horror of being Black in America. To put it bluntly, Malcolm X identified much more with the mind-set of Richard Wright's Bigger Thomas in *Native Son* than with that of Ralph Ellison's protagonist in *Invisible Man*.

Malcolm X's deep pessimism about the capacity and possibility of white Americans to shed their racism led him, ironically, to downplay the past and present bonds between Blacks and whites. For if the two groups were, as Martin Luther King, Jr., put it, locked into "one garment of destiny," then the very chances for Black freedom were nil. Malcolm X's pessimism also kept him ambivalent about American democracy—for if the majority were racist, how could the Black minority ever be free? His definition of a "nigger" was "a victim of American democracy"— had not the *Herrenvolk* democracy of the United States made Black people noncitizens or anticitizens of the republic? Of course, the aim of a constitutional democracy is to safeguard the rights of the minority and avoid the tyranny of the majority. Yet the concrete practice of the U.S. legal system from 1883 to 1964 promoted a tyranny of the white majority much more than a safeguarding of the rights of Black Americans. In fact, these tragic facts drove Malcolm X to look elsewhere for the promotion and protection of Black people's rights—to institutions such as the United Nations and the Organization of African Unity. One impulse behind his internalization of the Black Freedom struggle in the United States was a deep pessimism about America's will to racial justice, no matter how democratic the nation was or is.

Malcolm X's fear of cultural hybridity also rested on a third concern: his own personal hybridity as the grandson of a white man, which blurred the very boundaries so rigidly policed by white supremacist authorities. For Malcolm X, the distinctive feature of American culture was not its cross-cultural syncretism but rather its enforcement of a racial caste system that defined any product of this syncretism as abnormal, alien, and other to both Black and white communities. Like Garvey, Malcolm X saw such hybridity—for example, mulattoes—as symbols of weakness and confusion. The very idea of not "fitting in" the U.S. discourse of whiteness and blackness meant one was subject to exclusion and marginalization by both whites and Blacks. For Malcolm X, in a racist society, this was a form of social death.

One would think that Malcolm X's second conversion, in 1964, might have allayed his fear of cultural hybridity. Yet there seems to be little evidence that he revised his understanding of the radically culturally hybrid character of Black life. Furthermore, his deep pessimism toward American democracy continued after his second conversion—though no longer on mythological grounds but solely on the historical experiences of Africans in the modern world. It is no accident that the non-Black persons Malcolm X encountered who helped change his mind about the capacity of white people to be human were outside of America and Europe—Muslims in the Middle East. Needless to say, Malcolm found the most striking feature of the Islamic regimes not to be their undemocratic practices but their acceptance of his Black humanity. This great prophet of Black rage—with all his brilliance, courage, and conviction—remained blind to basic structures of domination based on class, gender, and sexual orientation in the Middle East.

The contemporary focus on Malcolm X, especially among Black youth, can be understood as both the open articulation of Black rage (as in film videos and on tapes targeted at whites, Jews, Koreans, Black women, Black men, and others), and desperate attempts to channel this rage into something more than a marketable commodity for the culture industry. The young Black generation is up against forces of death, destruction, and disease unprecedented in the everyday life of Black urban people. This raw reality of drugs and guns, despair and decrepitude generates a raw rage that, among past Black spokespersons, only Malcolm X was able to approximate. The issues of psychic conversion, cultural hybridity, Black supremacy, authoritarian organization, borders and boundaries in sexuality, and other matters all loom large at present—the same issues Malcolm X left dangling at the end of the short life in which he articulated Black rage and affirmed Black humanity.

If we are to build on the best of Malcolm X, we must preserve and expand his notion of psychic conversion (best seen in the works of bell hooks) that cements networks and groups in which Black community, humanity, love, care, and concern can take root and grow. These spaces—beyond Black music and Black religion—reject Manichean ideologies and authoritarian arrangements in the name of moral visions, subtle analyses of wealth and power, and concrete strategies of principled coalitions and democratic alliances. These visions, analyses, and strategies never lose sight of Black rage, yet they focus this rage where it belongs: on any form of racism, patriarchy, homophobia, or economic injustice that impedes the opportunities of people to live lives of dignity and decency. Poverty is as much a target of rage as degraded identity.

Furthermore, the cultural hybrid character of Black life leads us to highlight a metaphor alien to Malcolm X's theology—yet consonant with his performances to audiences—namely, the metaphor of jazz. I use the term "jazz" here not so much as a term for a musical art-form as for a mode of being in the world, an improvisational mode of protean, fluid, and flexible dispositions toward reality suspicious of either/or viewpoints, dogmatic pronouncements, and supremacist ideologies. To be a jazz freedom fighter is to attempt to galvanize and energize world-weary people into forms of organization with accountable leadership that promotes critical exchange and broad reflection. The interplay of individuality and unity is not one of uniformity and unanimity imposed from above but rather of conflict among diverse groupings that reach a dynamic consensus subject to questioning and criticism. As with a soloist in a jazz quartet, quintet, or band, individuality is promoted in order to sustain and increase the *creative* tension with the group—a tension that yields higher levels of performance to achieve the aim of the collective project. This kind of critical and democratic sensibility flies in the face of any policing of borders and boundaries of "blackness," "maleness," "femaleness," or "whiteness." Black people's rage ought to target white supremacy but also realize that maleness can encompass feminists such as Frederick Douglass or W. E. B. Du Bois. Black people's rage should not overlook homophobia; it also should acknowledge that heterosexuality can be associated with so-called straight antihomophobes—just as the struggle against Black poverty can be supported by progressive elements of the well-to-do regardless of race, gender, or sexual orientation.

Malcolm X was the first great Black spokesperson who looked ferocious white racism in the eye, didn't blink, and lived long enough to tell America the truth about this glaring hypocrisy in a bold and defiant manner. Unlike Elijah Muhammad and Martin Luther King, Jr., he did not live long enough to forge his own distinctive ideas and ways of channeling Black rage in constructive channels to change American society. Only if we are as willing as Malcolm X to grow and confront the new challenges posed by the Black rage of our day will we take the Black freedom struggle to a new and higher level.

Questions for Reading and Analysis

1. How does West define Malcolm X's idea of "psychic conversion in black people"?

2. Why, according to West, would some members of the black middle and upper class resist Malcolm X's idea of psychic conversion?

3. What, according to West, did Elijah Muhammad and Martin Luther King, Jr., understand about black rage that Malcolm X did not understand?

4. How does West support his point that Malcolm X's idea of black supremacy is still indebted to white racism?

5. In what ways does West see black religion and music as a route to liberation from racism? How does he differ with Malcolm X on this point?

6. How does the metaphor of jazz serve to illustrate West's idea of overcoming "supremacist ideologies" and the fear of "cultural hybridity"?

Wiesenfeld laments the "disgruntled consumer approach" that many college students use to confront professors who give them grades they don't like, but he acknowledges a "weird innocence" in the attitude that grades are not linked to performance and that higher ones might be acquired through pleading. His essay appeared in the "My Turn" column in Newsweek *on June 17, 1996.*

Making the Grade

Many Students Wheedle for a Degree as if It Were a Freebie T Shirt

Kurt Wiesenfeld

It was a rookie error. After 10 years I should have known better, but I went to my office the day after final grades were posted. There was a tentative knock on the door. "Professor Wiesenfeld? I took your Physics 2121 class? I flunked it? I wonder if there's anything I can do to improve my grade?" I thought: "Why are you asking me? Isn't it too late to worry about it? Do you dislike making declarative statements?"

After the student gave his tale of woe and left, the phone rang. "I got a D in your class. Is there any way you can change it to 'Incomplete'?" Then the e-mail assault began: "I'm shy about coming in to talk to you, but I'm not shy about asking for a better grade. Anyway, it's worth a try." The next day I had three phone messages from students asking *me* to call *them*. I didn't.

Time was, when you received a grade, that was it. You might groan and moan, but you accepted it as the outcome of your efforts or lack thereof (and, yes, sometimes a tough grader). In the last few years, however, some students have developed a disgruntled-consumer approach. If they don't like their grade, they go to the "return" counter to trade it in for something better.

What alarms me is their indifference toward grades as an indication of personal effort and performance. Many, when pressed about why they think they deserve a better grade, admit they don't deserve one but would like one anyway. Having been raised on gold stars for effort and smiley faces for self-esteem, they've learned that they can get by without hard work and real talent if they can talk the professor into giving them a break. This attitude is beyond cynicism. There's a weird innocence to the assumption that one expects (even deserves) a better grade simply by begging for it. With that outlook, I guess I shouldn't be as flabbergasted as I was that 12 students asked me to change their grades *after* final grades were posted.

That's 10 percent of my class who let three months of midterms, quizzes and lab reports slide until long past remedy. My graduate student calls it hyperrational thinking: if effort and intelligence don't matter, why should deadlines? What matters is getting a better grade through an unearned bonus, the academic equivalent of a freebie T shirt or toaster giveaway. Rewards are disconnected from the quality of one's work. An act and its consequences are unrelated, random events.

Their arguments for wheedling better grades often ignore academic performance. Perhaps they feel it's not relevant. "If my grade isn't raised to a D, I'll lose my scholarship." "If you don't give me a C, I'll flunk out." One sincerely overwrought student pleaded, "If I don't pass, my life is over." This is tough stuff to deal with. Apparently, I'm responsible for someone's losing a scholarship, flunking out or deciding whether life has meaning. Perhaps these students see me as a commodities broker with something they want—a grade. Though intrinsically worthless, grades, if properly manipulated, can be traded for what has value: a degree, which means a job, which means money. The one thing college actually offers—a chance to learn—is considered irrelevant, even less than worthless, because of the long hours and hard work required.

In a society saturated with surface values, love of knowledge for its own sake does sound eccentric. The benefits of fame and wealth are more obvious. So is it right to blame students for reflecting the superficial values saturating our society?

Yes, of course it's right. These guys had better take themselves seriously now, because our country will be forced to take them seriously later, when the stakes are much higher. They must recognize that their attitude is not only self-destructive, but socially destructive. The erosion of quality control—giving appropriate grades for actual accomplishments—is a major concern in my department. One colleague noted that a physics major could obtain a degree without ever answering a written exam question completely. How? By pulling in enough partial credit and extra credit. And by getting breaks on grades.

But what happens once she or he graduates and gets a job? That's when the misfortunes of eroding academic standards multiply. We lament that schoolchildren get "kicked upstairs" until they graduate from high school despite being illiterate and mathematically inept, but we seem unconcerned with college graduates whose less blatant deficiencies are far more harmful if their accreditation exceeds their qualifications.

Most of my students are science and engineering majors. If they're good at getting partial credit but not at getting the answer right, then the new bridge breaks or the new drug doesn't work. One finds examples here in Atlanta. Last year a light tower in the Olympic Stadium collapsed, killing a worker. It collapsed because an engineer miscalculated how much weight it could hold. A new 12-story dormitory could develop dangerous cracks due to a foundation that's uneven by more than six inches. The error resulted from incorrect data being fed into a computer. I drive past that dorm daily on my way to work, wondering if a foundation crushed under kilotons of weight is repairable or if this structure will have to be demolished. Two 10,000-pound steel beams at the new natatorium collapsed in March, crashing into the student athletic complex. (Should we give partial credit since no one was hurt?) Those are real-world consequences of errors and lack of expertise.

But the lesson is lost on the grade-grousing 10 percent. Say that you won't (not can't, but won't) change the grade they deserve to what they want, and they're frequently bewildered or angry. They don't think it's fair that they're judged according to their performance, not their desires or "potential." They don't think it's fair that they should jeopardize their scholarships or be in danger of flunking out simply because they could not or did not do their work. But it's more than fair; it's necessary to help preserve a minimum standard of quality that our society needs to maintain safety and integrity. I don't know if the 13th-hour students will learn that lesson, but I've learned mine. From now on, after final grades are posted, I'll lie low until the next quarter starts.

Questions for Reading and Analysis

1. What does Wiesenfeld mean when he says, "Rewards are disconnected from the quality of one's work. An act and its consequences are unrelated, random events." How does this statement explain his students' behavior as he sees it?

2. What is Wiesenfeld's thesis? Where in the essay does he state it? What are the arguments Wiesenfeld gives to support his thesis?

3. How do the last sentence of the essay and the introduction connect? What is the effect of this connection?

4. Who is the intended audience for Wiesenfeld's essay? Do you, a student, feel included in this audience? Why or why not?

*W*inner of six Nebula and six Hugo awards, Connie Willis (b. 1945) wrote "Ado" when, she says, "political correctness was still a gleam in some activist's eye." First published in 1988, "Ado" was reprinted in 1994 in Willis's collection Impossible Things, *when its take on the dangers of censorship was eerily timely, blurring the distinction between science fiction and non-fiction.*

Ado

Connie Willis

The Monday before spring break I told my English lit class we were going to do Shakespeare. The weather in Colorado is usually wretched this time of year. We get all the snow the ski resorts needed in December, use up our scheduled snow days, and end up going an extra week in June. The forecast on the *Today* show hadn't predicted any snow till Saturday, but with luck it would arrive sooner.

My announcement generated a lot of excitement. Paula dived for her corder and rewound it to make sure she'd gotten my every word, Edwin Sumner looked smug, and Delilah snatched up her books and stomped out, slamming the door so hard it woke Rick up. I passed out the release/refusal slips and told them they had to have them back in by Wednesday. I gave one to Sharon to give Delilah.

"Shakespeare is considered one of our greatest writers, possibly *the* greatest," I said for the benefit of Paula's corder. "On Wednesday I will be talking about Shakespeare's life, and on Thursday and Friday we will be reading his work."

Wendy raised her hand. "Are we going to read all the plays?"

I sometimes wonder where Wendy has been the last few years—certainly not in this school, possibly not in this universe. "What we're studying hasn't been decided yet," I said. "The principal and I are meeting tomorrow."

"It had better be one of the tragedies," Edwin said darkly.

By lunch the news was all over the school. "Good luck," Greg Jefferson, the biology teacher, said in the teachers' lounge. "I just got done doing evolution."

"Is it really that time of year again?" Karen Miller said. She teaches American lit across the hall. "I'm not even up to the Civil War yet."

"It's that time of year again," I said. "Can you take my class during your free period tomorrow? I've got to meet with Harrows."

"I can take them all morning. Just have your kids come into my room tomorrow. We're doing 'Thanatopsis.' Another thirty kids won't matter."

"'Thanatopsis'?" I said, impressed. "The whole thing?"

"All but lines ten and sixty-eight. It's a terrible poem, you know. I don't think anybody understands it well enough to protest. And I'm not telling anybody what the title means."

"Cheer up," Greg said. "Maybe we'll have a blizzard."

Tuesday was clear, with a forecast of temps in the sixties. Delilah was outside the school when I got there, wearing a red "Seniors Against Devil Worship in the Schools" T-shirt and shorts. She was carrying a picket sign that said, "Shakespeare is Satan's Spokesman." "Shakespeare" and "Satan" were both misspelled.

"We're not starting Shakespeare till tomorrow," I told her. "There's no reason for you not to be in class. Ms. Miller is teaching 'Thanatopsis.'"

"Not lines ten and sixty-eight, she's not. Besides, Bryant was a Theist, which is the same thing as a Satanist." She handed me her refusal slip and a fat manila envelope. "Our protests are in there." She lowered her voice. "What does the word 'thanatopsis' really mean?"

"It's an Indian word. It means, 'One who uses her religion to ditch class and get a tan.'"

I went inside, got Shakespeare out of the vault in the library, and went into the office. Ms. Harrows already had the Shakespeare file and her box of Kleenex out. "Do you have to do this?" she said, blowing her nose.

"As long as Edwin Sumner's in my class, I do. His mother's head of the President's Task Force on Lack of Familiarity with the Classics." I added Delilah's list of protests to the stack and sat down at the computer.

"Well, it may be easier than we think," she said. "There have been a lot of suits since last year, which takes care of *Macbeth, The Tempest, Midsummer Night's Dream, The Winter's Tale,* and *Richard III.*"

"Delilah's been a busy girl," I said. I fed in the unexpurgated disk and the excise and reformat programs. "I don't remember there being any witchcraft in *Richard III.*"

She sneezed and grabbed for another Kleenex. "There's not. That was a slander suit. Filed by his great-great-grand-something. He claims there's no conclusive proof that Richard III killed the little princes. It doesn't matter anyway. The Royal Society for the Restoration of Divine Right of Kings has an injunction against all the history plays. What's the weather supposed to be like?"

"Terrible," I said. "Warm and sunny." I called up the catalog and deleted *Henry IV, Parts I and II,* and the rest of her list. "*The Taming of the Shrew?*"

"Angry Women's Alliance. Also *Merry Wives of Windsor, Romeo and Juliet,* and *Love's Labour's Lost.*"

"*Othello?* Never mind. I know that one. *The Merchant of Venice?* The Anti-Defamation League?"

"No. American Bar Association. And Morticians International. They object to the use of the word 'casket' in Act III." She blew her nose.

It took us first and second period to deal with the plays and most of the third to finish the sonnets. "I've got a class fourth period and then lunch duty," I said. "We'll have to finish up the rest of them this afternoon."

"Is there anything left for this afternoon?" Ms. Harrows asked.

"*As You Like It* and *Hamlet*," I said. "Good heavens, how did they miss *Hamlet*?"

"Are you sure about *As You Like It*?" Ms. Harrows said, leafing through her stack. "I thought somebody'd filed a restraining order against it."

"Probably the Mothers Against Transvestites," I said. "Rosalind dresses up like a man in Act II."

"No, here it is. The Sierra Club. 'Destructive attitudes toward the environment.'" She looked up. "What destructive attitudes?"

"Orlando carves Rosalind's name on a tree." I leaned back in my chair so I could see out the window. The sun was still shining maliciously down. "I guess we go with *Hamlet*. This should make Edwin and his mother happy."

"We've still got the line-by-lines to go," Ms. Harrows said. "I think my throat is getting sore."

I got Karen to take my afternoon classes. It was sophomore lit and we'd been doing Beatrix Potter—all she had to do was pass out a worksheet on *Squirrel Nutkin*. I had outside lunch duty. It was so hot I had to take my jacket off. The College Students for Christ were marching around the school carrying picket signs that said, "Shakespeare was a Secular Humanist."

Delilah was lying on the front steps, reeking of sun tan oil. She waved her "Shakespeare is Satan's Spokesman" sign languidly at me. "'Ye have sinned a great sin,'" she quoted. "'Blot me, I pray thee, out of thy book which thou hast written.' Exodus Chapter 32, Verse 30."

"First Corinthians 13:3," I said. "'Though I give my body to be burned and have not charity, it profiteth me nothing.'"

"I called the doctor," Ms. Harrows said. She was standing by the window looking out at the blazing sun. "He thinks I might have pneumonia."

I sat down at the computer and fed in *Hamlet*. "Look on the bright side. At least we've got the E and R programs. We don't have to do it by hand the way we used to."

She sat down behind the stack. "How shall we do this? By group or by line?"

"We might as well take it from the top."

"Line one. 'Who's there?' The National Coalition Against Contractions."

"Let's do it by group," I said.

"All right. We'll get the big ones out of the way first. The Commission on Poison Prevention feels the 'graphic depiction of poisoning in the murder of Hamlet's father may lead to copycat crimes.' They cite a case in New Jersey where a sixteen-year-old poured Drano in his father's ear after reading the play. Just a minute. Let me get a Kleenex. The Literature Liberation Front objects to the phrases, 'Frailty, thy name is woman,' and 'O, most pernicious woman,' the 'What a piece of work is man' speech, and the queen."

"The whole queen?"

She checked her notes. "Yes. All lines, references, and allusions." She felt under her jaw, first one side, then the other. "I think my glands are swollen. Would that go along with pneumonia?"

Greg Jefferson came in, carrying a grocery sack. "I thought you could use some combat rations. How's it going?"

"We lost the queen," I said. "Next?"

"The National Cutlery Council objects to the depiction of swords as deadly weapons. 'Swords don't kill people. People kill people.' The Copenhagen Chamber of Commerce objects to the line, 'Something is rotten in the state of Denmark.' Students Against Suicide, the International Federation of Florists, and the Red Cross object to Ophelia's drowning."

Greg was setting out the bottles of cough syrup and cold tablets on the desk. He handed me a bottle of Valium. "The International Federation of Florists?" he said.

"She fell in picking flowers," I said. "What was the weather like out there?"

"Just like summer," he said. "Delilah's using an aluminum sun reflector."

"Ass," Ms. Harrows said.

"Beg pardon?" Greg said.

"ASS, the Association of Summer Sunbathers, objects to the line, 'I am too much i' the sun,' Ms. Harrows said, and took a swig from the bottle of cough syrup.

We were only half-finished by the time school let out. The Nuns' Network objected to the line "Get thee to a nunnery," Fat and Proud of It wanted the passage beginning "Oh, that this too too solid flesh should melt" removed, and we didn't even get to Delilah's list, which was eight pages long.

"What play are we going to do?" Wendy asked me on my way out.

"*Hamlet*," I said.

"Hamlet?" she said. "Is that the one about the guy whose uncle murders the king and then the queen marries the uncle?"

"Not anymore," I said.

Delilah was waiting for me outside. "'Many of them brought their books together and burned them,'" she quoted. "Acts 19:19."

"'Look not upon me, because I am black, because the sun hath looked upon me,'" I said.

It was overcast Wednesday but still warm. The Veterans for a Clean America and the Subliminal Seduction Sentinels were picnicking on the lawn. Delilah had on a halter top. "That thing you said yesterday about the sun turning people black, what was that from?"

"The Bible," I said. "Song of Solomon. Chapter 1, Verse 6."

"Oh," she said, relieved. "That's not in the Bible anymore. We threw it out."

Ms. Harrows had left a note for me. She was at the doctor's. I was supposed to meet with her third period.

"Do we get to start today?" Wendy asked.

"If everybody remembered to bring in their slips. I'm going to lecture on Shakespeare's life," I said. "You don't know what the forecast for today is, do you?"

"Yeah, it's supposed to be great."

I had her collect the refusal slips while I went over my notes. Last year Delilah's sister Jezebel had filed a grievance halfway through the lecture for "trying to preach promiscuity, birth control, and abortion by saying Anne Hathaway got pregnant before she got married." "Promiscuity," "abortion," "pregnant," and "before" had all been misspelled.

Everybody had remembered their slips. I sent the refusals to the library and started to lecture.

"Shakespeare—" I said. Paula's corder clicked on. "William Shakespeare was born on April twenty-third, 1564, in Stratford-on-Avon."

Rick, who hadn't raised his hand all year or even given an indication that he was sentient, raised his hand. "Do you intend to give equal time to the Baconian theory?" he said. "Bacon was not born on April twenty-third, 1564. He was born on January twenty-second, 1561."

Ms. Harrows wasn't back from the doctor's by third period, so I started on Delilah's list. She objected to forty-three references to spirits, ghosts, and related matters, twenty-one obscene words ("obscene" misspelled), and seventy-eight others that she thought might be obscene, such as pajock and cockles.

Ms. Harrows came in as I was finishing the list and threw her briefcase down. "Stress-induced!" she said. "I have pneumonia, and he says my symptoms are stress-induced!"

"Is it still cloudy out?"

"It is seventy-two degrees out. Where are we?"

"Morticians International," I said. "Again. 'Death presented as universal and inevitable.'" I peered at the paper. "That doesn't sound right."

Ms. Harrows took the paper away from me. "That's their 'Thanatopsis' protest. They had their national convention last week. They filed a whole set at once, and I haven't had a chance to sort through them." She rummaged around in her stack. "Here's the one on *Hamlet*. 'Negative portrayal of interment-preparation personnel—'"

"The gravedigger."

"'—And inaccurate representation of burial regulations. Neither a hermetically sealed coffin nor a vault appears in the scene.'"

We worked until five o'clock. The Society for the Advancement of Philosophy considered the line "There are more things in heaven and earth, Horatio, than are dreamt of in your philosophy" a slur on their profession. The Actors' Guild challenged Hamlet's hiring of nonunion employees, and the Drapery Defense League objected to Polonius being stabbed while hiding behind a curtain. "The clear implication of the scene is that the arras is dangerous," they had written in their brief. "Draperies don't kill people. People kill people."

Ms. Harrows put the paper down on top of the stack and took a swig of cough syrup. "And that's it. Anything left?"

"I think so," I said, punching *reformat* and scanning the screen. "Yes, a couple of things. How about, 'There is a willow grows aslant a brook / That shows his hoar leaves in the glassy stream.'

"You'll never get away with 'hoar,'" Ms. Harrows said.

Thursday I got to school at seven-thirty to print out thirty copies of *Hamlet* for my class. It had turned colder and even cloudier in the night. Delilah was wearing a parka and mittens. Her face was a deep scarlet, and her nose had begun to peel.

"'Hath the Lord as great delight in burnt offerings as in obeying the voice of the Lord?'" I asked. "First Samuel 15:22." I patted her on the shoulder.

"Yeow," she said.

I passed out *Hamlet* and assigned Wendy and Rick to read the parts of Hamlet and Horatio.

"'The air bites shrewdly; it is very cold,'" Wendy read.

"Where are we?" Rick said. I pointed out the place to him. "Oh. 'It is a nipping and an eager air.'"

"'What hour now?'" Wendy read.

"'I think it lacks of twelve.'"

Wendy turned her paper over and looked at the back. "That's it?" she said. "That's all there is to *Hamlet*? I thought his uncle killed his father and then the ghost told him his mother was in on it and he said 'To be or not to be' and Ophelia killed herself and stuff." She turned the paper back over. "This can't be the whole play."

"It better not be the whole play," Delilah said. She came in, carrying her picket sign. "There'd better not be any ghosts in it. Or cockles."

"Did you need some Solarcaine, Delilah?" I asked her.

"I *need* a Magic Marker," she said with dignity.

I got her one out of the desk. She left, walking a little stiffly, as if it hurt to move.

"You can't just take parts of the play out because somebody doesn't like them," Wendy said. "If you do, the play doesn't make any sense. I bet if Shakespeare were here, he wouldn't let you just take things out—"

"Assuming Shakespeare wrote it," Rick said. "If you take every other letter in line two except the first three and the last six, they spell 'pig,' which is obviously a code word for Bacon."

"Snow day!" Ms. Harrows said over the intercom. Everybody raced to the windows. "We will have early dismissal today at nine-thirty."

I looked at the clock. It was 9:28.

"The Overprotective Parents Organization has filed the following protest: 'It is now snowing, and as the forecast predicts more snow, and as snow can result in slippery streets, poor visibility, bus accidents, frostbite, and avalanches, we demand that school be closed today and tomorrow so as not to endanger our children.' Buses will leave at nine thirty-five. Have a nice spring break!"

"The snow isn't even sticking on the ground," Wendy said. "Now we'll never get to do Shakespeare."

Delilah was out in the hall, on her knees next to her picket sign, crossing out the word "man" in "Spokesman."

"The Feminists for a Fair Language are here," she said disgustedly. "They've got a court order." She wrote "person" above the crossed-out "man." "A court order! Can you believe that? I mean, what's happening to our right to freedom of speech?"

"You misspelled 'person,'" I said.

Questions for Reading and Analysis

1. In a sentence, what is the message in Willis's story?

2. While Willis's story reads like satire of the PC movement and a litigation-happy society, what examples come close to depicting actual events? Can you cite examples from the news in recent years that have borne out Willis's concerns?

3. What or whom does Wendy represent in the story?

4. What is the significance of the names of Delilah and her sister Jezebel? Are any other character names significant or symbolic?

5. What is the point of the narrator's noting the various misspelled words in the signs and petitions of Delilah and Jezebel?

Known for both her poetry and her feminist writings about female beauty and the women's movement, Naomi Wolf argues in "Promiscuities" that we need to find ways to initiate young women into sexual adulthood other than just teaching them how to avoid unwanted pregnancy. Her suggestion is to appoint "Womanhood Guides," adult women who will teach girls the ethical, social, and emotional aspects of sexuality besides its strictly biological side.

Promiscuities: The Secret Struggle Toward Womanhood

Naomi Wolf

He and I could have been a poster couple for the liberal ideal of responsible teen sexuality—and, paradoxically, this was reflected in the lack of drama and meaning that I felt crossing this threshold. Conscientious students who were mapping out our college applications and scheduling our after-school jobs to save up for tuition, we were the sort of kids who Planned Ahead. But even the preparations for losing one's virginity felt barren of larger social significance.

When Martin and I went together to a clinic to arrange for contraception some weeks before the actual deed, no experience could have been flatter. He waited, reading old copies of *Scientific American*, while I was fitted for a diaphragm ("the method with one of the highest effectiveness levels if we are very careful, and the fewest risks to you," Martin had explained after looking it up). The offices were full of high school couples. If the management intended the mood to be welcoming to adolescents, they had done an excellent job. Cartoon strips about contraception were displayed in several rooms. The staff members were straight-talking, and they did not patronize. The young, bearded doctor who fitted me treated it all as if he were explaining to me a terrific new piece of equipment for some hearty activity such as camping or rock climbing.

In terms of the mechanics of servicing teenage desire safely in a secular, materialistic society, the experience was impeccable. The technology worked and was either cheap or free. But when we walked out, I still felt there was something important missing. It was weird to have these adults just hand you the keys to the kingdom, ask, "Any questions?" wave, and return to their paperwork. They did not even have us wait until we could show we had learned something concrete—until we could answer some of their questions. It was easier than getting your learner's permit to drive a car. Now, giving us a moral context was not their job. They had enough to handle, and they were doing so valiantly. Indeed, their work seems in retrospect like one of the few backstops we encountered to society's abdication of us within our sexuality. But from visiting the clinic in the absence of any other adults giving us a moral framework in which to learn about sexuality, the message we got was: "You can be adults without trying. The only meaning this has is the meaning you give it." There was a sense, I recall in retrospect, that the adults who were the gatekeepers to society had once again failed to initiate us in any way.

For not at the clinic, at school, in our synagogue, or anywhere in pop culture did this message come through clearly to us: sexual activity comes with responsibilities that are deeper than personal. If our parents did say this, it was scarcely reinforced outside the home. No one said, at the clinic, "You must use this diaphragm or this condom, not only because that is how you will avoid the personal disaster of unwanted pregnancy but because if you have sex without using protection you are doing something antisocial and morally objectionable. If you, boy or girl, initiate a pregnancy out of carelessness, that is dumb, regrettable behavior." Nothing morally significant about the transfer of power from adults to teenagers was represented in that technology. It was like going to the vet: as if we were being processed not on a social but on an animal level.

•　　•　　•

Unsurprisingly, the more forbidden women are to own their sexuality lest they become "sluts," the more inclined they are to project an out-of-control sexuality onto men. The more a woman's "appropriate" sexual persona is defined as being for others, the more the demon lover stands in her mind as promising a sexuality that can be, subversively, for herself.

Losing our virginity was supposed to pass for attaining sexual maturity. But it was too easy, what we did, and it didn't matter enough to satisfy us more than physically. The end of our virginity passed unmarked, neither mourned nor celebrated: the worldview we inherited told us that what we gained by becoming fully sexual was infinitely valuable and what we lost by leaving behind our virgin state was less than negligible. In other cultures I have looked at, older women, who upheld the values of femaleness, decided when a girl could join them in womanhood. Their decision was based on whether the girl had attained the level of wisdom and self-discipline that would benefit her, her family, and the society. Those older women alone, through their deliberations, had the power to bestow womanhood on the initiates.

In our culture, men were deciding for us if we were women. Heck: *teenage boys* were deciding for us if we were women.

Instead we should be telling girls what they already know but rarely see affirmed: that the lives they lead inside their own self-contained bodies, the skills they attain through their own concentration and rigor, and the unique phase in their lives during which they may explore boys and eroticism at their own pace—these are magical. And they constitute the entrance point to a life cycle of a sexuality that should be held sacred.

•　　•　　•

If one is allowed to grow up being proud of one's sexual womanhood as it develops day by day, one may acquire that "sureness" that Margaret Mead[1] spoke of, and be far less susceptible to the blandishment of industries or ideologies that promise to bestow a sexual womanhood, as well as being less susceptible to the pressures in the marketplace that stand ready to stigmatize women for any hint of their sexuality.

Obviously, girls need better rites of passage in our culture. Such rituals, we have seen, require rigor, separation from males and from the daily environment, and the exchange of privileged information. It is important, in such rituals, for grown women outside the family to do the initiating. I'd like to propose that groups of friends with children sign one another up, upon the birth of a daughter, for the responsibility of becoming part of small groups—Womanhood Guides. Instead or in addition to the familiar role of godparent, someone who signs on for such a task will join with a few other women, and a small cohort of girls, in the girls' thirteenth year, for a retreat into the wilderness—something as simple as a trip to a state park, organized through the schools, church groups, or through individual family groups. There, amid stories, songs, and hikes the older women would pass on to the younger everything they have learned about womanhood, and answer *every single question* the girls want to ask—questions that will be far more trusting and substantive than those asked in the constrained, public environment of a sex education class. The older women can certainly, depending on the religious and cultural sensitivities of the group, show the girls birth control devices and explain how they work. They would explain a sexual ethic that, as women initiates, the girls would be asked to commit to—an ethic that might include committing never to do anything one does not fully consent to do; never to use sex to get something (love, status, money) that one should seek in other ways; never to have sex without consciousness—not to use drugs or alcohol to mask one's sexual intention and responsibility; to practice saying what one wants; to practice saying what one doesn't want; to seek conscientiously, with every means at one's disposal, to avoid having to undergo an abortion or to bring into the world a child one is not ready to parent; never to degrade or violate one's own sexuality, or tolerate others' degrading or violating it. But their most important task—one that the culture would value these women for undertaking—would be to explain to the girls, in clear, compassionate terms, just how to explore female sexual desire in such a way as to postpone intercourse until they are really, truly, feeling safe, sensually aware, and ready; until, that is, whether the marker is their eighteenth birthday or their engagement or their marriage, they feel ready to undertake such a profound step not as curious, passionate, half certain girls, but as *empowered, self-knowing, mature women*. When the retreat is over and the girls have proven to the older women that they have mastered some of the skills and knowledge of womanhood—the rudiments of taking care of themselves professionally and sexually, and understanding what it means to take care of children—they return to their neighborhoods and a great big party is thrown to welcome them back and celebrate their changed status.

In addition to the sexual education, a family's friends can commit to being part of a wisdom initiation: transmitting their professional skills to the girl whom they are assigned to guide. I have, for instance, such a commitment of exchange from the scientist parents of a two-year-old girl; as my daughter grows up, they have agreed to teach her about earth sciences, show her experiments, and explain to her the jobs that one can do in that field—something in which I have no expertise— and I in turn have committed to working with their daughter on writing. In this way, through these commitments of mentoring exchanges, girls feel specially valued not only by their families but by the extended community—the locus of the initiation tension, and the possibilities of what they might love and become good at expands, and these skills are undertaken at the special time when they begin to cross the border into womanhood. "Privilege knowledge" associated with becoming women need not be sexual; through adolescent exchange relationships, that hunger for a special women's wisdom is filled.

Endnote

1. Margaret Mead (1901–1978) was an American anthropologist whose classic *Coming of Age in Samoa* (1928) describes adolescent girls in a largely noncompetitive and permissive culture.

Questions for Reading and Analysis

1. What conclusions does Wolf draw from the experience of visiting the birth control clinic with her boyfriend before they became sexually active?

2. What, according to Wolf, is *not* taught at these clinics? What does this say about our culture's attitude toward sexuality? How does this lack of knowledge harm young women?

3. What does Wolf suggest we do to teach young women about their sexuality?

4. Do you think her idea of appointing "Womanhood Guides" (or, by extension, "Manhood Guides") to initiate girls (boys) into womanhood (manhood) could really work in the lives of everyday Americans? Why or why not?

In A Room of One's Own, *a mainstay of feminist commentary first published in 1928, Virginia Woolf (1882–1941) argues that for a woman to really write, she must have her own money and her own room. In* Professions for Women, *originally a paper delivered to the Women's Service League in 1930, the essayist and novelist adds that a woman writer must also exorcise the "Angel of the House," a deferential demon that serves to suppress a woman's own ideas and desires.*

Professions for Women

Virginia Woolf

When your secretary invited me to come here, she told me that your Society is concerned with the employment of women and she suggested that I might tell you something about my own professional experiences. It is true I am a woman; it is true I am employed; but what professional experiences have I had? It is difficult to say. My profession is literature; and in that profession there are fewer experiences for women than in any other, with the exception of the stage—fewer, I mean, that are peculiar to women. For the road was cut many years ago—by Fanny Burney, by Aphra Behn, by Harriet Martineau, by Jane Austen, by George Eliot—many famous women, and many more unknown and forgotten, have been before me, making the path smooth, and regulating my steps. Thus, when I came to write, there were very few material obstacles in my way. Writing was a reputable and harmless occupation. The family peace was not broken by the scratching of a pen. No demand was made upon the family purse. For ten and sixpence one can buy paper enough to write all the plays of Shakespeare—if one has a mind that way. Pianos and models, Paris, Vienna, and Berlin, masters and mistresses, are not needed by a writer. The cheapness of writing paper is, of course, the reason why women have succeeded as writers before they have succeeded in the other professions.

But to tell you my story—it is a simple one. You have only got to figure to yourselves a girl in a bedroom with a pen in her hand. She had only to move that pen from left to right—from ten o'clock to one. Then it occurred to her to do what is simple and cheap enough after all—to slip a few of those pages into an envelope, fix a penny stamp in the corner, and drop the envelope into the red box at the corner. It was thus that I became a journalist; and my effort was rewarded on the first day of the following month—a very glorious day it was for me—by a letter from an editor containing a cheque for one pound ten shillings and sixpence. But to show you how little I deserve to be called a professional woman, how little I know of the struggles and difficulties of such lives, I have to admit that instead of spending that sum upon bread and butter, rent, shoes and stockings, or butcher's bills, I went out and bought a cat—a beautiful cat, a Persian cat, which very soon involved me in bitter disputes with my neighbours.

What could be easier than to write articles and to buy Persian cats with the profits? But wait a moment. Articles have to be about something. Mine, I seem to remember, was about a novel by a famous man. And while I was writing this review, I discovered that if I were going to review books I should need to do battle with a certain phantom. And the phantom was a woman, and when I came to know her better I called her after the heroine of a famous poem, The Angel in the House. It was she who used to come between me and my paper when I was writing reviews. It was she who bothered me and wasted my time and so tormented me that at last I killed her. You who come of a younger and happier generation may not have heard of her—you may not know what I mean by the Angel in the House. I will describe her as shortly as I can. She was intensely sympathetic. She was immensely charming. She was utterly unselfish. She excelled in the difficult arts of family life. She sacrificed herself daily. If there was chicken, she took the leg; if there was a draught she sat in it—in short she was so constituted that she never had a mind or a wish of her own, but preferred to sympathize always with the minds and wishes of others. Above all—I need not say it—she was pure. Her purity was supposed to be her chief beauty—her blushes, her great grace. In those days—the last of Queen Victoria—every house had its Angel. And when I came to write I encountered her with the very first words. The shadow of her wings fell on my page; I heard the rustling of her skirts in the room. Directly, that is to say, I took my pen in my hand to review that novel by a famous man, she slipped behind me and whispered: "My dear, you are a young woman. You are writing about a book that has been written by a man. Be sympathetic; be tender; flatter; deceive; use all the arts and wiles of our sex. Never let anybody guess that you have a mind of your own. Above all, be pure." And she made as if to guide my pen. I now record the one act for which I take some credit to myself, though the credit rightly belongs to some excellent ancestors of mine who left me a certain sum of money—shall we say five hundred pounds a year?—so that it was not necessary for me to depend solely on charm for my living. I turned upon her and caught her by the throat. I did my best to kill her. My excuse if I were to be had up in a court of law, would be that I acted in self-defence. Had I not killed her she would have killed me. She would have plucked the heart out of my writing. For, as I found, directly I put pen to paper, you cannot review even a novel without having a mind of your own, without expressing what you think to be the truth about human relations, morality, sex. And all these questions, according to the Angel of the House, cannot be dealt with freely and openly by women; they must charm, they must conciliate, they must—to put it bluntly—tell lies if they are to succeed. Thus, whenever I felt the shadow of her wing or the radiance of her halo upon my page, I took up the inkpot and flung it at her. She died hard. Her fictitious nature was of great assistance to her. It is far harder to kill a phantom than a reality. She was always creeping back when I thought I had despatched her. Though I flatter myself that I killed her in the end, the struggle was severe; it took much time that had better have been spent upon learning Greek grammar; or in roaming the world in search of adventures. But it was a real experience; it was an experience that was bound to befall all women writers at that time. Killing the Angel in the House was part of the occupation of a woman writer.

But to continue my story. The Angel was dead; what then remained? You may say that what remained was a simple and common object—a young woman in a bedroom with an inkpot. In other words, now that she had rid herself of false-hood, that young woman had only to be herself. Ah, but what is "herself"? I mean, what is a woman? I assure you, I do not know. I do not believe that you know. I do not believe that anybody can know until she has expressed herself in all the arts and professions open to human skill. That indeed is one of the reasons why I have come here—out of respect for you, who are in process of showing us by your experiments what a woman is, who are in process of providing us, by your failures and successes, with that extremely important piece of information.

But to continue the story of my professional experiences. I made one pound ten and six by my first review; and I bought a Persian cat with the proceeds. Then I grew ambitious. A Persian cat is all very well, I said; but a Persian cat is not enough. I must have a motorcar. And it was thus that I became a novelist—for it is a very strange thing that people will give you a motorcar if you will tell them a story. It is a still stranger thing that there is nothing so delightful in the world as telling stories. It is far pleasanter than writing reviews of famous novels. And yet, if I am to obey your secretary and tell you my professional experiences as a novelist, I must tell you about a very strange experience that befell me as a novelist. And to understand it you must try first to imagine a novelist's state of mind. I hope I am not giving away professional secrets if I say that a novelist's chief desire is to be as unconscious as possible. He has to induce in himself a state of perpetual lethargy. He wants life to proceed with the utmost quiet and regularity. He wants to see the same faces, to read the same books, to do the same things day after day, month after month, while he is writing, so that nothing may break the illusion in which he is living—so that nothing may disturb or disquiet the mysterious nosings about, feel-ings round, darts, dashes, and sudden discoveries of that very shy and illusive spirit, the imagination. I suspect that this state is the same both for men and women. Be that as it may, I want you to imagine me writing a novel in a state of trance. I want you to figure to yourselves a girl sitting with a pen in her hand, which for min-utes, and indeed for hours, she never dips into the inkpot. The image that comes to my mind when I think of this girl is the image of a fisherman lying sunk in dreams on the verge of a deep lake with a rod held out over the water. She was let-ting her imagination sweep unchecked round every rock and cranny of the world that lies submerged in the depths of our unconscious being. Now came the expe-rience, the experience that I believe to be far commoner with women writers than with men. The line raced through the girl's fingers. Her imagination had rushed away. It had sought the pools, the depths, the dark places where the largest fish slumber. And then there was a smash. There was an explosion. There was foam and confusion. The imagination had dashed itself against something hard. The girl was roused from her dream. She was indeed in a state of the most acute and difficult distress. To speak without figure, she had thought of something, something about the body, about the passion which it was unfitting for her as a woman to say. Men, her reason told her, would be shocked. The consciousness of what men will say of a woman who speaks the truth about her passions had roused her from her artist's state of unconsciousness. She could write no more. The trance was over. Her imagination could work no longer. This I believe to be a very common experience with women writers—they are impeded by the extreme conventionality of the other sex. For though men sensibly allow themselves great freedom in these respects, I doubt that they realize or can control the extreme severity with which they condemn such freedom in women.

These then were two very genuine experiences of my own. These were two of the adventures of my professional life. The first—killing the Angel in the House— I think I solved. She died. But the second, telling the truth about my own experiences as a body, I do not think I solved. I doubt that any woman has solved it yet. The obstacles against her are still immensely powerful—and yet they are very difficult to define. Outwardly, what is simpler than to write books? Outwardly, what obstacles are there for a woman rather than for a man? Inwardly, I think, the case is very different; she has still many ghosts to fight, many prejudices to overcome. Indeed it will be a long time still, I think, before a woman can sit down to write a book without finding a phantom to be slain, a rock to be dashed against. And if this is so in literature, the freest of all professions for women, how is it in the new professions which you are now for the first time entering?

Those are the questions that I should like, had I time, to ask you. And indeed, if I have laid stress upon these professional experiences of mine, it is because I believe that they are, though in different forms, yours also. Even when the path is nominally open—when there is nothing to prevent a woman from being a doctor, a lawyer, a civil servant—there are many phantoms and obstacles, as I believe, looming in her way. To discuss and define them is I think of great value and importance; for thus only can the labour be shared, the difficulties be solved. But besides this, it is necessary also to discuss the ends and the aims for which we are fighting, for which we are doing battle with these formidable obstacles. Those aims cannot be taken for granted; they must be perpetually questioned and examined. The whole position, as I see it—here in this hall surrounded by women practising for the first time in history I know not how many different professions—is one of extraordinary interest and importance. You have won rooms of your own in the house hitherto exclusively owned by men. You are able, though not without great labour and effort, to pay the rent. You are earning your five hundred pounds a year. But this freedom is only a beginning; the room is your own, but it is still bare. It has to be furnished; it has to be decorated; it has to be shared. How are you going to furnish it, how are you going to decorate it? With whom are you going to share it, and upon what terms? These, I think are questions of the utmost importance and interest. For the first time in history you are able to ask them; for the first time you are able to decide for yourselves what the answers should be. Willingly would I stay and discuss those questions and answers—but not tonight. My time is up; and I must cease.

Questions for Reading and Analysis

1. In your own words, describe Woolf's concept of "The Angel of the House." How did it interfere with her writing book reviews?

2. Woolf's essay was originally delivered as a speech to the Women's Service League in 1930. In what ways does she anticipate and cater to her audience?

3. Is Woolf's essay relevant today, some 70 years after the original speech?

Elizabeth Wurtzel, a member of the much-hyped and much-maligned "Generation X," is the author of the bestseller Prozac Nation *and the recent* Bitch: In Praise of Difficult Women. *Winner of the 1986* Rolling Stone *College Journalism Award, she has also penned music criticism for* The New Yorker *and* New York *magazine. In "Parental Guidance Suggested," Wurtzel laments the effects of the culture of divorce, which she regards as a generational phenomenon. Children of divorce and neglect, she argues, are forced to construct families among their peers.*

Parental Guidance Suggested

Elizabeth Wurtzel

It is the spring of my junior year of college, I am lying in a near-catatonic state in a mental ward, I have just been given an industrial-strength antipsychotic—the kind they give to schizophrenics—because I have not been able to stop crying and shaking and wailing for hours, and the doctor is afraid that I might, quite literally, choke on my own tears. The pill they've given me—some variation on Thorazine—has knocked me into a silent state of submission that would be perfectly blissful if only the therapist on duty would stop trying to get me to talk to her. She wants to know what's wrong; she wants to know what I am experiencing that is so potent and profound that it takes a brain-draining drug to make it go away.

I don't know, is all I keep saying. I don't know, I don't know, I don't know.

What have you lost? she asks, trying a new approach.

I know I better come up with something. I better think of an answer before they start trying out other things on me—different drugs, electroconvulsive therapy (known in the vernacular as *shock*), whatever.

I think it's got something to do with summer camp, I say.

She looks at me blankly.

It's like this, I begin: I'm from New York City, my mom is Jewish and middle class, my dad is solidly white trash, they divorced when I was two, my mom was always unemployed or marginally employed and my dad was always uninvolved or marginally involved in raising me, there was never enough money for anything, we lived in state-subsidized housing, I went to private schools on scholarships, and my childhood, as I recall it, was one big flurry of application forms for financial aid or for special rates on this thing or that thing that my mother thought I should really have because she didn't want me to be deprived of anything.

My mom really did her best.

But then, as soon as I was old enough, my mother decided that I had to go to sleep-away camp for the summers. She was overextended as a parent throughout the school year, my dad wasn't willing to take care of me, and there was nothing for a girl like me to do in New York City during the long hot summer except get into trouble with the neighborhood kids. So it was off to camp. That was that.

I went to camp for five years in a row—a different one each year, a different setup in a different rural town in the Poconos or the Catskills or the Berkshires or wherever I could enroll at a discount rate. And the funny thing is, I explain to the therapist, after my mother had sent me off to these places that I thought were so lonesome and horrible, instead of hating her for it, I just spent all summer missing her. All my waking and sleeping energy was devoted to missing this rather minimal and unstable home I came from. Starting on June 28, or whatever day it was that I got to camp, and never even achieving a brief reprieve until I'd come home on August 24 or so, I would devote myself fully to the task of getting back home. I'd spend hours each day writing my mom letters, calling her on the phone, just making sure that she'd know exactly where and when to pick me up at the bus when it was time to return. I would run to the camp administrative offices to make sure that notices about the location of the return trip would be sent to my mother so that she'd know where to find me. I'd extract promises that she'd arrive there one or two hours early. I'd even call my dad and get him to promise to be there at least a half hour before the estimated time of arrival. I'd talk to the head counselor and express my concern that I might be put on a bus to New Jersey or Long Island and somehow end up in the wrong place and never find my way back home. I would ask other New Yorkers in my bunk if I could go home with them if my mother failed to materialize at the bus stop. I would call grandparents, aunts, uncles, and baby-sitters—always collect—to find out where they would be on August 24, just in case I had to go to one of their homes, in case my parents didn't show up to get me.

Instead of discovering the virtues of tennis and volleyball, or of braiding lanyards and weaving potholders, I would devote a full eight weeks of my summer to planning for a two-hour trip back home.

The therapist looks at me kind of strangely, as if this doesn't quite make sense, that summer camp was so long ago and I'll never have to go back again, so why is this still bothering me? There's no way, I realize, to ever make her understand that homesickness is just a state of mind for me, that I'm always missing someone or some place or something, I'm always trying to get back to some imaginary somewhere. My life has been one long longing.

And I'm sick of it. And I can't move. And I've a feeling, I tell the therapist, that I might as well lie here congealed to this hospital bed forever because there's no place in the world that's at all like a home to me and I'd rather be dead than spend another minute in this life as an emotional nomad.

A few days later, having lost all hope of anything else working, a psychiatrist gives me a prescription for a new, virtually untried antidepressant that she thinks might help. It's called flouxetine hydrochloride, brand name Prozac. A few weeks later, I am better, much better, as I have been ever since.

But there's just one small problem. They can give me all sorts of drugs to stabilize my moods, to elevate the downs, to flatten the ups, to make me function in this world like any other normal, productive person who works, pays rent, has affairs, waters her own plants. They can make it all feel pretty much all right most of the time. But they can't do anything for the homesickness. There's no pill they can come up with that can cure the longing I feel to be in a place that feels like home. There's no cure for the strange estrangedness, and if there were, I am sure my body would resist it.

Since I first began taking Prozac, the pill has become one of the most commonly prescribed drugs in the country, with 650,000 orders filled each month. Back in 1990, the story of this wonder drug made the cover of periodicals like *Newsweek* and *New York*, while *Rolling Stone* deemed Prozac the "hot yuppie upper," and all the major network news-magazines and daytime talk shows began to do their Prozac-saved-my-life segments. While a backlash of reports linked Prozac with incidents of suicide and murder, the many people whom it relieved from symptoms of depression had nothing but praise: Cheryl Wheeler, a Nashville folkie, even wrote a song called "Is It Peace or Is It Prozac?"

Yet this is not just about Prozac: it's about the mainstreaming of mental illness—it's about the way a state of mind that was once considered tragic has become completely commonplace. Talk of depression as the mental disease of our times has been very much in the air in the last few years, to the point where it has almost become a political issue: As Hillary Rodham Clinton campaigned on behalf of what she deemed "The Politics of Meaning," it was hard not to notice that her references to a "sleeping sickness of the soul," to "alienation and despair and hopelessness," to a "crisis of meaning," and to a "spiritual vacuum" seemed to imply that the country's problems have less to do with taxes and unemployment than with the simple fact that we were in one big collective bad mood. It is almost as if, perhaps, the next time half a million people gather for a protest march in Washington it will not be for abortion rights or gay liberation but because we're all just so bummed out.

Of course, one of the striking elements of this depression outbreak is the extent to which it has gotten such a strong hold on so many young people. The Valium addicts of the fifties and sixties, the housewives reaching for their mother's little helpers, the strung-out junkies and crackheads who litter the gutters of the Bowery or the streets of Harlem or the Skid Row of any town—all these people were stereotyped as wasted, dissipated, or middle-aged. What is fascinating about depression this time around is the extent to which it is affecting those who have so much to look forward to and to hope for, who are, as one might say of a bright young thing about to make her debut into the world, so full of promise.

Recently, I was reading a magazine on an airplane, and I chanced upon an article titled "The Plot Sickens," in which a college writing instructor sees the gruesome, pessimistic nature of the work that her students produce as an indication of a wave of youth malaise like none she'd ever noticed before in twenty-one years of teaching. "To read their work, you'd think they were a generation that was starved, beaten, raped, arrested, addicted, and war-torn. Inexplicable intrusions of random tragedy break up the otherwise good life of the characters," the author writes. "The figures in their fictions are victims of hideous violence by accident; they commit crimes, but only for the hell of it; they hate, not understanding why they hate; they are loved or abused or depressed, and don't know why. . . . Randomness rules."

Perhaps for the author of that article, the nature of her students' work is surprising. For me, and for everyone I know my age, it just seems normal, peculiarly ordinary. I mean: Randomness *does* rule.

A few years ago, I wrote an article about my bout with depression for *Mademoiselle*. I was rather alarmed when the piece generated more mail than anything else they'd run in several years and was somewhat heartened but also terribly saddened to see that I had touched such a raw, exposed nerve in so many young women. Shortly after the article ran, I was on the phone with my editor, and she suddenly asked, "I wonder what Prozac would do for regular people—I mean, not clinical cases like you, but just the rest of us who are normally depressed."

Once again, that word *normally* seemed to be creeping up in a place where it oughtn't be. Since when is it *normal* to be depressed? What kind of world do we live in that someone can refer to depression as a *normal* state?

Christopher Ricks[1] once wrote an essay about the difference between "disenchanted" and "unenchanted," the former describing someone sprung by reality from an enchanted state, while the latter is a person who was never enchanted to begin with. And that's me. And that's what society's come to: the spate of depression that I have come into contact with is not among people who've been disappointed by life—it's among those who have given up on it before they've even given it a real go. So many of us who are in our twenties now were born into homes that had already fallen apart, fathers on the lam, mothers on the floor, no sense of security and safety, no sense of home at all. So we muddle through our adult lives wandering around, kind of dazed, kind of wasted, looking like lost children who are still waiting to be claimed at the security office of the shopping mall or amusement park or supermarket where our parents last lost track of us. When Sonic Youth titled its 1989 album *Daydream Nation*, I think they must have been referring to this youth cadre of the walking wounded, of people who spend so many of their waking hours lost in thought, distraction, and abstraction, trying to get a grip on the hopes—on the dreams—that they dare not have in their conscious minds. Sleep is no relief because they are always sort of asleep. All these young people are homesick and in a reverie for an enchanted place they've never known.

While I often get the sense that many older people look back on their childhoods with a sense of sorrow that they had to grow up and say good-bye to all that, most of my friends could not wait to come of age and get out of the house because the house was not a home. The lucky among us had two active, participating parents and had to spend a lot of time schlepping between two households, always lugging an overnight bag or wondering whether the black-and-white saddle shoes and box of Legos were at Mommy's or Daddy's. In my case, only my mother really cared for me, and she had a really hard time just making ends meet; she seemed forever on the verge of a nervous breakdown, so I spent much of my time just trying to keep her calm. My dad used Valium and pretty much managed to sleep through my whole childhood (when I was nine, we went to see *The Last Waltz*, he fell asleep, and we ended up sitting through the movie three times because I couldn't get him to wake up); our Saturday-afternoon visits mostly involved his putting me in front of the television set to watch "Star Trek" reruns or college basketball while he dozed off.

But these are only the incidental, aftershock effects that divorce has on children—far more terrifying is the violent rupture it creates in any young person's life because any sense of home is ripped asunder, any sense of a safe haven in a cruel world is taken away. We did not learn about bitterness and hatred on the streets (the supposed source of all terror)—we learned from watching our parents try to kill each other. We didn't learn to break promises and (marriage) vows from big bad bullies at school—we learned from watching our parents deny every word they once said to each other. And we learned from them that it is not just acceptable, but virtually normal, to realize that love does not last forever. There are certainly plenty of kids whose parents will stay together until death do they part and who haven't experienced the symptoms I've just described. But even they are affected by the divorce revolution because it colors their worldview, too. They know that their own marriages might end in divorce. They know that the family unit is not sacred, and this adds a degree of uncertainty to their own plans.

But I don't want to get too down on divorce. It has become all too facile a neoconservative impulse to blame divorce or the decline of so-called family values for all the ills of our society. Even more troubling is how easy it has become for people in my age group to blame the lack of a structured family life when they were growing up for all their problems as adults. If I allowed myself to express the full extent of the bitterness I feel toward my parents for not, shall we say, having their shit together while they were raising me, I fear that I might start to sound like an ally of Dan Quayle. And I don't want to do that. The main reason: it is precisely those family values that Dan Quayle referred to in his famous anti-Murphy Brown speech that drove my parents, and so many of my friends' parents, into marriages they were not ready for and bearing children they were not capable of properly nurturing.

It was the family imperative, the sense that life happens in a simple series of steps (something like: adolescence-college-marriage-kids) that all sane and decent people must adhere to that got our parents in trouble to begin with. Remember, the progenitors of people in my age group are not, for the most part, those free-wheeling, wild baby boomers who took it upon themselves to transform our society in the late sixties and early seventies. Our parents were, on the whole, a little too old for that, they are people who were done with college and had moved on to the work world by the early sixties—several years before the campus uprisings, the antiwar activities, and the emerging sex-drugs-and-rock-and-roll culture had become a pervasive force. By the time the radical sixties hit our home bases, we were already born, and our parents found themselves stuck between an entrenched belief that children needed to be raised in a traditional household and a new sense that anything was possible, that the alternative lifestyle was out there for the asking. A little too old to take full advantage of the cultural revolution of the sixties, our parents just got all the fallout. Instead of waiting later to get married, our parents got divorced; instead of becoming feminists, our mothers were left as displaced homemakers. A lot of already existent unhappy situations were dissolved by people who were not quite young or free (read: childless) enough to start again. And their discontent—their stuck-ness—was played out on their children.

My parents are I perfect case in point. Lord knows whatever possessed them to get married in the first place. It probably had something to do with the fact that my mom was raised with many of her first cousins, and all of them were getting married, so it seemed like the thing to do. And from her point of view, back in the early sixties, marriage was the only way she could get out of her parents' house. She'd gone to Cornell, wanting to be an architect, but her mother told her all she could be was an architect's *secretary*, so she majored in art history with that goal in mind. She'd spent a junior year abroad at the Sorbonne and did all the studiedly adventurous things a nice Jewish girl from Long Island can do in Paris —rented a moped, wore a black cape, dated some nobleman type—but once she got out of college, she moved back home and was expected to stay there until she moved into her husband's house. (Certainly there were many bolder women who defied this expectation, who took efficiencies and railroad flats with girlfriends in safe neighborhoods in the city, who worked and dated and went to theater openings and lectures—but my mom was not one of them.) She took a job in the executive training program at Macy's, and one day while she was riding the escalator up from the main floor to the mezzanine, she passed my father, who was riding down. They got married less than a year later, even though he hadn't gone to college, had no ambition, and was considered a step down for a girl like my mom.

My parents did weird things after they got married. My dad got a job at IBM and they moved to Poughkeepsie, New York, where my mom went nuts with boredom and bought herself a pet monkey named Percy. Eventually she got pregnant with me, decided a baby was better than a monkey, and she moved down to New York City because she could not bear another day in a town that was half Vassar College, half IBM. My father followed, I was born, they fought, they were miserable, he refused to get a college degree, they fought some more, and then one day I wouldn't stop crying. My mom called my dad at work to say that if he didn't come home immediately and figure out how to get me to calm down, she was going to defenestrate me. Whatever my father did when he got to the apartment must have worked, because I'm still alive today, but I think that moment marked the end of their marriage.

This was a marriage that could have peacefully ceased to be one fine day with an understanding that it was just a mistake, they were just two foolish kids playing house. Problem was, they had a child, and for many years after they split up, I became the battlefield on which they fought through all their ideological differences. This was New York City in the late sixties, Harlem had burned down, my mom was petrified about being a single mother with a deadbeat ex-husband, so she sent me to the synagogue nursery school, thinking this would provide me with some sense of community and stability. My dad would turn up to see me about once a week, and he would talk to me about atheism and insist I eat lobster and ham and other nonkosher foods that I was taught in school were not allowed. For years, my mom was tugging toward trying to give me a solid, middle-class, traditional upbringing, while my father would tell me that I should just be an artist or a poet or live off the land, or some such thing. She was desperate to keep at least a toehold in the bourgeoisie, and he was working overtime (or actually, not *gainfully* working at all) to stay the hell out of it. Back and forth this went for years, until it felt clear that all three of us were caught mostly in the confusing cross fire of changing times, and what little foundation my parents could possibly give me was shattered and scattered by conflict.

When I was ten or eleven, I really cracked up, started hiding in the locker room at school, crying for hours, or walking around the corridors saying, *Everything is plastic, we're all gonna die anyway, so why does anything matter?* I'd read this phrase in a picture of some graffiti in a magazine article about punk rock, which I decided was definitely a great invention. When I stopped talking, stopped eating, stopped going to school, and started spending my time cutting my legs up with razor blades while listening to dumb rock music like Foreigner on a little Panasonic tape recorder, my parents agreed I needed psychiatric help. To make a very long and complicated story short, my mom found a therapist for me, my dad didn't like him and kept trying to sneak me off to others, I never got terribly effective treatment, my father refused to file an insurance claim for the psychiatrist I was seeing, and the whole scenario concluded with me as messed up as ever, but with all the adults involved suing one another. My mom sued my dad for unpaid alimony and child support, my psychiatrist sued my dad for unpaid bills, and after years of lawyers everywhere, my father finally fled to Florida when I was fourteen years old and did not turn up in my life again until my freshman year at Harvard.

By the time I actually did grow up, I was so grateful to be out of my parents' firing range and not stuck in between them or torn apart like an overstretched rubber band they each tugged at for years that my depression actually began to lift. For me, growing up was not about coming face-to-face with the cruelties of the world; it was about relief.

Obviously, divorce is inevitable and at this point there is joint custody and divorce counseling and all sorts of other things to make the process less painful for the children and for the adults. Which might mean that things are better now, although I think things must be so much worse if divorce is being normalized— because let's face it, all these strangely pieced together families of half siblings and stepparents and all that are not natural. At one time, a kid got two parents who did their best to get it right, but now, taking stepparents into account, he can have twice as many guardians—along with nannies, therapists, tutors, and whatnot— but somehow, all these people put together can't seem to raise a child decently. It's like having ninety-two channels of cable and nothing to watch.

* * *

Despite the exhaustion, I still think that adulthood has been a lot better for me than growing up was. And I believe the task of a lifetime for my generation will be to reinvent the family unit in a way that works and endures. Perhaps critics will say, *Those twentysomethings, all they ever worry about is their private lives*, but I for one believe our private lives deserve some thoughtful attention. If anyone had bothered to give our development as human beings some constructive thought while we were still young enough to receive the benefits passively, we wouldn't have to think about our personal lives so damn much now.

I have heard it said that in our modern world, twelve-step fellowships have become a substitute for family, that the rooms of alcoholics and junkies offering each other support in church basements and community centers is the closest thing anyone has to a familial setup. I have also heard that the neo-Nazi kids in modern Germany, the inner-city youth who join gangs in Los Angeles like the Bloods and the Crips, the homeboys hanging out on the corner—all these movements and loosely bound organizations are about young people trying to find a place in this world to call home, trying to find people in this world to call family. The interesting thing about the attraction of something like AA is that an organization like that involves such a large group of people—not just a few random friends but a big collection of helpful people. And I think we all need some version of that. In the worst moments of my depression, I used to wish I were a drug addict—I used to think it would be so nice if it were simply a matter of getting heroin or alcohol out of my life—because then I could walk into a meeting of fellow sufferers and feel that I'd arrived home at last.

But I'd hate to think that I'd have to become a junkie in order to find my place in this world. And I don't think that is the case. In fact, I think one of the ways many of us twentysomethings have come to deal with our rootlessness has been by turning friends into family. For those of us without addictions, those of us who are just run-of-the-mill parasites on society, our alliances are all that's left. For many of my friends, the world feels like one big orphanage—we're so far from our families, or without families at all, or without families that are able to serve a familial role, and here we get thrown into this lot of life together. Of course, some pundits make fun of us for turning friends and ex-lovers into pseudo-family members, but I believe this is an arrangement that actually works. (Besides, if anyone has a better idea, I'm glad to listen. Joining the Moonies, hooking up with the Branch Davidians, or running off to Esalen are *not* acceptable substitutes.)

And obviously, the theme of friends-as-family seems to resonate in the media a great deal: whether it's in the Banana Republic advertising campaign that pictures several versions of "Your Chosen Family," or it's in the United Colors of Benetton billboards and print ads that try to depict an international loving brotherhood of all races and nations. It's in MTV's attempt at *cinema vérité*[2] with "The Real World," a series that shows a group of young people living in a loft together and puttering their way through the tribulations of everyday; and it's in the way the typical television drama or sitcom of today is likely to revolve around the odd connections and acquaintances made by single people or one-parent families in their apartment complex or subdivision, not on the freestanding biological family that was the center of almost every show thirty years ago. It's in all the press that surrounded the Clinton-Gore bus campaign that attempted to portray the two candidate couples—Al and Tipper and Bill and Hillary—as a little fun-loving family on a perpetual double date rolling its way across the country; and it was in Clinton's beckoning speech at the Democratic convention, in which he invited everyone out there to "join our family." All these examples just amount to a manipulation of Americans' simplest desire to imagine the possibility of home, and yet even as I know my emotions are being toyed with, I still appreciate all these public attempts to define family as something that's got nothing to do with blood.

All my friends, inadequately parented as we seem to have been, spend as much time looking after one another as we do just hanging out and having fun. . . . Insofar as I'm now able to get work done, to make attempts at having relationships, to live a life that is fruitful and productive at all, I attribute it completely to the friends that I have turned into my family.

And if anyone finds that pathetic, I don't care. I don't want to spend another minute of my life supine and suffering in a hospital bed, praying to God for any form of relief he can give to a mind—not even a body—in terrible pain. I don't ever want to endure another morning of the orderlies coming in at 7:00 to take a blood sample and take my temperature because that is the routine in a health-care facility—even though the only thing that's wrong with me is in my head. I don't want to roam the streets at all hours of the day and night, feeling crazy from the heat in the middle of January, running like hell from the voices in my head. I don't want to live life as a sicko. And the friendships I have developed as an adult are probably the only thing standing between me and Bellevue.[3] More to the point, they are the only thing standing between me and suicide. The hole in my heart that was left by a grievous lack of family connections has in some ways been patched over, if not altogether filled, by a sense of family I've found in the last few years.

But I must say, I'm sure my friends and I often seem like these sad lost people who are scared to grow up. I sometimes worry that the clinginess of our relationships is kind of a sorry thing, that we often seem to be holding on tight because of the depth of our desperation and need—and perhaps this just isn't healthy. We often spend time together in large groups of people, and I keep thinking we all really should be out on dates in couples, but it doesn't seem as though any of us is quite ready even to think about getting into deeply committed relationships. I have plenty of friends who have been going out with the same person for years, but none of them is showing signs of heading to the altar. We're all just much too frightened.

And it is this nervousness, this lack of trust, that makes this generation seem ineffectual to many older people on so many fronts.

But we are trying our best to take care of one another. And it is my hope that when we finally do have kids of our own, the sense of community we have created for ourselves will be passed along to them. I hope my children know that their father and I are not the only adults in their lives who can be counted on—I hope they feel that Christine, Jason, Mark, Larissa, Tom, Heather, Ronnie, and Sharon are as much a part of their family as they are part of mine. I hope my friends' children will play with my kids, and I hope they all grow up understanding that they too can choose families of their own. I hope they don't ever think that their world and their expectations are limited by two people who just happen to be their parents, and might do some really stupid, silly things along the way.

These days we all sit around, drinking Rolling Rock and smoking pot late into the night as if we were still in our college dormitory rooms, and sometimes we talk about how it will be to have kids someday. And we all say the same thing: we can't wait to bring children into the world and do everything right that our parents did wrong. Of course, I suspect that our parents had the same idea themselves, and look where it got them.

But still, I've got to believe I can do better. I've already brought up myself, so surely I ought to be able to raise someone else.

I think.

Endnotes

1. British literary critic (b. 1933), now teaching at Boston University.
2. Literally, cinema of fact or cinema of truth: a style of filmmaking that stresses unbiased realism.
3. Hospital in New York City with a large psychiatric ward.

Questions for Reading and Analysis

1. What kinds of problems does Wurtzel suggest are peculiar to her generation?
2. What does Wurtzel mean by "homesickness"?
3. Describe Wurtzel's tone. What words and phrases reveal her youth?
4. Do you agree with Wurtzel's arguments? Would the experiences of your generation lend support to Wurtzel's claims?

In this famous excerpt from his autobiography, Malcolm X (1925–65) explains how, in prison, he got a "homemade education," learning to read by copying out of the dictionary. His newfound reading ability, he writes, awoke a "long dormant craving to be mentally alive," and reinforced the teachings of Elijah Muhammad, the Black Muslim leader. Malcolm X left the Black Muslim movement to form his own organization in 1964; he was assassinated in 1965.

From The Autobiography of Malcolm X

Malcolm X

It was because of my letters that I happened to stumble upon starting to acquire some kind of a homemade education.

I became increasingly frustrated at not being able to express what I wanted to convey in letters that I wrote, especially those to Mr. Elijah Muhammad.[1] In the street, I had been the most articulate hustler out there—I had commanded attention when I said something. But now, trying to write simple English, I not only wasn't articulate, I wasn't even functional. How would I sound writing in slang, the way I would *say* it, something such as, "Look, daddy, let me pull your coat about a cat, Elijah Muhammad—"

Many who today hear me somewhere in person, or on television, or those who read something I've said, will think I went to school far beyond the eighth grade. This impression is due entirely to my prison studies.

It had really begun back in the Charlestown Prison, when Bimbi[2] first made me feel envy of his stock of knowledge. Bimbi had always taken charge of any conversations he was in, and I had tried to emulate him. But every book I picked up had few sentences which didn't contain anywhere from one to nearly all of the words that might as well have been in Chinese. When I just skipped those words, of course, I really ended up with little idea of what the book said. So I had come to the Norfolk Prison Colony still going through only book-reading motions. Pretty soon, I would have quit even these motions, unless I had received the motivation that I did.

I saw that the best thing I could do was get hold of a dictionary—to study, to learn some words. I was lucky enough to reason also that I should try to improve my penmanship. It was sad. I couldn't even write in a straight line. It was both ideas together that moved me to request a dictionary along with some tablets and pencils from the Norfolk Prison Colony school.

I spent two days just riffling uncertainly through the dictionary's pages. I'd never realized so many words existed! I didn't know *which* words I needed to learn. Finally, just to start some kind of action, I began copying.

In my slow, painstaking, ragged handwriting, I copied into my tablet everything printed on that first page, down to the punctuation marks.

I believe it took me a day. Then, aloud, I read back, to myself, everything I'd written on the table. Over and over, aloud, to myself, I read my own handwriting.

I woke up the next morning, thinking about those words—immensely proud to realize that not only had I written so much at one time, but I'd written words that I never knew were in the world. Moreover, with a little effort, I also could remember what many of these words meant. I reviewed the words whose meanings I didn't remember. Funny thing, from the dictionary first page right now, that "aardvark" springs to my mind. The dictionary had a picture of it, a long-tailed, long-eared, burrowing African mammal, which lives off termites caught by sticking out its tongue as an anteater does for ants.

I was so fascinated that I went on—I copied the dictionary's next page. And the same experience came when I studied that. With every succeeding page, I also learned of people and places and events from history. Actually the dictionary is like a miniature encyclopedia. Finally the dictionary's *A* section had filled a whole tablet—and I went on into the *B's.* That was the way I started copying what eventually became the entire dictionary. It went a lot faster after so much practice helped me to pick up handwriting speed. Between what I wrote in my tablet, and writing letters, during the rest of my time in prison I would guess I wrote a million words.

I suppose it was inevitable that as my word-base broadened, I could for the first time pick up a book and read and now begin to understand what the book was saying. Anyone who has read a great deal can imagine the new world that opened. Let me tell you something: From then until I left that prison, in every free moment I had, if I was not reading in the library, I was reading on my bunk. You couldn't have gotten me out of books with a wedge. Between Mr. Muhammad's teachings, my correspondence, my visitors—usually Ella and Reginald—and my reading of books, months passed without my even thinking about being imprisoned. In fact, up to then, I never had been so truly free in my life.

The Norfolk Prison Colony's library was in the school building. A variety of classes was taught there by instructors who came from such places as Harvard and Boston universities. The weekly debates between inmate teams were also held in the school building. You would be astonished to know how worked up convict debaters and audiences would get over subjects like "Should Babies Be Fed Milk?"

Available on the prison library's shelves were books on just about every general subject. Much of the big private collection that Parkhurst had willed to the prison was still in crates and boxes in the back of the library—thousands of old books. Some of them looked ancient: covers faded, old-time parchment-looking binding. Parkhurst . . . seemed to have been principally interested in history and religion. He had the money and the special interest to have a lot of books that you wouldn't have in general circulation. Any college library would have been lucky to get that collection.

As you can imagine, especially in a prison where there was heavy emphasis on rehabilitation, an inmate was smiled upon if he demonstrated an unusually intense interest in books. There was a sizable number of well-read inmates, especially the popular debaters. Some were said by many to be practically walking encyclopedias. They were almost celebrities. No university would ask any student to devour literature as I did when this new world opened to me, of being able to read and *understand*.

I read more in my room than in the library itself. An inmate who was known to read a lot could check out more than the permitted maximum number of books. I preferred reading in the total isolation of my own room.

When I had progressed to really serious reading, every night at about ten P.M. I would be outraged with the "lights out." It always seemed to catch me right in the middle of something engrossing.

Fortunately, right outside my door was a corridor light that cast a glow into my room. The glow was enough to read by, once my eyes adjusted to it. So when "lights out" came, I would sit on the floor where I could continue reading in that glow.

At one-hour intervals the night guards paced past every room. Each time I heard the approaching footsteps, I jumped into bed and feigned sleep. And as soon as the guard passed, I got back out of bed onto the floor area of that light-glow, where I would read for another fifty-eight minutes—until the guard approached again. That went on until three or four every morning. Three or four hours of sleep a night was enough for me. Often in the years in the streets I had slept less than that.

The teachings of Mr. Muhammad stressed how history had been "whitened"— when white men had written history books, the black man simply had been left out. Mr. Muhammad couldn't have said anything that would have struck me much harder. I had never forgotten how when my class, me and all of those whites, had studied seventh-grade United States history back in Mason, the history of the Negro had been covered in one paragraph, and the teacher had gotten a big laugh with his joke, "Negroes' feet are so big that when they walk, they leave a hole in the ground."

This is one reason why Mr. Muhammad's teachings spread so swiftly all over the United States, among *all* Negroes, whether or not they became followers of Mr. Muhammad. The teachings ring true—to every Negro. You can hardly show me a black adult in America—or a white one, for that matter—who knows from the history books anything like the truth about the black man's role. In my own case, once I heard of the "glorious history of the black man," I took special pains to hunt in the library for books that would inform me on details about black history.

I can remember accurately the very first set of books that really impressed me. I have since bought that set of books and I have it at home for my children to read as they grow up. It's called *Wonders of the World*. It's full of pictures of archeological finds, statues that depict, usually, non-European people.

I found books like Will Durant's *Story of Civilization*. I read H. G. Wells's *Outline of History*. *Souls of Black Folk* by W. E. B. Du Bois gave me a glimpse into the black people's history before they came to this country. Carter G. Woodson's *Negro History* opened my eyes about black empires before the black slave was brought to the United States, and the early Negro struggles for freedom.

J. A. Rogers's three volumes of *Sex and Race* told about race-mixing before Christ's time; about Aesop being a black man who told fables; about Egypt's Pharaohs; about the great Coptic Christian Empires; about Ethiopia, the earth's oldest continuous black civilization, as China is the oldest continuous civilization.

Mr. Muhammad's teaching about how the white man had been created led me to *Findings in Genetics* by Gregor Mendel. (The dictionary's *G* section was where I had learned what "genetics" meant.) I really studied this book by the Austrian monk. Reading it over and over, especially certain sections, helped me to understand that if you started with a black man, a white man could be produced; but starting with a white man, you never could produce a black man—because the white chromosome is recessive. And since no one disputes that there was but one Original Man, the conclusion is clear.

During the last year or so, in the *New York Times*, Arnold Toynbee used the word "bleached" in describing the white man. (His words were: "White (i.e., bleached) human beings of North European origin. . . .") Toynbee also referred to the European geographic area as only a peninsula of Asia. He said there is no such thing as Europe. And if you look at the globe, you will see for yourself that America is only an extension of Asia. (But at the same time Toynbee is among those who have helped to bleach history. He has written that Africa was the only continent that produced no history. He won't write that again. Every day now, the truth is coming to light.)

I never will forget how shocked I was when I began reading about slavery's total horror. It made such an impact upon me that it later became one of my favorite subjects when I became a minister of Mr. Muhammad's. The world's most monstrous crime, the sin and the blood on the white man's hands, are almost impossible to believe. Books like the one by Frederick Olmstead opened my eyes to the horrors suffered when the slave was landed in the United States. The European woman, Fanny Kemble, who had married a Southern white slave-owner, described how human beings were degraded. Of course I read *Uncle Tom's Cabin*. In fact, I believe that's the only novel I have ever read since I started serious reading.

Parkhurst's collection also contained some bound pamphlets of the Abolitionist Anti-Slavery Society of New England. I read descriptions of atrocities, saw those illustrations of black slave women tied up and flogged with whips; of black mothers watching their babies being dragged off, never to be seen by their mothers again; of dogs after slaves, and of the fugitive slave catchers, evil white men with whips and clubs and chains and guns. I read about the slave preacher Nat Turner, who put the fear of God into the white slavemaster. Nat Turner wasn't going around preaching pie-in-the-sky and "nonviolent" freedom for the black man. There in Virginia one night in 1831, Nat and seven other slaves started out at his master's home and through the night they went from one plantation "big house" to the next, killing, until by the next morning 57 white people were dead and Nat had about 70 slaves following him. White people, terrified for their lives, fled from their homes, locked themselves up in public buildings, hid in the woods, and some even left the state. A small army of soldiers took two months to catch and hang Nat Turner. Somewhere I have read where Nat Turner's example is said to have inspired John Brown to invade Virginia and attack Harpers Ferry nearly thirty years later, with thirteen white men and five Negroes.

I read Herodotus, "the father of History," or, rather, I read about him. And I read the histories of various nations, which opened my eyes gradually, then wider and wider, to how the whole world's white men had indeed acted like devils, pillaging and raping and bleeding and draining the whole world's non-white people. I remember, for instance, books such as Will Durant's *The Story of Oriental Civilization*, and Mahatma Ghandi's accounts of the struggle to drive the British out of India.

Book after book showed me how the white man had brought upon the world's black, brown, red, and yellow peoples every variety of the sufferings of exploitation. I saw how since the sixteenth century, the so-called "Christian trader" white man began to ply the seas in his lust for Asian and African empires, and plunder, and power. I read, I saw, how the white man never has gone among the non-white peoples bearing the Cross in the true manner and spirit of Christ's teachings—meek, humble, and Christlike.

I perceived, as I read, how the collective white man had been actually nothing but a piratical opportunist who used Faustian machinations to make his own Christianity his initial wedge in criminal conquests. First, always "religiously," he branded "heathen" and "pagan" labels upon ancient non-white cultures and civilizations. The stage thus set, he then turned upon his non-white victims his weapons of war.

I read how, entering India—half a *billion* deeply religious brown people—the British white man, by 1759, through promises, trickery and manipulations, controlled much of India through Great Britain's East India Company. The parasitical British administration kept tentacling out to half of the subcontinent. In 1857, some of the desperate people of India finally mutinied—and, excepting the African slave trade, nowhere has history recorded any more unnecessary bestial and ruthless human carnage than the British suppression of the non-white Indian people.

Over 115 million African blacks—close to the 1930s population of the United States—were murdered or enslaved during the slave trade. And I read how when the slave market was glutted, the cannibalistic white powers of Europe next carved up, as their colonies, the richest areas of the black continent. And Europe's chancelleries for the next century played a chess game of naked exploitation and power from Cape Horn to Cairo.

Ten guards and the warden couldn't have torn me out of those books. Not even Elijah Muhammad could have been more eloquent than those books were in providing indisputable proof that the collective white man had acted like a devil in virtually every contact he had with the world's collective non-white man. I listen today to the radio, and watch television, and read the headlines about the collective white man's fear and tension concerning China. When the white man professes ignorance about why the Chinese hate him so, my mind can't help flashing back to what I read, there in prison, about how the blood forebears of this same white man raped China at a time when China was trusting and helpless. Those original white "Christian traders" sent into China millions of pounds of opium. By 1839, so many of the Chinese were addicts that China's desperate government destroyed twenty thousand chests of opium. The first Opium War was promptly declared by the white man. Imagine! Declaring *war* upon someone who objects to be narcotized! The Chinese were severely beaten, with Chinese-invented gunpowder.

The Treaty of Nanking made China pay the British white man for the destroyed opium: forced open China's major ports to British trade; forced China to abandon Hong Kong; fixed China's import tariffs so low that cheap British articles soon flooded in, maiming China's industrial development.

After a second Opium War, the Tientsin Treaties legalized the ravaging opium trade, legalized a British-French-American control of China's customs. China tried delaying that Treaty's ratification; Peking was looted and burned.

"Kill the foreign white devils!" was the 1901 Chinese war cry in the Boxer Rebellion. Losing again, this time the Chinese were driven from Peking's choicest areas. The vicious, arrogant white man put up the famous signs, "Chinese and dogs not allowed."

Red China after World War II closed its doors to the Western white world. Massive Chinese agricultural, scientific, and industrial efforts are described in a book that *Life* magazine recently published. Some observers inside Red China have reported that the world never has known such a hate-white campaign as is now going on in this non-white country where, present birth-rates continuing, in fifty more years Chinese will be half the earth's population. And it seems that some Chinese chickens will soon come home to roost, with China's recent successful nuclear tests.

Let us face reality. We can see in the United Nations a new world order being shaped, along color lines—an alliance among the non-white nations. America's U.N. Ambassador Adlai Stevenson complained not long ago that in the United Nations "a skin game" was being played. He was right. He was facing reality. A "skin game" *is* being played. But Ambassador Stevenson sounded like Jesse James accusing the marshal of carrying a gun. Because who in the world's history ever has played a worse "skin game" than the white man?

Mr. Muhammad, to whom I was writing daily, had no idea of what a new world had opened up to me through my efforts to document his teachings in books.

When I discovered philosophy, I tried to touch all the landmarks of philosophical development. Gradually, I read most of the old philosophers, Occidental and Oriental. The Oriental philosophers were the ones I came to prefer; finally, my impression was that most Occidental philosophy had largely been borrowed from the Oriental thinkers. Socrates, for instance, traveled in Egypt. Some sources even say that Socrates was initiated into some of the Egyptian mysteries. Obviously Socrates got some of his wisdom among the East's wise men.

I have often reflected upon the new vistas that reading opened to me. I knew right there in prison that reading had changed forever the course of my life. As I see it today, the ability to read awoke inside me some long dormant craving to be mentally alive. I certainly wasn't seeking any degree, the way a college confers a status symbol upon its students. My homemade education gave me, with every additional book that I read, a little bit more sensitivity to the deafness, dumbness, and blindness that was afflicting the black race in America. Not long ago, an English writer telephoned me from London, asking questions. One was, "What's your alma mater?" I told him, "Books." "You will never catch me with a free fifteen minutes in which I'm not studying something I feel might be able to help the black man.

Yesterday I spoke in London, and both ways on the plane across the Atlantic I was studying a document about how the United Nations proposes to insure the human rights of the oppressed minorities of the world. The American black man is the world's most shameful case of minority oppression. What makes the black man think of himself as only an internal United States issue is just a catch-phrase, two words, "civil rights." How is the black man going to get "civil rights" before first he wins his *human* rights? If the American black man will start thinking about his *human* rights, and then start thinking of himself as part of one of the world's great peoples, he will see he has a case for the United Nations.

I can't think of a better case! Four hundred years of black blood and sweat invested here in America, and the white man still has the black man begging for what every immigrant fresh off the ship can take for granted the minute he walks down the gangplank.

But I'm digressing. I told the Englishman that my alma mater was books, a good library. Every time I catch a plane, I have with me a book that I want to read—and that's a lot of books these days. If I weren't out here every day battling the white man, I could spend the rest of my life reading, just satisfying my curiosity—because you can hardly mention anything I'm not curious about. I don't think anybody ever got more out of going to prison than I did. In fact, prison enabled me to study far more intensively than I would have if my life had gone differently and I had attended some college. I imagine that one of the biggest troubles with colleges is there are too many distractions, too much panty-raiding, fraternities, and boola-boola and all of that. Where else but in a prison could I have attacked my ignorance by being able to study intensely sometimes as much as fifteen hours a day?

Endnotes

1. *Elijah Muhammad*: U.S. clergyman (1897–1975); leader of the Black Muslims 1934–1975.
2. *Bimbi*: A fellow inmate.

Questions for Reading and Analysis

1. What distinction does the writer make, early in the selection, between spoken language and written language?

2. Why does Malcolm X decide to pursue an education? How does he set out to accomplish his goal?

3. Despite his physical imprisonment, Malcolm X claims that upon discovering language, he feels freer than at any other time in his life. In what sense does language liberate him?

4. Malcolm X seems to assert the superiority of his "homemade education" over a more formal education. Are there limitations to his approach?

In his 1997 essay "The Undying Problem of the Death Penalty,"
Hiller B. Zobel, a Fellow of the Society of American Historians and
a judge on the Massachusetts Superior Court, analyzes a 1901 murder
case, claiming that the concerns about the death penalty have changed
very little in the almost 100 years since.

The Undying Problem of
the Death Penalty

Hiller B. Zobel

Can it be fair? Humane? Deter crime? These very current questions troubled Americans just as much in the day of the Salem witch trials as in the day of Timothy McVeigh.

Chief Justice Oliver Wendell Holmes of the Massachusetts Supreme Judicial Court spent part of May 6, 1901, writing about the death penalty, and specifically about electrocution. Earlier that day lawyers for Luigi Storti, a twenty-seven-year-old Italian laborer without a family in America, convicted for the murder of a fellow immigrant in Boston's North End, had argued that electrocution was punishment "cruel or unusual," proscribed by the Massachusetts Declaration of Rights, a charter nine years older than the federal Bill of Rights.

Until 1898 the mode of capital punishment in Massachusetts, as in almost every other state that inflicted death, had been the gallows. The electric chair was supposed to eliminate the uncertainty and pain of hanging (where miscalculation of the "drop" distance might result in slow strangulation or ripping the head from the body), with the aid of the nineteenth century's secular deity, science, and that newly harnessed miracle, electricity.

Although Storti was to be the first person ever to die in Massachusetts's electric chair, he naturally cared less about the method of execution than about mere survival. His lawyers' first move after the guilty verdict had been a straight forward review by the Massachusetts high court focusing on claims of legal error, such as that the statements he had made to the police were not voluntary. That appeal had failed, and so had an effort to obtain an executive commutation and a legislative attempt to abolish the death penalty completely. Then, days before his execution, Storti developed pulmonary hemorrhages, probably from tuberculosis, that left him so weak he would have to be carried to the electric chair. Unwilling to execute a dying man—and hoping for a natural death that would solve everyone's problems—Gov. Murray Crane stayed the execution until May 11.

Then Storti's health began to improve, and his lawyers presented the petition that Holmes and his colleagues had just considered. With less than an a week remaining before execution, Holmes—a fast worker under any circumstances—set out the Court's views promptly so that, as he put it, "we may avoid delaying the course of the law and raising false hopes in [Storti's] mind."

The planned execution, Storti's lawyers had argued, was cruel or unusual punishment because the procedure involved not only pain and death but also psychological anguish. No, replied Holmes, electrocution was "devised for the purpose of reaching the end proposed as swiftly and painlessly as possible." Any mental suffering, he added, "is due not to its being more horrible to be struck by lightning than to be hanged with the chance of slowly strangling, but to the general fear of death. The suffering due to that fear the law does not seek to spare. It means that it shall be felt." Holmes was merely saying in his elegant, direct way that the death penalty sought as much to deter future criminals as to punish current ones.

Storti's lawyers immediately petitioned for a federal writ of *habeas corpus*, this time arguing that Storti's detention somehow violated a treaty between Italy and the United States. Impatiently the federal circuit court in Boston denied the petition and even (as lower federal judges were permitted to do) prohibited the right to appeal to the United States Supreme Court.

Undaunted, counsel for Storti persuaded United States Supreme Court Justice Horace Gray to allow the appeal to proceed, meanwhile lodging another appeal, which Holmes quickly rejected, arguing that irreconcilable laws were requiring both "special" and "solitary" confinement before execution. On December 2, 1901, the Supreme Court permanently ended Storti's procedural odyssey. The grounds purporting to justify Storti's release, said Justice David Brewer for a unanimous Court, were "wholly without foundation." He called the case "another of the numerous instances" in which applications and appeals were taken "quite destitute of meritorious grounds, and operating only to delay the administration of justice."

It is difficult to tell whether the exertions on Storti's behalf drew their inspiration from the death penalty itself or from the fearsome new technology. New York had enacted the first electrocution statute in 1888, responding to the report of a special commission that it represented "the most humane and practical method known to modern science of carrying into effect the sentence of death."

We tend to consider misgivings about the death penalty a late-twentieth century concern. In fact, in 1794 Pennsylvania abolished death as a punishment for all crimes except "willful, deliberate, and premeditated" killing. Even earlier, in the colonies as in Britain, the courts had applied a concept called "benefit of clergy" to decapitalize manslaughter—that is, killing without malice. In medieval England clerics could insist on being tried in ecclesiastical courts; they proved their status by demonstrating literacy (because, generally, only they knew how to read). Later the "benefit" became available to any demonstrated reader. By 1707 even an illiterate first offender could escape the noose, after being branded on the thumb to preclude any subsequent application. Louisiana passed an abolitional legislative resolution in 1830 and revoked it in 1846. Also in 1846 Michigan abolished capital punishment for all crimes but treason; in 1853 Wisconsin abolished it absolutely.

Other states tried to deal with the problem by giving the jury power to recommend against death. It became common also to classify murder by degrees.

Typically, first-degree murder entailed not only malice—unjustified killing—but also premeditation, defined, not very helpfully, as reflection, even if for only a few seconds, followed by the decision to kill and then by the killing. In essence, the jury could decide life or death according to its own view of the facts, and in all cases, of course, the jurors retained the unsanctioned but uncontrollable right to disregard even compelling evidence and acquit: jury nullification. As Holmes said in another context, jurors can "let a little popular prejudice into the administration of law (in violation of their oath)." Indeed, repeated demonstrations of jurors' reluctance to render a verdict that would mandate the death sentence led, as early as the 1830s, to an editorial lament in a Rhode Island newspaper with an unintended irony: "Unless the prisoner, from his color or extraction, is cut off from ordinary sympathy, he is almost sure of an acquittal."

The fact is that, historically, we have never regarded the death penalty placidly. Curtis Bok, a judge in Pennsylvania on both the trial and the appellate benches, once asked, "Why is the State so ashamed of its process that it must kill at dead of night in an isolated place and on an unnamed day?" The man who pulls the switch generally stands hidden from everyone's view. When Storti died, the press account pointedly noted the anonymity of the executioner. Even when death comes by a firing squad, the round in one of the rifles is blank, presumably so that no one will know for certain that his was a fatal shot.

The death penalty provokes in us dreadfully conflicted feelings, beginning with recognition of the need for a fair procedure in determining guilt and imposing punishment. Like Francis Bacon four centuries ago, we know that "revenge is a kind of wild justice, which the more man's nature runs to, the more ought law to weed it out." Thus we recoil from lynch law, either in fact (Leo Frank and Emmett Till) or in fiction (The Ox-Bow Incident).

Yet even as we insist on due process, we express impatience with the inhibitions that fair procedure imposes. In part an appellate court's role is to restrain the mob spirit; still, what judges see as ensuring constitutional and legal rights, the public and the victim's family often denounce as legal technicalities. Certainly, when a client's life is at stake, a good, honest lawyer will try every available argument, just as Storti's did. Hope does ever bloom; remember, too, what Samuel Johnson once advised Boswell: "An argument which does not convince yourself, may convince the judge to whom you urge it." It was also Johnson who said, "When a man knows he is to be hanged in a fortnight, it concentrates his mind [and, one might add, his lawyer's mind] wonderfully."

Counsel's ingenuity and desperate effort do not always sit well with the appellate courts. Justice Brewer's impatience with Storti has found echoes in our own time, when Supreme Court justices have expressed similar unhappiness with not only defendants and lawyers but also some lower court judges. Nonetheless the Court as an institution and the justices themselves have found the implications of the death penalty not so easy to fathom. Furman v. Georgia, the 1972 decision that for a time eliminated executions in this country, produced no fewer than nine separate opinions, one per justice: five concurring with the one-page anonymous *per curium* order, four dissenting. Two of the "majority" justices thought the death penalty cruel and unusual punishment per se; the others thought it unconstitutionally disparate in its effects: Most of those executed were poor, young, ignorant, and perhaps the victims of racial discrimination.

Eight years later, when the Massachusetts Supreme Judicial Court struck down the commonwealth's new Furman-shaped death penalty statute, it condemned the psychological agony inherent in the punishment, directly refuting Holmes's tough words to Storti. "Mental pain," Chief Justice Edward Hennessey wrote, quoting Justice Brennan in Furman, "is an inseparable part of our practice of punishing criminals by death, for the prospect of pending execution exacts a frightful toll during the inevitable long wait between the imposition of sentence and the actual infliction of death." Of course, part of the waiting period results from the drawn-out appellate process.

If the mental-pain view prevails, no form of execution can ever pass constitutional muster. After all, even lethal injection, supposedly the most painless method, still involves the "long wait" following conviction while the legal process tries to ensure that death, the one punishment not subject to revision, comes only to the truly guilty. And electrocution, whose supposed absence of pain so attracted the Victorians, has turned out to hold its own horrors. Lewis E. Lawes, for many years the warden at Sing Sing Prison, had this to say about what happens in the electric chair: "The [prisoner] leaps as if to break the strong leather straps that hold [him]. Sometimes a thin wisp of smoke pushes itself out from under the helmet that holds the head electrode, followed by a faint odor of burning flesh. [The body heats to 130 degrees—a little less than rare roast beef.] The hands turn red, then white, and the cords of the neck stand out like steel bands."

The newspaper account of Storti's death omitted some of the details, but the reporter had certainly seen the same sights that Warden Lawes had: "The body of Storti surged up against the tightly buckled straps, which creaked and strained under the pressure, the veins in his neck and wrists and face swelled." Afterward, the reporter wrote, "none of the other witnesses would say anything of particular interest about the execution, except that nothing could be more sudden or certain in producing death than electricity as it is applied in the prison."

Deliberately using the power of the state to take a human life continues to raise moral and political issues that legislators find uncomfortable to face and judges find impossible to solve. Whether today's out-of-sight executions more effectively deter crime than did the public spectacles of hangings in earlier times is not the only question. Over the last twenty years society has become more willing to recognize the interests of victims or (in cases of murder) their families in the punishment process. Elected local prosecutors, when deciding, for example, to explore the possibility of a plea to second-degree murder or manslaughter, pay careful attention to the survivors' desires. Beyond that, at sentencing time, even when the judge has no discretion, many states give family representatives the right to vent their feelings in open court.

In short, although revenge may indeed be a kind of wild justice, we are now coming to think that perhaps the law needs not to root it out but to regulate it. Whether that regulation should involve the latter-day gallows tree is a question that is anything but new, yet that remains and will remain for all of us to ponder and—however we can—answer.

Questions for Reading and Analysis

1. What are the "dreadfully conflicted feelings" that have always haunted capital punishment cases? What problems have repeatedly arisen in the administration of the death penalty?

2. What conclusions does he reach about the issue of revenge?

3. As a Massachusetts Superior Court judge, Zobel is an expert talking to an audience of non-lawyers. In what way is his analysis different from other essays you have read about the death penalty?

4. Judges in both the past and the present look at the "psychological pain" the criminal experiences as part of the punishment of the death penalty. While many complain about the time it takes to actually execute somebody who has been found guilty, one might argue that the delays in the process also intensify a criminal's mental pain and thus his punishment. Do you think the argument about psychological pain is a legitimate reason to speed up the appeals process in capital punishment cases?

Appendix A:
Selected Student Writing

Four Student Essays

1999 & 2000 Schwing Award Essays

Three Successful Proficiency Exam Responses

Four Student Essays

The following essays by James Derouen, Ricky Hervey, Jennifer Ponti, and Philip A. Soulet, Jr. are responses to 1158 writing assignments, all deemed exemplary by their teachers.

Clean Up T.V.—Turn It Off

James Derouen

Classroom discussion of the South Park episode we viewed last week revealed that some viewers definitely found the show offensive. While this response to shows such as *South Park* can be expected (and is perhaps even understandable), to suggest that the response warrants stricter regulation or a "clean up" of a private industry is invalid and potentially dangerous. If programs such as *South Park* have negative ramifications on society (a questionable hypothesis in itself), then perhaps we should examine our society's dependence on television as the root of the problem.

Perhaps the most obvious counter-argument for the stricter regulation of television is the inherent subjectivity of such regulations. What I mean by this is that to regulate, we must devise standards with which to regulate. Whose standards will we use? What my neighbor in this class finds offensive may not offend me, and vice versa. One could argue that there are publicly accepted standards of decency that could be used, but we've tried this with poorly devised obscenity laws that are already on the books and prove hard to enforce. The fact is that what one group or individual finds offensive may not offend another group or individual. This becomes more true as our world becomes better connected and we are increasingly exposed to other cultures and subcultures. It is foolish to think that we could ever devise a set of standards with which to regulate that would satisfy a significant majority, much less everybody.

In addition, even if we could agree upon a set of standards to regulate television, would it be our job? I don't think it would. With the exception of public television, television programs are privately funded ventures. Even public television does not receive the majority of its funding from the government. If television opts to censor or regulate itself, as it often does, based on the demands of the public, that is one issue. However, to call for regulation of television in general by the government or any other group is censorship. The federal communications commission already regulates what words can be said and what images can be shown on network television and radio. It could be argued that this is censorship in itself. The fact remains that television is a private industry. The makers of television programs should be allowed the creative license to produce what they wish, in addition, they should be able to air what they wish. Viewers aren't forced to watch.

This statement addresses a final point. Television is viewed by choice. There is no required minimum viewing time per day, although a newcomer to our society might think otherwise. If television programs really do inspire violence, dishonesty, anger and other negative attributes, then perhaps we shouldn't watch. If parents don't have enough time to monitor what their children watch, then they should make time. If prospective parents don't feel they'll have time, then perhaps they should reconsider being parents.

Taking offense or being shocked by what one views on television is understandable. People cannot help their feelings and they are certainly entitled to them. However, as the old saying goes, "one person's trash is another's treasure." Increasing the regulation of television in order to "clean it up" is not a viable option or even one that is within our rights. If it offends you, that's understandable. Just turn it off.

Modern Television: A Mirror of Reality

Ricky Hervey

Standards of American television have changed drastically since its introduction in the 1950's. Television originally consisted of a mere three channels that dealt conservatively with the adult issues of sex and violence. As a result, early television presented a limited description of American life. For example, at one time Elvis was not allowed to shake his hips on *The Ed Sullivan Show*, outraging teenage girls across America. Gradually, however, broadcasters loosened their restrictions to accommodate the growing interests of the American public. Suddenly, *The Brady Bunch* admitted it was acceptable for a married couple to share a bed. Today we have shock artists such as Howard Stern parading half-naked pornographic stars around while speaking about his miniature penis. *South Park* features animated grammar school children uttering such profanity as "Bitch" and "You bastard," while poking fun at political correctness in religion and government. However, on the opposite end of the spectrum are programs such as *Seventh Heaven* that emphasize strong moral values and children's channels such as the Disney Channel. While some content in television programs today does indeed border on the obscene, these programs are the exception rather than the rule. Television does provide an accurate representation of our society.

While sex, violence, and profanity may seem to dominate the television industry, many programs and even networks provide wholesome entertainment for the entire family. Children can watch cartoons 24 hours a day on the Cartoon Network. The Disney Channel and Nickelodeon similarly provide entertainment for children that parents can trust. While PBS airs programs such as *Sesame Street* and *Barney*, which provide education for children, the *History Channel* and the *Learning Channel* provide education for adults. Indeed, basic cable provides close to one hundred channels to choose from, allowing viewers to find wholesome programming 24 hours a day.

As a matter of fact, television manufacturers and networks are currently working together to assist parents in controlling what their children are exposed to on television without infringing on the media's freedom of speech. Networks have developed a ratings system to aid parents in monitoring what their children watch. According to *The Times Picayune TV Focus*, programs are rated for all children (TVY), for older children (TVY7), or for a general audience (TVG). Programs involving more mature content can suggest viewing for mature audiences on (TVMA). In addition to this rating system, new televisions come equipped with a "parental control" feature. This feature allows parents to block out programs according to their rating. Adults have the right to chose when entertainment becomes offensive, and now we can more effectively make these choices for our children.

Even if we choose not to watch television shows that we view to be overly offensive, we must acknowledge the importance of their social role. Many dramas, such as *NYPD Blue* and HBO's *Oz*, portray the violence that so many Americans would like to ignore. Howard Stern consistently tests his limits by being as crude as possible. He teaches us how not to act by being the most hated man in America. *South Park* carries a strong political message with every episode. In one episode, one of the children unknowingly comes close to sexual abuse through the internet. While offensive and even perverse, this episode serves the dual purpose of bringing awareness to the very real problem of child abuse on the internet and exposing an organization of pedophiles (NAMBLA, or the National Man-Boy Love Association). Above all, even offensive television provides entertainment. After all, the criterion by which "offensiveness" is judged varies greatly from person to person.

Undoubtedly, some viewers will find aspects of modern television offensive. Coming from the most culturally diverse society on the globe, this is simply an unavoidable evil. However, as Americans, we have the right to choose which television shows are right for us. Networks have even developed rating systems in order to establish a criterion by which to judge which shows are right for children and which are solely for adult entertainment. Rather than attempt to place restrictions, we must respect each other's right to freedom of expression. After all, television is merely a mirror of American life.

A Rhetorical Success of Martin Luther King, Jr.

Jennifer Ponti

Rhetorical success, as set forth in Wayne C. Booth's "The Rhetorical Stance," is partially dependent upon audience awareness and voice (the implied character of the speaker). Booth's critical elements are obvious in Martin Luther King's 1963 "Letter from Birmingham Jail." King is responding to eight white clergymen who oppose "unwise and untimely" Negro demonstrations in Alabama. From the content and tone of their letter, King realizes that he will respond to well-educated southern men who are devout Christians, students of the Bible, fearful of violence and extremism from Negro demonstrations and, in all likelihood, prejudiced. With this audience awareness, he chooses to address his audience in "patient and reasonable terms." King's well-chosen voice and acute awareness of his audience make his 1963 "Letter from Birmingham Jail" rhetorically successful.

King could have understandably been infuriated by the accusations and criticisms of the eight white clergymen. If he had chosen to respond in a belligerent voice, his letter would not have been rhetorically effective. In all likelihood, the clergymen would have considered his remarks as the rantings of an imprisoned extremist. Cognizant of his audience, King, therefore, responds in a congenial voice. In the first paragraph, King calls the clergymen "men of good will." Throughout his letter, King appeals to his audience with peaceful terms such as "my friends," "my fellow brethren," and "my Christian and Jewish brothers." In the penultimate paragraph, a humble King seeks tolerance for his shortcomings from the clergymen: "If I have said anything in my letter that overstates the truth and indicates an unreasonable patience, I beg you to forgive me." King concludes his letter with a final offer of good will: "I also hope that circumstances will soon make it possible for me to meet each of you, not as an integrationist or a civil-rights leader but as a fellow clergyman and a Christian brother." As in all rhetorically successful writing, King has chosen a voice that, as Booth says, "engages the audience in the process of thinking—and feeling—it [the subject] through."

What better way to engage an audience into thinking and feeling about a subject than to focus on what is most familiar to the audience. King is keenly aware of his audience's clerical background and knowledge of the Bible, and he utilizes this awareness superbly. In his explanation of just and unjust laws, King defines just laws in terms of "moral law or the law of God." He quotes St. Augustine and St. Thomas Aquinas to defend his position on this issue. He effectively uses the biblical example of Shadrach, Meshach, and Abednego to support his acts of civil disobedience. Acutely aware of his audience of clergymen, he expresses his disappointment with the white religious leadership of the community and desperately appeals to the clergymen to break loose "from the paralyzing chains of conformity and join us as active partners in the struggle for freedom." King defends his acts of extremism with reference to St. Paul, Amos, and Jesus. Just as St. Paul carried the gospel throughout the Greco-Roman world, so King feels compelled to spread the gospel of freedom throughout America. Some may argue that King damages his rhetorical efforts by likening himself to Jesus and St. Paul. A close analysis, however, indicates that King utilizes these analogies to defend his actions rather than elevate his status. In line with Booth's rhetorical stance, King has identified the area and scope of his audience's knowledge, and has effectively appealed to that knowledge with biblical and clerical references.

King is aware of his audience's limitations, i.e., he recognizes what his audience does not know. He knows that his audience has little knowledge of what it means to be a Negro in America. It is important to King that his audience vicariously feels the persecution and oppression of the Negroes; therefore, he proceeds to educate the clergymen. With a 305-word, emotionally composed sentence, King describes what it means to be a Negro, segregated, and "plunged into the abyss of despair." This is not a man who wishes to place himself above his audience: This is a humble man who is appealing to the fair-mindedness and Christian background/career of his audience. In this same commentary, in conformity with Booth's rhetorical stance, King expresses his conviction to improve the plight of the Negro, his deep concern for his subject, and logic in conveying his frustration with delayed justice. This one lengthy sentence exemplifies the voice of King's letter—it is rhetoric at its best!

King's letter is a profound example of the proper use of audience awareness and voice. It would be interesting to know how deeply (if at all) the eight white clergymen from Alabama were affected by King's "Letter from Birmingham Jail." It is hard to imagine that they were not persuaded to take up King's cause after reading his rhetorically successful letter.

The Changing Roles of Gays on Television

Philip A. Soulet, Jr.

This year's new line-up of television shows boasts of many gay characters, some being introduced on old favorites while others are appearing on entirely new programs. This is a relatively new phenomenon as evidenced by the fact that it was only in the 1970's that gay issues began being discussed publicly. Until that time even an inference of homosexuality could have caused the cancellation of a program or kept it from ever being produced. Over the last thirty or so years, gay characters on television have gone from nonexistent to people to be feared to the central figures in some highly popular sitcoms.[1]

When the very successful sitcom *My Three Sons* was first pitched to the networks, a major concern of the executives was that the American public would find it unsettling to see an all-male household. They feared that it would look like the two adults were in a romantic sort of relationship and that people would balk at the idea. Fortunately, the American people were not so easily frightened and the show became a huge success, running in syndication for years.

In the 1970's, the cult film star Divine made several appearances on *All in the Family*. Divine's character, Beverly, was a transvestite first introduced in an episode in which Archie had given her mouth to mouth resuscitation. Archie was appalled when he realized that she was a he, but the rest of the family was much more open toward her. That may have been America's first introduction to an as yet invisible portion of the population.

Also in the seventies, Billy Crystal portrayed a gay man, a recurring character on the sitcom *Soap*. While stereotyping him as effeminate was a useful prop for many punch lines, the series did include his character being accepted by the family and even romantically involved with a professional football player. If it could be considered groundbreaking to have an openly gay character on a television, then it must have been earth-shattering to include one who didn't fit the usual mold.

During the Reagan/Bush years of the eighties, gay characters again disappeared from network television. The exception was the occasional movie of the week featuring an AIDS patient. The AIDS movies did bring about a greater awareness of gays in society, and certainly helped raise awareness of that dreaded disease, but they also emphasized a differentness and sense of tragedy instead of the normalization which had begun on the earlier sitcoms and would return in the 1990's.

Roseanne opened the door wider for gay characters on television in the nineties, with a much-hyped coming out of the character portrayed by Sandra Bernhardt. The series later had another much publicized scene in which Roseanne was kissed by another woman. In its later years, a recurring character played by Martin Moll had an openly gay relationship, and his partner made frequent appearances on the show as well.

Soon after *Roseanne* opened the door, Ellen Degeneres came out both in and out of character on her show *Ellen*. This stirred quite a public debate, especially in the more conservative sectors of society. Ultimately, *Ellen* was cancelled, though the network claimed a lack of sponsor support to be the reason.

Gay characters have since appeared on several series including *NYPD Blue*, *Dawson's Creek*, and *Spin City* (which holds claim to having the only gay person of color currently on television). *Will and Grace*, which began airing just last year, features not one, but two central characters who are gay. And the coming season, according to *The Advocate*, promises five new gay characters gracing the airwaves of the networks.

In the last thirty years of network programming, roles for gay characters have gone from zero to a sprinkling to the current culmination in gay-themed sitcoms. This tremendous change can be traced to a few brave individuals, including some farsighted executives, and thanks to them, America's favorite form of entertainment is now a little more varied. And, as we've all been told, variety is the spice of life.

Endnote

1. It might be wise to mention here that for the sake of simplicity, in this essay the term gay will be applied to both males and females.

Reading Matters

Schwing Award Essays
1999 & 2000

The following essay, penned by Elizabeth A. Underwood, won the Ella V. Schwing Award, an annual award for the best essay written in a freshman English class at UNO, in 1999. Underwood's essay responds to an 1158 class assignment asking students to consider a group of people that has been the victim of unfair stereotyping, integrating personal experience and at least two print sources.

The Grief of Grief

Elizabeth A. Underwood

When I was nineteen my mother died, just six months after my father's death. They were both relatively young and died suddenly. The shock of this double loss was acute, not to mention crippling. I did not have the emotional maturity to seek out the proper resources for coping. I had no clue that what I was feeling had its own laws, its own needs, and was even completely natural. At the time of my mother's death, I was working as kennel assistant for a local veterinarian. Just three days after her burial I was told to come back to work or I would lose my job. Numb, I complied. No one there mentioned my loss; their silence implied that things for me should be back to normal. My employer requested my help with the euthanasia of a client's dog. I tried to get out of it but it was impossible. My boss didn't think this should be too difficult for me. He said, "Come on, we've got work to do." Those words left a lasting impression; they communicated what was expected of me—to buckle down, be a soldier, and get on with the business of life. The owner of the dog was a sparrow of a woman, spindly and white-haired, putting her spindly and white-haired poodle to rest. I held the ancient dog as the needle went in and the owner stroked and cooed through tears, giving her old pet some last comforts. The pain this stranger felt hit me especially hard. It was clear what I could expect if I kept this job. I quit the next day. I can't say I handled my grief as effectively. My boss' attitude was merely symbolic of the repressiveness I encountered elsewhere; it took me years to work out the grief I suppressed as a reaction to it.

Death is a natural and constant part of life, yet its aftermath, grief, is a phenomenon that is sorely misunderstood. Those who experience it will have to endure

520

numerous stereotypes that range from being labeled as abnormal, if one speaks openly about its symptoms, to having one's grief dismissed when it is connected with the less socially accepted types of loss. Also, our standards for the duration of the mourning period itself are frequently unrealistic. These stereotypes are often the result of a basic discomfort about the topic of death. We're squeamish about our mortality, and as a topic of conversation, it's considered taboo. That we're not immortal is a difficult truth to comprehend, much less accept and embrace. I've known people so angry about their lack of control over their mortality that they treat death as if it were an offense, an unfair misfortune. Ironically, death is the great equalizer, the one event in life that we're all promised—regardless of gender, race, religion, or class. Still, a code of silence about death is encouraged, as we're convinced that it is one of the rotten aspects of life we're better off ignoring. Elisabeth Kubler-Ross notes, "We have as much distaste for talking about personal death as for thinking about it. It is an indelicacy, like talking in mixed company about venereal disease or abortion in the old days" (qtd. in Tatlebaum 13). Out of this aversion come many myths that can prevent the bereaved from processing their loss in a healthy way.

The most common assumptions about grief are that it is an independent, simple emotion and that it follows the same general patterns for everyone. In actuality, grief affects one's entire world; how it influences one personally is an extremely idiosyncratic process. There are psychological effects (fear, depression, anger, guilt, confusion, despair), social effects (withdrawal, excessive neediness), and physical effects (weight loss or gain, exhaustion, nausea, dizziness, apathy, insomnia). Grief is mystifying in its utter disregard for boundaries; human beings are surprising in their expectations of them. Dr. Theresa Rando addresses this problem in her book *How To Go On Living When Someone You Love Dies.* "I have found that the myths and unrealistic expectations that society maintains for grievers are some of the worst problems a griever has"(7).

The concept of a boundary that separates grief from the rest of one's life is arbitrary. A person never forgets the loss of a father, for example; his absence will be felt, in varying degrees, for the rest of one's life. Why is it that people have such false expectations for the period of mourning itself? Rando stresses that "The duration of your grief . . . will depend upon you and the death you have experienced. This is why there is no set time period for how long it should take"(77). Time-line myths create incredible stress for the grief-stricken. It's demeaning to be confronted with the judgment that loss can or should be processed in a preordained amount of time; after that time is up, a person is considered inadequate if the trauma continues to have effect.

Another destructive stereotype the bereaved endure is having their loss socially invalidated. A shocking number of mourners suffer such experiences. For example, some people believe that an abortion shouldn't affect the woman who chooses it because the choice must prove she has no attachment to the fetus. Often the death of a young child or infant is not expected to cause extreme grief as the child didn't live long enough to warrant it. Numerous types of relationships aren't sanctioned as being valuable enough to mourn. That vet I worked for maintained a cold demeanor toward anyone expressing emotion over the death of a pet. I know a lot of people who have had their grief over losing a pet belittled. As definitions of what makes "a family" evolve, our requirements for what grants someone the right to grieve remain archaic. Rando writes, "The importance of a death in our life is not determined exclusively by bloodlines" (58). The loss of a cat, ex-lover, aunt, co-worker, or best friend can hurt as intensely as a father's death.

The death of someone socially devalued (the mentally ill or handicapped, AIDS victims, criminals, addicts) brings up frustrating problems for grievers. Rando illustrates, "The severing of any of these relationships is a major and traumatic loss which must be understood and responded to as such. Our failure to do so as individuals and as a society only predisposes these people to poorer bereavement outcomes" (61). If peers don't share one's conviction that your brother is worth loving despite the fact that he's been arrested for selling drugs, one cannot count on them for support if he dies.

A young man I worked with here in New Orleans was murdered a little over a year ago. His sister, Martha*, also worked with me; she and I had become close. When news of Elvin's* murder reached my boss, she did not tell any of the staff. To her, his death just wasn't worth the fuss. Elvin had quit the restaurant a month prior, and it was rumored he'd been selling pot. The circumstances of his death were also unsavory—he'd been shot eight times while in the Desire housing projects. I found out about his death by seeing it written up in the local newspaper. (Martha, of course, had not been coming to work.) When I approached my boss to talk about it, she was nonchalant. "How is Martha?" I asked. My boss casually replied, "Oh, she's fine. You do know that her and Elvin weren't that close." This was a gross over-simplification, a way not only to devalue this young man but to label any grief over his murder as inappropriate. It goes without saying that his family was, and still is, devastated; not just by the violence of their loss but also the lack of social validation and support.

Reluctant to confront issues of mortality, some people grope for any excuse to distance themselves from evidence of it. This may be why so many people are ill equipped to cope with it when it strikes. In her book, *The Courage To Grieve,* Judy Tatlebaum writes, "One consequence of the denial of death in our society is that we are often ignorant and unskilled with coping with loss . . . having no idea what to do when we hear of a death, many of us run away from helping the bereaved" (73). This ignorance exhibits itself in distressing ways that only intensify if one has suffered a series of losses. The stereotype is that one must be attracting death in some way. The truism "bad things happen to good people" morphs into a paranoia that death is a virus one catches and carries like a contagion.

Tobey and his life-long friend, Arun, were big factors in my decision to move to New Orleans. They were brothers to me, in the spiritual sense of the word. They let me live with them until I got my own apartment. We shared uncanny connections; there was nothing we wouldn't do for each other. All of this evaporated when Tobey committed suicide in their apartment; Arun and I found his body. In the aftermath of that ugly day, my energy was focused on Arun's well-being. My grief would have to wait for attention. When I found Arun dead just three months later, I was totally crushed. My unresolved grief from losing Tobey was only compounded by the loss of Arun and the horrific nature of what I'd witnessed.

*Names have been changed

I do not mean to dismiss the support I have gotten through the years. I may not have survived any of these traumas without the compassion and strength of those who have cared for me. As deeply moved by that as I am, it's been the discriminations I've suffered that I still struggle to comprehend. After the most recent losses, my closest friend "couldn't see me anymore"; my grief reminded her of things she needed to "put behind her." A guy I'd been dating told me he believed I was clinically insane because of the intensity of my emotional distress. He dumped me.

Two weeks after Arun's funeral I went back to my waitressing job. The diner was a safe haven, providing consistency in my life when I desperately needed it. My co-workers were incredibly supportive. On the other hand, the manager treated me as if I were guilty of some crime, a pariah, full of bad luck and trouble. She never once addressed what happened to me. The innocent banter we used to share was now reduced to stiff greetings and averted eyes. I called in sick one day, feeling on the verge of a nervous breakdown, a fact I made clear when I asked for the day off. When I returned, the manager said, "Feeling better?" In her best Snow White voice. I was honest. "No, this is all so hard on me." She answered, fallen, "Oh, I thought you just had a cold." Two weeks later she fired me, using a flimsy excuse. I took it extremely hard. Luckily, I was blessed with good friends for co-workers who rallied around me and got me my job back. Sadly, some damage was already done. It was obvious that the only way I could be an acceptable employee would be to keep the truth of my grief to myself.

These examples may seem extreme, yet they are more common than we care to admit. Sit in on a group therapy session for survivors of loss to see just how ordinary these circumstance and reactions are. The general attitude is that death is a curse, a nightmare to be avoided at all costs, even to the point of turning your back on someone who is suffering. Yet death is the one experience that undeniably links us all. Grief processing should be a place of common ground; the arena in which we can meet, unite, nurture, and be nurtured.

Survivors of loss are not lepers to be avoided nor are they weaklings needing to be rushed through their mourning process. Rather, they are living proof that death is something that can be endured and handled with grace. The aftermath of loss will be more tolerable when there is less ignorance and more compassion in our dealings with its survivors. Though the experience of losing someone you love is bound to leave lasting scars, it is possible to gain profound insight by openly and honestly facing grief and death. I learned this from Tobey's mother, Mimi, who confided in me late one night, "I used to be afraid all the time, especially of the dark. When Tobey was born I wasn't afraid of the dark anymore but I still had a lot of fear in me, fear of death. I thought I could control the world, that I could change the world. That's how I would keep my children safe. When Tobey died, I was liberated from that illusion. I was set free. In a way, his death set me free."

Works Cited

Rando, Theresa A. *How To Go On Living When Someone You Love Dies.* 1988. New York: Bantam, 1991.

Tatlebaum, Judy. *The Courage to Grieve: Creative Living, Recovery, and Growth Through Grief.* New York: Harper, 1980.

*T**he following untitled essay by Steven Dominick won the Ella V. Schwing Award, an annual award for the best essay written in a freshman English class at UNO, in 2000. Dominick's essay responds to an 1158 class assignment asking students to answer this question: Is it just to sentence as adults juveniles who have been convicted of crimes such as armed robbery or murder?*

Untitled

Steven Dominick

In a 1975 address, Marian Wright Edelman expressed the ambiguity of America's views concerning the fate of juvenile offenders when she observed that, "We are willing to spend the least amount of money to keep a kid at home, more to put him in a foster home, and the most to institutionalize him." Her views have been crystallized, twenty-five years later, in the troubling murder trial of a thirteen-year-old Michigan boy, Nathaniel Abraham, who stands accused of first degree murder. Throughout the country, courts, district attorneys, and communities are looking at this trial as a case study in how to deal with the adult crimes of juveniles. In an attempt to gain a measure of control over the spiraling problem of juvenile crime, the criminal justice system has increasingly sought to try youthful lawbreakers in adult courts. As is often the case, however, with rash attempts at solving complex societal problems with overly simplistic one-dimensional solutions, true justice is not the end product. This being the very goal of the court system, attempts to try youths as adults stand diametrically opposed to the stated mission of the criminal justice system. Blanket approaches such as these may create a false sense of action and security, but when held up to the unforgiving light of objective analysis, they do little to foster the cause of justice for either the accused or society.

Nathaniel Abraham is an unlikely candidate to be the poster boy for juvenile tort reform. His life prior to age eleven had been filled with violent episodes. In those years before he became a murderer, police intervention in Nathaniel's life was required twenty-two times. After the shooting, which left an eighteen-year-old dead, he bragged to his friends about his actions with no apparent remorse. When confronted by authorities and explained the gravity of his actions, Nathaniel could not fully comprehend the consequences that he might face. This is often the response observed when those that have not yet reached the age of majority are confronted with the possibility of adult penalties to be paid for their crimes. In the past, a separate system of laws and punishment was established for juveniles. The emphasis was on reform and rehabilitation. Usually, when the youth turned eighteen or twenty-one the juvenile arrest record was wiped clean. It was the hope of the court that the new adult would be able to lead a productive life from that point forward.

At some point in the latter half of the twentieth-century the emphasis shifted away from reform and towards public safety. With this shift came the production of a new generation of hardened juvenile criminals. These youths knew early in their lives that whatever crimes they committed would hang like an albatross around their necks. Youths hardened by the criminal justice system, like Nathaniel Abraham, are not offered an out. Rather, they are confronted with a society prepared to see them fail.

The justice that this society demands is often elusive. In its stead, political decisions are rendered with little regard for justice but with maximum appeal for the masses. The reality is that rarely is there a convergence of justice and popular opinion. District attorneys argue that the court system has failed in its duty to protect the citizens and, therefore, they must step in with new prosecutorial strategies, such as the trying of juveniles as adults. The result is that those youths accused of certain crimes must give up their rights to be tried according to their age because adults in charge of their rehabilitation have abdicated their responsibility. In the Michigan case the prosecutor has been accused of pandering to a public already outraged by the growing wave of juvenile violence. His decision to charge Abraham as an adult is seen as a nod to that portion of the public.

Perhaps overlooked by this approach is the issue of justice as it relates to Nathaniel and other juveniles charged as adults. The possibility of selective use of this aspect of prosecution is cause for concern. What is unknown are the variables used to assign the case to either juvenile or adult court. Factors as subjective as race, economic standing, gender, and publicity are presently sources of contention in all courtrooms. Placing the power to assign the gravity of the crime solely in the hands of prosecutors, as the Michigan law does, removes an important layer of judicial protection that is essential to the cause of justice. In fact, this law is an attempt to circumvent an already established juvenile court system approved of by the voters in the state constitution.

Increasingly prevalent in courthouses around the country is the use of blended sentencing patterns as a means of punishing juvenile offenders. In these cases the youth is sentenced as a juvenile and his behavior during the duration of his juvenile sentence is monitored. If he does not live up to the terms of his punishment he is expected to serve the rest of his adult time. Unfortunately, the improvement, or rehabilitation, is contingent upon programs that emphasize reform. These are the very programs that do not exist because the decision was made to shift to punishment of juvenile criminals rather than preparation for reentry into society. At the completion of this vicious cycle is a hardened youthful offender more likely to have gotten into trouble during his incarceration than to have improved his life. It is the fairness component of justice that is missing from this illogical approach.

Providing security for the people is one of the primary duties of any government. To do so while providing justice for all is the greatest challenge every government faces. The trying of the youngest members of American society as adults, regardless of the severity of their crimes, reduces the courts to agents of injustice. The removal of youths from the court system designed specifically to handle such cases is an attempt to divert blame and attention from the true problems. As Marian Edelman argued, it is most beneficial for society to deal with its root problems rather than to wait until they flower. Unfortunately, some of these flowers bear poison fruit, like Nathaniel Abraham.

Three Successful Proficiency Exam Responses

The following essays, written by UNO students Morgan Bowman, Breen R. Stevens, and Jason Waguespack, are examples of passing proficiency exam responses. Each essay responds to a different proficiency prompt.

PROMPT #1: Nancy Mairs concludes her essay "On Being A Cripple" by explaining that living as a "cripple . . . opened and enriched my life enormously." Writers like Brigid Brophy and Natalie Kusz, on the other hand, suggest that being treated as the outcast is oppressive. Is there ever an advantage to being the one outside the mainstream?

Difference as Impetus to Cultural Evolution

Morgan Bowman

To take a cursory glance at modern media is to come away with the notion that we live in an enlightened society. Our self-image is one of tolerance and political correctness. We fancy ourselves to be more forward thinking, less biased, and more accepting of differences than our forefathers. These are lies that we tell ourselves and our children, unwilling to face the reality that we are no more visionary than we have ever been, that differences are still met with division, and that the ideas and trends we tout as being evidence of our wonderful enlightenment are little more than watered down victims of the necessary and infinite process of cultural evolution.

This type of evolution has been ongoing for centuries, since, most likely, the beginning of humanity. It is a cycle, an often painful process that begins, most commonly, with one revolutionary, or sect of revolutionaries, who defy the cultural norm, who by their difference force us to think beyond that norm. Often, they are persecuted, derided, or shunned for their bravery, but always, in the end, society gains a wider vision from their efforts. What was once so shocking becomes, with time, not so shocking. A new norm is established; evolution has occurred, and, unfortunately, with the evolution of this norm the boundaries are reset, our definition of the average is altered only slightly. In this way, humanity creeps ever forward—a petulant child crying out against every jolt, holding its hand over its ears until someone pries them away.

There are serious and not-so-serious examples of this evolutionary process. In the early 1920s, young women challenged society's expectations by raising their hemlines to shocking lengths. Prior to this time, a glimpse of a lady's ankle was thought to be risqué, but with the arrival of the prohibition era flapper, our attitudes about propriety began to change. Rock and roll, also, at its outset, was a reviled development. To the mothers and fathers of the 1940s and 50s it was a creation of the devil himself. It encouraged juvenile delinquency, was a crime against morality, and would, it was feared, do nothing but corrupt the minds of impressionable youth. Again, however, what was once so outrageous became, with time, accepted. By today's standards, the rock and roll of our parents' generation seems remarkably sedate.

An examination of the more serious events in our cultural evolution reveals the same patterns, even if accompanied by more virulent prejudices, more violent reactions. Martin Luther changed forever the face of Christianity on the day he nailed his theses to that door and was excommunicated for his trouble. His actions set in motion years of warfare and the emigration of countless people in search of religious tolerance. Because of him, protestant religions exist now in every corner of the globe.

In another well-known example, Aristotle was forced to drink hemlock for his crimes against the norm, yet despite this, thousands of students read his teachings each year. Darwin, also, brought change in the form of violent cultural upset, and in the wake of his upheaval, almost all modern biology textbooks are now based on his theories. The women's rights movement, along with the struggle for racial equality, brought with them widespread cultural upset, often violent reactions, and eventually, a revision of accepted standards in a process that is ongoing to this day.

Our society, now poised at the beginning of a new millennium, is no different, no more tolerant of differences than it has ever been. Each generation of teenage rebels fancies its struggle to be unique, its methods of expression to be more radical than the generations that came before. And each successive generation discovers that, in the end, its rebellion was no different that of their parents, that being "different" is just another type of conformity. Already, the radical methods adopted by my generation have become cliched. Today, you can walk the halls of any junior high school to find various body piercing, tattoos of every shape and size, and hair colors that cover the full spectrum of visible light. In our fervor to be different, we have established a new norm. The evolutionary process continues unabated and unacknowledged.

PROMPT #2: The legal system in the United States is often symbolized by a blindfolded figure, holding scales of justice, which supposedly represent everyone's right to fair and impartial treatment by the law, regardless of economic status, gender, race, religion, disability, age, or sexual orientation. Many argue, however, that true justice is more an ideal than a reality, and that some individuals are routinely judged more harshly than others, based not on their guilt or innocence, but upon factors beyond their control. These critics point out that money and fame often seem to buy freedom, and they use examples like President Clinton, O.J. Simpson, and the parents of JonBenet Ramsey to prove their case. Is our justice system unjust, or is it the best system available, despite its flaws?

Necessities

Breen R. Stevens

When we look at the justice system in America today, we see scores of allegedly guilty people being turned free. What we are not often seeing, however, are the cases of innocent citizens being released without conviction. I believe that this is a good working example of our legal system, and, although it is imperfect, is a justified necessity that follows, in principle, with what the founding fathers of our nation represented and fought for.

To see this, we only need to look at the Declaration of Independence. In this proclamation, Thomas Jefferson said that we accept as truths that all men are created equal, and are endowed by our Creator with certain inalienable rights. These include the rights of life, liberty, and the pursuit of happiness. He further went on to say that government is instituted among men to secure these rights. It is in the light of this reasoning that we come to the judicial philosophy that says an accused citizen is innocent until proven guilty.

This basic precept is what helps keep us from sentencing innocent people to imprisonment, or worse. Once judgment is passed down upon someone, the damage to them is irreparable. How do you apologize to a man who has just spent the last seventeen years of his life in prison, only to be released and absolved of his crime when new evidence proved he was innocent all along? How do you compensate a grieving family whose mother or father was wrongly executed? The fact that there is no possible form of reparations for stealing years off of someone's life, or their life altogether, is why our justice system exists as it does today.

Our courts rule according to the moral maxim that it is a greater injustice to err against an innocent man, than in favor of a guilty man, and rightfully so, for it is the job of our government to provide us with a system that seeks to protect us without infringing on the rights we cherish so deeply. This is not to say that the system cannot be altered. So long as it does not trample over our rights, we are free to change it. This is in light of the fact that man is also imperfect, and as such, can make mistakes. The ability of our government to amend and repeal laws is a testimony to this philosophy of progressive change.

Therefore, our justice system, though flawed, is a functional necessity, designed to maintain order in society without infringing upon our inalienable rights; it is a synthesis of our need for justice with our core values and beliefs. To act otherwise would be a direct contradiction to what people like Thomas Jefferson intended when they threw off the yoke of injustice, and founded this country.

PROMPT #3: *Presidential candidate George W. Bush has been criticized recently by both Republicans and Democrats for visiting the campus of Bob Jones University, a "fundamentalist" Christian university which does not allow interracial dating by its students. If we are to understand and accept the differences in our culture, should we also be more understanding and accepting of "fundamentalist" Christians (such as those running Bob Jones University) and their beliefs? Or should we openly reject groups who hold extreme views?*

Opposing Extremism

Jason Waguespack

Our nation's history has seen a long struggle to realize the goals of freedom and equality among different groups of people. Such struggles have been against extremists who stifle other people's freedoms. In large part we have been successful but we must continue to be vigilant in opposing extremism, for it can grow if left unchecked. To preserve freedom and equality for all, extremist groups must be openly rejected.

We must reject extremist groups when personal freedoms are being infringed upon. This is important because the infringement of personal rights will affect the whole nation. Like a virus, it will spread from one section of the nation to another if not opposed. At Bob Jones university, the right to date between races is impeded by fundamentalist Christians. This view is clearly extremist, considering that mainstream Christians are not opposed to interracial dating. Denouncing this view will set an example for those who try to impede personal freedom.

Groups that hold extreme views must be rejected to protect and promote equality. Ethnic groups and minorities have seen persecution for their differences, which directly interferes with our nation's image as a place where all have equal rights. Our nation's Constitution means nothing if it cannot protect all who are American citizens. Our nation cannot function without equality. The opposition of racist groups such as the Ku Klux Klan will ensure that minorities' rights are safe.

We should openly reject extremist groups to protect this nation and our freedoms. When extremist groups are left unchecked, it can lead to war and tragedy. Perhaps the greatest example is the rise of Nazi Germany. Adolf Hitler's brand of socialism and anti-Semitism caused the deaths of millions of Jews in the Holocaust and almost cost Europe and the rest of the world its freedom. If Hitler and his political party had been opposed and stopped before they could control Germany's government, the world would have been spared a great tragedy.

Our culture contains a multitude of different groups. Our society's survival is dependent on having an understanding and acceptance among all different groups of people, but if we allow extremist views to go unchecked, it could lead to the usurping of personal freedoms and perhaps even tragedy. That is not what our nation is about. Our constitution should guarantee the rights of all, for our nation was not founded by extremists.

Appendix B: Suggested Groupings for Assigned Readings

Arguments from Principle

Jane Bernstein *Victim of Circumstance*

Angela Bolte *Do Wedding Dresses Come in Lavender?*

E.M. Forster *What I Believe*

Nat Hentoff *When Nice People Burn Books*

Thomas Jefferson *The Declaration of Independence*

Martin Luther King, Jr. *Letter from Birmingham Jail*

Plato *The Allegory of the Cave*

Jonathan Swift *A Modest Proposal*

Henry David Thoreau *Civil Disobedience*

Debates

Angela Bolte *Do Wedding Dresses Come in Lavender?*

Lisa Duggan *Abolish Marriage!*

Judith Dunaway and K. H. Ginzel *Smoking for Others: Predicament of the Nonsmoker*

David Sedaris *Diary of a Smoker*

Paul Kingsnorth *Human Health on the Line*

Thomas Gale Moore *Happiness is a Warm Planet*

Themes

Coming of Age

Robert Bly *A World of Half-Adults*

Gish Jen *What Means Switch* [fiction]

William Severini Kowinski *Kids in the Mall: Growing Up Controlled*

Joan Nestle *A Restricted Country*

Richard Rodriguez *Complexion*

Naomi Wolf *Promiscuities: The Secret Struggle Toward Womanhood*

Crime and Punishment

Jane Bernstein *Victim of Circumstance*

Susan Glaspell *A Jury of Her Peers* [fiction]
George Orwell *A Hanging*
Henry David Thoreau *Civil Disobedience*
Hiller B. Zobel *The Undying Problem of the Death Penalty*

Education

Wayne Booth *Boring from Within: The Art of the Freshman Essay*
Christopher Buckley *Reunion Schedule*
Mark Edmundson *On the Uses of Education:*
    As Lite Entertainment for Bored College Students
Jonathan Kozol *The Disenfranchised: Silent and Unseen*
Lewis H. Lapham *School Bells*
Plato *The Allegory of the Cave*
Earl Shorris *On the Uses of a Liberal Education:*
    As a Weapon in the Hands of the Restless Poor
Alice Walker *Everyday Use*
Kurt Wiesenfeld *Making the Grade*
Connie Willis *Ado*
Virginia Woolf *Professions for Women*
Malcolm X from *The Autobiography of Malcolm X*

Gender

Sandra Cisneros *Woman Hollering Creek* [fiction]
Angela Davis *I Used To Be Your Sweet Mama:*
    Ideology, Sexuality, and Domesticity
Susan Faludi *Blame It on Feminism*
Susan Glaspell *A Jury of Her Peers* [fiction]
Ellen Goodman *Sorry, Nike, I Just Don't Get That Ad*
Kay Leigh Hagan *Bitches from Hell: The Politics of Self-Defense*
June Jordan *Report from the Bahamas*
Jody Raphael *Keeping Women Poor: How Domestic Violence Prevents*
    Women From Leaving Welfare and Entering the World of Work
Richard Rodriguez *Complexion*
Muriel R. Schulz *The Semantic Derogation of Women*
Deborah Tannen *Sex, Lies, and Conversation*
Nancy Updike *Hitting the Wall*
Naomi Wolf *Promiscuities: The Secret Struggle Toward Womanhood*
Virginia Woolf *Professions for Women*

Insiders and Outsiders

James Baldwin *Fifth Avenue, Uptown: A Letter from Harlem*

Shannon Bell *Tattooed: A Participant Observer's Exploration of Meaning*

Annie Dillard *Singing with the Fundamentalists*

Annie Downey *I Am Your Welfare Reform*

Gish Jen *What Means Switch* [fiction]

June Jordan *Report from the Bahamas*

Martin Luther King, Jr. *Letter from Birmingham Jail*

Jonathan Kozol *The Disenfranchised: Silent and Unseen*

C.S. Lewis *The Inner Ring*

Nancy Mairs *On Being a Cripple*

Joan Nestle *A Restricted Country*

Jody Raphael *Keeping Women Poor: How Domestic Violence Prevents Women From Leaving Welfare and Entering the World of Work*

Richard Rodriguez *Complexion*

Michael Sandel *Honor and Resentment*

Brent Staples *Black Men and Public Space*

Cornel West *Malcolm X and Black Rage*

Virginia Woolf *Professions for Women*

Malcolm X From *The Autobiography of Malcolm X*

Language

Stuart Chase *Gobbledygook*

George Orwell *Politics and the English Language*

Muriel R. Schulz *The Semantic Derogation of Women*

Deborah Tannen *Sex, Lies, and Conversation*

Malcolm X From *The Autobiography of Malcolm X*

Media

Harry Crews *Pages from the Life of a Georgia Innocent*

Barbara Ehrenreich *Spudding Out*

Ellen Goodman *Sorry, Nike, I Just Don't Get That Ad*

Pete Hamill *News is a Verb*

Neil Postman *Television News Narcosis*

Katie Roiphe *Adultery's Double Standard*

Nature and Science

Louise Erdrich *Skunk Dreams*

Paul Kingsnorth *Human Health on the Line*

Thomas Gale Moore *Happiness is a Warm Planet*
Michael Pollan *Why Mow? The Case Against Lawns*
Robert Pool *Struggling to Do Science for Society*
Theodore Roszak *The Nature of Serenity*
Scott Russell Sanders *The Common Life*
Brent Staples *Turning People Into Product*
Lewis Thomas *Crickets, Bats, Cats & Chaos*

Poverty
James Baldwin *Fifth Avenue, Uptown: A Letter from Harlem*
Annie Downey *I Am Your Welfare Reform*
Jonathan Kozol *The Disenfranchised: Silent and Unseen*
Jody Raphael *Keeping Women Poor: How Domestic Violence Prevents
    Women From Leaving Welfare and Entering the World of Work*
Earl Shorris *On the Uses of a Liberal Education:
    As a Weapon in the Hands of the Restless Poor*
Jonathan Swift *A Modest Proposal*

Relationships
Robert Bly *A World of Half-Adults*
Angela Bolte *Do Wedding Dresses Come in Lavender?*
Raymond Carver *Cathedral* [fiction]
Sandra Cisneros *Woman Hollering Creek* [fiction]
Angela Davis *I Used To Be Your Sweet Mama:
    Ideology, Sexuality, and Domesticity*
Lisa Duggan *Abolish Marriage!*
Barbara Ehrenreich *Spudding Out*
E.M. Forster *What I Believe*
Susan Glaspell *A Jury of Her Peers* [fiction]
Gish Jen *What Means Switch* [fiction]
Jody Raphael *Keeping Women Poor: How Domestic Violence Prevents
    Women From Leaving Welfare and Entering the World of Work*
Katie Roiphe *Adultery's Double Standard*
Scott Russell Sanders *The Common Life*
Deborah Tannen *Sex, Lies, and Conversation*
Alice Walker *Everyday Use* [fiction]
Naomi Wolf *Promiscuities: The Secret Struggle Toward Womanhood*
Elizabeth Wurtzel *Parental Guidance Suggested*

Women and Abuse
Sandra Cisneros *Woman Hollering Creek* [fiction]
Susan Glaspell *A Jury of Her Peers* [fiction]
Ellen Goodman *Sorry, Nike, I Just Don't Get That Ad*
Kay Leigh Hagan *Bitches from Hell: The Politics of Self-Defense*
June Jordan *Report from the Bahamas*
Jody Raphael *Keeping Women Poor: How Domestic Violence Prevents Women From Leaving Welfare and Entering the World of Work*
Muriel R. Schulz *The Semantic Derogation of Women*
Jane Slaughter *A Beaut of a Shiner*
Nancy Updike *Hitting the Wall*

Appendix C:
Suggested Writing Assignments

The following is a selection of writing assignments. Many different writing instructors shared their ideas and assignments for this edition of Reading Matters. *The result is a collection varied in style, format, goal, and degree of difficulty.*

- Write an essay in which you argue that education makes us free. Use your own experience and the essays you have been reading on the subject for support.

- When Louisiana tried to introduce a state-wide teacher evaluation program, the idea was rejected by most of the teachers who claimed that a standardized evaluation could not accurately measure the manifold duties of a successful teacher and that it would be unfair to deprive long-term employees of their livelihood if they did not measure up. Supporters of the test have argued that a standardized evaluation would weed out unqualified teachers and thus raise educational standards in our state. Where do you stand on the issue? Should Louisiana have state-wide teaching evaluations for primary and secondary schools?

- The State of Louisiana now awards TOPS scholarships to all high school graduates with grade point averages of 2.5 or higher. Considering that many businesses require college degrees of their job applicants, these scholarships have opened doors for many students who would otherwise not have been able to go to college. Because everybody needs a college degree and because (almost) everybody in our state can get one, many students go to college not so much by choice but out of necessity; some, unfortunately, have very little interest in higher education, and some lack the intellectual discipline to cope with academic requirements.

   Based on your experience and the readings you have done, write an essay in which you argue whether a college education in our day and age is a right or a privilege.

- The establishment of birth-control clinics and sex education classes in high schools has long been a heated controversy. In the light of what you have read in Naomi Wolf's and Robert Bly's essays, write an argument for or against the proposition to have clinics (and/or sex-ed classes) in high schools. Make sure you research the issue in the library before writing.

- In the manner of C.S. Lewis, write a commencement speech in which you defend the virtues of individualism against the "Good Ole Boys" network so prevalent in our local economy—or the other way round. Make sure you support your arguments with personal examples and ideas from your readings on the subject.

- In the style of Buckley, write an ironic itinerary for an "orientation weekend" for prospective students and their parents here at UNO. Make sure, though, that your satire contains some kernel of criticism of the way institutions of higher education market themselves.

- Lewis Lapham argues that, despite their campaign speeches to the contrary, political leaders prefer their voters uneducated yet "injected with the virus of unbridled appetite for goods and services they can't afford" because this "double bind instills the attitudes of passivity and apprehension, which in turn induce the fear of authority and the habits of obedience." In other words, poverty and illiteracy make good citizens. Does his statement accurately describe our social reality? After doing some research on the connection between education and criminality, write an essay in which you support or refute Lapham's theory.

- Compare Lewis Lapham's essay about the influence of consumerism on the public education system ("School Bells") to Kowinski's argument about shopping malls. What similarities do you detect?

- Write an argument in which you take a stand on educating young people to be consumers first and foremost. Do the advantages of consumerism outweigh the disadvantages? Use the essays by Kowinski, Bly, and Lapham for ideas and support.

- Considering the various ways in which people acquire educations, in or out of universities, write an essay in which you define what it means to be "educated."

- Kurt Wiesenfeld and Mark Edmundson point to the consequences as higher education becomes an increasingly competitive business. Because students (or their parents) are paying customers, universities often cater to their demands, afraid that they might take their money elsewhere. This new attitude has resulted in inflated grades, watered-down curricula, and teachers worrying incessantly about student evaluations. Central to this debate is how the university views its relationship with its students: are they its products or its customers? Write an essay in which you try to answer this question.

- In Earl Shorris's essay "On the Uses of a Liberal Education: As a Weapon in the Hands of the Restless Poor," a prison inmate suggests that Plato's allegory illustrates a way out of poverty: "The ghetto is the cave. Education is the light. Poor people can understand that." Do you agree with this contemporary interpretation of the story?

- Read Shelley's *Frankenstein* or watch *Blade Runner*. Then write an argument in which you support or refute Staples's thesis that futurist writers of the past accurately portrayed the conflicts we encounter now that the technology to create synthetic life is within reach.

- Using Kingsnorth's evidence, refute Moore's essay "Happiness is a Warm Planet."

- Write an essay in which you define and defend your position on the role of the scientist in our world. Should a scientist be mainly an analyst or does he/she have obligations to become an advocate if necessary? To make your essay more specific, choose an area of science in which you are interested (gene technology, for instance, or atomic weapons) and argue the scientists' position in this particular field. Make sure you research your topic carefully before you take a position.

- Take a scientist of the past (J. Robert Oppenheimer, for instance) whose research has had far-reaching (and destructive) consequences. Research the person and his/her work and argue whether or not this person is responsible for the consequences of his/her research. Draw a connection between this historic figure and the responsibilities of today's scientists.

- Both Roszak and Sanders talk about the necessity of reconnecting ourselves with nature, but they do not describe specific ways of doing so. Write an essay in which you propose and defend one practical way in which we, in our everyday lives, can contribute towards this goal. Support your argument with the ideas from the two essays and from some of your own research.

- Apply C.S. Lewis's theory to our contemporary teenage culture and argue whether or not what he says about the professional world applies to high school society.

- The Bible (Mt. 20:1–16) contains the parable of the workers in the vineyard, all of whom were hired at different times of the day to work on the landowner's property. At the end of the day, they were all paid the same wages, those that had worked all day and those that had worked only an hour at the end of the day. When one of the workers, who had worked all day, complained, the landowner replied that his complaint was groundless because he was not cheated out of the wage he had been promised. "Are you envious because I am generous?" the master asks the dissatisfied worker.

In its emphasis on equal rewards for unequal performance, the parable describes an incident similar to the Callie Smartt case. Putting aside the religious significance of the story, write an essay in which you argue whether or not the landowner had been fair to his workers and whether the disgruntled worker's complaints were justified. Back up your arguments with parallel cases from your own (work) experience.

- If you had to choose between doing work you like for very little money or work you endure for a lot of money, which would you choose? Write an essay in which you defend your choice.

- Taking ideas from Smiley, Sayers, and Sanders, write an essay in which you define what you think is "meaningful work." Make sure that your definition, like theirs, is grounded in some overall principle, philosophical or otherwise.

- Jane Bernstein in "Victim of Circumstance" touches on the responsibility a victim's family might have in determining whether a convicted criminal is eligible for parole. How does her view compare to Zobel's observations on justice and revenge at the end of his essay?

- Wolf's argument focuses on the sexual initiation of women. However, her ideas could easily be adapted to the education of young men as well. Write an argument for or against the establishment of "Manhood Guides" in addition to "Womanhood Guides" in the sense that Wolf describes it.

- Looking at the essays by Virginia Woolf and Susan Faludi, written more than half a century apart, do you think women have accomplished what the early feminists set out to do? Or are they still fighting many of the same battles? Write an essay in which you take a stand on this issue.

- Consider the roles men and women are faced with in their everyday lives. While one man might find it perfectly natural to cook, clean, and decorate, another finds those things effeminate and unmanly. One woman finds it in her nature to cook and care for her children while another feels like a failure to her sex because she has no inclination to do either. In short, many of the essays we read over the course of the semester suggest that men and women are still confined by the "bars" of society if they go against the stereotypical roles set out for them. As you head into adulthood (or continue through it) at the beginning of the 21st century, do you feel these roles are as prominent as the readings suggest they are? Which do you feel has more impact on the roles we take on for ourselves, nature or nurture?

- Taking Faludi's definition of feminism as your starting point, do you think it is possible today to be a feminist and a woman without giving up claims to romance, marriage and motherhood? Why? Why not? Back up your answer with examples from your own experience and from your reading!

- With divorce rates at an all-time high, with same-sex marriage still illegal in all fifty states, and with incidents of domestic violence and adultery increasing at an alarming rate, why would anyone want to marry? What does it even mean to be married? What purpose does a marriage serve? Does it have any benefit beyond a fancy piece of paper? What is the difference between marriage and a long-term or life commitment? What constitutes a marriage these days anyway? Why not do away with marriage altogether and eliminate these problems? Argue for or against doing away with marriage.

- If polygamy works for some and not for others, so be it. If same-sex marriages are what others want, so be it. If still others want traditional heterosexual marriages, so be it. Does who we spend our life with affect anyone else? Don't we have a right to the pursuit of happiness? Does anyone have the right to tell us whom we can and cannot marry, specifically the government? Why do they get to decide what is wrong and right for two consenting adults? Should the government be involved in marriages at all? Argue for or against the government's role in deciding what does and does not constitute a marriage.

- Without using the Bible or the dictionary as a defense, argue for or against same-sex marriage. To write an informed essay on the subject, you must go beyond personal opinion. Consider recent events surrounding the dilemma of same-sex marriage to build a stronger case for your position. Use plenty of specific details and be sure to clearly define and defend your stance on the issue.

- Assuming that Roiphe's observation is correct, write an essay in which you demonstrate that the double standard towards adultery, even though it might look like it supports sexual freedom for women, really perpetuates age-old stereotypes about women.

- Compare Lisa Duggan's "Abolish Marriage!" to Angela Bolte's essay. Where do the two authors agree with each other? Where do they disagree? Is a compromise between the two arguments possible?

- Research a current social problem (welfare, homelessness, etc.), but try to find sources that emphasize the human aspect of the problem (case stories, first-hand accounts of what it is like to be in this situation). On the basis of your findings, write an essay in which you show the human side of the problem in comparison (or contrast) to what public opinion and/or policy makers say about it.

- Several essays and stories in this collection—Carver, "Cathedral," Crews, "Pages from the Life of a Georgia Innocent," Dillard, "Singing with the Fundamentalists," Downey, "I Am Your Welfare Reform," Mairs, "On Being a Cripple," Staples, "Black Men and Public Space"—attempt to correct prevailing stereotypes and prejudices about certain groups in our society. The authors of these essays try to set the record straight on such diverse groups as dirt farmers in Georgia, religious fundamentalists, handicapped people, men, and women.

Pick a group of people that has been the target of unfair stereotyping and write an essay in which you prove those stereotypes to be wrong, developing your arguments with personal experience and/or material from your readings. (It would lend your essay quite a bit of personal credibility if you yourself were a member of this group, but you may certainly pick a group you do not belong to. Keep in mind, however, that whatever personal experience you use must be part of an argument against stereotypes: this essay is not merely a personal narrative.)

- Take some aspect of your own life that most people regard as a disadvantage (such as growing up poor or in a single-parent household, for example) and, like Nancy Mairs, write an essay in which you show that there are positive aspects about this situation that people often overlook. Your purpose is to educate your reader about a situation that you know intimately but your reader does not, to correct a prevailing prejudice about an aspect of your life.

- Have you ever read something or heard someone speak about something, and you asked yourself, "What gives him the right to say that? What does he know?" Well, this is your chance to take the stage and voice your beliefs. This is your chance to establish your credibility and show that you are an authority on your subject, to show your reader why you feel the way you do.

Beware: this is not your chance to rant. You must select a debatable topic, but you must also construct a sound argument. Take a side on the issue and support it with evidence—something to give your belief substance. Pick a subject you are an authority on, something you have been or are personally involved with. Write about something that counts. Make your reader care.

Understanding WHY YOU feel a certain way in regards to particular issues will help you to build more effective arguments. If you want your views to be understood by others, you must understand them first. Consider appeals to emotion, logic, and ethics as you select your supporting details and construct your essay. You should have at least one of each. You must have a thesis, and you should include plenty of specific details that will put the reader in your shoes and make him or her understand what makes you an authority on your subject, what gives YOU the right to have an opinion.

EX: Someone who vigorously supports helmet laws for motorcycles might have been influenced by the death or injury of a family member and also by statistics or news programs he has seen on the issue. He may even be a cyclist who enjoys feeling safe inside his helmet as he cruises his motorcycle along the I-10, or he may be a cyclist who survived serious injury because he was wearing a helmet.

The key to this assignment is that you must write about something that you've had concrete experience with. Don't write about SUVs being hazardous on the roads unless you were somehow involved in an accident with one. Don't write about the death penalty unless you were on death row or had or have a loved one on death row. Don't argue against gay marriage unless you were in one that went bad or were otherwise directly affected by one. If your father's didn't last, write about that. No intangible subjects. The everlasting effects of Kurt Cobain's death don't count unless you were there or otherwise personally involved with him. In other words, it's easy to talk the talk, but you've got to show that you've done the walk.

- In George Orwell's essay "Shooting an Elephant," he relates the story of how he was confronted with a moral dilemma and abandoned his morals to escape the mockery of the native Burmans. In fact, Orwell dreaded the mockery of the natives more than he dreaded the possibility of losing his life should the elephant attack him. In more general terms, he simply became "a puppet of the system." Can you think of a time you (or someone you know well) were forced to do something just because others thought you should or because you might lose something if you didn't? Maybe you cut your hair to get a job or you hid your beliefs to retain or achieve a certain standing or position. Is there ever sufficient justification for abandoning our morals? For going against what we believe is right in our hearts? (Stay away from typical peer pressure issues such as smoking, drugs, drinking, and sex.)

- Write an essay in which you argue for or against the suggestion that we can change people's attitudes and prejudices if we change (by law, if necessary) the language they use.

- Take a piece of art that has been criticized by many people and write an article defending its merit. Make sure your argument is based on a clearly stated definition of art. You might want to consult some reliable sources to help you with this definition. Make sure you hand in a picture or copy of the work of art you chose as the focus of your essay.

- Imagine you are a member of the jury in Minnie Wright's trial. The jury has been deliberating for a while, but you cannot come to any clear conclusion as to the verdict. Because you are an eloquent speaker, you decide to put the case to your fellow jurors as you see it. Write the speech in which you argue either for or against Minnie's guilt.

- Television has become a daily ritual, turning family members into immobile couch potatoes, according to Barbara Ehrenreich. Write an essay in which you argue whether or not television has a destructive influence on family life.

- In "Pages from the Life of a Georgia Innocent," Harry Crews argues that the media should not shield children from certain harsh realities of life. He suggests that it is actually far more damaging to children to expose them only to sugar-coated images that depict existence as warm and comfortable. To what extent do you agree with Crews? Should children be protected from reality or exposed to it through the media? At what ages? To which realities? Are there realities that children should not be exposed to under any circumstances? Why?

- Our discussion of *South Park* and other offensive shows suggested that television is flooded with offensive images. Is this necessarily a problem? Do you feel that measures need to be taken to "clean up" television? Or is it a viable, useful cultural presence as it currently is? Why?

- Write a formal revision of any one of your essays using the classical model of arrangement. Identify each of the seven parts by including a corresponding number in the margin. The paper should be typed, double spaced, and the essay being revised should be turned in as well—just attach it with a paper clip. Remember to focus on the purpose of each part of the model.

Classical Model for Argument

1. Opening statement: should have two functions—catching the reader's attention and establishing the writer's credibility and authority.

2. Background information: should set up the argument by providing important knowledge that the reader can use to better understand the thesis and argument. Remember the questions: "What is the cause of this issue?" "What effect has it created for those involved?"

3. Definition of subject matter or issue: how would you define the particular subject or issue in your own words? For example, what is a pet? What is "true freedom to become what you want?" What constitutes "dating a co-worker?"

4. Thesis: this includes your stance and then, after the rough draft, a statement that sums up the main idea behind the whole argument.

5. Proof: this includes examples from personal experience, the experience of others, and support from outside sources; it also includes the supporting logical reasons.

6. Refutation: a portion of the body where you respond to the opponents' main logical reasons with intelligence, virtue, and goodwill, but in the end make sure that you have downplayed the significance of each point.

7. Conclusion: should, at least, refresh the reader's memory of your examples and summarize the main points of the argument. It also could include a direct appeal to the audience, perhaps even suggesting a call to action or reform.